INDIA

D0988732

JUL 1 2 2005

3-09 (3)
7-12 (35)
11-15 (38)
7-18 (41)

INDIAN PRAIRIE PUBLIC LIBRARY
401 Plainfield Road
Darien, IL 60561

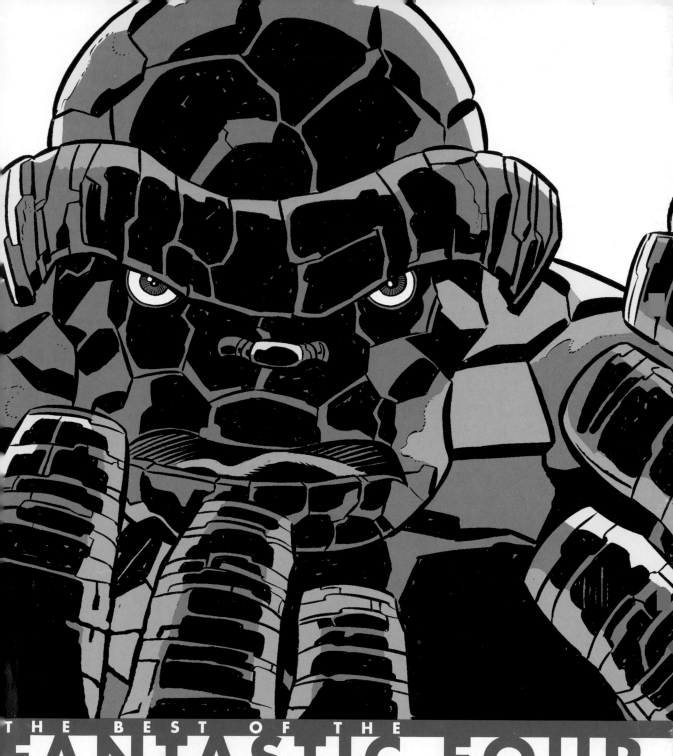

THE BEST OF THE
FANTASTIC FOUR
VOLUME ONE

INDIAN PRAIRIE PUBLIC LIBRARY
401 Plainfield Road
Darien, IL 60561

THE BEST OF THE FANTASTIC FOUR VOLUME ONE

"THE FANTASTIC FOUR!"
From *FANTASTIC FOUR #1* (Nov. 1961)
WRITER: Stan Lee
PENCILER: Jack Kirby
INKER: Unknown
LETTERER: Art Simek

"ORIGIN OF DOCTOR DOOM!"
From *FANTASTIC FOUR ANNUAL #2* (1964)
WRITER: Stan Lee
PENCILER: Jack Kirby
INKER: Chic Stone
LETTERER: Sam Rosen

"A BLIND MAN SHALL LEAD THEM!"
From *FANTASTIC FOUR #39* (June 1965)
WRITER: Stan Lee
PENCILER: Jack Kirby
INKER: Frank Giacoia
LETTERER: Art Simek

"THE BATTLE OF THE BAXTER BUILDING"
From *FANTASTIC FOUR #40* (July 1965)
WRITER: Stan Lee
PENCILER: Jack Kirby
INKER: Vince Colletta
LETTERER: Art Simek

"THIS MAN...THIS MONSTER!"
From *FANTASTIC FOUR #51* (June 1966)
WRITER: Stan Lee
PENCILER: Jack Kirby
INKER: Joe Sinnott
LETTERER: Art Simek

"THE LONG JOURNEY HOME!"
From *FANTASTIC FOUR #100* (July 1970)
WRITER: Stan Lee
CO-PLOT & PENCILER: Jack Kirby
INKER: Joe Sinnott
LETTERER: Sam Rosen

"THE ALIEN, THE ALLY, AND...ARMAGEDDON!"
From *FANTASTIC FOUR #116* (Nov. 1971)
WRITER: Archie Goodwin
PENCILER: John Buscema
INKER: Joe Sinnott
LETTERER: Art Simek

"IMPROBABLE AS IT MAY SEEM... THE IMPOSSIBLE MAN IS BACK IN TOWN!"
From *FANTASTIC FOUR #176* (Nov. 1976)
WRITER: Roy Thomas
PENCILER: George Pérez
INKER: Joe Sinnott
COLORIST: Michele Wolfman
LETTERER: Joe Rosen

"REMEMBRANCE OF THINGS PAST!"
From *MARVEL TWO-IN-ONE #50* (April 1979)
WRITER & PENCILER: John Byrne
INKER: Joe Sinnott
COLORIST: Francoise Mouly
LETTERER: Jim Novak

"TERROR IN A TINY TOWN"
From *FANTASTIC FOUR #236* (Nov. 1981)
WRITER & ARTIST: John Bryne
COLORIST: Glynis Wein
LETTERER: Jim Novak

"A SMALL LOSS"
From *FANTASTIC FOUR #267* (June 1984)
WRITER & ARTIST: John Byrne
COLORIST: Glynis Wein
LETTERER: Michael Higgins

"APRIL FOOL!!"
From *MARVEL FANFARE #15* (July 1984)
WRITER, ARTIST & COLORIST: Barry Windsor-Smith
LETTERER: Jim Novak

"REMEMBRANCE OF THINGS PAST"
From *FANTASTIC FOUR #56* (Aug. 2002)
WRITER: Karl Kesel
PENCILER: Stuart Immonen
INKER: Scott Koblish
COLORIST: Liquid! Graphics
LETTERER: Richard Starkings & Comicraft's Albert Deschesne

"INSIDE OUT"
From *FANTASTIC FOUR #60* (Oct. 2002)
WRITER: Mark Waid
PENCILER: Mike Wieringo
INKER: Karl Kesel
COLORIST: Paul Mounts
LETTERER: Richard Starkings & Comicraft's Albert Deschesne

"WOLF AT THE DOOR – PART 4"

From *MARVEL KNIGHTS 4 #4* (April 2004)

WRITER: Roberto Aguirre-Sacasa
PENCILER: Steve McNiven
INKER: Mark Morales
COLORIST: Morry Hollowell
LETTERER: Virtual Calligraphy's Randy Gentile

SELECT ART RECONSTRUCTION: Pond Scum & Mickey Ritter
SELECT COLOR RECONSTRUCTION: Digital Chameleon, Andy Yanchus, George Roussos, VLM & Jerron Quality Color

Special Thanks to Ralph Macchio & Pond Scum

COLLECTION EDITOR: Mark D. Beazley
ASSISTANT EDITOR: Jennifer Grünwald
SENIOR EDITOR, SPECIAL PROJECTS: Jeff Youngquist
CONSULTING EDITOR: Tom Brevoort
DIRECTOR OF SALES: David Gabriel
PRODUCTION: Jared Osborn, Jerry Kalinowski & Jerron Quality Color
BOOK DESIGNER: Patrick McGrath
CREATIVE DIRECTOR: Tom Marvelli

EDITOR IN CHIEF: Joe Quesada   PUBLISHER: Dan Buckley

IMAGINAUTS: Stan Lee & Jack Kirby

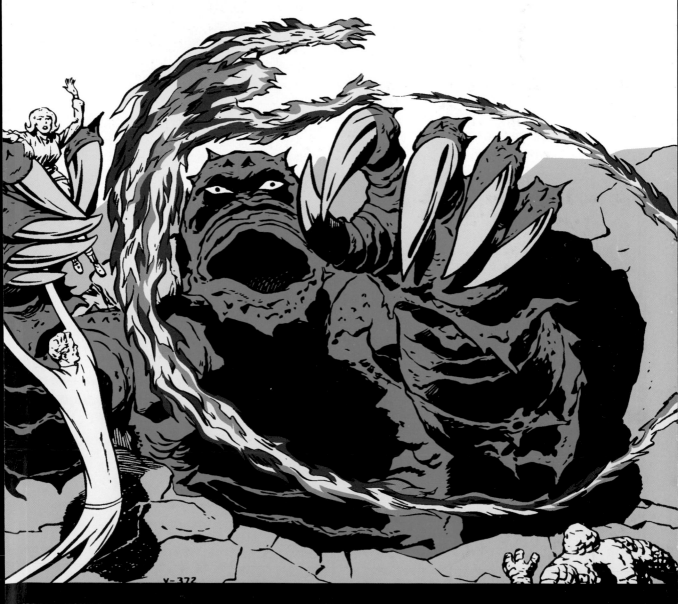

BEST OF THE FANTASTIC FOUR VOL. 1. Contains material originally published in magazine form as FANTASTIC FOUR #1, #39-40, #51, #100, #116, #176, #236, 267, Annual #2; FANTASTIC FOUR (Vol. 3) #56 and #60; MARVEL FANFARE #15, MARVEL TWO-IN-ONE #50; and MARVEL KNIGHTS 4 #4. First printing 2005. ISBN# 0-7851-1782-2. Published by MARVEL COMICS, a division of MARVEL ENTERTAINMENT GROUP, INC. OFFICE OF PUBLICATION: 10 East 40th Street, New York, NY 10016. Copyright © 1961, 1965, 1966, 1970, 1971, 1976, 1979, 1981, 1984, 2002, 2004 and 2005 Marvel Characters, Inc. All rights reserved. $29.99 per copy in the U.S. and $48.00 in Canada (GST #R127032852); Canadian Agreement #40668537. All characters featured in this issue and the distinctive names and likenesses thereof, and all related indicia are trademarks of Marvel Characters, Inc. No similarity between any of the names, characters, persons, and/or institutions in this magazine with those of any living or dead person or institution is intended, and any such similarity which may exist is purely coincidental. **Printed in the U.S.A.** AVI ARAD, Chief Creative Officer; ALAN FINE, President & CEO of Toy Biz and Marvel Publishing; DAN CARR, Director of Production; ELAINE CALLENDER, Director of Manufacturing; DAVID BOGART, Managing Editor; STAN LEE, Chairman Emeritus. For information regarding advertising in Marvel Comics or on Marvel.com, please contact Joe Maimone, Advertising Director, at jmaimone@marvel.com or 212-576-8534.

10 9 8 7 6 5 4 3 2 1

INTRODUCTION

It's difficult to realize, from a distance of over forty years from the day in which it was published, what a revolution in the world of comic books was ushered in by Marvel in the early 1960s—and embodied in its flagship title, THE FANTASTIC FOUR. By almost any standard, that initial issue which went to press on August 8, 1961 seems crude and hurried, as though rushed out hastily in order to try to catch cultural lightning in a bottle. Indeed, legend has it that Marvel's publisher Martin Goodman, having played golf with one of his distributor's field-men and learned through the course of conversation that rival DC's new series, JUSTICE LEAGUE OF AMERICA, was achieving a staggering 97% sell-through on magazine racks across the country, ordered editor Stan Lee to quickly assemble his own team of supermen to try to capture some of that market.

Whether by accident or by design—and most probably some combination of the two—Stan and artist/co-creator Jack Kirby (there is much disagreement in knowledgeable fan circles as to how much each man contributed to the final product) developed a model that far outstripped the competition, a model that reflected the changing values of '60s society in a way that DC's staid, traditional crimebusters never could. Lee and Kirby's initial stories most closely resembled the formulaic monster tales they'd been peddling for the previous several years, stories in which drab scientists would overcome extraterrestrial menaces through some clever quirk of science. But even there, the seeds of the Marvel style were in evidence.

The Fantastic Four were like no super heroes before them. Sure, they had colorful super powers and went on exciting adventures. But there was an air of ambivalence that ran through the series, personified most readily in Ben Grimm, the Thing. Here was a super hero for whom the acquisition of superhuman abilities was an inconvenience, a cross to be borne. For unlike the typical costumed champion of the era, the Thing's powers and the horrific countenance that came with them alienated him from his fellow man, prevented him from living a normal life between world-threatening crises. And Grimm wasn't shy about letting you know that—in the very early days, much of the series' tension came from wondering when the Thing was going to snap and polish off his three companions in a fit of rage.

It was this sort of soap opera conflict that quickly became the hallmark of the book. The Fantastic Four were often at odds with one another, almost more so than the villains they fought. By the third issue, the youthful Human Torch had had enough, and quit the group—they would have to seek him out and lure him back the following month. This was the first time the Fantastic Four came close to breaking up, but it was far from the last. Team leader Reed Richards had his own problems. The love of his life, Sue Storm, the Invisible Girl, seemed smitten with one of their arch-foes, the regal Sub-Mariner, and this threatened his dreams of suburban tranquility. The romantic triangle would play itself out over several years, culminating in the first wedding in comics, an affair to rival that of Charles and Lady Di twenty years before the fact.

At the very beginning, the Fantastic Four wore no uniforms, due to concerns that DC, who then distributed the tiny Marvel line of books, might object to competition in the costumed-hero arena. Fan response quickly changed this, as the kids who wrote in clearly preferred their super-doers clad in colorful skintight attire—and what a revelation to Lee and Kirby that there were kids reading this stuff, and who cared enough about it to respond. Lee reacted to this interest by instituting fan pages and Bullpen Bulletins in his books, creating a cult of personality around himself and the various Marvel artists. Marvel was quickly seen as the with-it place to be, a publisher that was more in tune with what its readers' lives were about.

The Marvel books were also more visceral than anything else on the stands. In the aftermath of the comic-book witch hunts of the 1950s, culminating in Senate hearings on the correlation between comic-book reading and juvenile delinquency, super-hero stories had been well and properly neutered. The typical super hero of the day seldom used his great powers to grapple with an enemy directly, but instead relied on them to solve intricate puzzles provided by the villain, or to safeguard the secret of their dual identities. But the Fantastic Four had no dual identities—their true names were known to one and all. As was their address—in an inspired move, after a short false start, Lee and Kirby set the FF's adventures against the backdrop of New York City, rather than a fictitious Gotham or Metropolis.

And the FF were less about puzzle-solving and more about action. Boundless action-flying, grappling, punching, smashing, hurling, falling—always at the outer edge of the extreme, always with as much kineticism as could be mustered. Where the DC super heroes had been about intellect and restraint, the Marvel characters were all about emotion and impact and release. This struck quite a chord with a whole generation that was slowly making its way out of the conformist '50s into the free-spirited '60s.

As the decade went on, Kirby's work in particular grew bigger and broader. He was a font of ideas, almost always with a super-scientific backdrop, almost always mind-blowing in their scale. Reading FANTASTIC FOUR was like taking your drug of choice, and being transported to realms beyond the everyday, where anything was possible. And yet, within that, the core essence of the characters was always allowed to shine through. The fact that this was, in essence, a white-collar middle American family was never lost along the way, and the big moments were always balanced by the small touches of humanity. Lee maintained a level of irreverent humor in his scripting, a satiric voice that communicated a knowing wink to the reader, despite all of the Sturm und Drang, that he wasn't taking all of these goings-on completely seriously.

Now, more than forty years have passed, and the innovations wrought by FANTASTIC FOUR in its heyday have become the underpinnings of industry standard. Time has moved on, and the Fantastic Four have moved with it, in four

decades of monthly releases telling their tales. It's difficult for any one volume to capture the sum totality of a series so long-lived, but we hope our meager assemblage of stories conveys at least a portion of the heights to which it has ascended over the years. For, as Stan first christened it on an early issue, and despite more modern titles that might momentarily eclipse it, FANTASTIC FOUR remains "The World's Greatest Comic Magazine."

Tom Brevoort
Editor, Fantastic Four

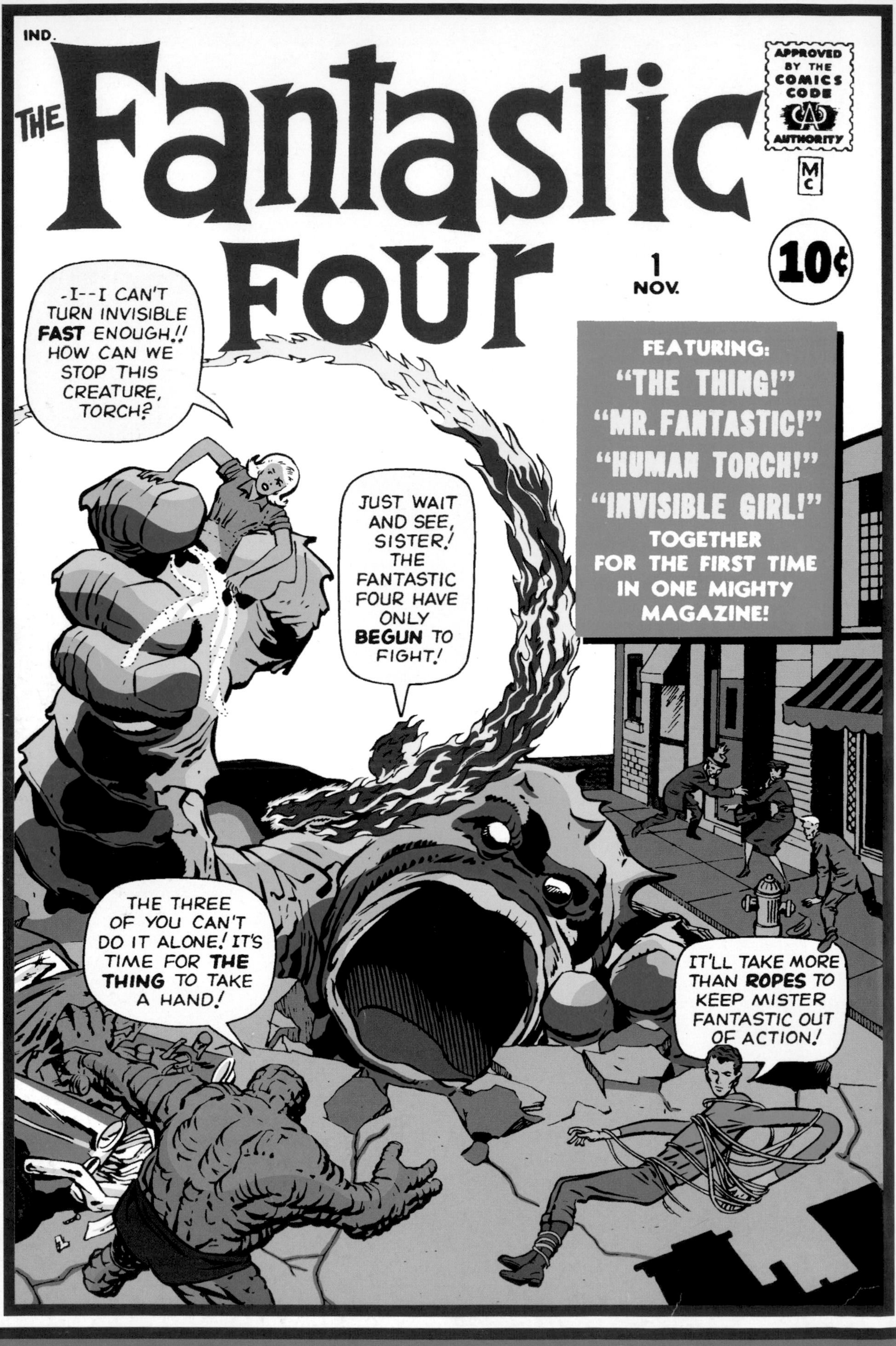

IND.
THE Fantastic FOUR
APPROVED BY THE COMICS CODE AUTHORITY
MC
1 NOV.
10¢
-I--I CAN'T TURN INVISIBLE FAST ENOUGH!! HOW CAN WE STOP THIS CREATURE, TORCH?
FEATURING: "THE THING!" "MR. FANTASTIC!" "HUMAN TORCH!" "INVISIBLE GIRL!" TOGETHER FOR THE FIRST TIME IN ONE MIGHTY MAGAZINE!
JUST WAIT AND SEE, SISTER! THE FANTASTIC FOUR HAVE ONLY BEGUN TO FIGHT!
THE THREE OF YOU CAN'T DO IT ALONE! IT'S TIME FOR THE THING TO TAKE A HAND!
IT'LL TAKE MORE THAN ROPES TO KEEP MISTER FANTASTIC OUT OF ACTION!

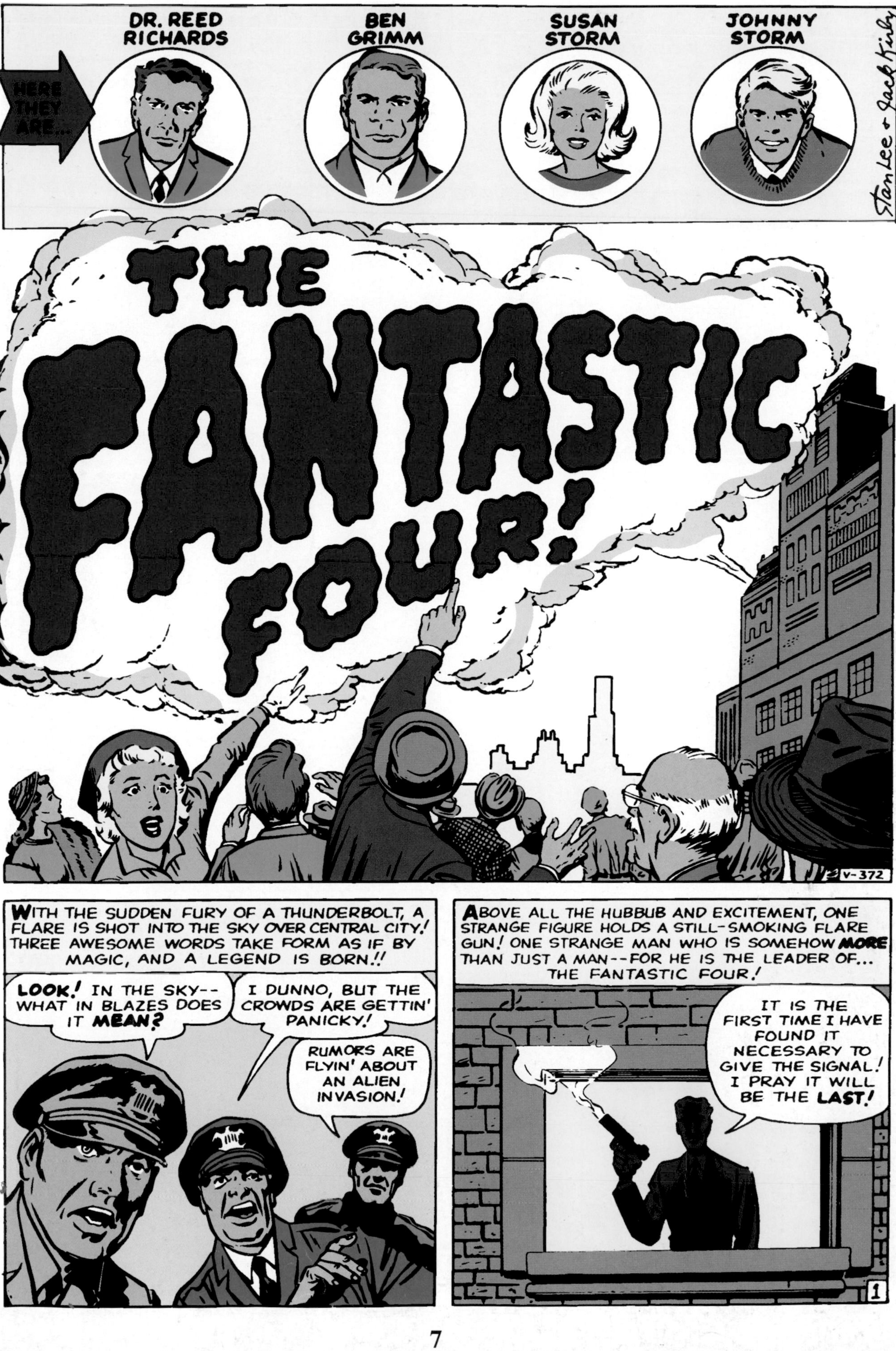
DR. REED RICHARDS
BEN GRIMM
SUSAN STORM
JOHNNY STORM
HERE THEY ARE...
Stan Lee + Jack Kirby
THE FANTASTIC FOUR!
V-372
WITH THE SUDDEN FURY OF A THUNDERBOLT, A FLARE IS SHOT INTO THE SKY OVER CENTRAL CITY! THREE AWESOME WORDS TAKE FORM AS IF BY MAGIC, AND A LEGEND IS BORN!!
LOOK! IN THE SKY-- WHAT IN BLAZES DOES IT MEAN?
I DUNNO, BUT THE CROWDS ARE GETTIN' PANICKY!
RUMORS ARE FLYIN' ABOUT AN ALIEN INVASION!
ABOVE ALL THE HUBBUB AND EXCITEMENT, ONE STRANGE FIGURE HOLDS A STILL-SMOKING FLARE GUN! ONE STRANGE MAN WHO IS SOMEHOW MORE THAN JUST A MAN--FOR HE IS THE LEADER OF... THE FANTASTIC FOUR!
IT IS THE FIRST TIME I HAVE FOUND IT NECESSARY TO GIVE THE SIGNAL! I PRAY IT WILL BE THE LAST!
1

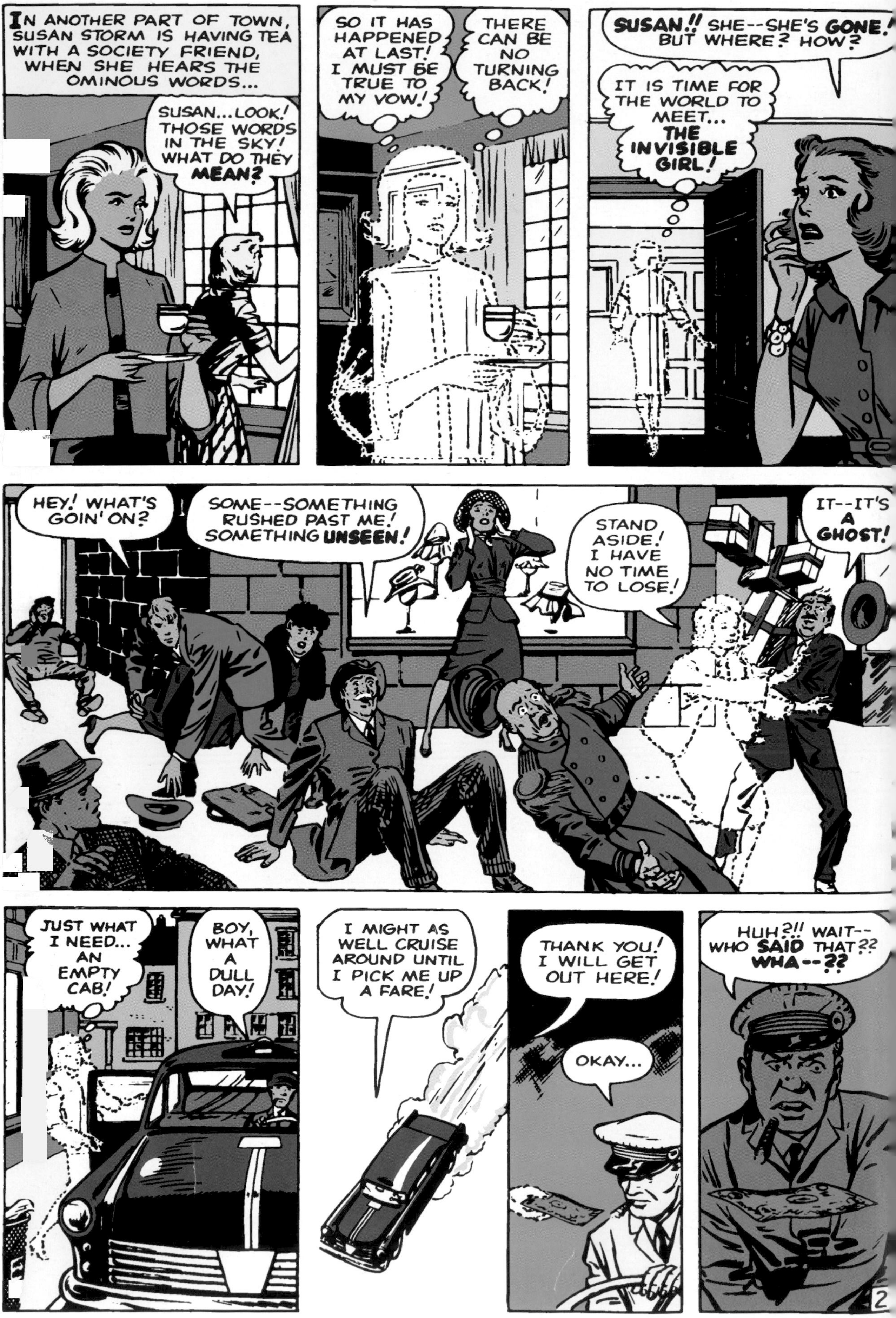
IN ANOTHER PART OF TOWN, SUSAN STORM IS HAVING TEA WITH A SOCIETY FRIEND, WHEN SHE HEARS THE OMINOUS WORDS...
SUSAN...LOOK! THOSE WORDS IN THE SKY! WHAT DO THEY MEAN?
SO IT HAS HAPPENED AT LAST! I MUST BE TRUE TO MY VOW!
THERE CAN BE NO TURNING BACK!
SUSAN!! SHE--SHE'S GONE! BUT WHERE? HOW?
IT IS TIME FOR THE WORLD TO MEET... THE INVISIBLE GIRL!
HEY! WHAT'S GOIN' ON?
SOME--SOMETHING RUSHED PAST ME! SOMETHING UNSEEN!
STAND ASIDE! I HAVE NO TIME TO LOSE!
IT--IT'S A GHOST!
JUST WHAT I NEED... AN EMPTY CAB!
BOY, WHAT A DULL DAY!
I MIGHT AS WELL CRUISE AROUND UNTIL I PICK ME UP A FARE!
THANK YOU! I WILL GET OUT HERE!
OKAY...
HUH?!! WAIT-- WHO SAID THAT?? WHA--??
2

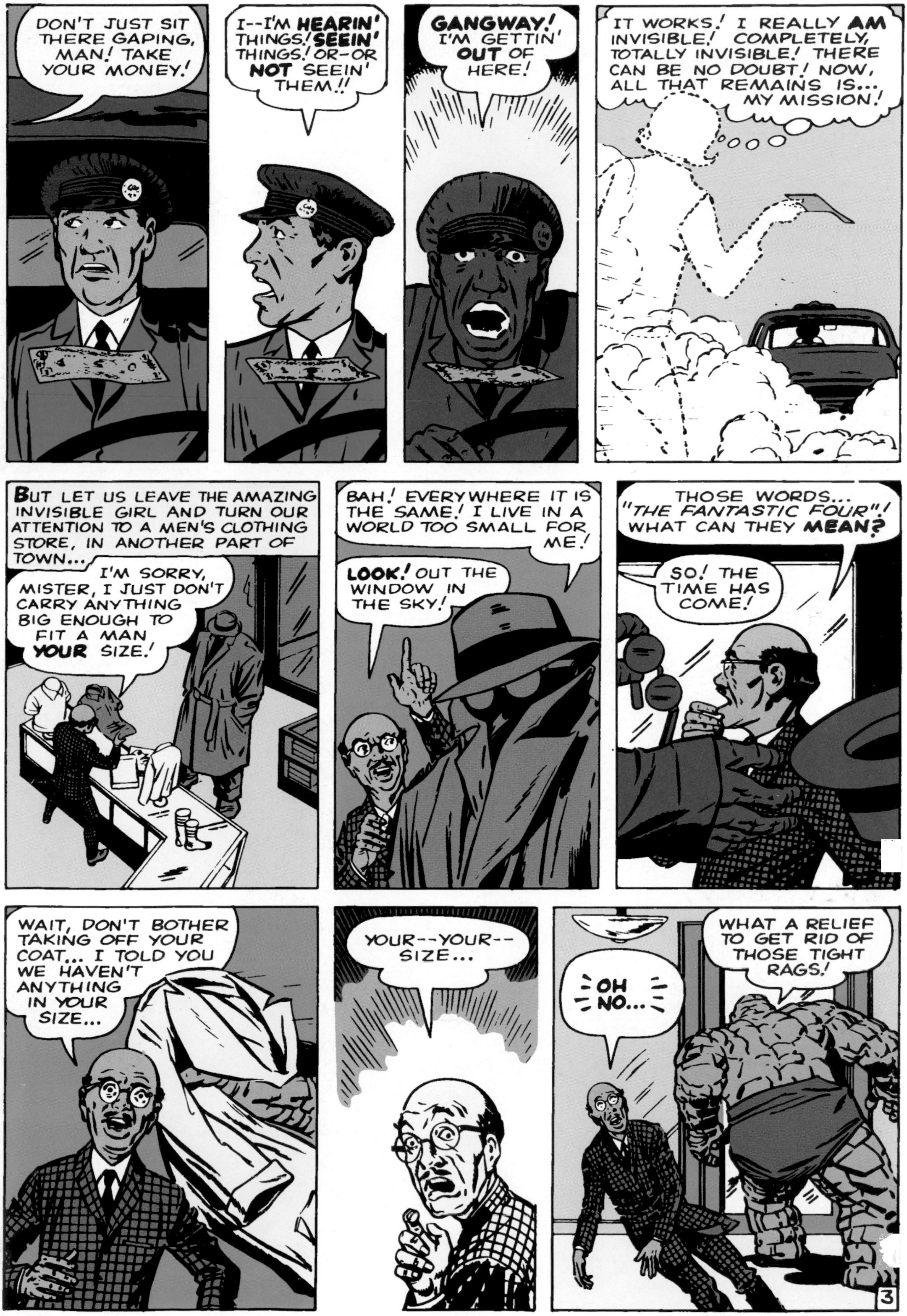
DON'T JUST SIT THERE GAPING, MAN! TAKE YOUR MONEY!
I--I'M HEARIN' THINGS! SEEIN' THINGS! OR--OR NOT SEEIN' THEM!!
GANGWAY! I'M GETTIN' OUT OF HERE!
IT WORKS! I REALLY AM INVISIBLE! COMPLETELY, TOTALLY INVISIBLE! THERE CAN BE NO DOUBT! NOW, ALL THAT REMAINS IS... MY MISSION!
BUT LET US LEAVE THE AMAZING INVISIBLE GIRL AND TURN OUR ATTENTION TO A MEN'S CLOTHING STORE, IN ANOTHER PART OF TOWN...
I'M SORRY, MISTER, I JUST DON'T CARRY ANYTHING BIG ENOUGH TO FIT A MAN YOUR SIZE!
BAH! EVERYWHERE IT IS THE SAME! I LIVE IN A WORLD TOO SMALL FOR ME!
LOOK! OUT THE WINDOW IN THE SKY!
THOSE WORDS... "THE FANTASTIC FOUR"! WHAT CAN THEY MEAN?
SO! THE TIME HAS COME!
WAIT, DON'T BOTHER TAKING OFF YOUR COAT... I TOLD YOU WE HAVEN'T ANYTHING IN YOUR SIZE...
YOUR--YOUR--SIZE...
OH NO...
WHAT A RELIEF TO GET RID OF THOSE TIGHT RAGS!
3

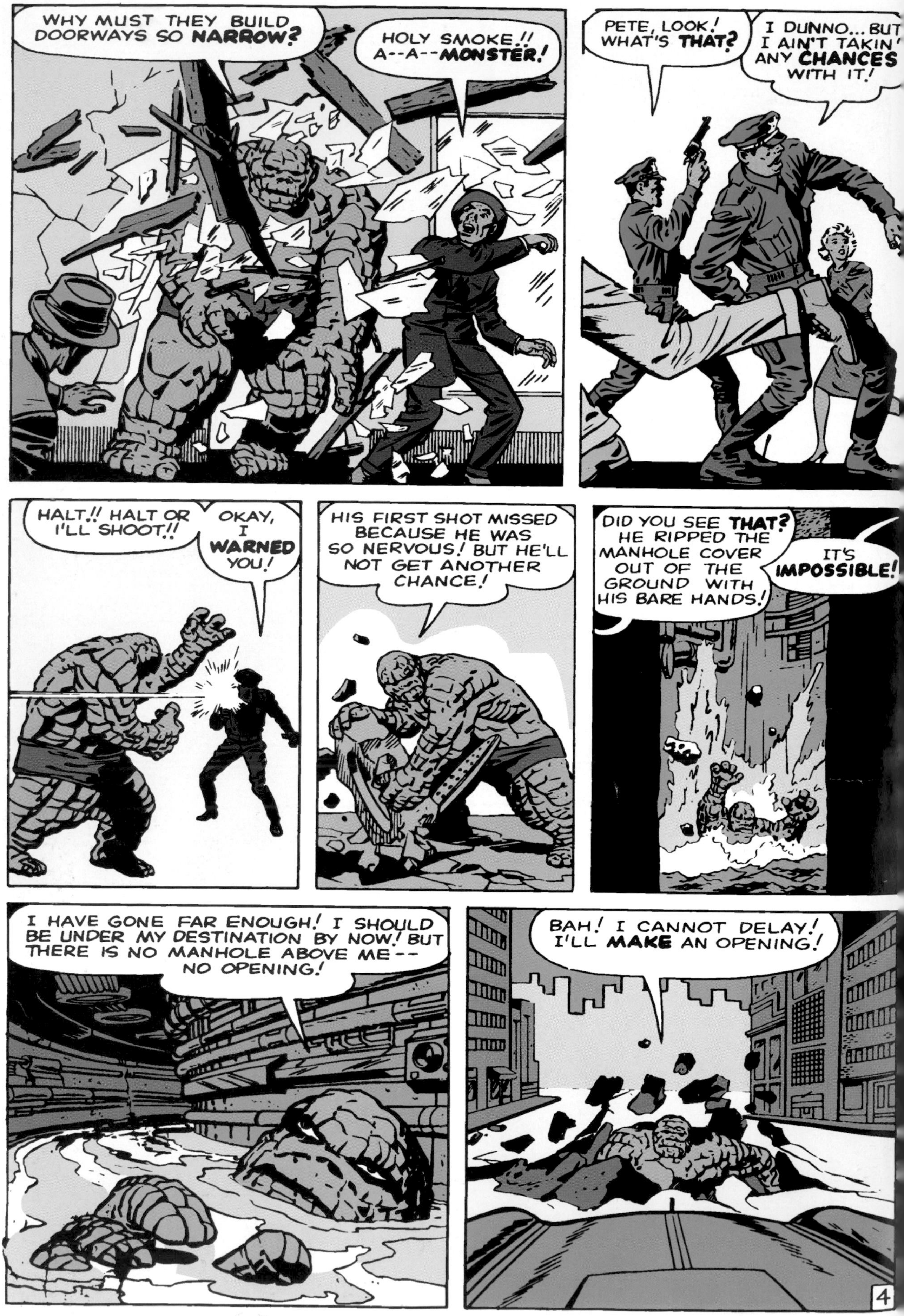
WHY MUST THEY BUILD DOORWAYS SO NARROW?
HOLY SMOKE!! A--A--MONSTER!
PETE, LOOK! WHAT'S THAT?
I DUNNO... BUT I AIN'T TAKIN' ANY CHANCES WITH IT!
HALT!! HALT OR I'LL SHOOT!!
OKAY, I WARNED YOU!
HIS FIRST SHOT MISSED BECAUSE HE WAS SO NERVOUS! BUT HE'LL NOT GET ANOTHER CHANCE!
DID YOU SEE THAT? HE RIPPED THE MANHOLE COVER OUT OF THE GROUND WITH HIS BARE HANDS!
IT'S IMPOSSIBLE!
I HAVE GONE FAR ENOUGH! I SHOULD BE UNDER MY DESTINATION BY NOW! BUT THERE IS NO MANHOLE ABOVE ME-- NO OPENING!
BAH! I CANNOT DELAY! I'LL MAKE AN OPENING!
4

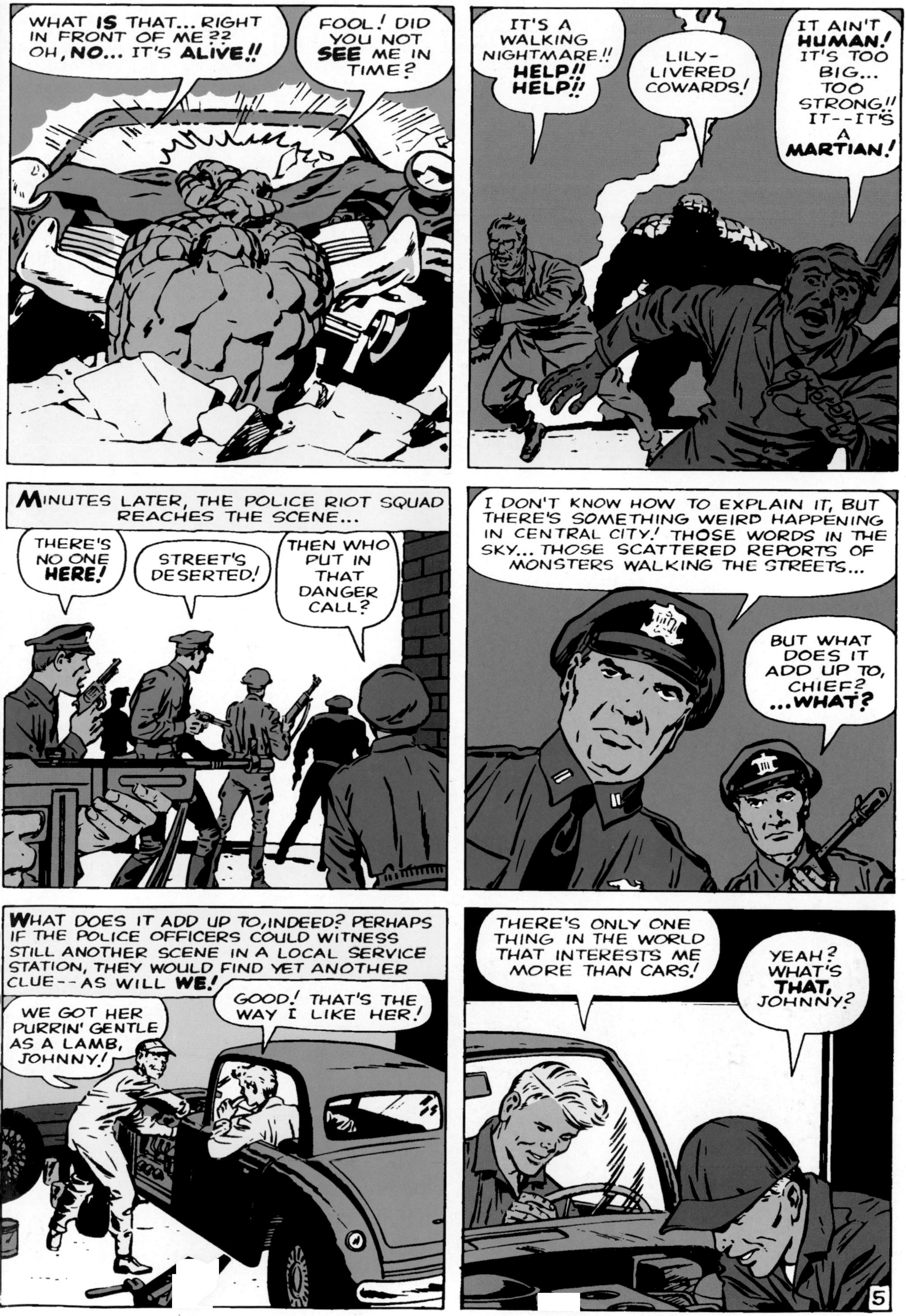
WHAT IS THAT... RIGHT IN FRONT OF ME?? OH, NO... IT'S ALIVE!!
FOOL! DID YOU NOT SEE ME IN TIME?
IT'S A WALKING NIGHTMARE!! HELP!! HELP!!
LILY-LIVERED COWARDS!
IT AIN'T HUMAN! IT'S TOO BIG... TOO STRONG!! IT--IT'S A MARTIAN!
MINUTES LATER, THE POLICE RIOT SQUAD REACHES THE SCENE...
THERE'S NO ONE HERE!
STREET'S DESERTED!
THEN WHO PUT IN THAT DANGER CALL?
I DON'T KNOW HOW TO EXPLAIN IT, BUT THERE'S SOMETHING WEIRD HAPPENING IN CENTRAL CITY! THOSE WORDS IN THE SKY... THOSE SCATTERED REPORTS OF MONSTERS WALKING THE STREETS...
BUT WHAT DOES IT ADD UP TO, CHIEF? ...WHAT?
WHAT DOES IT ADD UP TO, INDEED? PERHAPS IF THE POLICE OFFICERS COULD WITNESS STILL ANOTHER SCENE IN A LOCAL SERVICE STATION, THEY WOULD FIND YET ANOTHER CLUE--AS WILL WE!
WE GOT HER PURRIN' GENTLE AS A LAMB, JOHNNY!
GOOD! THAT'S THE WAY I LIKE HER!
THERE'S ONLY ONE THING IN THE WORLD THAT INTERESTS ME MORE THAN CARS!
YEAH? WHAT'S THAT, JOHNNY?
5

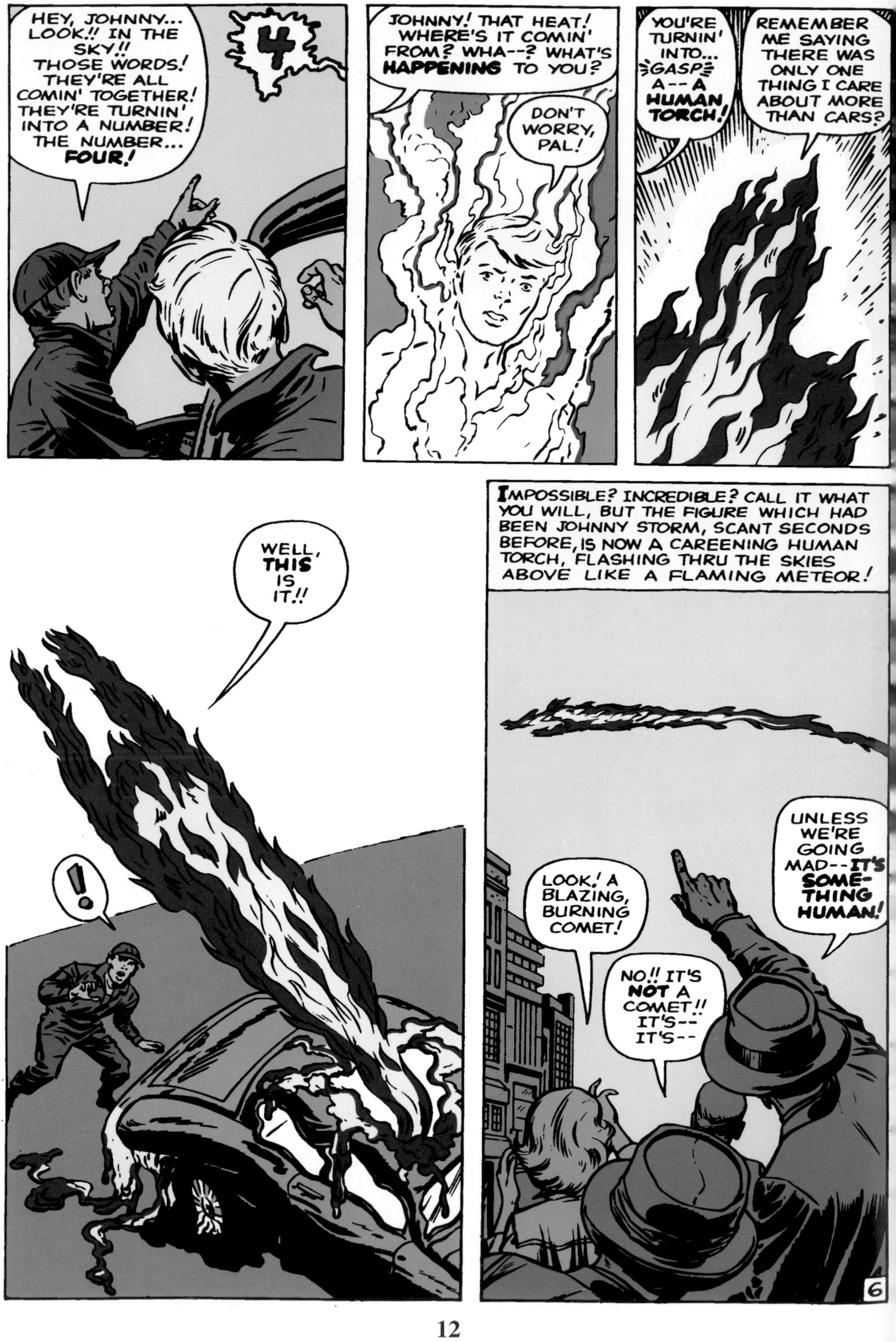
HEY, JOHNNY... LOOK!! IN THE SKY!! THOSE WORDS! THEY'RE ALL COMIN' TOGETHER! THEY'RE TURNIN' INTO A NUMBER! THE NUMBER... FOUR!
4
JOHNNY! THAT HEAT! WHERE'S IT COMIN' FROM? WHA--? WHAT'S HAPPENING TO YOU?
DON'T WORRY, PAL!
YOU'RE TURNIN' INTO... GASP A--A HUMAN TORCH!
REMEMBER ME SAYING THERE WAS ONLY ONE THING I CARE ABOUT MORE THAN CARS?
WELL, THIS IS IT!!
!
IMPOSSIBLE? INCREDIBLE? CALL IT WHAT YOU WILL, BUT THE FIGURE WHICH HAD BEEN JOHNNY STORM, SCANT SECONDS BEFORE, IS NOW A CAREENING HUMAN TORCH, FLASHING THRU THE SKIES ABOVE LIKE A FLAMING METEOR!
LOOK! A BLAZING, BURNING COMET!
NO!! IT'S NOT A COMET!! IT'S-- IT'S--
UNLESS WE'RE GOING MAD--IT'S SOMETHING HUMAN!
6

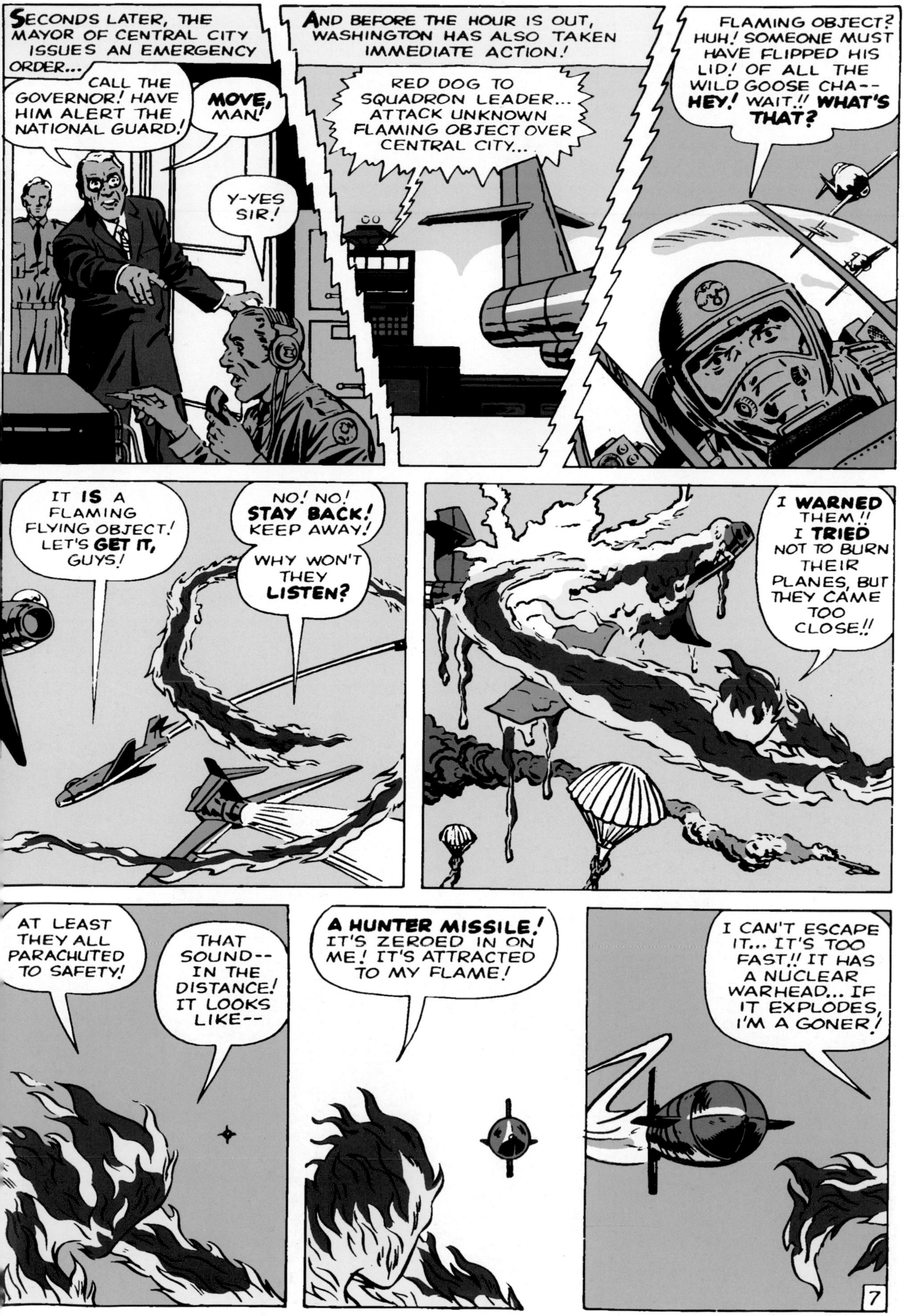
SECONDS LATER, THE MAYOR OF CENTRAL CITY ISSUES AN EMERGENCY ORDER...
CALL THE GOVERNOR! HAVE HIM ALERT THE NATIONAL GUARD!
MOVE, MAN!
Y-YES SIR!
AND BEFORE THE HOUR IS OUT, WASHINGTON HAS ALSO TAKEN IMMEDIATE ACTION!
RED DOG TO SQUADRON LEADER... ATTACK UNKNOWN FLAMING OBJECT OVER CENTRAL CITY...
FLAMING OBJECT? HUH! SOMEONE MUST HAVE FLIPPED HIS LID! OF ALL THE WILD GOOSE CHA-- HEY! WAIT!! WHAT'S THAT?
IT IS A FLAMING FLYING OBJECT! LET'S GET IT, GUYS!
NO! NO! STAY BACK! KEEP AWAY!
WHY WON'T THEY LISTEN?
I WARNED THEM!! I TRIED NOT TO BURN THEIR PLANES, BUT THEY CAME TOO CLOSE!!
AT LEAST THEY ALL PARACHUTED TO SAFETY!
THAT SOUND-- IN THE DISTANCE! IT LOOKS LIKE--
A HUNTER MISSILE! IT'S ZEROED IN ON ME! IT'S ATTRACTED TO MY FLAME!
I CAN'T ESCAPE IT... IT'S TOO FAST!! IT HAS A NUCLEAR WARHEAD... IF IT EXPLODES, I'M A GONER!
7

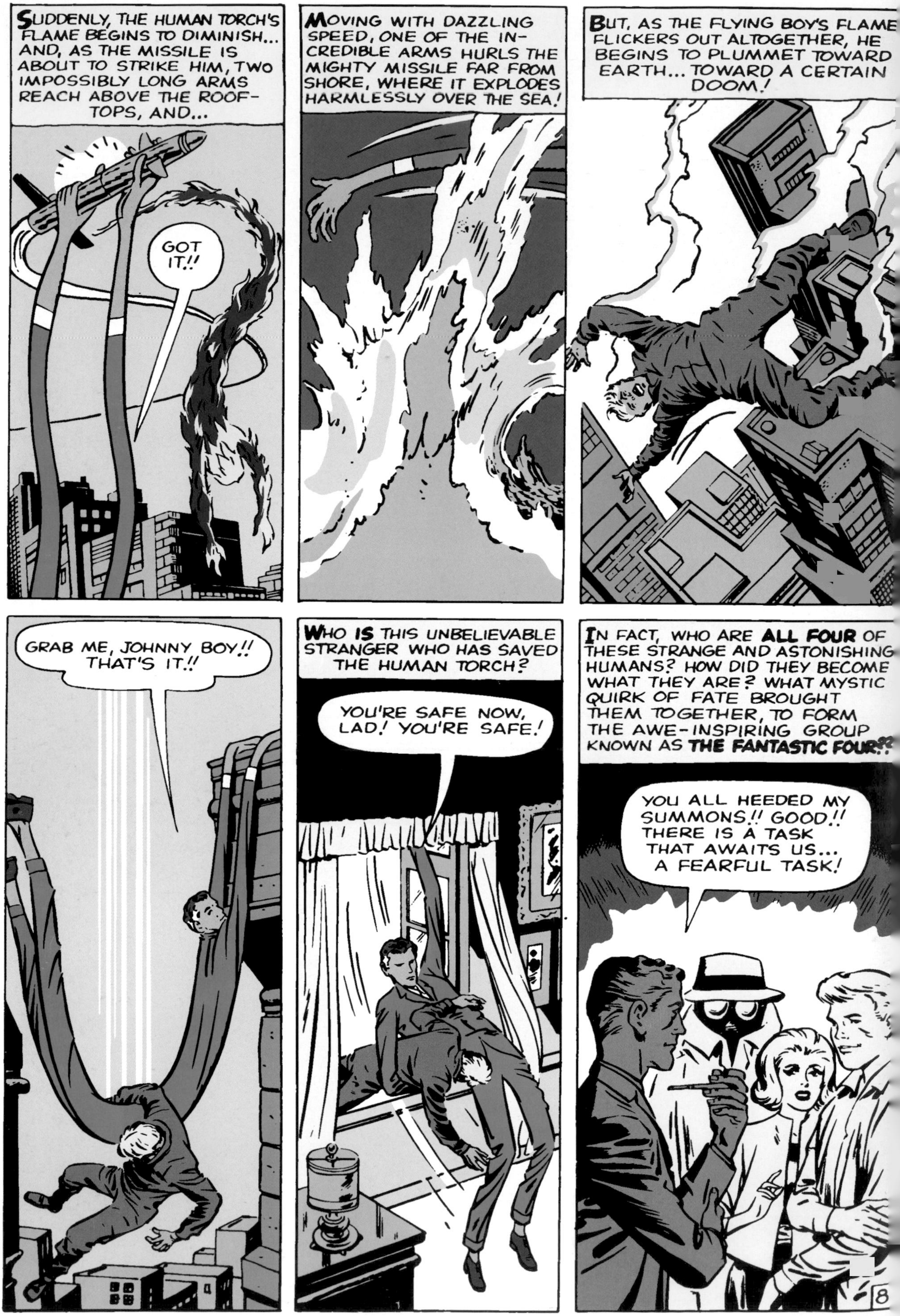
SUDDENLY, THE HUMAN TORCH'S FLAME BEGINS TO DIMINISH... AND, AS THE MISSILE IS ABOUT TO STRIKE HIM, TWO IMPOSSIBLY LONG ARMS REACH ABOVE THE ROOF-TOPS, AND...
GOT IT!!
MOVING WITH DAZZLING SPEED, ONE OF THE IN-CREDIBLE ARMS HURLS THE MIGHTY MISSILE FAR FROM SHORE, WHERE IT EXPLODES HARMLESSLY OVER THE SEA!
BUT, AS THE FLYING BOY'S FLAME FLICKERS OUT ALTOGETHER, HE BEGINS TO PLUMMET TOWARD EARTH... TOWARD A CERTAIN DOOM!
GRAB ME, JOHNNY BOY!! THAT'S IT!!
WHO IS THIS UNBELIEVABLE STRANGER WHO HAS SAVED THE HUMAN TORCH?
YOU'RE SAFE NOW, LAD! YOU'RE SAFE!
IN FACT, WHO ARE ALL FOUR OF THESE STRANGE AND ASTONISHING HUMANS? HOW DID THEY BECOME WHAT THEY ARE? WHAT MYSTIC QUIRK OF FATE BROUGHT THEM TOGETHER, TO FORM THE AWE-INSPIRING GROUP KNOWN AS THE FANTASTIC FOUR??
YOU ALL HEEDED MY SUMMONS!! GOOD!! THERE IS A TASK THAT AWAITS US... A FEARFUL TASK!
8

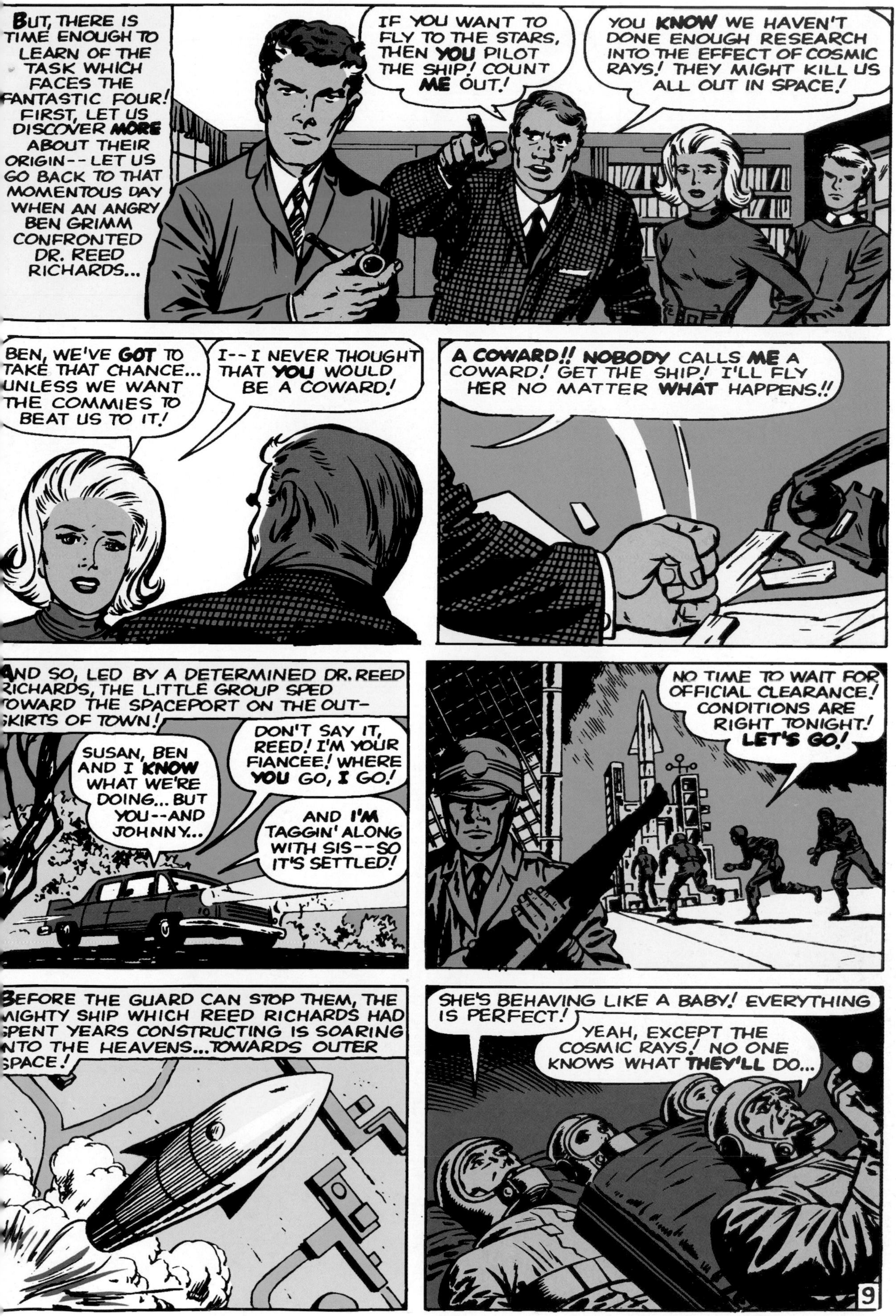
BUT, THERE IS TIME ENOUGH TO LEARN OF THE TASK WHICH FACES THE FANTASTIC FOUR! FIRST, LET US DISCOVER MORE ABOUT THEIR ORIGIN-- LET US GO BACK TO THAT MOMENTOUS DAY WHEN AN ANGRY BEN GRIMM CONFRONTED DR. REED RICHARDS...
IF YOU WANT TO FLY TO THE STARS, THEN YOU PILOT THE SHIP! COUNT ME OUT!
YOU KNOW WE HAVEN'T DONE ENOUGH RESEARCH INTO THE EFFECT OF COSMIC RAYS! THEY MIGHT KILL US ALL OUT IN SPACE!
BEN, WE'VE GOT TO TAKE THAT CHANCE... UNLESS WE WANT THE COMMIES TO BEAT US TO IT!
I-- I NEVER THOUGHT THAT YOU WOULD BE A COWARD!
A COWARD!! NOBODY CALLS ME A COWARD! GET THE SHIP! I'LL FLY HER NO MATTER WHAT HAPPENS!!
AND SO, LED BY A DETERMINED DR. REED RICHARDS, THE LITTLE GROUP SPED TOWARD THE SPACEPORT ON THE OUTSKIRTS OF TOWN!
SUSAN, BEN AND I KNOW WHAT WE'RE DOING... BUT YOU--AND JOHNNY...
DON'T SAY IT, REED! I'M YOUR FIANCEE! WHERE YOU GO, I GO!
AND I'M TAGGIN' ALONG WITH SIS--SO IT'S SETTLED!
NO TIME TO WAIT FOR OFFICIAL CLEARANCE! CONDITIONS ARE RIGHT TONIGHT! LET'S GO!
BEFORE THE GUARD CAN STOP THEM, THE MIGHTY SHIP WHICH REED RICHARDS HAD SPENT YEARS CONSTRUCTING IS SOARING INTO THE HEAVENS... TOWARDS OUTER SPACE!
SHE'S BEHAVING LIKE A BABY! EVERYTHING IS PERFECT!
YEAH, EXCEPT THE COSMIC RAYS! NO ONE KNOWS WHAT THEY'LL DO...
9

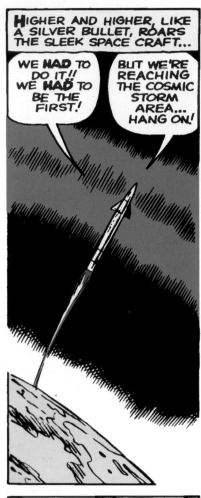

HIGHER AND HIGHER, LIKE A SILVER BULLET, ROARS THE SLEEK SPACE CRAFT...

WE **HAD** TO DO IT!! WE **HAD** TO BE THE FIRST!

BUT WE'RE REACHING THE COSMIC STORM AREA... HANG ON!

RAK TAC TAC TAC TAC

HEAR **THAT**?? IT'S THE **COSMIC RAYS**!! I--I **WARNED** YOU ABOUT 'EM.!!

THEY'RE PENETRATING THE SHIP!! OUR SHIELDING ISN'T STRONG ENOUGH!

BUT I DON'T **F-EL** ANYTHING!

NATURALLY. THEY'RE ONLY RAYS OF LIGHT! YOU CAN'T FEEL 'EM-- BUT THEY'LL AFFECT YOU JUST THE SAME!

MY HEAD!! IT--IT'S POUNDING AS THOUGH IT'S ABOUT TO BURST!!

BEN WAS **RIGHT!!** WE SHOULD HAVE **WAITED**... SHOULD HAVE GOTTEN HEAVIER SHIELDING!

JOHNNY! WHAT **IS** IT? WHAT'S HAPPENING TO YOU?

I DON'T KNOW, SIS! MY BODY FEELS HOT-- LIKE IT'S ON FIRE!! I-I FEEL LIKE I'M BURNING UP!!

UGH.!! LISTEN TO ME...

...SOMEBODY **ELSE** TAKE THE CONTROLS... I CAN'T HANDLE THE SHIP ANY MORE! MY-- MY ARMS ARE HEAVY-- TOO HEAVY-- CAN'T MOVE-- TOO HEAVY-- GOT TO LIE DOWN-- CAN'T MOVE!!

BEN!

10

16

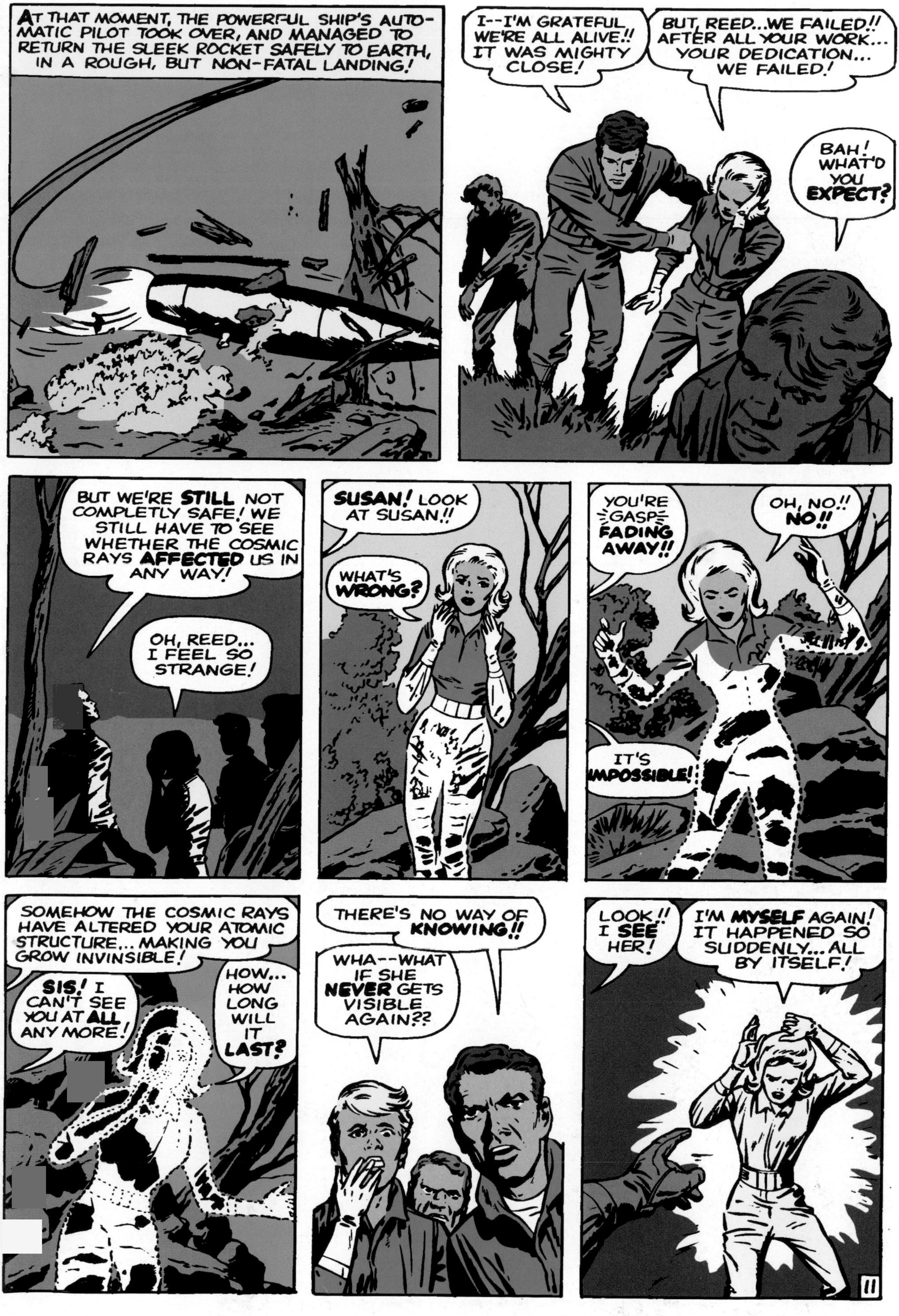
AT THAT MOMENT, THE POWERFUL SHIP'S AUTOMATIC PILOT TOOK OVER, AND MANAGED TO RETURN THE SLEEK ROCKET SAFELY TO EARTH, IN A ROUGH, BUT NON-FATAL LANDING!
I--I'M GRATEFUL WE'RE ALL ALIVE!! IT WAS MIGHTY CLOSE!
BUT, REED...WE FAILED!! AFTER ALL YOUR WORK... YOUR DEDICATION... WE FAILED!
BAH! WHAT'D YOU EXPECT?
BUT WE'RE STILL NOT COMPLETLY SAFE! WE STILL HAVE TO SEE WHETHER THE COSMIC RAYS AFFECTED US IN ANY WAY!
OH, REED... I FEEL SO STRANGE!
SUSAN! LOOK AT SUSAN!!
WHAT'S WRONG?
YOU'RE -GASP- FADING AWAY!!
OH, NO!! NO!!
IT'S IMPOSSIBLE!
SOMEHOW THE COSMIC RAYS HAVE ALTERED YOUR ATOMIC STRUCTURE...MAKING YOU GROW INVINSIBLE!
SIS! I CAN'T SEE YOU AT ALL ANY MORE!
HOW... HOW LONG WILL IT LAST?
THERE'S NO WAY OF KNOWING!!
WHA--WHAT IF SHE NEVER GETS VISIBLE AGAIN??
LOOK!! I SEE HER!
I'M MYSELF AGAIN! IT HAPPENED SO SUDDENLY...ALL BY ITSELF!
11

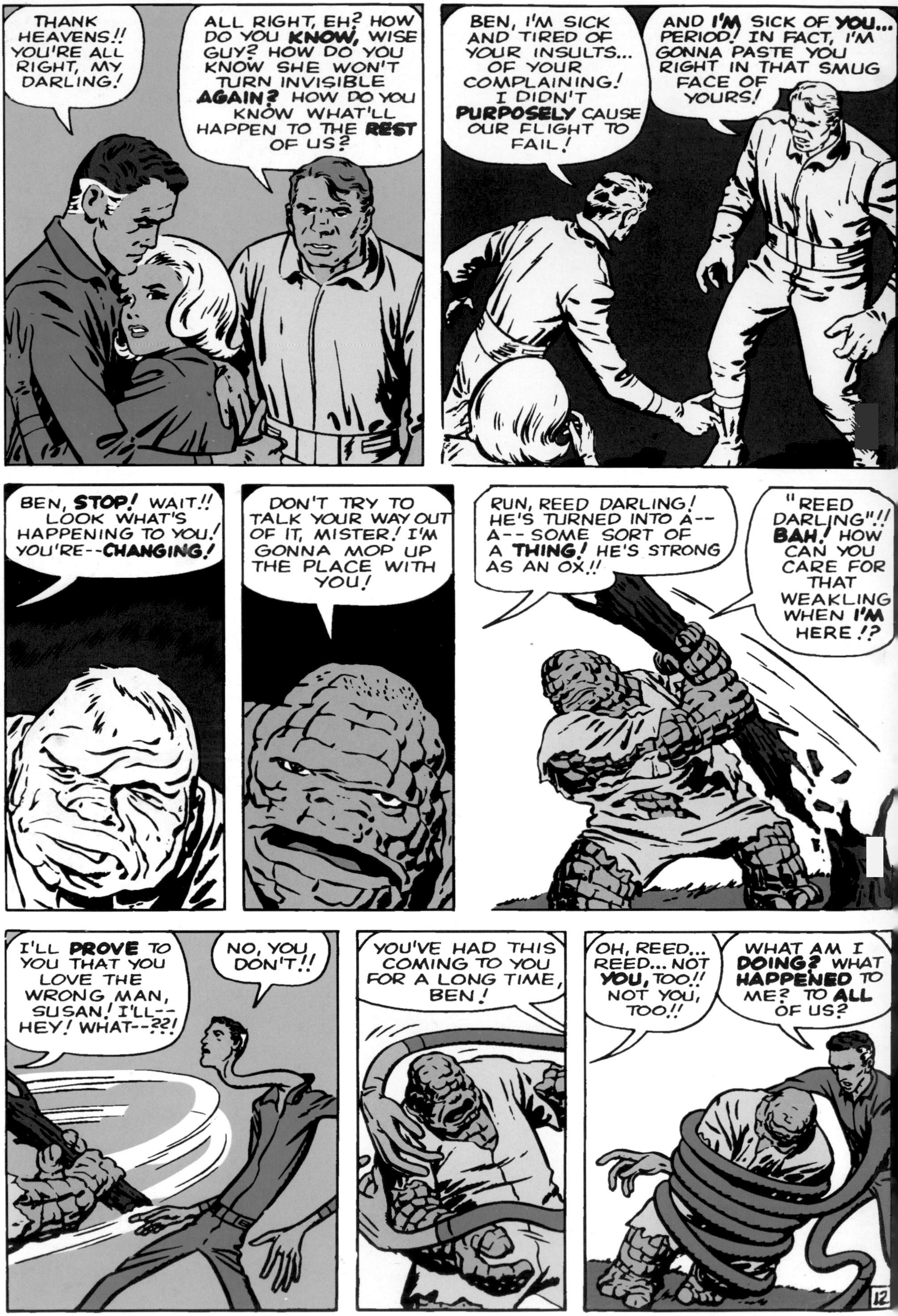
THANK HEAVENS!! YOU'RE ALL RIGHT, MY DARLING!
ALL RIGHT, EH? HOW DO YOU KNOW, WISE GUY? HOW DO YOU KNOW SHE WON'T TURN INVISIBLE AGAIN? HOW DO YOU KNOW WHAT'LL HAPPEN TO THE REST OF US?
BEN, I'M SICK AND TIRED OF YOUR INSULTS... OF YOUR COMPLAINING! I DIDN'T PURPOSELY CAUSE OUR FLIGHT TO FAIL!
AND I'M SICK OF YOU... PERIOD! IN FACT, I'M GONNA PASTE YOU RIGHT IN THAT SMUG FACE OF YOURS!
BEN, STOP! WAIT!! LOOK WHAT'S HAPPENING TO YOU! YOU'RE--CHANGING!
DON'T TRY TO TALK YOUR WAY OUT OF IT, MISTER! I'M GONNA MOP UP THE PLACE WITH YOU!
RUN, REED DARLING! HE'S TURNED INTO A-- A--SOME SORT OF A THING! HE'S STRONG AS AN OX!!
"REED DARLING"!! BAH! HOW CAN YOU CARE FOR THAT WEAKLING WHEN I'M HERE!?
I'LL PROVE TO YOU THAT YOU LOVE THE WRONG MAN, SUSAN! I'LL-- HEY! WHAT--??!
NO, YOU DON'T!!
YOU'VE HAD THIS COMING TO YOU FOR A LONG TIME, BEN!
OH, REED... REED... NOT YOU, TOO!! NOT YOU, TOO!!
WHAT AM I DOING? WHAT HAPPENED TO ME? TO ALL OF US?
12

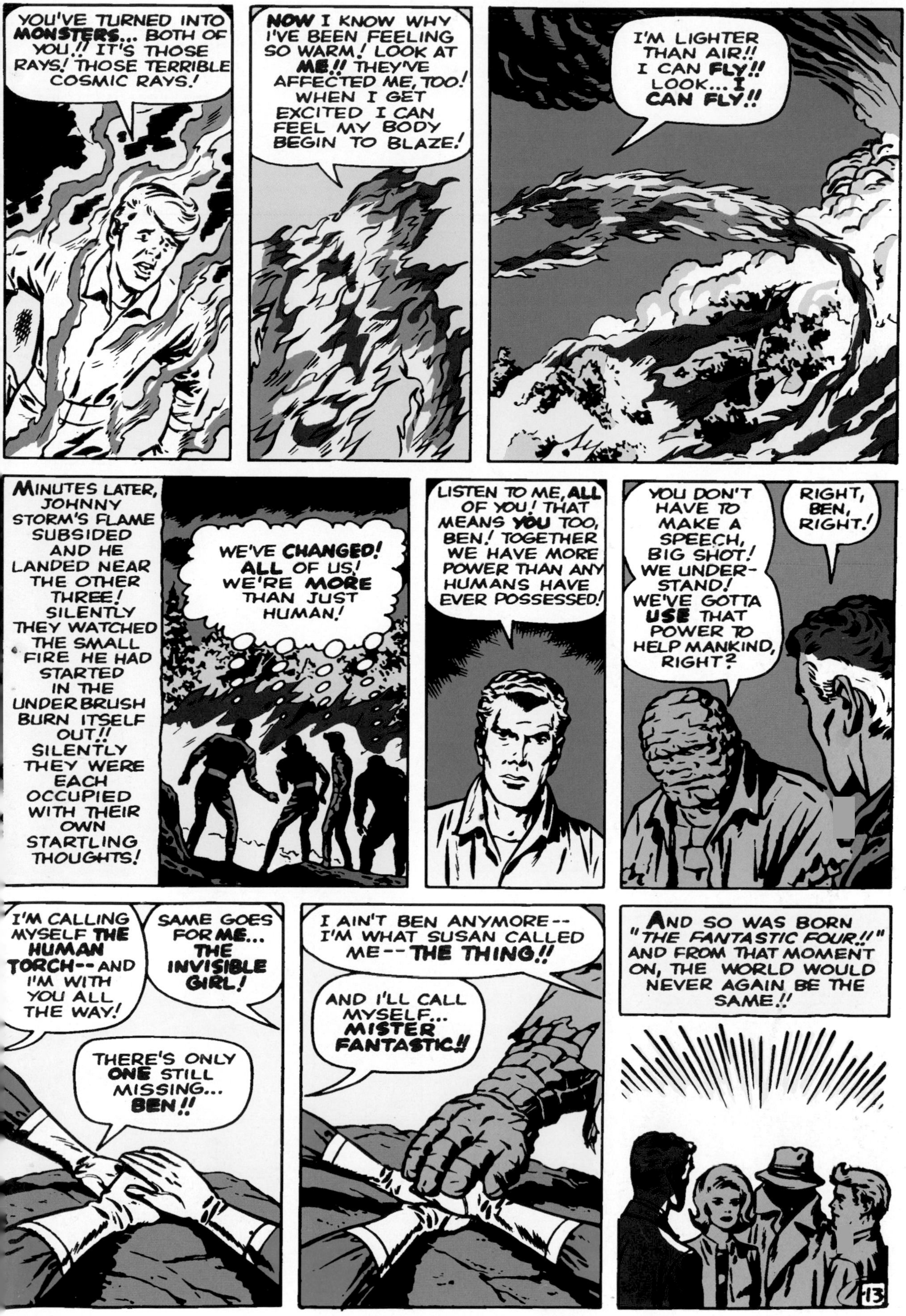

YOU'VE TURNED INTO MONSTERS... BOTH OF YOU!! IT'S THOSE RAYS! THOSE TERRIBLE COSMIC RAYS!
NOW I KNOW WHY I'VE BEEN FEELING SO WARM! LOOK AT ME!! THEY'VE AFFECTED ME, TOO! WHEN I GET EXCITED I CAN FEEL MY BODY BEGIN TO BLAZE!
I'M LIGHTER THAN AIR!! I CAN FLY!! LOOK... I CAN FLY!!
MINUTES LATER, JOHNNY STORM'S FLAME SUBSIDED AND HE LANDED NEAR THE OTHER THREE! SILENTLY THEY WATCHED THE SMALL FIRE HE HAD STARTED IN THE UNDERBRUSH BURN ITSELF OUT!! SILENTLY THEY WERE EACH OCCUPIED WITH THEIR OWN STARTLING THOUGHTS!
WE'VE CHANGED! ALL OF US! WE'RE MORE THAN JUST HUMAN!
LISTEN TO ME, ALL OF YOU! THAT MEANS YOU TOO, BEN! TOGETHER WE HAVE MORE POWER THAN ANY HUMANS HAVE EVER POSSESSED!
YOU DON'T HAVE TO MAKE A SPEECH, BIG SHOT! WE UNDER-STAND! WE'VE GOTTA USE THAT POWER TO HELP MANKIND, RIGHT?
RIGHT, BEN, RIGHT!
I'M CALLING MYSELF THE HUMAN TORCH-- AND I'M WITH YOU ALL THE WAY!
SAME GOES FOR ME... THE INVISIBLE GIRL!
THERE'S ONLY ONE STILL MISSING... BEN!!
I AIN'T BEN ANYMORE-- I'M WHAT SUSAN CALLED ME-- THE THING!!
AND I'LL CALL MYSELF... MISTER FANTASTIC!!
AND SO WAS BORN "THE FANTASTIC FOUR!!" AND FROM THAT MOMENT ON, THE WORLD WOULD NEVER AGAIN BE THE SAME!!
13

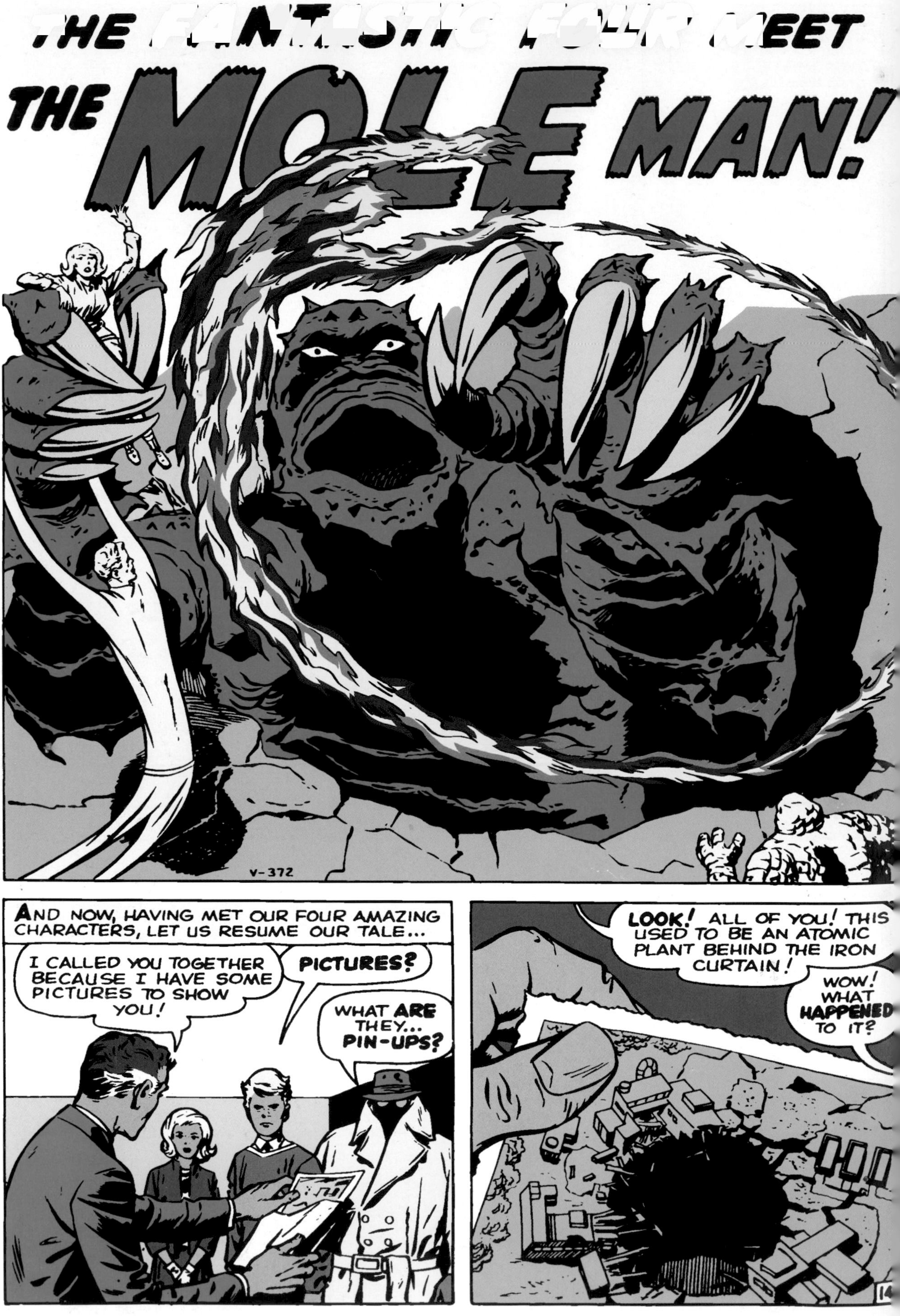
THE FANTASTIC FOUR MEET
THE MOLE MAN!
V-372
AND NOW, HAVING MET OUR FOUR AMAZING CHARACTERS, LET US RESUME OUR TALE...
I CALLED YOU TOGETHER BECAUSE I HAVE SOME PICTURES TO SHOW YOU!
PICTURES?
WHAT ARE THEY... PIN-UPS?
LOOK! ALL OF YOU! THIS USED TO BE AN ATOMIC PLANT BEHIND THE IRON CURTAIN!
WOW! WHAT HAPPENED TO IT?
14

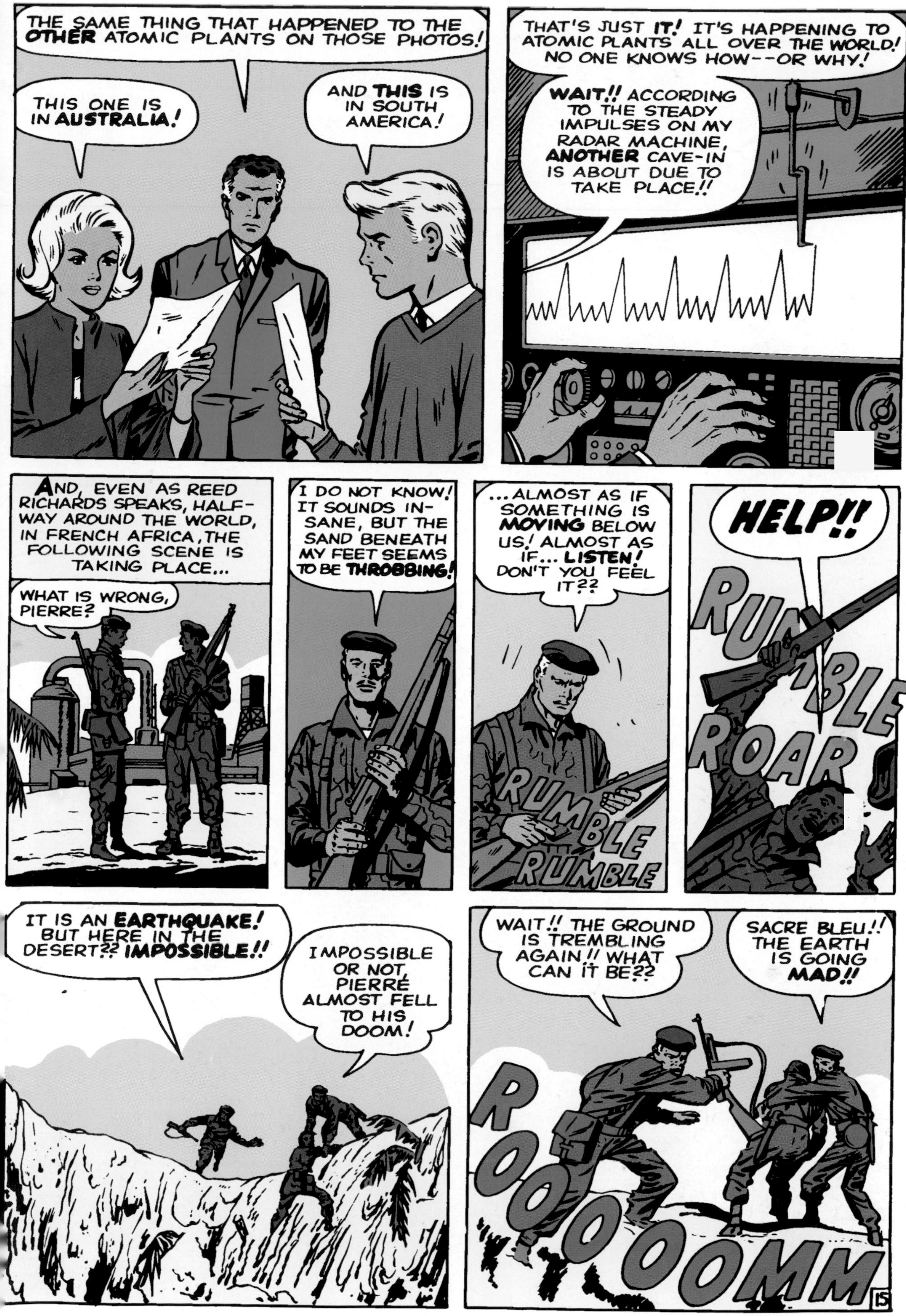
THE SAME THING THAT HAPPENED TO THE OTHER ATOMIC PLANTS ON THOSE PHOTOS!
THIS ONE IS IN AUSTRALIA!
AND THIS IS IN SOUTH AMERICA!
THAT'S JUST IT! IT'S HAPPENING TO ATOMIC PLANTS ALL OVER THE WORLD! NO ONE KNOWS HOW--OR WHY!
WAIT!! ACCORDING TO THE STEADY IMPULSES ON MY RADAR MACHINE, ANOTHER CAVE-IN IS ABOUT DUE TO TAKE PLACE!!
AND, EVEN AS REED RICHARDS SPEAKS, HALF-WAY AROUND THE WORLD, IN FRENCH AFRICA, THE FOLLOWING SCENE IS TAKING PLACE...
WHAT IS WRONG, PIERRE?
I DO NOT KNOW! IT SOUNDS IN-SANE, BUT THE SAND BENEATH MY FEET SEEMS TO BE THROBBING!
...ALMOST AS IF SOMETHING IS MOVING BELOW US! ALMOST AS IF... LISTEN! DON'T YOU FEEL IT??
RUMBLE
RUMBLE
HELP!!
RUMBLE
ROAR
IT IS AN EARTHQUAKE! BUT HERE IN THE DESERT?? IMPOSSIBLE!!
IMPOSSIBLE OR NOT, PIERRE ALMOST FELL TO HIS DOOM!
WAIT!! THE GROUND IS TREMBLING AGAIN!! WHAT CAN IT BE??
SACRE BLEU!! THE EARTH IS GOING MAD!!
ROOOOOOMM
15

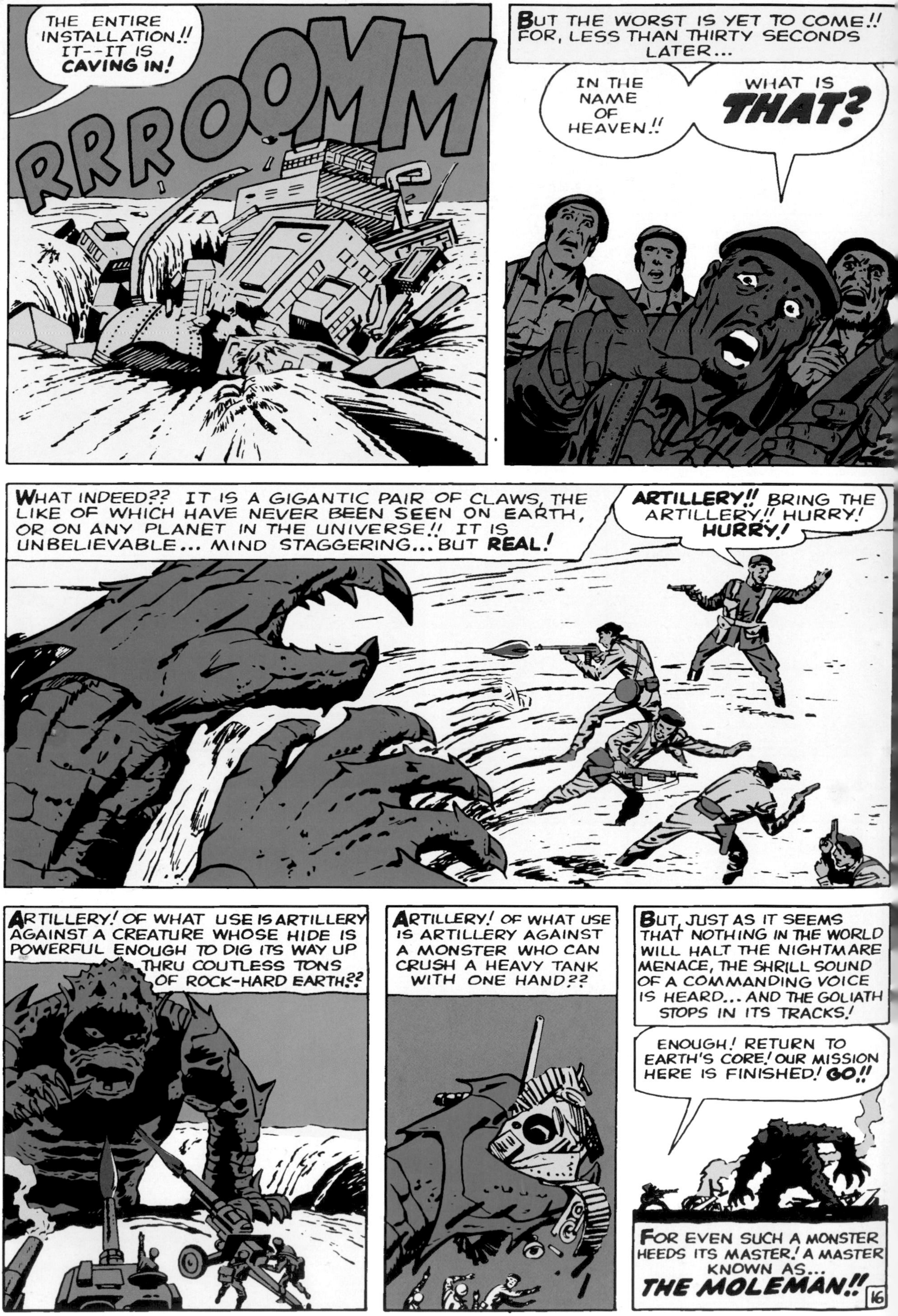
THE ENTIRE INSTALLATION!! IT--IT IS CAVING IN!
RRROOMMM
BUT THE WORST IS YET TO COME!! FOR, LESS THAN THIRTY SECONDS LATER...
IN THE NAME OF HEAVEN!!
WHAT IS THAT?
WHAT INDEED?? IT IS A GIGANTIC PAIR OF CLAWS, THE LIKE OF WHICH HAVE NEVER BEEN SEEN ON EARTH, OR ON ANY PLANET IN THE UNIVERSE!! IT IS UNBELIEVABLE... MIND STAGGERING... BUT REAL!
ARTILLERY!! BRING THE ARTILLERY!! HURRY! HURRY!
ARTILLERY! OF WHAT USE IS ARTILLERY AGAINST A CREATURE WHOSE HIDE IS POWERFUL ENOUGH TO DIG ITS WAY UP THRU COUTLESS TONS OF ROCK-HARD EARTH??
ARTILLERY! OF WHAT USE IS ARTILLERY AGAINST A MONSTER WHO CAN CRUSH A HEAVY TANK WITH ONE HAND??
BUT, JUST AS IT SEEMS THAT NOTHING IN THE WORLD WILL HALT THE NIGHTMARE MENACE, THE SHRILL SOUND OF A COMMANDING VOICE IS HEARD... AND THE GOLIATH STOPS IN ITS TRACKS!
ENOUGH! RETURN TO EARTH'S CORE! OUR MISSION HERE IS FINISHED! GO!!
FOR EVEN SUCH A MONSTER HEEDS ITS MASTER! A MASTER KNOWN AS... THE MOLEMAN!!
16

BUT WE SHALL RETURN TO THE MOLEMAN BEFORE LONG.! FIRST, LET US TURN OUR ATTENTION BACK TO THE FANTASTIC FOUR, AS THEY GAZE IN ASTONISHMENT AT DR. REED RICHARDS' SUPER-SENSITIVE RADARSCOPE...

THERE! IT HAS HAPPENED AGAIN! THIS TIME IN FRENCH EQUITORIAL AFRICA!

BUT HOW? WHY?

THAT'S WHAT WE'VE GOT TO FIND OUT!

BY STUDYING THE CAVE-INS CAREFULLY, I'VE PIN-POINTED AN ISLAND LOCATED EXACTLY BETWEEN THEM! THAT IS WHERE WE WILL FIND OUR ANSWER! IT IS KNOWN AS MONSTER ISLE!

MONSTER ISLE! THAT'S JUST A FAIRY TALE! THERE'S NO SUCH PLACE!

ONLY ONE WAY TO FIND OUT, BEN!

AND FIND OUT THEY DO! HOURS LATER, ABOARD THEIR SMALL, PRIVATE JET, THE FANTASTIC FOUR SEE A STRANGE MOUNTAIN RISING FROM THE SEA, LIKE AN UNEARTHLY GROTESQUE FACE!! THEY HAVE FOUND... MONSTER ISLE!

THERE IT IS!

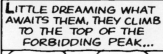

LITTLE DREAMING WHAT AWAITS THEM, THEY CLIMB TO THE TOP OF THE FORBIDDING PEAK...

IF THIS IS JUST A WILD GOOSE CHASE, MISTER, I'LL MAKE SURE YOU LIVE TO REGRET IT!

SAVE YOUR BREATH FOR THE CLIMB, GRUESOME!

HOLD IT!! I HEAR SOMETHING!!

IT'S COMING FROM BELOW!

LOOK!! THOSE EYES...

SUDDENLY, A LIVING THREE-HEADED NIGHTMARE HURLS ITSELF AT THEM FROM OVER THE EDGE OF THE PEAK OF MONSTER ISLE!

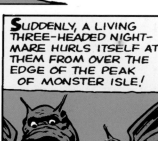

17

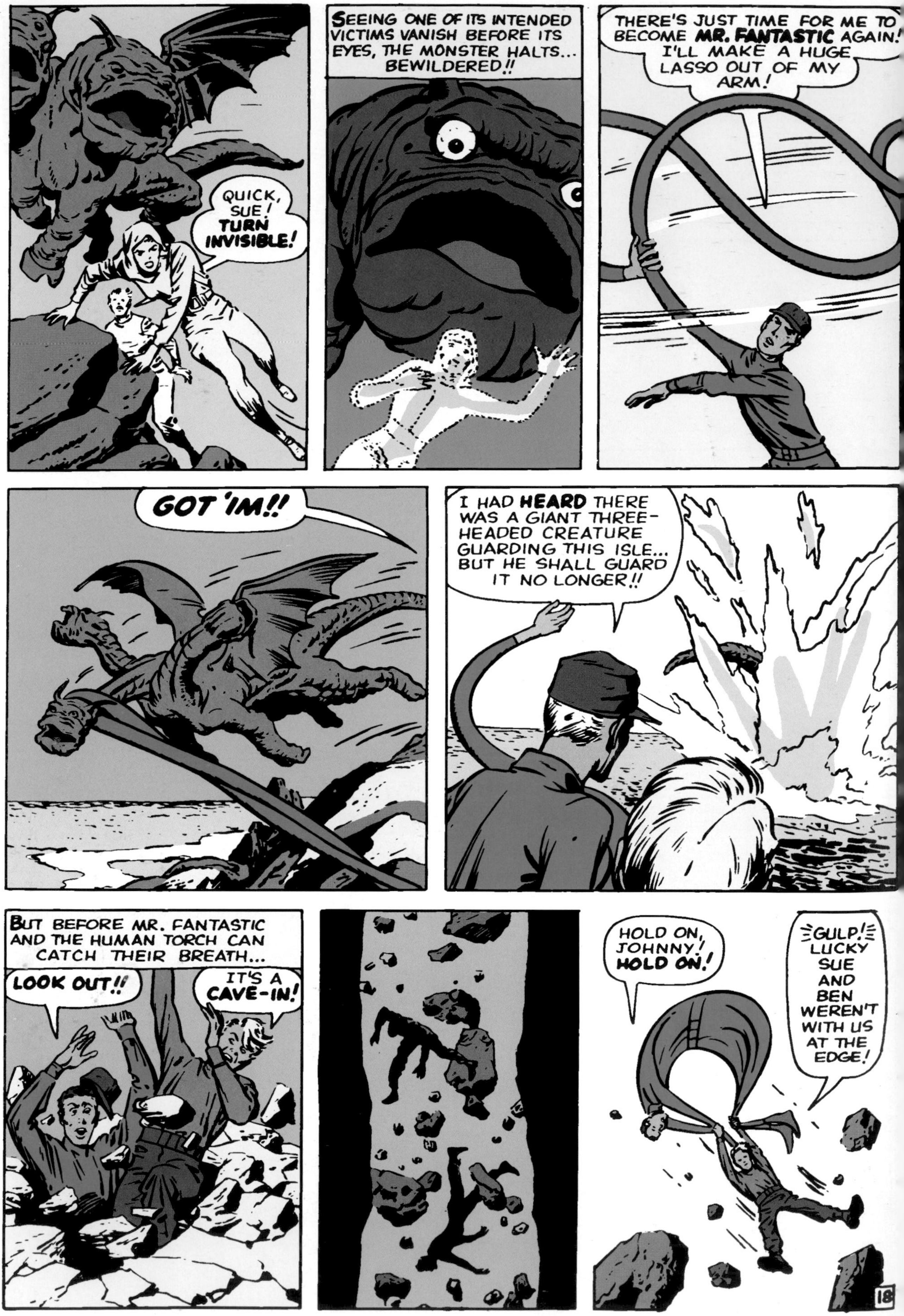
QUICK, SUE! TURN INVISIBLE!
SEEING ONE OF ITS INTENDED VICTIMS VANISH BEFORE ITS EYES, THE MONSTER HALTS... BEWILDERED!!
THERE'S JUST TIME FOR ME TO BECOME MR. FANTASTIC AGAIN! I'LL MAKE A HUGE LASSO OUT OF MY ARM!
GOT 'IM!!
I HAD HEARD THERE WAS A GIANT THREE-HEADED CREATURE GUARDING THIS ISLE... BUT HE SHALL GUARD IT NO LONGER!!
BUT BEFORE MR. FANTASTIC AND THE HUMAN TORCH CAN CATCH THEIR BREATH...
LOOK OUT!!
IT'S A CAVE-IN!
HOLD ON, JOHNNY! HOLD ON!
GULP! LUCKY SUE AND BEN WEREN'T WITH US AT THE EDGE!
18

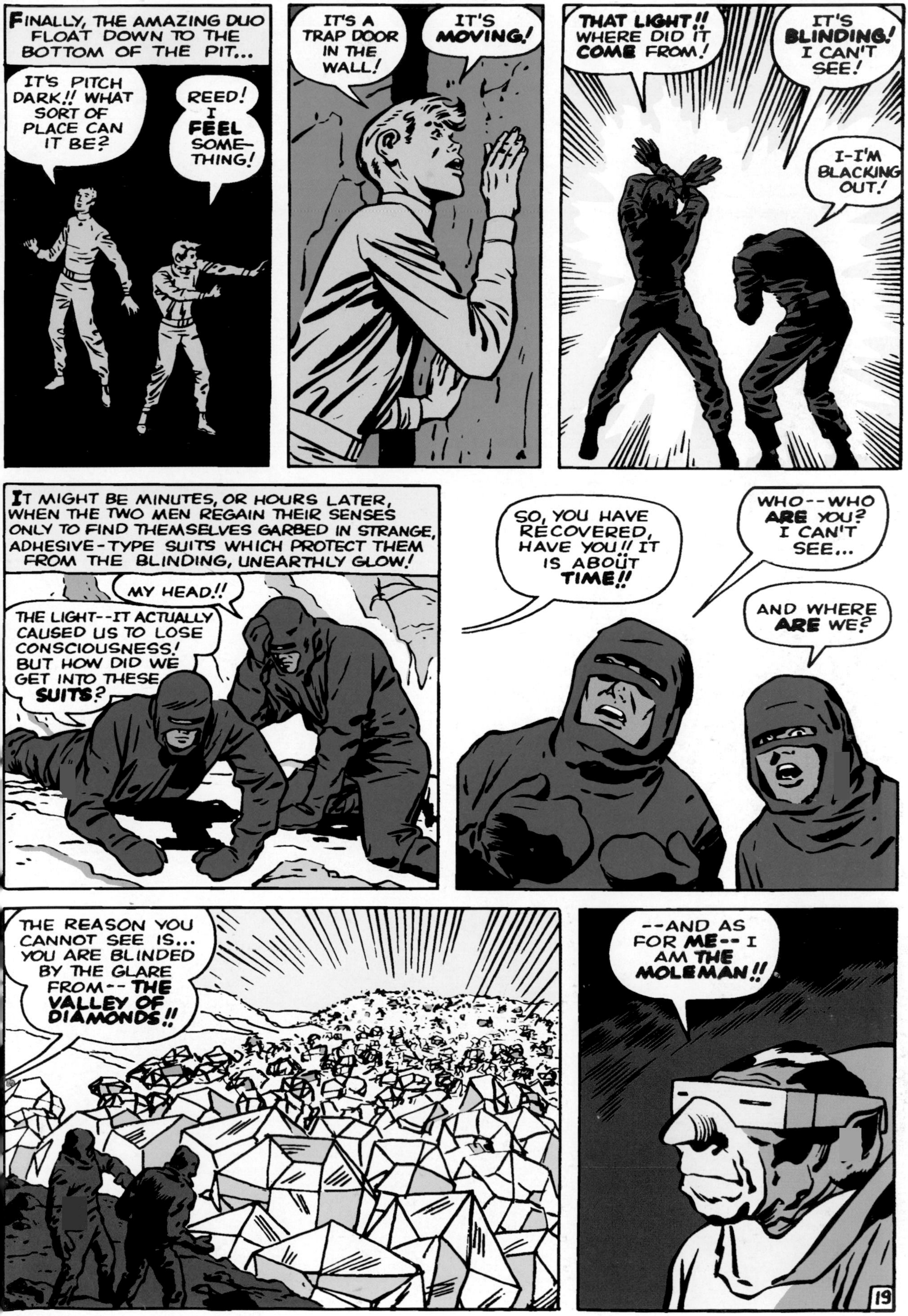
FINALLY, THE AMAZING DUO FLOAT DOWN TO THE BOTTOM OF THE PIT...
IT'S PITCH DARK!! WHAT SORT OF PLACE CAN IT BE?
REED! I FEEL SOME-THING!
IT'S A TRAP DOOR IN THE WALL!
IT'S MOVING!
THAT LIGHT!! WHERE DID IT COME FROM!
IT'S BLINDING! I CAN'T SEE!
I-I'M BLACKING OUT!
IT MIGHT BE MINUTES, OR HOURS LATER, WHEN THE TWO MEN REGAIN THEIR SENSES ONLY TO FIND THEMSELVES GARBED IN STRANGE, ADHESIVE-TYPE SUITS WHICH PROTECT THEM FROM THE BLINDING, UNEARTHLY GLOW!
MY HEAD!!
THE LIGHT--IT ACTUALLY CAUSED US TO LOSE CONSCIOUSNESS! BUT HOW DID WE GET INTO THESE SUITS?
SO, YOU HAVE RECOVERED, HAVE YOU!! IT IS ABOUT TIME!!
WHO--WHO ARE YOU? I CAN'T SEE...
AND WHERE ARE WE?
THE REASON YOU CANNOT SEE IS... YOU ARE BLINDED BY THE GLARE FROM-- THE VALLEY OF DIAMONDS!!
--AND AS FOR ME-- I AM THE MOLEMAN!!
19

THE MOLEMAN'S SECRET!

BEFORE WE WITNESS THE BREATH-TAKING CONCLUSION OF OUR AMAZING TALE, LET US GATHER TOGETHER ALL THE LOOSE ENDS! LET US RETURN TO THE TWO MEMBERS OF THE FANTASTIC FOUR WHO DID NOT FALL BELOW DURING THE CAVE-IN...

REED... AND JOHNNY... GOT TO FIND THEM!!

WAIT! THAT NOISE -- BEHIND ME!! WHAT--??

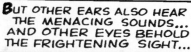

BUT OTHER EARS ALSO HEAR THE MENACING SOUNDS... AND OTHER EYES BEHOLD THE FRIGHTENING SIGHT...

THE EYES OF... **THE THING!!**

DUCK, SUE! OUT OF THE WAY!

LET **ME** HANDLE 'IM!

20

THE SECOND GIGANTIC GUARDIAN OF MONSTER ISLE IS POWERFUL BEYOND BELIEF...BUT HE IS FIGHTING AN ENEMY WHOSE EVERY ATOM HAS BEEN CHARGED WITH COSMIC RAYS...AN ENEMY WHO **CAN'T BE STOPPED!**

YOU'VE DONE IT, BEN! YOU'VE BEATEN HIM!

WHAT DID YOU **EXPECT??**

I'M **THE THING,** AIN'T I??

NOW LET'S GO AND FIND THAT SKINNY, LOUD-MOUTHED BOY-FRIEND OF YOURS!

OH, BEN-- IF ONLY YOU COULD STOP HATING REED FOR WHAT HAPPENED TO YOU!

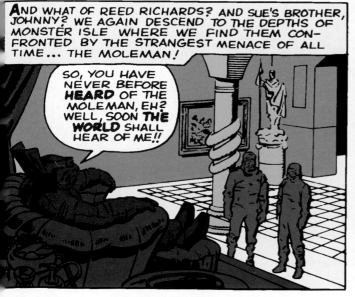

AND WHAT OF REED RICHARDS? AND SUE'S BROTHER, JOHNNY? WE AGAIN DESCEND TO THE DEPTHS OF MONSTER ISLE WHERE WE FIND THEM CONFRONTED BY THE STRANGEST MENACE OF ALL TIME... THE MOLEMAN!

SO, YOU HAVE NEVER BEFORE **HEARD** OF THE MOLEMAN, EH? WELL, SOON **THE WORLD** SHALL HEAR OF ME!!

FOR SOON, THE MOLEMAN WILL HAVE THE ENTIRE WORLD IN HIS **POWER!**

HOW DID YOU **GET** HERE? WHAT **IS** THIS PLACE?

21

27

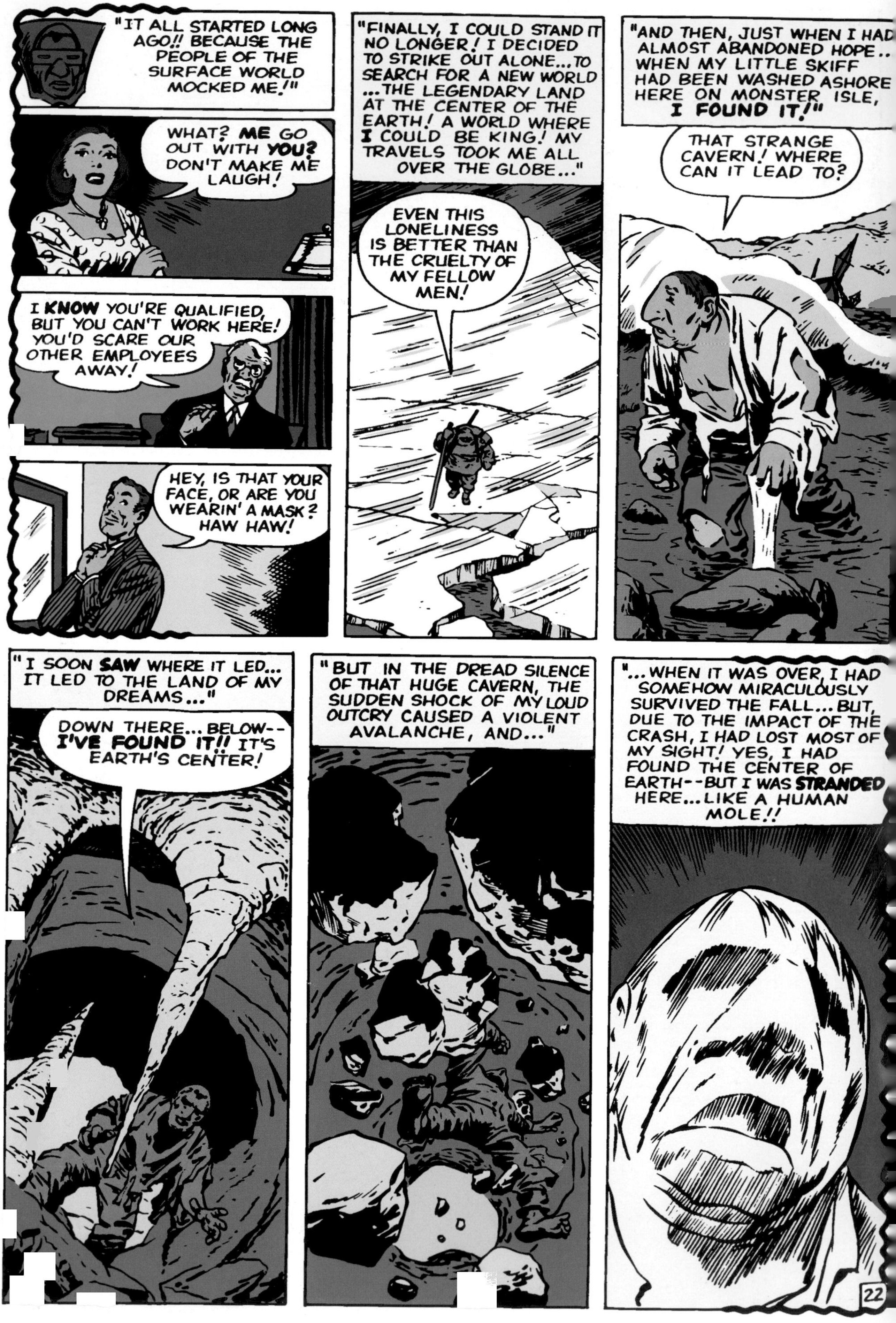

"IT ALL STARTED LONG AGO!! BECAUSE THE PEOPLE OF THE SURFACE WORLD MOCKED ME!"
WHAT? ME GO OUT WITH YOU? DON'T MAKE ME LAUGH!
I KNOW YOU'RE QUALIFIED, BUT YOU CAN'T WORK HERE! YOU'D SCARE OUR OTHER EMPLOYEES AWAY!
HEY, IS THAT YOUR FACE, OR ARE YOU WEARIN' A MASK? HAW HAW!
"FINALLY, I COULD STAND IT NO LONGER! I DECIDED TO STRIKE OUT ALONE...TO SEARCH FOR A NEW WORLD ...THE LEGENDARY LAND AT THE CENTER OF THE EARTH! A WORLD WHERE I COULD BE KING! MY TRAVELS TOOK ME ALL OVER THE GLOBE..."
EVEN THIS LONELINESS IS BETTER THAN THE CRUELTY OF MY FELLOW MEN!
"AND THEN, JUST WHEN I HAD ALMOST ABANDONED HOPE.. WHEN MY LITTLE SKIFF HAD BEEN WASHED ASHORE HERE ON MONSTER ISLE, I FOUND IT!"
THAT STRANGE CAVERN! WHERE CAN IT LEAD TO?
"I SOON SAW WHERE IT LED... IT LED TO THE LAND OF MY DREAMS..."
DOWN THERE... BELOW-- I'VE FOUND IT!! IT'S EARTH'S CENTER!
"BUT IN THE DREAD SILENCE OF THAT HUGE CAVERN, THE SUDDEN SHOCK OF MY LOUD OUTCRY CAUSED A VIOLENT AVALANCHE, AND..."
"...WHEN IT WAS OVER, I HAD SOMEHOW MIRACULOUSLY SURVIVED THE FALL... BUT, DUE TO THE IMPACT OF THE CRASH, I HAD LOST MOST OF MY SIGHT! YES, I HAD FOUND THE CENTER OF EARTH--BUT I WAS STRANDED HERE...LIKE A HUMAN MOLE!!
22

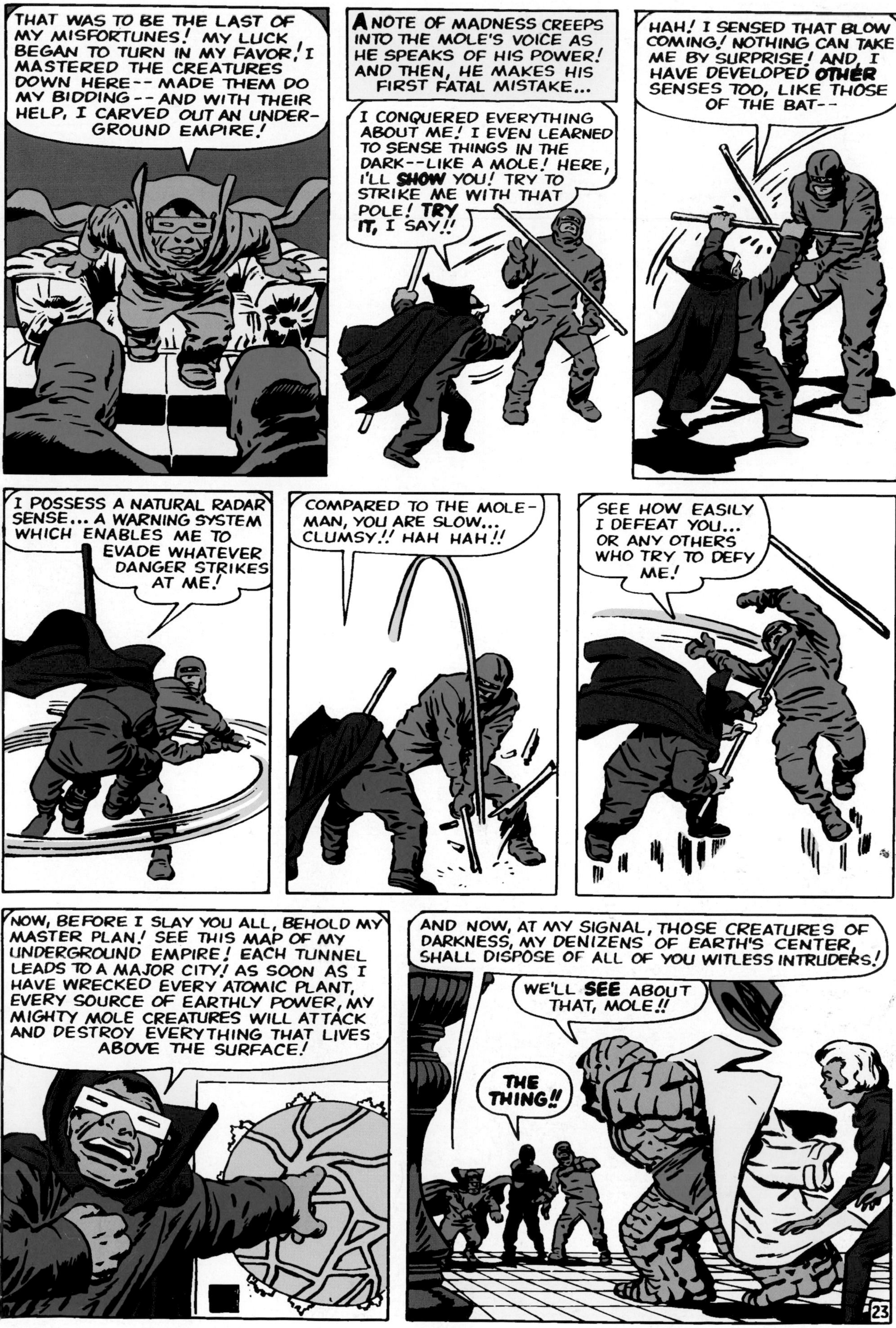
THAT WAS TO BE THE LAST OF MY MISFORTUNES! MY LUCK BEGAN TO TURN IN MY FAVOR! I MASTERED THE CREATURES DOWN HERE -- MADE THEM DO MY BIDDING -- AND WITH THEIR HELP, I CARVED OUT AN UNDERGROUND EMPIRE!
A NOTE OF MADNESS CREEPS INTO THE MOLE'S VOICE AS HE SPEAKS OF HIS POWER! AND THEN, HE MAKES HIS FIRST FATAL MISTAKE...
I CONQUERED EVERYTHING ABOUT ME! I EVEN LEARNED TO SENSE THINGS IN THE DARK--LIKE A MOLE! HERE, I'LL SHOW YOU! TRY TO STRIKE ME WITH THAT POLE! TRY IT, I SAY!!
HAH! I SENSED THAT BLOW COMING! NOTHING CAN TAKE ME BY SURPRISE! AND, I HAVE DEVELOPED OTHER SENSES TOO, LIKE THOSE OF THE BAT--
I POSSESS A NATURAL RADAR SENSE... A WARNING SYSTEM WHICH ENABLES ME TO EVADE WHATEVER DANGER STRIKES AT ME!
COMPARED TO THE MOLE-MAN, YOU ARE SLOW... CLUMSY!! HAH HAH!!
SEE HOW EASILY I DEFEAT YOU... OR ANY OTHERS WHO TRY TO DEFY ME!
NOW, BEFORE I SLAY YOU ALL, BEHOLD MY MASTER PLAN! SEE THIS MAP OF MY UNDERGROUND EMPIRE! EACH TUNNEL LEADS TO A MAJOR CITY! AS SOON AS I HAVE WRECKED EVERY ATOMIC PLANT, EVERY SOURCE OF EARTHLY POWER, MY MIGHTY MOLE CREATURES WILL ATTACK AND DESTROY EVERYTHING THAT LIVES ABOVE THE SURFACE!
AND NOW, AT MY SIGNAL, THOSE CREATURES OF DARKNESS, MY DENIZENS OF EARTH'S CENTER, SHALL DISPOSE OF ALL OF YOU WITLESS INTRUDERS!
WE'LL SEE ABOUT THAT, MOLE!!
THE THING!!
23

TOO LATE, FOOL! THE DIE IS CAST! THERE IS NO TURNING BACK.!!

THING.!! LOOK OUT... BEHIND YOU!

BONG! BONG!

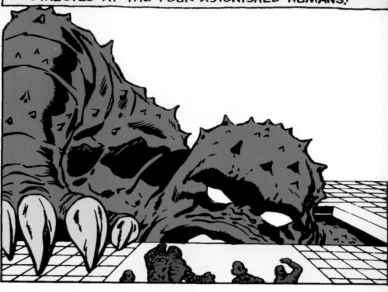

HEARING THE MOLE'S SIGNAL, THE LARGEST AND MOST DEADLY OF HIS UNDERGROUND CREATURES PONDEROUSLY RAISES ITSELF INTO THE ROOM... ITS BRAINLESS RAGE DIRECTED AT THE FOUR ASTONISHED HUMANS!

AND THEN, THE FANTASTIC FOUR FLY INTO BLAZING ACTION...

LOOK OUT, REED! I'M GONNA BURN MY WAY OUTTA THIS MONKEY SUIT!

GOOD BOY, TORCH!

STAND ASIDE, GANG! IT'S GONNA GET MIGHTY **WARM** AROUND HERE!

BACK AND FORTH, BUZZING AROUND THE MONSTER'S HEAD LIKE A HORNET, FLIES THE HUMAN TORCH, AS THE GIGANTIC CREATURE VAINLY TRIES TO GRASP HIS FIERY FOE!

REED! THE MOLE MAN! HE'S ESCAPING!

NOT IF **I** CAN HELP IT, SUE!

AND HELP IT I **CAN!**

24

30

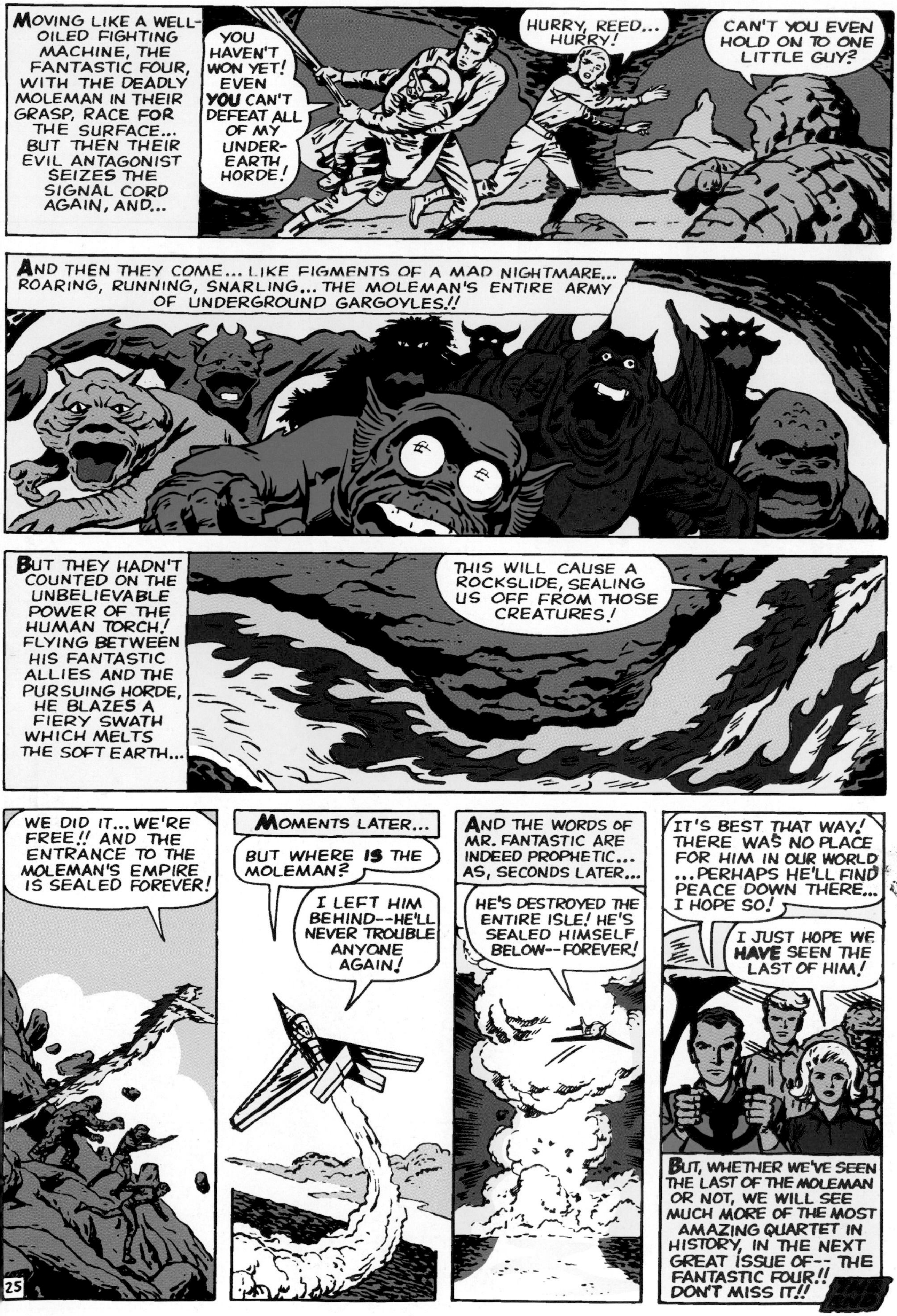
MOVING LIKE A WELL-OILED FIGHTING MACHINE, THE FANTASTIC FOUR, WITH THE DEADLY MOLEMAN IN THEIR GRASP, RACE FOR THE SURFACE... BUT THEN THEIR EVIL ANTAGONIST SEIZES THE SIGNAL CORD AGAIN, AND...
YOU HAVEN'T WON YET! EVEN YOU CAN'T DEFEAT ALL OF MY UNDER-EARTH HORDE!
HURRY, REED... HURRY!
CAN'T YOU EVEN HOLD ON TO ONE LITTLE GUY?
AND THEN THEY COME... LIKE FIGMENTS OF A MAD NIGHTMARE... ROARING, RUNNING, SNARLING... THE MOLEMAN'S ENTIRE ARMY OF UNDERGROUND GARGOYLES!!
BUT THEY HADN'T COUNTED ON THE UNBELIEVABLE POWER OF THE HUMAN TORCH! FLYING BETWEEN HIS FANTASTIC ALLIES AND THE PURSUING HORDE, HE BLAZES A FIERY SWATH WHICH MELTS THE SOFT EARTH...
THIS WILL CAUSE A ROCKSLIDE, SEALING US OFF FROM THOSE CREATURES!
WE DID IT... WE'RE FREE!! AND THE ENTRANCE TO THE MOLEMAN'S EMPIRE IS SEALED FOREVER!
25
MOMENTS LATER...
BUT WHERE IS THE MOLEMAN?
I LEFT HIM BEHIND--HE'LL NEVER TROUBLE ANYONE AGAIN!
AND THE WORDS OF MR. FANTASTIC ARE INDEED PROPHETIC... AS, SECONDS LATER...
HE'S DESTROYED THE ENTIRE ISLE! HE'S SEALED HIMSELF BELOW--FOREVER!
IT'S BEST THAT WAY! THERE WAS NO PLACE FOR HIM IN OUR WORLD ...PERHAPS HE'LL FIND PEACE DOWN THERE... I HOPE SO!
I JUST HOPE WE HAVE SEEN THE LAST OF HIM!
BUT, WHETHER WE'VE SEEN THE LAST OF THE MOLEMAN OR NOT, WE WILL SEE MUCH MORE OF THE MOST AMAZING QUARTET IN HISTORY, IN THE NEXT GREAT ISSUE OF-- THE FANTASTIC FOUR!! DON'T MISS IT!!
THE END

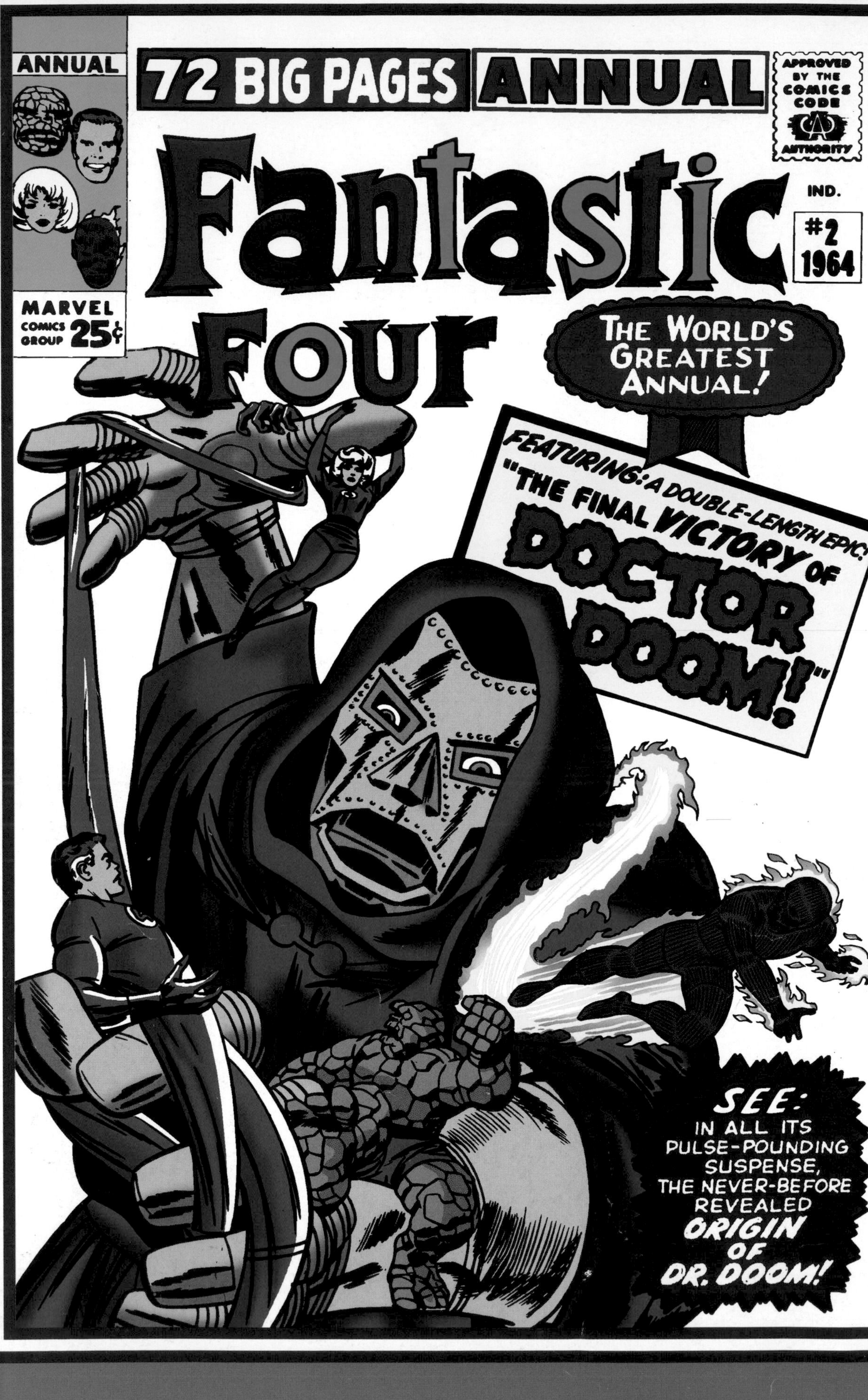
ANNUAL
72 BIG PAGES
ANNUAL
APPROVED BY THE COMICS CODE AUTHORITY
Fantastic Four
IND.
#2
1964
MARVEL COMICS GROUP 25¢
THE WORLD'S GREATEST ANNUAL!
FEATURING: A DOUBLE-LENGTH EPIC!
"THE FINAL VICTORY OF DOCTOR DOOM!"
SEE: IN ALL ITS PULSE-POUNDING SUSPENSE, THE NEVER-BEFORE REVEALED ORIGIN OF DR. DOOM!

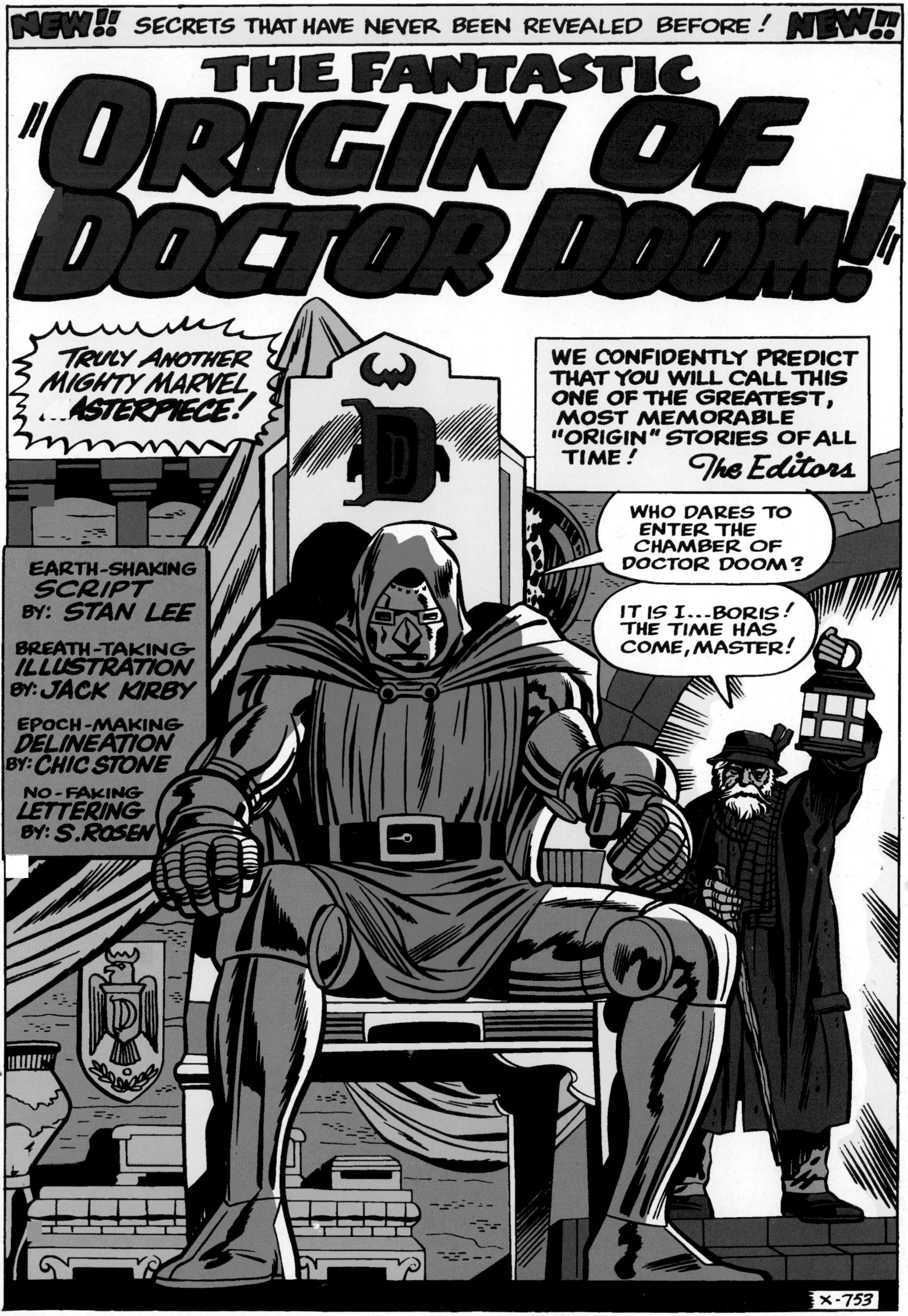
NEW!! SECRETS THAT HAVE NEVER BEEN REVEALED BEFORE! NEW!!
THE FANTASTIC "ORIGIN OF DOCTOR DOOM!"
TRULY ANOTHER MIGHTY MARVEL MASTERPIECE!
WE CONFIDENTLY PREDICT THAT YOU WILL CALL THIS ONE OF THE GREATEST, MOST MEMORABLE "ORIGIN" STORIES OF ALL TIME! The Editors
WHO DARES TO ENTER THE CHAMBER OF DOCTOR DOOM?
IT IS I...BORIS! THE TIME HAS COME, MASTER!
EARTH-SHAKING SCRIPT BY: STAN LEE
BREATH-TAKING ILLUSTRATION BY: JACK KIRBY
EPOCH-MAKING DELINEATION BY: CHIC STONE
NO-FAKING LETTERING BY: S. ROSEN
X-753

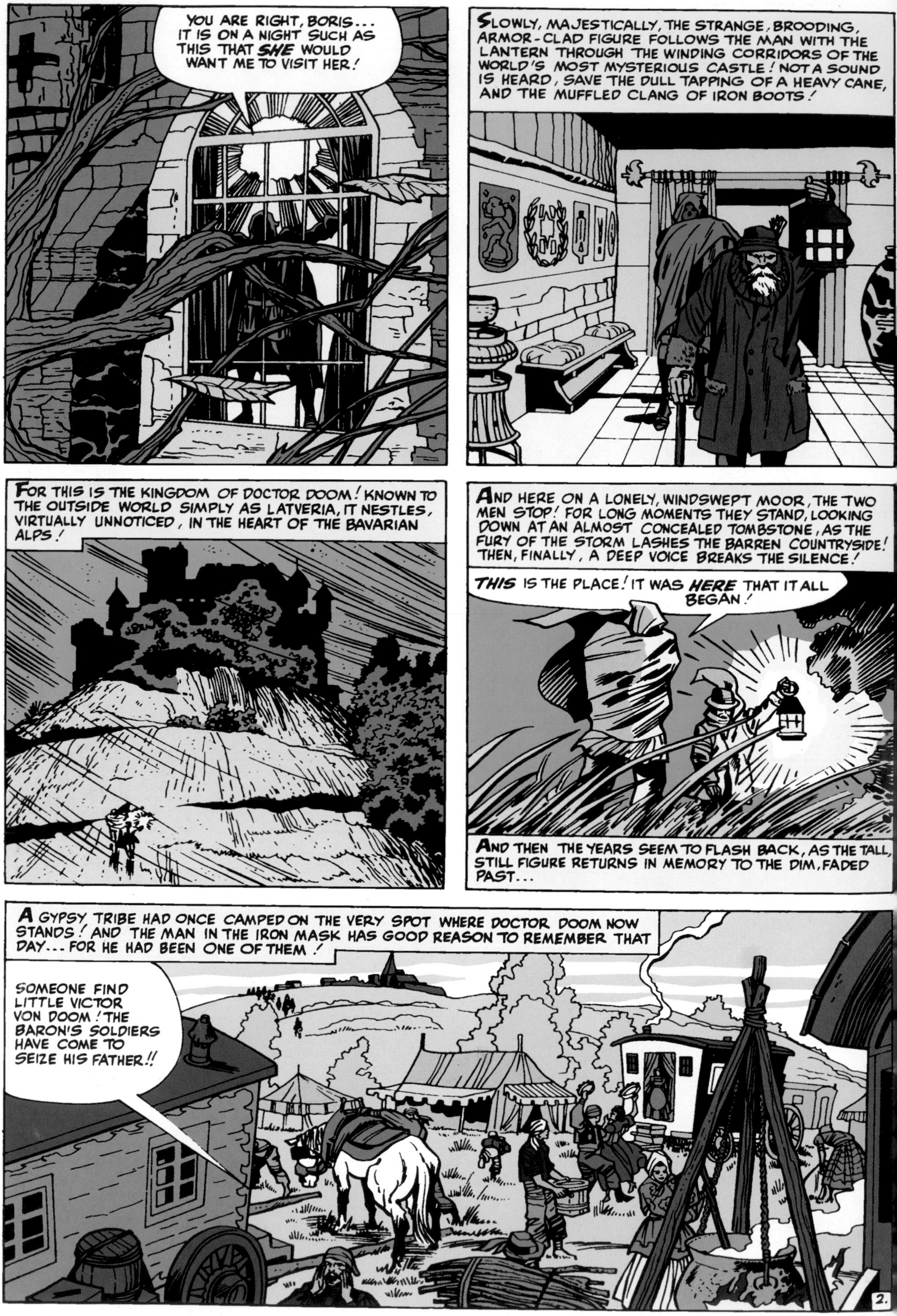

YOU ARE RIGHT, BORIS... IT IS ON A NIGHT SUCH AS THIS THAT SHE WOULD WANT ME TO VISIT HER!
SLOWLY, MAJESTICALLY, THE STRANGE, BROODING, ARMOR-CLAD FIGURE FOLLOWS THE MAN WITH THE LANTERN THROUGH THE WINDING CORRIDORS OF THE WORLD'S MOST MYSTERIOUS CASTLE! NOT A SOUND IS HEARD, SAVE THE DULL TAPPING OF A HEAVY CANE, AND THE MUFFLED CLANG OF IRON BOOTS!
FOR THIS IS THE KINGDOM OF DOCTOR DOOM! KNOWN TO THE OUTSIDE WORLD SIMPLY AS LATVERIA, IT NESTLES, VIRTUALLY UNNOTICED, IN THE HEART OF THE BAVARIAN ALPS!
AND HERE ON A LONELY, WINDSWEPT MOOR, THE TWO MEN STOP! FOR LONG MOMENTS THEY STAND, LOOKING DOWN AT AN ALMOST CONCEALED TOMBSTONE, AS THE FURY OF THE STORM LASHES THE BARREN COUNTRYSIDE! THEN, FINALLY, A DEEP VOICE BREAKS THE SILENCE!
THIS IS THE PLACE! IT WAS HERE THAT IT ALL BEGAN!
AND THEN THE YEARS SEEM TO FLASH BACK, AS THE TALL, STILL FIGURE RETURNS IN MEMORY TO THE DIM, FADED PAST...
A GYPSY TRIBE HAD ONCE CAMPED ON THE VERY SPOT WHERE DOCTOR DOOM NOW STANDS! AND THE MAN IN THE IRON MASK HAS GOOD REASON TO REMEMBER THAT DAY... FOR HE HAD BEEN ONE OF THEM!
SOMEONE FIND LITTLE VICTOR VON DOOM! THE BARON'S SOLDIERS HAVE COME TO SEIZE HIS FATHER!!
2.

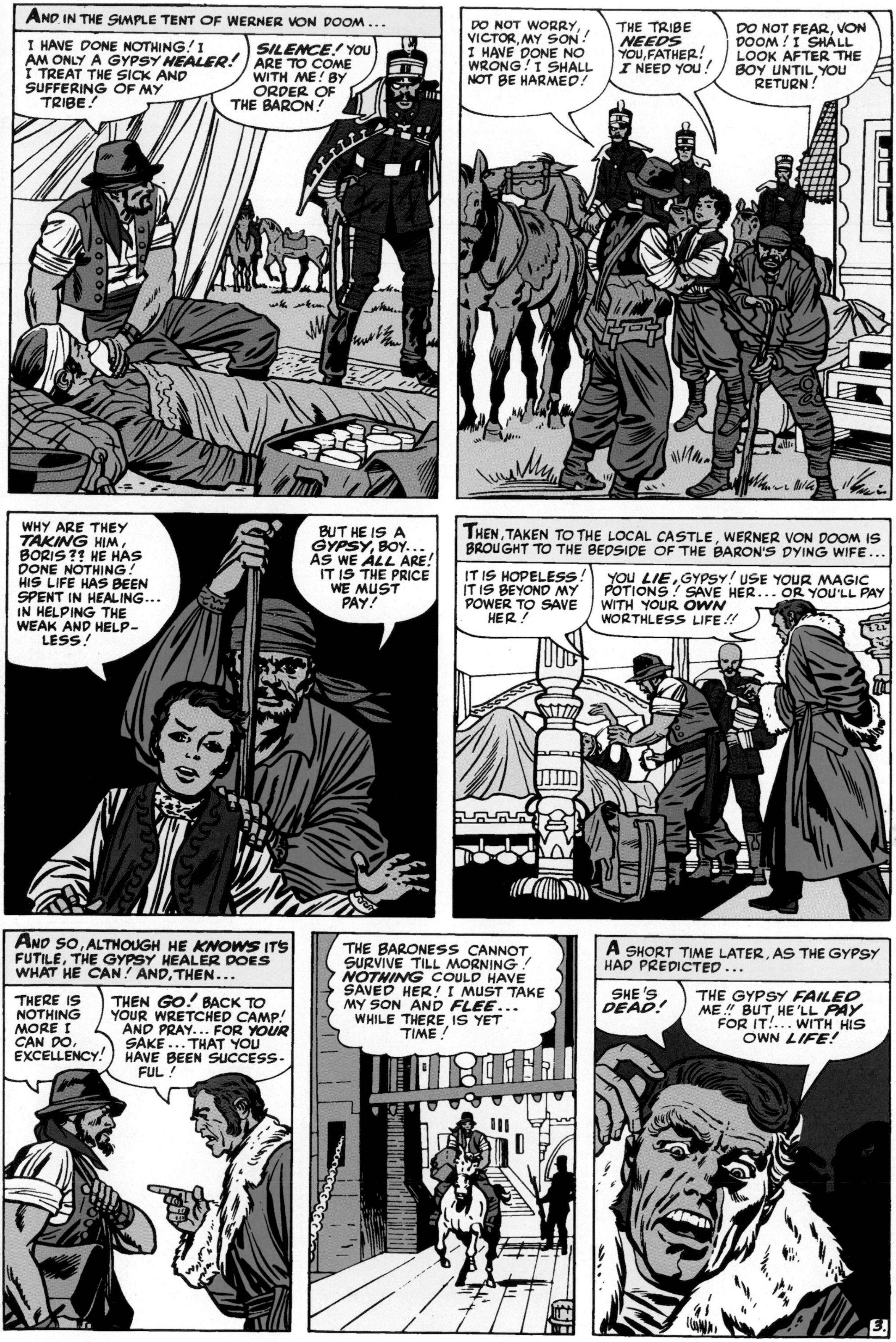
AND IN THE SIMPLE TENT OF WERNER VON DOOM...
I HAVE DONE NOTHING! I AM ONLY A GYPSY HEALER! I TREAT THE SICK AND SUFFERING OF MY TRIBE!
SILENCE! YOU ARE TO COME WITH ME! BY ORDER OF THE BARON!
DO NOT WORRY, VICTOR, MY SON! I HAVE DONE NO WRONG! I SHALL NOT BE HARMED!
THE TRIBE NEEDS YOU, FATHER! I NEED YOU!
DO NOT FEAR, VON DOOM! I SHALL LOOK AFTER THE BOY UNTIL YOU RETURN!
WHY ARE THEY TAKING HIM, BORIS?? HE HAS DONE NOTHING! HIS LIFE HAS BEEN SPENT IN HEALING... IN HELPING THE WEAK AND HELPLESS!
BUT HE IS A GYPSY, BOY... AS WE ALL ARE! IT IS THE PRICE WE MUST PAY!
THEN, TAKEN TO THE LOCAL CASTLE, WERNER VON DOOM IS BROUGHT TO THE BEDSIDE OF THE BARON'S DYING WIFE...
IT IS HOPELESS! IT IS BEYOND MY POWER TO SAVE HER!
YOU LIE, GYPSY! USE YOUR MAGIC POTIONS! SAVE HER... OR YOU'LL PAY WITH YOUR OWN WORTHLESS LIFE!!
AND SO, ALTHOUGH HE KNOWS IT'S FUTILE, THE GYPSY HEALER DOES WHAT HE CAN! AND, THEN...
THERE IS NOTHING MORE I CAN DO, EXCELLENCY!
THEN GO! BACK TO YOUR WRETCHED CAMP! AND PRAY... FOR YOUR SAKE... THAT YOU HAVE BEEN SUCCESSFUL!
THE BARONESS CANNOT SURVIVE TILL MORNING! NOTHING COULD HAVE SAVED HER! I MUST TAKE MY SON AND FLEE... WHILE THERE IS YET TIME!
A SHORT TIME LATER, AS THE GYPSY HAD PREDICTED...
SHE'S DEAD!
THE GYPSY FAILED ME!! BUT HE'LL PAY FOR IT!... WITH HIS OWN LIFE!
3.

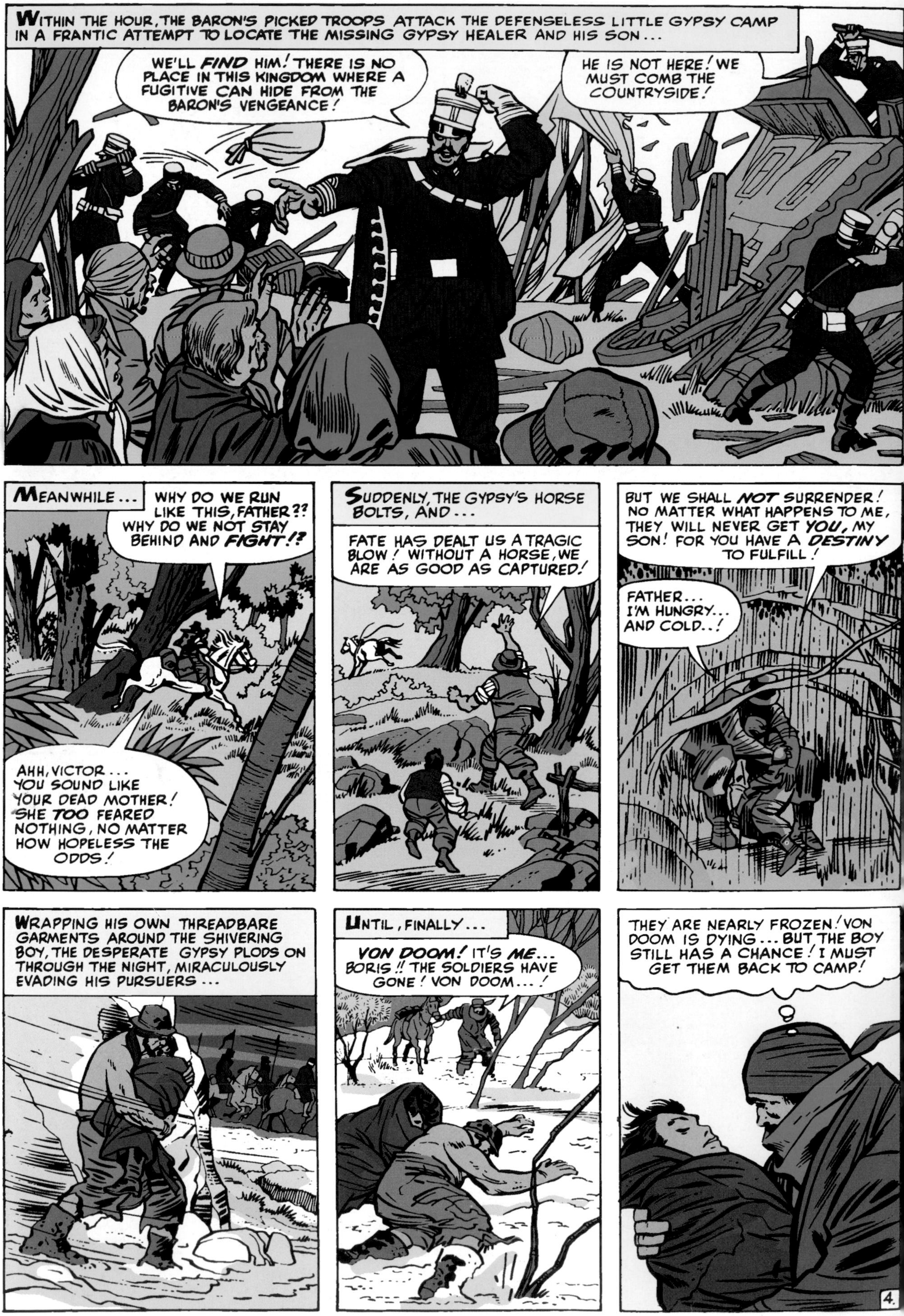

WITHIN THE HOUR, THE BARON'S PICKED TROOPS ATTACK THE DEFENSELESS LITTLE GYPSY CAMP IN A FRANTIC ATTEMPT TO LOCATE THE MISSING GYPSY HEALER AND HIS SON...
WE'LL FIND HIM! THERE IS NO PLACE IN THIS KINGDOM WHERE A FUGITIVE CAN HIDE FROM THE BARON'S VENGEANCE!
HE IS NOT HERE! WE MUST COMB THE COUNTRYSIDE!
MEANWHILE...
WHY DO WE RUN LIKE THIS, FATHER?? WHY DO WE NOT STAY BEHIND AND FIGHT!?
AHH, VICTOR... YOU SOUND LIKE YOUR DEAD MOTHER! SHE TOO FEARED NOTHING, NO MATTER HOW HOPELESS THE ODDS!
SUDDENLY, THE GYPSY'S HORSE BOLTS, AND...
FATE HAS DEALT US A TRAGIC BLOW! WITHOUT A HORSE, WE ARE AS GOOD AS CAPTURED!
BUT WE SHALL NOT SURRENDER! NO MATTER WHAT HAPPENS TO ME, THEY WILL NEVER GET YOU, MY SON! FOR YOU HAVE A DESTINY TO FULFILL!
FATHER... I'M HUNGRY... AND COLD..!
WRAPPING HIS OWN THREADBARE GARMENTS AROUND THE SHIVERING BOY, THE DESPERATE GYPSY PLODS ON THROUGH THE NIGHT, MIRACULOUSLY EVADING HIS PURSUERS...
UNTIL, FINALLY...
VON DOOM! IT'S ME... BORIS!! THE SOLDIERS HAVE GONE! VON DOOM...!
THEY ARE NEARLY FROZEN! VON DOOM IS DYING... BUT THE BOY STILL HAS A CHANCE! I MUST GET THEM BACK TO CAMP!
4.

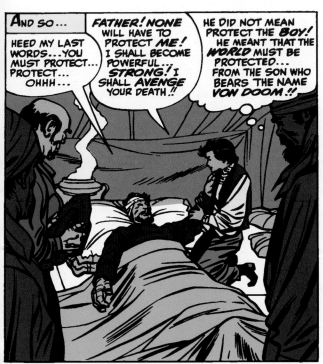

AND SO...

HEED MY LAST WORDS...YOU MUST PROTECT... PROTECT... OHHH...

FATHER! NONE WILL HAVE TO PROTECT *ME!* I SHALL BECOME POWERFUL... *STRONG!* I SHALL *AVENGE* YOUR DEATH.!!

HE DID NOT MEAN PROTECT THE *BOY!* HE MEANT THAT THE *WORLD* MUST BE PROTECTED... FROM THE SON WHO BEARS THE NAME *VON DOOM.!!*

THEY MURDERED MY MOTHER... WHEN I WAS BUT AN INFANT!! AND NOW THEY HAVE SLAIN MY FATHER!! THEY'LL *PAY* FOR THAT!! ALL OF *MANKIND* SHALL PAY!!

WE NEVER TOLD HIM THAT HIS MOTHER WAS A MYSTIC *SORCERESS.!!* AND HER BLOOD RUNS IN HIS OWN VEINS! I PRAY HE NEVER LEARNS OF HIS *DARK HERITAGE!*

BUT, AFTER THE OTHERS HAVE GONE...

THESE ARE YOUR FATHER'S HERBS AND REMEDIES! REMEMBER, LAD... HE USED THEM ONLY FOR *GOOD!*

AND MEN REPAID HIS KINDNESS BY *HOUNDING* HIM... *SLAYING* HIM!!

THEN, AFTER FAITHFUL BORIS DEPARTS...

WHAT HAVE I *FOUND*...HIDDEN HERE BENEATH THESE HEIRLOOMS! A STRANGE *CHEST!*

THAT *NAME!* CAN IT *BE?* IT BELONGED TO...MY *MOTHER!*

MAGIC POTIONS!! STRANGE SCIENTIFIC SECRETS! WHY DID I NEVER SUSPECT?? MY MOTHER WAS A *WITCH!*

AND NOW *I* CAN LEARN HER SECRETS!!

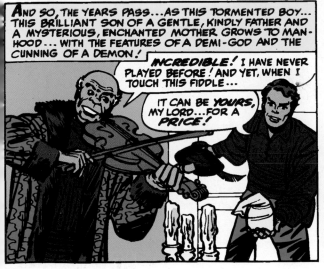

AND SO, THE YEARS PASS...AS THIS TORMENTED BOY... THIS BRILLIANT SON OF A GENTLE, KINDLY FATHER AND A MYSTERIOUS, ENCHANTED MOTHER GROWS TO MANHOOD...WITH THE FEATURES OF A DEMI-GOD AND THE CUNNING OF A DEMON!

INCREDIBLE! I HAVE NEVER PLAYED BEFORE! AND YET, WHEN I TOUCH THIS FIDDLE...

IT CAN BE *YOURS,* MY LORD...FOR A *PRICE!*

BUT VICTOR, WHY WOULD HE PAY A SMALL FORTUNE FOR A WORTHLESS FIDDLE?

IT IS *WORTH* IT, BORIS, BECAUSE OF THIS LITTLE DEVICE! FOR *THIS* IS WHAT CAUSES THE FIDDLE TO PLAY!

5.

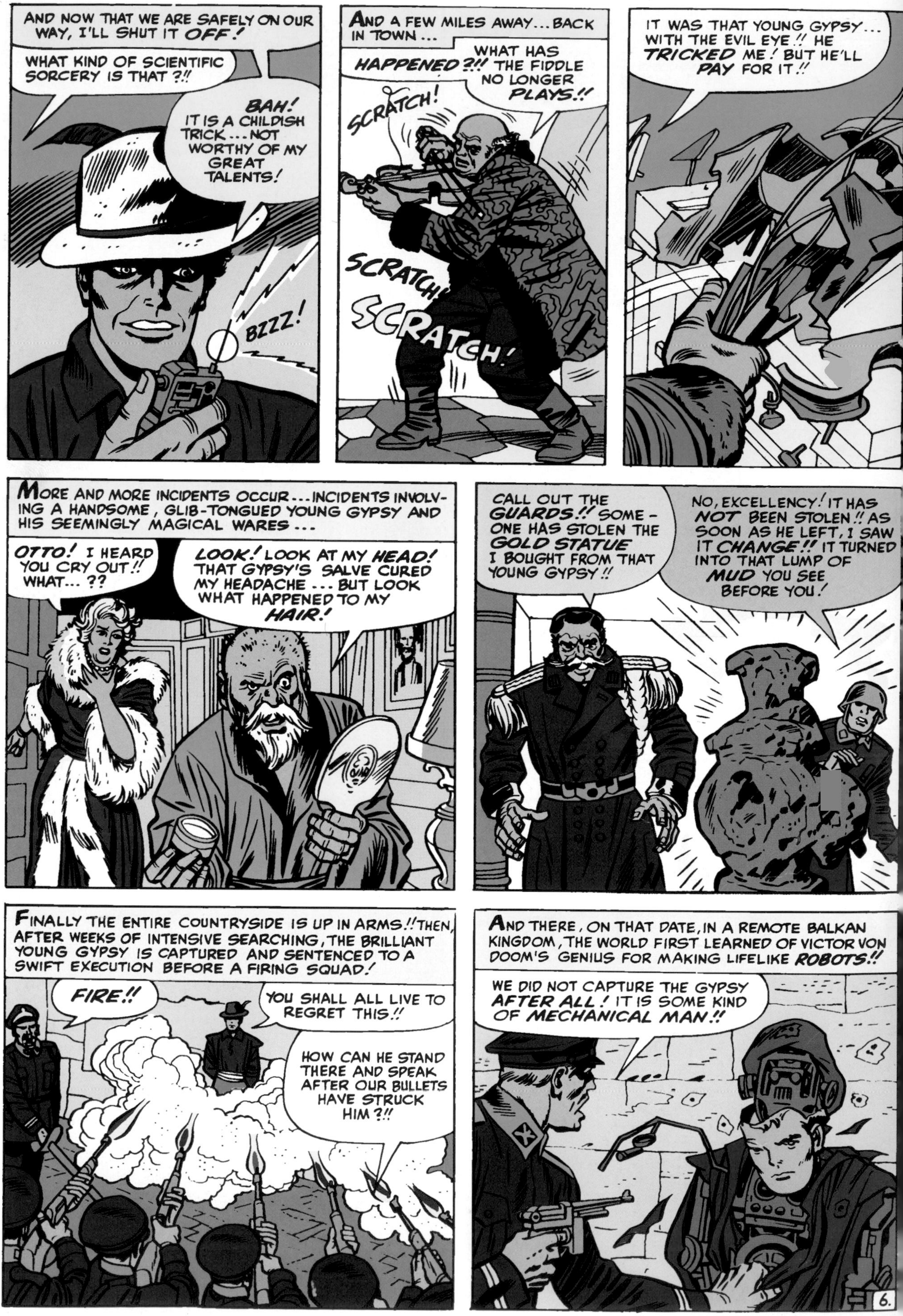
AND NOW THAT WE ARE SAFELY ON OUR WAY, I'LL SHUT IT OFF!
WHAT KIND OF SCIENTIFIC SORCERY IS THAT ?!!
BAH! IT IS A CHILDISH TRICK... NOT WORTHY OF MY GREAT TALENTS!
BZZZ!
AND A FEW MILES AWAY... BACK IN TOWN...
WHAT HAS HAPPENED ?!! THE FIDDLE NO LONGER PLAYS!!
SCRATCH!
SCRATCH!
SCRATCH!
IT WAS THAT YOUNG GYPSY... WITH THE EVIL EYE!! HE TRICKED ME! BUT HE'LL PAY FOR IT!!
MORE AND MORE INCIDENTS OCCUR... INCIDENTS INVOLVING A HANDSOME, GLIB-TONGUED YOUNG GYPSY AND HIS SEEMINGLY MAGICAL WARES...
OTTO! I HEARD YOU CRY OUT!! WHAT... ??
LOOK! LOOK AT MY HEAD! THAT GYPSY'S SALVE CURED MY HEADACHE... BUT LOOK WHAT HAPPENED TO MY HAIR!
CALL OUT THE GUARDS!! SOMEONE HAS STOLEN THE GOLD STATUE I BOUGHT FROM THAT YOUNG GYPSY!!
NO, EXCELLENCY! IT HAS NOT BEEN STOLEN!! AS SOON AS HE LEFT, I SAW IT CHANGE!! IT TURNED INTO THAT LUMP OF MUD YOU SEE BEFORE YOU!
FINALLY THE ENTIRE COUNTRYSIDE IS UP IN ARMS!! THEN, AFTER WEEKS OF INTENSIVE SEARCHING, THE BRILLIANT YOUNG GYPSY IS CAPTURED AND SENTENCED TO A SWIFT EXECUTION BEFORE A FIRING SQUAD!
FIRE!!
YOU SHALL ALL LIVE TO REGRET THIS!!
HOW CAN HE STAND THERE AND SPEAK AFTER OUR BULLETS HAVE STRUCK HIM ?!!
AND THERE, ON THAT DATE, IN A REMOTE BALKAN KINGDOM, THE WORLD FIRST LEARNED OF VICTOR VON DOOM'S GENIUS FOR MAKING LIFELIKE ROBOTS!!
WE DID NOT CAPTURE THE GYPSY AFTER ALL! IT IS SOME KIND OF MECHANICAL MAN!!
6.

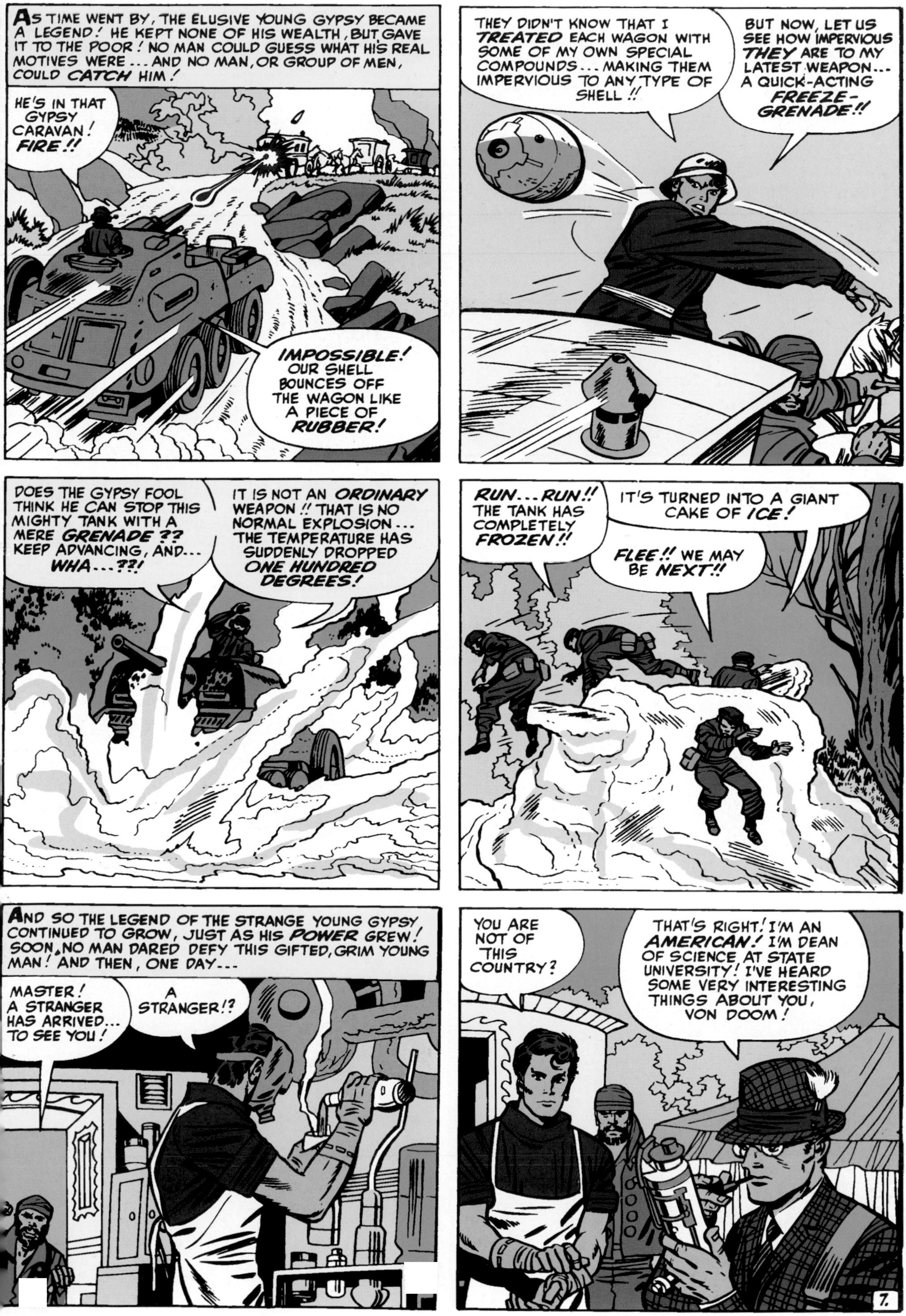
AS TIME WENT BY, THE ELUSIVE YOUNG GYPSY BECAME A LEGEND! HE KEPT NONE OF HIS WEALTH, BUT GAVE IT TO THE POOR! NO MAN COULD GUESS WHAT HIS REAL MOTIVES WERE... AND NO MAN, OR GROUP OF MEN, COULD CATCH HIM!
HE'S IN THAT GYPSY CARAVAN! FIRE!!
IMPOSSIBLE! OUR SHELL BOUNCES OFF THE WAGON LIKE A PIECE OF RUBBER!
THEY DIDN'T KNOW THAT I TREATED EACH WAGON WITH SOME OF MY OWN SPECIAL COMPOUNDS... MAKING THEM IMPERVIOUS TO ANY TYPE OF SHELL!!
BUT NOW, LET US SEE HOW IMPERVIOUS THEY ARE TO MY LATEST WEAPON... A QUICK-ACTING FREEZE-GRENADE!!
DOES THE GYPSY FOOL THINK HE CAN STOP THIS MIGHTY TANK WITH A MERE GRENADE?? KEEP ADVANCING, AND... WHA...??!
IT IS NOT AN ORDINARY WEAPON!! THAT IS NO NORMAL EXPLOSION... THE TEMPERATURE HAS SUDDENLY DROPPED ONE HUNDRED DEGREES!
RUN... RUN!! THE TANK HAS COMPLETELY FROZEN!!
IT'S TURNED INTO A GIANT CAKE OF ICE!
FLEE!! WE MAY BE NEXT!!
AND SO THE LEGEND OF THE STRANGE YOUNG GYPSY CONTINUED TO GROW, JUST AS HIS POWER GREW! SOON, NO MAN DARED DEFY THIS GIFTED, GRIM YOUNG MAN! AND THEN, ONE DAY---
MASTER! A STRANGER HAS ARRIVED... TO SEE YOU!
A STRANGER!?
YOU ARE NOT OF THIS COUNTRY?
THAT'S RIGHT! I'M AN AMERICAN! I'M DEAN OF SCIENCE AT STATE UNIVERSITY! I'VE HEARD SOME VERY INTERESTING THINGS ABOUT YOU, VON DOOM!
7.

IT'S TAKEN ME *MONTHS* TO FIND YOU! BUT AFTER SEEING SOME OF YOUR INVENTIONS, IT WAS WELL *WORTH* IT!

I'M PREPARED TO OFFER YOU A *SCHOLAR-SHIP* AT MY UNIVERSITY!

THAT WOULD ALLOW ME TO HAVE THE LATEST SCIENTIFIC APPARATUS AT MY DISPOSAL! HMMM....

YOU REMAIN HERE, BORIS, WITH THE OTHERS! I SHALL RETURN ONE DAY, TO REWARD YOU FOR YOUR LOYALTY!

AS YOU WISH, MASTER! NOTHING SHALL CHANGE UNTIL YOU COME BACK TO US!!

BEFORE THE DAY HAD ENDED, VICTOR VON DOOM WAS ABOARD A PLANE, HEADING FOR A NEW WORLD, AND A NEW DESTINY!

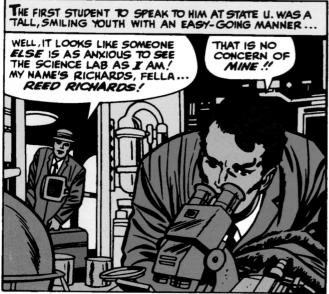

THE FIRST STUDENT TO SPEAK TO HIM AT STATE U. WAS A TALL, SMILING YOUTH WITH AN EASY-GOING MANNER...

WELL, IT LOOKS LIKE SOMEONE *ELSE* IS AS ANXIOUS TO SEE THE SCIENCE LAB AS *I* AM! MY NAME'S RICHARDS, FELLA... *REED RICHARDS!*

THAT IS NO CONCERN OF *MINE!!*

LOOK, I DON'T KNOW WHY YOU'VE GOT THAT KING-SIZED CHIP ON YOUR SHOULDER, BUT BEING WE'RE *BOTH* HERE ON SCIENCE SCHOLARSHIPS, HOW ABOUT US *ROOMING* TOGETHER!?

I HAVE NO WISH TO SHARE A ROOM WITH *ANY-ONE!* I DESIRE *PRIVACY!!*

WELL, IT'S NONE OF MY BUSINESS, BUT AREN'T YOU CARRYING THIS "MAD SCIENTIST" BIT A LITTLE TOO FAR?

MEN ALWAYS THINK THAT THEIR SUPERIORS ARE MAD!

I HAVE SAID *ENOUGH!* NOW I SHALL FIND MY OWN QUARTERS!

I'M GLAD HE *DIDN'T* ACCEPT MY OFFER! THERE'S SOME-THING *OMINOUS* ABOUT HIM... I CAN *SENSE* IT!!

8.

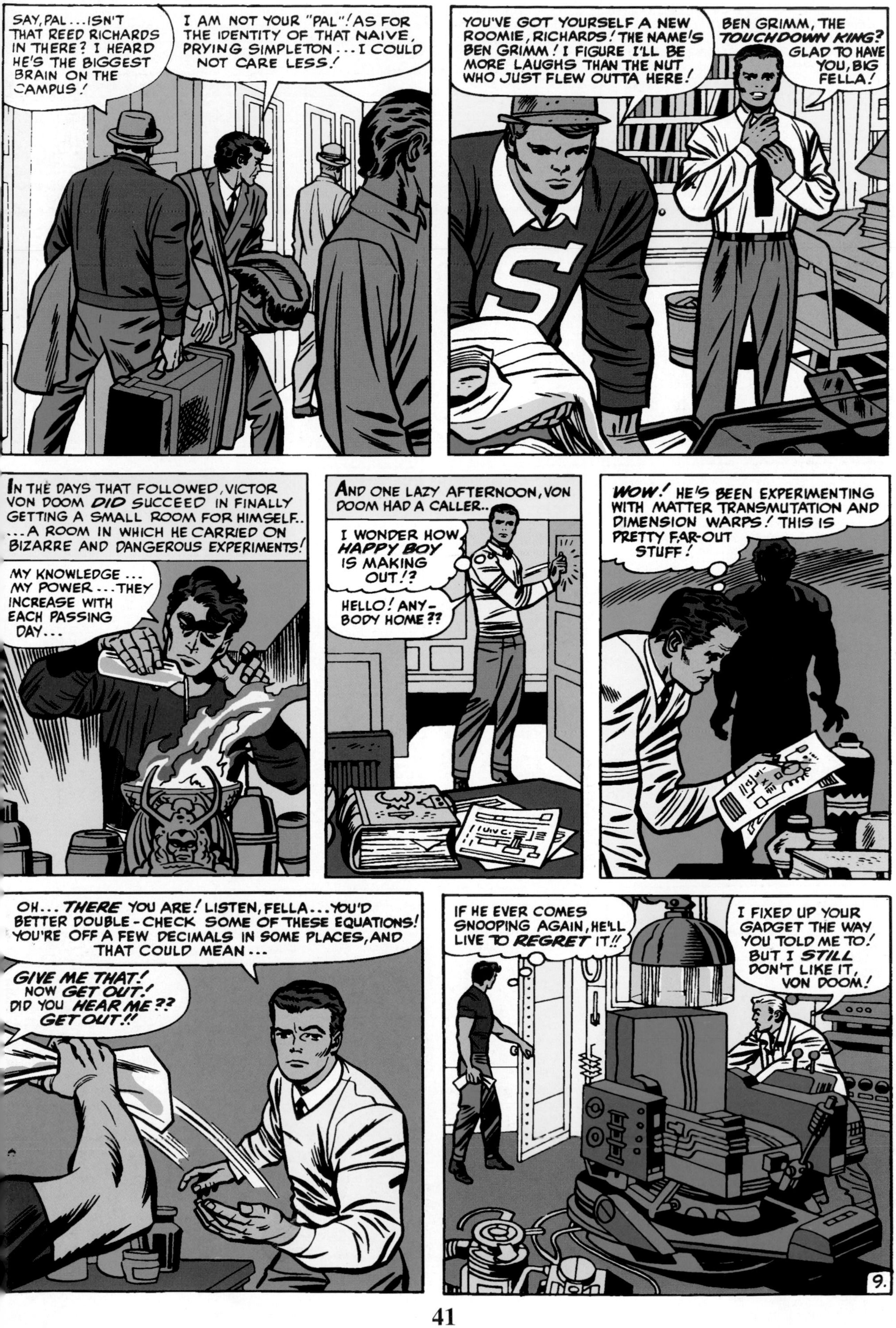
SAY, PAL... ISN'T THAT REED RICHARDS IN THERE? I HEARD HE'S THE BIGGEST BRAIN ON THE CAMPUS!
I AM NOT YOUR "PAL"! AS FOR THE IDENTITY OF THAT NAIVE, PRYING SIMPLETON... I COULD NOT CARE LESS!
YOU'VE GOT YOURSELF A NEW ROOMIE, RICHARDS! THE NAME'S BEN GRIMM! I FIGURE I'LL BE MORE LAUGHS THAN THE NUT WHO JUST FLEW OUTTA HERE!
BEN GRIMM, THE *TOUCHDOWN KING?* GLAD TO HAVE YOU, BIG FELLA!
IN THE DAYS THAT FOLLOWED, VICTOR VON DOOM *DID* SUCCEED IN FINALLY GETTING A SMALL ROOM FOR HIMSELF.. ...A ROOM IN WHICH HE CARRIED ON BIZARRE AND DANGEROUS EXPERIMENTS!
MY KNOWLEDGE... MY POWER... THEY INCREASE WITH EACH PASSING DAY...
AND ONE LAZY AFTERNOON, VON DOOM HAD A CALLER..
I WONDER HOW *HAPPY BOY* IS MAKING OUT!?
HELLO! ANY-BODY HOME??
WOW! HE'S BEEN EXPERIMENTING WITH MATTER TRANSMUTATION AND DIMENSION WARPS! THIS IS PRETTY FAR-OUT STUFF!
OH... *THERE* YOU ARE! LISTEN, FELLA... YOU'D BETTER DOUBLE-CHECK SOME OF THESE EQUATIONS! YOU'RE OFF A FEW DECIMALS IN SOME PLACES, AND THAT COULD MEAN...
GIVE ME THAT! NOW *GET OUT!* DID YOU *HEAR ME??* *GET OUT!!*
IF HE EVER COMES SNOOPING AGAIN, HE'LL LIVE TO *REGRET* IT!!
I FIXED UP YOUR GADGET THE WAY YOU TOLD ME TO! BUT I *STILL* DON'T LIKE IT, VON DOOM!
9.

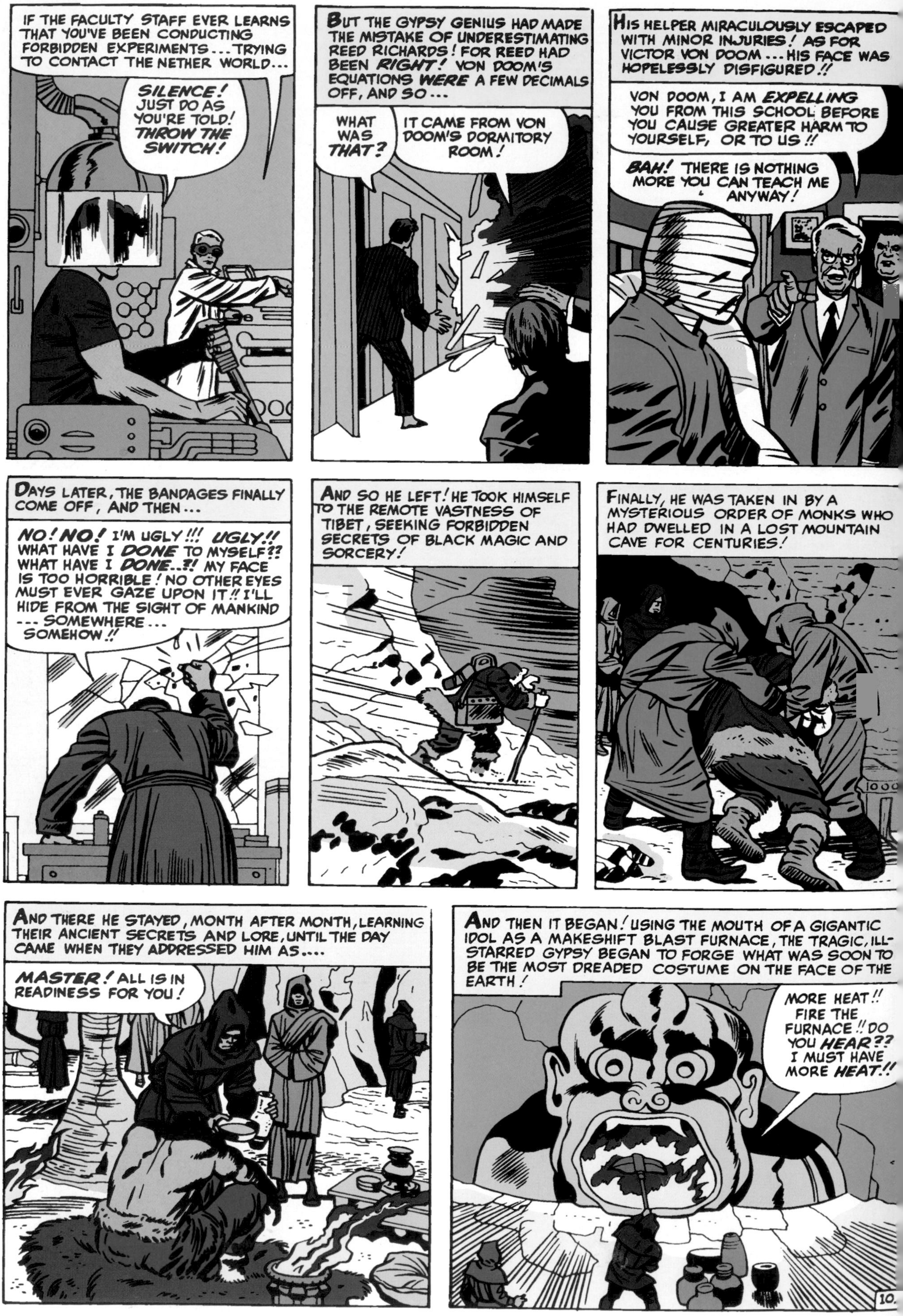
IF THE FACULTY STAFF EVER LEARNS THAT YOU'VE BEEN CONDUCTING FORBIDDEN EXPERIMENTS... TRYING TO CONTACT THE NETHER WORLD...
SILENCE! JUST DO AS YOU'RE TOLD! THROW THE SWITCH!
BUT THE GYPSY GENIUS HAD MADE THE MISTAKE OF UNDERESTIMATING REED RICHARDS! FOR REED HAD BEEN RIGHT! VON DOOM'S EQUATIONS WERE A FEW DECIMALS OFF, AND SO...
WHAT WAS THAT?
IT CAME FROM VON DOOM'S DORMITORY ROOM!
HIS HELPER MIRACULOUSLY ESCAPED WITH MINOR INJURIES! AS FOR VICTOR VON DOOM... HIS FACE WAS HOPELESSLY DISFIGURED!!
VON DOOM, I AM EXPELLING YOU FROM THIS SCHOOL BEFORE YOU CAUSE GREATER HARM TO YOURSELF, OR TO US!!
BAH! THERE IS NOTHING MORE YOU CAN TEACH ME ANYWAY!
DAYS LATER, THE BANDAGES FINALLY COME OFF, AND THEN...
NO! NO! I'M UGLY!!! UGLY!! WHAT HAVE I DONE TO MYSELF?? WHAT HAVE I DONE..?! MY FACE IS TOO HORRIBLE! NO OTHER EYES MUST EVER GAZE UPON IT!! I'LL HIDE FROM THE SIGHT OF MANKIND --- SOMEWHERE --- SOMEHOW!!
AND SO HE LEFT! HE TOOK HIMSELF TO THE REMOTE VASTNESS OF TIBET, SEEKING FORBIDDEN SECRETS OF BLACK MAGIC AND SORCERY!
FINALLY, HE WAS TAKEN IN BY A MYSTERIOUS ORDER OF MONKS WHO HAD DWELLED IN A LOST MOUNTAIN CAVE FOR CENTURIES!
AND THERE HE STAYED, MONTH AFTER MONTH, LEARNING THEIR ANCIENT SECRETS AND LORE, UNTIL THE DAY CAME WHEN THEY ADDRESSED HIM AS....
MASTER! ALL IS IN READINESS FOR YOU!
AND THEN IT BEGAN! USING THE MOUTH OF A GIGANTIC IDOL AS A MAKESHIFT BLAST FURNACE, THE TRAGIC, ILL-STARRED GYPSY BEGAN TO FORGE WHAT WAS SOON TO BE THE MOST DREADED COSTUME ON THE FACE OF THE EARTH!
MORE HEAT!! FIRE THE FURNACE!! DO YOU HEAR?? I MUST HAVE MORE HEAT!!
10

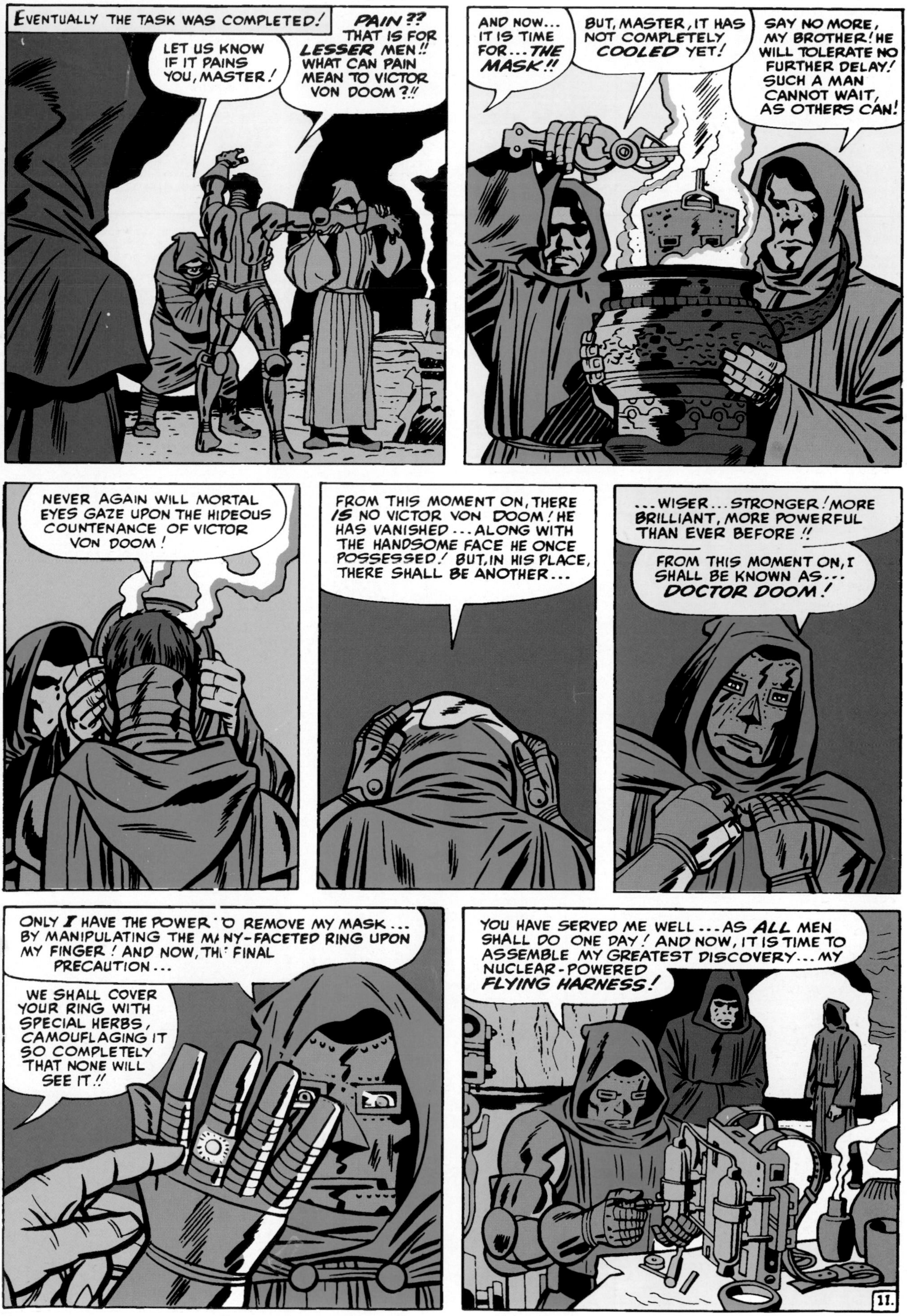

EVENTUALLY THE TASK WAS COMPLETED!
LET US KNOW IF IT PAINS YOU, MASTER!
PAIN?? THAT IS FOR LESSER MEN!! WHAT CAN PAIN MEAN TO VICTOR VON DOOM?!!
AND NOW... IT IS TIME FOR... THE MASK!!
BUT, MASTER, IT HAS NOT COMPLETELY COOLED YET!
SAY NO MORE, MY BROTHER! HE WILL TOLERATE NO FURTHER DELAY! SUCH A MAN CANNOT WAIT, AS OTHERS CAN!
NEVER AGAIN WILL MORTAL EYES GAZE UPON THE HIDEOUS COUNTENANCE OF VICTOR VON DOOM!
FROM THIS MOMENT ON, THERE IS NO VICTOR VON DOOM! HE HAS VANISHED... ALONG WITH THE HANDSOME FACE HE ONCE POSSESSED! BUT, IN HIS PLACE, THERE SHALL BE ANOTHER...
...WISER... STRONGER! MORE BRILLIANT, MORE POWERFUL THAN EVER BEFORE!!
FROM THIS MOMENT ON, I SHALL BE KNOWN AS... DOCTOR DOOM!
ONLY I HAVE THE POWER TO REMOVE MY MASK... BY MANIPULATING THE MANY-FACETED RING UPON MY FINGER! AND NOW, THE FINAL PRECAUTION...
WE SHALL COVER YOUR RING WITH SPECIAL HERBS, CAMOUFLAGING IT SO COMPLETELY THAT NONE WILL SEE IT!!
YOU HAVE SERVED ME WELL... AS ALL MEN SHALL DO ONE DAY! AND NOW, IT IS TIME TO ASSEMBLE MY GREATEST DISCOVERY... MY NUCLEAR-POWERED FLYING HARNESS!
11.

HE HAS LEFT US! WILL HE EVER RETURN?

NONE CAN TRULY SAY! FOR, SUCH A MAN MUST FOLLOW HIS DESTINY, NO MATTER WHERE IT MAY LEAD!

WOE TO THE WORLD, NOW THAT *DOCTOR DOOM* IS BORN!!

AND HUMANITY SOON LEARNS, TO ITS SHOCKED DISMAY, OF THE AWESOME MENACE WHICH IS IN ITS MIDST...!

DAILY ALARM
DOCTOR DOOM ISSUES ULTIMATUM TO EUROPE!

EVENING TR

THE POST
DOCTOR DOOM EVIL GENIUS, CREATES NEW WEAPON

FANTASTIC FOUR IN NEW BATTLE WITH DOCTOR DOOM!

DAILY TELEG

DOCTOR DOOM MAKES BID FOR POWER!

News-Record

DOCTOR DOOM WORLD MENACE! FANTASTIC FOUR ASK PUBLIC NOT TO PANIC! GOVERNMENT ISSUES NEW REPORT!

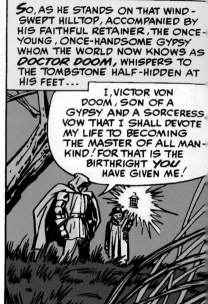

SO, AS HE STANDS ON THAT WIND-SWEPT HILLTOP, ACCOMPANIED BY HIS FAITHFUL RETAINER, THE ONCE-YOUNG, ONCE-HANDSOME GYPSY WHOM THE WORLD NOW KNOWS AS *DOCTOR DOOM*, WHISPERS TO THE TOMBSTONE HALF-HIDDEN AT HIS FEET...

I, VICTOR VON DOOM, SON OF A GYPSY AND A SORCERESS, VOW THAT I SHALL DEVOTE MY LIFE TO BECOMING THE MASTER OF ALL MAN-KIND! FOR THAT IS THE BIRTHRIGHT *YOU* HAVE GIVEN ME!

WITHOUT ANOTHER WORD, THE DRAMATIC BEING WHO HAS BECOME ABSOLUTE MONARCH OF THE KINGDOM OF LATVERIA, TURNS ON HIS HEEL AND WALKS THROUGH THE TINY VILLAGE, NEITHER SPEAKING NOR LOOKING LEFT NOR RIGHT!

GOOD DAY TO YOU, HERR DOCTOR!

MAY YOU ENJOY GOOD HEALTH, MASTER!

OURS HAS BEEN A PROSPEROUS LAND SINCE HE HAS RULED US!

MOMMY, *LOOK!* ISN'T THAT...?

HUSH, DEAR! YOU MUST BE SILENT WHEN THE *MASTER* PASSES!

AND SO, THE AWESOME FIGURE CONTINUES HIS WALK, SHOWING HIMSELF TO HIS SUBJECTS, WHILE HIS MIND DWELLS ON MATTERS WHICH ARE FAR BEYOND THEIR SIMPLE COMPREHENSION! AND THEN...

NOW WE SHALL RETURN TO THE CASTLE!

YES, MASTER!

AGAIN HE LOCKS HIMSELF WITHIN HIS LABORATORY! AND, WHEN HE EMERGES ONCE MORE, WHO KNOWS WHAT NEW MENACE WILL HAVE BEEN CREATED, TO THREATEN MANKIND!??

THROUGH THE LONG, SILENT NIGHTS, IN THAT BARREN CASTLE, HALF-HIDDEN IN THE ISOLATED KINGDOM OF LATVERIA, DOCTOR DOOM WORKS, AND PLANS, AND BROODS! AND, WHEN HIS WORK IS FINALLY FINISHED---THEN LET THE WORLD BEWARE!!

12

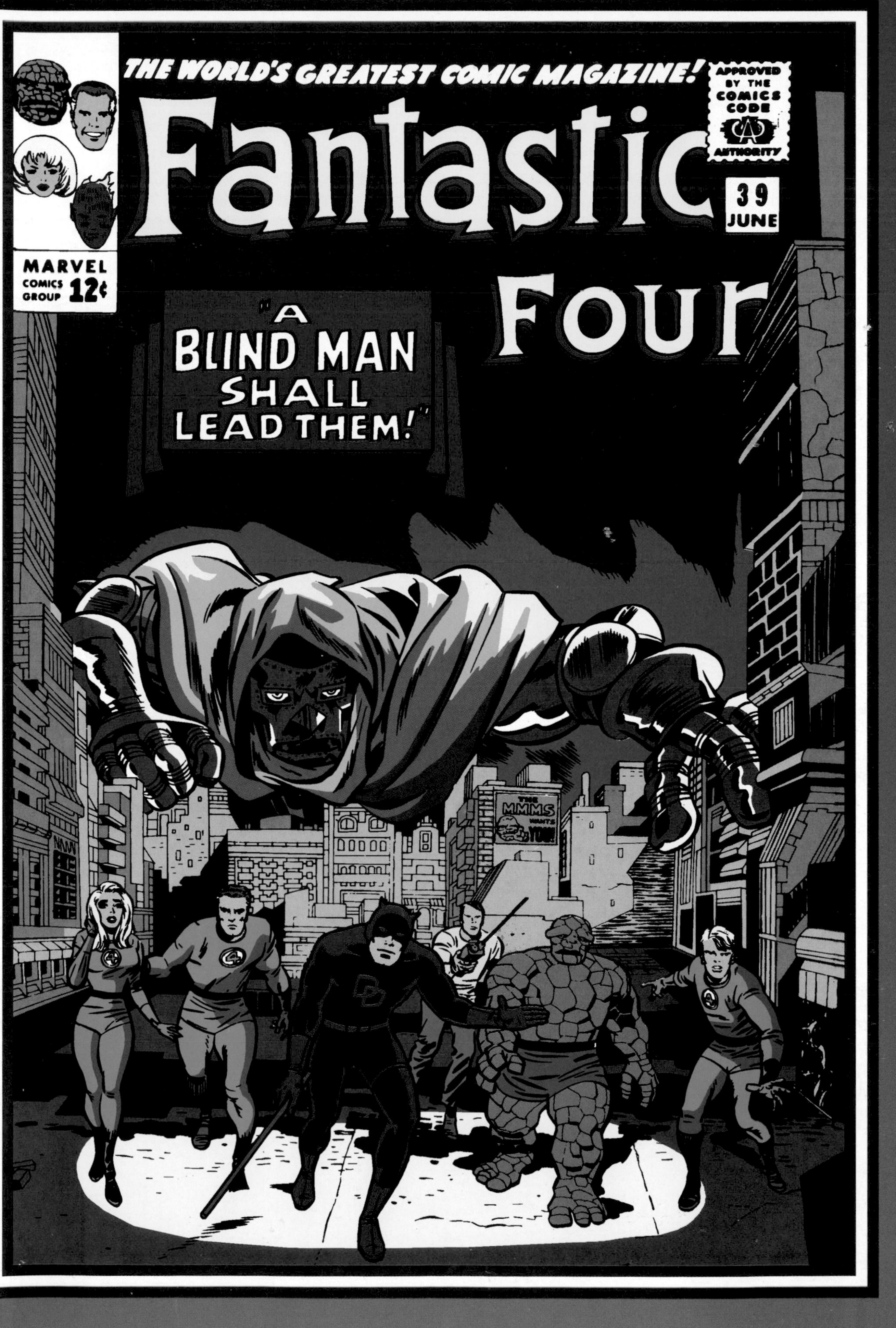
THE WORLD'S GREATEST COMIC MAGAZINE!
APPROVED BY THE COMICS CODE AUTHORITY
Fantastic Four
39
JUNE
MARVEL COMICS GROUP 12¢
"A BLIND MAN SHALL LEAD THEM!"
THE MMMS WANTS YOU!

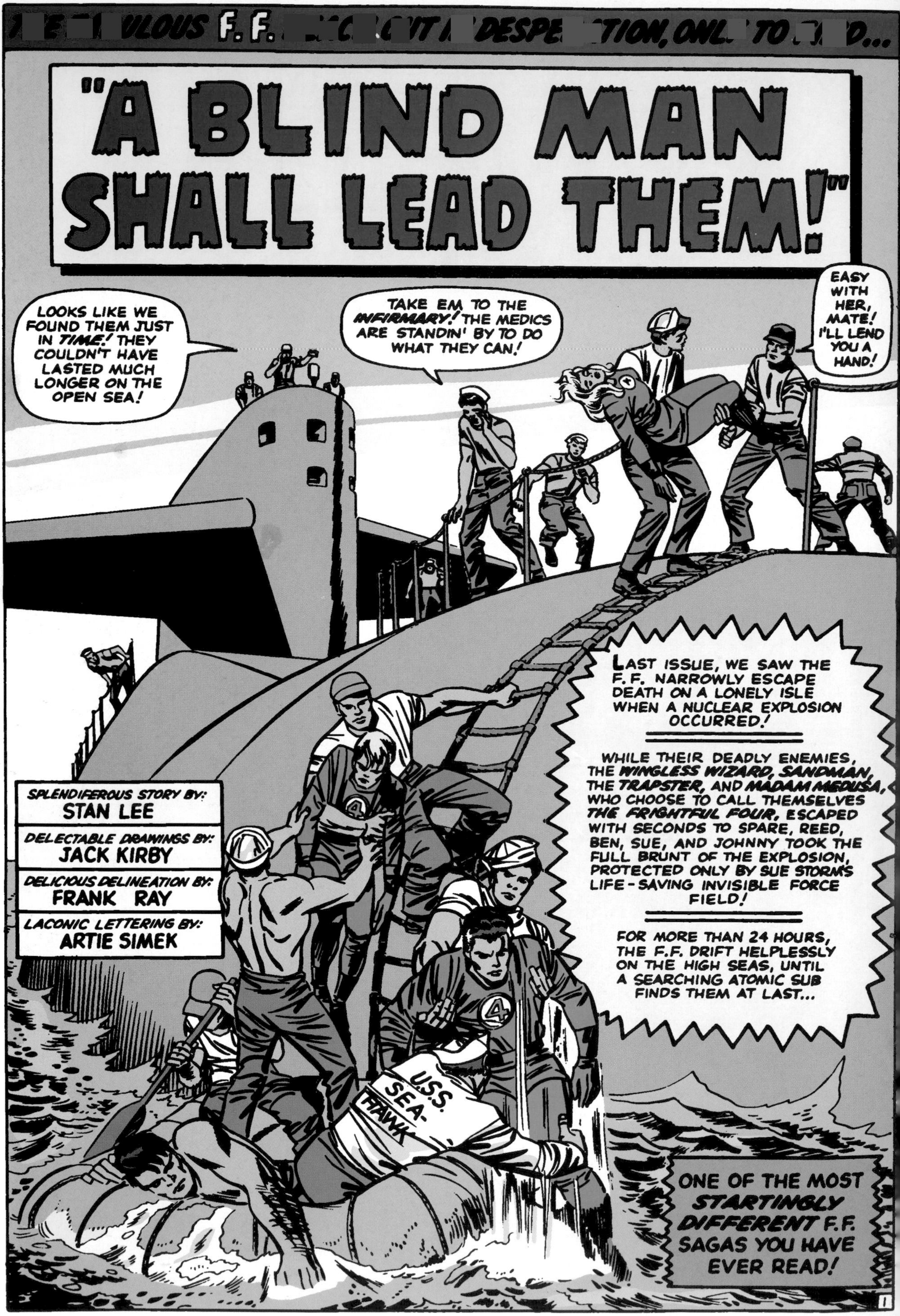

...VULOUS F.F. ...IT ... DESPE...TION, ONL... TO ...D...
"A BLIND MAN SHALL LEAD THEM!"
LOOKS LIKE WE FOUND THEM JUST IN TIME! THEY COULDN'T HAVE LASTED MUCH LONGER ON THE OPEN SEA!
TAKE EM TO THE INFIRMARY! THE MEDICS ARE STANDIN' BY TO DO WHAT THEY CAN!
EASY WITH HER, MATE! I'LL LEND YOU A HAND!
LAST ISSUE, WE SAW THE F.F. NARROWLY ESCAPE DEATH ON A LONELY ISLE WHEN A NUCLEAR EXPLOSION OCCURRED!
WHILE THEIR DEADLY ENEMIES, THE WINGLESS WIZARD, SANDMAN, THE TRAPSTER, AND MADAM MEDUSA, WHO CHOOSE TO CALL THEMSELVES THE FRIGHTFUL FOUR, ESCAPED WITH SECONDS TO SPARE, REED, BEN, SUE, AND JOHNNY TOOK THE FULL BRUNT OF THE EXPLOSION, PROTECTED ONLY BY SUE STORM'S LIFE-SAVING INVISIBLE FORCE FIELD!
FOR MORE THAN 24 HOURS, THE F.F. DRIFT HELPLESSLY ON THE HIGH SEAS, UNTIL A SEARCHING ATOMIC SUB FINDS THEM AT LAST...
SPLENDIFEROUS STORY BY: STAN LEE
DELECTABLE DRAWINGS BY: JACK KIRBY
DELICIOUS DELINEATION BY: FRANK RAY
LACONIC LETTERING BY: ARTIE SIMEK
U.S.S. SEA-HAWK
ONE OF THE MOST STARTINGLY DIFFERENT F.F. SAGAS YOU HAVE EVER READ!
1

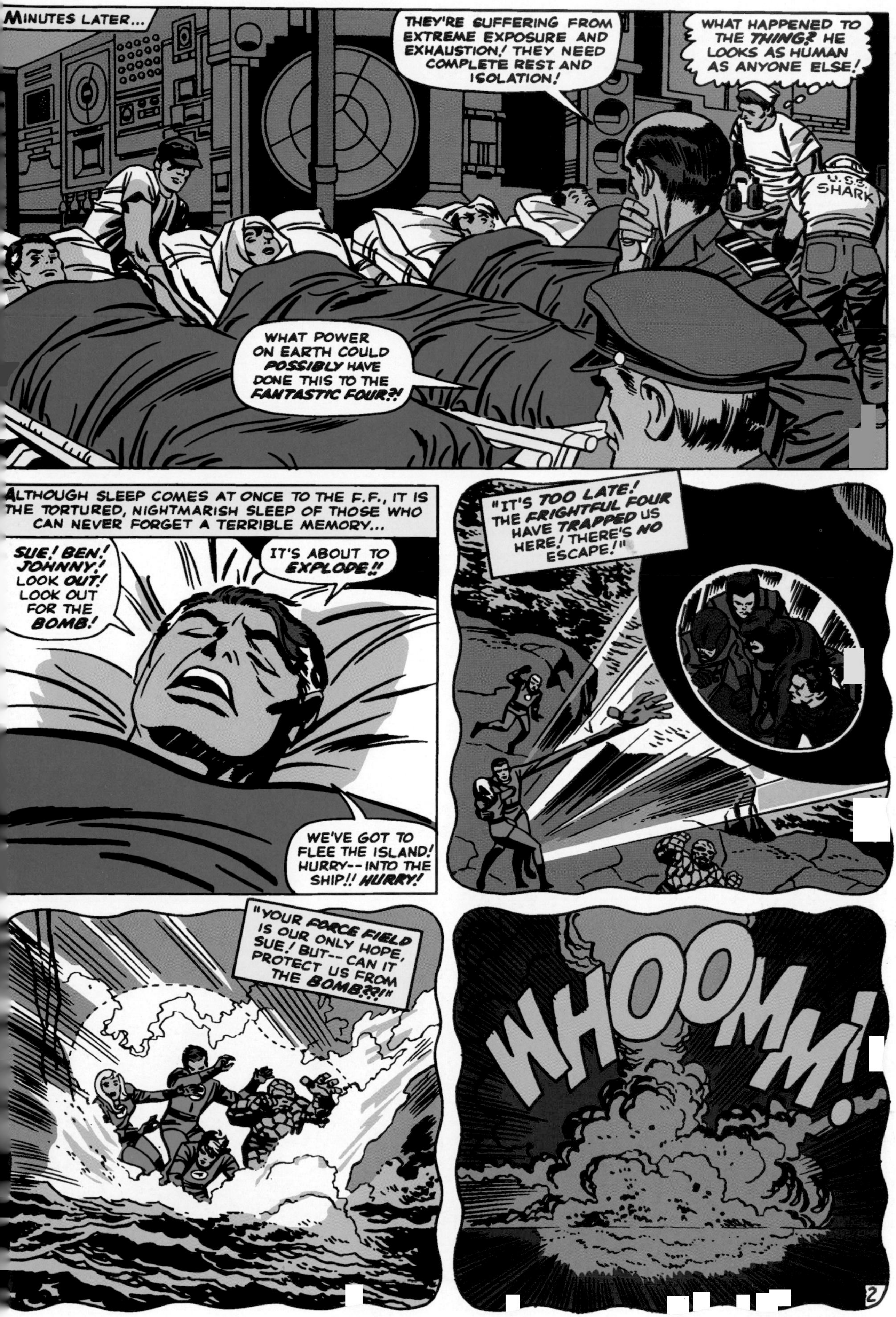
MINUTES LATER...
THEY'RE SUFFERING FROM EXTREME EXPOSURE AND EXHAUSTION! THEY NEED COMPLETE REST AND ISOLATION!
WHAT HAPPENED TO THE THING? HE LOOKS AS HUMAN AS ANYONE ELSE!
U.S.S. SHARK
WHAT POWER ON EARTH COULD POSSIBLY HAVE DONE THIS TO THE FANTASTIC FOUR?!
ALTHOUGH SLEEP COMES AT ONCE TO THE F.F., IT IS THE TORTURED, NIGHTMARISH SLEEP OF THOSE WHO CAN NEVER FORGET A TERRIBLE MEMORY...
SUE! BEN! JOHNNY! LOOK OUT! LOOK OUT FOR THE BOMB!
IT'S ABOUT TO EXPLODE!!
WE'VE GOT TO FLEE THE ISLAND! HURRY--INTO THE SHIP!! HURRY!
"IT'S TOO LATE! THE FRIGHTFUL FOUR HAVE TRAPPED US HERE! THERE'S NO ESCAPE!"
"YOUR FORCE FIELD IS OUR ONLY HOPE, SUE! BUT-- CAN IT PROTECT US FROM THE BOMB??!"
WHOOMM!
2

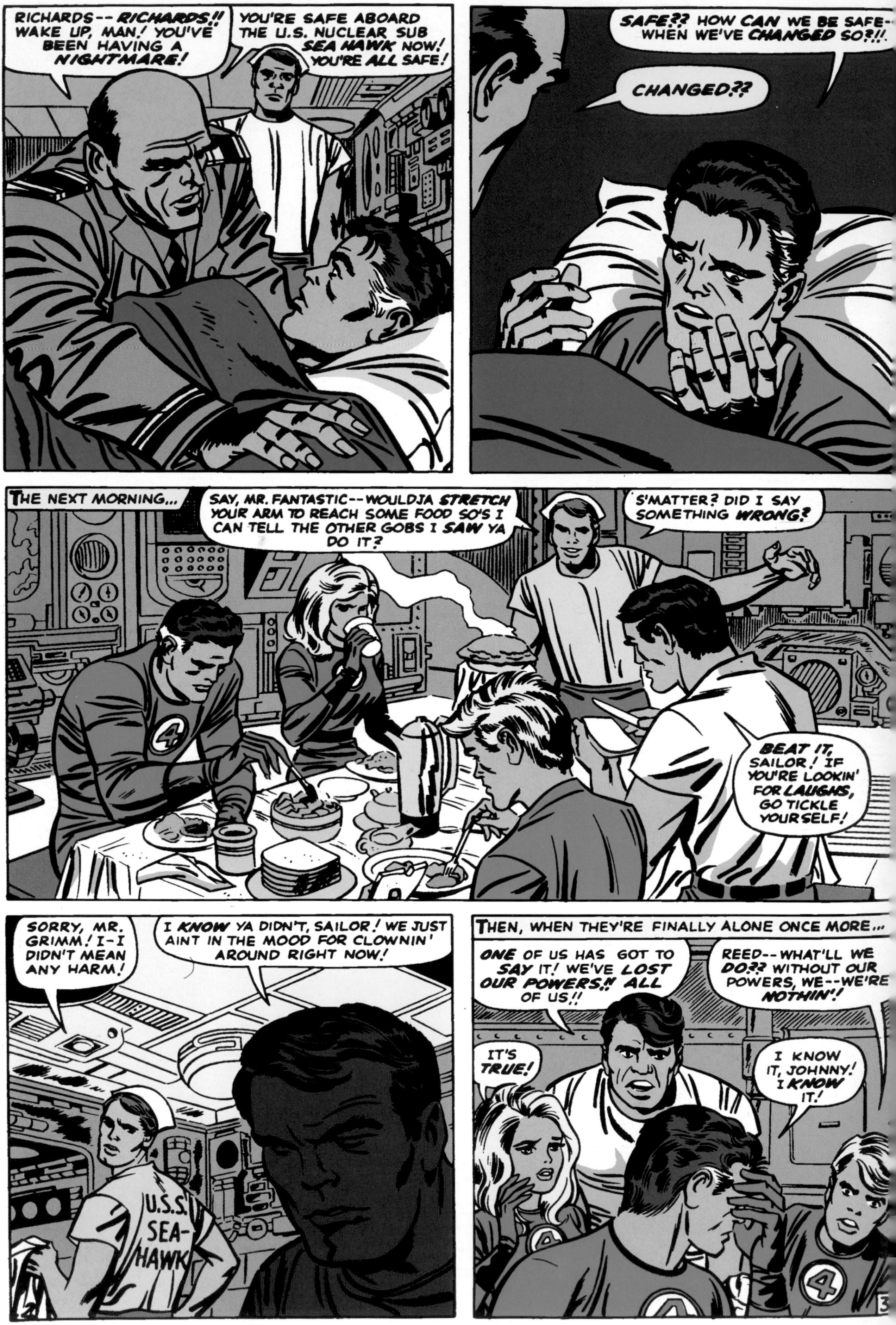
RICHARDS--RICHARDS!! WAKE UP, MAN! YOU'VE BEEN HAVING A NIGHTMARE!
YOU'RE SAFE ABOARD THE U.S. NUCLEAR SUB SEA HAWK NOW! YOU'RE ALL SAFE!
SAFE?? HOW CAN WE BE SAFE-- WHEN WE'VE CHANGED SO?!!
CHANGED??
THE NEXT MORNING...
SAY, MR. FANTASTIC--WOULDJA STRETCH YOUR ARM TO REACH SOME FOOD SO'S I CAN TELL THE OTHER GOBS I SAW YA DO IT?
S'MATTER? DID I SAY SOMETHING WRONG?
BEAT IT, SAILOR! IF YOU'RE LOOKIN' FOR LAUGHS, GO TICKLE YOURSELF!
SORRY, MR. GRIMM! I-I DIDN'T MEAN ANY HARM!
I KNOW YA DIDN'T, SAILOR! WE JUST AINT IN THE MOOD FOR CLOWNIN' AROUND RIGHT NOW!
U.S.S. SEA-HAWK
THEN, WHEN THEY'RE FINALLY ALONE ONCE MORE...
ONE OF US HAS GOT TO SAY IT! WE'VE LOST OUR POWERS!! ALL OF US!!
REED--WHAT'LL WE DO?? WITHOUT OUR POWERS, WE--WE'RE NOTHIN'!
IT'S TRUE!
I KNOW IT, JOHNNY! I KNOW IT!
3

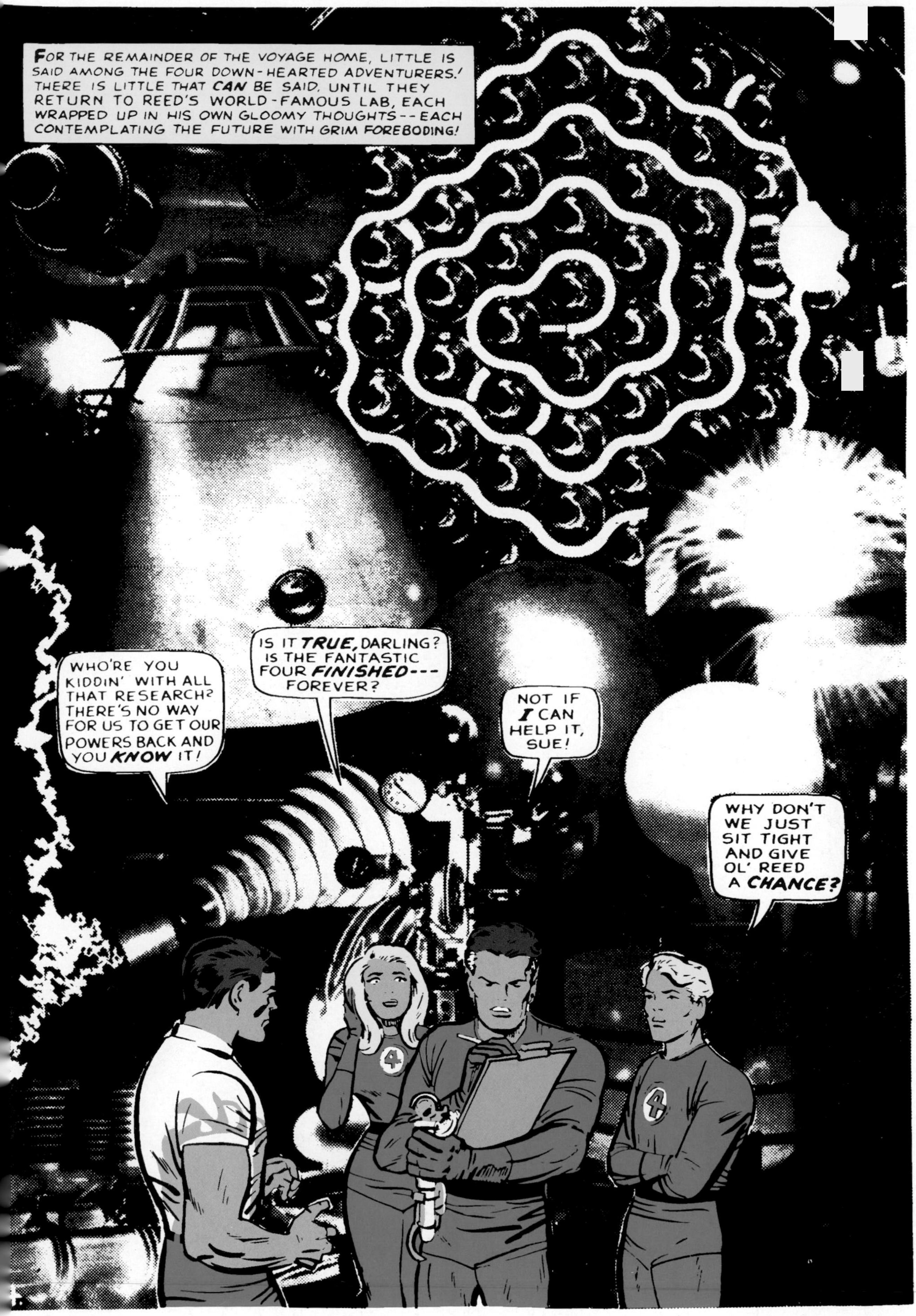
FOR THE REMAINDER OF THE VOYAGE HOME, LITTLE IS SAID AMONG THE FOUR DOWN-HEARTED ADVENTURERS! THERE IS LITTLE THAT CAN BE SAID, UNTIL THEY RETURN TO REED'S WORLD-FAMOUS LAB, EACH WRAPPED UP IN HIS OWN GLOOMY THOUGHTS-- EACH CONTEMPLATING THE FUTURE WITH GRIM FOREBODING!
WHO'RE YOU KIDDIN' WITH ALL THAT RESEARCH? THERE'S NO WAY FOR US TO GET OUR POWERS BACK AND YOU KNOW IT!
IS IT TRUE, DARLING? IS THE FANTASTIC FOUR FINISHED--- FOREVER?
NOT IF I CAN HELP IT, SUE!
WHY DON'T WE JUST SIT TIGHT AND GIVE OL' REED A CHANCE?

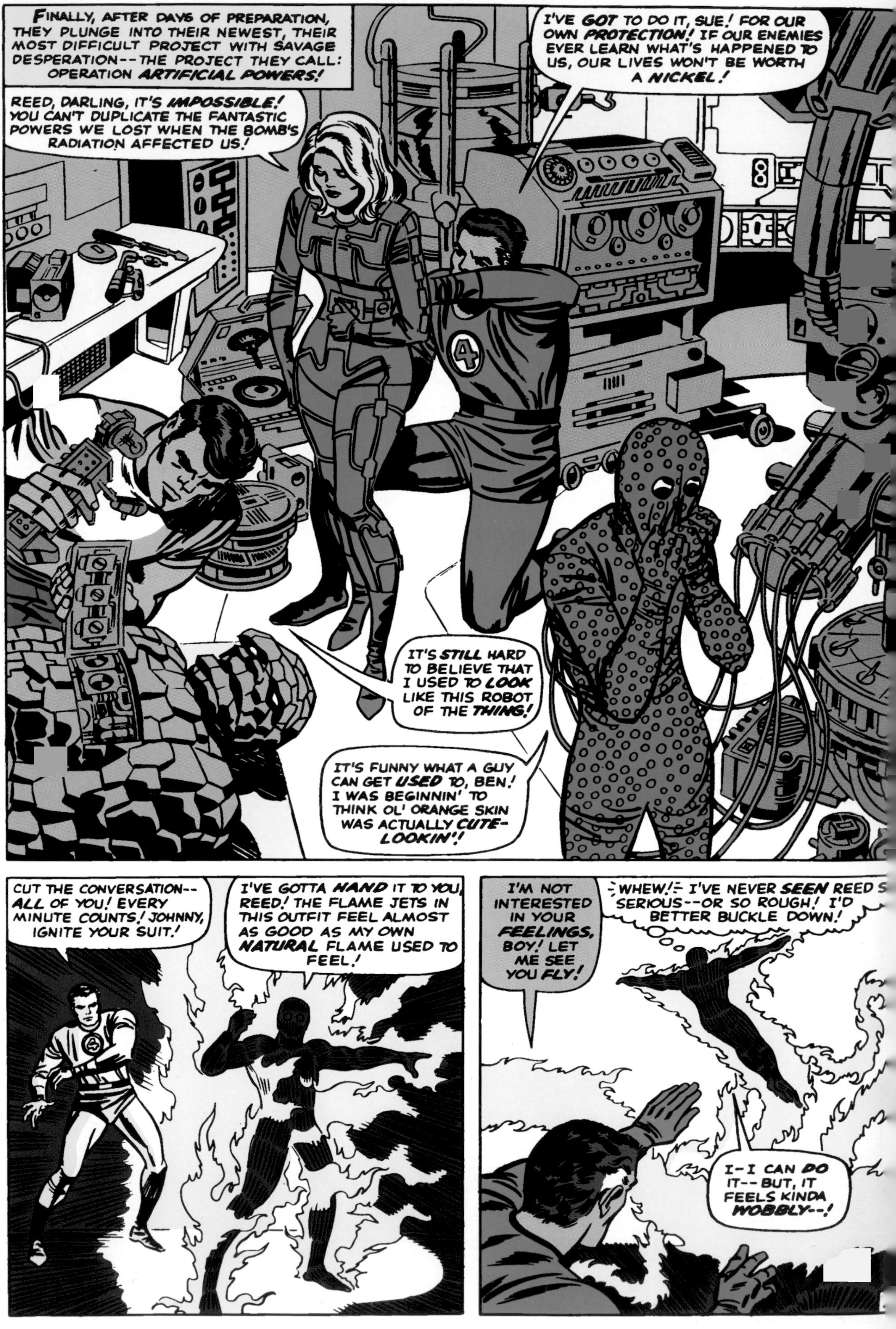
FINALLY, AFTER DAYS OF PREPARATION, THEY PLUNGE INTO THEIR NEWEST, THEIR MOST DIFFICULT PROJECT WITH SAVAGE DESPERATION--THE PROJECT THEY CALL: OPERATION ARTIFICIAL POWERS!
REED, DARLING, IT'S IMPOSSIBLE! YOU CAN'T DUPLICATE THE FANTASTIC POWERS WE LOST WHEN THE BOMB'S RADIATION AFFECTED US!
I'VE GOT TO DO IT, SUE! FOR OUR OWN PROTECTION! IF OUR ENEMIES EVER LEARN WHAT'S HAPPENED TO US, OUR LIVES WON'T BE WORTH A NICKEL!
IT'S STILL HARD TO BELIEVE THAT I USED TO LOOK LIKE THIS ROBOT OF THE THING!
IT'S FUNNY WHAT A GUY CAN GET USED TO, BEN! I WAS BEGINNIN' TO THINK OL' ORANGE SKIN WAS ACTUALLY CUTE-LOOKIN'!
CUT THE CONVERSATION--ALL OF YOU! EVERY MINUTE COUNTS! JOHNNY, IGNITE YOUR SUIT!
I'VE GOTTA HAND IT TO YOU, REED! THE FLAME JETS IN THIS OUTFIT FEEL ALMOST AS GOOD AS MY OWN NATURAL FLAME USED TO FEEL!
I'M NOT INTERESTED IN YOUR FEELINGS, BOY! LET ME SEE YOU FLY!
WHEW! I'VE NEVER SEEN REED S SERIOUS--OR SO ROUGH! I'D BETTER BUCKLE DOWN!
I-I CAN DO IT--BUT, IT FEELS KINDA WOBBLY--!

I CAN'T STAY ALOFT! LOOK OUT--*UNHHH!*

DON'T *QUIT*, KID! WE'RE NOT PLAYING *GAMES* NOW! KEEP PRACTICING TILL YOU *GET* IT! YOUR *LIFE* MAY DEPEND ON IT!

HEY, REED-- WHAT ABOUT *ME?*

YOU? UH, NOW LET'S SEE-- WHAT DID I HAVE IN MIND FOR YOU--?

LOOK, FELLA-- YOU HAVEN'T RESTED FOR *DAYS!* YA CAN'T KEEP DRIVIN' YOURSELF THIS WAY! WHY DON'T YOU--?

NO! WE CAN'T STOP *NOW!* GRAB THAT ROBOT CONTROL! MANIPULATE IT THE WAY I *TELL* YOU TO!

OKAY-- IF YOU *SAY* SO!

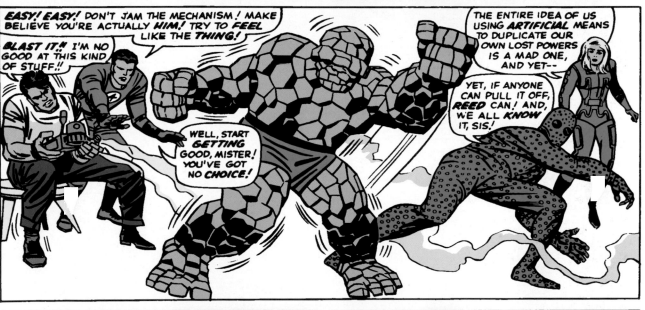

EASY! EASY! DON'T JAM THE MECHANISM! MAKE BELIEVE YOU'RE ACTUALLY *HIM!* TRY TO *FEEL* LIKE THE *THING!*

BLAST IT! I'M NO GOOD AT THIS KIND OF STUFF!!

WELL, START *GETTING* GOOD, MISTER! YOU'VE GOT NO *CHOICE!*

THE ENTIRE IDEA OF US USING *ARTIFICIAL* MEANS TO DUPLICATE OUR OWN LOST POWERS IS A MAD ONE, AND YET--

YET, IF ANYONE CAN PULL IT OFF, *REED* CAN! AND, WE ALL *KNOW* IT, SIS!

HEY, REED-- I FORGOT HOW TO *STOP* THE BLAMED THING! WHAT DO I DO NOW?

REVERSE THE VECTOR LEVER!! BEN, *LISTEN* TO ME, YOU CLUMSY BUMBLER!! GIVE ME THAT CONTROL!!

CRASH!

NOW DON'T BLOW A GASKET, STRETCH! I DID MY BEST! BUT MAYBE YA BETTER HIRE A *PUPPETEER!*

NO! ONLY *YOU* CAN KNOW WHAT THE THING WOULD DO UNDER ANY GIVEN CIRCUM-STANCE! IT MUST BE *YOU* WHO OPERATES THE ROBOT!

6

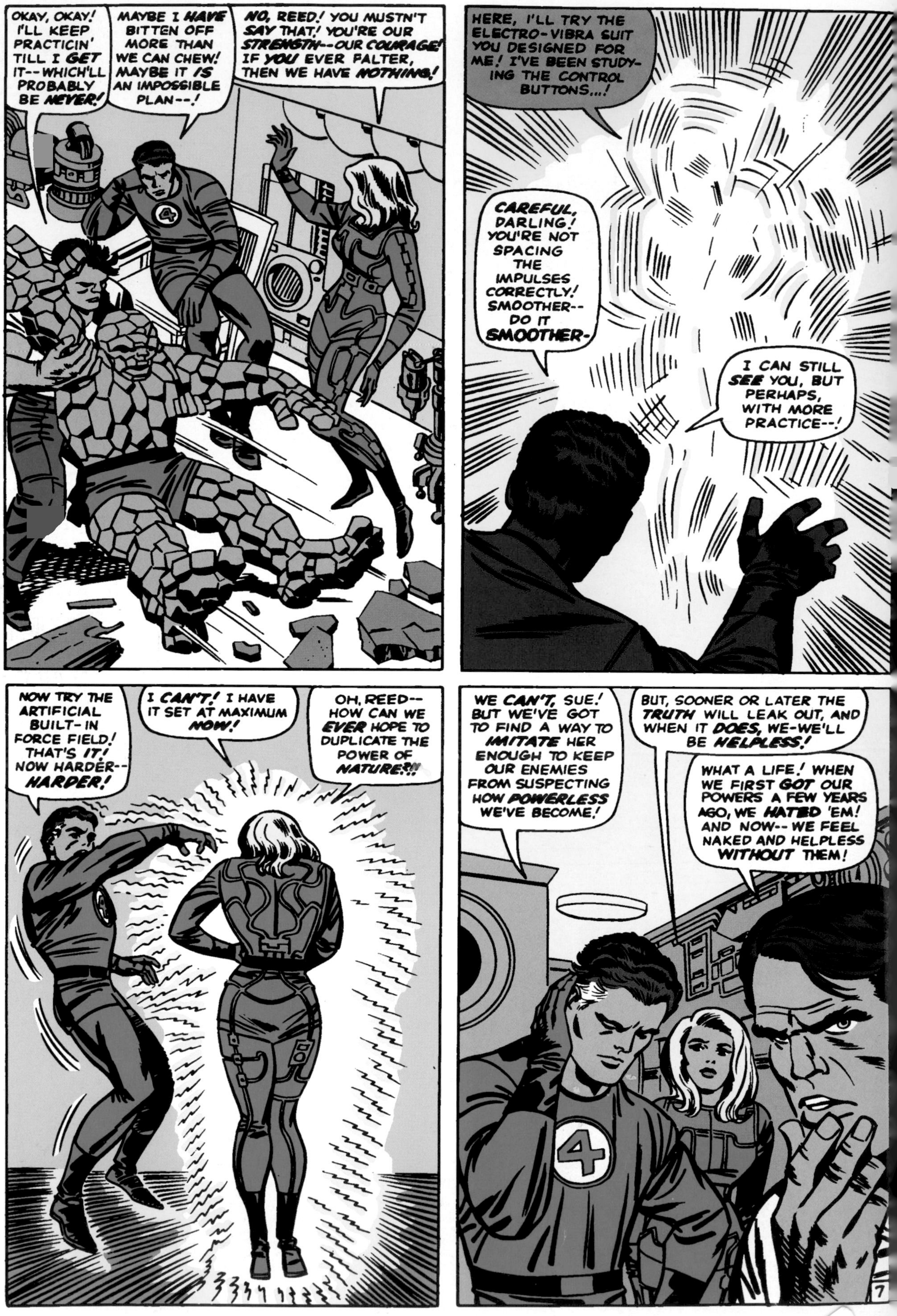
OKAY, OKAY! I'LL KEEP PRACTICIN' TILL I GET IT--WHICH'LL PROBABLY BE NEVER!
MAYBE I HAVE BITTEN OFF MORE THAN WE CAN CHEW! MAYBE IT IS AN IMPOSSIBLE PLAN--!
NO, REED! YOU MUSTN'T SAY THAT! YOU'RE OUR STRENGTH--OUR COURAGE! IF YOU EVER FALTER, THEN WE HAVE NOTHING!
HERE, I'LL TRY THE ELECTRO-VIBRA SUIT YOU DESIGNED FOR ME! I'VE BEEN STUDYING THE CONTROL BUTTONS...!
CAREFUL, DARLING! YOU'RE NOT SPACING THE IMPULSES CORRECTLY! SMOOTHER--DO IT SMOOTHER-
I CAN STILL SEE YOU, BUT PERHAPS, WITH MORE PRACTICE--!
NOW TRY THE ARTIFICIAL BUILT-IN FORCE FIELD! THAT'S IT! NOW HARDER--HARDER!
I CAN'T! I HAVE IT SET AT MAXIMUM NOW!
OH, REED--HOW CAN WE EVER HOPE TO DUPLICATE THE POWER OF NATURE?!!
WE CAN'T, SUE! BUT WE'VE GOT TO FIND A WAY TO IMITATE HER ENOUGH TO KEEP OUR ENEMIES FROM SUSPECTING HOW POWERLESS WE'VE BECOME!
BUT, SOONER OR LATER THE TRUTH WILL LEAK OUT, AND WHEN IT DOES, WE-WE'LL BE HELPLESS!
WHAT A LIFE! WHEN WE FIRST GOT OUR POWERS A FEW YEARS AGO, WE HATED 'EM! AND NOW-- WE FEEL NAKED AND HELPLESS WITHOUT THEM!
7

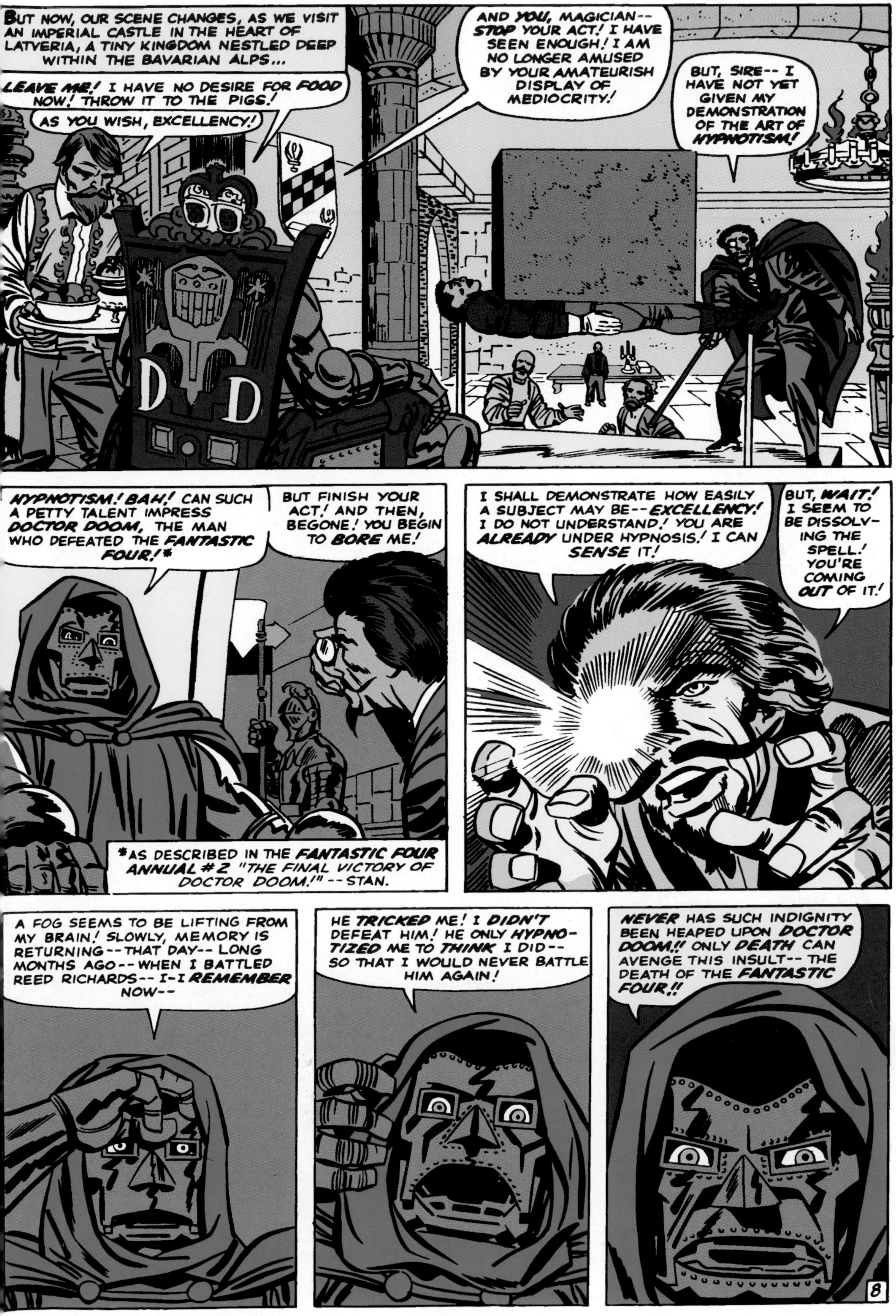

BUT NOW, OUR SCENE CHANGES, AS WE VISIT AN IMPERIAL CASTLE IN THE HEART OF LATVERIA, A TINY KINGDOM NESTLED DEEP WITHIN THE BAVARIAN ALPS...
LEAVE ME! I HAVE NO DESIRE FOR FOOD NOW! THROW IT TO THE PIGS!
AS YOU WISH, EXCELLENCY!
AND YOU, MAGICIAN-- STOP YOUR ACT! I HAVE SEEN ENOUGH! I AM NO LONGER AMUSED BY YOUR AMATEURISH DISPLAY OF MEDIOCRITY!
BUT, SIRE-- I HAVE NOT YET GIVEN MY DEMONSTRATION OF THE ART OF HYPNOTISM!
D D
HYPNOTISM! BAH! CAN SUCH A PETTY TALENT IMPRESS DOCTOR DOOM, THE MAN WHO DEFEATED THE FANTASTIC FOUR!*
BUT FINISH YOUR ACT! AND THEN, BEGONE! YOU BEGIN TO BORE ME!
*AS DESCRIBED IN THE FANTASTIC FOUR ANNUAL #2 "THE FINAL VICTORY OF DOCTOR DOOM!" --STAN.
I SHALL DEMONSTRATE HOW EASILY A SUBJECT MAY BE--EXCELLENCY! I DO NOT UNDERSTAND! YOU ARE ALREADY UNDER HYPNOSIS! I CAN SENSE IT!
BUT, WAIT! I SEEM TO BE DISSOLVING THE SPELL! YOU'RE COMING OUT OF IT!
A FOG SEEMS TO BE LIFTING FROM MY BRAIN! SLOWLY, MEMORY IS RETURNING--THAT DAY-- LONG MONTHS AGO--WHEN I BATTLED REED RICHARDS-- I-I REMEMBER NOW--
HE TRICKED ME! I DIDN'T DEFEAT HIM! HE ONLY HYPNOTIZED ME TO THINK I DID-- SO THAT I WOULD NEVER BATTLE HIM AGAIN!
NEVER HAS SUCH INDIGNITY BEEN HEAPED UPON DOCTOR DOOM!! ONLY DEATH CAN AVENGE THIS INSULT-- THE DEATH OF THE FANTASTIC FOUR!!
8

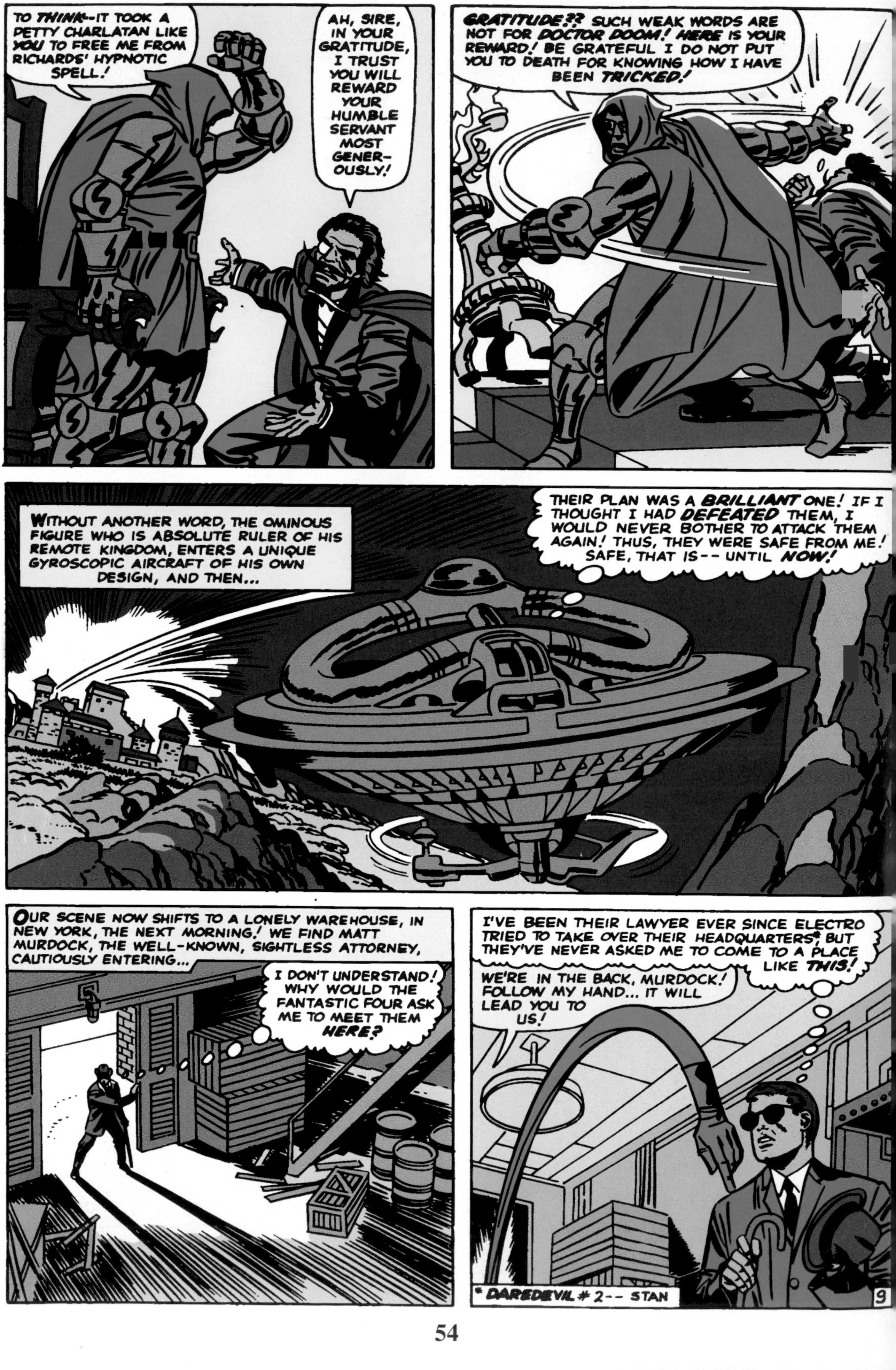
TO THINK--IT TOOK A PETTY CHARLATAN LIKE YOU TO FREE ME FROM RICHARDS' HYPNOTIC SPELL!
AH, SIRE, IN YOUR GRATITUDE, I TRUST YOU WILL REWARD YOUR HUMBLE SERVANT MOST GENEROUSLY!
GRATITUDE?? SUCH WEAK WORDS ARE NOT FOR DOCTOR DOOM! HERE IS YOUR REWARD! BE GRATEFUL I DO NOT PUT YOU TO DEATH FOR KNOWING HOW I HAVE BEEN TRICKED!
WITHOUT ANOTHER WORD, THE OMINOUS FIGURE WHO IS ABSOLUTE RULER OF HIS REMOTE KINGDOM, ENTERS A UNIQUE GYROSCOPIC AIRCRAFT OF HIS OWN DESIGN, AND THEN...
THEIR PLAN WAS A BRILLIANT ONE! IF I THOUGHT I HAD DEFEATED THEM, I WOULD NEVER BOTHER TO ATTACK THEM AGAIN! THUS, THEY WERE SAFE FROM ME! SAFE, THAT IS-- UNTIL NOW!
OUR SCENE NOW SHIFTS TO A LONELY WAREHOUSE, IN NEW YORK, THE NEXT MORNING! WE FIND MATT MURDOCK, THE WELL-KNOWN, SIGHTLESS ATTORNEY, CAUTIOUSLY ENTERING...
I DON'T UNDERSTAND! WHY WOULD THE FANTASTIC FOUR ASK ME TO MEET THEM HERE?
I'VE BEEN THEIR LAWYER EVER SINCE ELECTRO TRIED TO TAKE OVER THEIR HEADQUARTERS*, BUT THEY'VE NEVER ASKED ME TO COME TO A PLACE LIKE THIS!
WE'RE IN THE BACK, MURDOCK! FOLLOW MY HAND... IT WILL LEAD YOU TO US!
* DAREDEVIL # 2-- STAN
9

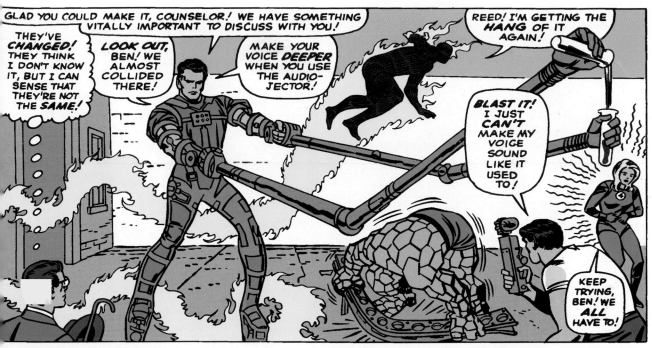

GLAD YOU COULD MAKE IT, COUNSELOR! WE HAVE SOMETHING VITALLY IMPORTANT TO DISCUSS WITH YOU!

THEY'VE CHANGED! THEY THINK I DON'T KNOW IT, BUT I CAN SENSE THAT THEY'RE NOT THE SAME!

LOOK OUT, BEN! WE ALMOST COLLIDED THERE!

MAKE YOUR VOICE DEEPER WHEN YOU USE THE AUDIO-JECTOR!

REED! I'M GETTING THE HANG OF IT AGAIN!

BLAST IT! I JUST CAN'T MAKE MY VOICE SOUND LIKE IT USED TO!

KEEP TRYING, BEN! WE ALL HAVE TO!

SOMETHING TERRIBLE MUST HAVE HAPPENED TO THEM! THEY'RE IN GREAT DANGER! THEY NEED HELP!

NOW LISTEN CAREFULLY, MURDOCK-- THERE ISN'T MUCH TIME! AND, WHAT-EVER I TELL YOU IS CONFIDENTIAL!

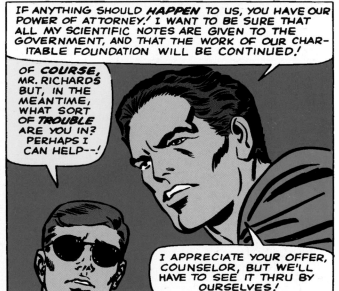

IF ANYTHING SHOULD HAPPEN TO US, YOU HAVE OUR POWER OF ATTORNEY! I WANT TO BE SURE THAT ALL MY SCIENTIFIC NOTES ARE GIVEN TO THE GOVERNMENT, AND THAT THE WORK OF OUR CHAR-ITABLE FOUNDATION WILL BE CONTINUED!

OF COURSE, MR. RICHARDS BUT, IN THE MEANTIME, WHAT SORT OF TROUBLE ARE YOU IN? PERHAPS I CAN HELP--!

I APPRECIATE YOUR OFFER, COUNSELOR, BUT WE'LL HAVE TO SEE IT THRU BY OURSELVES!

BUT THEN, SUDDENLY...

AN EXPLOSION! SOMEONE'S ATTACKIN' US!

MURDOCK, THIS IS NO PLACE FOR YOU! TRY TO ESCAPE! IT ISN'T YOUR PROBLEM!

WHOEVER CAUSED THAT EXPLOSION IS JUST TOYING WITH US! IT WASN'T POWERFUL ENOUGH TO CAUSE SERIOUS INJURY!

NOW WE'RE BEING PEPPERED WITH SMALL STUN-BLASTS-- JUST STRONG ENOUGH TO KEEP US OFF-BALANCE!

10

BEN! ONLY THE *THING'S* STRENGTH CAN HELP US NOW! BEN, DO YOU *HEAR* ME??

WHO CAN IT *BE?* WHO WOULD ATTACK US *HERE?*

YEAH! YEAH! SHUDDUP AND LEMME *CONCENTRATE!*

WHEN I FIND OUT, I'LL LETCHA *KNOW!*

NOW RUN FOR COVER WHILE I HOLD THIS BLAMED *WALL* UP!

WONDERFUL! YOU SOUNDED JUST *LIKE* THE THING!

WHO'D YA *EXPECT* ME TO SOUND LIKE-- *GOMER PYLE?!*

UNNHHH--! CAN'T *HOLD* IT ANY LONGER--!!

BUT, UNNOTICED AMONGST THE CONFUSION AND CARNAGE, A *NEW* FIGURE SUDDENLY APPEARS! WHERE MATT MURDOCK, SIGHTLESS LAWYER, HAD JUST STOOD, A LIGHTNING-FAST CHANGE OF CLOTHES NOW REVEALS-- *DAREDEVIL,* THE MAN WITHOUT FEAR!!

SOMETHING HAS HAPPENED TO THE F.F.! THEY'VE LOST THEIR NATURAL POWERS! I CAN HELP THEM MORE AS *DAREDEVIL* THAN AS THEIR *LAWYER* NOW!

ALTHOUGH DEPRIVED OF THE GIFT OF SIGHT, THE FEARLESS ADVENTURER'S *OTHER* SENSES ARE SO HIGHLY DEVELOPED THAT NO LIVING BEING HAS EVER SUSPECTED THAT DAREDEVIL IS ACTUALLY A *BLIND* MAN!

UHHHHH....!

THAT *SOUND!* THE TORCH IS HURT!

SPAT!

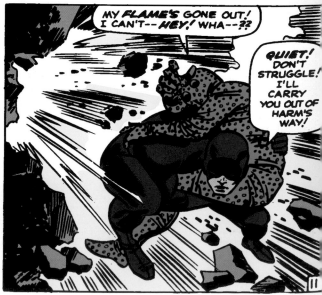

MY *FLAME'S* GONE OUT! I CAN'T-- *HEY!* WHA--??

QUIET! DON'T STRUGGLE! I'LL CARRY YOU OUT OF HARM'S WAY!

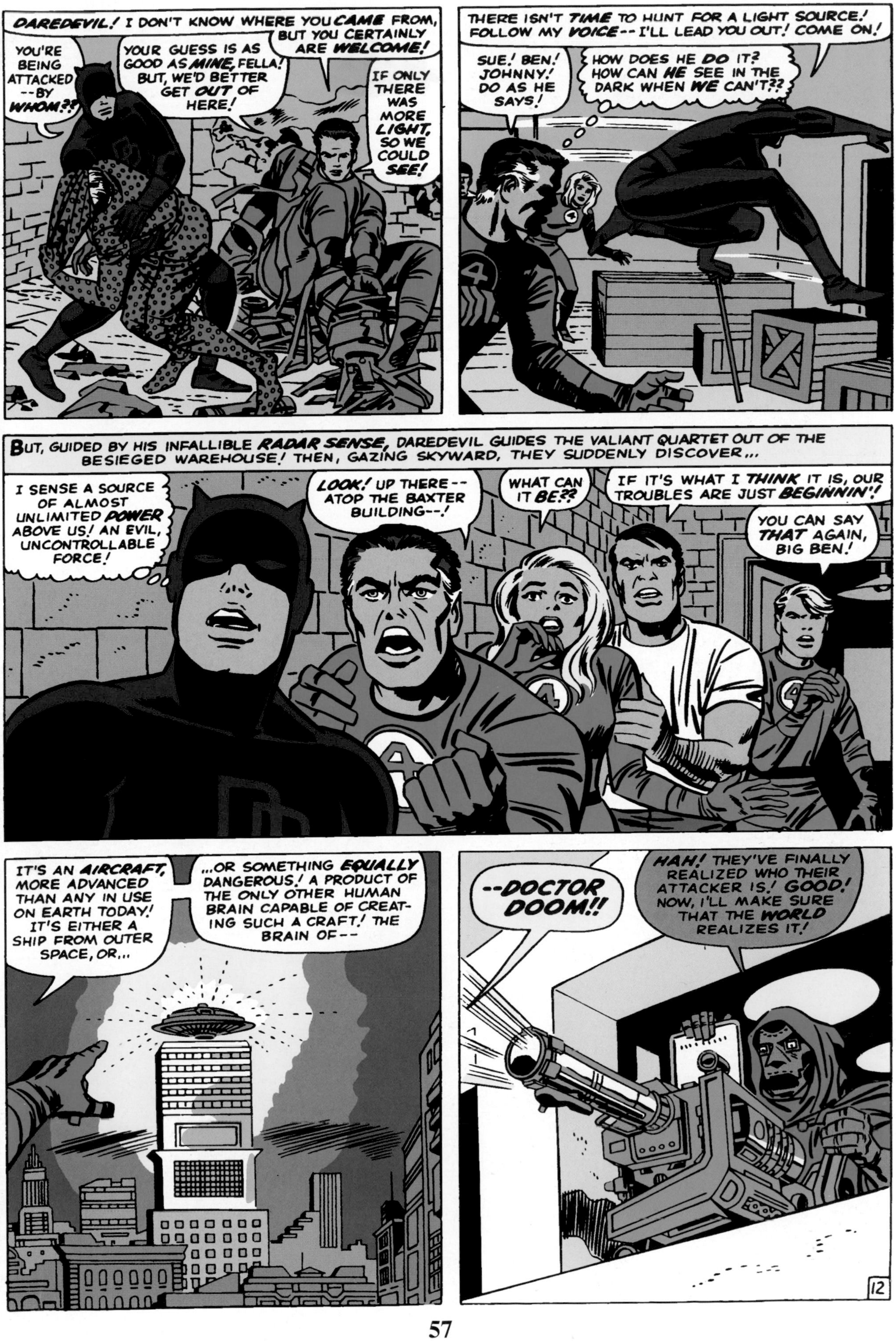

DAREDEVIL! I DON'T KNOW WHERE YOU CAME FROM, BUT YOU CERTAINLY ARE WELCOME!
YOU'RE BEING ATTACKED --BY WHOM??
YOUR GUESS IS AS GOOD AS MINE, FELLA! BUT, WE'D BETTER GET OUT OF HERE!
IF ONLY THERE WAS MORE LIGHT, SO WE COULD SEE!
THERE ISN'T TIME TO HUNT FOR A LIGHT SOURCE! FOLLOW MY VOICE -- I'LL LEAD YOU OUT! COME ON!
SUE! BEN! JOHNNY! DO AS HE SAYS!
HOW DOES HE DO IT? HOW CAN HE SEE IN THE DARK WHEN WE CAN'T??
BUT, GUIDED BY HIS INFALLIBLE RADAR SENSE, DAREDEVIL GUIDES THE VALIANT QUARTET OUT OF THE BESIEGED WAREHOUSE! THEN, GAZING SKYWARD, THEY SUDDENLY DISCOVER...
I SENSE A SOURCE OF ALMOST UNLIMITED POWER ABOVE US! AN EVIL, UNCONTROLLABLE FORCE!
LOOK! UP THERE -- ATOP THE BAXTER BUILDING--!
WHAT CAN IT BE??
IF IT'S WHAT I THINK IT IS, OUR TROUBLES ARE JUST BEGINNIN'!
YOU CAN SAY THAT AGAIN, BIG BEN!
IT'S AN AIRCRAFT, MORE ADVANCED THAN ANY IN USE ON EARTH TODAY! IT'S EITHER A SHIP FROM OUTER SPACE, OR...
...OR SOMETHING EQUALLY DANGEROUS! A PRODUCT OF THE ONLY OTHER HUMAN BRAIN CAPABLE OF CREATING SUCH A CRAFT! THE BRAIN OF --
--DOCTOR DOOM!!
HAH! THEY'VE FINALLY REALIZED WHO THEIR ATTACKER IS! GOOD! NOW, I'LL MAKE SURE THAT THE WORLD REALIZES IT!
12

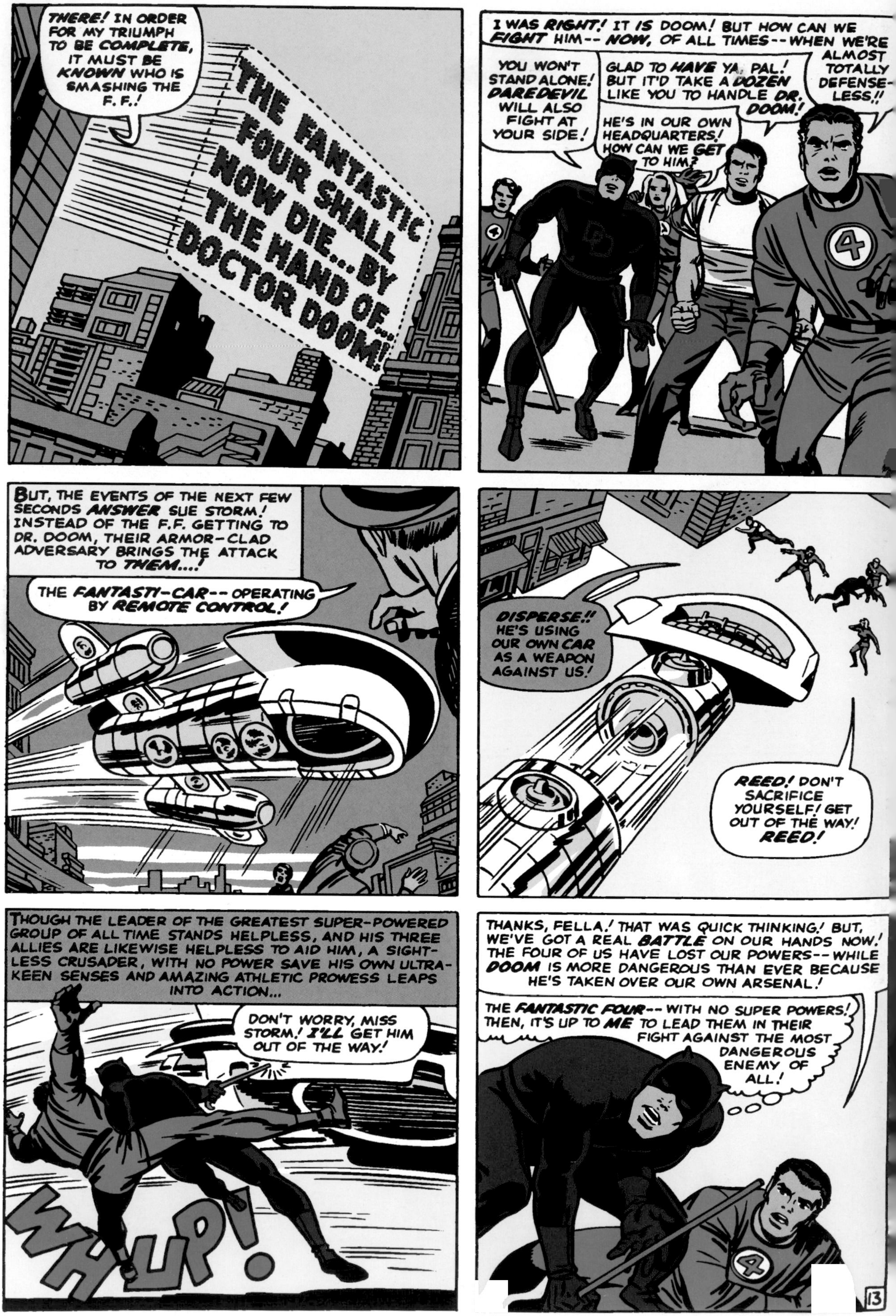
THERE! IN ORDER FOR MY TRIUMPH TO BE COMPLETE, IT MUST BE KNOWN WHO IS SMASHING THE F.F.!
THE FANTASTIC FOUR SHALL NOW DIE...BY THE HAND OF... DOCTOR DOOM!
I WAS RIGHT! IT IS DOOM! BUT HOW CAN WE FIGHT HIM-- NOW, OF ALL TIMES--WHEN WE'RE ALMOST TOTALLY DEFENSELESS!!
YOU WON'T STAND ALONE! DAREDEVIL WILL ALSO FIGHT AT YOUR SIDE!
GLAD TO HAVE YA, PAL! BUT IT'D TAKE A DOZEN LIKE YOU TO HANDLE DR. DOOM!
HE'S IN OUR OWN HEADQUARTERS! HOW CAN WE GET TO HIM?
BUT, THE EVENTS OF THE NEXT FEW SECONDS ANSWER SUE STORM! INSTEAD OF THE F.F. GETTING TO DR. DOOM, THEIR ARMOR-CLAD ADVERSARY BRINGS THE ATTACK TO THEM....!
THE FANTASTI-CAR-- OPERATING BY REMOTE CONTROL!
DISPERSE!! HE'S USING OUR OWN CAR AS A WEAPON AGAINST US!
REED! DON'T SACRIFICE YOURSELF! GET OUT OF THE WAY! REED!
THOUGH THE LEADER OF THE GREATEST SUPER-POWERED GROUP OF ALL TIME STANDS HELPLESS, AND HIS THREE ALLIES ARE LIKEWISE HELPLESS TO AID HIM, A SIGHTLESS CRUSADER, WITH NO POWER SAVE HIS OWN ULTRA-KEEN SENSES AND AMAZING ATHLETIC PROWESS LEAPS INTO ACTION...
DON'T WORRY, MISS STORM! I'LL GET HIM OUT OF THE WAY!
WHUP!
THANKS, FELLA! THAT WAS QUICK THINKING! BUT, WE'VE GOT A REAL BATTLE ON OUR HANDS NOW! THE FOUR OF US HAVE LOST OUR POWERS--WHILE DOOM IS MORE DANGEROUS THAN EVER BECAUSE HE'S TAKEN OVER OUR OWN ARSENAL!
THE FANTASTIC FOUR-- WITH NO SUPER POWERS! THEN, IT'S UP TO ME TO LEAD THEM IN THEIR FIGHT AGAINST THE MOST DANGEROUS ENEMY OF ALL!
13

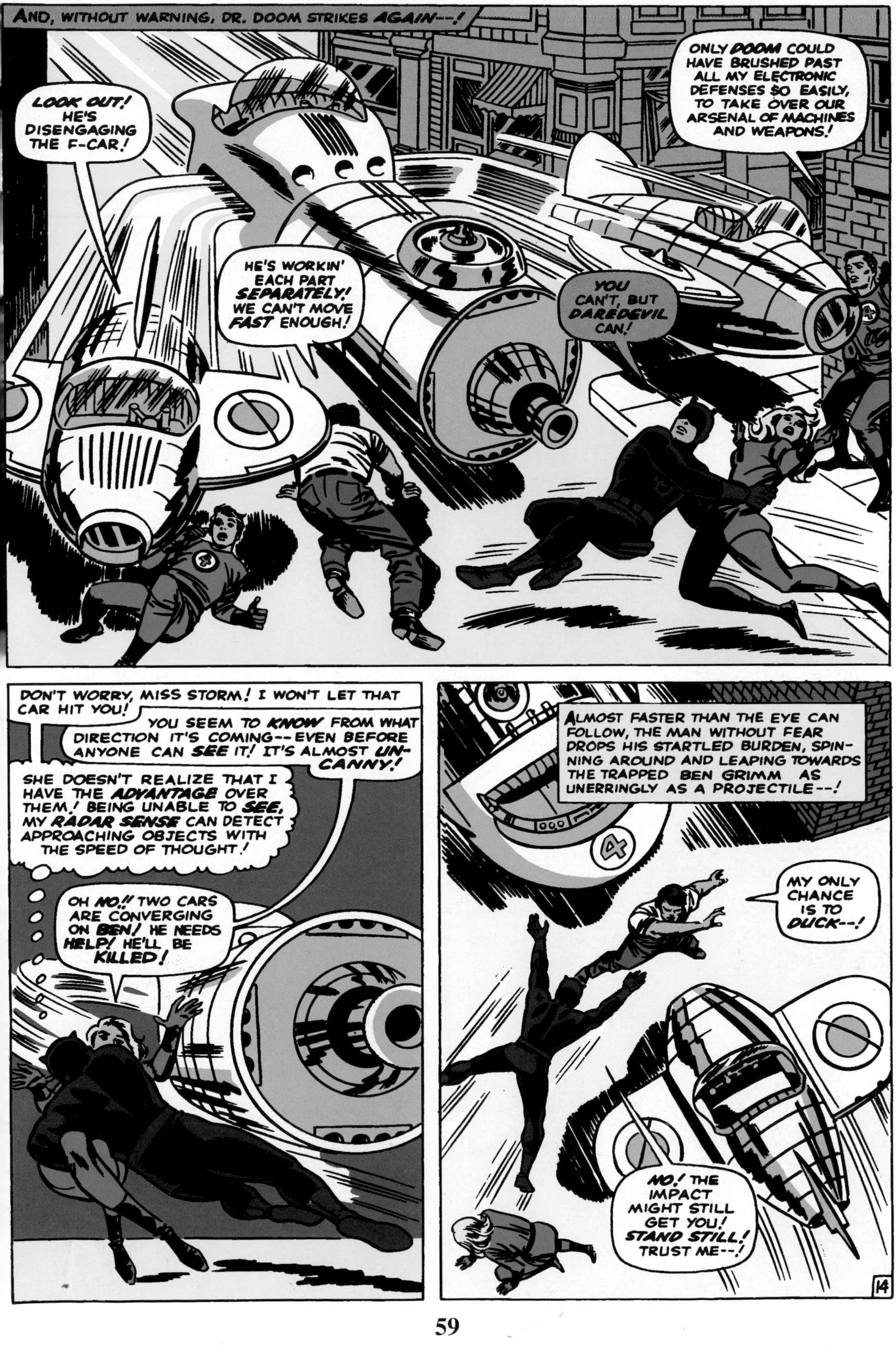
AND, WITHOUT WARNING, DR. DOOM STRIKES AGAIN--!
LOOK OUT! HE'S DISENGAGING THE F-CAR!
ONLY DOOM COULD HAVE BRUSHED PAST ALL MY ELECTRONIC DEFENSES SO EASILY, TO TAKE OVER OUR ARSENAL OF MACHINES AND WEAPONS!
HE'S WORKIN' EACH PART SEPARATELY! WE CAN'T MOVE FAST ENOUGH!
YOU CAN'T, BUT DAREDEVIL CAN!
DON'T WORRY, MISS STORM! I WON'T LET THAT CAR HIT YOU!
YOU SEEM TO KNOW FROM WHAT DIRECTION IT'S COMING--EVEN BEFORE ANYONE CAN SEE IT! IT'S ALMOST UN-CANNY!
SHE DOESN'T REALIZE THAT I HAVE THE ADVANTAGE OVER THEM! BEING UNABLE TO SEE, MY RADAR SENSE CAN DETECT APPROACHING OBJECTS WITH THE SPEED OF THOUGHT!
OH NO!! TWO CARS ARE CONVERGING ON BEN! HE NEEDS HELP! HE'LL BE KILLED!
ALMOST FASTER THAN THE EYE CAN FOLLOW, THE MAN WITHOUT FEAR DROPS HIS STARTLED BURDEN, SPIN-NING AROUND AND LEAPING TOWARDS THE TRAPPED BEN GRIMM AS UNERRINGLY AS A PROJECTILE--!
MY ONLY CHANCE IS TO DUCK--!
NO! THE IMPACT MIGHT STILL GET YOU! STAND STILL! TRUST ME--!
14

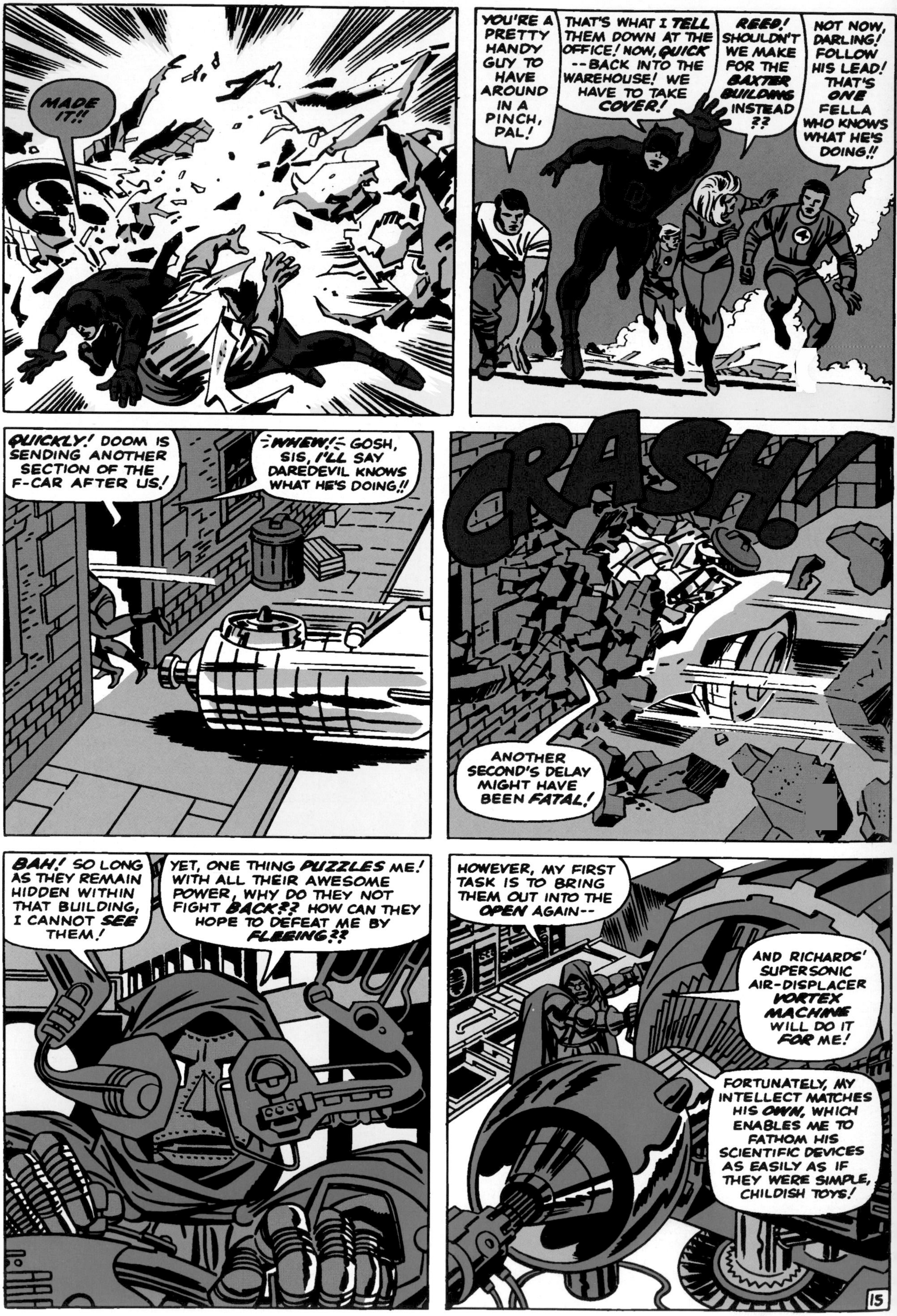
MADE IT!!
YOU'RE A PRETTY HANDY GUY TO HAVE AROUND IN A PINCH, PAL!
THAT'S WHAT I TELL THEM DOWN AT THE OFFICE! NOW, QUICK --BACK INTO THE WAREHOUSE! WE HAVE TO TAKE COVER!
REED! SHOULDN'T WE MAKE FOR THE BAXTER BUILDING INSTEAD??
NOT NOW, DARLING! FOLLOW HIS LEAD! THAT'S ONE FELLA WHO KNOWS WHAT HE'S DOING!!
QUICKLY! DOOM IS SENDING ANOTHER SECTION OF THE F-CAR AFTER US!
WHEW! GOSH, SIS, I'LL SAY DAREDEVIL KNOWS WHAT HE'S DOING!!
CRASH!
ANOTHER SECOND'S DELAY MIGHT HAVE BEEN FATAL!
BAH! SO LONG AS THEY REMAIN HIDDEN WITHIN THAT BUILDING, I CANNOT SEE THEM!
YET, ONE THING PUZZLES ME! WITH ALL THEIR AWESOME POWER, WHY DO THEY NOT FIGHT BACK?? HOW CAN THEY HOPE TO DEFEAT ME BY FLEEING??
HOWEVER, MY FIRST TASK IS TO BRING THEM OUT INTO THE OPEN AGAIN--
AND RICHARDS' SUPERSONIC AIR-DISPLACER VORTEX MACHINE WILL DO IT FOR ME!
FORTUNATELY, MY INTELLECT MATCHES HIS OWN, WHICH ENABLES ME TO FATHOM HIS SCIENTIFIC DEVICES AS EASILY AS IF THEY WERE SIMPLE, CHILDISH TOYS!
15

THUS, THE POWERFUL VORTEX RAY, WHICH CAN GENERATE THE FORCE OF A DOZEN HURRICANES-- CREATED BY *MR. FANTASTIC* AS AN AID IN WEATHER CONTROL, BECOMES A DEADLY *WEAPON* UNDER THE EVIL GUIDANCE OF *DR. DOOM...!*

WHRRRRRR

WITHIN SECONDS, THE CONDEMNED WAREHOUSE, IN WHICH THE F.F. AND DAREDEVIL HAD SOUGHT SHELTER, BECOMES A MASS OF WHIRLING BRICK AND RUBBLE....!

AT A TIME LIKE *THIS*, THERE IS NO SUBSTITUTE FOR *VISION!* I *KNOW* THE BUILDING IS BEING DESTROYED --BUT I CANNOT SENSE THE *MEANS* BY WHICH IT IS BEING DONE!

THIS POWERFUL AIR PRESSURE-- THE FLYING DEBRIS-- IT MEANS ONLY ONE THING! DOOM IS USING MY *VORTEX MACHINE!* WE CAN'T STAY HERE-- WE HAVE TO *SEPARATE--!*

GOOD! THAT TELLS ME WHAT I WANTED TO KNOW!

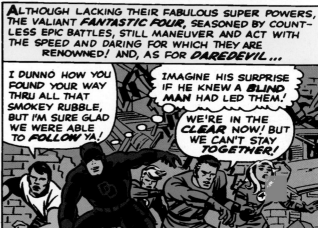

ALTHOUGH LACKING THEIR FABULOUS SUPER POWERS, THE VALIANT *FANTASTIC FOUR*, SEASONED BY COUNT- LESS EPIC BATTLES, STILL MANEUVER AND ACT WITH THE SPEED AND DARING FOR WHICH THEY ARE RENOWNED! AND, AS FOR *DAREDEVIL...*

I DUNNO HOW YOU FOUND YOUR WAY THRU ALL THAT SMOKEY RUBBLE, BUT I'M SURE GLAD WE WERE ABLE TO *FOLLOW* YA!

IMAGINE HIS SURPRISE IF HE KNEW A *BLIND MAN* HAD LED THEM!

WE'RE IN THE *CLEAR* NOW! BUT WE CAN'T STAY *TOGETHER!*

LISTEN *CLOSELY!* THERE'S NO TIME FOR QUESTIONS! SEPARATE IMMEDIATELY! WE'LL EACH RETURN TO THE BAXTER BUILDING FROM A DIFFERENT DIRECTION! IT'S OUR ONLY CHANCE!

DOOM MIGHT BE WATCHING US RIGHT *NOW!*

BUT WHAT CAN THE FOUR OF US *DO--* WITHOUT OUR *POWERS??*

YOU MEAN THE *FIVE* OF YOU, TORCH! *DARE- DEVIL* ISN'T DESERTING YOU *NOW!* READY, RICHARDS?

READY! TAKE CARE, MY DEAREST! DON'T LOSE YOUR HEAD! WE'LL WIN OUT *SOMEHOW!*

WHETHER WE DO OR NOT, DARLING-- REMEMBER HOW I LOVE YOU--!

LET 'ER *GO,* REED! MOVE IT!

C'MON, SIS! HEARTS 'N FLOWERS WON'T STOP *DOOM!*

16

THEN, BEN'S WARNING COMES NOT A SECOND TOO SOON...

SCATTER!

SIS! FOLLOW ME!

I WILL, JOHNNY!

THE VORTEX IS BACK!

THIS WAY, DAREDEVIL! I HAVE A PLAN!!

TELL ME QUICKLY! EVERY SECOND COUNTS!

WE'VE GOT TO SMASH DOOM'S WEAPONS AS HE USES THEM! THE OTHERS SHOULD BE SAFE FOR NOW--I'M SURE HE'S AFTER ME!

I SEE WHAT WE NEED IN FRONT OF A CONSTRUCTION SITE ACROSS THE STREET. IF WE CAN JUST MAKE IT--!

HERE THEY ARE-- GAS CYLINDERS WHICH ARE USED TO FURNISH ACCESSORY POWER! THEY'LL DO THE TRICK!

GAS CYLINDERS-- AGAINST A DEADLY TORNADO VORTEX? HOW--?

DON'T FORGET --THE VORTEX IS MY CREATION! I KNOW THE ELEMENTS OF WHICH IT'S COMPOSED!

AND GAS IS THE ONLY ELEMENT THAT WILL SHATTER IT! NO MORE TIME-- THROW IT-- NOW!

EVEN WITHOUT YOUR FABLED SUPER POWERS, I WOULD NEVER WANT TO HAVE YOU FOR AN ENEMY, RICHARDS!

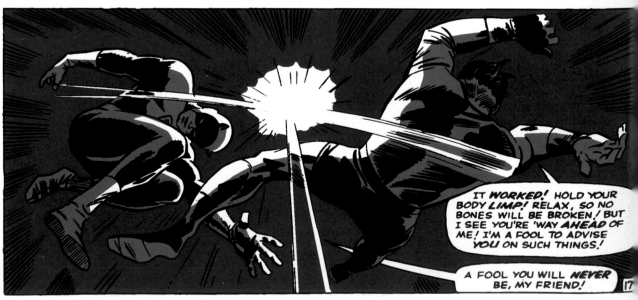

IT WORKED! HOLD YOUR BODY LIMP! RELAX, SO NO BONES WILL BE BROKEN! BUT I SEE YOU'RE 'WAY AHEAD OF ME! I'M A FOOL TO ADVISE YOU ON SUCH THINGS!

A FOOL YOU WILL NEVER BE, MY FRIEND!

17

THE VORTEX IS DESTROYED! AGAIN THEY'VE ESCAPED ME! BUT, I'LL FIND ANOTHER WEAPON TO USE AGAINST THEM!

HOWEVER, THE MAIN PROBLEM IS STILL UN-SOLVED-- WHY DO THEY KEEP FLEEING? WHY DON'T THEY ATTACK?

IF I DID NOT KNOW BETTER, I'D THINK THEY POSSESSED NO SUPER POWERS WITH WHICH TO STRIKE BACK AT ME!

AND THAT OTHER-- WHO FIGHTS WITH THEM--HE SEEMS TO BE THE ONE WHO HAS TAKEN THE LEAD! BUT-- THAT IS IMPOSSIBLE!! OR --IS IT??

IT MUST BE THE ANSWER! IT'S THE ONLY EXPLANATION! I'VE BEEN SUSPECTING A TRICK-- I WAS TOO CAUTIOUS TO REALIZE THE OBVIOUS-- THE FANTASTIC FOUR ARE POWERLESS!

NOW, ALL I NEED DO IS FOCUS RICHARDS' OWN TV RADAR TRACKER COMPONENTS ON EACH OF THEM, AND PICK THEM OFF EFFORTLESSLY, AT MY LEISURE!

NO! THAT WILL BE TOO EASY! I'LL TOY WITH THEM A WHILE LONGER! THIS IS TOO GLORIOUS A SITUATION--IT MUST LAST AS LONG AS POSSIBLE!

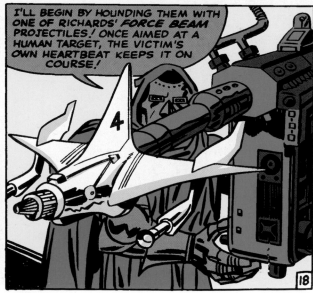

I'LL BEGIN BY HOUNDING THEM WITH ONE OF RICHARDS' FORCE BEAM PROJECTILES! ONCE AIMED AT A HUMAN TARGET, THE VICTIM'S OWN HEARTBEAT KEEPS IT ON COURSE!

18

HAD I *MYSELF* CREATED THIS RATHER OBVIOUS DEVICE, IT WOULD HAVE BEEN FAR MORE SOPHISTICATED--FAR MORE EFFICIENT! HOWEVER, EVEN IN ITS PRESENT *CUMBERSOME* FORM, IT SHOULD SERVE MY PURPOSE ADMIRABLY!

DAREDEVIL--*DUCK!* ONE OF MY FORCE BEAM MISSILES IS COMING TOWARDS US! IT'LL CONTINUE TO BLAST US UNLESS SOMETHING DIVERTS IT!

THANKS FOR THE BRIEFING, MISTER! MY *BILLY CLUB* WILL BE DIVERSION ENOUGH!

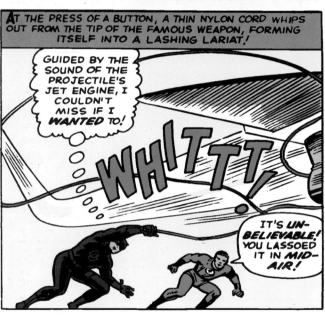

AT THE PRESS OF A BUTTON, A THIN NYLON CORD WHIPS OUT FROM THE TIP OF THE FAMOUS WEAPON, FORMING ITSELF INTO A LASHING LARIAT!

GUIDED BY THE SOUND OF THE PROJECTILE'S JET ENGINE, I COULDN'T MISS IF I *WANTED* TO!

WHITTT!

IT'S *UN-BELIEVABLE!* YOU LASSOED IT IN *MID-AIR!*

IT WOULD HAVE BEEN *MORE* UNBELIEVABLE IF I'D *MISSED!*

NOW, I'LL JUST SWING IT IN A WIDE ARC, BEFORE IT BREAKS FREE OF MY LARIAT--*THERE!* IT'S *FINISHED!*

DAREDEVIL, FOR A FELLA WITH NO SUPER POWERS THAT I CAN TELL, YOU'RE THE MOST INCREDIBLY *CAPABLE* FIGHTER I KNOW OF! HOW--?

IT MUST BE THAT FOUR-LEAF CLOVER I CARRY AROUND! NOW LISTEN-- I'VE GOT AN IDEA!

YOU'LL HAVE A BETTER CHANCE TO MAKE IT TO YOUR HQ IF I MAKE DOOM CONCENTRATE ON *ME!* SO GO TO IT, WHILE I DRAW HIS FIRE!

WAIT--!

IF WE DON'T MEET AGAIN, IT WAS SWELL KNOWING YOU! YOU'RE A REAL *FUN* GROUP!

19

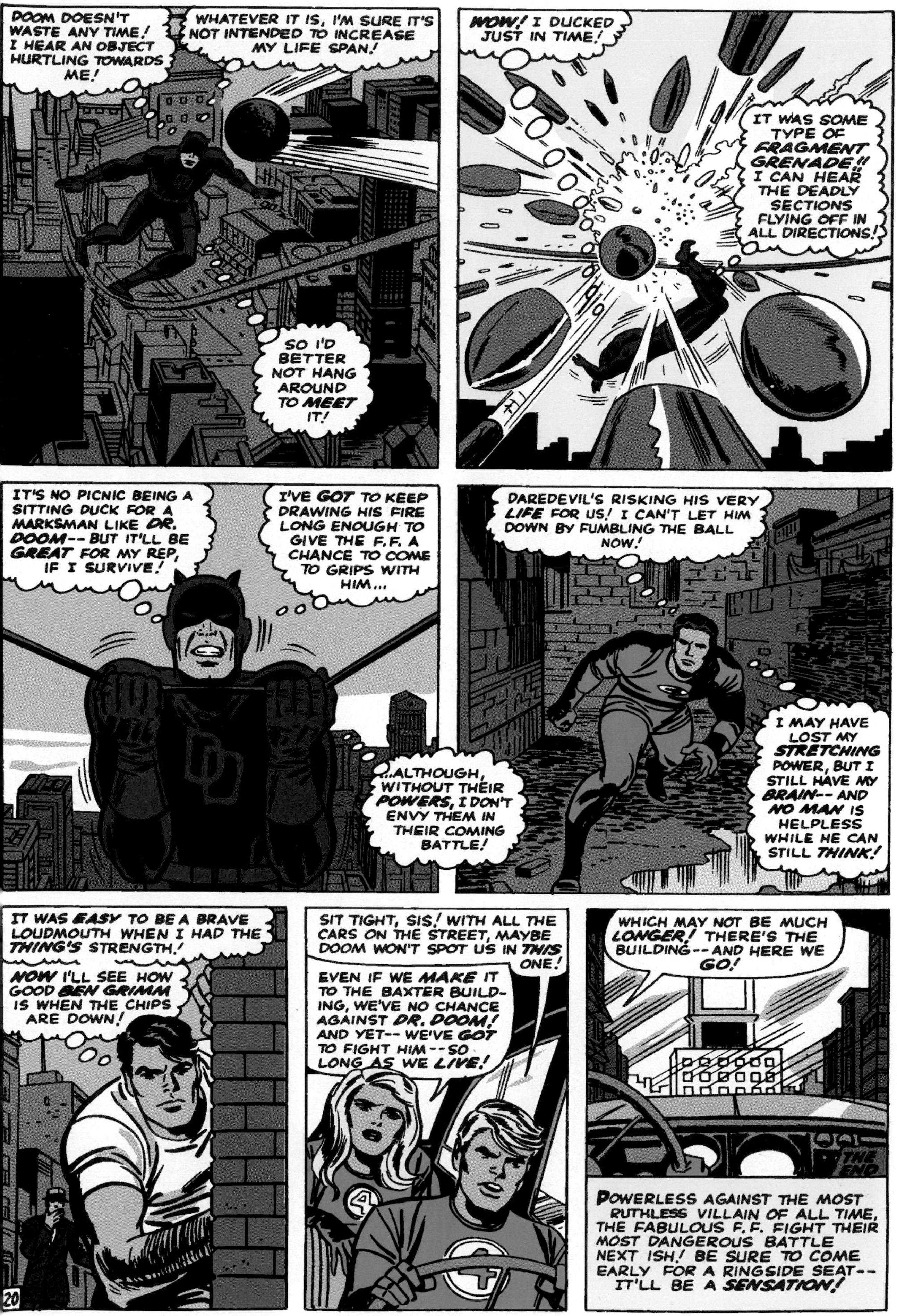
DOOM DOESN'T WASTE ANY TIME! I HEAR AN OBJECT HURTLING TOWARDS ME!
WHATEVER IT IS, I'M SURE IT'S NOT INTENDED TO INCREASE MY LIFE SPAN!
SO I'D BETTER NOT HANG AROUND TO MEET IT!
WOW! I DUCKED JUST IN TIME!
IT WAS SOME TYPE OF FRAGMENT GRENADE!! I CAN HEAR THE DEADLY SECTIONS FLYING OFF IN ALL DIRECTIONS!
IT'S NO PICNIC BEING A SITTING DUCK FOR A MARKSMAN LIKE DR. DOOM-- BUT IT'LL BE GREAT FOR MY REP, IF I SURVIVE!
I'VE GOT TO KEEP DRAWING HIS FIRE LONG ENOUGH TO GIVE THE F.F. A CHANCE TO COME TO GRIPS WITH HIM...
...ALTHOUGH, WITHOUT THEIR POWERS, I DON'T ENVY THEM IN THEIR COMING BATTLE!
DAREDEVIL'S RISKING HIS VERY LIFE FOR US! I CAN'T LET HIM DOWN BY FUMBLING THE BALL NOW!
I MAY HAVE LOST MY STRETCHING POWER, BUT I STILL HAVE MY BRAIN-- AND NO MAN IS HELPLESS WHILE HE CAN STILL THINK!
IT WAS EASY TO BE A BRAVE LOUDMOUTH WHEN I HAD THE THING'S STRENGTH!
NOW I'LL SEE HOW GOOD BEN GRIMM IS WHEN THE CHIPS ARE DOWN!
20
SIT TIGHT, SIS! WITH ALL THE CARS ON THE STREET, MAYBE DOOM WON'T SPOT US IN THIS ONE!
EVEN IF WE MAKE IT TO THE BAXTER BUILDING, WE'VE NO CHANCE AGAINST DR. DOOM! AND YET-- WE'VE GOT TO FIGHT HIM--SO LONG AS WE LIVE!
WHICH MAY NOT BE MUCH LONGER! THERE'S THE BUILDING--AND HERE WE GO!
THE END
POWERLESS AGAINST THE MOST RUTHLESS VILLAIN OF ALL TIME, THE FABULOUS F.F. FIGHT THEIR MOST DANGEROUS BATTLE NEXT ISH! BE SURE TO COME EARLY FOR A RINGSIDE SEAT-- IT'LL BE A SENSATION!

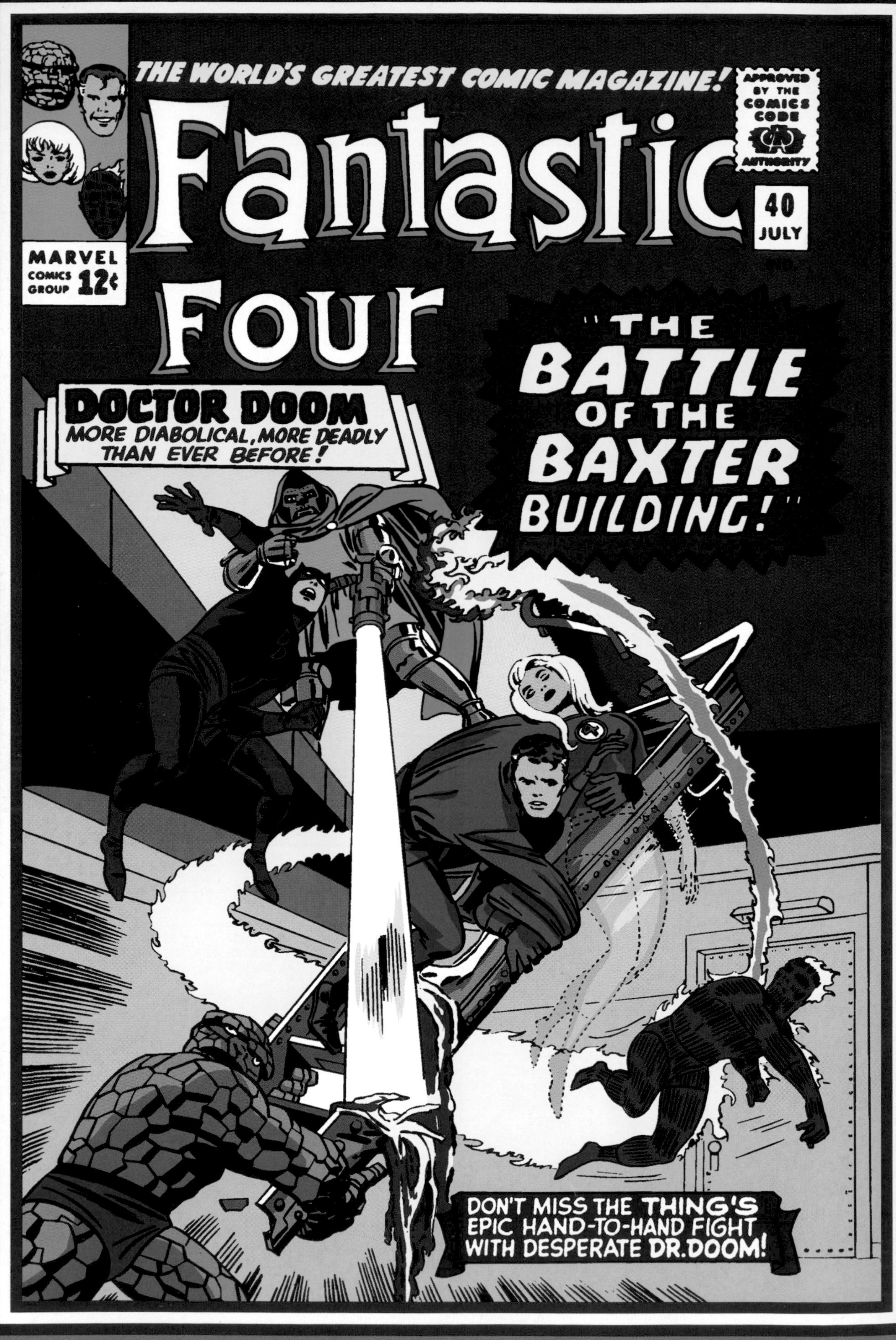
THE WORLD'S GREATEST COMIC MAGAZINE!
APPROVED BY THE COMICS CODE AUTHORITY
Fantastic Four
40 JULY
MARVEL COMICS GROUP 12¢
DOCTOR DOOM
MORE DIABOLICAL, MORE DEADLY THAN EVER BEFORE!
"THE BATTLE OF THE BAXTER BUILDING!"
DON'T MISS THE THING'S EPIC HAND-TO-HAND FIGHT WITH DESPERATE DR. DOOM!

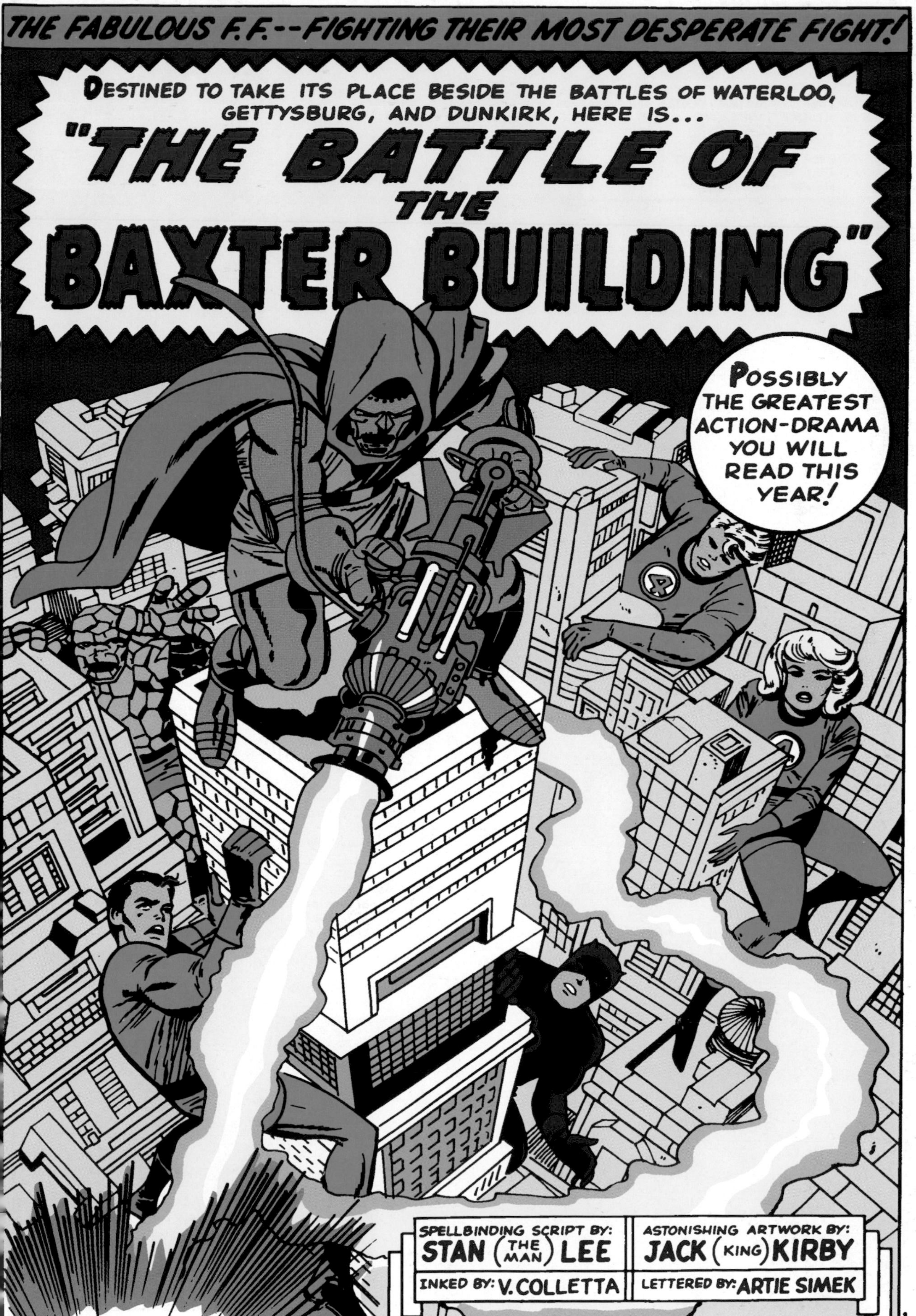
THE FABULOUS F.F.--FIGHTING THEIR MOST DESPERATE FIGHT!
DESTINED TO TAKE ITS PLACE BESIDE THE BATTLES OF WATERLOO, GETTYSBURG, AND DUNKIRK, HERE IS...
"THE BATTLE OF THE BAXTER BUILDING"
POSSIBLY THE GREATEST ACTION-DRAMA YOU WILL READ THIS YEAR!
SPELLBINDING SCRIPT BY: STAN (THE MAN) LEE
ASTONISHING ARTWORK BY: JACK (KING) KIRBY
INKED BY: V. COLLETTA
LETTERED BY: ARTIE SIMEK
1.

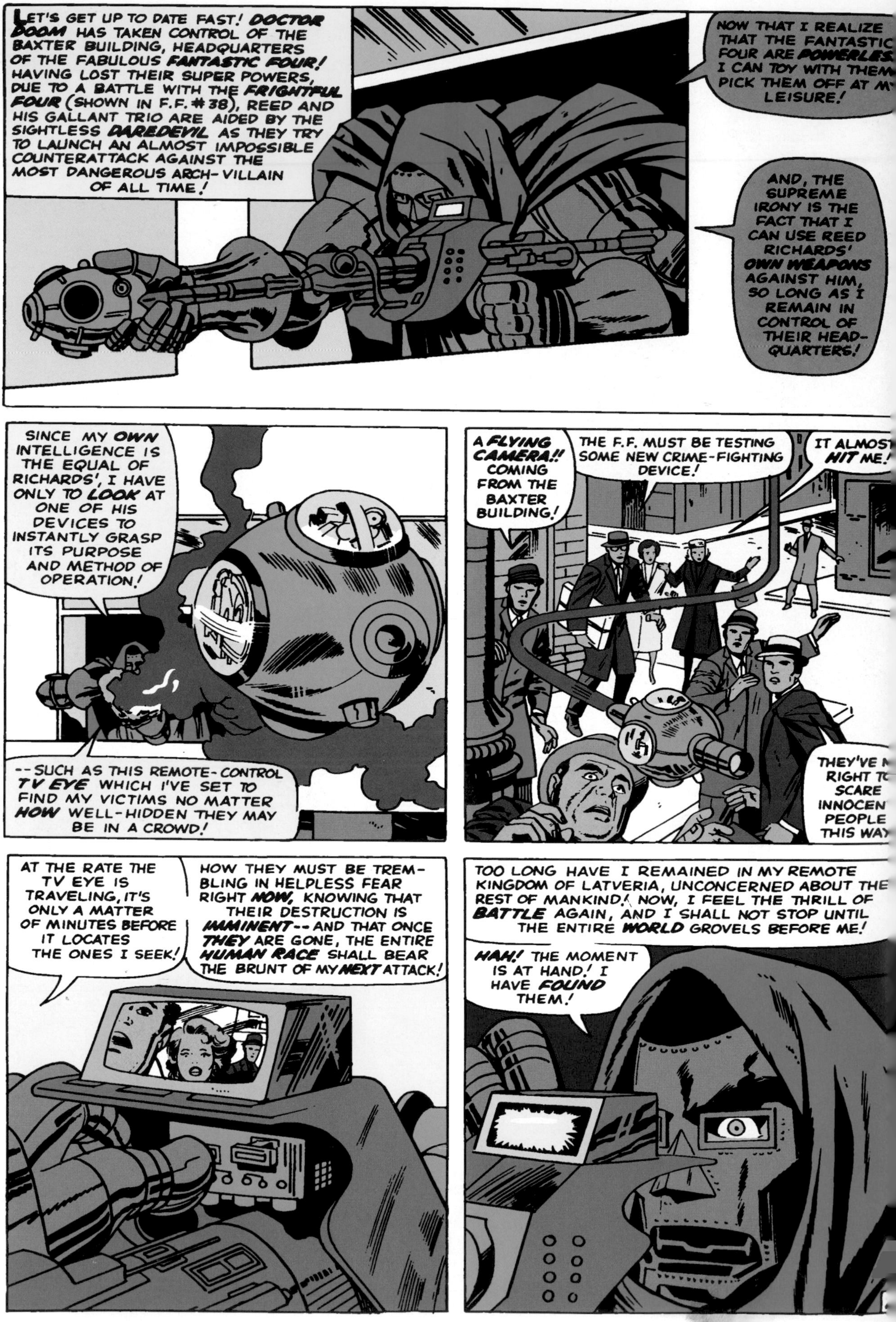
LET'S GET UP TO DATE FAST! DOCTOR DOOM HAS TAKEN CONTROL OF THE BAXTER BUILDING, HEADQUARTERS OF THE FABULOUS FANTASTIC FOUR! HAVING LOST THEIR SUPER POWERS, DUE TO A BATTLE WITH THE FRIGHTFUL FOUR (SHOWN IN F.F. #38), REED AND HIS GALLANT TRIO ARE AIDED BY THE SIGHTLESS DAREDEVIL AS THEY TRY TO LAUNCH AN ALMOST IMPOSSIBLE COUNTERATTACK AGAINST THE MOST DANGEROUS ARCH-VILLAIN OF ALL TIME!
NOW THAT I REALIZE THAT THE FANTASTIC FOUR ARE POWERLESS I CAN TOY WITH THEM PICK THEM OFF AT MY LEISURE!
AND, THE SUPREME IRONY IS THE FACT THAT I CAN USE REED RICHARDS' OWN WEAPONS AGAINST HIM, SO LONG AS I REMAIN IN CONTROL OF THEIR HEAD-QUARTERS!
SINCE MY OWN INTELLIGENCE IS THE EQUAL OF RICHARDS', I HAVE ONLY TO LOOK AT ONE OF HIS DEVICES TO INSTANTLY GRASP ITS PURPOSE AND METHOD OF OPERATION!
--SUCH AS THIS REMOTE-CONTROL TV EYE WHICH I'VE SET TO FIND MY VICTIMS NO MATTER HOW WELL-HIDDEN THEY MAY BE IN A CROWD!
A FLYING CAMERA!! COMING FROM THE BAXTER BUILDING!
THE F.F. MUST BE TESTING SOME NEW CRIME-FIGHTING DEVICE!
IT ALMOST HIT ME!
THEY'VE N RIGHT TO SCARE INNOCEN PEOPLE THIS WAY
AT THE RATE THE TV EYE IS TRAVELING, IT'S ONLY A MATTER OF MINUTES BEFORE IT LOCATES THE ONES I SEEK!
HOW THEY MUST BE TREMBLING IN HELPLESS FEAR RIGHT NOW, KNOWING THAT THEIR DESTRUCTION IS IMMINENT--AND THAT ONCE THEY ARE GONE, THE ENTIRE HUMAN RACE SHALL BEAR THE BRUNT OF MY NEXT ATTACK!
TOO LONG HAVE I REMAINED IN MY REMOTE KINGDOM OF LATVERIA, UNCONCERNED ABOUT THE REST OF MANKIND! NOW, I FEEL THE THRILL OF BATTLE AGAIN, AND I SHALL NOT STOP UNTIL THE ENTIRE WORLD GROVELS BEFORE ME!
HAH! THE MOMENT IS AT HAND! I HAVE FOUND THEM!

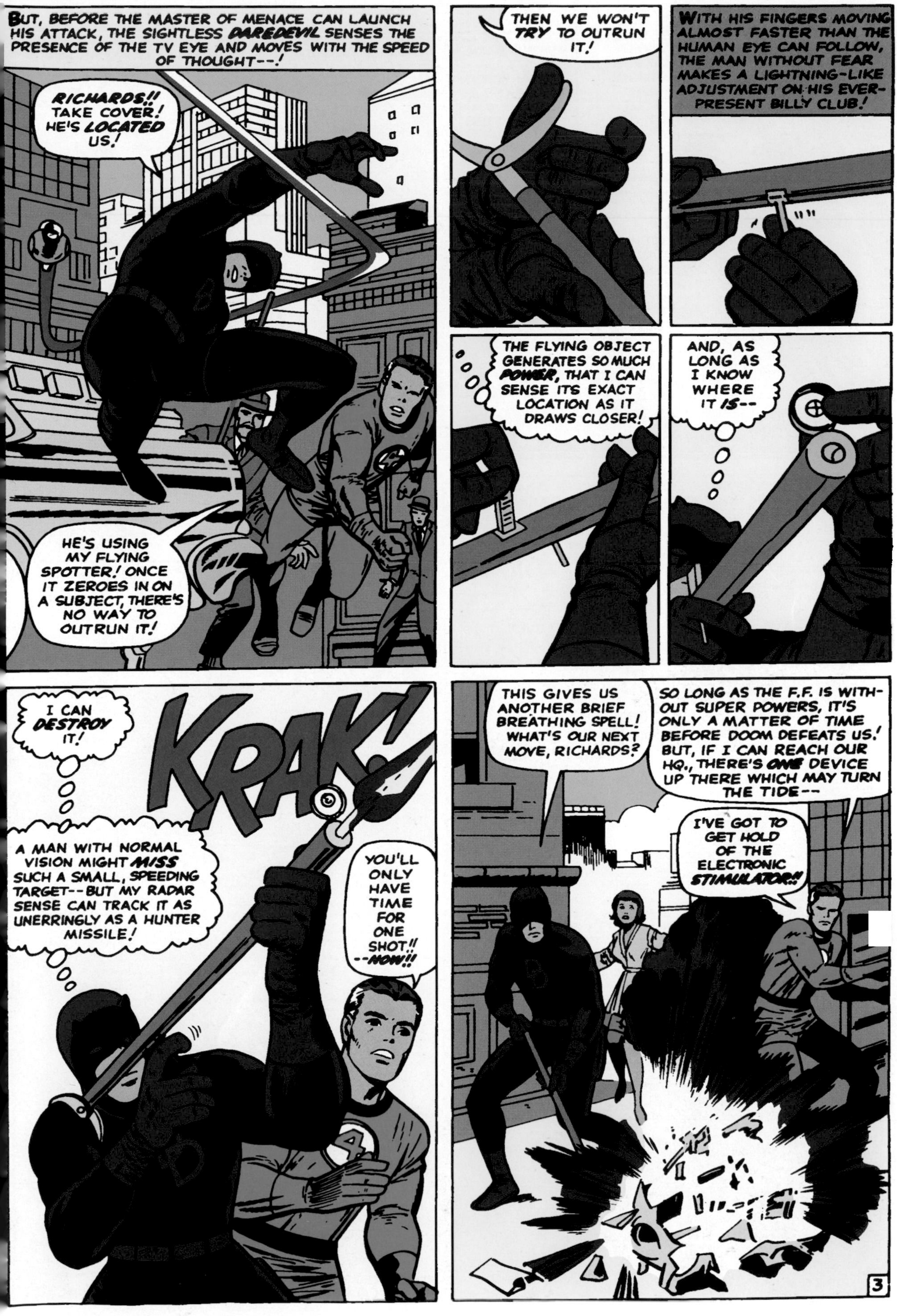
BUT, BEFORE THE MASTER OF MENACE CAN LAUNCH HIS ATTACK, THE SIGHTLESS DAREDEVIL SENSES THE PRESENCE OF THE TV EYE AND MOVES WITH THE SPEED OF THOUGHT--!
RICHARDS!! TAKE COVER! HE'S LOCATED US!
HE'S USING MY FLYING SPOTTER! ONCE IT ZEROES IN ON A SUBJECT, THERE'S NO WAY TO OUTRUN IT!
THEN WE WON'T TRY TO OUTRUN IT!
WITH HIS FINGERS MOVING ALMOST FASTER THAN THE HUMAN EYE CAN FOLLOW, THE MAN WITHOUT FEAR MAKES A LIGHTNING-LIKE ADJUSTMENT ON HIS EVER-PRESENT BILLY CLUB!
THE FLYING OBJECT GENERATES SO MUCH POWER, THAT I CAN SENSE ITS EXACT LOCATION AS IT DRAWS CLOSER!
AND, AS LONG AS I KNOW WHERE IT IS--
I CAN DESTROY IT!
KRAK!
A MAN WITH NORMAL VISION MIGHT MISS SUCH A SMALL, SPEEDING TARGET--BUT MY RADAR SENSE CAN TRACK IT AS UNERRINGLY AS A HUNTER MISSILE!
YOU'LL ONLY HAVE TIME FOR ONE SHOT!! --NOW!!
THIS GIVES US ANOTHER BRIEF BREATHING SPELL! WHAT'S OUR NEXT MOVE, RICHARDS?
SO LONG AS THE F.F. IS WITHOUT SUPER POWERS, IT'S ONLY A MATTER OF TIME BEFORE DOOM DEFEATS US! BUT, IF I CAN REACH OUR HQ., THERE'S ONE DEVICE UP THERE WHICH MAY TURN THE TIDE--
I'VE GOT TO GET HOLD OF THE ELECTRONIC STIMULATOR!!
3

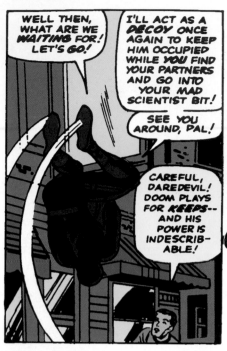

WELL THEN, WHAT ARE WE *WAITING* FOR! LET'S *GO!*

I'LL ACT AS A *DECOY* ONCE AGAIN TO KEEP HIM OCCUPIED WHILE *YOU* FIND YOUR PARTNERS AND GO INTO YOUR *MAD SCIENTIST* BIT!

SEE YOU AROUND, PAL!

CAREFUL, DAREDEVIL! DOOM PLAYS FOR *KEEPS*-- AND HIS POWER IS INDESCRIBABLE!

BE *CAREFUL??* YOU'RE TALKING TO THE WRONG BOY, MISTER! IF I WAS THE CAUTIOUS TYPE, I'D BE BUYING BACK MY INTRODUCTION TO YOU RIGHT *NOW!*

IF WE SURVIVE THIS BATTLE, I'LL OWE THAT MAN A DEBT THAT CAN NEVER BE REPAID!

WELL, HAPPY DAYS!

TWANNNGGG!

ARE YOU *WATCHING*, DOOMSIE? READY OR NOT, HERE I *COME!*

I HOPE I'M STILL ALIVE AND KICKING IF AND WHEN THEY REGAIN THEIR POWERS--

--BECAUSE *THEN* THE BATTLE BETWEEN *THEM* AND *DOOM* WILL BE SOMETHING TO TALK ABOUT FOR *YEARS!*

AND, AS DAREDEVIL TAUNTS THE MENACING DR. DOOM FROM THE NEARBY ROOFTOPS, A COMMANDEERED TAXI SPEEDS UP TO THE DESPERATELY RUNNING REED RICHARDS...

REED, DARLING! THANK HEAVENS YOU'RE STILL UNHARMED! BUT-- WHERE'S *DARE-DEVIL!*

I'LL EXPLAIN LATER, SUE! OPEN THE DOOR --QUICK!

THEN, AFTER GIVING SUE AND JOHNNY A QUICK BRIEFING...

THIS IS *IT!* GIVE 'ER THE *GUN*, JOHNNY! WE'VE *GOT* TO REACH THE *STIMULATOR!*

IT SEEMS SO *HOPELESS!* EVEN *WITH* OUR POWERS, DR. DOOM WAS ALMOST UNBEATABLE! BUT *NOW--!*

KNOCK IT OFF, SIS! THAT KINDA TALK WE CAN DO *WITHOUT!*

I WONDER WHERE OL' *BEN* DISAPPEARED TO??

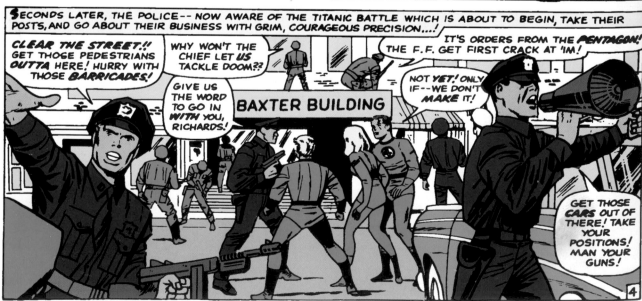

SECONDS LATER, THE POLICE-- NOW AWARE OF THE TITANIC BATTLE WHICH IS ABOUT TO BEGIN, TAKE THEIR POSTS, AND GO ABOUT THEIR BUSINESS WITH GRIM, COURAGEOUS PRECISION...!

CLEAR THE STREET!! GET THOSE PEDESTRIANS *OUTTA* HERE! HURRY WITH THOSE *BARRICADES!*

WHY WON'T THE CHIEF LET *US* TACKLE DOOM??

GIVE US THE WORD TO GO IN *WITH* YOU, RICHARDS!

IT'S ORDERS FROM THE *PENTAGON!* THE F.F. GET FIRST CRACK AT 'IM!

NOT *YET!* ONLY IF-- WE DON'T *MAKE* IT!

BAXTER BUILDING

GET THOSE *CARS* OUT OF THERE! TAKE YOUR POSITIONS! MAN YOUR GUNS!

4

AND SO-- *IT BEGINS!!*

EASY! DOOM IS PROBABLY WATCHING OUR EVERY MOVE WITH ONE OF MY AUTOMATIC SCANNERS!

WHEW! TALK ABOUT *HOPELESS ODDS!*

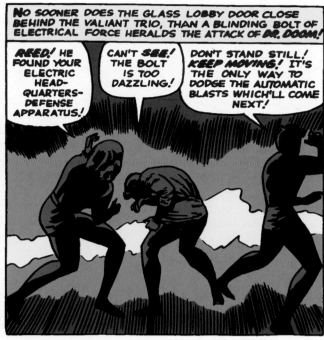

NO SOONER DOES THE GLASS LOBBY DOOR CLOSE BEHIND THE VALIANT TRIO, THAN A BLINDING BOLT OF ELECTRICAL FORCE HERALDS THE ATTACK OF *DR. DOOM!*

REED! HE FOUND YOUR ELECTRIC HEAD-QUARTERS-DEFENSE APPARATUS!

CAN'T *SEE!* THE BOLT IS TOO DAZZLING!

DON'T STAND STILL! *KEEP MOVING!* IT'S THE ONLY WAY TO DODGE THE AUTOMATIC BLASTS WHICH'LL COME NEXT!

HEAD FOR THE *ELEVATOR,* JOHNNY! TAKE A ZIG-ZAG ROUTE! I'LL TRY TO KEEP *SUE* OUT OF HARM'S WAY!

BUT, REED-- I'LL SLOW YOU DOWN! *YOU'LL* BE HIT BECAUSE OF *ME!*

MAYBE *NOT!* DON'T FORGET I ARRANGED THE *SEQUENCE* OF THE BLASTS! IF I CAN JUST *REMEMBER* THEM--!

NOT *THERE,* JOHNNY! SIDESTEP TO YOUR LEFT-- *NOW!* THAT'S IT! ANOTHER INCH WOULD HAVE *TRAPPED* YOU!

EVEN WITH *SIS* IN HIS ARMS-- DODGING FOR HIS *OWN* LIFE-- HE'S ABLE TO SAVE *ME!* THERE'S *NEVER* BEEN A GUY LIKE REED BEFORE!

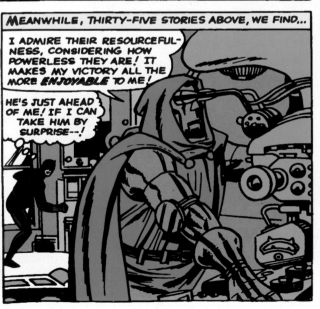

MEANWHILE, THIRTY-FIVE STORIES ABOVE, WE FIND...

I ADMIRE THEIR RESOURCEFUL-NESS, CONSIDERING HOW POWERLESS THEY ARE! IT MAKES MY VICTORY ALL THE MORE *ENJOYABLE* TO ME!

HE'S JUST AHEAD OF ME! IF I CAN TAKE HIM BY SURPRISE--!

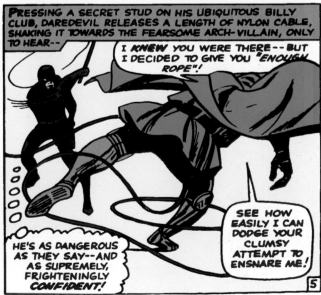

PRESSING A SECRET STUD ON HIS UBIQUITOUS BILLY CLUB, DAREDEVIL RELEASES A LENGTH OF NYLON CABLE, SHAKING IT TOWARDS THE FEARSOME ARCH-VILLAIN, ONLY TO HEAR--

I *KNEW* YOU WERE THERE-- BUT I DECIDED TO GIVE YOU "ENOUGH *ROPE*"!

SEE HOW EASILY I CAN DODGE YOUR *CLUMSY* ATTEMPT TO ENSNARE ME!

HE'S AS DANGEROUS AS THEY SAY-- AND AS SUPREMELY, FRIGHTENINGLY *CONFIDENT!*

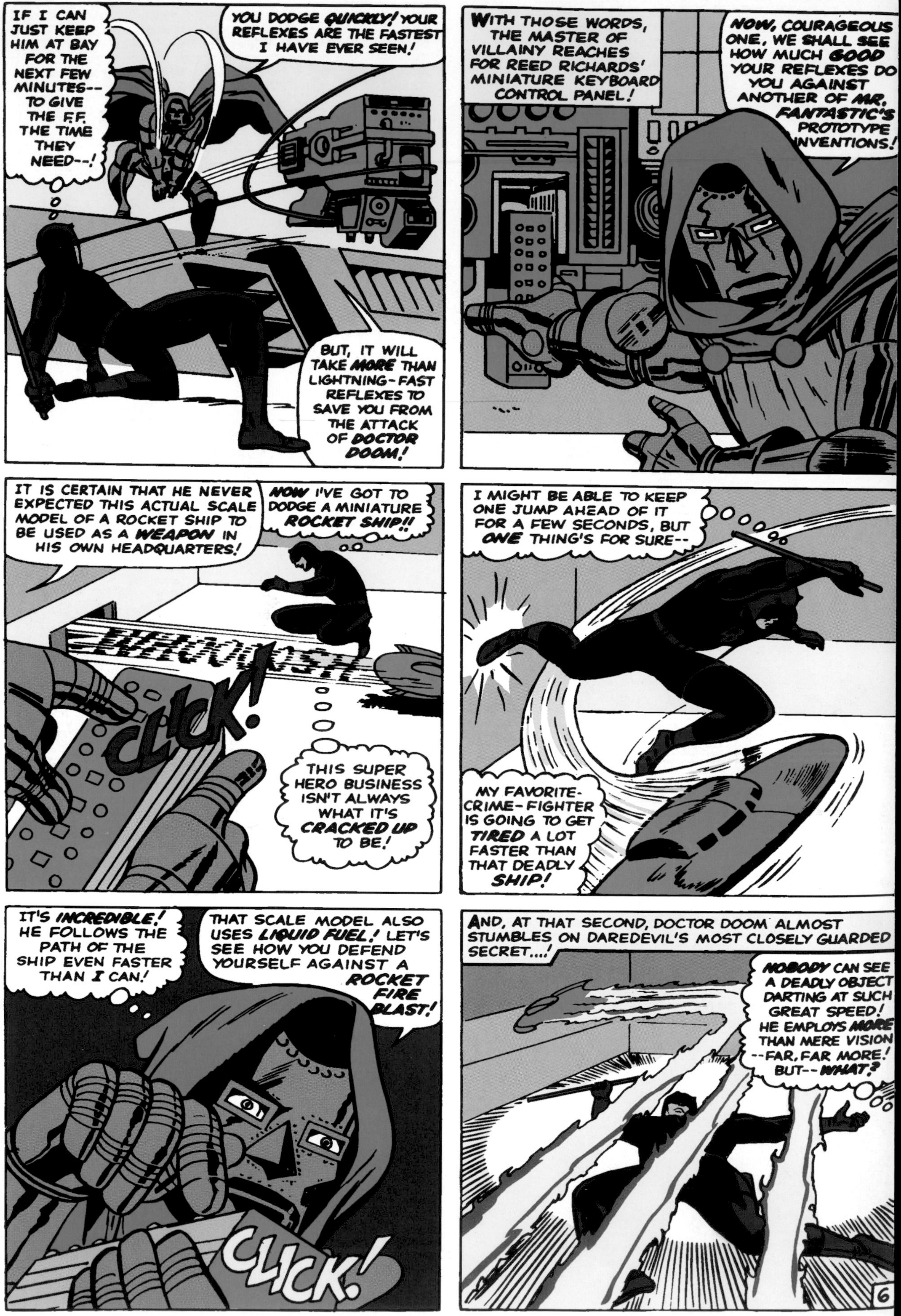
IF I CAN JUST KEEP HIM AT BAY FOR THE NEXT FEW MINUTES-- TO GIVE THE F.F. THE TIME THEY NEED--!
YOU DODGE QUICKLY! YOUR REFLEXES ARE THE FASTEST I HAVE EVER SEEN!
BUT, IT WILL TAKE MORE THAN LIGHTNING-FAST REFLEXES TO SAVE YOU FROM THE ATTACK OF DOCTOR DOOM!
WITH THOSE WORDS, THE MASTER OF VILLAINY REACHES FOR REED RICHARDS' MINIATURE KEYBOARD CONTROL PANEL!
NOW, COURAGEOUS ONE, WE SHALL SEE HOW MUCH GOOD YOUR REFLEXES DO YOU AGAINST ANOTHER OF MR. FANTASTIC'S PROTOTYPE INVENTIONS!
IT IS CERTAIN THAT HE NEVER EXPECTED THIS ACTUAL SCALE MODEL OF A ROCKET SHIP TO BE USED AS A WEAPON IN HIS OWN HEADQUARTERS!
NOW I'VE GOT TO DODGE A MINIATURE ROCKET SHIP!!
WHOOSH!
CLICK!
THIS SUPER HERO BUSINESS ISN'T ALWAYS WHAT IT'S CRACKED UP TO BE!
I MIGHT BE ABLE TO KEEP ONE JUMP AHEAD OF IT FOR A FEW SECONDS, BUT ONE THING'S FOR SURE--
MY FAVORITE CRIME-FIGHTER IS GOING TO GET TIRED A LOT FASTER THAN THAT DEADLY SHIP!
IT'S INCREDIBLE! HE FOLLOWS THE PATH OF THE SHIP EVEN FASTER THAN I CAN!
THAT SCALE MODEL ALSO USES LIQUID FUEL! LET'S SEE HOW YOU DEFEND YOURSELF AGAINST A ROCKET FIRE BLAST!
CLICK!
AND, AT THAT SECOND, DOCTOR DOOM ALMOST STUMBLES ON DAREDEVIL'S MOST CLOSELY GUARDED SECRET....!
NOBODY CAN SEE A DEADLY OBJECT DARTING AT SUCH GREAT SPEED! HE EMPLOYS MORE THAN MERE VISION --FAR, FAR MORE! BUT--WHAT?
6

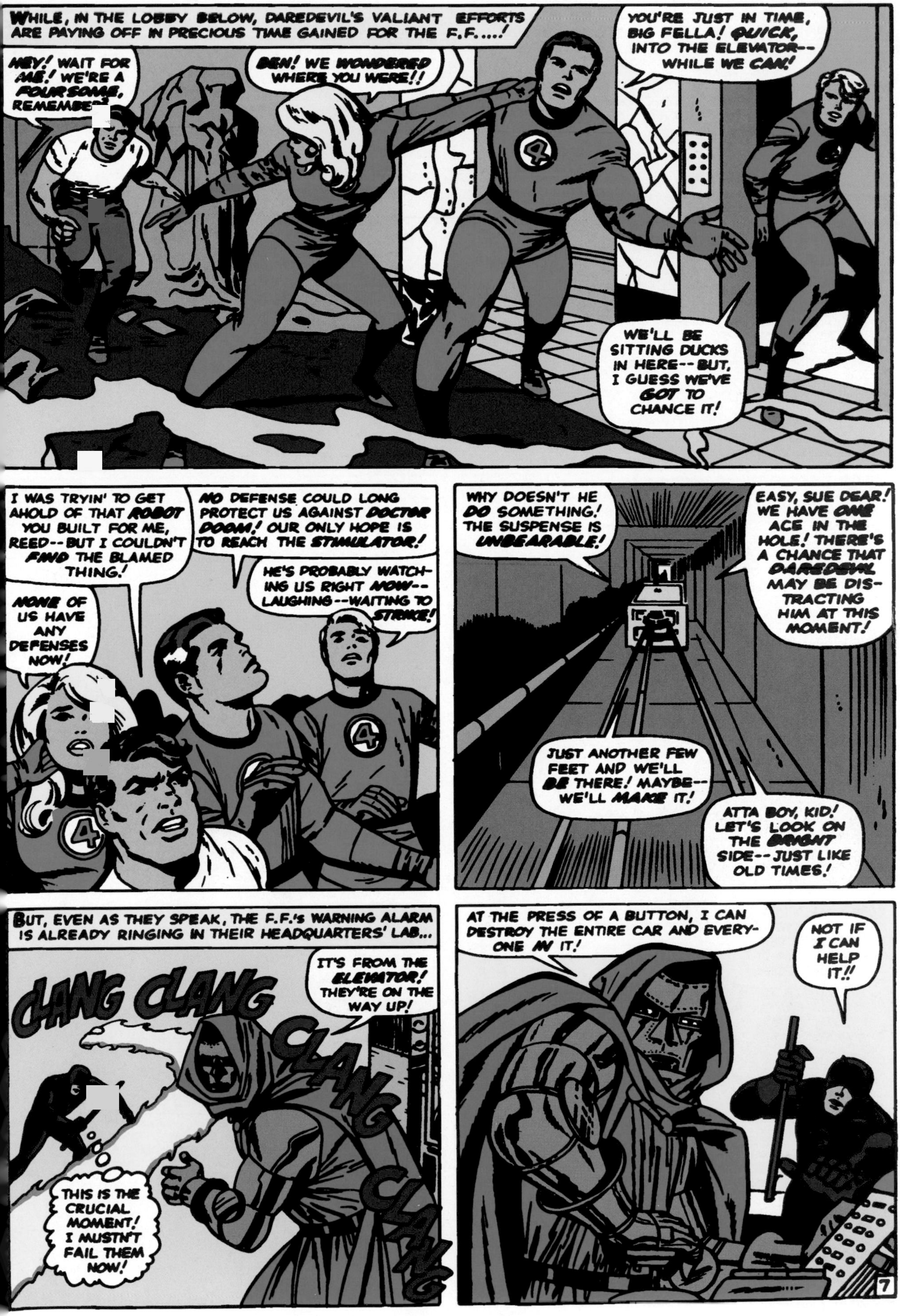

WHILE, IN THE LOBBY BELOW, DAREDEVIL'S VALIANT EFFORTS ARE PAYING OFF IN PRECIOUS TIME GAINED FOR THE F.F....!
HEY! WAIT FOR ME! WE'RE A FOURSOME, REMEMBER?
BEN! WE WONDERED WHERE YOU WERE!!
YOU'RE JUST IN TIME, BIG FELLA! QUICK, INTO THE ELEVATOR-- WHILE WE CAN!
WE'LL BE SITTING DUCKS IN HERE--BUT, I GUESS WE'VE GOT TO CHANCE IT!
I WAS TRYIN' TO GET AHOLD OF THAT ROBOT YOU BUILT FOR ME, REED--BUT I COULDN'T FIND THE BLAMED THING!
NO DEFENSE COULD LONG PROTECT US AGAINST DOCTOR DOOM! OUR ONLY HOPE IS TO REACH THE STIMULATOR!
NONE OF US HAVE ANY DEFENSES NOW!
HE'S PROBABLY WATCHING US RIGHT NOW-- LAUGHING--WAITING TO STRIKE!
WHY DOESN'T HE DO SOMETHING! THE SUSPENSE IS UNBEARABLE!
EASY, SUE DEAR! WE HAVE ONE ACE IN THE HOLE! THERE'S A CHANCE THAT DAREDEVIL MAY BE DISTRACTING HIM AT THIS MOMENT!
JUST ANOTHER FEW FEET AND WE'LL BE THERE! MAYBE-- WE'LL MAKE IT!
ATTA BOY, KID! LET'S LOOK ON THE BRIGHT SIDE--JUST LIKE OLD TIMES!
BUT, EVEN AS THEY SPEAK, THE F.F.'s WARNING ALARM IS ALREADY RINGING IN THEIR HEADQUARTERS' LAB...
CLANG CLANG
IT'S FROM THE ELEVATOR! THEY'RE ON THE WAY UP!
CLANG
CLANG
CLANG
THIS IS THE CRUCIAL MOMENT! I MUSTN'T FAIL THEM NOW!
AT THE PRESS OF A BUTTON, I CAN DESTROY THE ENTIRE CAR AND EVERYONE IN IT!
NOT IF I CAN HELP IT!!
7

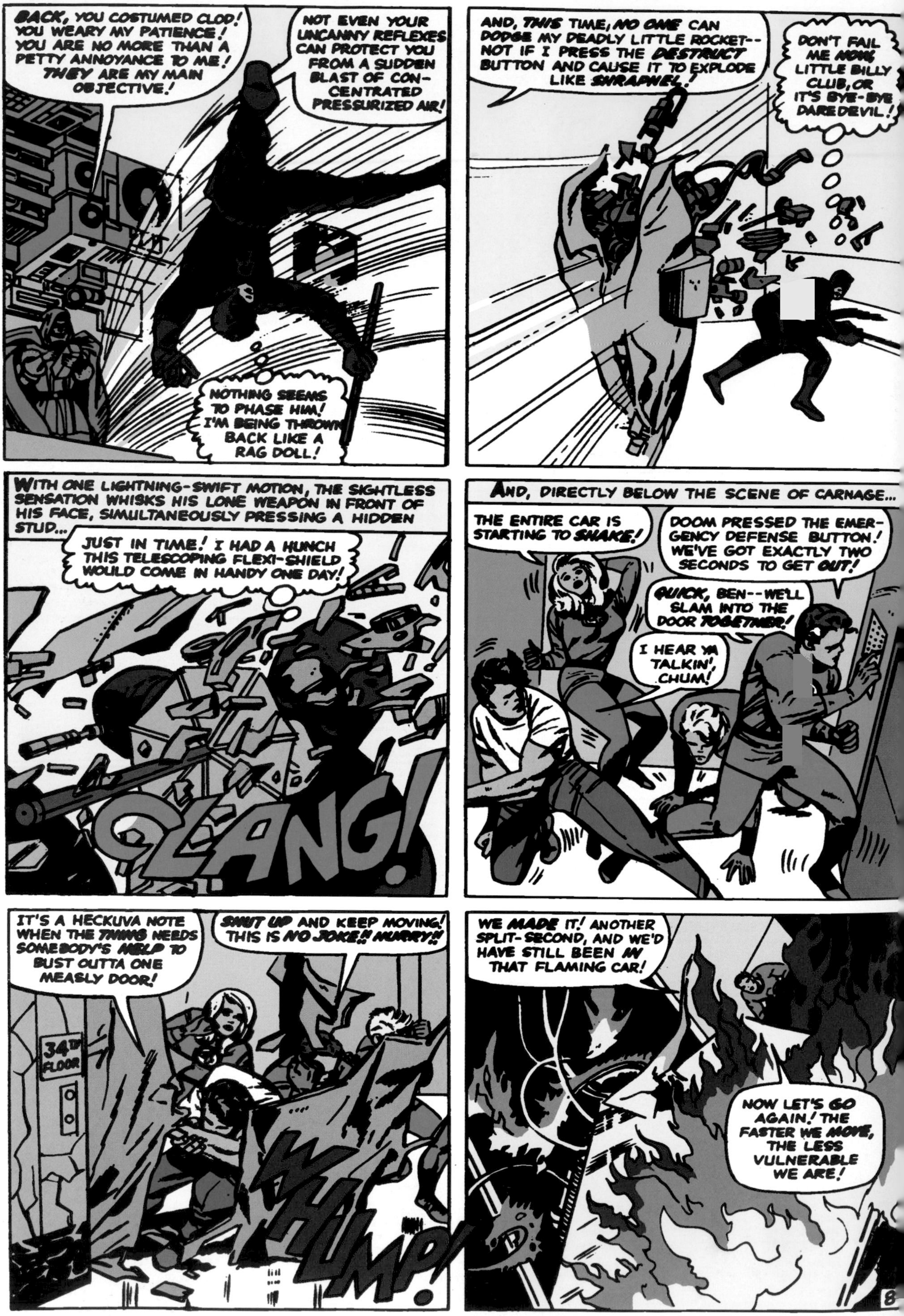

BACK, YOU COSTUMED CLOD! YOU WEARY MY PATIENCE! YOU ARE NO MORE THAN A PETTY ANNOYANCE TO ME! THEY ARE MY MAIN OBJECTIVE!
NOT EVEN YOUR UNCANNY REFLEXES CAN PROTECT YOU FROM A SUDDEN BLAST OF CON-CENTRATED PRESSURIZED AIR!
NOTHING SEEMS TO PHASE HIM! I'M BEING THROWN BACK LIKE A RAG DOLL!
AND, THIS TIME, NO ONE CAN DODGE MY DEADLY LITTLE ROCKET-- NOT IF I PRESS THE DESTRUCT BUTTON AND CAUSE IT TO EXPLODE LIKE SHRAPNEL!
DON'T FAIL ME NOW, LITTLE BILLY CLUB, OR IT'S BYE-BYE DAREDEVIL!
WITH ONE LIGHTNING-SWIFT MOTION, THE SIGHTLESS SENSATION WHISKS HIS LONE WEAPON IN FRONT OF HIS FACE, SIMULTANEOUSLY PRESSING A HIDDEN STUD...
JUST IN TIME! I HAD A HUNCH THIS TELESCOPING FLEXI-SHIELD WOULD COME IN HANDY ONE DAY!
CLANG!
AND, DIRECTLY BELOW THE SCENE OF CARNAGE...
THE ENTIRE CAR IS STARTING TO SHAKE!
DOOM PRESSED THE EMER-GENCY DEFENSE BUTTON! WE'VE GOT EXACTLY TWO SECONDS TO GET OUT!
QUICK, BEN--WE'LL SLAM INTO THE DOOR TOGETHER!
I HEAR YA TALKIN', CHUM!
IT'S A HECKUVA NOTE WHEN THE THING NEEDS SOMEBODY'S HELP TO BUST OUTTA ONE MEASLY DOOR!
SHUT UP AND KEEP MOVING! THIS IS NO JOKE!! HURRY!!
34TH FLOOR
WHUMP!
WE MADE IT! ANOTHER SPLIT-SECOND, AND WE'D HAVE STILL BEEN IN THAT FLAMING CAR!
NOW LET'S GO AGAIN! THE FASTER WE MOVE, THE LESS VULNERABLE WE ARE!
8

LUCKY WE GOT AS FAR AS THE 34TH FLOOR! NOW THERE'S ONLY ONE FLIGHT TO GO!

LUCKY!? SHEEESH!! WE'RE ONLY A FEW FEET AWAY FROM FACING THE MOST DANGEROUS MENACE OF ALL TIME--WITHOUT OUR SUPER POWERS--WITHOUT ONE SINGLE WEAPON!

IF THAT'S LUCK, YOU CAN HAVE IT, PAL!

STEADY-- ALL OF YOU! THERE'S NO TURN- ING BACK NOW!

STAY BEHIND ME! WHAT- EVER HAPPENS, I'LL TAKE IT FIRST AND-- LOOK OUT!!

HE FOUND YOUR STAIRWAY ATTACK BUTTON! WE'RE IN FOR IT NOW!

REED!!

I'LL LET THEM GET STILL CLOSER--LET THEM THINK THEY HAVE A CHANCE! AHH, THE EXQUISITE TRIUMPH OF THIS MOMENT IS BEYOND DESCRIP- TION!

HE'S TURNED AWAY FROM ME AGAIN!

RELEASE THAT MACHINE, DOOM!

YOU DARE ATTACK ME PHYSICALLY?? YOU DARE LAY A HAND ON ME!!?

WHY NOT? I EVEN WALK IN THE RAIN WITHOUT MY BOOTIES SOMETIMES!

THAT'S WHY THEY CALL ME DAREDEVIL!!

DAREDEVIL--BAH! SEE HOW EASILY I BREAK YOUR GRIP WITH MY STEEL-SHOD FINGERS!

I'M DONE TOYING WITH YOU NOW! YOU SHALL LEARN WHAT IT MEANS TO INCUR THE WRATH OF DOCTOR DOOM!

WHERE DO YOU DIG UP THAT DIALOGUE OF YOURS-- IN CORN FLAKES BOXES? ¡UHMMH¡!

I TRUST YOU ENJOYED THAT WITTICISM--FOR IT IS THE LAST YOU SHALL EVER UTTER!

HE'S NOT KIDDING! IT'S LIKE BEING HELD BY A BULLDOZER!

9

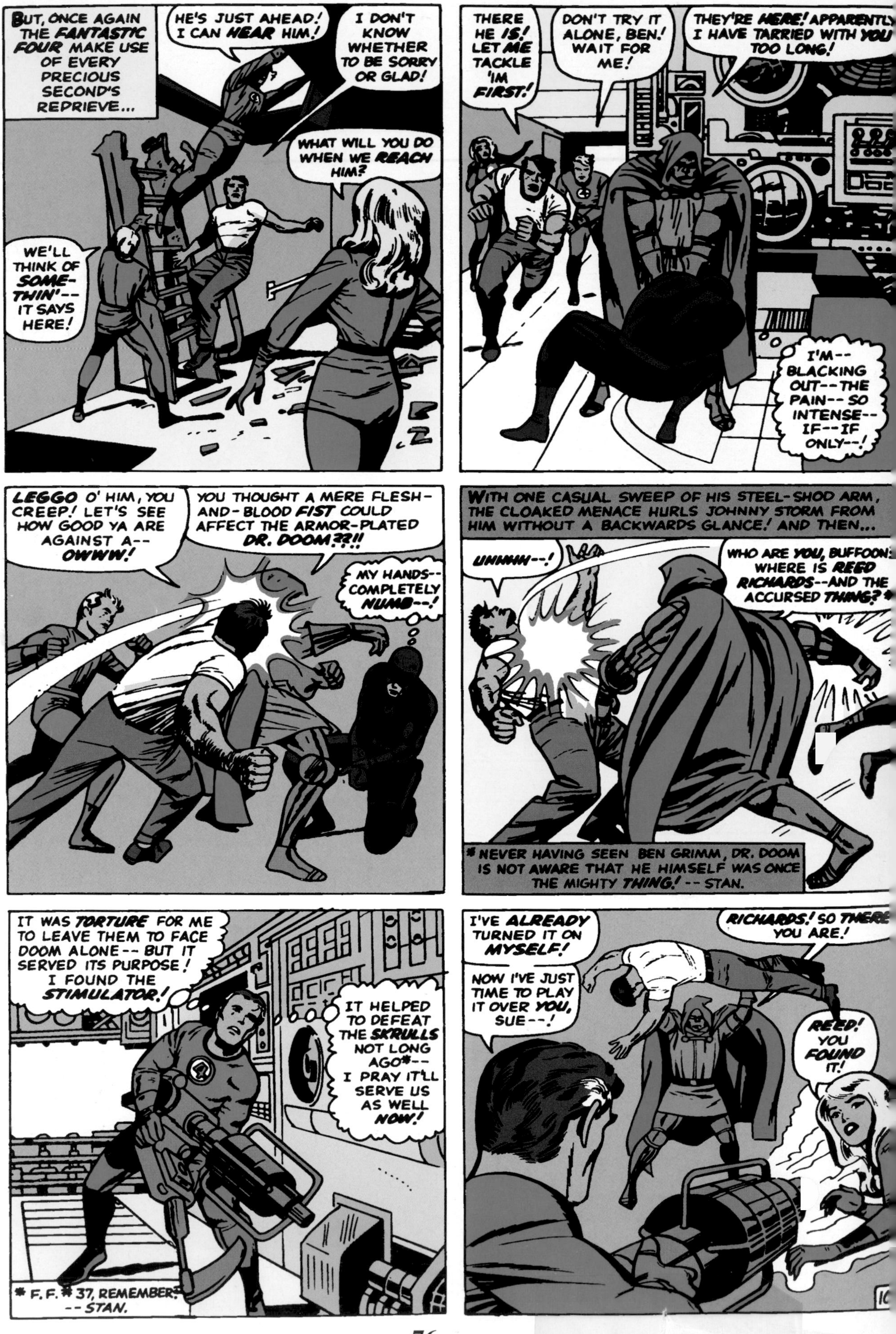
BUT, ONCE AGAIN THE FANTASTIC FOUR MAKE USE OF EVERY PRECIOUS SECOND'S REPRIEVE...
HE'S JUST AHEAD! I CAN HEAR HIM!
I DON'T KNOW WHETHER TO BE SORRY OR GLAD!
WHAT WILL YOU DO WHEN WE REACH HIM?
WE'LL THINK OF SOME-THIN'-- IT SAYS HERE!
THERE HE IS! LET ME TACKLE 'IM FIRST!
DON'T TRY IT ALONE, BEN! WAIT FOR ME!
THEY'RE HERE! APPARENTLY I HAVE TARRIED WITH YOU TOO LONG!
I'M-- BLACKING OUT-- THE PAIN-- SO INTENSE-- IF-- IF ONLY--!
LEGGO O' HIM, YOU CREEP! LET'S SEE HOW GOOD YA ARE AGAINST A-- OWWW!
YOU THOUGHT A MERE FLESH-AND-BLOOD FIST COULD AFFECT THE ARMOR-PLATED DR. DOOM??!!
MY HANDS-- COMPLETELY NUMB--!
WITH ONE CASUAL SWEEP OF HIS STEEL-SHOD ARM, THE CLOAKED MENACE HURLS JOHNNY STORM FROM HIM WITHOUT A BACKWARDS GLANCE! AND THEN...
UHHHHH--!
WHO ARE YOU, BUFFOON? WHERE IS REED RICHARDS--AND THE ACCURSED THING?*
* NEVER HAVING SEEN BEN GRIMM, DR. DOOM IS NOT AWARE THAT HE HIMSELF WAS ONCE THE MIGHTY THING! -- STAN.
IT WAS TORTURE FOR ME TO LEAVE THEM TO FACE DOOM ALONE -- BUT IT SERVED ITS PURPOSE! I FOUND THE STIMULATOR!
IT HELPED TO DEFEAT THE SKRULLS NOT LONG AGO*-- I PRAY IT'LL SERVE US AS WELL NOW!
* F.F. # 37, REMEMBER? -- STAN.
I'VE ALREADY TURNED IT ON MYSELF!
NOW I'VE JUST TIME TO PLAY IT OVER YOU, SUE--!
RICHARDS! SO THERE YOU ARE!
REED! YOU FOUND IT!
10

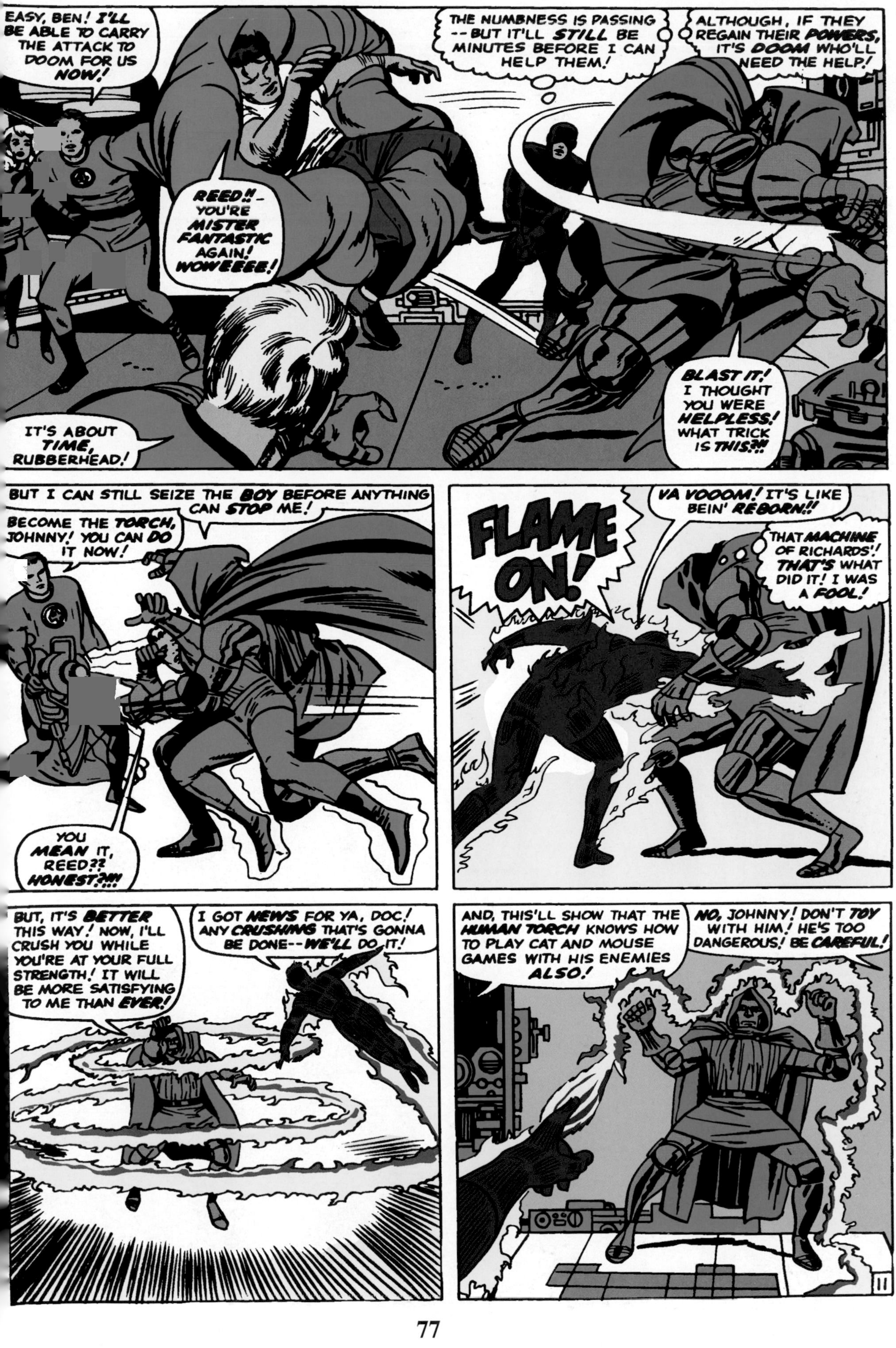

EASY, BEN! I'LL BE ABLE TO CARRY THE ATTACK TO DOOM FOR US NOW!
THE NUMBNESS IS PASSING -- BUT IT'LL STILL BE MINUTES BEFORE I CAN HELP THEM!
ALTHOUGH, IF THEY REGAIN THEIR POWERS, IT'S DOOM WHO'LL NEED THE HELP!
REED!! - YOU'RE MISTER FANTASTIC AGAIN! WOWEEEE!
IT'S ABOUT TIME, RUBBERHEAD!
BLAST IT! I THOUGHT YOU WERE HELPLESS! WHAT TRICK IS THIS?!!
BUT I CAN STILL SEIZE THE BOY BEFORE ANYTHING CAN STOP ME!
BECOME THE TORCH, JOHNNY! YOU CAN DO IT NOW!
YOU MEAN IT, REED?? HONEST?!!!
FLAME ON!
VA VOOOM! IT'S LIKE BEIN' REBORN!!
THAT MACHINE OF RICHARDS'! THAT'S WHAT DID IT! I WAS A FOOL!
BUT, IT'S BETTER THIS WAY! NOW, I'LL CRUSH YOU WHILE YOU'RE AT YOUR FULL STRENGTH! IT WILL BE MORE SATISFYING TO ME THAN EVER!
I GOT NEWS FOR YA, DOC! ANY CRUSHING THAT'S GONNA BE DONE--WE'LL DO IT!
AND, THIS'LL SHOW THAT THE HUMAN TORCH KNOWS HOW TO PLAY CAT AND MOUSE GAMES WITH HIS ENEMIES ALSO!
NO, JOHNNY! DON'T TOY WITH HIM! HE'S TOO DANGEROUS! BE CAREFUL!
11

AW, WHO'RE YOU KIDDIN', REED! HIS NUMBER'S UP NOW, AND HE KNOWS IT!

JOHNNY! HIS FOOT--IT'S STEPPING ON THAT LEVER! LOOK OUT!

BUT, SUE'S FRENZIED WARNING COMES A SPLIT-SECOND TOO LATE--!

TAKE COVER, JOHNNY! HE ACTIVATED THE IN-FLOOR REFRIGERATION UNIT-- YOUR FLAME'S DYING OUT!

WE'VE GOT TO REACH HIM BEFORE HE CAN PLAN A NEW ATTACK!

I'LL TURN INVISIBLE-- GET AS CLOSE AS POSSIBLE!

THE NEARER I AM, THE MORE EFFECTIVE MY FORCE FIELD WILL--OHHH!

WHAT'S HAPPENING TO ME??

BY SETTING THE FREEZING UNIT ON FULL, I CAN TRAP THE THREE OF YOU WITH YOUR OWN DEVICE!

HOW EASY IT WAS FOR ME, AFTER ALL!

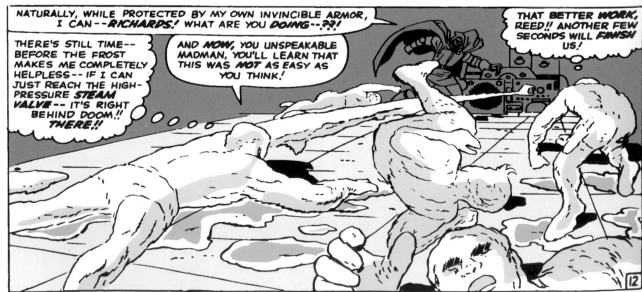

NATURALLY, WHILE PROTECTED BY MY OWN INVINCIBLE ARMOR, I CAN--RICHARDS! WHAT ARE YOU DOING--??!

THERE'S STILL TIME-- BEFORE THE FROST MAKES ME COMPLETELY HELPLESS--IF I CAN JUST REACH THE HIGH-PRESSURE STEAM VALVE-- IT'S RIGHT BEHIND DOOM!! THERE!!

AND NOW, YOU UNSPEAKABLE MADMAN, YOU'LL LEARN THAT THIS WAS NOT AS EASY AS YOU THINK!

THAT BETTER WORK, REED!! ANOTHER FEW SECONDS WILL FINISH US!

12

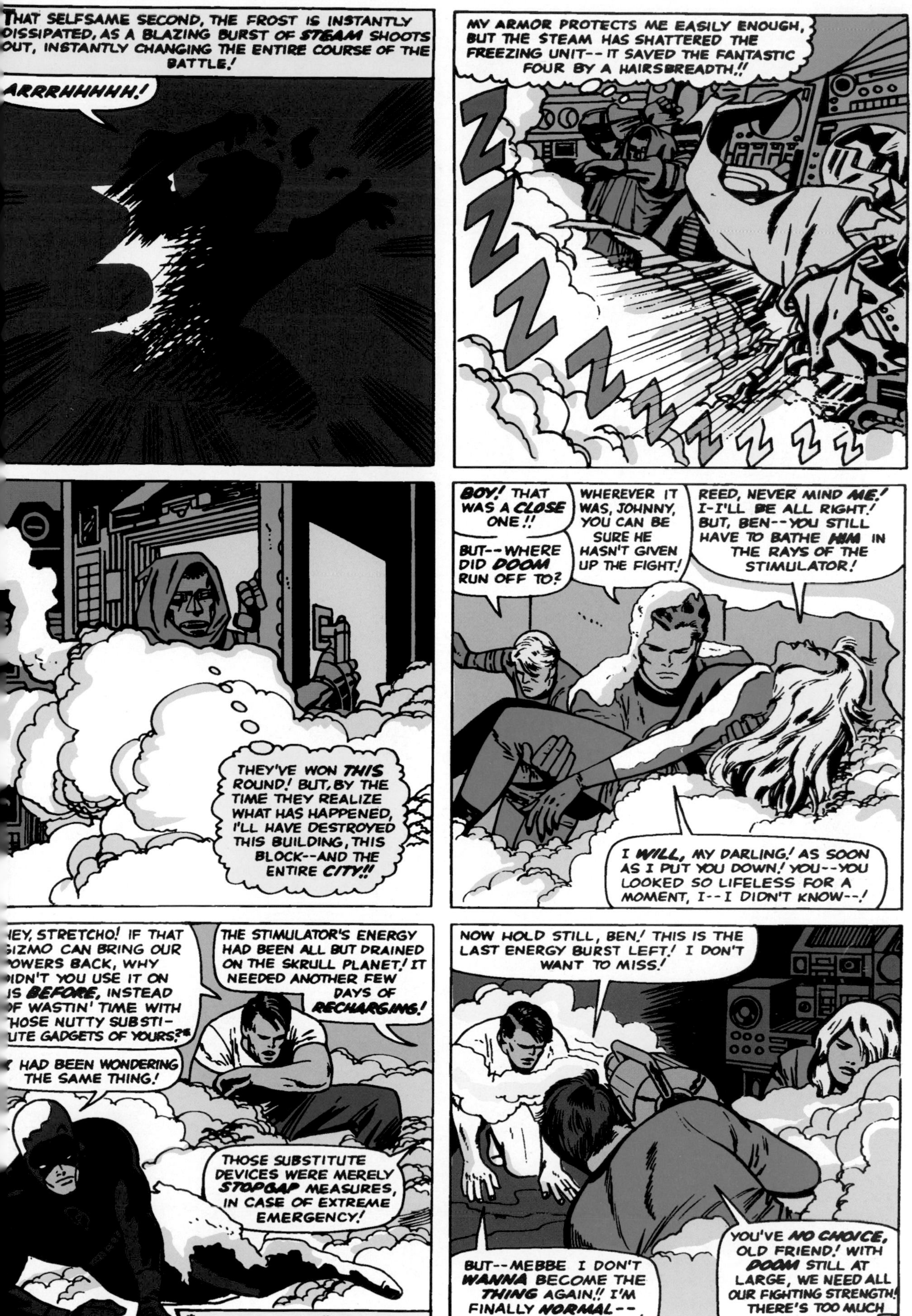
THAT SELFSAME SECOND, THE FROST IS INSTANTLY DISSIPATED, AS A BLAZING BURST OF STEAM SHOOTS OUT, INSTANTLY CHANGING THE ENTIRE COURSE OF THE BATTLE!
ARRRHHHHH!
MY ARMOR PROTECTS ME EASILY ENOUGH, BUT THE STEAM HAS SHATTERED THE FREEZING UNIT-- IT SAVED THE FANTASTIC FOUR BY A HAIRSBREADTH!!
THEY'VE WON THIS ROUND! BUT, BY THE TIME THEY REALIZE WHAT HAS HAPPENED, I'LL HAVE DESTROYED THIS BUILDING, THIS BLOCK--AND THE ENTIRE CITY!!
BOY! THAT WAS A CLOSE ONE!!
BUT--WHERE DID DOOM RUN OFF TO?
WHEREVER IT WAS, JOHNNY, YOU CAN BE SURE HE HASN'T GIVEN UP THE FIGHT!
REED, NEVER MIND ME! I-I'LL BE ALL RIGHT! BUT, BEN--YOU STILL HAVE TO BATHE HIM IN THE RAYS OF THE STIMULATOR!
I WILL, MY DARLING! AS SOON AS I PUT YOU DOWN! YOU--YOU LOOKED SO LIFELESS FOR A MOMENT, I--I DIDN'T KNOW--!
EY, STRETCHO! IF THAT GIZMO CAN BRING OUR POWERS BACK, WHY DIDN'T YOU USE IT ON US BEFORE, INSTEAD OF WASTIN' TIME WITH THOSE NUTTY SUBSTITUTE GADGETS OF YOURS?*
THE STIMULATOR'S ENERGY HAD BEEN ALL BUT DRAINED ON THE SKRULL PLANET! IT NEEDED ANOTHER FEW DAYS OF RECHARGING!
I HAD BEEN WONDERING THE SAME THING!
THOSE SUBSTITUTE DEVICES WERE MERELY STOPGAP MEASURES, IN CASE OF EXTREME EMERGENCY!
*AS SEEN IN F.F. #39 -- STAN.
NOW HOLD STILL, BEN! THIS IS THE LAST ENERGY BURST LEFT! I DON'T WANT TO MISS!
BUT--MEBBE I DON'T WANNA BECOME THE THING AGAIN!! I'M FINALLY NORMAL-- LIKE ANYONE ELSE!
YOU'VE NO CHOICE, OLD FRIEND! WITH DOOM STILL AT LARGE, WE NEED ALL OUR FIGHTING STRENGTH! THERE'S TOO MUCH AT STAKE!
13

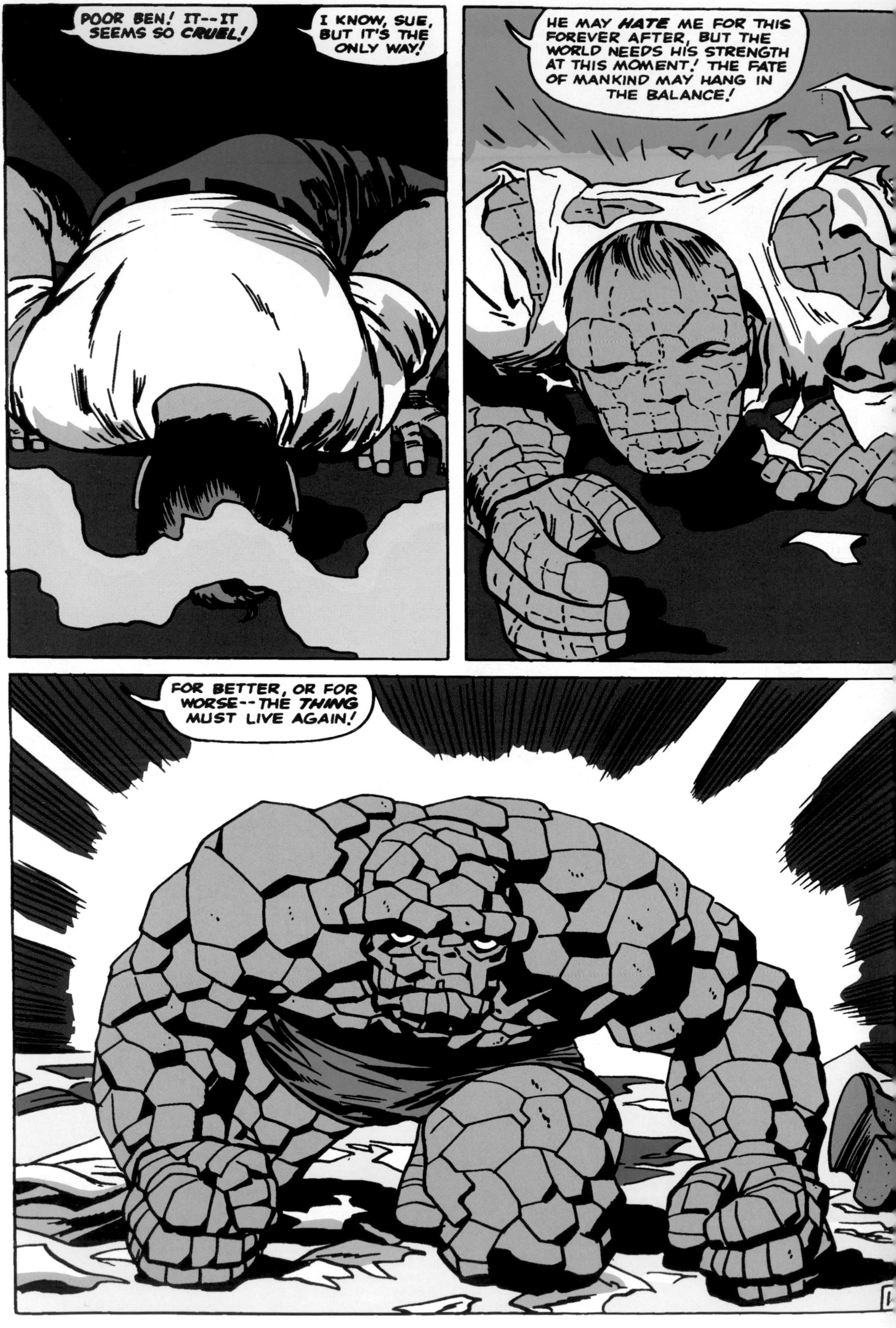
POOR BEN! IT--IT SEEMS SO CRUEL!
I KNOW, SUE, BUT IT'S THE ONLY WAY!
HE MAY HATE ME FOR THIS FOREVER AFTER, BUT THE WORLD NEEDS HIS STRENGTH AT THIS MOMENT! THE FATE OF MANKIND MAY HANG IN THE BALANCE!
FOR BETTER, OR FOR WORSE--THE THING MUST LIVE AGAIN!

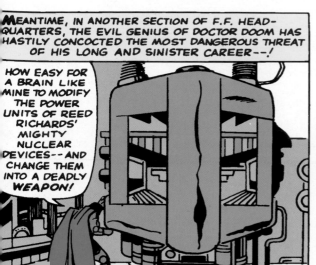

MEANTIME, IN ANOTHER SECTION OF F.F. HEAD-QUARTERS, THE EVIL GENIUS OF DOCTOR DOOM HAS HASTILY CONCOCTED THE MOST DANGEROUS THREAT OF HIS LONG AND SINISTER CAREER--!

HOW EASY FOR A BRAIN LIKE MINE TO MODIFY THE POWER UNITS OF REED RICHARDS' MIGHTY NUCLEAR DEVICES-- AND CHANGE THEM INTO A DEADLY WEAPON!

I'VE CREATED A *TIME BOMB* WHICH WILL DESTROY EVERYTHING IN SIGHT!

ALL I NEED DO IS GET SAFELY OUT OF RANGE AND AWAIT THE FATAL MOMENT! MORE THAN EVER HAVE I INSURED THAT THE NAME OF *DOCTOR DOOM* SHALL FOREVER LIVE IN *INFAMY!*

AND NOW, TO TAKE MY LEAVE! THE FANTASTIC FOUR HAVE WON THE BATTLE-- BUT LOST THE WAR! *WAIT-- WHAT'S THAT?!*

WHOOM

YOU!! IT'S BECAUSE OF *YOU* THAT I'M THE *THING* AGAIN!! YOU'RE GONNA *PAY* FOR THAT, DO YA HEAR?? I'M GONNA *DEMOLISH* YOU!!

AHHH! AT LAST-- THE BRAINLESS, BLABBERING *THING!* I'VE BEEN *WAITING* FOR YOU!

AND YA WON'T HAVETA WAIT ANY *LONGER!*

WOKK

Y-YER STILL *STANDIN'??!*....!

NATURALLY! MY ARMOR'S FORCE FIELD CAN GENERATE 100,000 MEGAVOLTS OF PURE ENERGY! THE MIRACLE IS THAT *YOU* HAVE NOT DESTROYED *YOURSELF!*

15

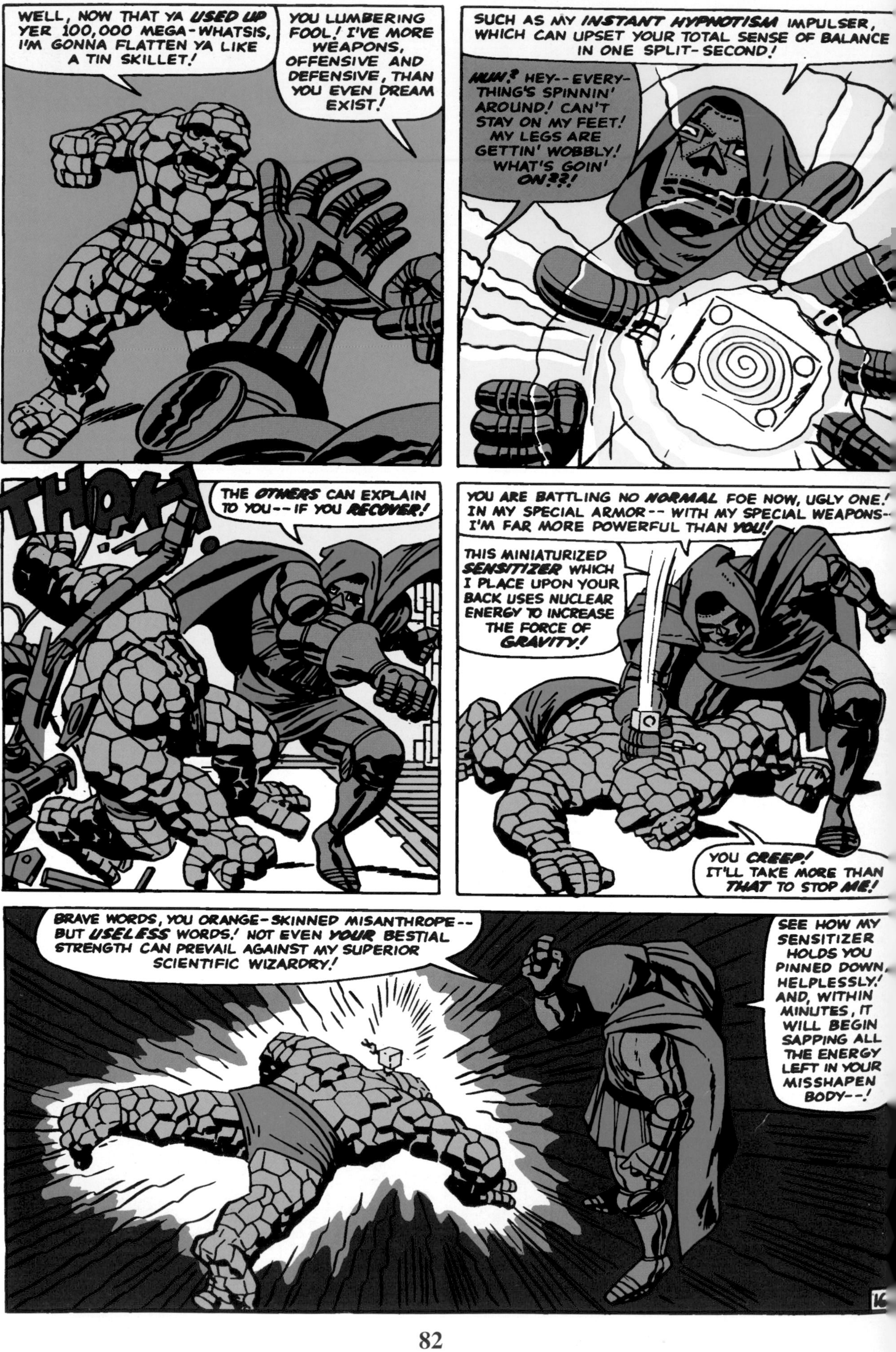
WELL, NOW THAT YA USED UP YER 100,000 MEGA-WHATSIS, I'M GONNA FLATTEN YA LIKE A TIN SKILLET!
YOU LUMBERING FOOL! I'VE MORE WEAPONS, OFFENSIVE AND DEFENSIVE, THAN YOU EVEN DREAM EXIST!
SUCH AS MY INSTANT HYPNOTISM IMPULSER, WHICH CAN UPSET YOUR TOTAL SENSE OF BALANCE IN ONE SPLIT-SECOND!
HUH? HEY--EVERYTHING'S SPINNIN' AROUND! CAN'T STAY ON MY FEET! MY LEGS ARE GETTIN' WOBBLY! WHAT'S GOIN' ON??!
THPAK!
THE OTHERS CAN EXPLAIN TO YOU--IF YOU RECOVER!
YOU ARE BATTLING NO NORMAL FOE NOW, UGLY ONE! IN MY SPECIAL ARMOR-- WITH MY SPECIAL WEAPONS-- I'M FAR MORE POWERFUL THAN YOU!
THIS MINIATURIZED SENSITIZER WHICH I PLACE UPON YOUR BACK USES NUCLEAR ENERGY TO INCREASE THE FORCE OF GRAVITY!
YOU CREEP! IT'LL TAKE MORE THAN THAT TO STOP ME!
BRAVE WORDS, YOU ORANGE-SKINNED MISANTHROPE--BUT USELESS WORDS! NOT EVEN YOUR BESTIAL STRENGTH CAN PREVAIL AGAINST MY SUPERIOR SCIENTIFIC WIZARDRY!
SEE HOW MY SENSITIZER HOLDS YOU PINNED DOWN, HELPLESSLY! AND, WITHIN MINUTES, IT WILL BEGIN SAPPING ALL THE ENERGY LEFT IN YOUR MISSHAPEN BODY--!
16

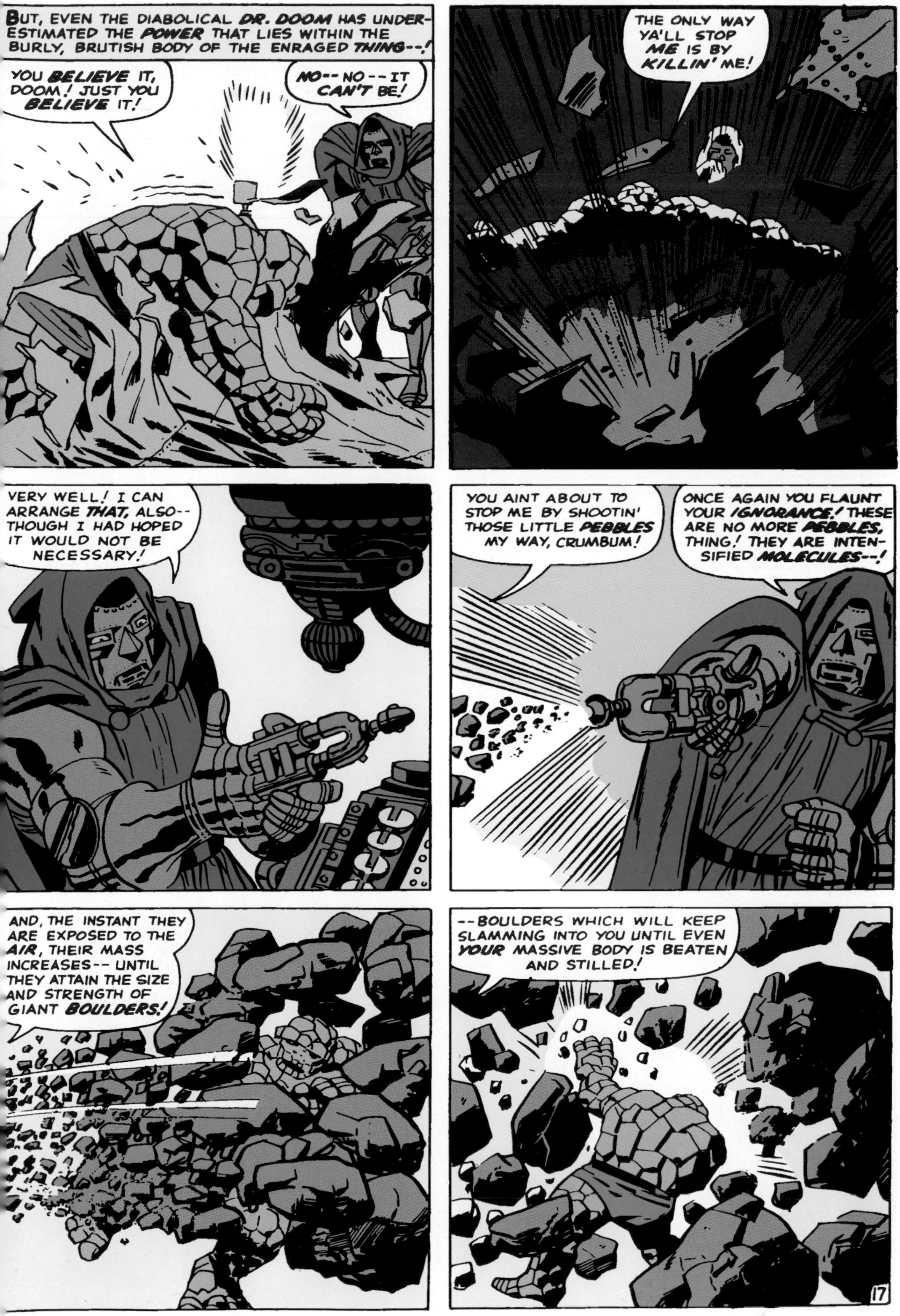

BUT, EVEN THE DIABOLICAL DR. DOOM HAS UNDERESTIMATED THE POWER THAT LIES WITHIN THE BURLY, BRUTISH BODY OF THE ENRAGED THING--!
YOU BELIEVE IT, DOOM! JUST YOU BELIEVE IT!
NO-- NO -- IT CAN'T BE!
THE ONLY WAY YA'LL STOP ME IS BY KILLIN' ME!
VERY WELL! I CAN ARRANGE THAT, ALSO-- THOUGH I HAD HOPED IT WOULD NOT BE NECESSARY!
YOU AINT ABOUT TO STOP ME BY SHOOTIN' THOSE LITTLE PEBBLES MY WAY, CRUMBUM!
ONCE AGAIN YOU FLAUNT YOUR IGNORANCE! THESE ARE NO MORE PEBBLES, THING! THEY ARE INTENSIFIED MOLECULES--!
AND, THE INSTANT THEY ARE EXPOSED TO THE AIR, THEIR MASS INCREASES-- UNTIL THEY ATTAIN THE SIZE AND STRENGTH OF GIANT BOULDERS!
--BOULDERS WHICH WILL KEEP SLAMMING INTO YOU UNTIL EVEN YOUR MASSIVE BODY IS BEATEN AND STILLED!
17

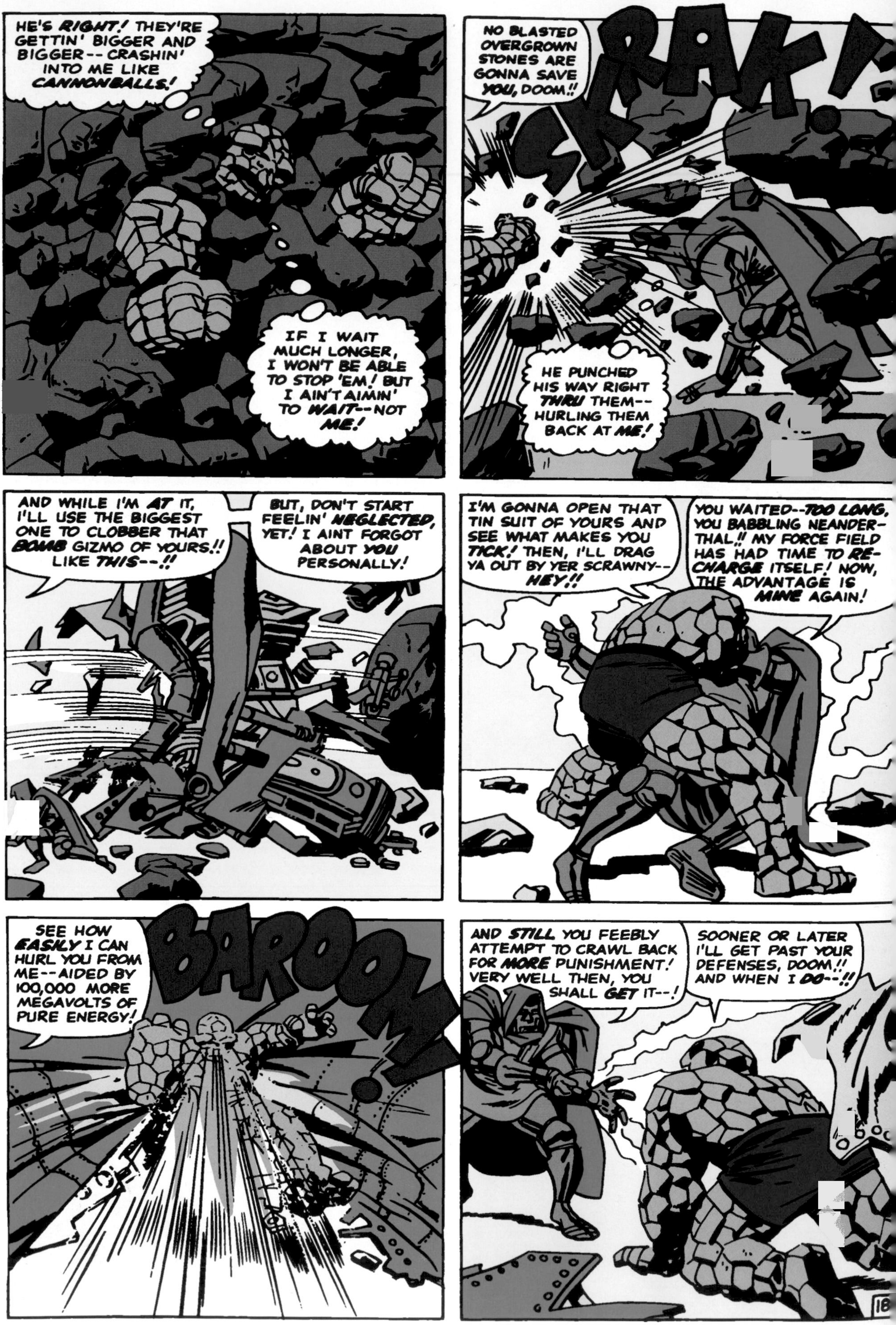
HE'S RIGHT! THEY'RE GETTIN' BIGGER AND BIGGER--CRASHIN' INTO ME LIKE CANNONBALLS!
IF I WAIT MUCH LONGER, I WON'T BE ABLE TO STOP 'EM! BUT I AIN'T AIMIN' TO WAIT--NOT ME!
NO BLASTED OVERGROWN STONES ARE GONNA SAVE YOU, DOOM!!
SKRAK!!
HE PUNCHED HIS WAY RIGHT THRU THEM--HURLING THEM BACK AT ME!
AND WHILE I'M AT IT, I'LL USE THE BIGGEST ONE TO CLOBBER THAT BOMB GIZMO OF YOURS!! LIKE THIS--!!
BUT, DON'T START FEELIN' NEGLECTED, YET! I AINT FORGOT ABOUT YOU PERSONALLY!
I'M GONNA OPEN THAT TIN SUIT OF YOURS AND SEE WHAT MAKES YOU TICK! THEN, I'LL DRAG YA OUT BY YER SCRAWNY--HEY!!
YOU WAITED--TOO LONG, YOU BABBLING NEANDERTHAL!! MY FORCE FIELD HAS HAD TIME TO RE-CHARGE ITSELF! NOW, THE ADVANTAGE IS MINE AGAIN!
SEE HOW EASILY I CAN HURL YOU FROM ME--AIDED BY 100,000 MORE MEGAVOLTS OF PURE ENERGY!
BAROOM!
AND STILL YOU FEEBLY ATTEMPT TO CRAWL BACK FOR MORE PUNISHMENT! VERY WELL THEN, YOU SHALL GET IT--!
SOONER OR LATER I'LL GET PAST YOUR DEFENSES, DOOM!! AND WHEN I DO--!!
18

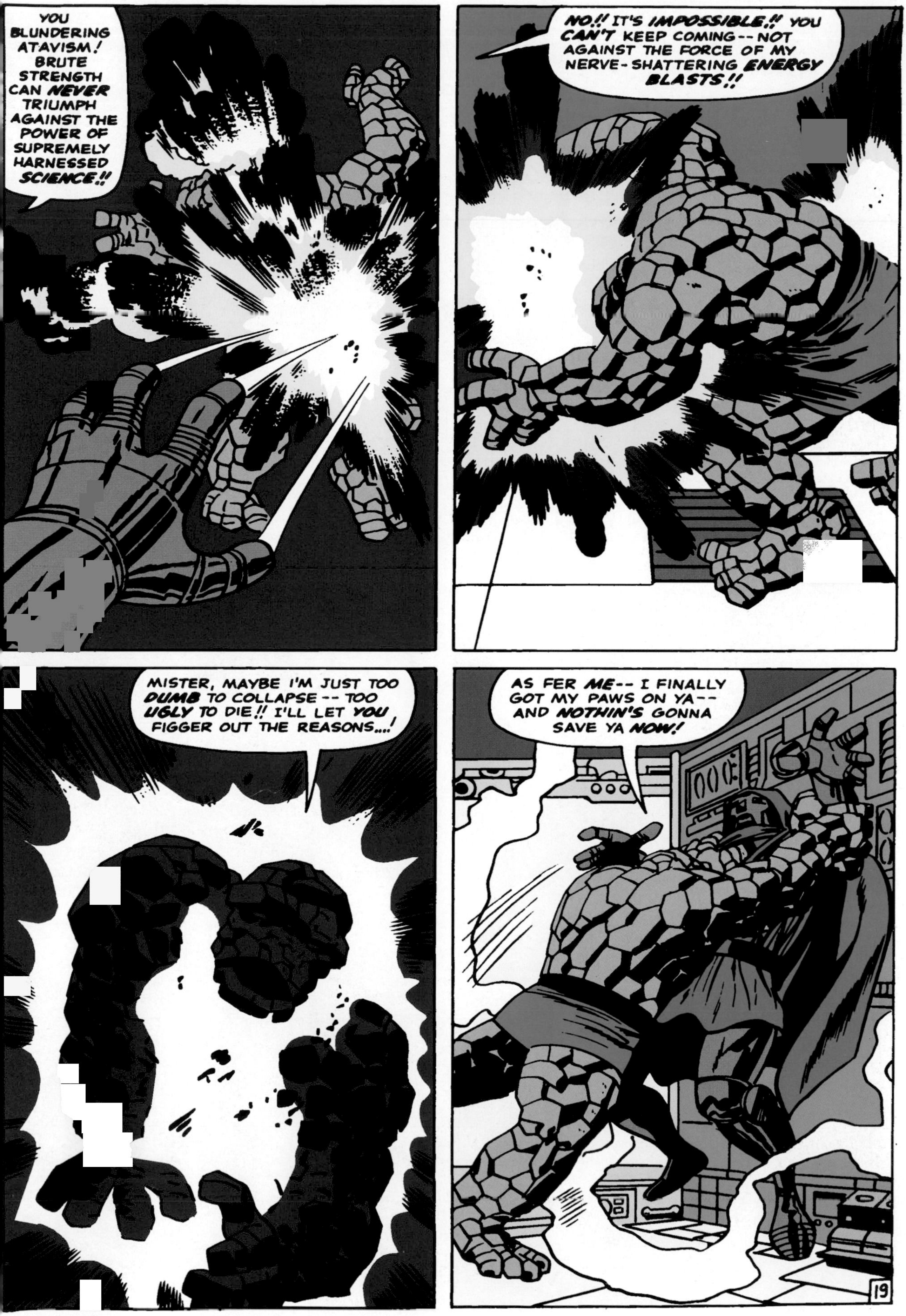
YOU BLUNDERING ATAVISM! BRUTE STRENGTH CAN NEVER TRIUMPH AGAINST THE POWER OF SUPREMELY HARNESSED SCIENCE!!
NO!! IT'S IMPOSSIBLE!! YOU CAN'T KEEP COMING--NOT AGAINST THE FORCE OF MY NERVE-SHATTERING ENERGY BLASTS!!
MISTER, MAYBE I'M JUST TOO DUMB TO COLLAPSE -- TOO UGLY TO DIE!! I'LL LET YOU FIGGER OUT THE REASONS....!
AS FER ME-- I FINALLY GOT MY PAWS ON YA-- AND NOTHIN'S GONNA SAVE YA NOW!
19

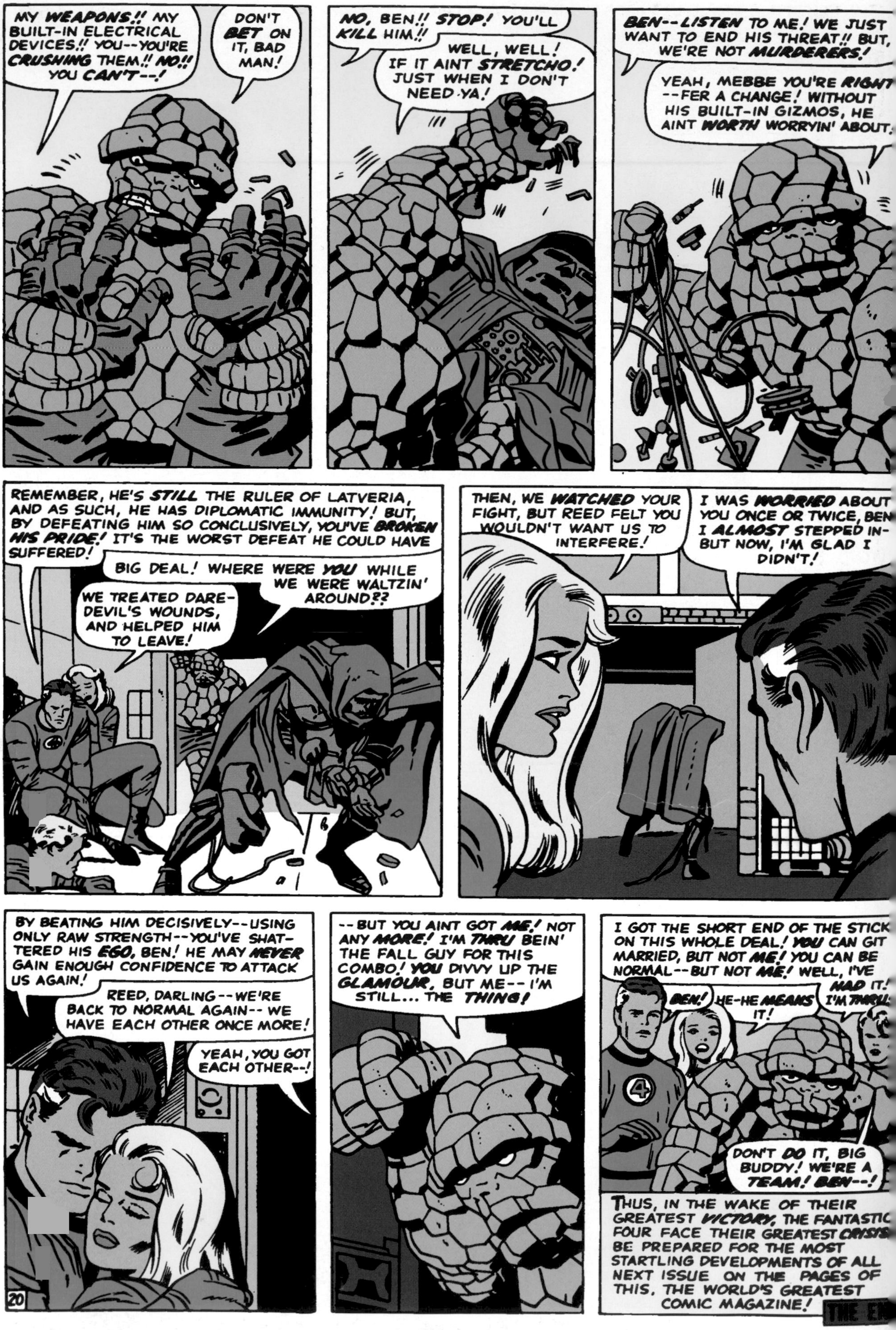

MY WEAPONS!! MY BUILT-IN ELECTRICAL DEVICES!! YOU--YOU'RE CRUSHING THEM!! NO!! YOU CAN'T--!
DON'T BET ON IT, BAD MAN!
NO, BEN!! STOP! YOU'LL KILL HIM!!
WELL, WELL! IF IT AINT STRETCHO! JUST WHEN I DON'T NEED YA!
BEN--LISTEN TO ME! WE JUST WANT TO END HIS THREAT!! BUT, WE'RE NOT MURDERERS!
YEAH, MEBBE YOU'RE RIGHT --FER A CHANGE! WITHOUT HIS BUILT-IN GIZMOS, HE AINT WORTH WORRYIN' ABOUT!
REMEMBER, HE'S STILL THE RULER OF LATVERIA, AND AS SUCH, HE HAS DIPLOMATIC IMMUNITY! BUT, BY DEFEATING HIM SO CONCLUSIVELY, YOU'VE BROKEN HIS PRIDE! IT'S THE WORST DEFEAT HE COULD HAVE SUFFERED!
BIG DEAL! WHERE WERE YOU WHILE WE WERE WALTZIN' AROUND?!?
WE TREATED DAREDEVIL'S WOUNDS, AND HELPED HIM TO LEAVE!
THEN, WE WATCHED YOUR FIGHT, BUT REED FELT YOU WOULDN'T WANT US TO INTERFERE!
I WAS WORRIED ABOUT YOU ONCE OR TWICE, BEN! I ALMOST STEPPED IN--BUT NOW, I'M GLAD I DIDN'T!
BY BEATING HIM DECISIVELY--USING ONLY RAW STRENGTH--YOU'VE SHATTERED HIS EGO, BEN! HE MAY NEVER GAIN ENOUGH CONFIDENCE TO ATTACK US AGAIN!
REED, DARLING--WE'RE BACK TO NORMAL AGAIN--WE HAVE EACH OTHER ONCE MORE!
YEAH, YOU GOT EACH OTHER--!
20
--BUT YOU AINT GOT ME! NOT ANY MORE! I'M THRU BEIN' THE FALL GUY FOR THIS COMBO! YOU DIVVY UP THE GLAMOUR, BUT ME--I'M STILL... THE THING!
I GOT THE SHORT END OF THE STICK ON THIS WHOLE DEAL! YOU CAN GIT MARRIED, BUT NOT ME! YOU CAN BE NORMAL--BUT NOT ME! WELL, I'VE HAD IT! I'M THRU!
BEN!
HE-HE MEANS IT!
DON'T DO IT, BIG BUDDY! WE'RE A TEAM! BEN--!
THUS, IN THE WAKE OF THEIR GREATEST VICTORY, THE FANTASTIC FOUR FACE THEIR GREATEST CRISIS! BE PREPARED FOR THE MOST STARTLING DEVELOPMENTS OF ALL NEXT ISSUE ON THE PAGES OF THIS, THE WORLD'S GREATEST COMIC MAGAZINE!
THE EN

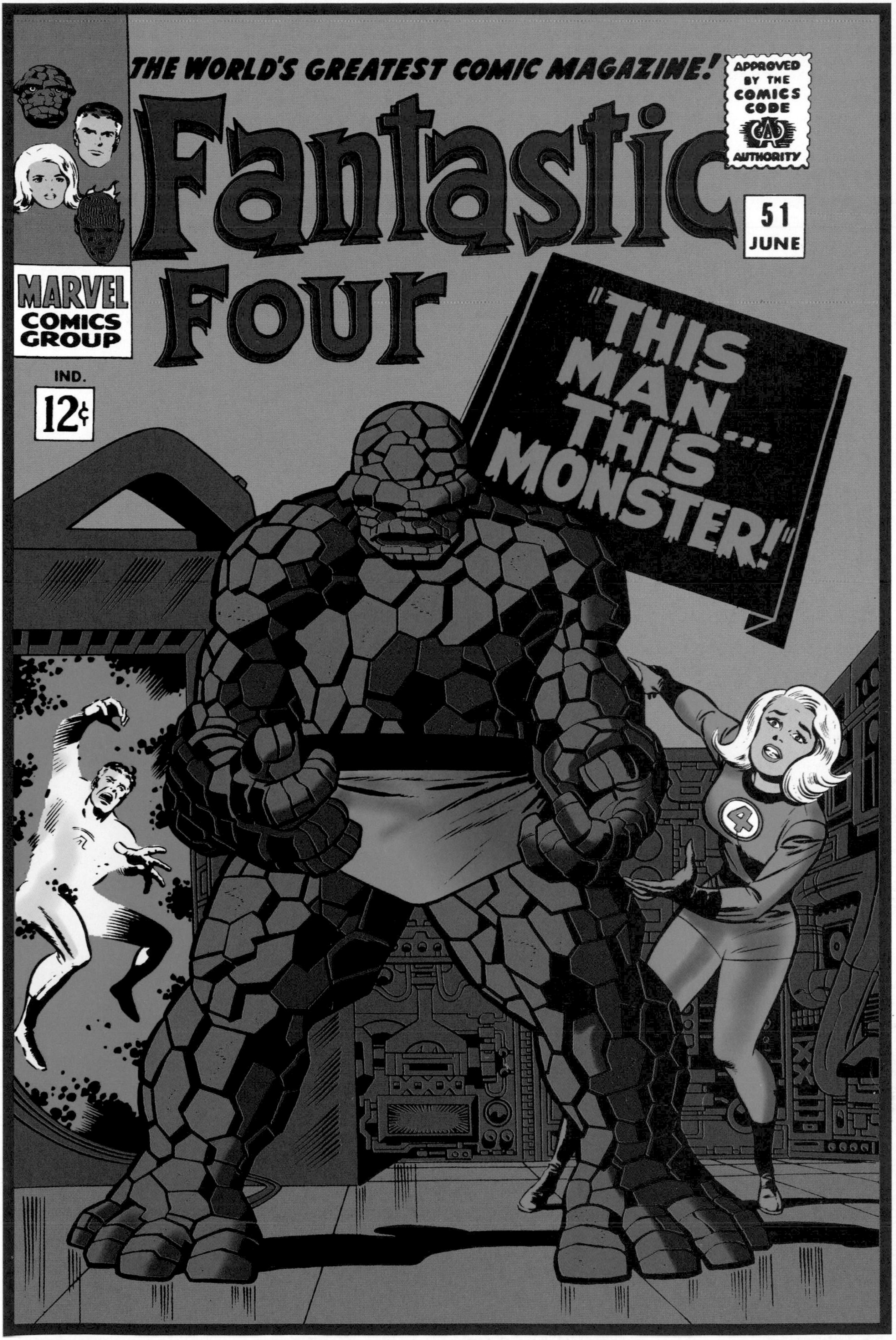
THE WORLD'S GREATEST COMIC MAGAZINE!
APPROVED BY THE COMICS CODE AUTHORITY
Fantastic Four
51
JUNE
MARVEL COMICS GROUP
IND.
12¢
"THIS MAN... THIS MONSTER!"

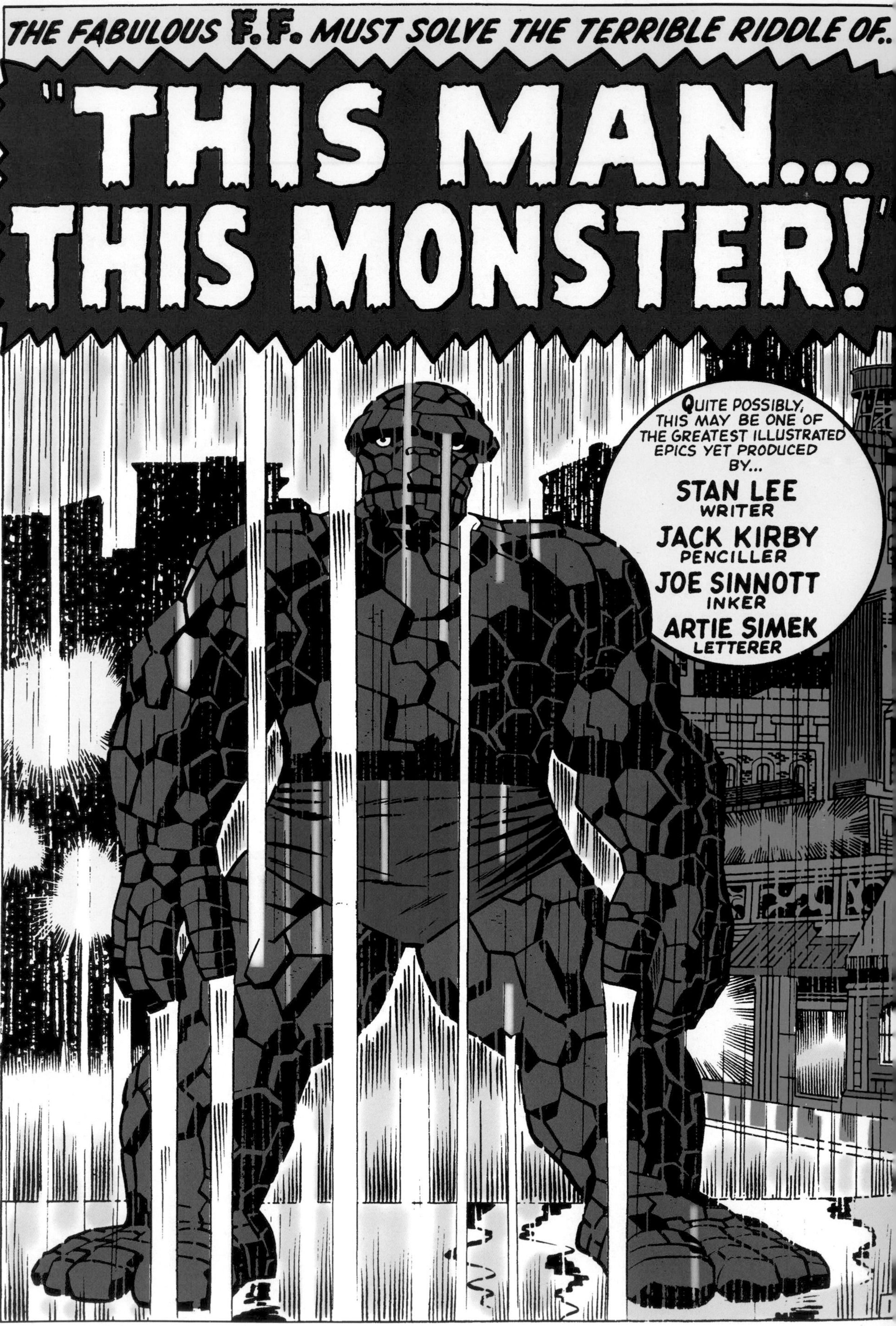
THE FABULOUS F.F. MUST SOLVE THE TERRIBLE RIDDLE OF..
"THIS MAN... THIS MONSTER!"
QUITE POSSIBLY, THIS MAY BE ONE OF THE GREATEST ILLUSTRATED EPICS YET PRODUCED BY...
STAN LEE WRITER
JACK KIRBY PENCILLER
JOE SINNOTT INKER
ARTIE SIMEK LETTERER

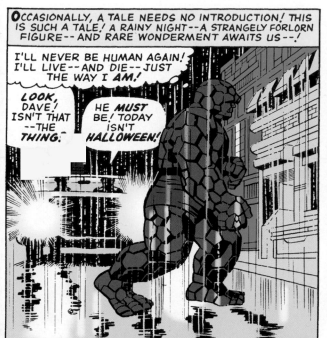

OCCASIONALLY, A TALE NEEDS NO INTRODUCTION! THIS IS SUCH A TALE! A RAINY NIGHT--A STRANGELY FORLORN FIGURE--AND RARE WONDERMENT AWAITS US--!

I'LL NEVER BE HUMAN AGAIN! I'LL LIVE--AND DIE--JUST THE WAY I *AM*!

LOOK, DAVE! ISN'T THAT --THE *THING*?

HE *MUST* BE! TODAY ISN'T *HALLOWEEN*!

WANT A *LIFT*, BIG FELLA? A GUY CAN CATCH A *COLD* THAT WAY!

IS ANYTHING *WRONG*? YOU LOOK KINDA *BEAT*!

A *NORMAL* GUY, Y'MEAN! WEATHER DON'T BOTHER *ME*!

SO WOULD *YOU*, IF YA HAD A FACE LIKE *MINE*!

AWW, DON'T MIND *ME*! I'M OKAY! EVERYTHIN'S COMIN' UP ROSES! SEE YA AROUND!

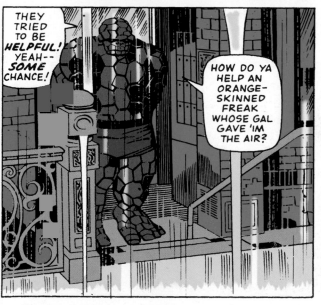

THEY TRIED TO BE *HELPFUL*! YEAH-- *SOME* CHANCE!

HOW DO YA HELP AN ORANGE-SKINNED FREAK WHOSE GAL GAVE 'IM THE AIR?

I WONDER WHAT MADE ME WALK TA *THIS* NEIGHBORHOOD? ALMOST LIKE SOMETHIN' WAS PULLIN'-- *HEY*!

I *SAW* YOU OUT THERE IN THE RAIN! WHY NOT COME IN WHERE IT'S WARM AND DRY?

WHAT *IS* THIS--"BE NICE TO GARGOYLES" WEEK, OR SOMETHIN'?

I CAN UNDERSTAND YOUR BITTERNESS-- AND SYMPATHIZE WITH IT! I, TOO, KNOW HOW IT FEELS TO BE LONELY-- AND SAD OF HEART!

HE STILL SUSPECTS *NOTHING*! I MUST BE CAREFUL--SO VERY CAREFUL--!

I'LL JUST SIT HERE FER A MINUTE! I'M TIRED'A WALKIN'-- TIRED'A THINKIN'--!

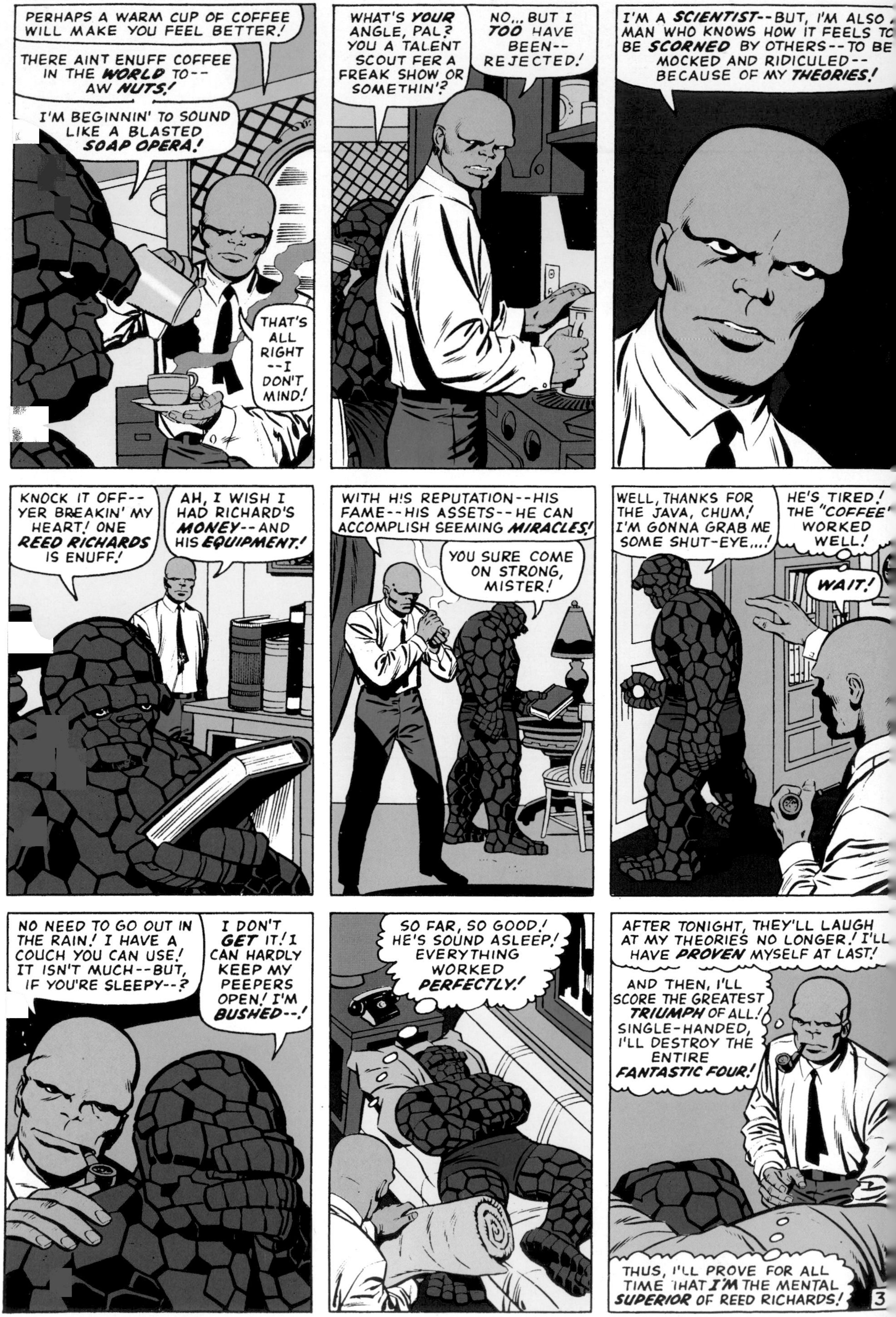
PERHAPS A WARM CUP OF COFFEE WILL MAKE YOU FEEL BETTER!
THERE AINT ENUFF COFFEE IN THE WORLD TO-- AW NUTS!
I'M BEGINNIN' TO SOUND LIKE A BLASTED SOAP OPERA!
THAT'S ALL RIGHT --I DON'T MIND!
WHAT'S YOUR ANGLE, PAL? YOU A TALENT SCOUT FER A FREAK SHOW OR SOMETHIN'?
NO... BUT I TOO HAVE BEEN--REJECTED!
I'M A SCIENTIST--BUT, I'M ALSO A MAN WHO KNOWS HOW IT FEELS TO BE SCORNED BY OTHERS--TO BE MOCKED AND RIDICULED--BECAUSE OF MY THEORIES!
KNOCK IT OFF--YER BREAKIN' MY HEART! ONE REED RICHARDS IS ENUFF!
AH, I WISH I HAD RICHARD'S MONEY--AND HIS EQUIPMENT!
WITH HIS REPUTATION--HIS FAME--HIS ASSETS--HE CAN ACCOMPLISH SEEMING MIRACLES!
YOU SURE COME ON STRONG, MISTER!
WELL, THANKS FOR THE JAVA, CHUM! I'M GONNA GRAB ME SOME SHUT-EYE...!
HE'S TIRED! THE "COFFEE" WORKED WELL!
WAIT!
NO NEED TO GO OUT IN THE RAIN! I HAVE A COUCH YOU CAN USE! IT ISN'T MUCH--BUT, IF YOU'RE SLEEPY--?
I DON'T GET IT! I CAN HARDLY KEEP MY PEEPERS OPEN! I'M BUSHED--!
SO FAR, SO GOOD! HE'S SOUND ASLEEP! EVERYTHING WORKED PERFECTLY!
AFTER TONIGHT, THEY'LL LAUGH AT MY THEORIES NO LONGER! I'LL HAVE PROVEN MYSELF AT LAST!
AND THEN, I'LL SCORE THE GREATEST TRIUMPH OF ALL! SINGLE-HANDED, I'LL DESTROY THE ENTIRE FANTASTIC FOUR!
THUS, I'LL PROVE FOR ALL TIME THAT I'M THE MENTAL SUPERIOR OF REED RICHARDS!
3

I'VE SPENT A *LIFETIME* CREATING MY *DUPLICATION APPARATUS!*

AND, IT'S TAKEN LONG MONTHS OF PATIENT PLANNING TO LURE THE *THING* INTO THIS ROOM, BY USING MY SHORT-RANGE SUBLIMINAL INFLUENCER!

BUT NOW, ALL THE LABOR, ALL THE WAITING, ALL THE SCHEMING, WILL PAY OFF AT *LAST!* I'M *THRU* BEING A LOSER-- *THIS* TIME I'VE GOT THE *WINNING HAND!*

AS FOR THE *THING*--- THERE'S *NO WAY* HE CAN EVER *STOP* ME!

HE WAS THE PERFECT CHOICE FOR MY EXPERIMENT, BECAUSE OF OUR SLIGHT SKELETAL RESEMBLANCE...

THAT FACT WILL MAKE THE *DUPLICATION PROCESS* ALL THE MORE EFFECTIVE!

AND NOW--LET IT *BEGIN!*

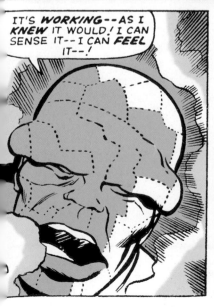

IT'S *WORKING*--AS I *KNEW* IT WOULD! I CAN SENSE IT--I CAN *FEEL* IT--!

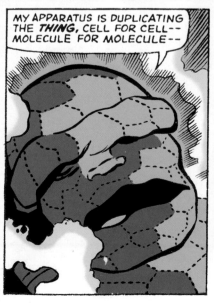

MY APPARATUS IS DUPLICATING THE *THING*, CELL FOR CELL-- MOLECULE FOR MOLECULE--

IT'S *OVER!* I'M AN EXACT *REPLICA* OF HIM!

NOW, ALL HIS *FAME*--AND HIS *POWER*--ARE *MINE!*

4

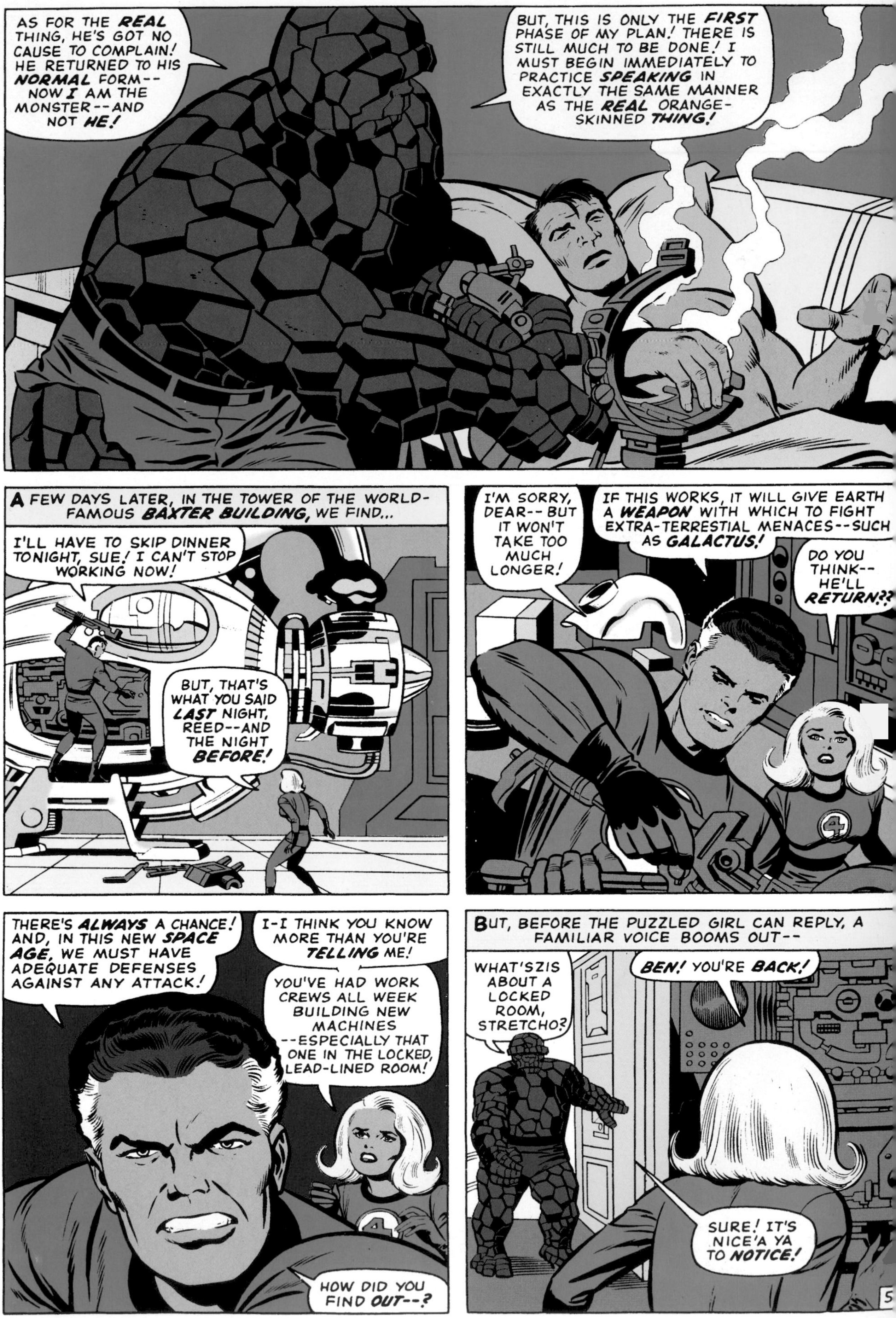
AS FOR THE REAL THING, HE'S GOT NO CAUSE TO COMPLAIN! HE RETURNED TO HIS NORMAL FORM-- NOW I AM THE MONSTER--AND NOT HE!
BUT, THIS IS ONLY THE FIRST PHASE OF MY PLAN! THERE IS STILL MUCH TO BE DONE! I MUST BEGIN IMMEDIATELY TO PRACTICE SPEAKING IN EXACTLY THE SAME MANNER AS THE REAL ORANGE-SKINNED THING!
A FEW DAYS LATER, IN THE TOWER OF THE WORLD-FAMOUS BAXTER BUILDING, WE FIND...
I'LL HAVE TO SKIP DINNER TONIGHT, SUE! I CAN'T STOP WORKING NOW!
BUT, THAT'S WHAT YOU SAID LAST NIGHT, REED--AND THE NIGHT BEFORE!
I'M SORRY, DEAR-- BUT IT WON'T TAKE TOO MUCH LONGER!
IF THIS WORKS, IT WILL GIVE EARTH A WEAPON WITH WHICH TO FIGHT EXTRA-TERRESTIAL MENACES--SUCH AS GALACTUS!
DO YOU THINK-- HE'LL RETURN??
THERE'S ALWAYS A CHANCE! AND, IN THIS NEW SPACE AGE, WE MUST HAVE ADEQUATE DEFENSES AGAINST ANY ATTACK!
I-I THINK YOU KNOW MORE THAN YOU'RE TELLING ME!
YOU'VE HAD WORK CREWS ALL WEEK BUILDING NEW MACHINES --ESPECIALLY THAT ONE IN THE LOCKED, LEAD-LINED ROOM!
HOW DID YOU FIND OUT--?
BUT, BEFORE THE PUZZLED GIRL CAN REPLY, A FAMILIAR VOICE BOOMS OUT--
WHAT'SZIS ABOUT A LOCKED ROOM, STRETCHO?
BEN! YOU'RE BACK!
SURE! IT'S NICE'A YA TO NOTICE!
5

WHERE HAVE YOU *BEEN*, BEN? WE HAVEN'T HEARD FROM YOU FOR *DAYS!*

I HAD ME SOME *THINKIN'* TO DO!

I HOPE YOU GOT WHATEVER WAS BOTHERING YOU OUT OF YOUR SYSTEM...

WE'VE NO TIME FOR *PRIMA DONNAS* HERE!

RELAX, HAMBONE! I'M OKAY NOW! HEY, WHERE'S THE *TORCH?*

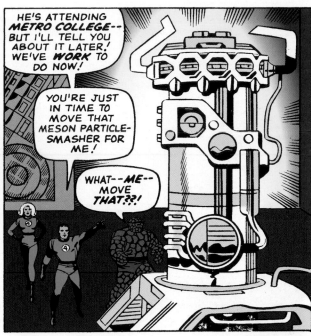

HE'S ATTENDING *METRO COLLEGE*-- BUT I'LL TELL YOU ABOUT IT LATER! WE'VE *WORK* TO DO NOW!

YOU'RE JUST IN TIME TO MOVE THAT MESON PARTICLE-SMASHER FOR ME!

WHAT--*ME*--MOVE *THAT??!*

QUIT CLOWNING, BEN! I'M WORKING AGAINST TIME! EVERY MINUTE COUNTS!

OH--YEAH, SURE! OKAY-- I GUESS I CAN LIFT IT-- IF YA *WANT* ME TO!

OF *COURSE* YOU CAN! YOU'VE DONE IT *DOZENS* OF TIMES BEFORE!

SURE! SURE! I JUST *FORGOT!*

HEY! HOW *ABOUT* THAT?!! WITH *ONE* HAND, YET!

OVER *HERE*, BEN! C'MON-- STEP ON IT!

WHAT'S GOTTEN *INTO* YOU, BIG FELLA?

CAN'T YOU *GUESS* WHAT'S GOTTEN INTO HIM, BIG BRAIN??

THAT--THAT SOUNDS LIKE *BEN!*

WATCH YOURSELF, STRETCH! THAT GUY'S A *FAKE!* HE AINT THE THING --*I* AM!

REED! IT--IT ISN'T *POSSIBLE!* BUT--*LOOK!*

EASY! THERE *MUST* BE AN ANSWER!

AWRIGHT, SMART GUY-- *TALK!* HOW'D YA *DO* IT?? HOW'D YOU TURN YOURSELF INTO THE *THING?*

I SAID *TALK!*

WAIT'LL I STOP *TREMBLIN'*, SONNY!

6

LOOK, I DUNNO WHO THIS NUT IS, BUT IF HE DON'T STOP BREATHIN' IN MY FACE--!

HE *KNOWS* WHO I AM, ALL RIGHT! HE--HE *DUPLICATED* ME, SOMEHOW! *HE* TURNED INTO THE *THING*--AND *I* TURNED BACK TO *BEN GRIMM!* WE GOTTA MAKE 'IM *ADMIT* IT!

NOW *HOLD ON,* MISTER! THE *THING* ISN'T EXACTLY AN EASY MAN TO *IMITATE!*

HE'S NOT *IMITATING* ME--HE *IS* ME! I MEAN--!

STEP ASIDE, EGG-HEAD! I'LL SETTLE THIS BEFORE YA CAN SAY AUNT PETUNIA!

NO, BEN! HAVE YOU GONE *MAD??* YOU CAN'T *ATTACK* HIM WITH THAT TITANIUM STEEL BAR!

YOU GOTTA BE *KIDDIN'!* IF I WANTED TO CLOBBER 'IM, I WOULDN'T NEED ANY *BAR!*

I JUST WANNA PUT ON A LITTLE *SHOW* FOR YA--!

NOW, IF I AINT REALLY THE *THING,* THEN WHO'S DOIN'-- *THIS??!*

BRRN-CH!

ANY QUESTIONS?

LOOK, FRIEND, I'LL ADMIT YOU BEAR AN UNCANNY RESEMBLANCE TO *BEN GRIMM,* BUT I DON'T KNOW HOW YOU CAN EXPECT TO GET AWAY WITH SUCH A FOOLISH CLAIM!

Y-YOU MEAN YOU DON'T *BELIEVE* ME??!

YA CATCH ON REAL QUICK, BUB!

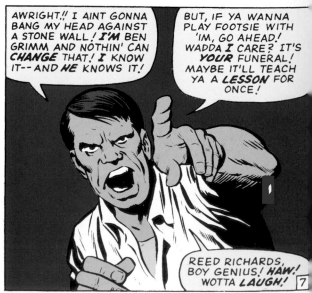

AWRIGHT!! I AINT GONNA BANG MY HEAD AGAINST A STONE WALL! *I'M* BEN GRIMM AND NOTHIN' CAN *CHANGE* THAT! *I* KNOW IT-- AND *HE* KNOWS IT!

BUT, IF YA WANNA PLAY FOOTSIE WITH 'IM, GO AHEAD! WADDA *I* CARE? IT'S *YOUR* FUNERAL! MAYBE IT'LL TEACH YA A *LESSON* FOR ONCE!

REED RICHARDS, BOY GENIUS! *HAW!* WOTTA *LAUGH!*

7

94

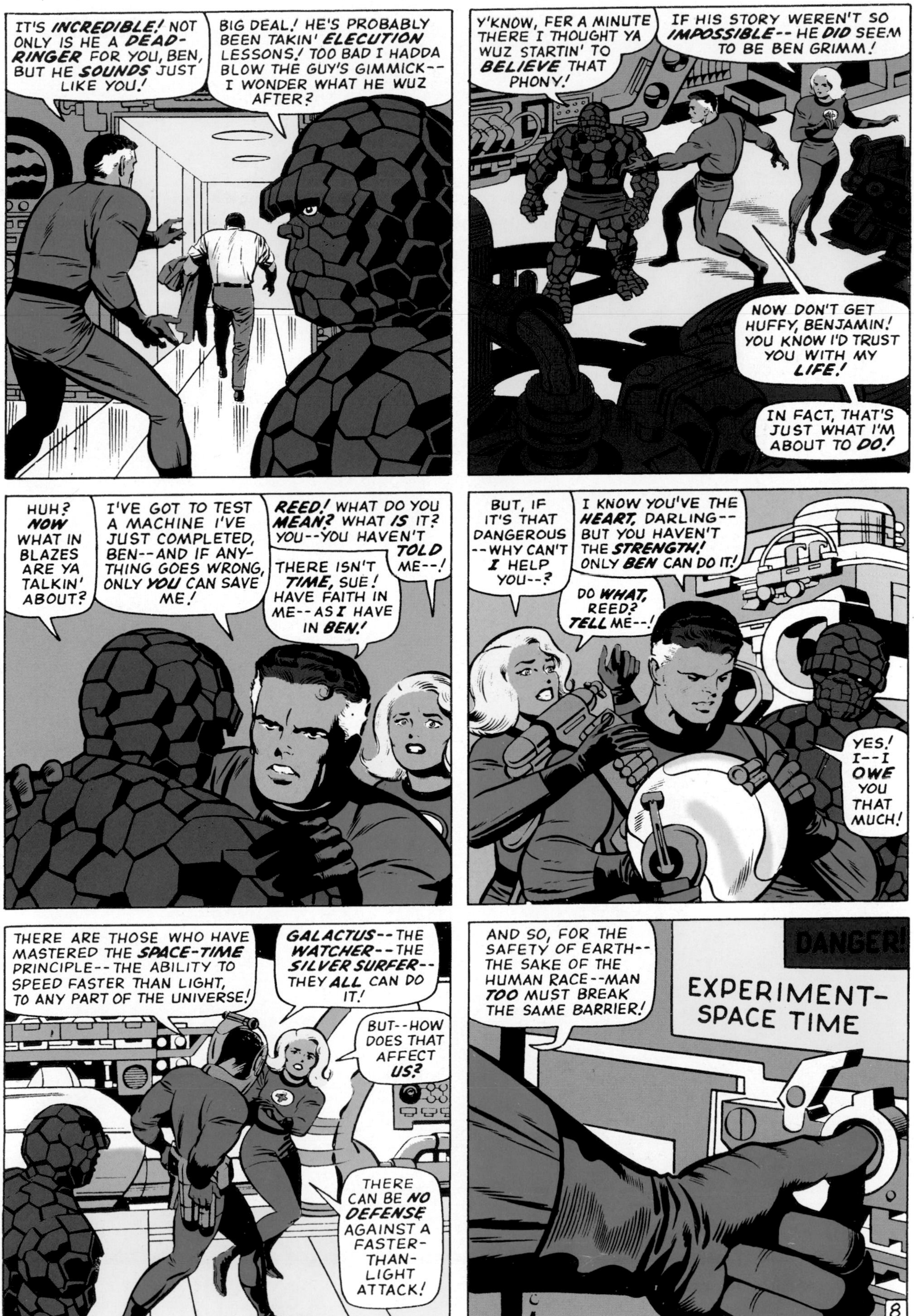
IT'S INCREDIBLE! NOT ONLY IS HE A DEAD-RINGER FOR YOU, BEN, BUT HE SOUNDS JUST LIKE YOU!
BIG DEAL! HE'S PROBABLY BEEN TAKIN' ELECUTION LESSONS! TOO BAD I HADDA BLOW THE GUY'S GIMMICK-- I WONDER WHAT HE WUZ AFTER?
Y'KNOW, FER A MINUTE THERE I THOUGHT YA WUZ STARTIN' TO BELIEVE THAT PHONY!
IF HIS STORY WEREN'T SO IMPOSSIBLE-- HE DID SEEM TO BE BEN GRIMM!
NOW DON'T GET HUFFY, BENJAMIN! YOU KNOW I'D TRUST YOU WITH MY LIFE!
IN FACT, THAT'S JUST WHAT I'M ABOUT TO DO!
HUH? NOW WHAT IN BLAZES ARE YA TALKIN' ABOUT?
I'VE GOT TO TEST A MACHINE I'VE JUST COMPLETED, BEN--AND IF ANY-THING GOES WRONG, ONLY YOU CAN SAVE ME!
REED! WHAT DO YOU MEAN? WHAT IS IT? YOU--YOU HAVEN'T TOLD ME--!
THERE ISN'T TIME, SUE! HAVE FAITH IN ME--AS I HAVE IN BEN!
BUT, IF IT'S THAT DANGEROUS--WHY CAN'T I HELP YOU--?
I KNOW YOU'VE THE HEART, DARLING--BUT YOU HAVEN'T THE STRENGTH! ONLY BEN CAN DO IT!
DO WHAT, REED? TELL ME--!
YES! I--I OWE YOU THAT MUCH!
THERE ARE THOSE WHO HAVE MASTERED THE SPACE-TIME PRINCIPLE--THE ABILITY TO SPEED FASTER THAN LIGHT, TO ANY PART OF THE UNIVERSE!
GALACTUS--THE WATCHER--THE SILVER SURFER--THEY ALL CAN DO IT!
BUT--HOW DOES THAT AFFECT US?
THERE CAN BE NO DEFENSE AGAINST A FASTER-THAN-LIGHT ATTACK!
AND SO, FOR THE SAFETY OF EARTH--THE SAKE OF THE HUMAN RACE--MAN TOO MUST BREAK THE SAME BARRIER!
DANGER!
EXPERIMENT-SPACE TIME
8

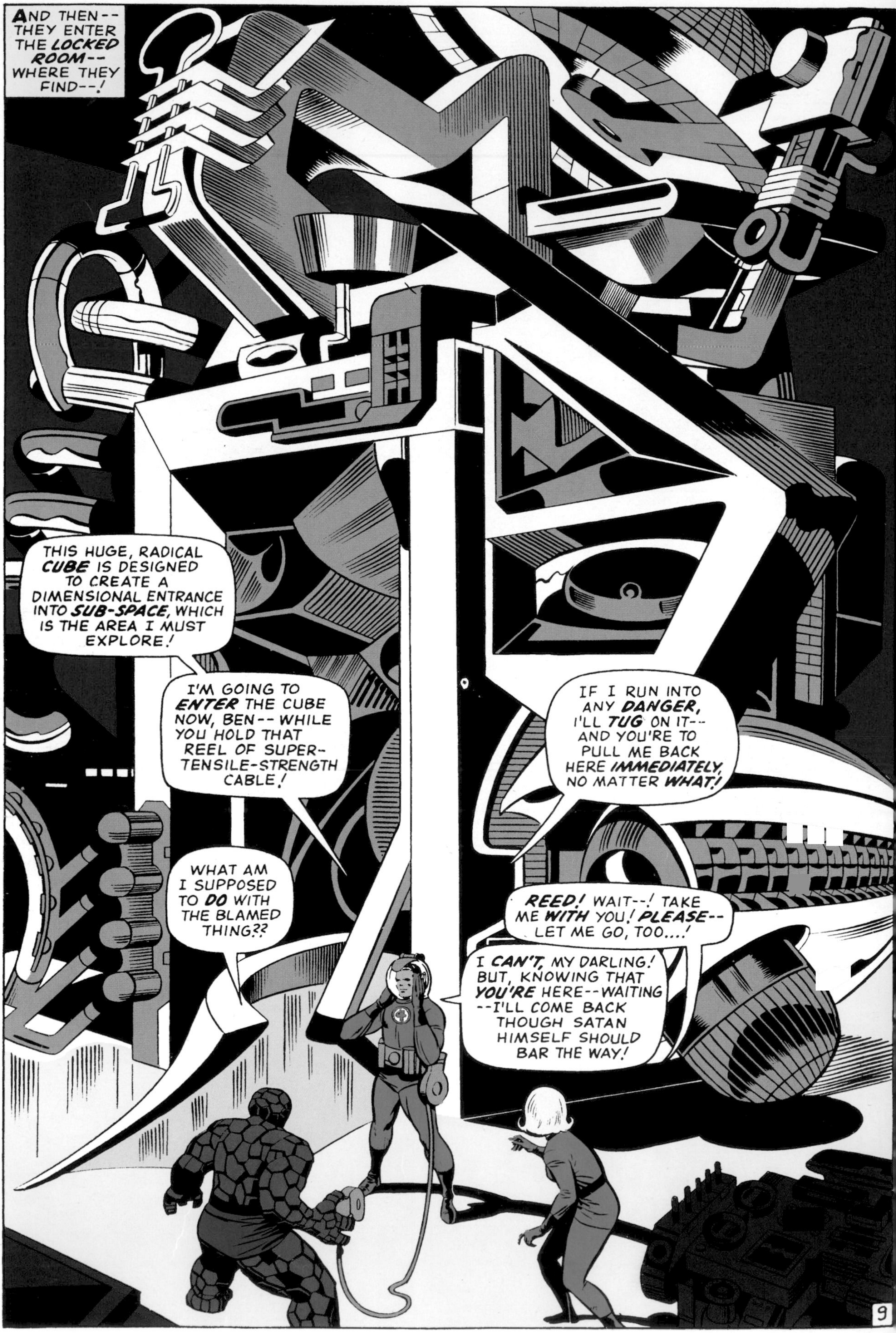
AND THEN-- THEY ENTER THE LOCKED ROOM-- WHERE THEY FIND--!
THIS HUGE, RADICAL CUBE IS DESIGNED TO CREATE A DIMENSIONAL ENTRANCE INTO SUB-SPACE, WHICH IS THE AREA I MUST EXPLORE!
I'M GOING TO ENTER THE CUBE NOW, BEN-- WHILE YOU HOLD THAT REEL OF SUPER-TENSILE-STRENGTH CABLE!
IF I RUN INTO ANY DANGER, I'LL TUG ON IT-- AND YOU'RE TO PULL ME BACK HERE IMMEDIATELY, NO MATTER WHAT!
WHAT AM I SUPPOSED TO DO WITH THE BLAMED THING??
REED! WAIT--! TAKE ME WITH YOU! PLEASE-- LET ME GO, TOO....!
I CAN'T, MY DARLING! BUT, KNOWING THAT YOU'RE HERE--WAITING --I'LL COME BACK THOUGH SATAN HIMSELF SHOULD BAR THE WAY!
9

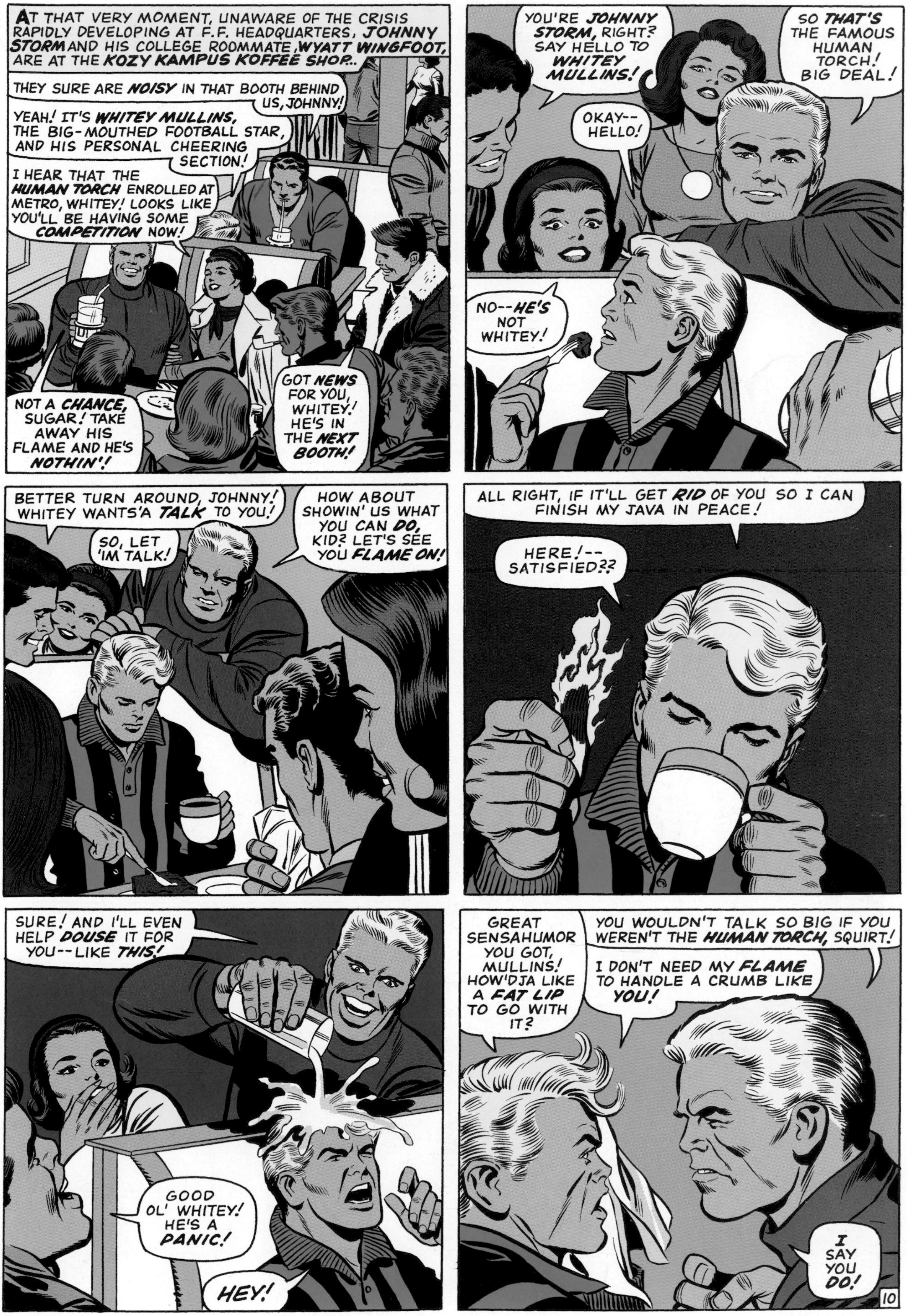
AT THAT VERY MOMENT, UNAWARE OF THE CRISIS RAPIDLY DEVELOPING AT F.F. HEADQUARTERS, JOHNNY STORM AND HIS COLLEGE ROOMMATE, WYATT WINGFOOT, ARE AT THE KOZY KAMPUS KOFFEE SHOP..
THEY SURE ARE NOISY IN THAT BOOTH BEHIND US, JOHNNY!
YEAH! IT'S WHITEY MULLINS, THE BIG-MOUTHED FOOTBALL STAR, AND HIS PERSONAL CHEERING SECTION!
I HEAR THAT THE HUMAN TORCH ENROLLED AT METRO, WHITEY! LOOKS LIKE YOU'LL BE HAVING SOME COMPETITION NOW!
NOT A CHANCE, SUGAR! TAKE AWAY HIS FLAME AND HE'S NOTHIN'!
GOT NEWS FOR YOU, WHITEY! HE'S IN THE NEXT BOOTH!
YOU'RE JOHNNY STORM, RIGHT? SAY HELLO TO WHITEY MULLINS!
SO THAT'S THE FAMOUS HUMAN TORCH! BIG DEAL!
OKAY-- HELLO!
NO--HE'S NOT WHITEY!
BETTER TURN AROUND, JOHNNY! WHITEY WANTS'A TALK TO YOU!
HOW ABOUT SHOWIN' US WHAT YOU CAN DO, KID? LET'S SEE YOU FLAME ON!
SO, LET 'IM TALK!
ALL RIGHT, IF IT'LL GET RID OF YOU SO I CAN FINISH MY JAVA IN PEACE!
HERE!-- SATISFIED??
SURE! AND I'LL EVEN HELP DOUSE IT FOR YOU--LIKE THIS!
GOOD OL' WHITEY! HE'S A PANIC!
HEY!
GREAT SENSAHUMOR YOU GOT, MULLINS! HOW'DJA LIKE A FAT LIP TO GO WITH IT?
YOU WOULDN'T TALK SO BIG IF YOU WEREN'T THE HUMAN TORCH, SQUIRT!
I DON'T NEED MY FLAME TO HANDLE A CRUMB LIKE YOU!
I SAY YOU DO!
10

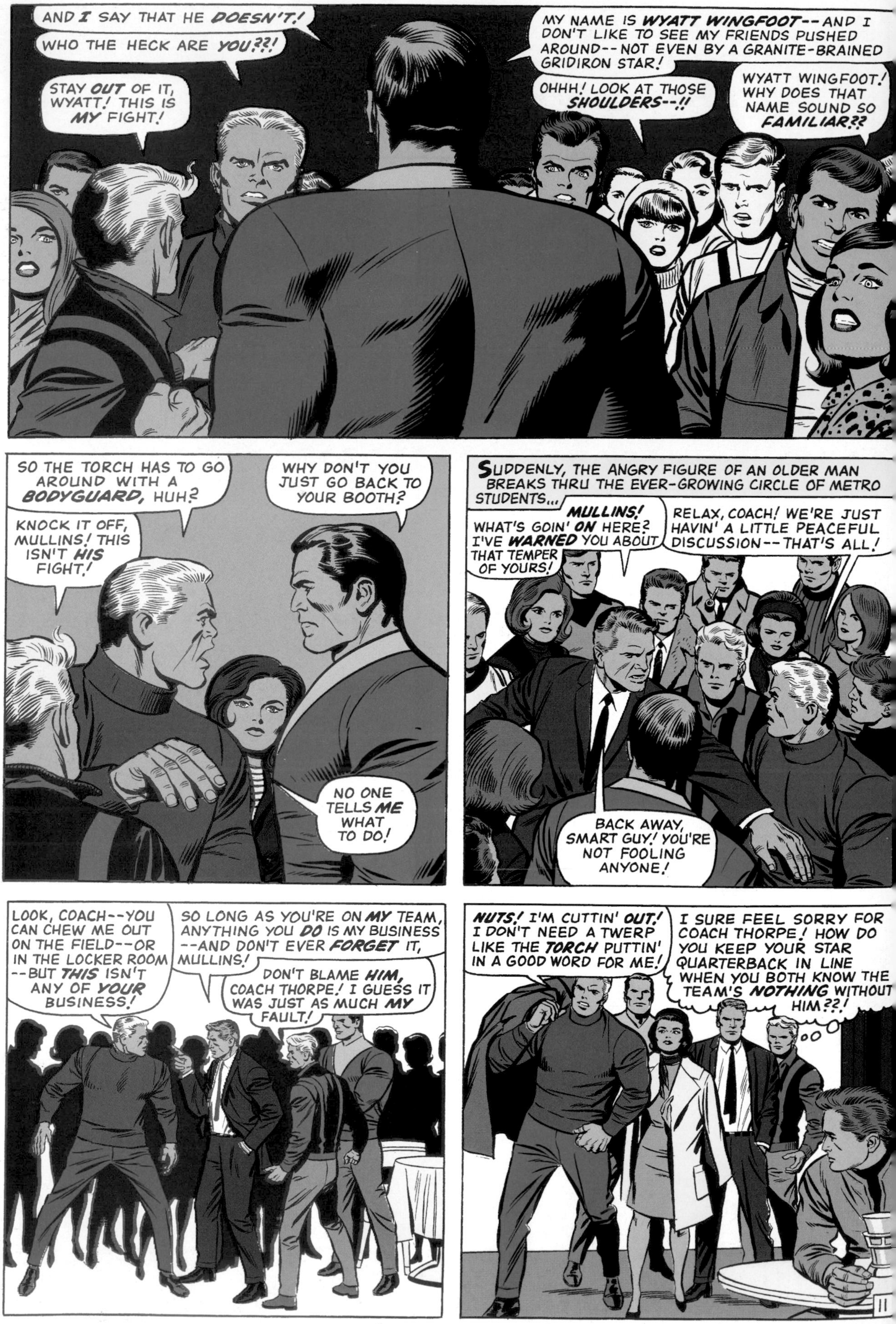

AND I SAY THAT HE DOESN'T!
WHO THE HECK ARE YOU??!
STAY OUT OF IT, WYATT! THIS IS MY FIGHT!
MY NAME IS WYATT WINGFOOT-- AND I DON'T LIKE TO SEE MY FRIENDS PUSHED AROUND-- NOT EVEN BY A GRANITE-BRAINED GRIDIRON STAR!
OHHH! LOOK AT THOSE SHOULDERS--!!
WYATT WINGFOOT! WHY DOES THAT NAME SOUND SO FAMILIAR??
SO THE TORCH HAS TO GO AROUND WITH A BODYGUARD, HUH?
KNOCK IT OFF, MULLINS! THIS ISN'T HIS FIGHT!
WHY DON'T YOU JUST GO BACK TO YOUR BOOTH?
NO ONE TELLS ME WHAT TO DO!
SUDDENLY, THE ANGRY FIGURE OF AN OLDER MAN BREAKS THRU THE EVER-GROWING CIRCLE OF METRO STUDENTS...
MULLINS! WHAT'S GOIN' ON HERE? I'VE WARNED YOU ABOUT THAT TEMPER OF YOURS!
RELAX, COACH! WE'RE JUST HAVIN' A LITTLE PEACEFUL DISCUSSION-- THAT'S ALL!
BACK AWAY, SMART GUY! YOU'RE NOT FOOLING ANYONE!
LOOK, COACH-- YOU CAN CHEW ME OUT ON THE FIELD-- OR IN THE LOCKER ROOM-- BUT THIS ISN'T ANY OF YOUR BUSINESS!
SO LONG AS YOU'RE ON MY TEAM, ANYTHING YOU DO IS MY BUSINESS-- AND DON'T EVER FORGET IT, MULLINS!
DON'T BLAME HIM, COACH THORPE! I GUESS IT WAS JUST AS MUCH MY FAULT!
NUTS! I'M CUTTIN' OUT! I DON'T NEED A TWERP LIKE THE TORCH PUTTIN' IN A GOOD WORD FOR ME!
I SURE FEEL SORRY FOR COACH THORPE! HOW DO YOU KEEP YOUR STAR QUARTERBACK IN LINE WHEN YOU BOTH KNOW THE TEAM'S NOTHING WITHOUT HIM??!
11

SORRY IF I'VE CAUSED ANY TROUBLE, COACH--!

FORGET IT, SON! SAY, WHAT'S *YOUR* NAME, BIG FELLA? I HAVEN'T SEEN YOU HERE BEFORE!

I AM--WYATT WINGFOOT, SIR--!

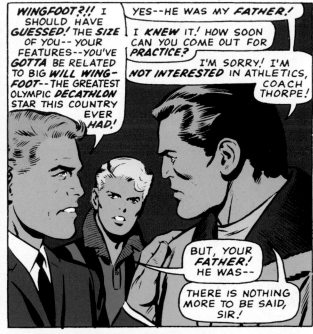

WINGFOOT?!! I SHOULD HAVE *GUESSED!* THE *SIZE* OF YOU-- YOUR *FEATURES*--YOU'VE *GOTTA* BE RELATED TO BIG *WILL WINGFOOT*--THE GREATEST OLYMPIC *DECATHLON* STAR THIS COUNTRY EVER *HAD!*

YES--HE WAS MY *FATHER!*

I *KNEW* IT! HOW SOON CAN YOU COME OUT FOR *PRACTICE?*

I'M SORRY! I'M *NOT INTERESTED* IN ATHLETICS, COACH THORPE!

BUT, YOUR *FATHER!* HE WAS--

THERE IS NOTHING MORE TO BE SAID, SIR!

WHAT'S *WRONG*, DEAR? YOU LOOK AS THOUGH YOU'VE SEEN A *GHOST!*

I ALMOST *HAVE!* THAT BOY IS WILL WINGFOOT'S *SON!* IF HE'S INHERITED EVEN A *FRACTION* OF HIS FATHER'S PROWESS--!

BUT, WHAT AM I *SAYING?* WHAT *DIFFERENCE* DOES IT MAKE?

HE DOESN'T *WANT* TO TRY OUT FOR THE TEAM! HE WON'T EVEN *DISCUSS* ATHLETICS!

DON'T WORRY, JIM-- THERE'LL BE *OTHER* PLAYERS--!

NO! NOT LIKE *HIM!* DON'T YOU *SEE*, BELLE? HIS *FATHER* AND I--WE WERE *GREAT* TOGETHER! AND NOW--FATE HAS SENT *WYATT* TO ME! IT'S MY BIG CHANCE--TO COACH THE GREATEST TEAM OF ALL, BEFORE I RETIRE!

I'VE *GOT* TO MAKE HIM PLAY!

BUT NOW, IT'S TIME TO RETURN TO THE *BAXTER BUILDING*, WHERE REED RICHARDS IS ABOUT TO UNDERTAKE ONE OF THE MOST DANGEROUS FEATS OF HIS CAREER--

REED--MY DARLING--DON'T *DO* IT! I-I HAVE A *PREMONITION*--OF DISASTER! OR, AT LEAST--LET ME COME *WITH* YOU--!

IT'S *IMPOSSIBLE*, SUE! BUT, I CAN'T TURN BACK NOW! SUB-SPACE *MUST* BE EXPLORED--AND CONQUERED--FOR THE GOOD OF MANKIND!

I ALWAYS THOUGHT HE WAS JUST A *GLAMOR-PANTS*--OUT FOR ALL THE DOUGH AND GLORY HE COULD GET! BUT HE'S TACKLIN' A JOB THAT WON'T NET HIM A PLUGGED NICKEL--

AND HE'S DOING IT WITHOUT ANY FANFARE--OR ANY PUBLICITY!

12

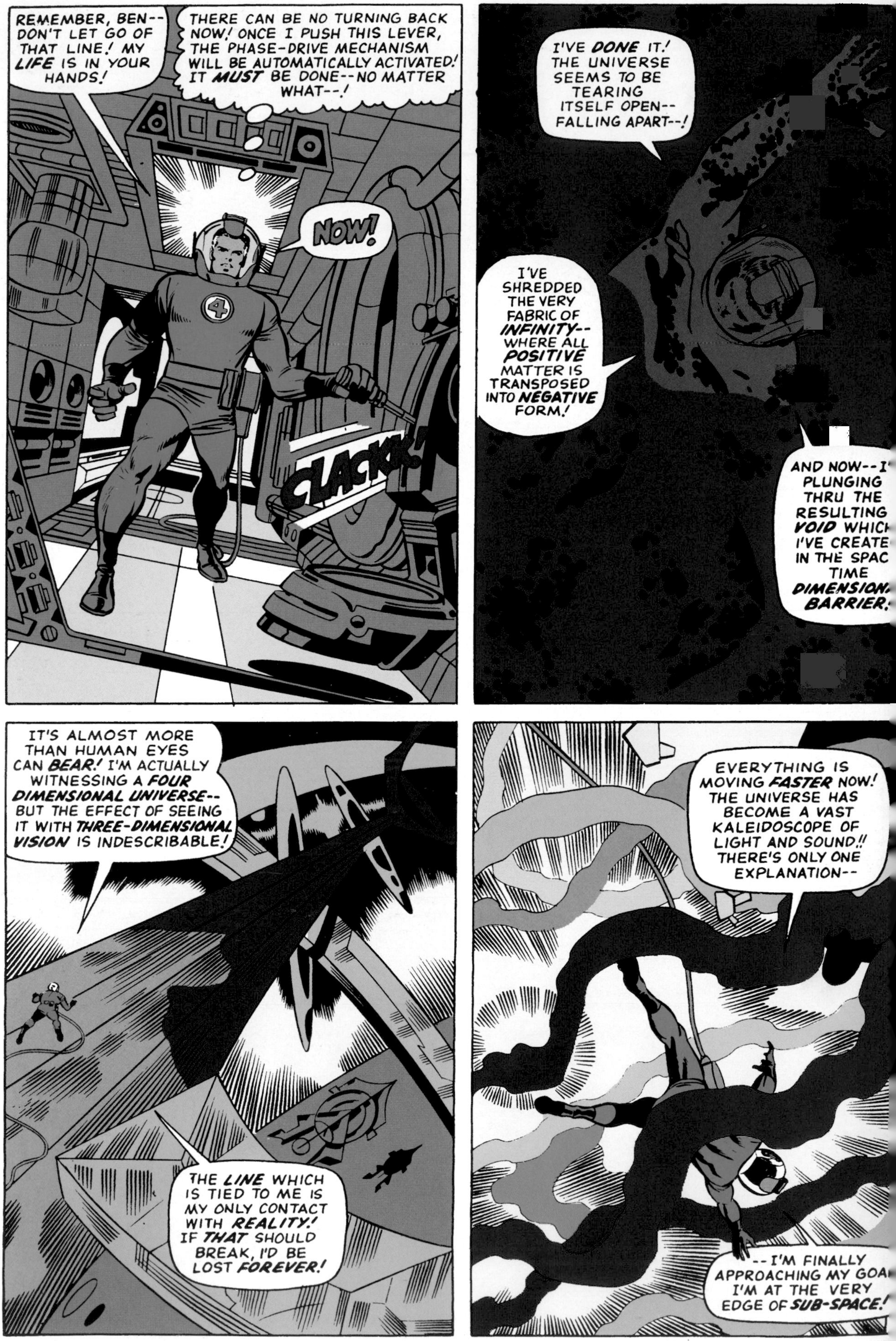
REMEMBER, BEN-- DON'T LET GO OF THAT LINE! MY LIFE IS IN YOUR HANDS!
THERE CAN BE NO TURNING BACK NOW! ONCE I PUSH THIS LEVER, THE PHASE-DRIVE MECHANISM WILL BE AUTOMATICALLY ACTIVATED! IT MUST BE DONE--NO MATTER WHAT--!
NOW!
CLACKK!
I'VE DONE IT! THE UNIVERSE SEEMS TO BE TEARING ITSELF OPEN-- FALLING APART--!
I'VE SHREDDED THE VERY FABRIC OF INFINITY-- WHERE ALL POSITIVE MATTER IS TRANSPOSED INTO NEGATIVE FORM!
AND NOW--I PLUNGING THRU THE RESULTING VOID WHIC I'VE CREATE IN THE SPAC TIME DIMENSION BARRIER
IT'S ALMOST MORE THAN HUMAN EYES CAN BEAR! I'M ACTUALLY WITNESSING A FOUR DIMENSIONAL UNIVERSE-- BUT THE EFFECT OF SEEING IT WITH THREE-DIMENSIONAL VISION IS INDESCRIBABLE!
THE LINE WHICH IS TIED TO ME IS MY ONLY CONTACT WITH REALITY! IF THAT SHOULD BREAK, I'D BE LOST FOREVER!
EVERYTHING IS MOVING FASTER NOW! THE UNIVERSE HAS BECOME A VAST KALEIDOSCOPE OF LIGHT AND SOUND!! THERE'S ONLY ONE EXPLANATION--
--I'M FINALLY APPROACHING MY GOA I'M AT THE VERY EDGE OF SUB-SPACE!

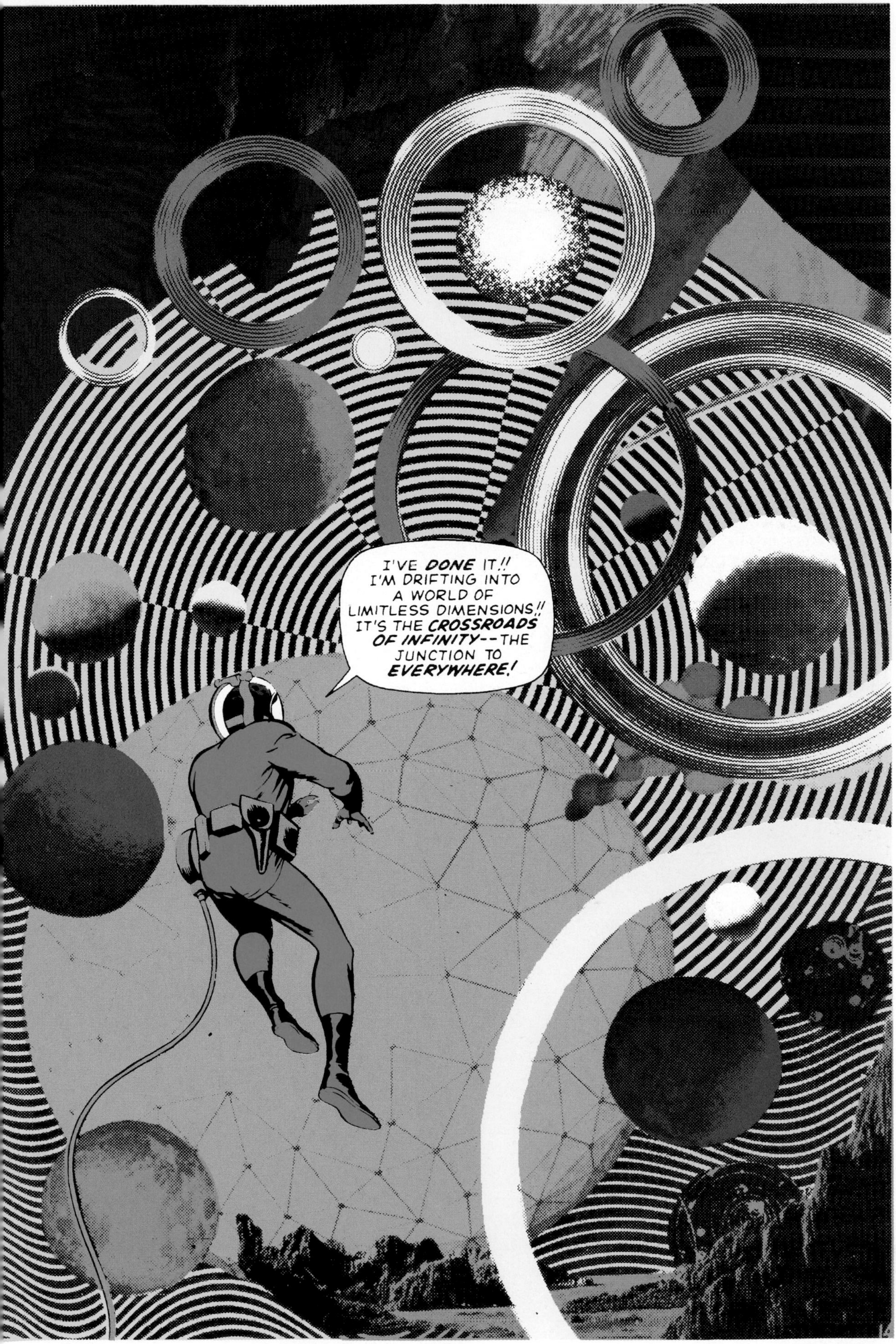
I'VE DONE IT!! I'M DRIFTING INTO A WORLD OF LIMITLESS DIMENSIONS!! IT'S THE CROSSROADS OF INFINITY--THE JUNCTION TO EVERYWHERE!

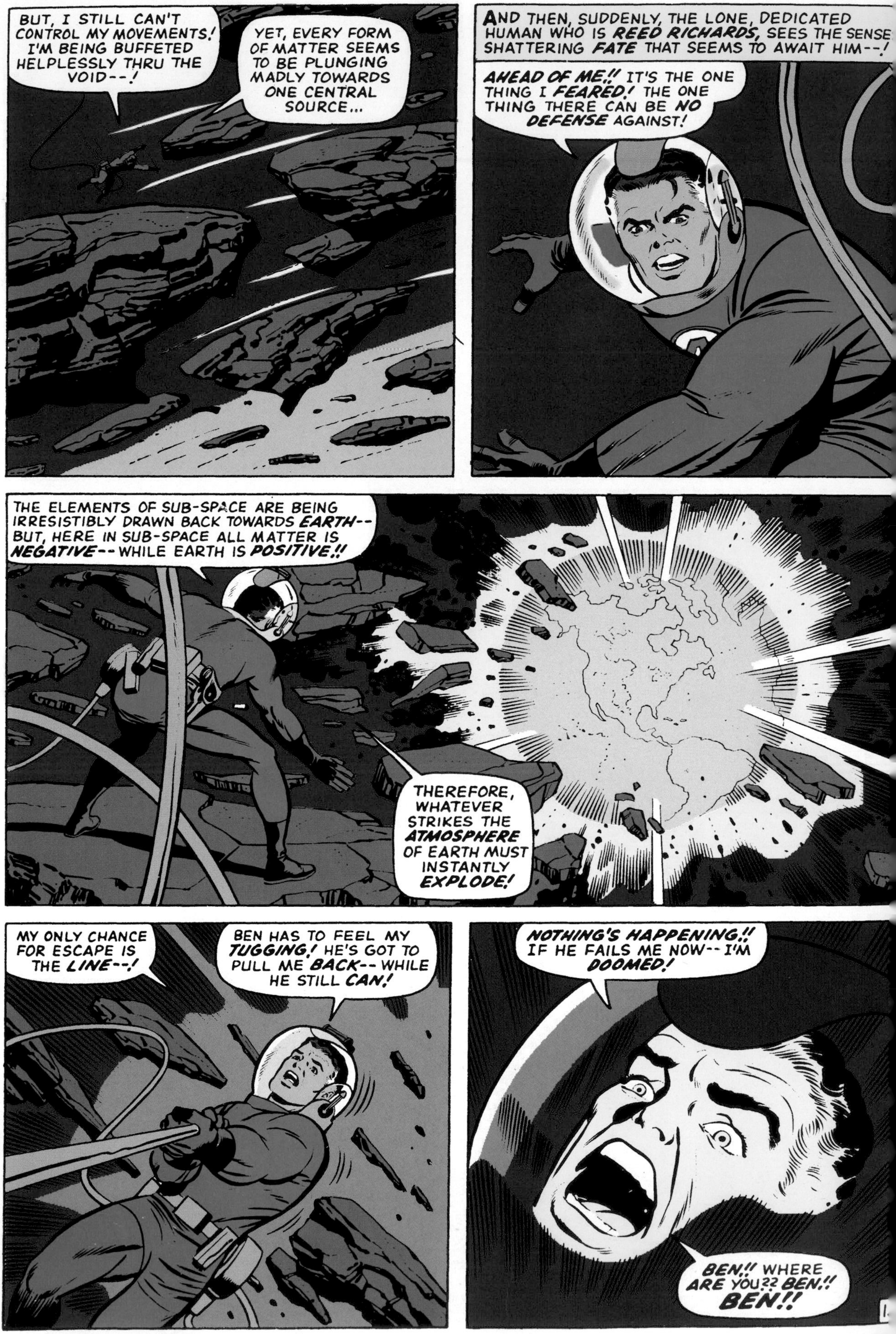
BUT, I STILL CAN'T CONTROL MY MOVEMENTS! I'M BEING BUFFETED HELPLESSLY THRU THE VOID--!
YET, EVERY FORM OF MATTER SEEMS TO BE PLUNGING MADLY TOWARDS ONE CENTRAL SOURCE...
AND THEN, SUDDENLY, THE LONE, DEDICATED HUMAN WHO IS REED RICHARDS, SEES THE SENSE SHATTERING FATE THAT SEEMS TO AWAIT HIM--!
AHEAD OF ME!! IT'S THE ONE THING I FEARED! THE ONE THING THERE CAN BE NO DEFENSE AGAINST!
THE ELEMENTS OF SUB-SPACE ARE BEING IRRESISTIBLY DRAWN BACK TOWARDS EARTH-- BUT, HERE IN SUB-SPACE ALL MATTER IS NEGATIVE-- WHILE EARTH IS POSITIVE!!
THEREFORE, WHATEVER STRIKES THE ATMOSPHERE OF EARTH MUST INSTANTLY EXPLODE!
MY ONLY CHANCE FOR ESCAPE IS THE LINE--!
BEN HAS TO FEEL MY TUGGING! HE'S GOT TO PULL ME BACK-- WHILE HE STILL CAN!
NOTHING'S HAPPENING!! IF HE FAILS ME NOW-- I'M DOOMED!
BEN!! WHERE ARE YOU?? BEN!! BEN!!

AND, AT THE OTHER END OF THE FATEFUL LINE, WE FIND--

HE'S *TUGGING!* ALL I GOTTA DO IS *IGNORE* HIM, AND I'LL HAVE *BEATEN* THE ONE MAN I'VE ALWAYS *ENVIED*--THE ONE MAN NO ONE *ELSE* COULD EVER DEFEAT!

BUT--ALL OF A SUDDEN, I *DON'T* ENVY HIM ANY MORE! I-I NEVER KNEW HOW *BRAVE* HE WAS --HOW UNSELFISH--!

BEN! THE LINE IS GROWING *TAUT!* IT'S *REED!* IT'S HIS *SIGNAL!*

ALL THESE YEARS--WHEN I THOUGHT I NEVER GOT THE BREAKS--NOW I KNOW THE *TRUTH!* IT WAS *MY* FAULT--NOBODY ELSE'S! I WOULDN'T WORK *HARD* ENOUGH--I WOULDN'T MAKE THE SACRIFICES THAT A *REED RICHARDS* WOULD--!

PULL HIM IN, BEN! QUICKLY-- *BEN!*

I NEVER *SAW* THINGS SO *CLEAR* BEFORE! IT--IT'S ALMOST LIKE I'VE *REALLY* BECOME THE *THING*--NOT JUST AN IMITATION!

BEN!! FOR THE LOVE OF *HEAVEN*--!

I NEVER DID A WORTHWHILE THING IN MY WHOLE LIFE!! BUT NOW--I'VE FINALLY GOT THE *CHANCE!* I CAN REALLY *BE* BEN GRIMM!

I'VE GOTTA *DO* IT! I'LL *SAVE* RICHARDS!!

DON'T WORRY, LADY!! I'LL GET 'IM-- *NOW!*

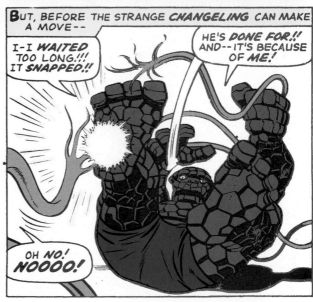

BUT, BEFORE THE STRANGE *CHANGELING* CAN MAKE A MOVE--

I-I *WAITED* TOO LONG.!!! IT *SNAPPED.!!*

HE'S *DONE FOR.!!* AND--IT'S BECAUSE OF *ME!*

OH *NO!* *NOOOO!*

I'VE GOT TO *GO* TO HIM!! HE CAN'T BE LEFT *ALONE* IN THERE!! HE *NEEDS* ME! HE *NEEDS* ME.!!

STAY BACK, DO Y'HEAR?? *STAY BACK!!* THERE'S NOTHIN' *YOU* CAN DO! WHATEVER'S HAPPENIN' TO 'IM IN THERE--ONLY A MASS OF *MUSCLE* CAN HELP!

YOU WAIT OUT *THERE* BABY! I'LL *WHISTLE* IF I NEED YA!

MEBBE, IF I'M *LUCKY,* I CAN STILL GRAB THAT BUSTED HUNK'A LINE--BEFORE IT'S TOO *LATE!*

16

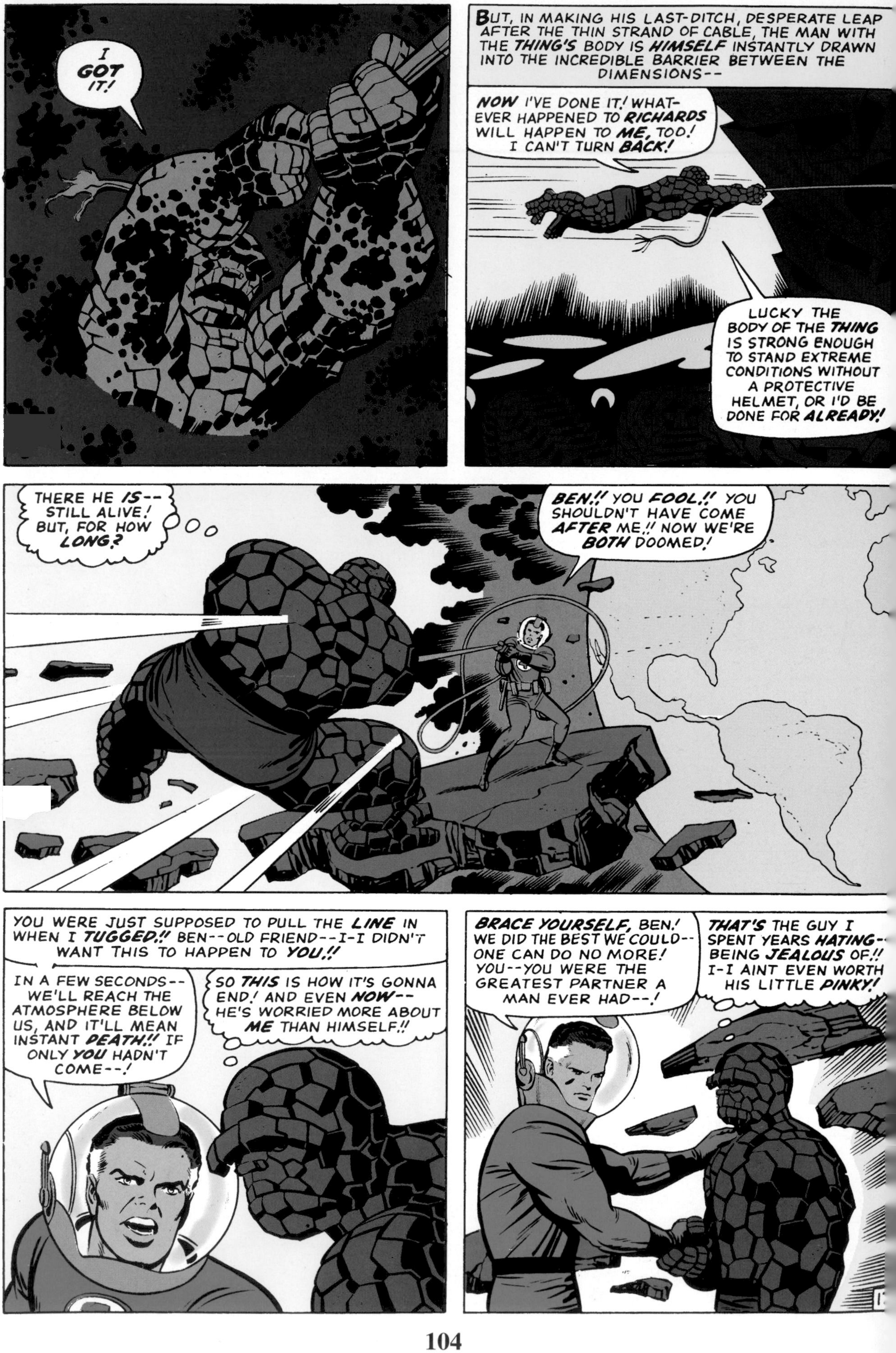

I GOT IT!
BUT, IN MAKING HIS LAST-DITCH, DESPERATE LEAP AFTER THE THIN STRAND OF CABLE, THE MAN WITH THE THING'S BODY IS HIMSELF INSTANTLY DRAWN INTO THE INCREDIBLE BARRIER BETWEEN THE DIMENSIONS--
NOW I'VE DONE IT! WHAT-EVER HAPPENED TO RICHARDS WILL HAPPEN TO ME, TOO! I CAN'T TURN BACK!
LUCKY THE BODY OF THE THING IS STRONG ENOUGH TO STAND EXTREME CONDITIONS WITHOUT A PROTECTIVE HELMET, OR I'D BE DONE FOR ALREADY!
THERE HE IS-- STILL ALIVE! BUT, FOR HOW LONG?
BEN!! YOU FOOL!! YOU SHOULDN'T HAVE COME AFTER ME!! NOW WE'RE BOTH DOOMED!
YOU WERE JUST SUPPOSED TO PULL THE LINE IN WHEN I TUGGED!! BEN--OLD FRIEND--I-I DIDN'T WANT THIS TO HAPPEN TO YOU!!
IN A FEW SECONDS-- WE'LL REACH THE ATMOSPHERE BELOW US, AND IT'LL MEAN INSTANT DEATH!! IF ONLY YOU HADN'T COME--!
SO THIS IS HOW IT'S GONNA END! AND EVEN NOW-- HE'S WORRIED MORE ABOUT ME THAN HIMSELF!!
BRACE YOURSELF, BEN! WE DID THE BEST WE COULD-- ONE CAN DO NO MORE! YOU--YOU WERE THE GREATEST PARTNER A MAN EVER HAD--!
THAT'S THE GUY I SPENT YEARS HATING-- BEING JEALOUS OF!! I-I AINT EVEN WORTH HIS LITTLE PINKY!

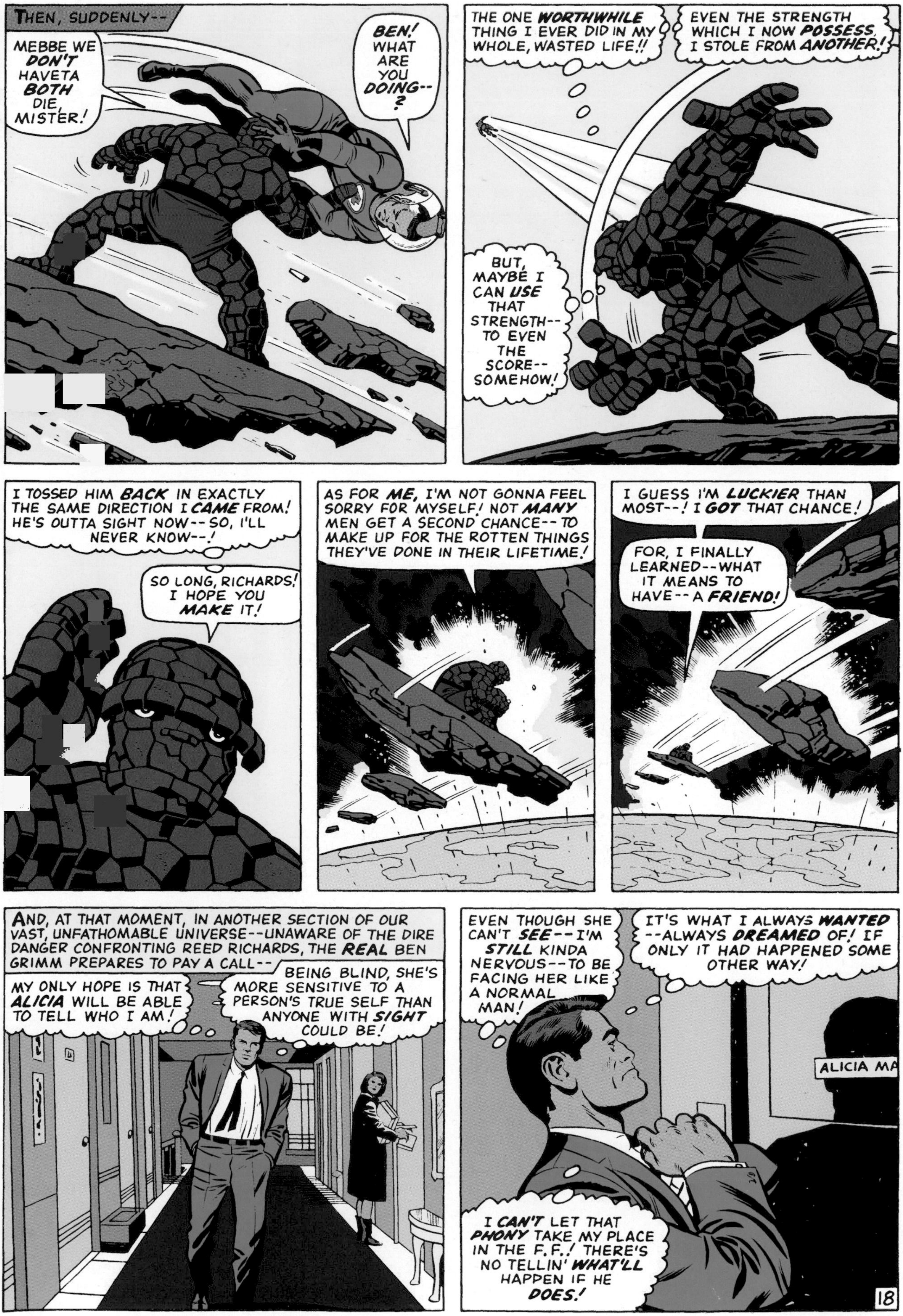
THEN, SUDDENLY--
MEBBE WE DON'T HAVETA BOTH DIE, MISTER!
BEN! WHAT ARE YOU DOING--?
THE ONE WORTHWHILE THING I EVER DID IN MY WHOLE, WASTED LIFE!!
EVEN THE STRENGTH WHICH I NOW POSSESS, I STOLE FROM ANOTHER!
BUT, MAYBE I CAN USE THAT STRENGTH-- TO EVEN THE SCORE-- SOMEHOW!
I TOSSED HIM BACK IN EXACTLY THE SAME DIRECTION I CAME FROM! HE'S OUTTA SIGHT NOW-- SO, I'LL NEVER KNOW--!
SO LONG, RICHARDS! I HOPE YOU MAKE IT!
AS FOR ME, I'M NOT GONNA FEEL SORRY FOR MYSELF! NOT MANY MEN GET A SECOND CHANCE-- TO MAKE UP FOR THE ROTTEN THINGS THEY'VE DONE IN THEIR LIFETIME!
I GUESS I'M LUCKIER THAN MOST--! I GOT THAT CHANCE!
FOR, I FINALLY LEARNED--WHAT IT MEANS TO HAVE-- A FRIEND!
AND, AT THAT MOMENT, IN ANOTHER SECTION OF OUR VAST, UNFATHOMABLE UNIVERSE--UNAWARE OF THE DIRE DANGER CONFRONTING REED RICHARDS, THE REAL BEN GRIMM PREPARES TO PAY A CALL--
MY ONLY HOPE IS THAT ALICIA WILL BE ABLE TO TELL WHO I AM!
BEING BLIND, SHE'S MORE SENSITIVE TO A PERSON'S TRUE SELF THAN ANYONE WITH SIGHT COULD BE!
EVEN THOUGH SHE CAN'T SEE-- I'M STILL KINDA NERVOUS-- TO BE FACING HER LIKE A NORMAL MAN!
IT'S WHAT I ALWAYS WANTED --ALWAYS DREAMED OF! IF ONLY IT HAD HAPPENED SOME OTHER WAY!
ALICIA MA
I CAN'T LET THAT PHONY TAKE MY PLACE IN THE F.F.! THERE'S NO TELLIN' WHAT'LL HAPPEN IF HE DOES!
18

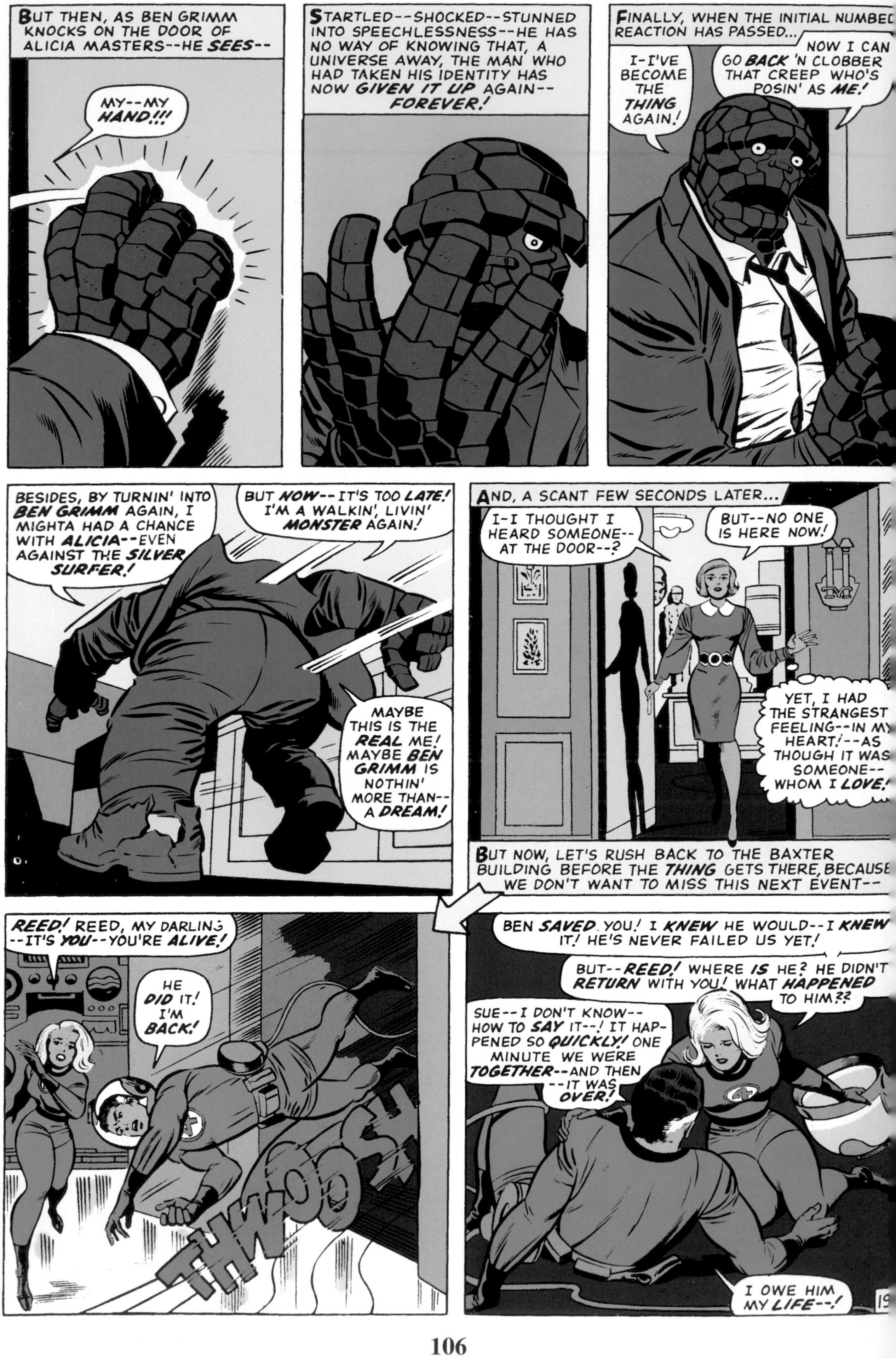

BUT THEN, AS BEN GRIMM KNOCKS ON THE DOOR OF ALICIA MASTERS--HE SEES--
MY--MY HAND!!!
STARTLED--SHOCKED--STUNNED INTO SPEECHLESSNESS--HE HAS NO WAY OF KNOWING THAT, A UNIVERSE AWAY, THE MAN WHO HAD TAKEN HIS IDENTITY HAS NOW GIVEN IT UP AGAIN--FOREVER!
FINALLY, WHEN THE INITIAL NUMBED REACTION HAS PASSED...
I-I'VE BECOME THE THING AGAIN!
NOW I CAN GO BACK 'N CLOBBER THAT CREEP WHO'S POSIN' AS ME!
BESIDES, BY TURNIN' INTO BEN GRIMM AGAIN, I MIGHTA HAD A CHANCE WITH ALICIA--EVEN AGAINST THE SILVER SURFER!
BUT NOW--IT'S TOO LATE! I'M A WALKIN', LIVIN' MONSTER AGAIN!
MAYBE THIS IS THE REAL ME! MAYBE BEN GRIMM IS NOTHIN' MORE THAN--A DREAM!
AND, A SCANT FEW SECONDS LATER...
I-I THOUGHT I HEARD SOMEONE--AT THE DOOR--?
BUT--NO ONE IS HERE NOW!
YET, I HAD THE STRANGEST FEELING--IN MY HEART!--AS THOUGH IT WAS SOMEONE--WHOM I LOVE!
BUT NOW, LET'S RUSH BACK TO THE BAXTER BUILDING BEFORE THE THING GETS THERE, BECAUSE WE DON'T WANT TO MISS THIS NEXT EVENT--
REED! REED, MY DARLING--IT'S YOU--YOU'RE ALIVE!
HE DID IT! I'M BACK!
THWOOSH
BEN SAVED YOU! I KNEW HE WOULD--I KNEW IT! HE'S NEVER FAILED US YET!
BUT--REED! WHERE IS HE? HE DIDN'T RETURN WITH YOU! WHAT HAPPENED TO HIM??
SUE--I DON'T KNOW--HOW TO SAY IT--! IT HAPPENED SO QUICKLY! ONE MINUTE WE WERE TOGETHER--AND THEN--IT WAS OVER!
I OWE HIM MY LIFE--!
19

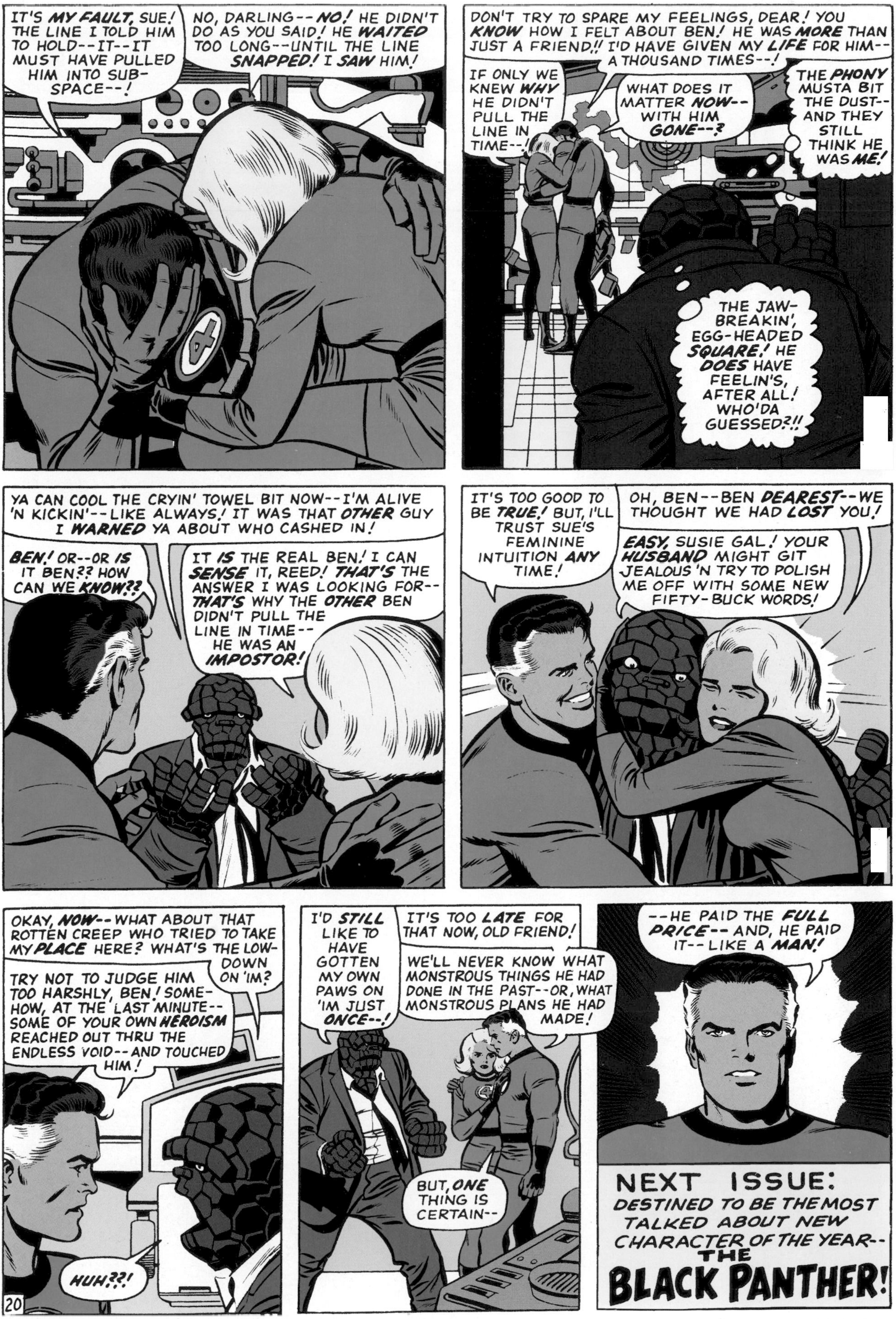
IT'S MY FAULT, SUE! THE LINE I TOLD HIM TO HOLD--IT--IT MUST HAVE PULLED HIM INTO SUB-SPACE--!
NO, DARLING--NO! HE DIDN'T DO AS YOU SAID! HE WAITED TOO LONG--UNTIL THE LINE SNAPPED! I SAW HIM!
DON'T TRY TO SPARE MY FEELINGS, DEAR! YOU KNOW HOW I FELT ABOUT BEN! HE WAS MORE THAN JUST A FRIEND!! I'D HAVE GIVEN MY LIFE FOR HIM--A THOUSAND TIMES--!
IF ONLY WE KNEW WHY HE DIDN'T PULL THE LINE IN TIME--!
WHAT DOES IT MATTER NOW--WITH HIM GONE--?
THE PHONY MUSTA BIT THE DUST--AND THEY STILL THINK HE WAS ME!
THE JAW-BREAKIN', EGG-HEADED SQUARE! HE DOES HAVE FEELIN'S, AFTER ALL! WHO'DA GUESSED?!!
YA CAN COOL THE CRYIN' TOWEL BIT NOW--I'M ALIVE 'N KICKIN'--LIKE ALWAYS! IT WAS THAT OTHER GUY I WARNED YA ABOUT WHO CASHED IN!
BEN! OR--OR IS IT BEN?? HOW CAN WE KNOW??
IT IS THE REAL BEN! I CAN SENSE IT, REED! THAT'S THE ANSWER I WAS LOOKING FOR--THAT'S WHY THE OTHER BEN DIDN'T PULL THE LINE IN TIME--HE WAS AN IMPOSTOR!
IT'S TOO GOOD TO BE TRUE! BUT, I'LL TRUST SUE'S FEMININE INTUITION ANY TIME!
OH, BEN--BEN DEAREST--WE THOUGHT WE HAD LOST YOU!
EASY, SUSIE GAL! YOUR HUSBAND MIGHT GIT JEALOUS 'N TRY TO POLISH ME OFF WITH SOME NEW FIFTY-BUCK WORDS!
OKAY, NOW--WHAT ABOUT THAT ROTTEN CREEP WHO TRIED TO TAKE MY PLACE HERE? WHAT'S THE LOW-DOWN ON 'IM?
TRY NOT TO JUDGE HIM TOO HARSHLY, BEN! SOME-HOW, AT THE LAST MINUTE--SOME OF YOUR OWN HEROISM REACHED OUT THRU THE ENDLESS VOID--AND TOUCHED HIM!
HUH??!
20
I'D STILL LIKE TO HAVE GOTTEN MY OWN PAWS ON 'IM JUST ONCE--!
IT'S TOO LATE FOR THAT NOW, OLD FRIEND!
WE'LL NEVER KNOW WHAT MONSTROUS THINGS HE HAD DONE IN THE PAST--OR, WHAT MONSTROUS PLANS HE HAD MADE!
BUT, ONE THING IS CERTAIN--
--HE PAID THE FULL PRICE--AND, HE PAID IT--LIKE A MAN!
NEXT ISSUE:
DESTINED TO BE THE MOST TALKED ABOUT NEW CHARACTER OF THE YEAR--THE
BLACK PANTHER!

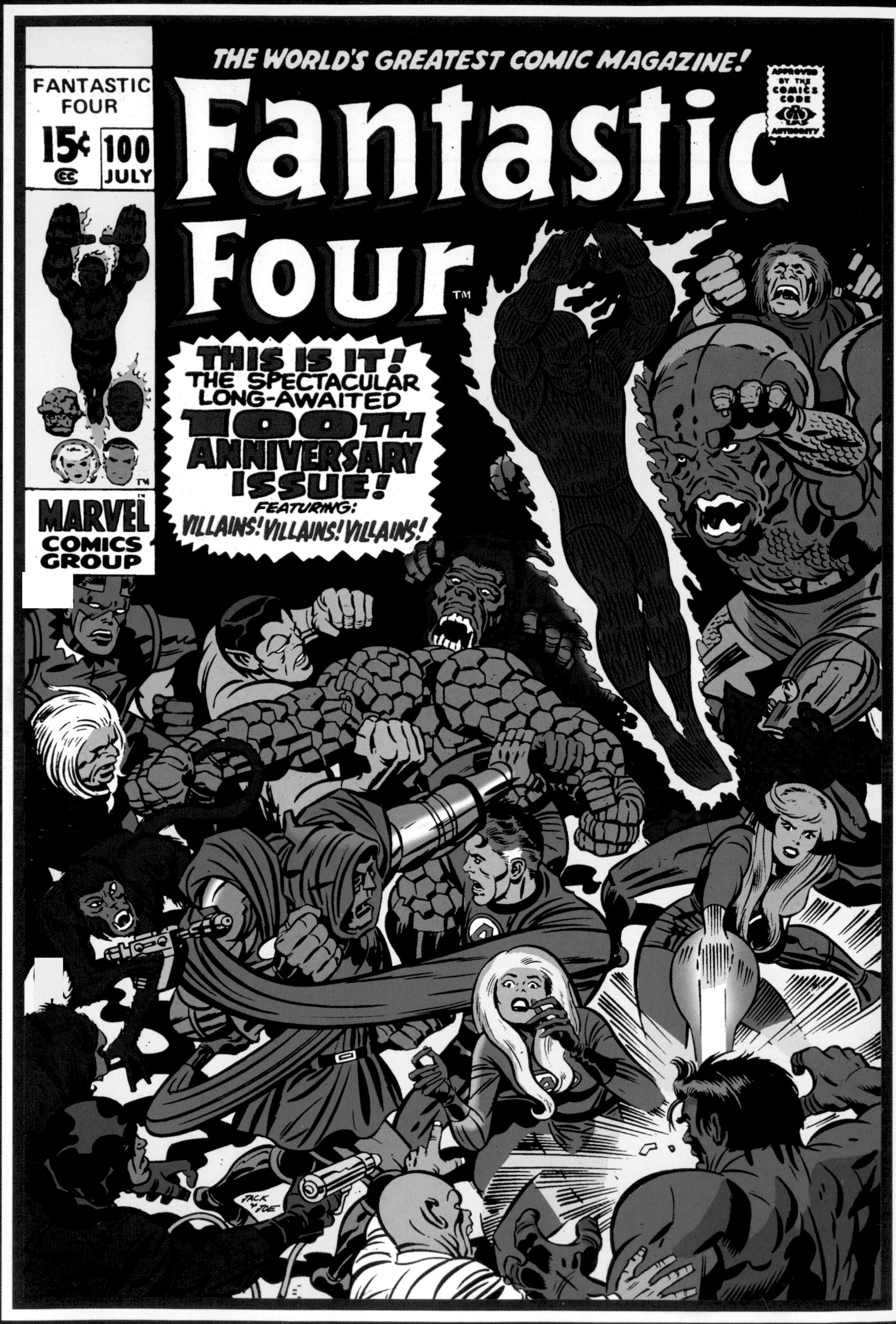
THE WORLD'S GREATEST COMIC MAGAZINE!
FANTASTIC FOUR
15¢
100
JULY
APPROVED BY THE COMICS CODE AUTHORITY
Fantastic Four
MARVEL COMICS GROUP
THIS IS IT! THE SPECTACULAR LONG-AWAITED 100TH ANNIVERSARY ISSUE!
FEATURING:
VILLAINS! VILLAINS! VILLAINS!
JACK & JOE

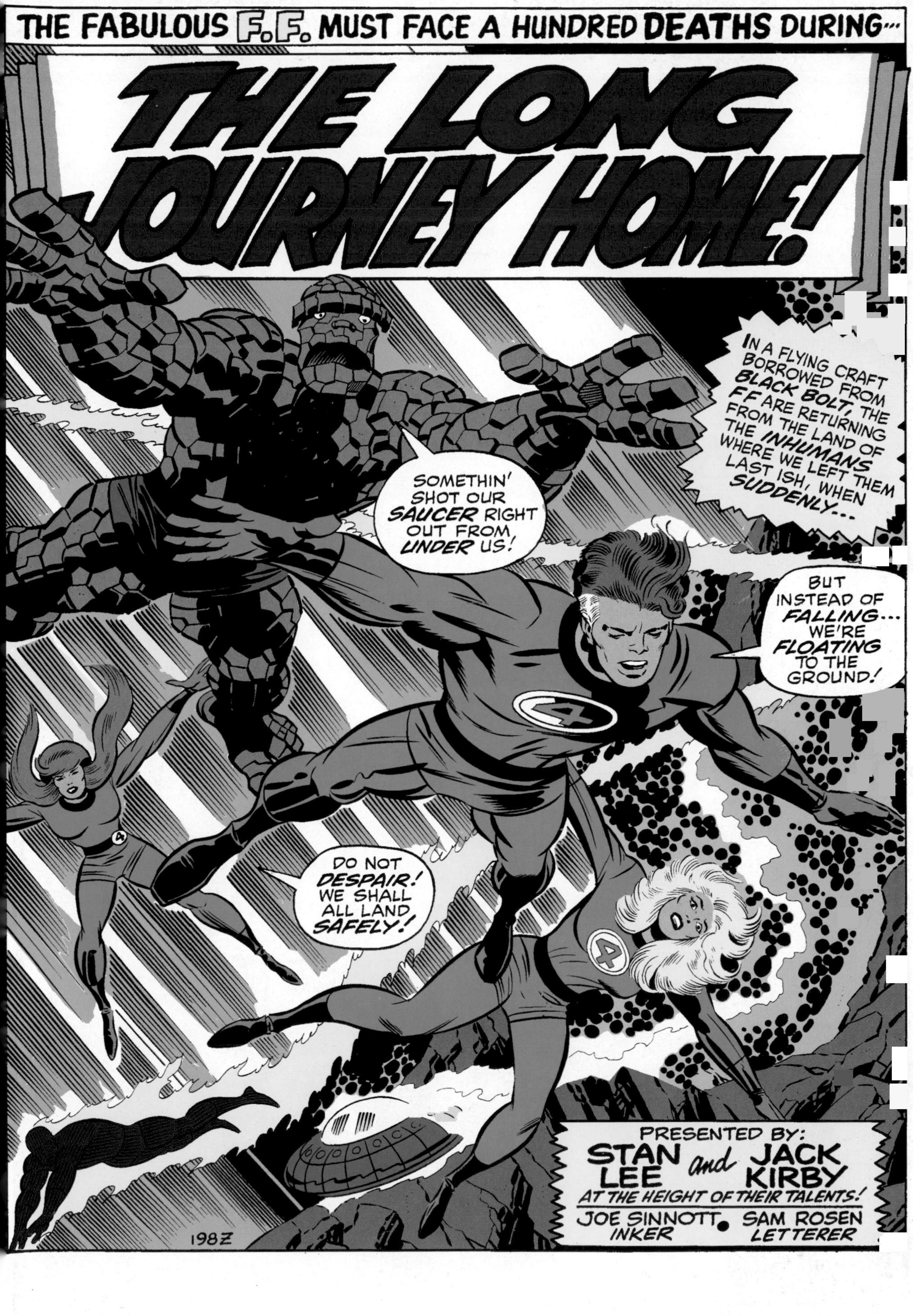
THE FABULOUS F.F. MUST FACE A HUNDRED DEATHS DURING...
THE LONG JOURNEY HOME!
IN A FLYING CRAFT BORROWED FROM BLACK BOLT, THE FF ARE RETURNING FROM THE LAND OF THE INHUMANS WHERE WE LEFT THEM LAST ISH, WHEN SUDDENLY...
SOMETHIN' SHOT OUR SAUCER RIGHT OUT FROM UNDER US!
BUT INSTEAD OF FALLING... WE'RE FLOATING TO THE GROUND!
DO NOT DESPAIR! WE SHALL ALL LAND SAFELY!
PRESENTED BY: STAN LEE and JACK KIRBY AT THE HEIGHT OF THEIR TALENTS!
JOE SINNOTT, INKER • SAM ROSEN LETTERER
198Z

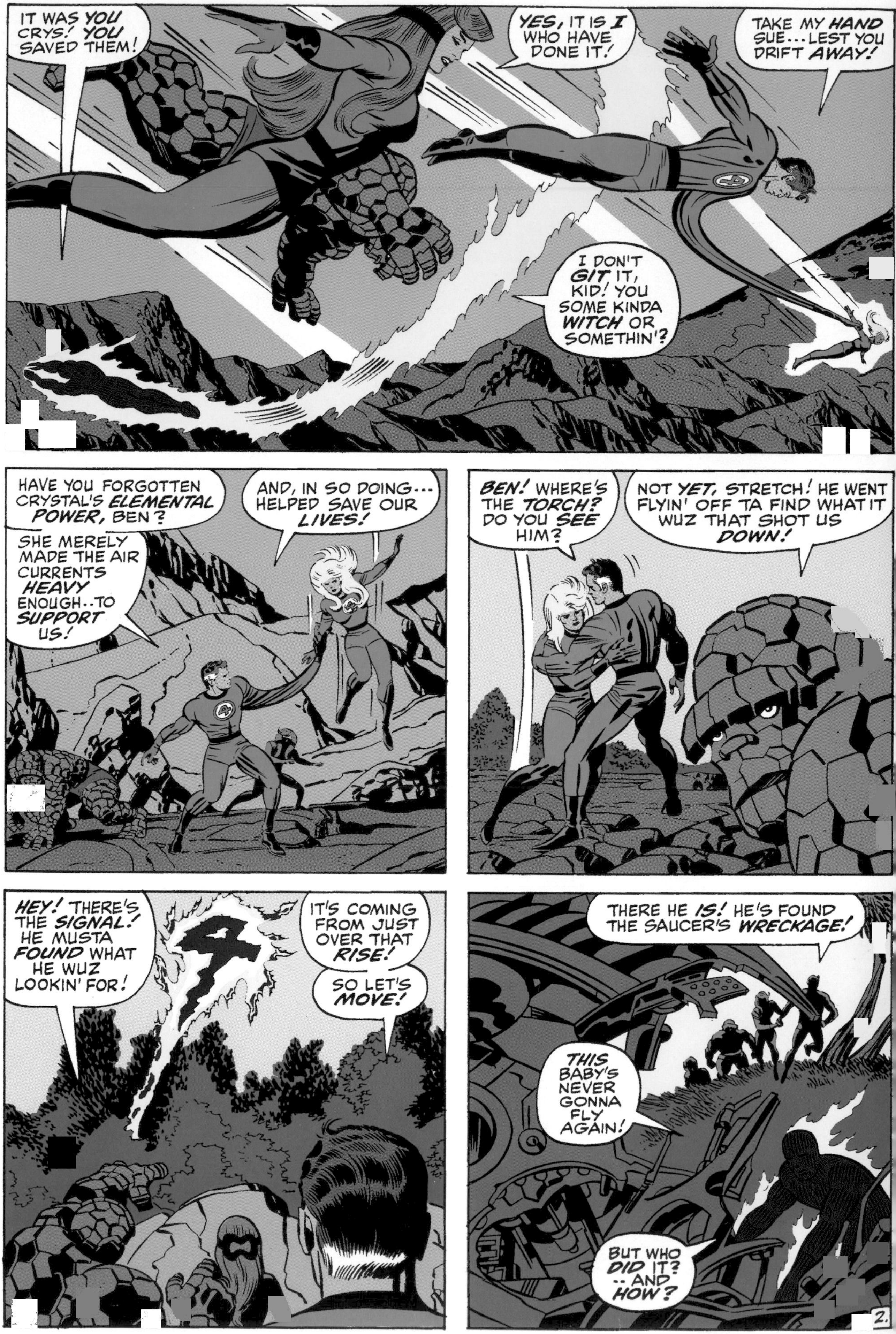
IT WAS YOU CRYS! YOU SAVED THEM!
YES, IT IS I WHO HAVE DONE IT!
TAKE MY HAND SUE...LEST YOU DRIFT AWAY!
I DON'T GIT IT, KID! YOU SOME KINDA WITCH OR SOMETHIN'?
HAVE YOU FORGOTTEN CRYSTAL'S ELEMENTAL POWER, BEN?
SHE MERELY MADE THE AIR CURRENTS HEAVY ENOUGH..TO SUPPORT US!
AND, IN SO DOING... HELPED SAVE OUR LIVES!
BEN! WHERE'S THE TORCH? DO YOU SEE HIM?
NOT YET, STRETCH! HE WENT FLYIN' OFF TA FIND WHAT IT WUZ THAT SHOT US DOWN!
HEY! THERE'S THE SIGNAL! HE MUSTA FOUND WHAT HE WUZ LOOKIN' FOR!
IT'S COMING FROM JUST OVER THAT RISE!
SO LET'S MOVE!
THERE HE IS! HE'S FOUND THE SAUCER'S WRECKAGE!
THIS BABY'S NEVER GONNA FLY AGAIN!
BUT WHO DID IT? .. AND HOW?
2.

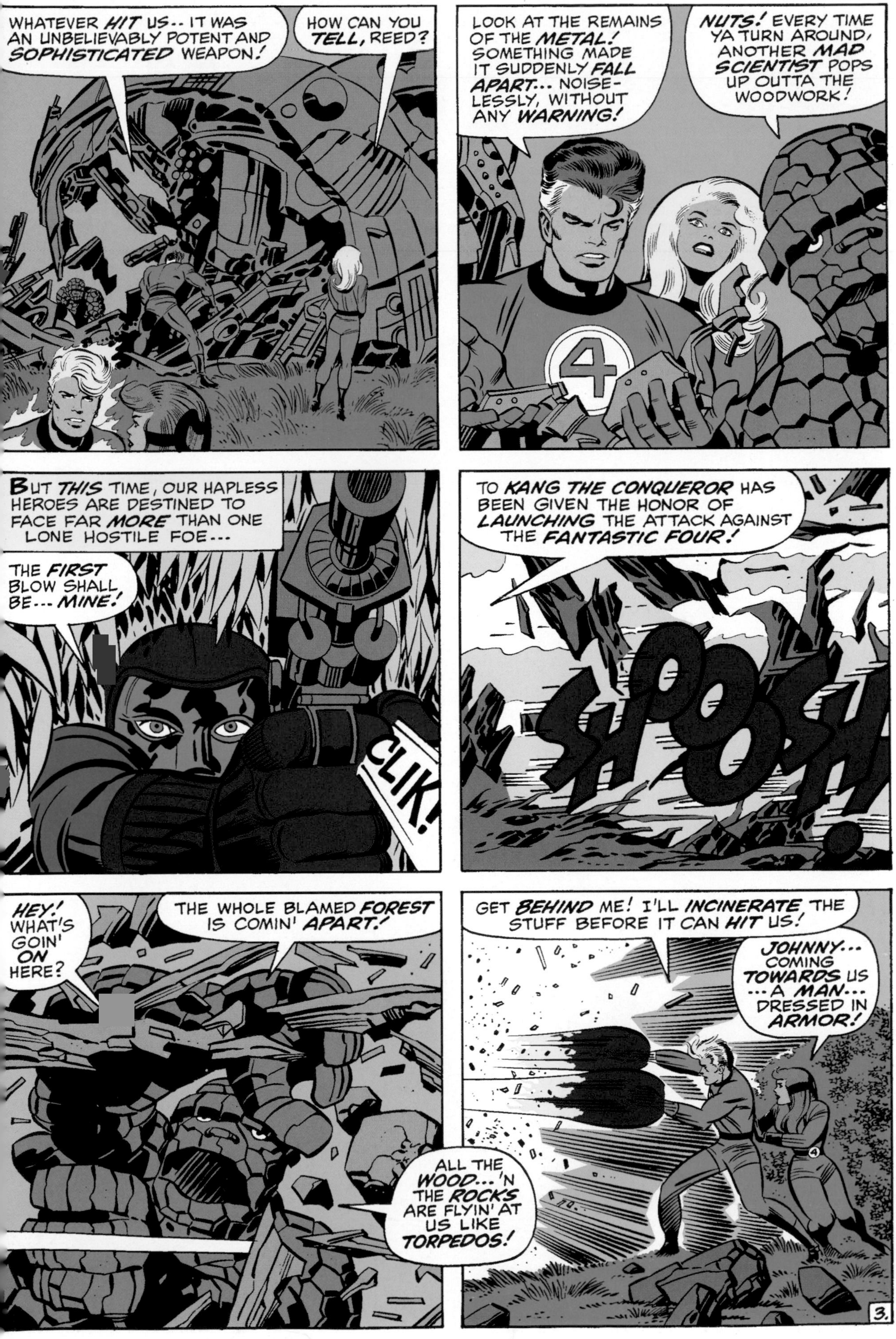
WHATEVER HIT US.. IT WAS AN UNBELIEVABLY POTENT AND SOPHISTICATED WEAPON!
HOW CAN YOU TELL, REED?
LOOK AT THE REMAINS OF THE METAL! SOMETHING MADE IT SUDDENLY FALL APART... NOISE-LESSLY, WITHOUT ANY WARNING!
NUTS! EVERY TIME YA TURN AROUND, ANOTHER MAD SCIENTIST POPS UP OUTTA THE WOODWORK!
BUT THIS TIME, OUR HAPLESS HEROES ARE DESTINED TO FACE FAR MORE THAN ONE LONE HOSTILE FOE---
THE FIRST BLOW SHALL BE--- MINE!
CLIK!
TO KANG THE CONQUEROR HAS BEEN GIVEN THE HONOR OF LAUNCHING THE ATTACK AGAINST THE FANTASTIC FOUR!
SHOOOSH!
HEY! WHAT'S GOIN' ON HERE?
THE WHOLE BLAMED FOREST IS COMIN' APART!
ALL THE WOOD... 'N THE ROCKS ARE FLYIN' AT US LIKE TORPEDOS!
GET BEHIND ME! I'LL INCINERATE THE STUFF BEFORE IT CAN HIT US!
JOHNNY... COMING TOWARDS US ...A MAN... DRESSED IN ARMOR!
3.

I SEE HIM *TOO!* IT... IT'S *KANG*... THE *CONQUEROR!*

I CAN DROP MY *FORCE FIELD* NOW, DARLING! THE FOREST IS *STILL* AGAIN!

BUT HOW WILL WE STRIKE *BACK* AT KANG?

LEAVE 'IM TA *ME*, SUSIE!

I'VE WAITED FER *YEARS* TA LEAN ON THE BUM!

BEN! *LOOK OUT!*

HEY! HOW DID HE DO THAT?

I DIDN'T TAKE MY *PEEPERS* OFFA HIM FER A *MINNIT!*

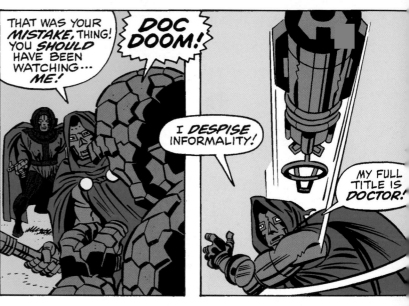

THAT WAS YOUR *MISTAKE,* THING! YOU *SHOULD* HAVE BEEN WATCHING... *ME!*

DOC DOOM!

I *DESPISE* INFORMALITY!

MY FULL TITLE IS *DOCTOR!*

NOW, WHILE YOU PONDER THE PROBLEM OF WHETHER *KANG* AND *MYSELF* ARE *TWO SEPARATE BEINGS...*

--- MY SELF-CONTAINED *MISSILE* SHALL CONCLUDE THIS CHARADE... *FOREVER!*

QUICK THINKING, MRS. RICHARDS!

BUT YOUR *FORCE FIELD* WILL BE *BROKEN* BY MY *NEXT* ATTACK!

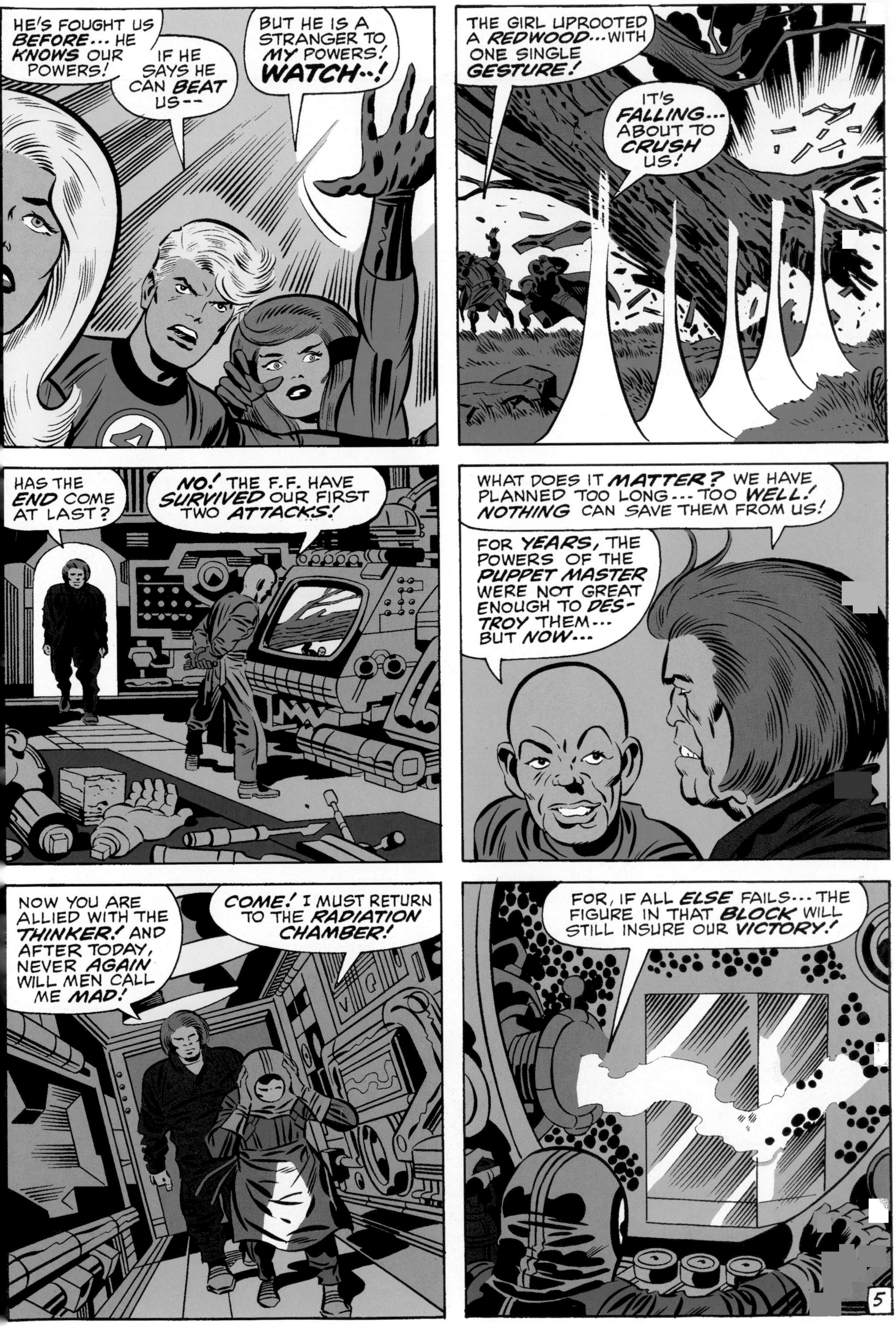
HE'S FOUGHT US BEFORE... HE KNOWS OUR POWERS!
IF HE SAYS HE CAN BEAT US--
BUT HE IS A STRANGER TO MY POWERS! WATCH..!
THE GIRL UPROOTED A REDWOOD...WITH ONE SINGLE GESTURE!
IT'S FALLING... ABOUT TO CRUSH US!
HAS THE END COME AT LAST?
NO! THE F.F. HAVE SURVIVED OUR FIRST TWO ATTACKS!
WHAT DOES IT MATTER? WE HAVE PLANNED TOO LONG--- TOO WELL! NOTHING CAN SAVE THEM FROM US!
FOR YEARS, THE POWERS OF THE PUPPET MASTER WERE NOT GREAT ENOUGH TO DESTROY THEM... BUT NOW...
NOW YOU ARE ALLIED WITH THE THINKER! AND AFTER TODAY, NEVER AGAIN WILL MEN CALL ME MAD!
COME! I MUST RETURN TO THE RADIATION CHAMBER!
FOR, IF ALL ELSE FAILS... THE FIGURE IN THAT BLOCK WILL STILL INSURE OUR VICTORY!
5

NOT EVEN THE SUPREMELY MASTERFUL *FANTASTIC FOUR* CAN SURVIVE...WHEN *ALL THE CARDS* ARE STACKED *AGAINST* THEM!

AND *HERE*... WITHIN THIS CHAMBER...IS THE MOST *POWERFUL* CARD OF ALL!

THIK!

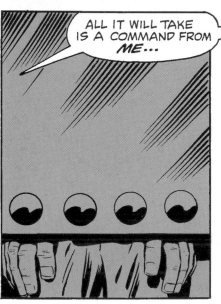

ALL IT WILL TAKE IS A COMMAND FROM *ME*...

...TO *WAKEN* HIM....AND THEN TO BRING HIM...

...TO *LIFE!*

*M*EANWHILE, HALF-WORLD AROUND THE WORLD...

THEY *AREN'T* DEAD! YOU CANNOT KILL...WHAT HAS NEVER *LIVED!*

REED! WHAT DO YOU *MEAN?*

THEY'RE *ANDROIDS,* SUE...POSSESSING THE *POWERS* AND *MEMORIES* OF THEIR HUMAN COUNTERPARTS!

ONLY *ONE MAN* CAN CREATE SUCH DEADLY *MONSTROSITIES*...!

6

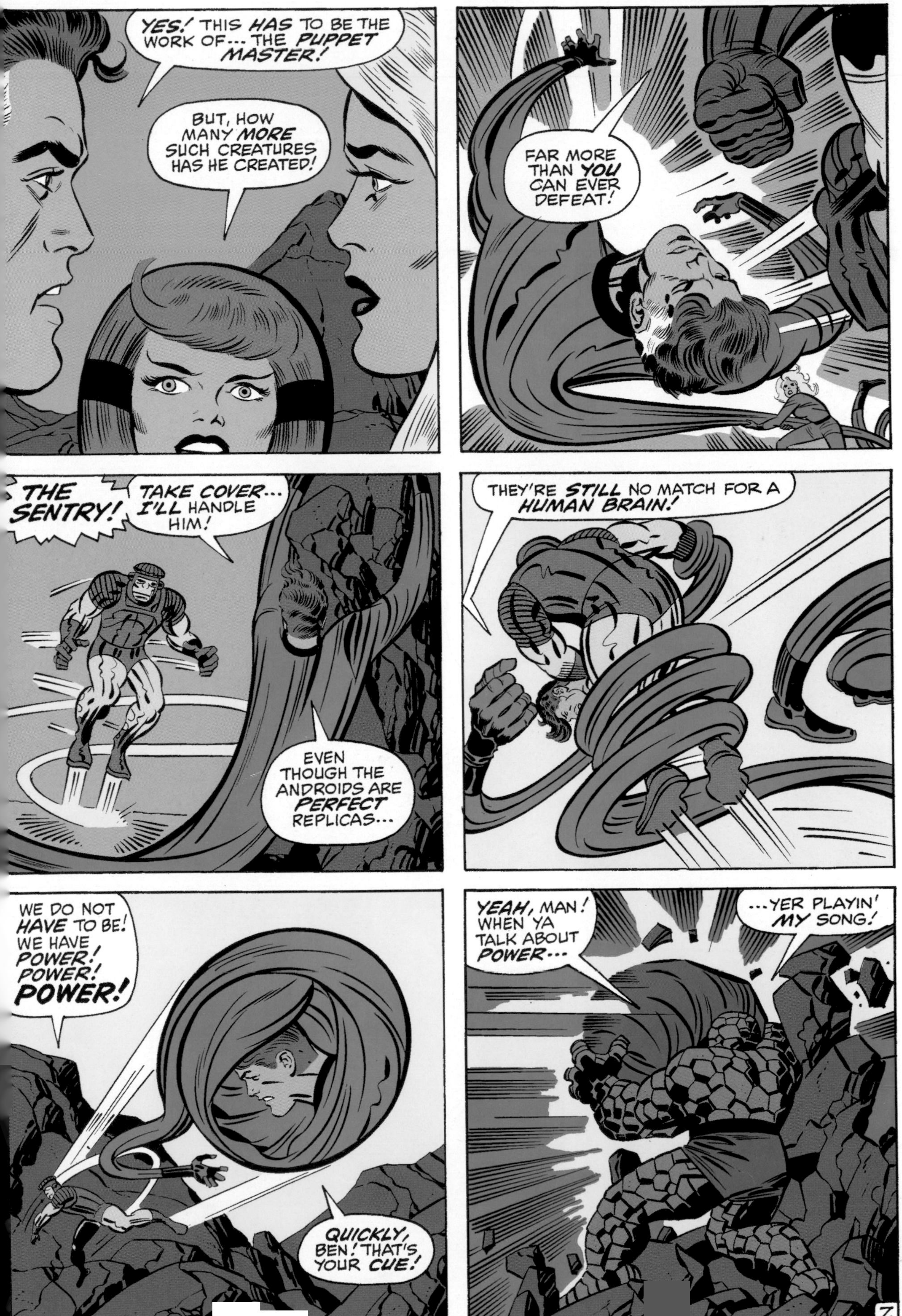
YES! THIS HAS TO BE THE WORK OF... THE PUPPET MASTER!
BUT, HOW MANY MORE SUCH CREATURES HAS HE CREATED!
FAR MORE THAN YOU CAN EVER DEFEAT!
THE SENTRY!
TAKE COVER... I'LL HANDLE HIM!
EVEN THOUGH THE ANDROIDS ARE PERFECT REPLICAS...
THEY'RE STILL NO MATCH FOR A HUMAN BRAIN!
WE DO NOT HAVE TO BE! WE HAVE POWER! POWER! POWER!
QUICKLY, BEN! THAT'S YOUR CUE!
YEAH, MAN! WHEN YA TALK ABOUT POWER...
...YER PLAYIN' MY SONG!
7.

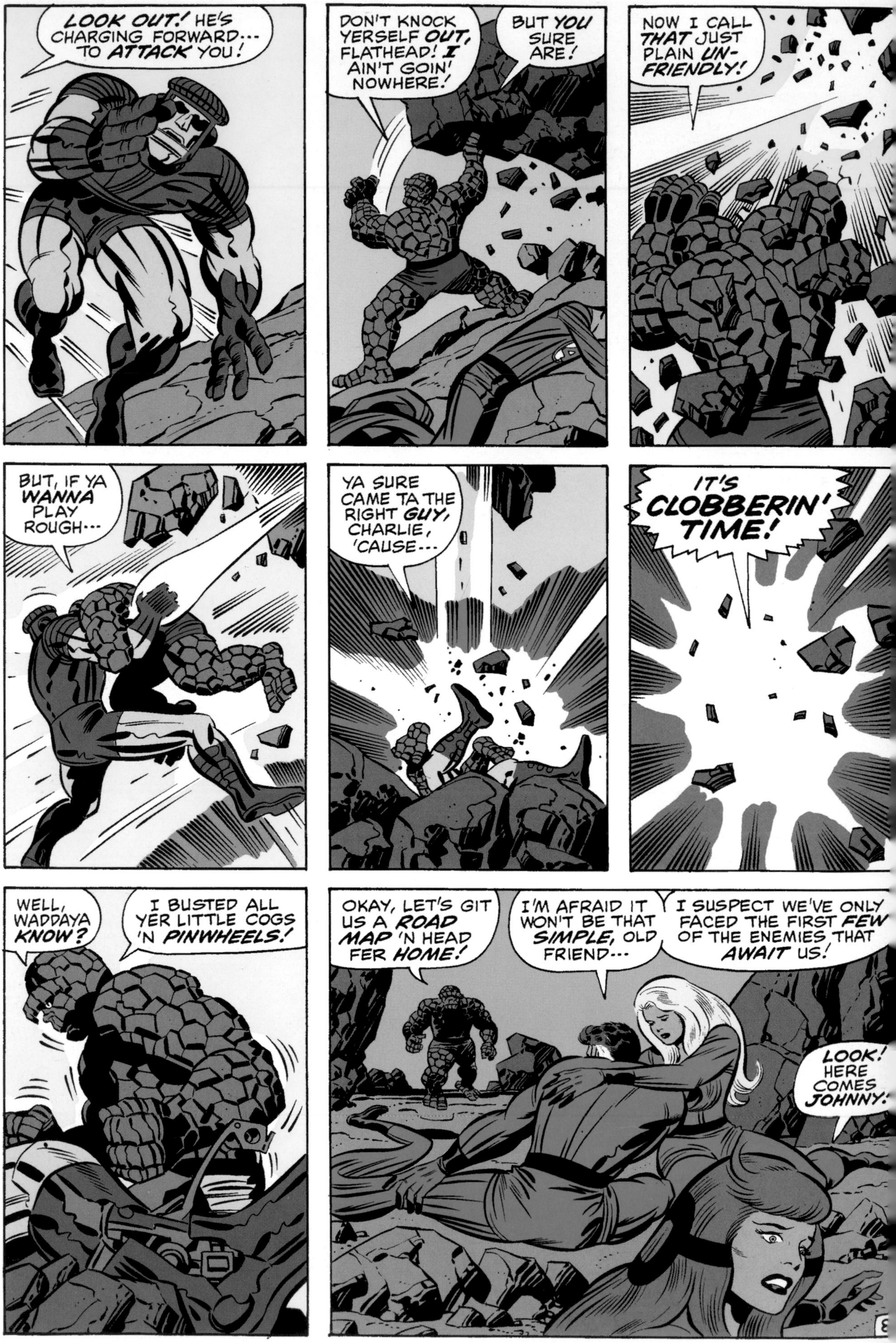
LOOK OUT! HE'S CHARGING FORWARD... TO ATTACK YOU!
DON'T KNOCK YERSELF OUT, FLATHEAD! I AIN'T GOIN' NOWHERE!
BUT YOU SURE ARE!
NOW I CALL THAT JUST PLAIN UN-FRIENDLY!
BUT, IF YA WANNA PLAY ROUGH...
YA SURE CAME TA THE RIGHT GUY, CHARLIE, 'CAUSE...
IT'S CLOBBERIN' TIME!
WELL, WADDAYA KNOW?
I BUSTED ALL YER LITTLE COGS 'N PINWHEELS!
OKAY, LET'S GIT US A ROAD MAP 'N HEAD FER HOME!
I'M AFRAID IT WON'T BE THAT SIMPLE, OLD FRIEND...
I SUSPECT WE'VE ONLY FACED THE FIRST FEW OF THE ENEMIES THAT AWAIT US!
LOOK! HERE COMES JOHNNY!
8

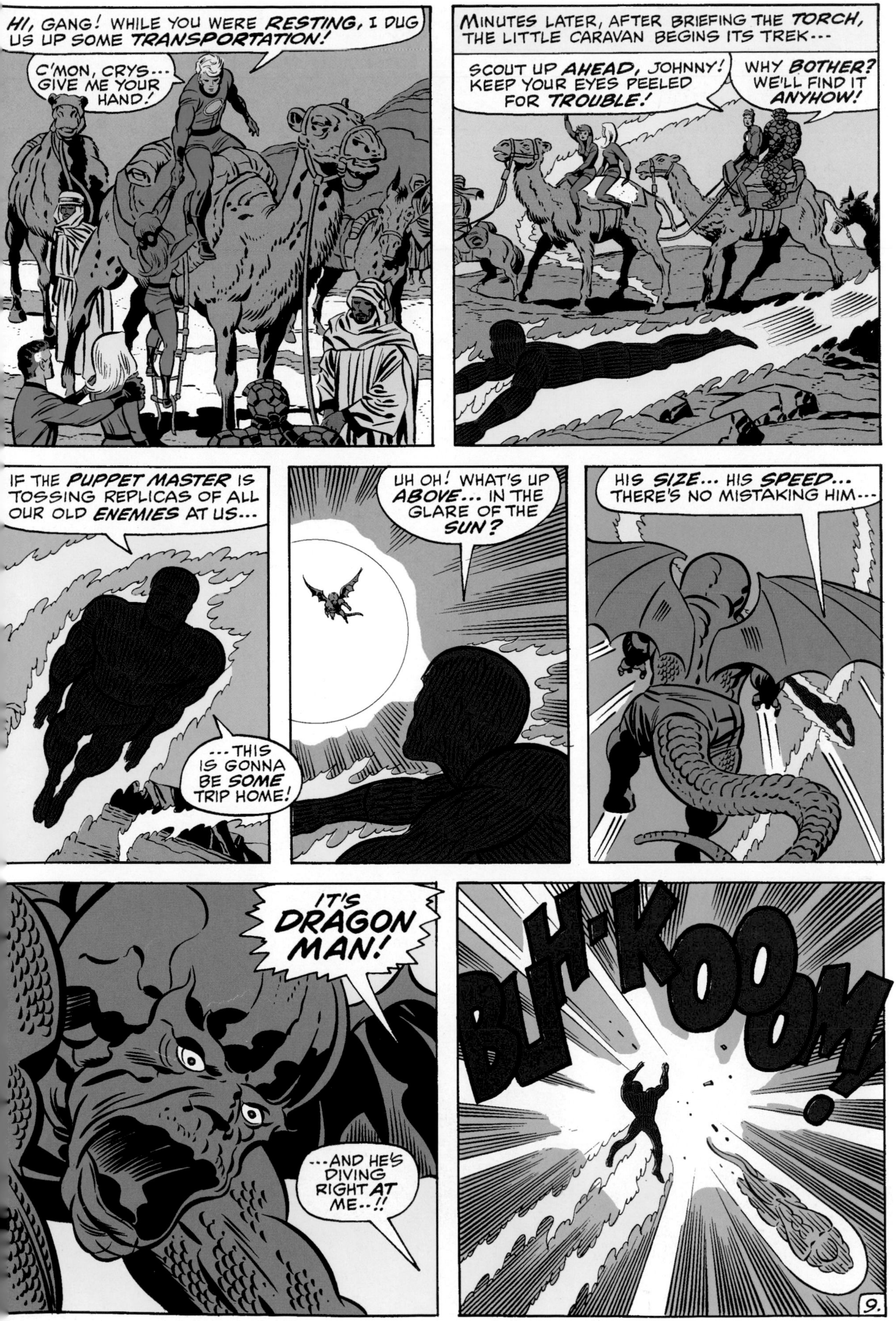
HI, GANG! WHILE YOU WERE RESTING, I DUG US UP SOME TRANSPORTATION!
C'MON, CRYS... GIVE ME YOUR HAND!
MINUTES LATER, AFTER BRIEFING THE TORCH, THE LITTLE CARAVAN BEGINS ITS TREK---
SCOUT UP AHEAD, JOHNNY! KEEP YOUR EYES PEELED FOR TROUBLE!
WHY BOTHER? WE'LL FIND IT ANYHOW!
IF THE PUPPET MASTER IS TOSSING REPLICAS OF ALL OUR OLD ENEMIES AT US...
---THIS IS GONNA BE SOME TRIP HOME!
UH OH! WHAT'S UP ABOVE... IN THE GLARE OF THE SUN?
HIS SIZE... HIS SPEED... THERE'S NO MISTAKING HIM---
IT'S DRAGON MAN!
---AND HE'S DIVING RIGHT AT ME--!!
BLH-KOOOM!
9.

FALL, TORCH--- INTO THE SNOW--- JUST AS I PLANNED!
IT WILL WEAKEN YOU! IT WILL DIM YOUR FLAME!
THUS MAKING YOU A PERFECT TARGET...
...FOR MY MOST LETHAL ATTACK!
DON'T COUNT ON IT, BIG SHOT!
...NOT WHILE I'VE ENOUGH HEAT LEFT TO FIRE ONE LAST BURST THRU THE MOUNTAIN...
...WHERE IT'LL BUILD UP ENOUGH PRESSURE... TO TRAP YOU---WHEN IT ERUPTS!
MADE IT! THE EXPLOSION CAUGHT HIM FLAT FOOTED!
BUT I'VE GOT TO REACH THE OTHERS NOW!
WON'T BE MUCH GOOD FOR ANY-THING--- TILL I CAN RECHARGE MY FLAME!
THERE THEY ARE NOW!
THEY'RE TRYING TO FORD THAT RIVER--- IN A NATIVE FIBER BOAT!
UH OH! THEY'RE CAUGHT IN A WHIRLPOOL...
AND MY FLAME'S TOO WEAK TO HELP!

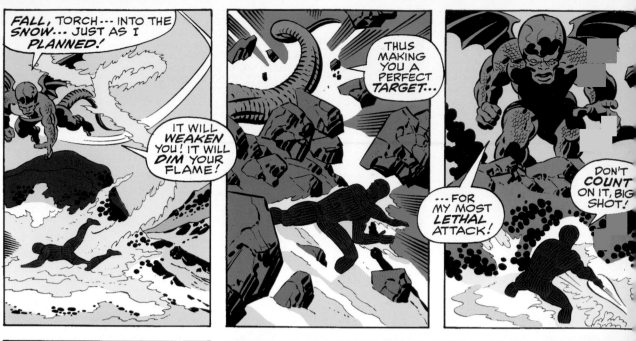

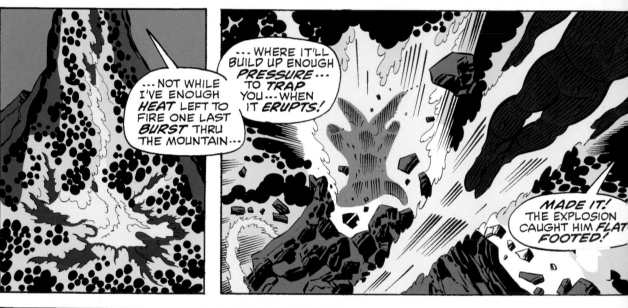

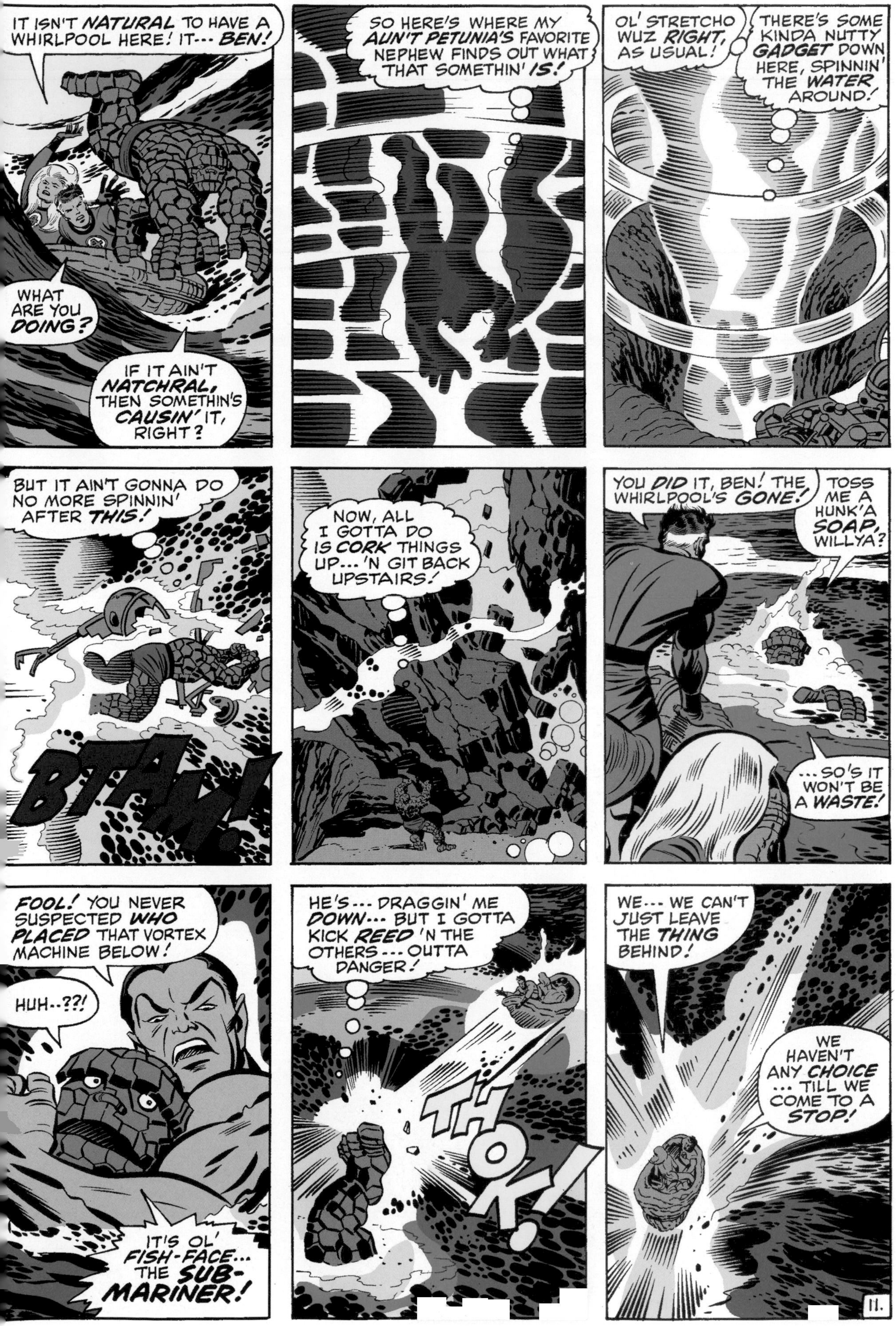
IT ISN'T NATURAL TO HAVE A WHIRLPOOL HERE! IT--- BEN!
WHAT ARE YOU DOING?
IF IT AIN'T NATCHRAL, THEN SOMETHIN'S CAUSIN' IT, RIGHT?
SO HERE'S WHERE MY AUN'T PETUNIA'S FAVORITE NEPHEW FINDS OUT WHAT THAT SOMETHIN' IS!
OL' STRETCHO WUZ RIGHT, AS USUAL!
THERE'S SOME KINDA NUTTY GADGET DOWN HERE, SPINNIN' THE WATER AROUND!
BUT IT AIN'T GONNA DO NO MORE SPINNIN' AFTER THIS!
BTAM!
NOW, ALL I GOTTA DO IS CORK THINGS UP... 'N GIT BACK UPSTAIRS!
YOU DID IT, BEN! THE WHIRLPOOL'S GONE!
TOSS ME A HUNK'A SOAP, WILLYA?
...SO'S IT WON'T BE A WASTE!
FOOL! YOU NEVER SUSPECTED WHO PLACED THAT VORTEX MACHINE BELOW!
HUH..??!
IT'S OL' FISH-FACE... THE SUB-MARINER!
HE'S... DRAGGIN' ME DOWN... BUT I GOTTA KICK REED 'N THE OTHERS... OUTTA DANGER!
THOK!
WE... WE CAN'T JUST LEAVE THE THING BEHIND!
WE HAVEN'T ANY CHOICE ... TILL WE COME TO A STOP!
11.

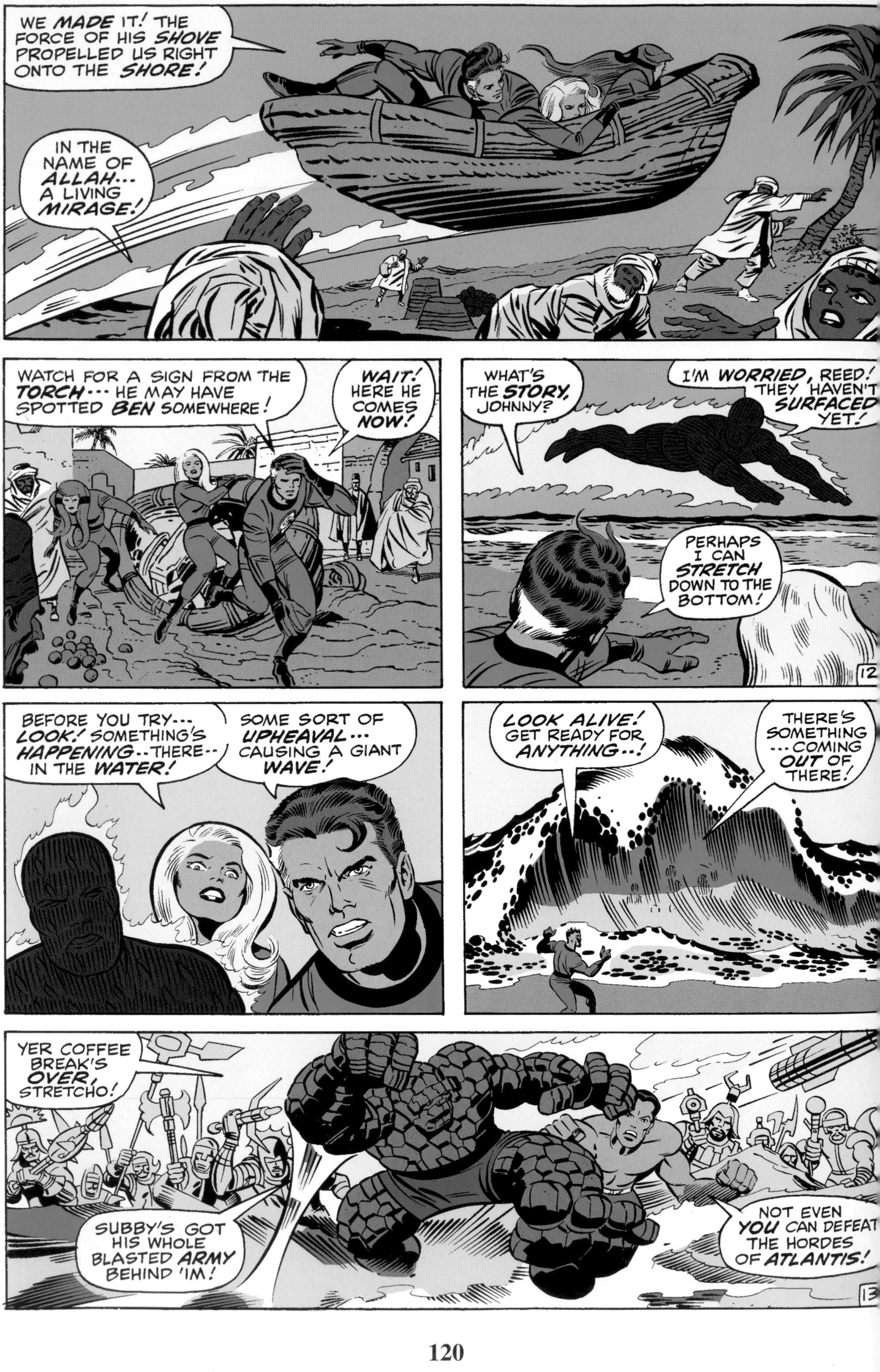
WE MADE IT! THE FORCE OF HIS SHOVE PROPELLED US RIGHT ONTO THE SHORE!
IN THE NAME OF ALLAH... A LIVING MIRAGE!
WATCH FOR A SIGN FROM THE TORCH... HE MAY HAVE SPOTTED BEN SOMEWHERE!
WAIT! HERE HE COMES NOW!
WHAT'S THE STORY, JOHNNY?
I'M WORRIED, REED! THEY HAVEN'T SURFACED YET!
PERHAPS I CAN STRETCH DOWN TO THE BOTTOM!
12
BEFORE YOU TRY... LOOK! SOMETHING'S HAPPENING.. THERE.. IN THE WATER!
SOME SORT OF UPHEAVAL... CAUSING A GIANT WAVE!
LOOK ALIVE! GET READY FOR ANYTHING..!
THERE'S SOMETHING ...COMING OUT OF THERE!
YER COFFEE BREAK'S OVER, STRETCHO!
SUBBY'S GOT HIS WHOLE BLASTED ARMY BEHIND 'IM!
NOT EVEN YOU CAN DEFEAT THE HORDES OF ATLANTIS!
13

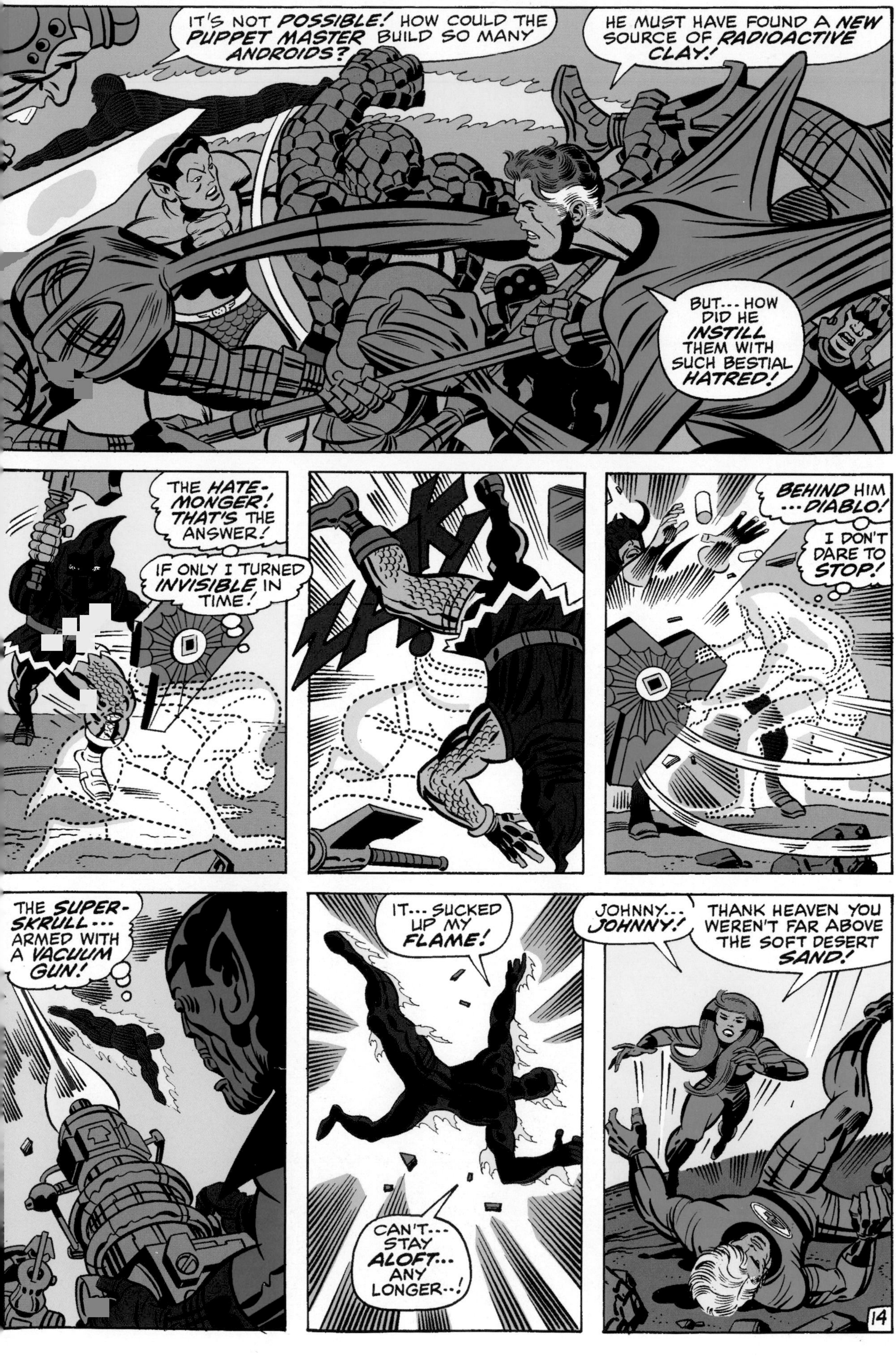
IT'S NOT POSSIBLE! HOW COULD THE PUPPET MASTER BUILD SO MANY ANDROIDS?
HE MUST HAVE FOUND A NEW SOURCE OF RADIOACTIVE CLAY!
BUT--- HOW DID HE INSTILL THEM WITH SUCH BESTIAL HATRED!
THE HATE-MONGER! THAT'S THE ANSWER!
IF ONLY I TURNED INVISIBLE IN TIME!
BEHIND HIM ---DIABLO!
I DON'T DARE TO STOP!
THE SUPER-SKRULL--- ARMED WITH A VACUUM GUN!
IT--- SUCKED UP MY FLAME!
CAN'T--- STAY ALOFT--- ANY LONGER--!
JOHNNY--- JOHNNY!
THANK HEAVEN YOU WEREN'T FAR ABOVE THE SOFT DESERT SAND!
14

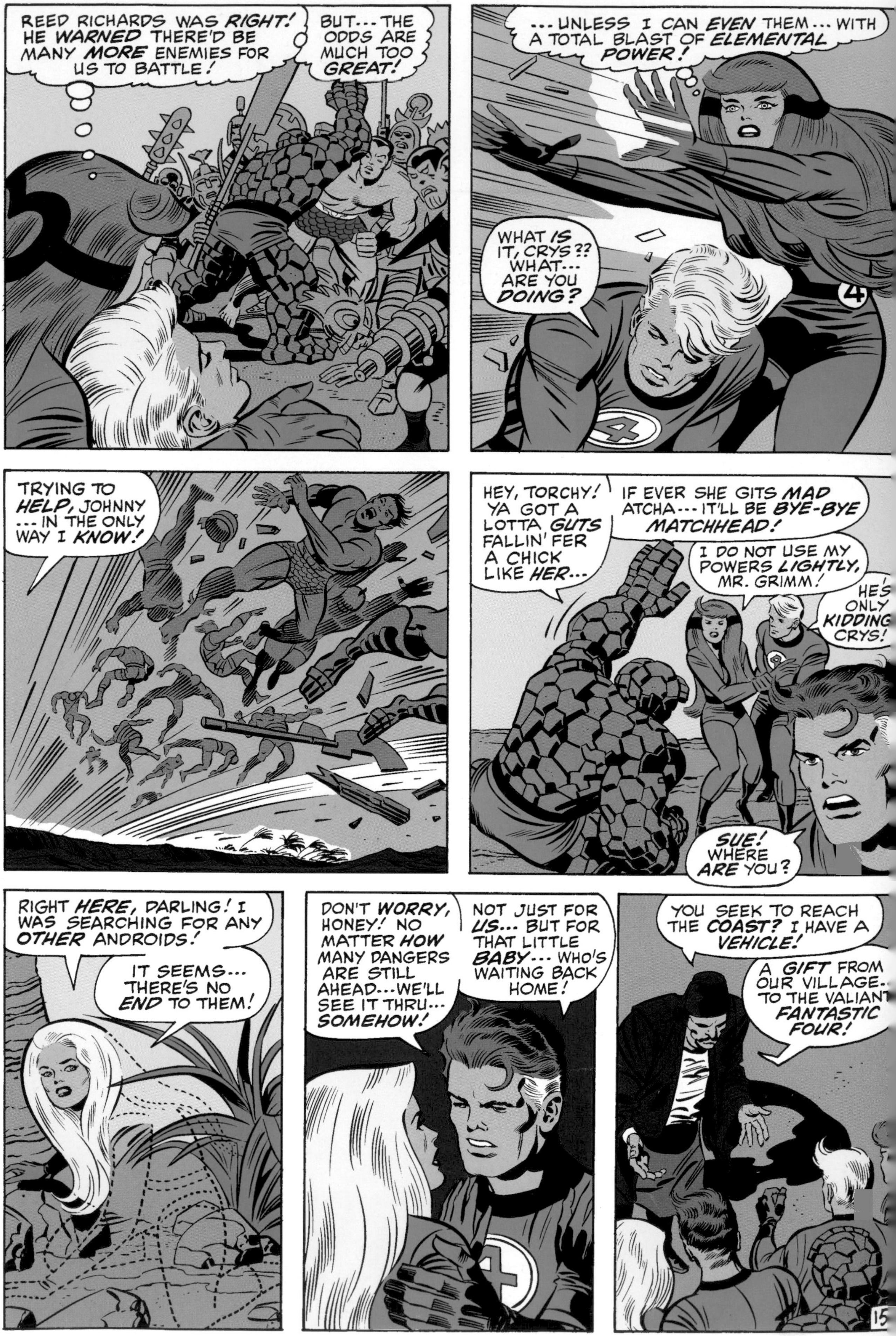
REED RICHARDS WAS RIGHT! HE WARNED THERE'D BE MANY MORE ENEMIES FOR US TO BATTLE!
BUT--- THE ODDS ARE MUCH TOO GREAT!
...UNLESS I CAN EVEN THEM... WITH A TOTAL BLAST OF ELEMENTAL POWER!
WHAT IS IT, CRYS?? WHAT... ARE YOU DOING?
TRYING TO HELP, JOHNNY ... IN THE ONLY WAY I KNOW!
HEY, TORCHY! YA GOT A LOTTA GUTS FALLIN' FER A CHICK LIKE HER...
IF EVER SHE GITS MAD ATCHA--- IT'LL BE BYE-BYE MATCHHEAD!
I DO NOT USE MY POWERS LIGHTLY, MR. GRIMM!
HE'S ONLY KIDDING CRYS!
SUE! WHERE ARE YOU?
RIGHT HERE, DARLING! I WAS SEARCHING FOR ANY OTHER ANDROIDS!
IT SEEMS... THERE'S NO END TO THEM!
DON'T WORRY, HONEY! NO MATTER HOW MANY DANGERS ARE STILL AHEAD---WE'LL SEE IT THRU--- SOMEHOW!
NOT JUST FOR US... BUT FOR THAT LITTLE BABY--- WHO'S WAITING BACK HOME!
YOU SEEK TO REACH THE COAST? I HAVE A VEHICLE!
A GIFT FROM OUR VILLAGE.. TO THE VALIANT FANTASTIC FOUR!
15

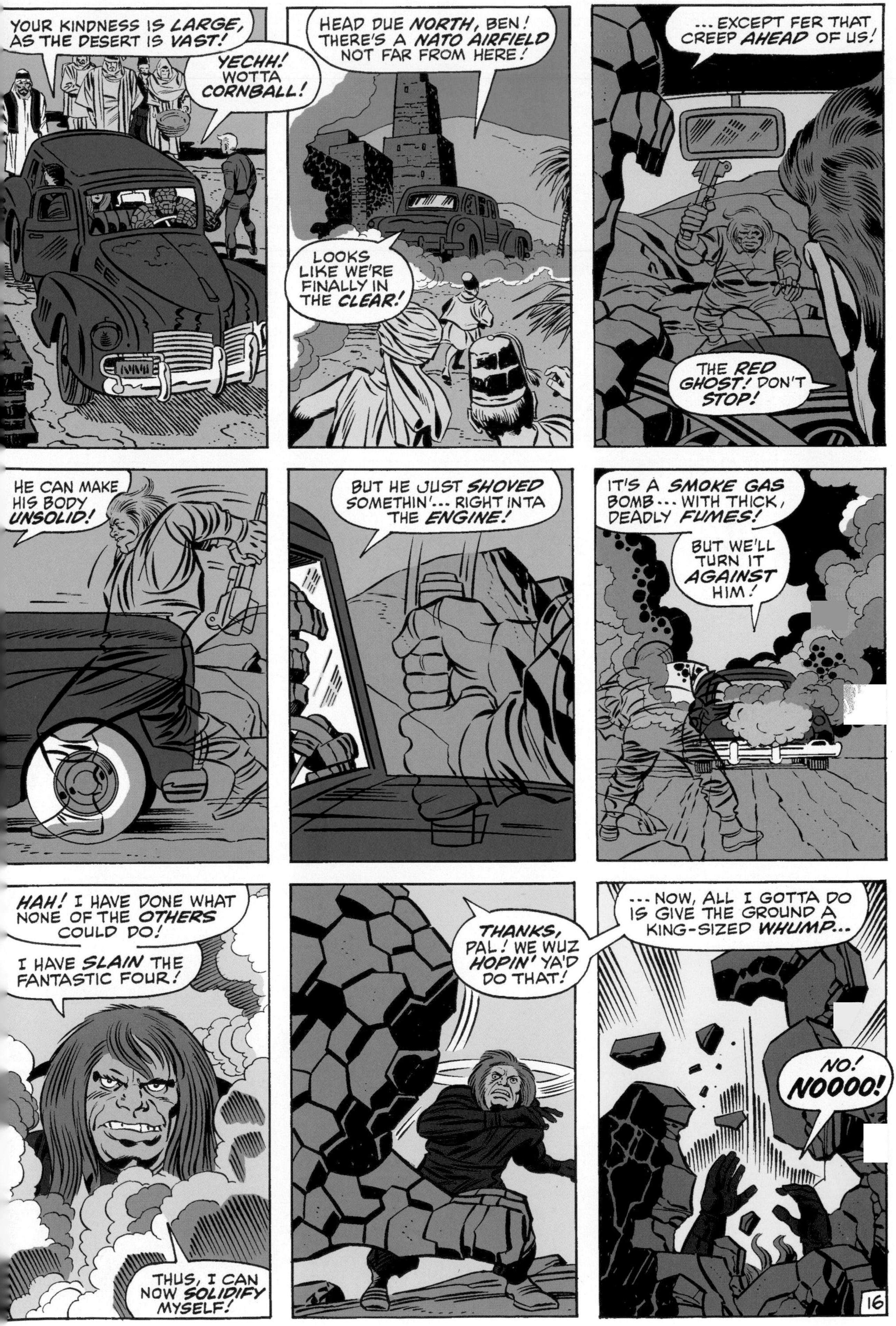
YOUR KINDNESS IS LARGE, AS THE DESERT IS VAST!
YECHH! WOTTA CORNBALL!
HEAD DUE NORTH, BEN! THERE'S A NATO AIRFIELD NOT FAR FROM HERE!
LOOKS LIKE WE'RE FINALLY IN THE CLEAR!
... EXCEPT FER THAT CREEP AHEAD OF US!
THE RED GHOST! DON'T STOP!
HE CAN MAKE HIS BODY UNSOLID!
BUT HE JUST SHOVED SOMETHIN'... RIGHT INTA THE ENGINE!
IT'S A SMOKE GAS BOMB... WITH THICK, DEADLY FUMES!
BUT WE'LL TURN IT AGAINST HIM!
HAH! I HAVE DONE WHAT NONE OF THE OTHERS COULD DO!
I HAVE SLAIN THE FANTASTIC FOUR!
THUS, I CAN NOW SOLIDIFY MYSELF!
THANKS, PAL! WE WUZ HOPIN' YA'D DO THAT!
... NOW, ALL I GOTTA DO IS GIVE THE GROUND A KING-SIZED WHUMP...
NO! NOOOO!
16

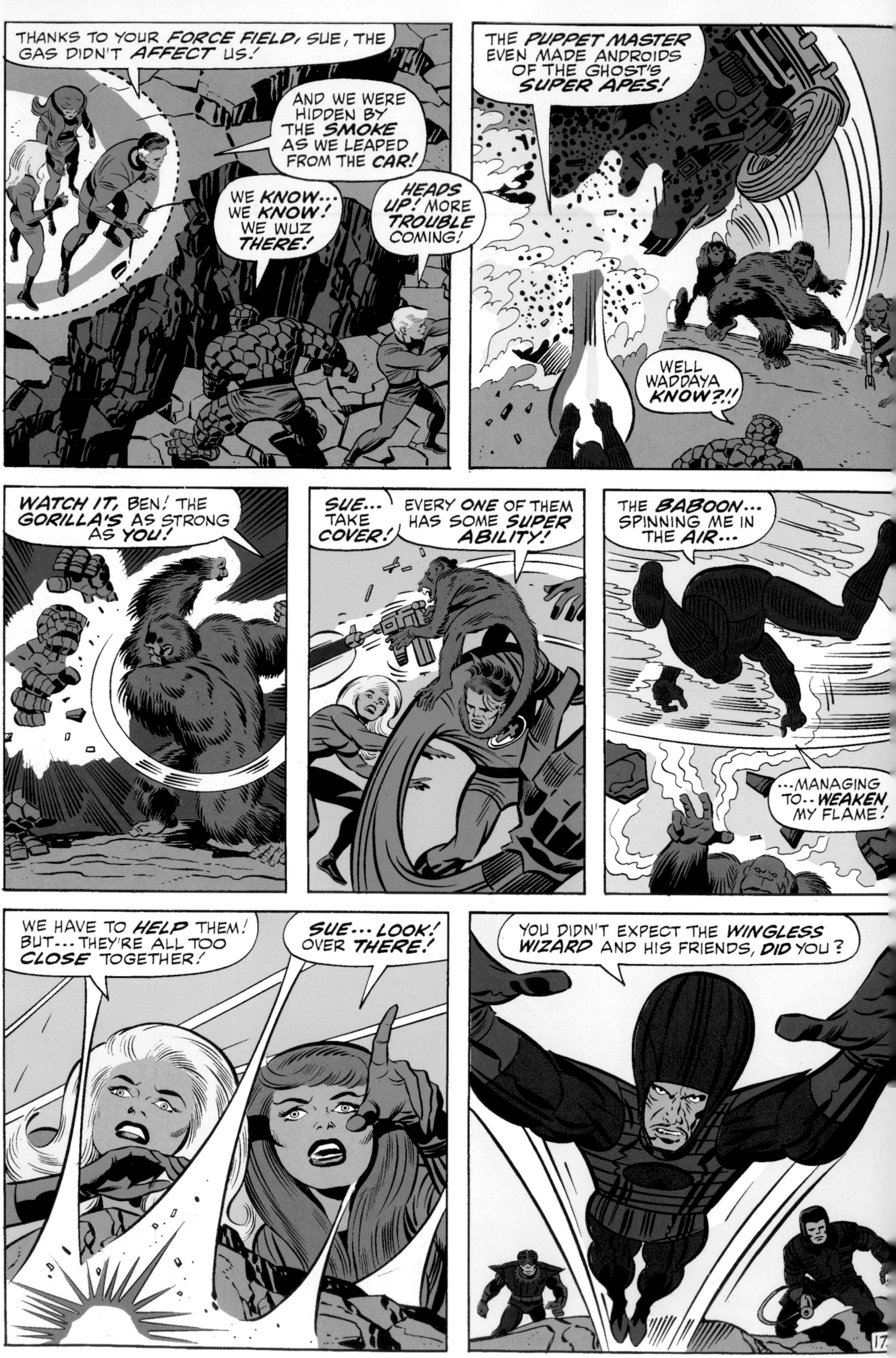
THANKS TO YOUR FORCE FIELD, SUE, THE GAS DIDN'T AFFECT US!
AND WE WERE HIDDEN BY THE SMOKE AS WE LEAPED FROM THE CAR!
WE KNOW... WE KNOW! WE WUZ THERE!
HEADS UP! MORE TROUBLE COMING!
THE PUPPET MASTER EVEN MADE ANDROIDS OF THE GHOST'S SUPER APES!
WELL WADDAYA KNOW?!!
WATCH IT, BEN! THE GORILLA'S AS STRONG AS YOU!
SUE... TAKE COVER!
EVERY ONE OF THEM HAS SOME SUPER ABILITY!
THE BABOON... SPINNING ME IN THE AIR...
...MANAGING TO.. WEAKEN MY FLAME!
WE HAVE TO HELP THEM! BUT--- THEY'RE ALL TOO CLOSE TOGETHER!
SUE... LOOK! OVER THERE!
YOU DIDN'T EXPECT THE WINGLESS WIZARD AND HIS FRIENDS, DID YOU?
17

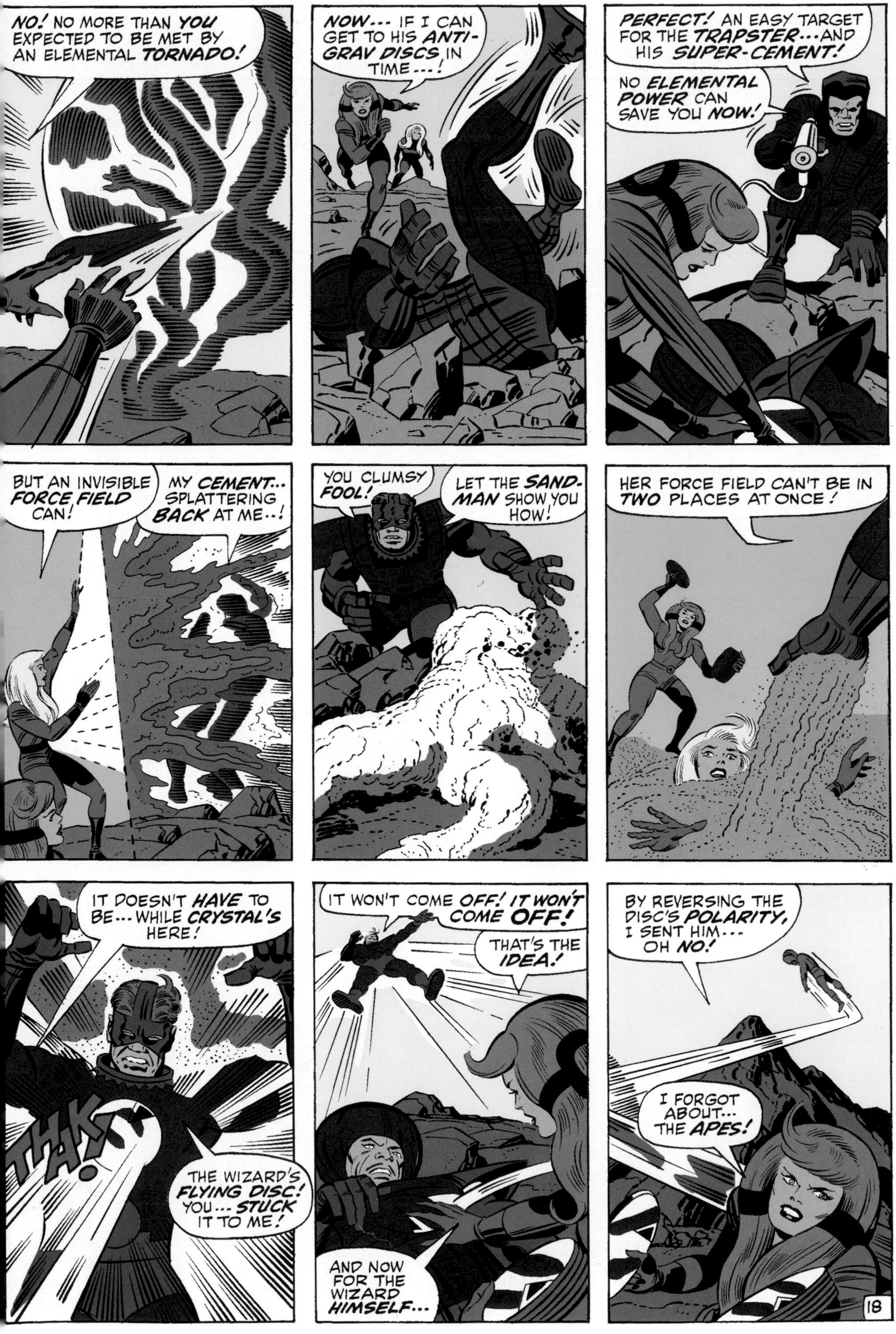
NO! NO MORE THAN YOU EXPECTED TO BE MET BY AN ELEMENTAL TORNADO!
NOW... IF I CAN GET TO HIS ANTI-GRAV DISCS IN TIME...!
PERFECT! AN EASY TARGET FOR THE TRAPSTER...AND HIS SUPER-CEMENT!
NO ELEMENTAL POWER CAN SAVE YOU NOW!
BUT AN INVISIBLE FORCE FIELD CAN!
MY CEMENT... SPLATTERING BACK AT ME..!
YOU CLUMSY FOOL!
LET THE SAND-MAN SHOW YOU HOW!
HER FORCE FIELD CAN'T BE IN TWO PLACES AT ONCE!
IT DOESN'T HAVE TO BE... WHILE CRYSTAL'S HERE!
THAK!
THE WIZARD'S FLYING DISC! YOU... STUCK IT TO ME!
IT WON'T COME OFF! IT WON'T COME OFF!
THAT'S THE IDEA!
AND NOW FOR THE WIZARD HIMSELF...
BY REVERSING THE DISC'S POLARITY, I SENT HIM... OH NO!
I FORGOT ABOUT... THE APES!
18

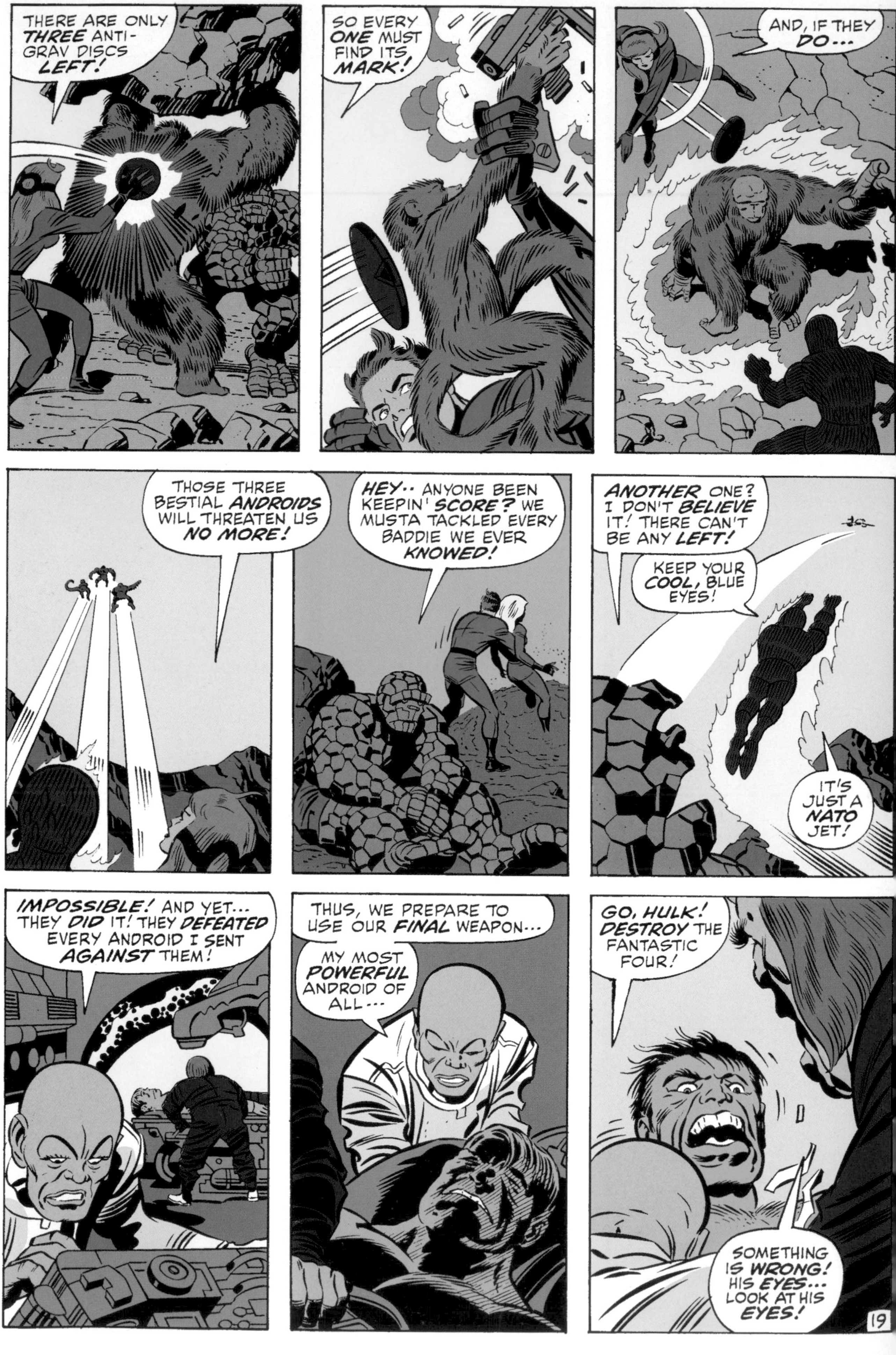
THERE ARE ONLY THREE ANTI-GRAV DISCS LEFT!
SO EVERY ONE MUST FIND ITS MARK!
AND, IF THEY DO...
THOSE THREE BESTIAL ANDROIDS WILL THREATEN US NO MORE!
HEY.. ANYONE BEEN KEEPIN' SCORE? WE MUSTA TACKLED EVERY BADDIE WE EVER KNOWED!
ANOTHER ONE? I DON'T BELIEVE IT! THERE CAN'T BE ANY LEFT!
KEEP YOUR COOL, BLUE EYES!
IT'S JUST A NATO JET!
IMPOSSIBLE! AND YET... THEY DID IT! THEY DEFEATED EVERY ANDROID I SENT AGAINST THEM!
THUS, WE PREPARE TO USE OUR FINAL WEAPON...
MY MOST POWERFUL ANDROID OF ALL...
GO, HULK! DESTROY THE FANTASTIC FOUR!
SOMETHING IS WRONG! HIS EYES... LOOK AT HIS EYES!
19

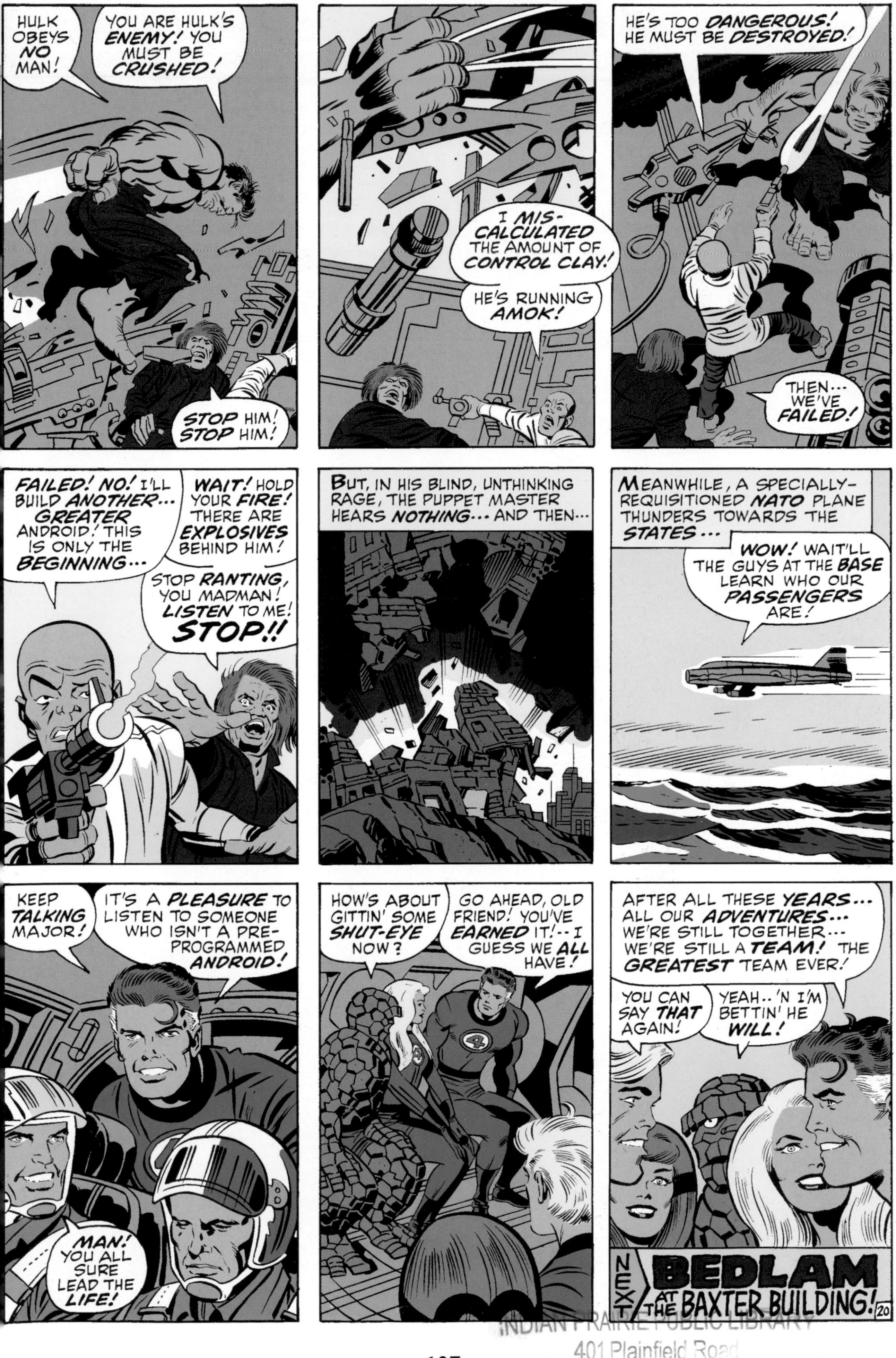
HULK OBEYS NO MAN!
YOU ARE HULK'S ENEMY! YOU MUST BE CRUSHED!
STOP HIM! STOP HIM!
I MIS-CALCULATED THE AMOUNT OF CONTROL CLAY!
HE'S RUNNING AMOK!
HE'S TOO DANGEROUS! HE MUST BE DESTROYED!
THEN... WE'VE FAILED!
FAILED! NO! I'LL BUILD ANOTHER... GREATER ANDROID! THIS IS ONLY THE BEGINNING...
WAIT! HOLD YOUR FIRE! THERE ARE EXPLOSIVES BEHIND HIM!
STOP RANTING, YOU MADMAN! LISTEN TO ME! STOP!!
BUT, IN HIS BLIND, UNTHINKING RAGE, THE PUPPET MASTER HEARS NOTHING... AND THEN...
MEANWHILE, A SPECIALLY-REQUISITIONED NATO PLANE THUNDERS TOWARDS THE STATES...
WOW! WAIT'LL THE GUYS AT THE BASE LEARN WHO OUR PASSENGERS ARE!
KEEP TALKING MAJOR!
IT'S A PLEASURE TO LISTEN TO SOMEONE WHO ISN'T A PRE-PROGRAMMED ANDROID!
MAN! YOU ALL SURE LEAD THE LIFE!
HOW'S ABOUT GITTIN' SOME SHUT-EYE NOW?
GO AHEAD, OLD FRIEND! YOU'VE EARNED IT!-- I GUESS WE ALL HAVE!
AFTER ALL THESE YEARS... ALL OUR ADVENTURES... WE'RE STILL TOGETHER... WE'RE STILL A TEAM! THE GREATEST TEAM EVER!
YOU CAN SAY THAT AGAIN!
YEAH.. 'N I'M BETTIN' HE WILL!
NEXT BEDLAM AT THE BAXTER BUILDING!
20

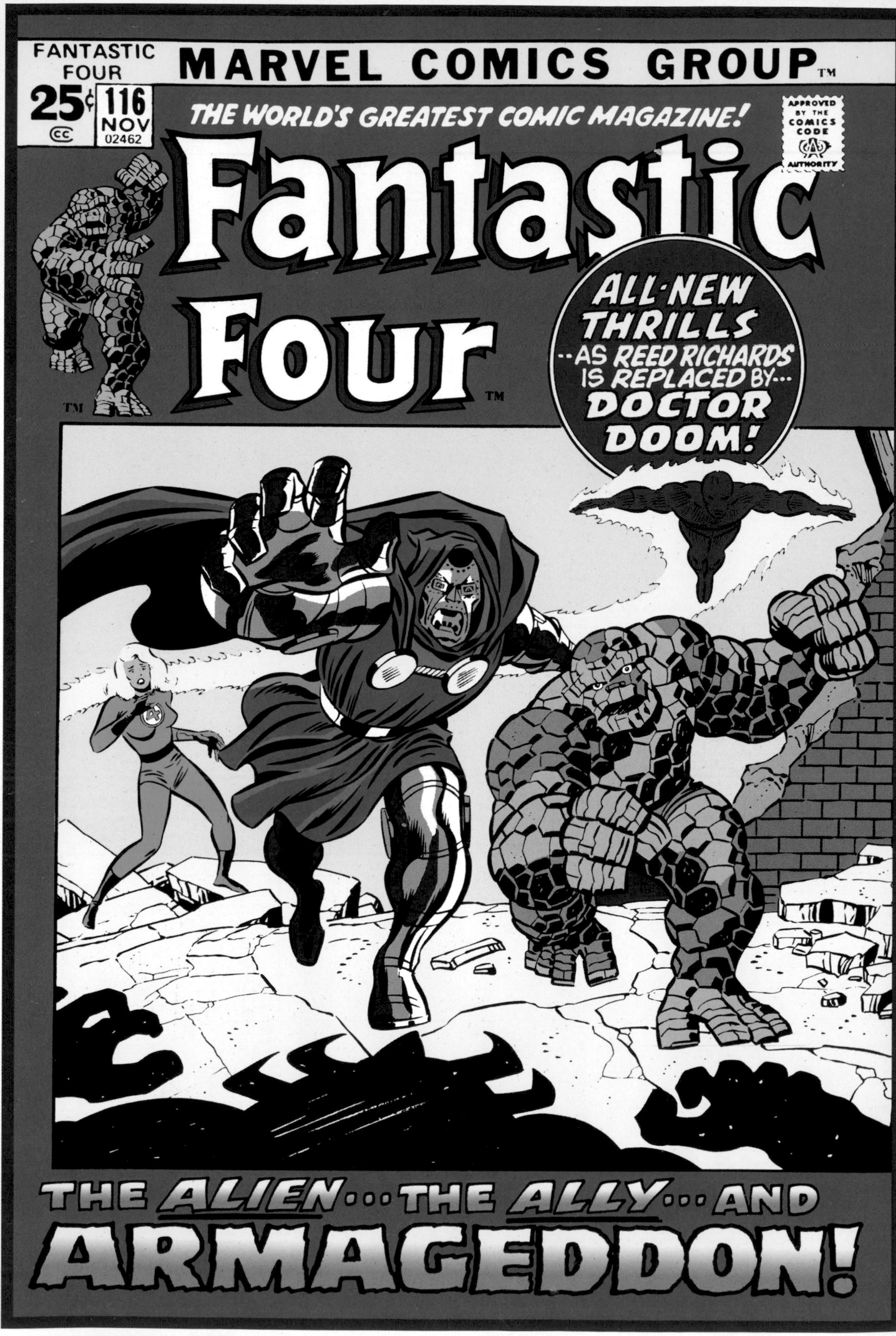
FANTASTIC FOUR
MARVEL COMICS GROUP TM
25¢ 116 NOV 02462
CC
THE WORLD'S GREATEST COMIC MAGAZINE!
APPROVED BY THE COMICS CODE AUTHORITY
Fantastic Four TM
TM
ALL-NEW THRILLS --AS REED RICHARDS IS REPLACED BY--- DOCTOR DOOM!
THE ALIEN... THE ALLY... AND
ARMAGEDDON!

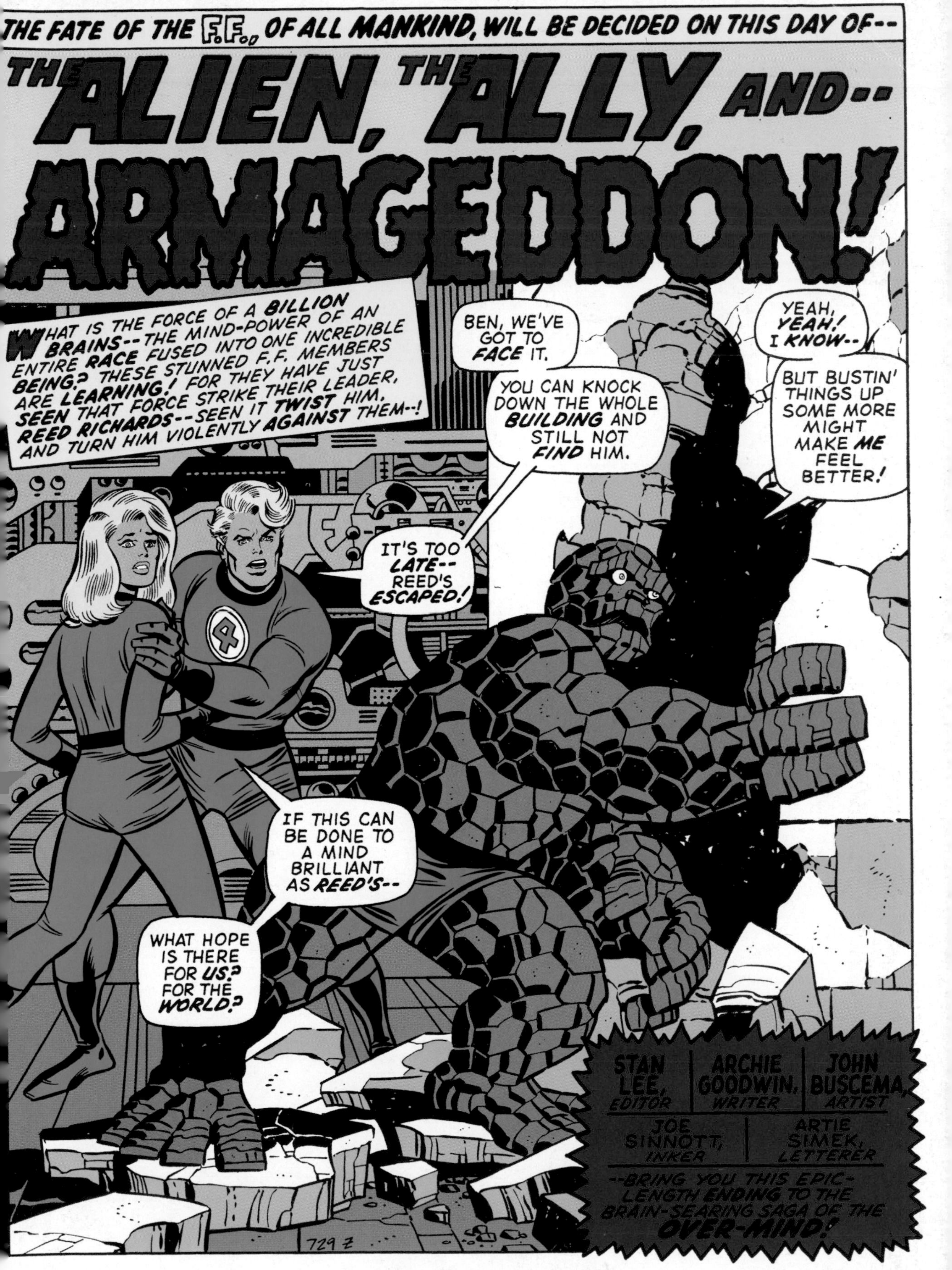
THE FATE OF THE F.F., OF ALL MANKIND, WILL BE DECIDED ON THIS DAY OF--
THE ALIEN, THE ALLY, AND-- ARMAGEDDON!
WHAT IS THE FORCE OF A BILLION BRAINS--THE MIND-POWER OF AN ENTIRE RACE FUSED INTO ONE INCREDIBLE BEING? THESE STUNNED F.F. MEMBERS ARE LEARNING! FOR THEY HAVE JUST SEEN THAT FORCE STRIKE THEIR LEADER, REED RICHARDS--SEEN IT TWIST HIM, AND TURN HIM VIOLENTLY AGAINST THEM--!
BEN, WE'VE GOT TO FACE IT.
YOU CAN KNOCK DOWN THE WHOLE BUILDING AND STILL NOT FIND HIM.
IT'S TOO LATE-- REED'S ESCAPED!
YEAH, YEAH! I KNOW--
BUT BUSTIN' THINGS UP SOME MORE MIGHT MAKE ME FEEL BETTER!
IF THIS CAN BE DONE TO A MIND BRILLIANT AS REED'S--
WHAT HOPE IS THERE FOR US? FOR THE WORLD?
STAN LEE, EDITOR
ARCHIE GOODWIN, WRITER
JOHN BUSCEMA, ARTIST
JOE SINNOTT, INKER
ARTIE SIMEK, LETTERER
--BRING YOU THIS EPIC-LENGTH ENDING TO THE BRAIN-SEARING SAGA OF THE OVER-MIND!
729 Z

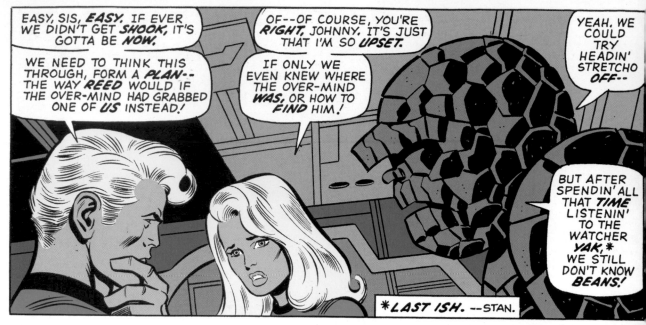

EASY, SIS, *EASY.* IF EVER WE DIDN'T GET *SHOOK,* IT'S GOTTA BE *NOW.*

WE NEED TO THINK THIS THROUGH, FORM A *PLAN*-- THE WAY *REED* WOULD IF THE OVER-MIND HAD GRABBED ONE OF *US* INSTEAD!

OF--OF COURSE, YOU'RE *RIGHT,* JOHNNY. IT'S JUST THAT I'M SO *UPSET.*

IF ONLY WE EVEN KNEW WHERE THE OVER-MIND *WAS,* OR HOW TO *FIND* HIM!

YEAH. WE COULD TRY HEADIN' *STRETCHO* OFF--

BUT AFTER SPENDIN' ALL THAT *TIME* LISTENIN' TO THE WATCHER *YAK,** WE STILL DON'T KNOW *BEANS!*

**LAST ISH.* --STAN.

JUST A LOTTA NUTTY STUFF 'BOUT THESE *ETERNAL* CREEPS, WHO TRIED TA TAKE OVER THE *UNIVERSE*--

--AN' GOT *SLAPPED-DOWN* FER IT--SO THEY ZAPPED ALL THEIR BRAIN-POWER INTO ONE GUY TO *GET EVEN* FOR 'EM--

--THE *OVERMIND!*

NOW MEBBE *ROD SERLING* COULD MAKE SUMPIN' OUTTA THAT, BUT US *WORLD-SAVERS* NEED--

EEEEEEEEEEEE

JOHNNY, *WHAT*--?

AN *ALARM!*

THE *MINI-REACTOR*--

IT'S STARTIN' TO LEAK *RADIOACTIVE PARTICLES!*

BEEN LEFT *ON* TOO LONG!

DON'T BLAME *ME,* HOT-STUFF.

YOU TURNED IT ON WHEN WE WUZ FIGHTIN' REED.

'COURSE I GOTTA *ADMIT.*

IT DROVE 'IM OUTTA *HIDIN'* THERE--

--JUST LIKE YA *FIGURED!*

BEN! *THAT'S IT!*

THE RADIO-ACTIVITY ISN'T ENOUGH TO *HARM* ANYONE--

BUT IF REED WAS EXPOSED *LONG* ENOUGH, IT MAY BE *TRACEABLE!*

2

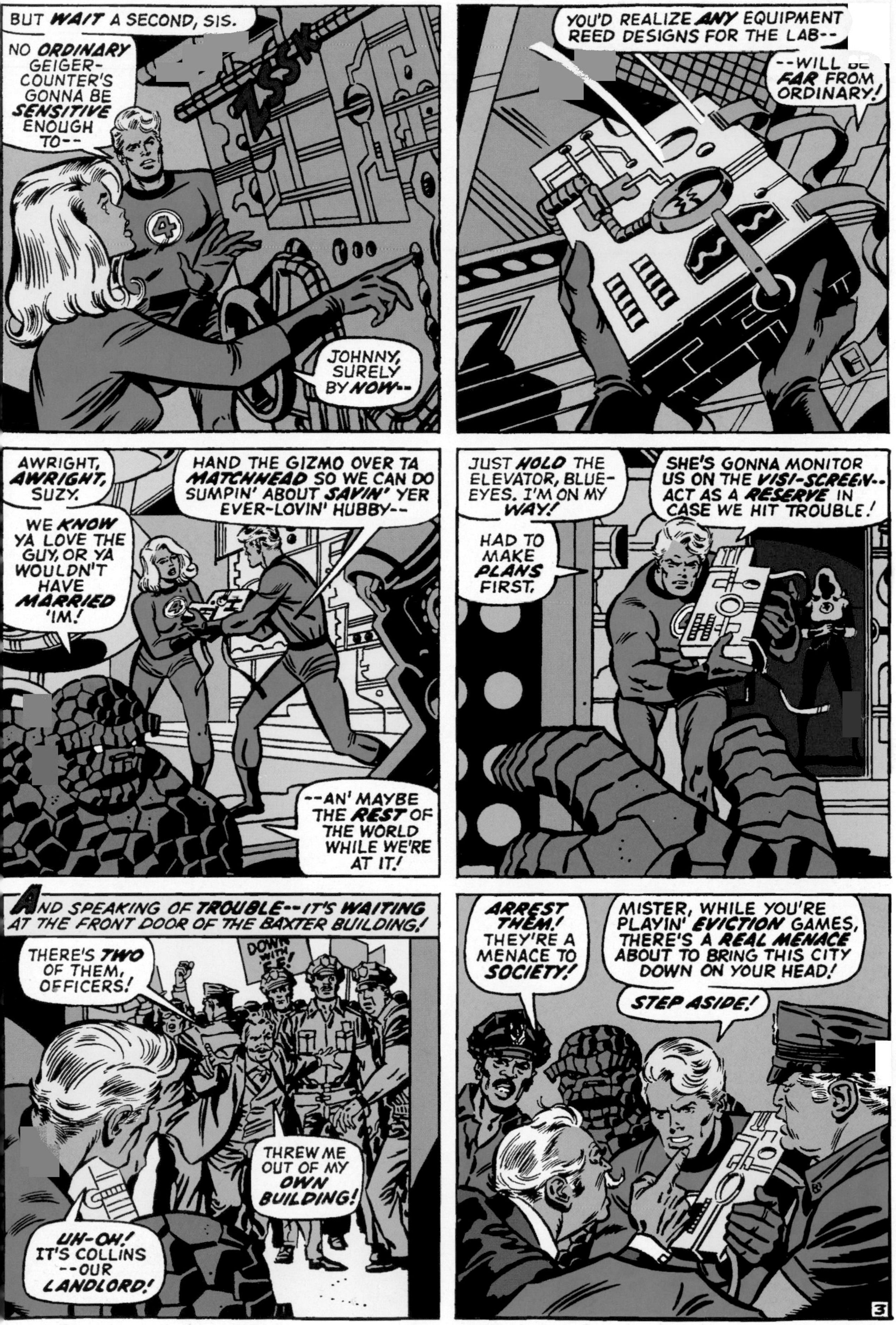
BUT WAIT A SECOND, SIS.
NO ORDINARY GEIGER-COUNTER'S GONNA BE SENSITIVE ENOUGH TO--
ZSSK
JOHNNY, SURELY BY NOW--
YOU'D REALIZE ANY EQUIPMENT REED DESIGNS FOR THE LAB--
--WILL BE FAR FROM ORDINARY!
AWRIGHT, AWRIGHT, SUZY.
WE KNOW YA LOVE THE GUY, OR YA WOULDN'T HAVE MARRIED 'IM!
HAND THE GIZMO OVER TA MATCHHEAD SO WE CAN DO SUMPIN' ABOUT SAVIN' YER EVER-LOVIN' HUBBY--
--AN' MAYBE THE REST OF THE WORLD WHILE WE'RE AT IT!
JUST HOLD THE ELEVATOR, BLUE-EYES. I'M ON MY WAY!
HAD TO MAKE PLANS FIRST.
SHE'S GONNA MONITOR US ON THE VISI-SCREEN--ACT AS A RESERVE IN CASE WE HIT TROUBLE!
AND SPEAKING OF TROUBLE--IT'S WAITING AT THE FRONT DOOR OF THE BAXTER BUILDING!
THERE'S TWO OF THEM, OFFICERS!
THREW ME OUT OF MY OWN BUILDING!
UH-OH! IT'S COLLINS--OUR LANDLORD!
ARREST THEM! THEY'RE A MENACE TO SOCIETY!
MISTER, WHILE YOU'RE PLAYIN' EVICTION GAMES, THERE'S A REAL MENACE ABOUT TO BRING THIS CITY DOWN ON YOUR HEAD!
STEP ASIDE!
3

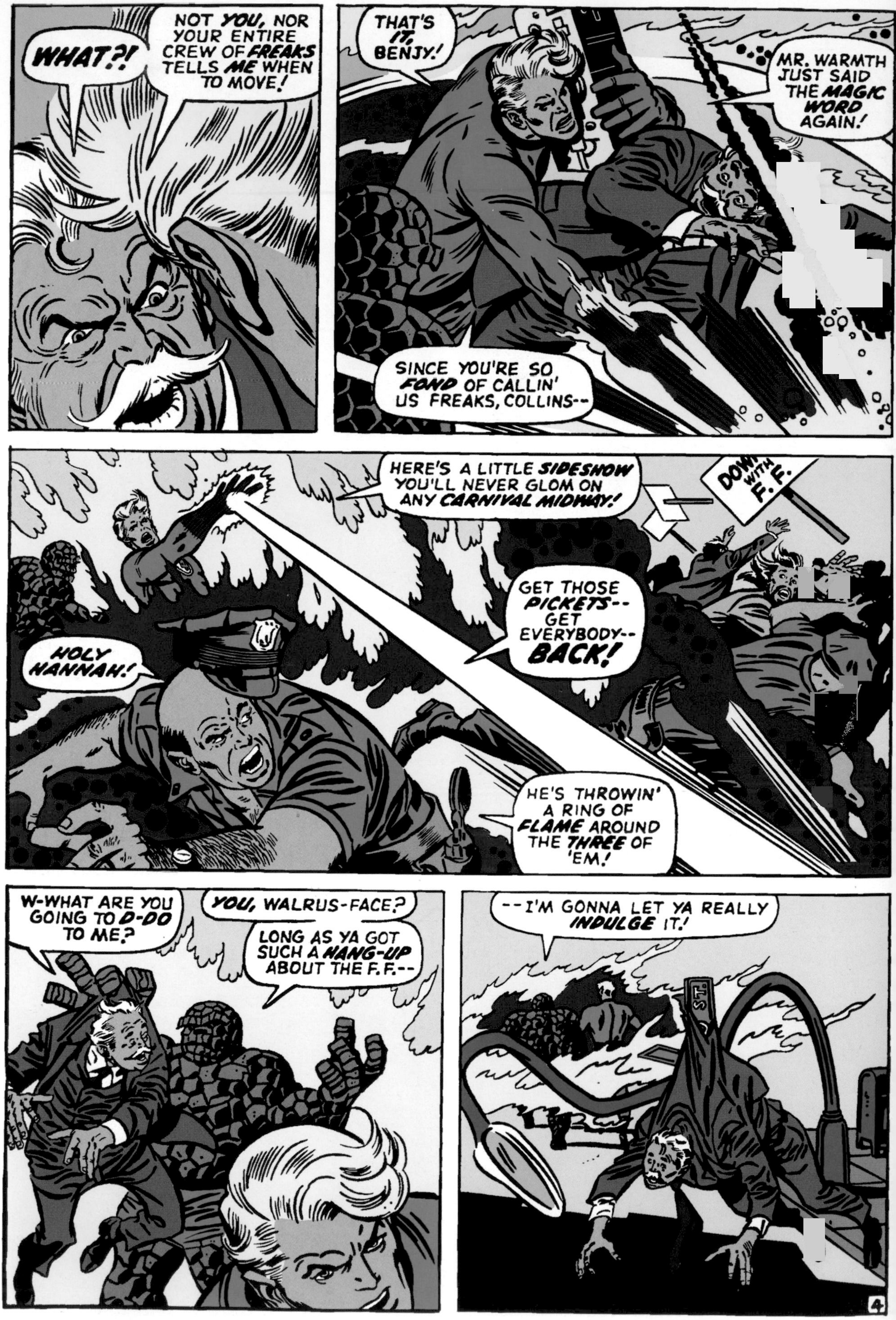
WHAT?!
NOT YOU, NOR YOUR ENTIRE CREW OF FREAKS TELLS ME WHEN TO MOVE!
THAT'S IT, BENJY!
MR. WARMTH JUST SAID THE MAGIC WORD AGAIN!
SINCE YOU'RE SO FOND OF CALLIN' US FREAKS, COLLINS--
HERE'S A LITTLE SIDESHOW YOU'LL NEVER GLOM ON ANY CARNIVAL MIDWAY!
WITH F.F.
GET THOSE PICKETS-- GET EVERYBODY-- BACK!
HOLY HANNAH!
HE'S THROWIN' A RING OF FLAME AROUND THE THREE OF 'EM!
W-WHAT ARE YOU GOING TO D-DO TO ME?
YOU, WALRUS-FACE?
LONG AS YA GOT SUCH A HANG-UP ABOUT THE F.F.--
--I'M GONNA LET YA REALLY INDULGE IT!
ST.
4

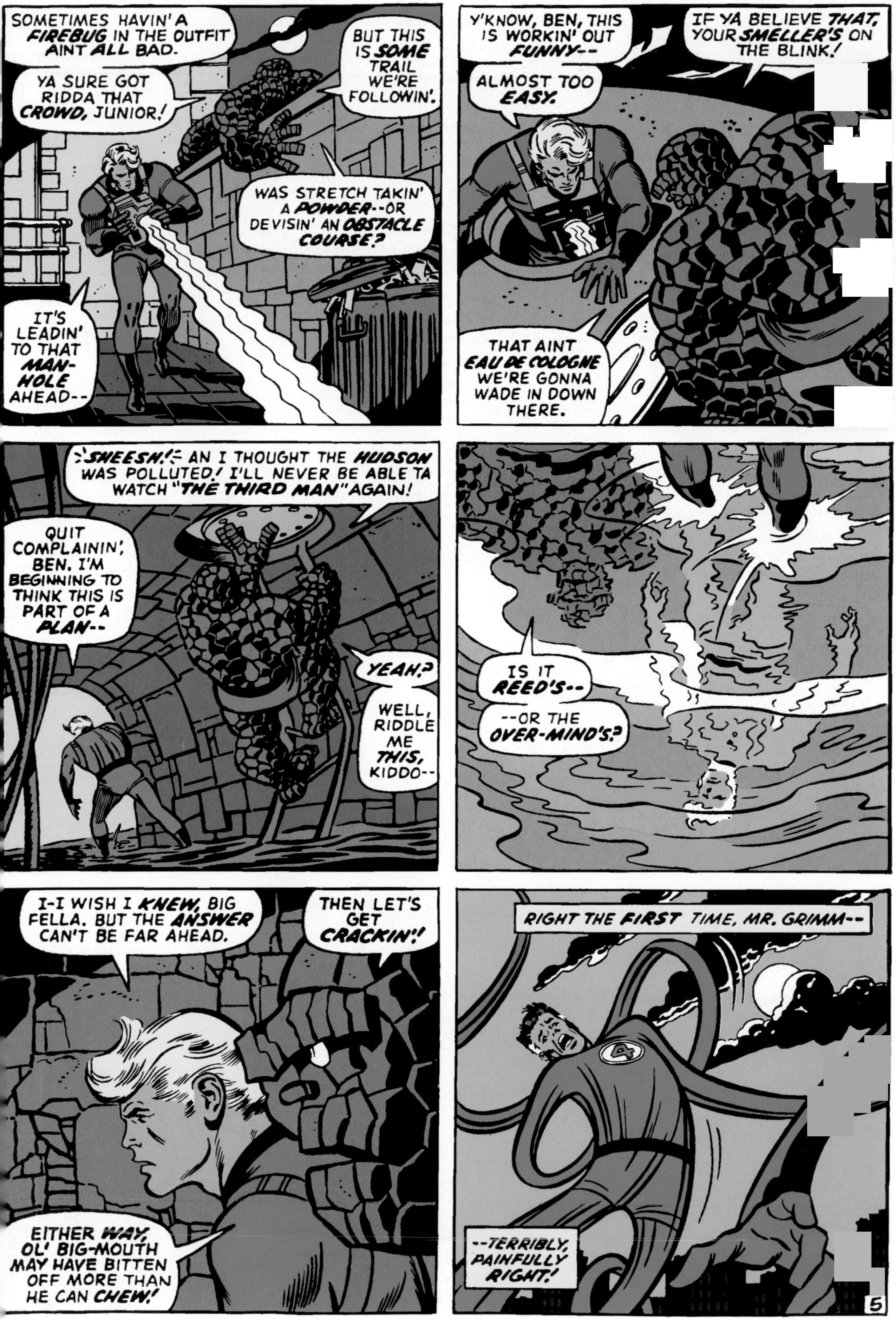
SOMETIMES HAVIN' A FIREBUG IN THE OUTFIT AINT ALL BAD.
YA SURE GOT RIDDA THAT CROWD, JUNIOR!
BUT THIS IS SOME TRAIL WE'RE FOLLOWIN'.
WAS STRETCH TAKIN' A POWDER--OR DEVISIN' AN OBSTACLE COURSE?
IT'S LEADIN' TO THAT MAN-HOLE AHEAD--
Y'KNOW, BEN, THIS IS WORKIN' OUT FUNNY--
ALMOST TOO EASY.
IF YA BELIEVE THAT, YOUR SMELLER'S ON THE BLINK!
THAT AINT EAU DE COLOGNE WE'RE GONNA WADE IN DOWN THERE.
SHEESH! AN I THOUGHT THE HUDSON WAS POLLUTED! I'LL NEVER BE ABLE TA WATCH "THE THIRD MAN" AGAIN!
QUIT COMPLAININ', BEN. I'M BEGINNING TO THINK THIS IS PART OF A PLAN--
YEAH?
WELL, RIDDLE ME THIS, KIDDO--
IS IT REED'S--
--OR THE OVER-MIND'S?
I-I WISH I KNEW, BIG FELLA. BUT THE ANSWER CAN'T BE FAR AHEAD.
THEN LET'S GET CRACKIN'!
EITHER WAY, OL' BIG-MOUTH MAY HAVE BITTEN OFF MORE THAN HE CAN CHEW!
RIGHT THE FIRST TIME, MR. GRIMM--
--TERRIBLY, PAINFULLY RIGHT!
5

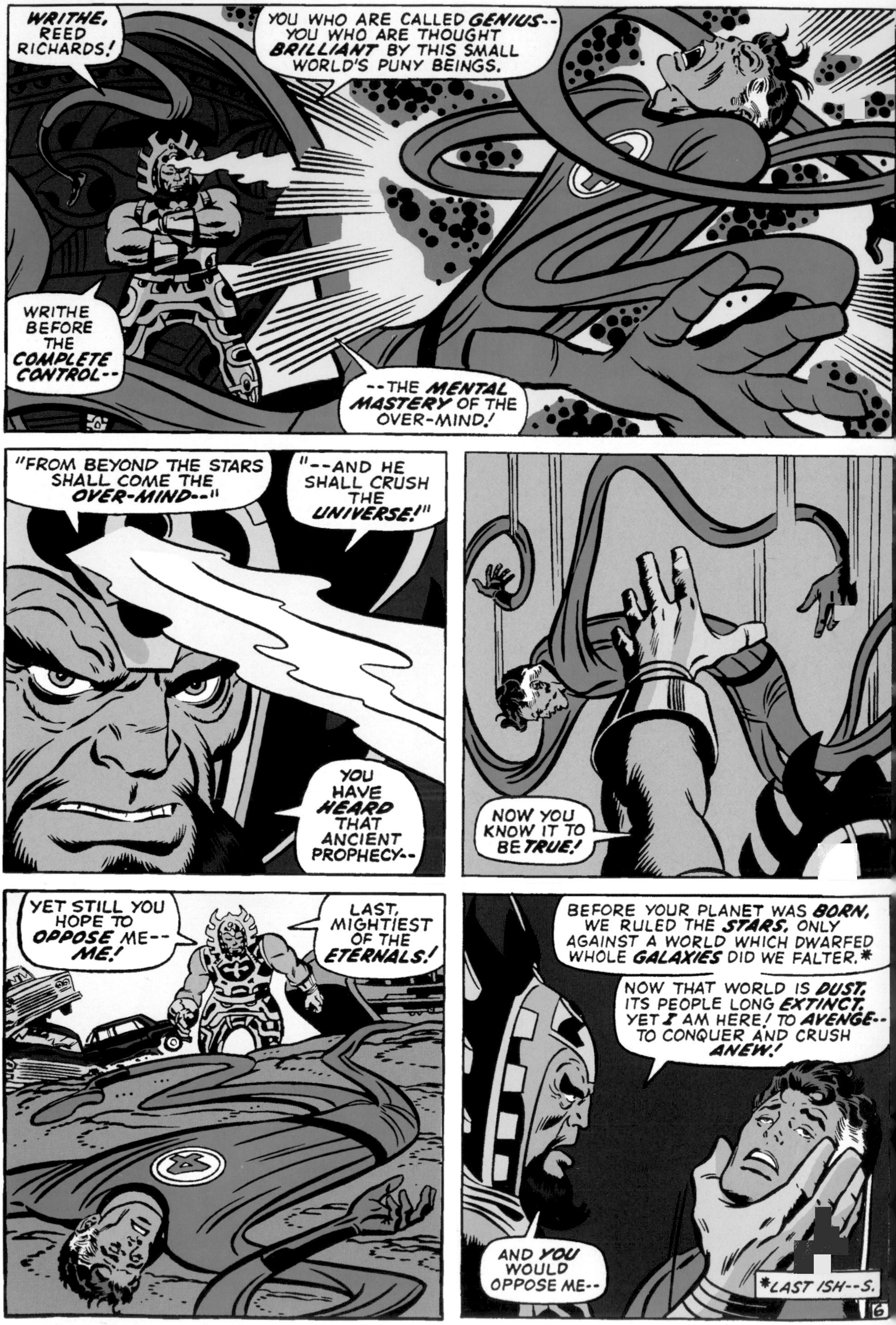
WRITHE, REED RICHARDS!
YOU WHO ARE CALLED GENIUS-- YOU WHO ARE THOUGHT BRILLIANT BY THIS SMALL WORLD'S PUNY BEINGS.
WRITHE BEFORE THE COMPLETE CONTROL--
--THE MENTAL MASTERY OF THE OVER-MIND!
"FROM BEYOND THE STARS SHALL COME THE OVER-MIND--"
"--AND HE SHALL CRUSH THE UNIVERSE!"
YOU HAVE HEARD THAT ANCIENT PROPHECY--
NOW YOU KNOW IT TO BE TRUE!
YET STILL YOU HOPE TO OPPOSE ME-- ME!
LAST, MIGHTIEST OF THE ETERNALS!
BEFORE YOUR PLANET WAS BORN, WE RULED THE STARS, ONLY AGAINST A WORLD WHICH DWARFED WHOLE GALAXIES DID WE FALTER.*
NOW THAT WORLD IS DUST, ITS PEOPLE LONG EXTINCT. YET I AM HERE! TO AVENGE-- TO CONQUER AND CRUSH ANEW!
AND YOU WOULD OPPOSE ME--
*LAST ISH--S.
6

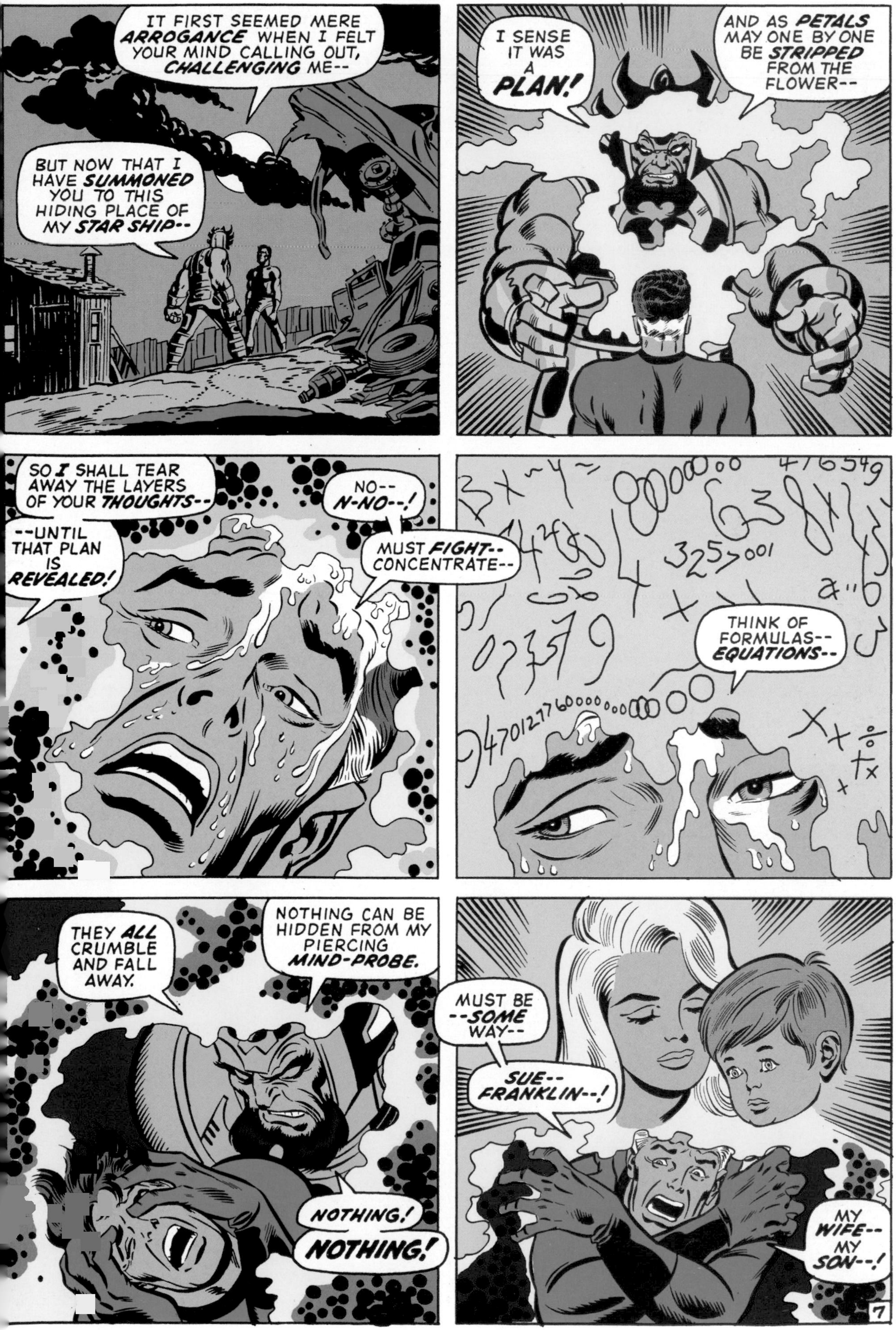
IT FIRST SEEMED MERE ARROGANCE WHEN I FELT YOUR MIND CALLING OUT, CHALLENGING ME--
BUT NOW THAT I HAVE SUMMONED YOU TO THIS HIDING PLACE OF MY STAR SHIP--
I SENSE IT WAS A PLAN!
AND AS PETALS MAY ONE BY ONE BE STRIPPED FROM THE FLOWER--
SO I SHALL TEAR AWAY THE LAYERS OF YOUR THOUGHTS--
--UNTIL THAT PLAN IS REVEALED!
NO-- N-NO--!
MUST FIGHT-- CONCENTRATE--
THINK OF FORMULAS-- EQUATIONS--
THEY ALL CRUMBLE AND FALL AWAY.
NOTHING CAN BE HIDDEN FROM MY PIERCING MIND-PROBE.
NOTHING! NOTHING!
MUST BE --SOME WAY--
SUE-- FRANKLIN--!
MY WIFE-- MY SON--!
7

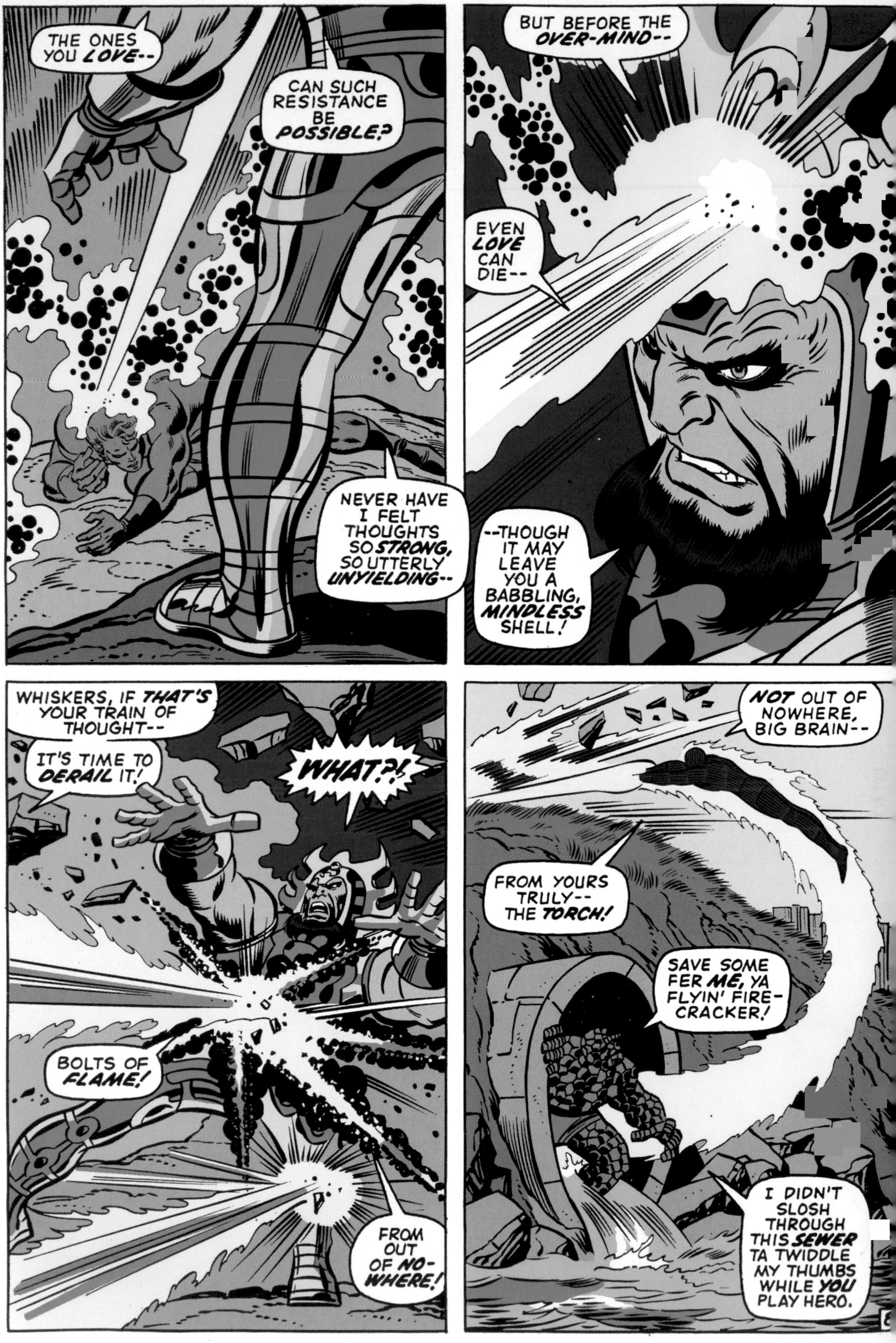
THE ONES YOU LOVE--
CAN SUCH RESISTANCE BE POSSIBLE?
NEVER HAVE I FELT THOUGHTS SO STRONG, SO UTTERLY UNYIELDING--
BUT BEFORE THE OVER-MIND--
EVEN LOVE CAN DIE--
--THOUGH IT MAY LEAVE YOU A BABBLING, MINDLESS SHELL!
WHISKERS, IF THAT'S YOUR TRAIN OF THOUGHT--
IT'S TIME TO DERAIL IT!
WHAT?!
BOLTS OF FLAME!
FROM OUT OF NO-WHERE!
NOT OUT OF NOWHERE, BIG BRAIN--
FROM YOURS TRULY-- THE TORCH!
SAVE SOME FER ME, YA FLYIN' FIRE-CRACKER!
I DIDN'T SLOSH THROUGH THIS SEWER TA TWIDDLE MY THUMBS WHILE YOU PLAY HERO.

THEN YOU BETTER **HURRY**, BIG BUDDY--

--'CAUSE I'M MAKIN' MY **MOVE**!

KRRAAK!

WADDA YA THINK **I'M** DOIN', GLORY-HOG?

IT IS NOT **GLORY** EITHER OF YOU WILL FIND IN **THIS** ENCOUNTER--

--BUT **DEFEAT**!

FOR, THE **PLAN** OF REED RICHARDS IS NOW **PLAIN** TO ME.

HE SUCCEEDED IN **RESISTING** MY POWER LONG ENOUGH FOR **YOU** TO FOLLOW ME HERE.

I WAS **CARELESS**, BUT STILL THE PLAN WILL **FAIL**--

UNGHH!

--AS WILL **YOU**!

MEBBE YA **KNOW** WHAT REED WUZ PLANNIN' AN' MEBBE YA **DON'T**, BUSHY-BROWS.

BUT IF **THAT** AN' TORCHY'S **FIREWORKS** AIN'T PANNIN' OUT--

IT'S TIME FER SOME **SERIOUS CLOBBERIN'**!

WHOM!

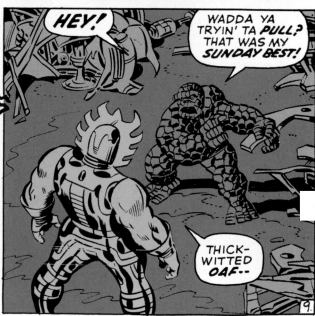

HEY!

WADDA YA TRYIN' TA **PULL**? THAT WAS MY **SUNDAY BEST**!

THICK-WITTED **OAF**--

137

DO YOU BELIEVE THE OVER-MIND'S *POWER* LIMITED TO HIS BRAIN *ALONE?*

WHEREVER YOU GET IT FROM, BUSTER-- IT TAKES *MORE* THAN A COUPL'A *SHOTS*--

--TO PUT THE *F.F.* OUT OF BUSINESS!

YOU *TELL* 'IM, KID.

BE RIGHT *WITH* YA--

SOON AS I DIG UP AN *ASPRIN!*

JOHNNY AND BEN HAVE *FOUND* THE OVER-MIND.

BUT HE SEEMS SO *POWERFUL*, SO *FORMIDABLE*--

THEY'RE *BARELY* HOLDING THEIR *OWN!*

I MUST *JOIN* THEM.

FOR, IF WE LOSE *THIS* BATTLE, *REED* --AND PERHAPS THE WHOLE *WORLD*--IS *LOST!*

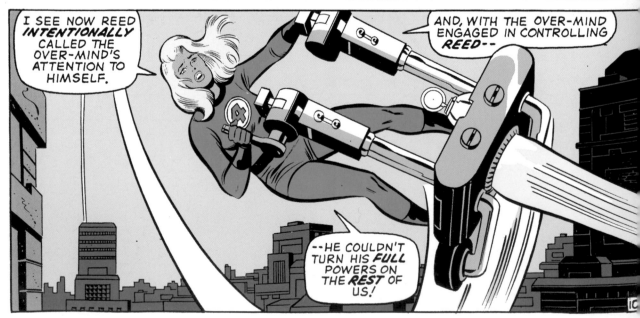

I SEE NOW REED *INTENTIONALLY* CALLED THE OVER-MIND'S ATTENTION TO HIMSELF.

AND, WITH THE OVER-MIND ENGAGED IN CONTROLLING *REED*--

--HE COULDN'T TURN HIS *FULL* POWERS ON THE *REST* OF US!

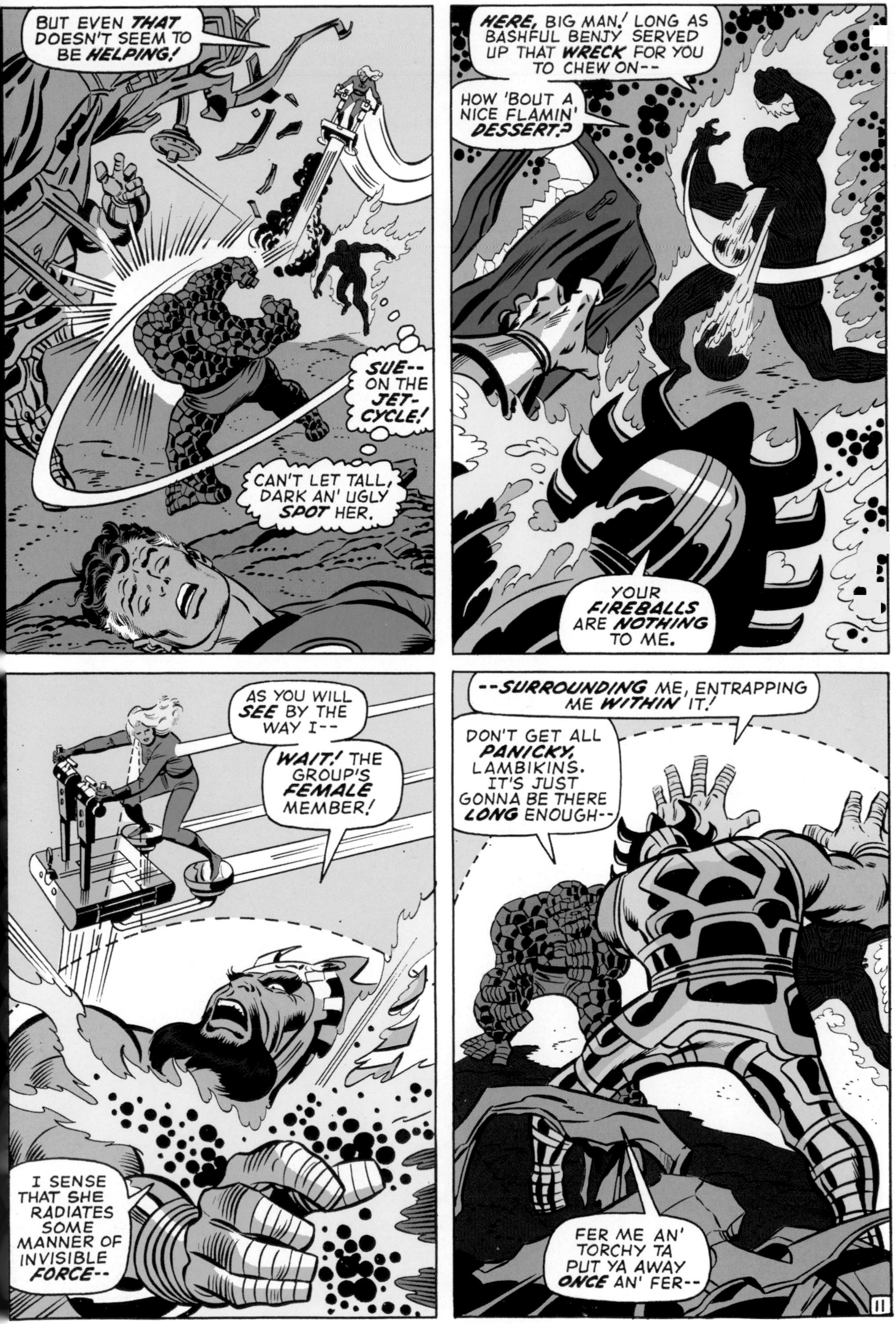

BUT EVEN THAT DOESN'T SEEM TO BE HELPING!
SUE-- ON THE JET-CYCLE!
CAN'T LET TALL, DARK AN' UGLY SPOT HER.
HERE, BIG MAN! LONG AS BASHFUL BENJY SERVED UP THAT WRECK FOR YOU TO CHEW ON--
HOW 'BOUT A NICE FLAMIN' DESSERT?
YOUR FIREBALLS ARE NOTHING TO ME.
AS YOU WILL SEE BY THE WAY I--
WAIT! THE GROUP'S FEMALE MEMBER!
I SENSE THAT SHE RADIATES SOME MANNER OF INVISIBLE FORCE--
--SURROUNDING ME, ENTRAPPING ME WITHIN IT!
DON'T GET ALL PANICKY, LAMBIKINS. IT'S JUST GONNA BE THERE LONG ENOUGH--
FER ME AN' TORCHY TA PUT YA AWAY ONCE AN' FER--
11

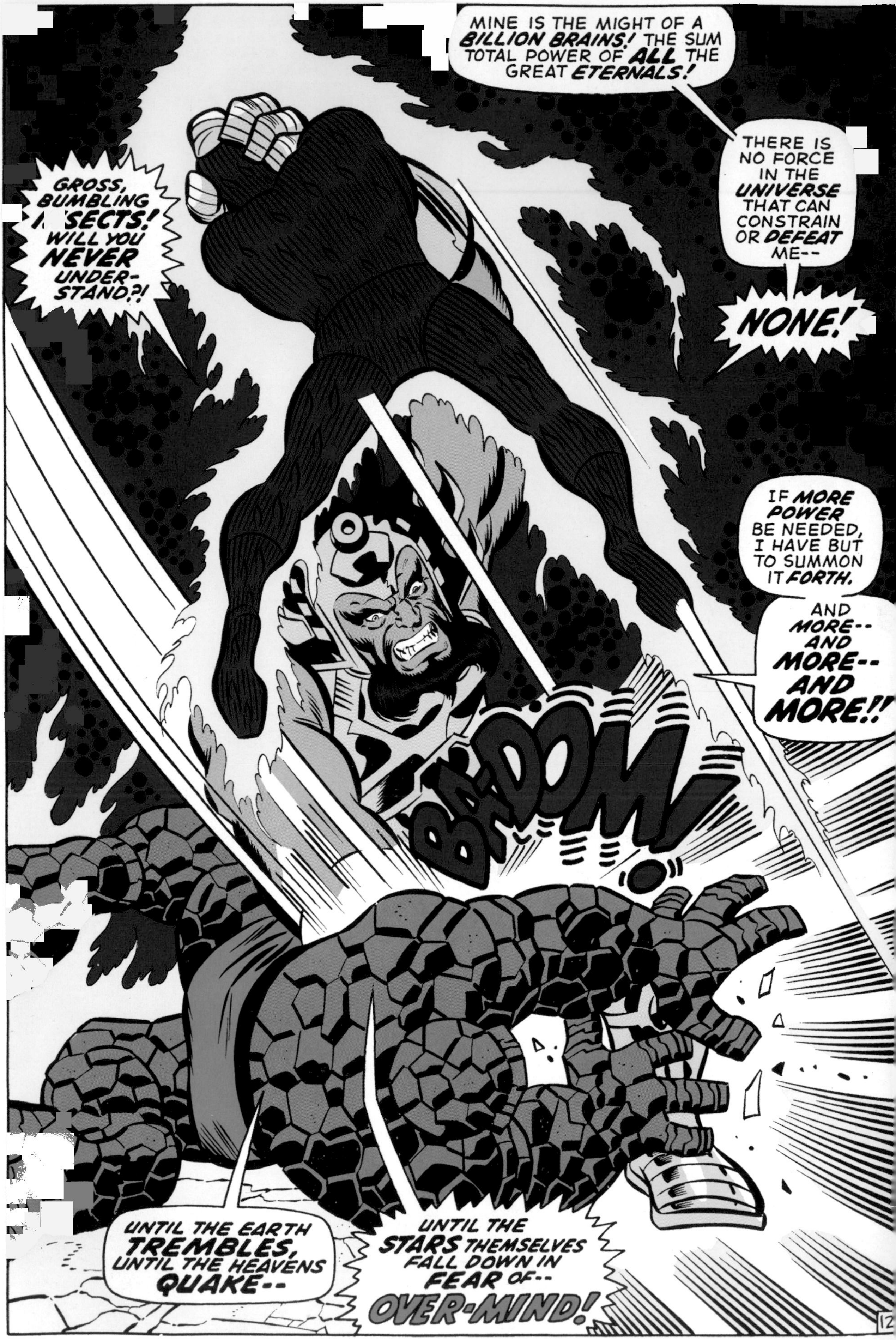
MINE IS THE MIGHT OF A BILLION BRAINS! THE SUM TOTAL POWER OF ALL THE GREAT ETERNALS!
THERE IS NO FORCE IN THE UNIVERSE THAT CAN CONSTRAIN OR DEFEAT ME--
NONE!
GROSS, BUMBLING INSECTS! WILL YOU NEVER UNDER-STAND?!
IF MORE POWER BE NEEDED, I HAVE BUT TO SUMMON IT FORTH.
AND MORE-- AND MORE-- AND MORE!!
BA-DOOM
UNTIL THE EARTH TREMBLES, UNTIL THE HEAVENS QUAKE--
UNTIL THE STARS THEMSELVES FALL DOWN IN FEAR OF--
OVER-MIND!
12

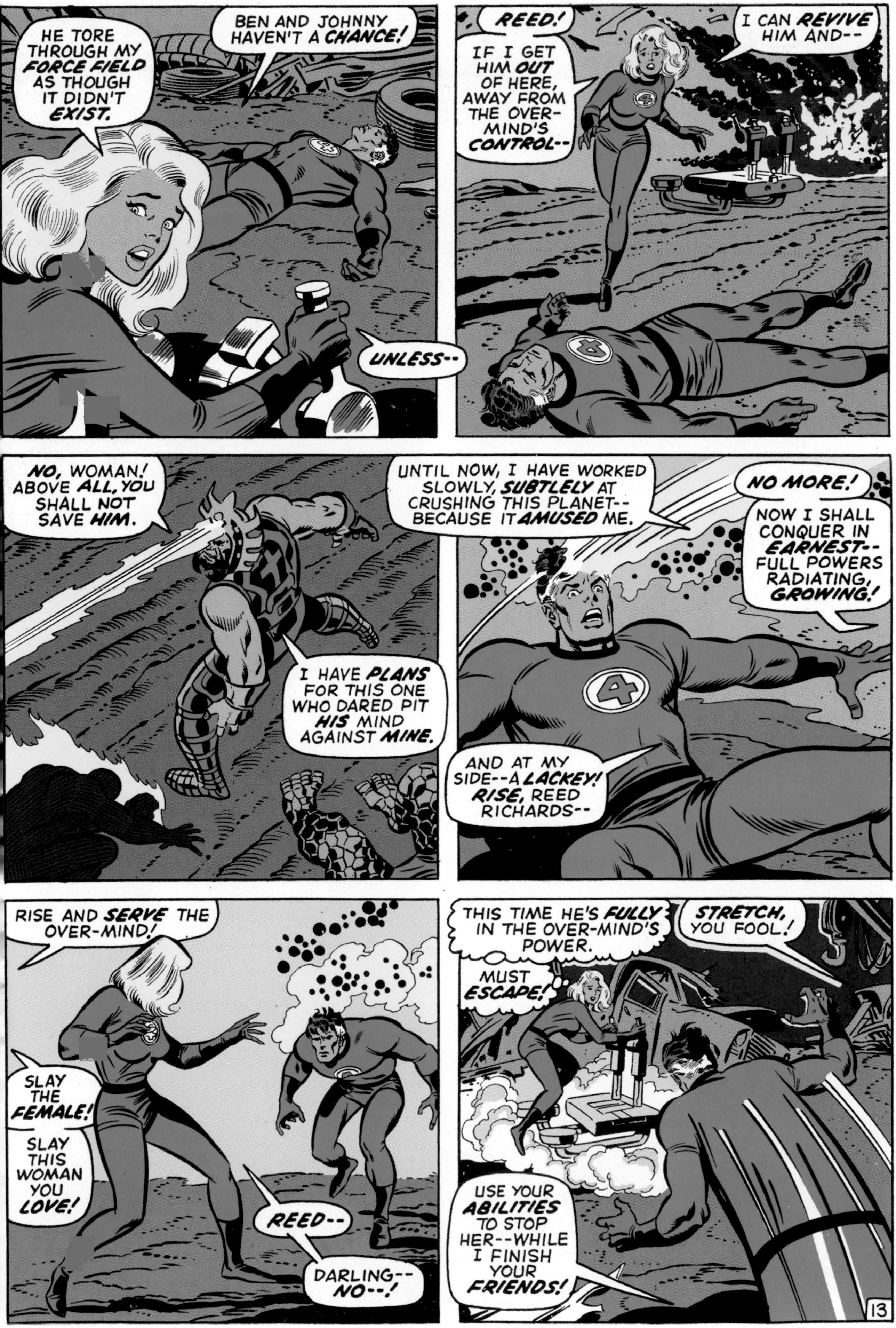

HE TORE THROUGH MY FORCE FIELD AS THOUGH IT DIDN'T EXIST.
BEN AND JOHNNY HAVEN'T A CHANCE!
UNLESS--
REED!
IF I GET HIM OUT OF HERE, AWAY FROM THE OVER-MIND'S CONTROL--
I CAN REVIVE HIM AND--
NO, WOMAN! ABOVE ALL, YOU SHALL NOT SAVE HIM.
I HAVE PLANS FOR THIS ONE WHO DARED PIT HIS MIND AGAINST MINE.
UNTIL NOW, I HAVE WORKED SLOWLY, SUBTLELY AT CRUSHING THIS PLANET-- BECAUSE IT AMUSED ME.
NO MORE!
NOW I SHALL CONQUER IN EARNEST-- FULL POWERS RADIATING, GROWING!
AND AT MY SIDE--A LACKEY! RISE, REED RICHARDS--
RISE AND SERVE THE OVER-MIND!
SLAY THE FEMALE!
SLAY THIS WOMAN YOU LOVE!
REED--
DARLING-- NO--!
THIS TIME HE'S FULLY IN THE OVER-MIND'S POWER.
MUST ESCAPE!
STRETCH, YOU FOOL!
USE YOUR ABILITIES TO STOP HER--WHILE I FINISH YOUR FRIENDS!
13

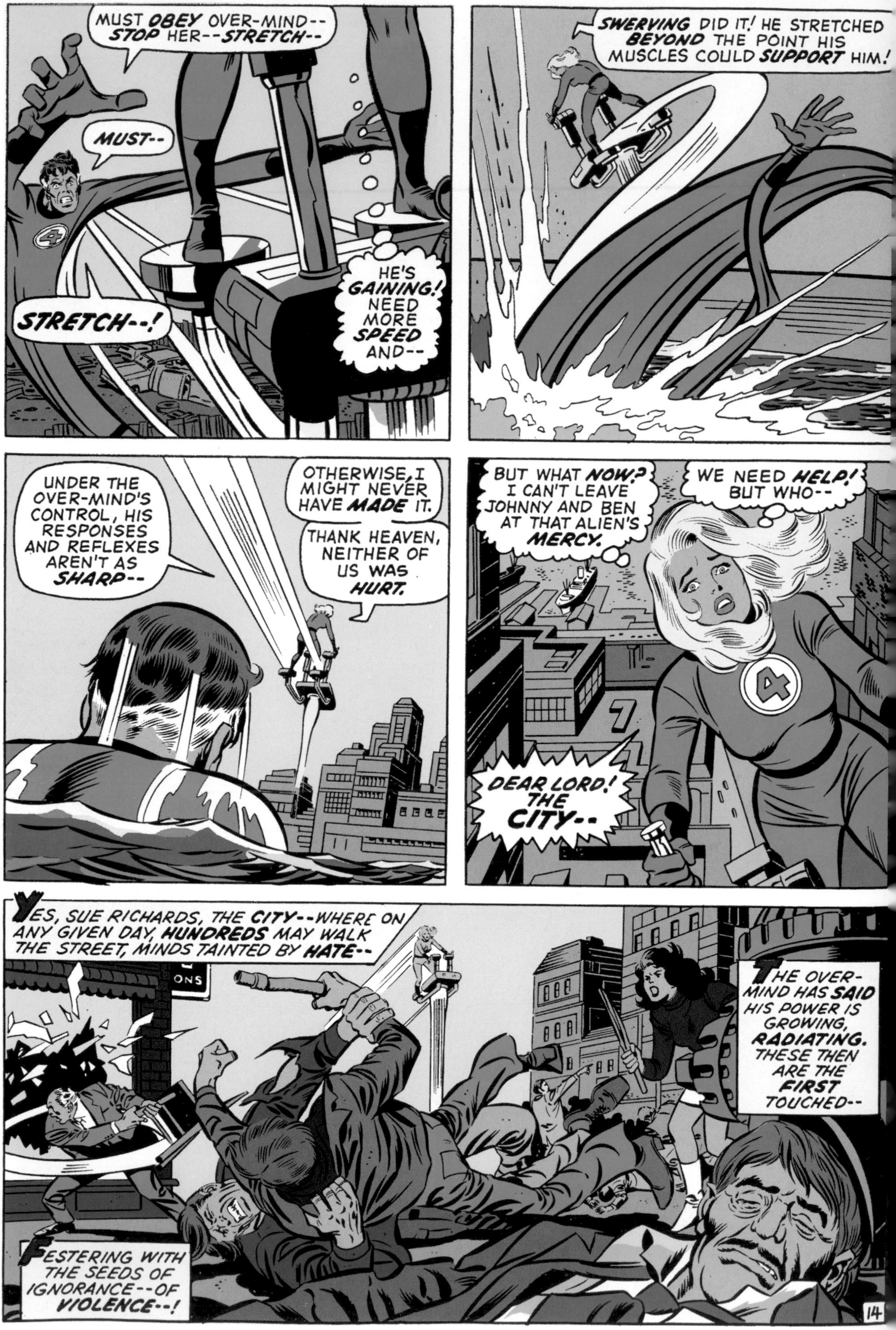

MUST OBEY OVER-MIND-- STOP HER--STRETCH--
MUST--
STRETCH--!
HE'S GAINING! NEED MORE SPEED AND--
SWERVING DID IT! HE STRETCHED BEYOND THE POINT HIS MUSCLES COULD SUPPORT HIM!
UNDER THE OVER-MIND'S CONTROL, HIS RESPONSES AND REFLEXES AREN'T AS SHARP--
OTHERWISE, I MIGHT NEVER HAVE MADE IT.
THANK HEAVEN, NEITHER OF US WAS HURT.
BUT WHAT NOW? I CAN'T LEAVE JOHNNY AND BEN AT THAT ALIEN'S MERCY.
WE NEED HELP! BUT WHO--
DEAR LORD! THE CITY--
YES, SUE RICHARDS, THE CITY--WHERE ON ANY GIVEN DAY, HUNDREDS MAY WALK THE STREET, MINDS TAINTED BY HATE--
THE OVER-MIND HAS SAID HIS POWER IS GROWING, RADIATING. THESE THEN ARE THE FIRST TOUCHED--
FESTERING WITH THE SEEDS OF IGNORANCE--OF VIOLENCE--!
14

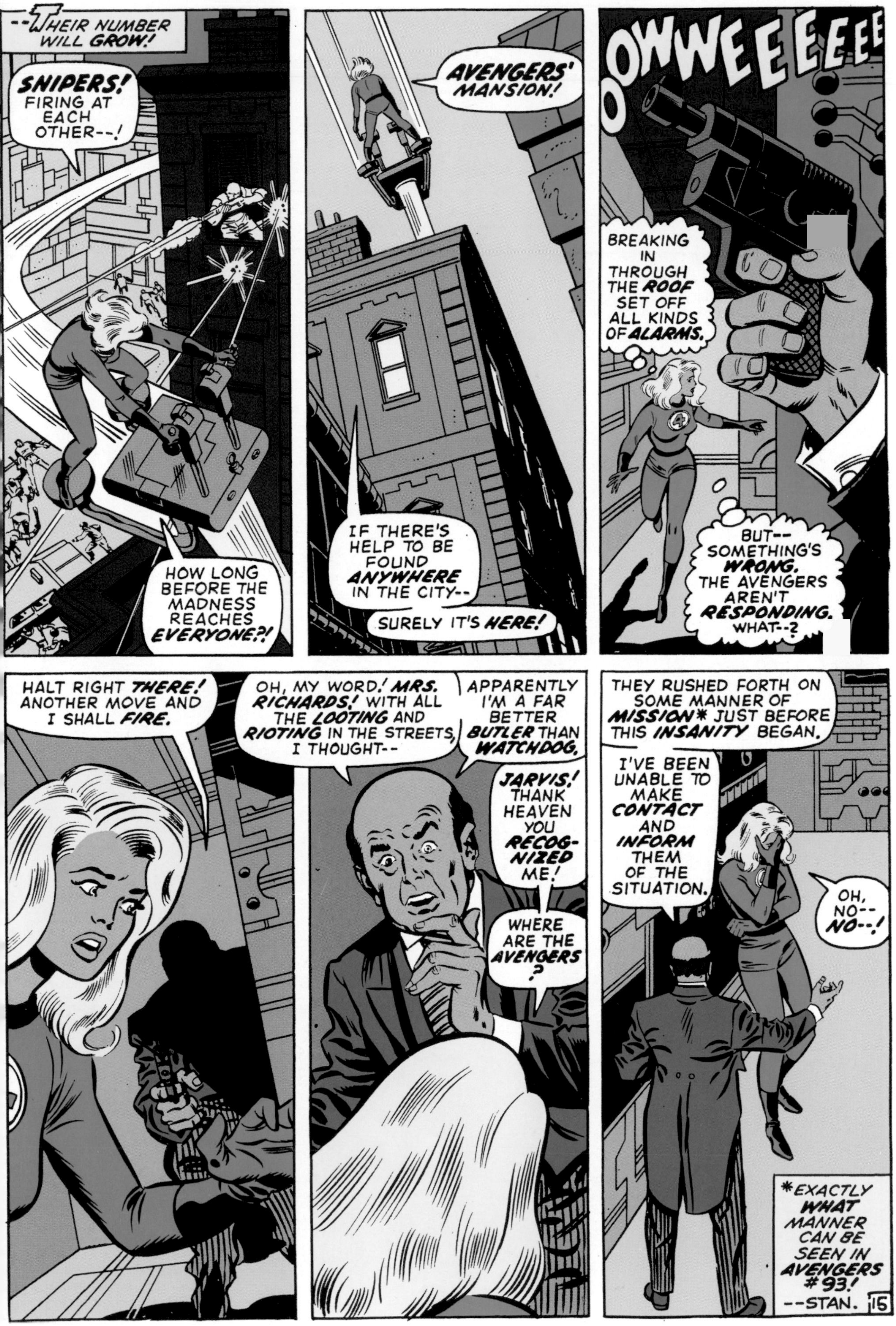
--THEIR NUMBER WILL GROW!
SNIPERS! FIRING AT EACH OTHER--!
HOW LONG BEFORE THE MADNESS REACHES EVERYONE?!
AVENGERS' MANSION!
IF THERE'S HELP TO BE FOUND ANYWHERE IN THE CITY--
SURELY IT'S HERE!
OOWWEEEEEE
BREAKING IN THROUGH THE ROOF SET OFF ALL KINDS OF ALARMS.
BUT--SOMETHING'S WRONG. THE AVENGERS AREN'T RESPONDING. WHAT--?
HALT RIGHT THERE! ANOTHER MOVE AND I SHALL FIRE.
OH, MY WORD! MRS. RICHARDS! WITH ALL THE LOOTING AND RIOTING IN THE STREETS, I THOUGHT--
APPARENTLY I'M A FAR BETTER BUTLER THAN WATCHDOG.
JARVIS! THANK HEAVEN YOU RECOGNIZED ME!
WHERE ARE THE AVENGERS?
THEY RUSHED FORTH ON SOME MANNER OF MISSION* JUST BEFORE THIS INSANITY BEGAN.
I'VE BEEN UNABLE TO MAKE CONTACT AND INFORM THEM OF THE SITUATION.
OH, NO--NO--!
*EXACTLY WHAT MANNER CAN BE SEEN IN AVENGERS #93! --STAN.
15

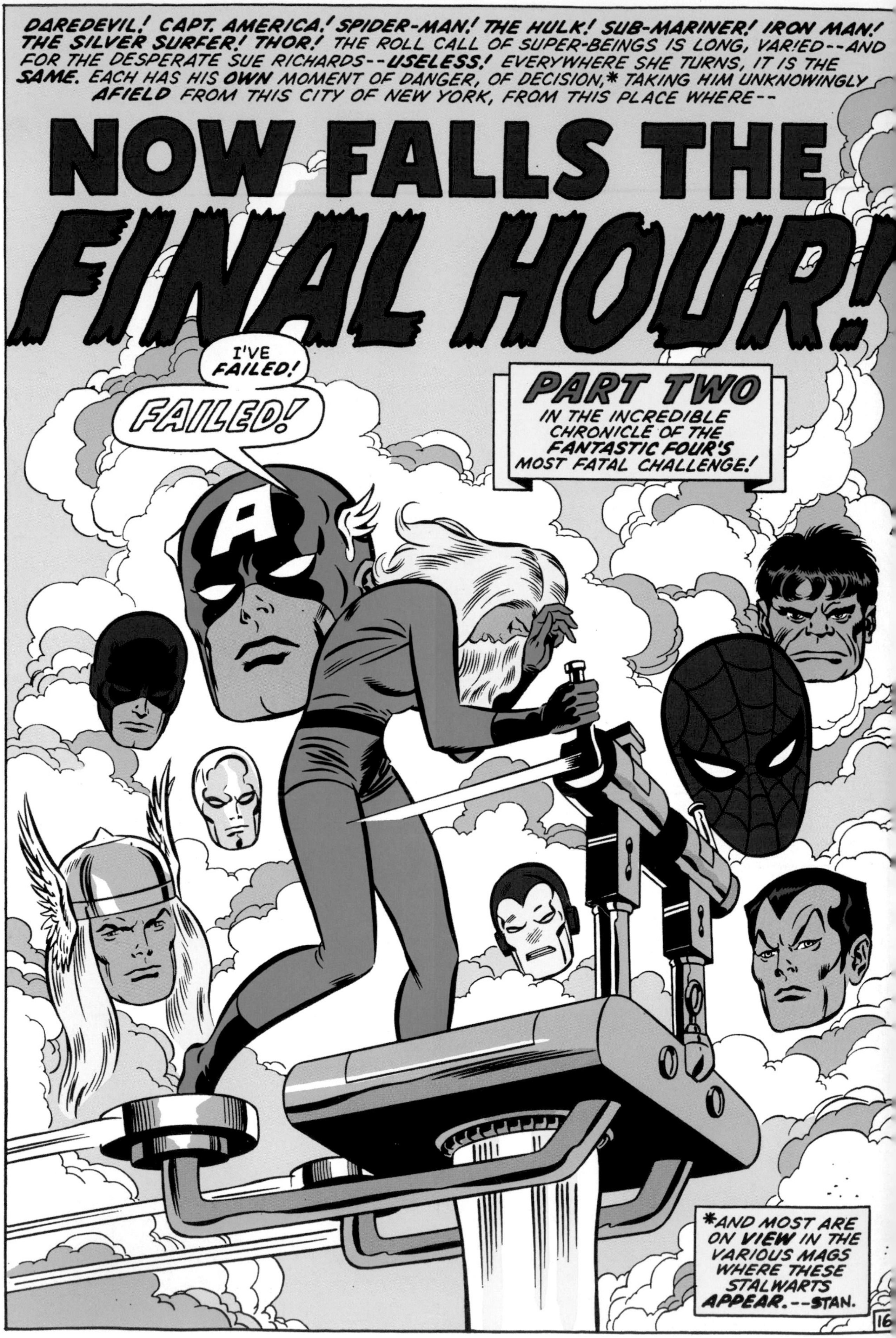
DAREDEVIL! CAPT. AMERICA! SPIDER-MAN! THE HULK! SUB-MARINER! IRON MAN! THE SILVER SURFER! THOR! THE ROLL CALL OF SUPER-BEINGS IS LONG, VARIED--AND FOR THE DESPERATE SUE RICHARDS--USELESS! EVERYWHERE SHE TURNS, IT IS THE SAME. EACH HAS HIS OWN MOMENT OF DANGER, OF DECISION,* TAKING HIM UNKNOWINGLY AFIELD FROM THIS CITY OF NEW YORK, FROM THIS PLACE WHERE--
NOW FALLS THE FINAL HOUR!
I'VE FAILED!
FAILED!
PART TWO IN THE INCREDIBLE CHRONICLE OF THE FANTASTIC FOUR'S MOST FATAL CHALLENGE!
*AND MOST ARE ON VIEW IN THE VARIOUS MAGS WHERE THESE STALWARTS APPEAR.--STAN.
16

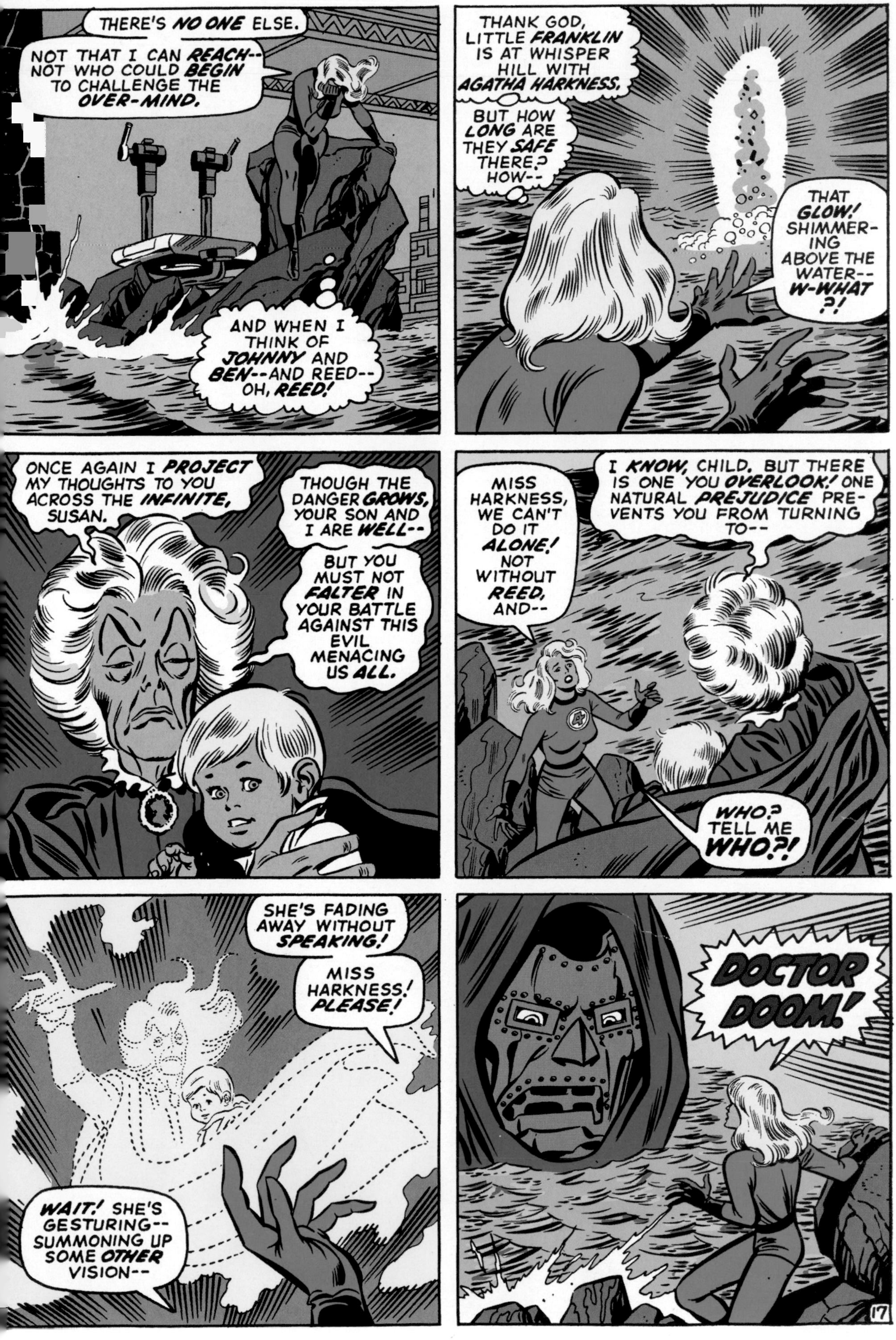
THERE'S NO ONE ELSE.
NOT THAT I CAN REACH-- NOT WHO COULD BEGIN TO CHALLENGE THE OVER-MIND.
AND WHEN I THINK OF JOHNNY AND BEN--AND REED-- OH, REED!
THANK GOD, LITTLE FRANKLIN IS AT WHISPER HILL WITH AGATHA HARKNESS.
BUT HOW LONG ARE THEY SAFE THERE? HOW--
THAT GLOW! SHIMMERING ABOVE THE WATER-- W-WHAT ?!
ONCE AGAIN I PROJECT MY THOUGHTS TO YOU ACROSS THE INFINITE, SUSAN.
THOUGH THE DANGER GROWS, YOUR SON AND I ARE WELL--
BUT YOU MUST NOT FALTER IN YOUR BATTLE AGAINST THIS EVIL MENACING US ALL.
MISS HARKNESS, WE CAN'T DO IT ALONE! NOT WITHOUT REED, AND--
I KNOW, CHILD. BUT THERE IS ONE YOU OVERLOOK! ONE NATURAL PREJUDICE PREVENTS YOU FROM TURNING TO--
WHO? TELL ME WHO?!
SHE'S FADING AWAY WITHOUT SPEAKING!
MISS HARKNESS! PLEASE!
WAIT! SHE'S GESTURING-- SUMMONING UP SOME OTHER VISION--
DOCTOR DOOM!
17

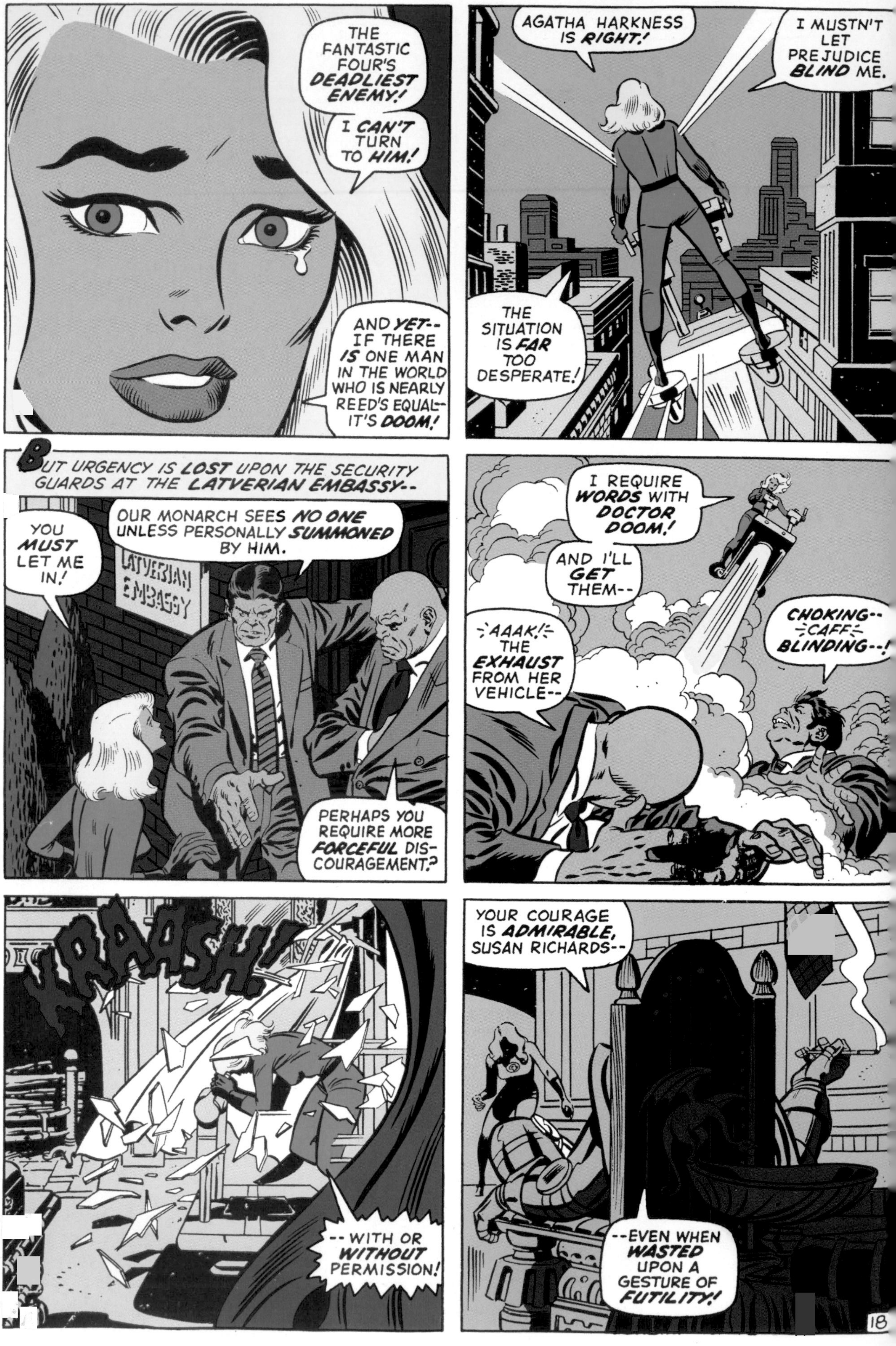
THE FANTASTIC FOUR'S DEADLIEST ENEMY!
I CAN'T TURN TO HIM!
AND YET-- IF THERE IS ONE MAN IN THE WORLD WHO IS NEARLY REED'S EQUAL-- IT'S DOOM!
AGATHA HARKNESS IS RIGHT!
I MUSTN'T LET PREJUDICE BLIND ME.
THE SITUATION IS FAR TOO DESPERATE!
BUT URGENCY IS LOST UPON THE SECURITY GUARDS AT THE LATVERIAN EMBASSY--
YOU MUST LET ME IN!
OUR MONARCH SEES NO ONE UNLESS PERSONALLY SUMMONED BY HIM.
LATVERIAN EMBASSY
PERHAPS YOU REQUIRE MORE FORCEFUL DISCOURAGEMENT?
I REQUIRE WORDS WITH DOCTOR DOOM!
AND I'LL GET THEM--
AAAK! THE EXHAUST FROM HER VEHICLE--
CHOKING-- CAFF BLINDING--!
KRAASH!
--WITH OR WITHOUT PERMISSION!
YOUR COURAGE IS ADMIRABLE, SUSAN RICHARDS--
--EVEN WHEN WASTED UPON A GESTURE OF FUTILITY!
18

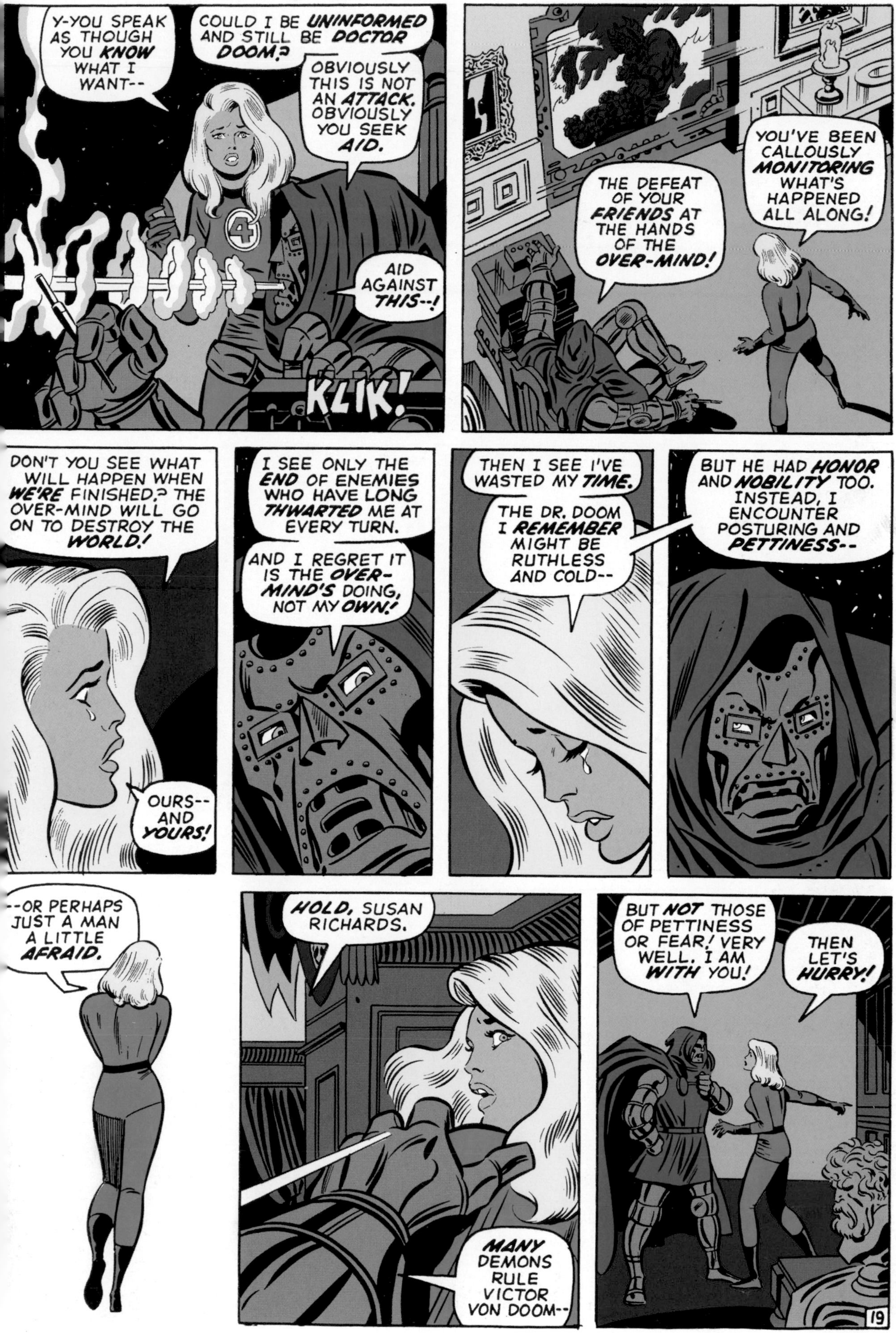
Y-YOU SPEAK AS THOUGH YOU KNOW WHAT I WANT--
COULD I BE UNINFORMED AND STILL BE DOCTOR DOOM?
OBVIOUSLY THIS IS NOT AN ATTACK. OBVIOUSLY YOU SEEK AID.
AID AGAINST THIS--!
KLIK!
YOU'VE BEEN CALLOUSLY MONITORING WHAT'S HAPPENED ALL ALONG!
THE DEFEAT OF YOUR FRIENDS AT THE HANDS OF THE OVER-MIND!
DON'T YOU SEE WHAT WILL HAPPEN WHEN WE'RE FINISHED? THE OVER-MIND WILL GO ON TO DESTROY THE WORLD!
OURS-- AND YOURS!
I SEE ONLY THE END OF ENEMIES WHO HAVE LONG THWARTED ME AT EVERY TURN.
AND I REGRET IT IS THE OVER-MIND'S DOING, NOT MY OWN!
THEN I SEE I'VE WASTED MY TIME.
THE DR. DOOM I REMEMBER MIGHT BE RUTHLESS AND COLD--
BUT HE HAD HONOR AND NOBILITY TOO. INSTEAD, I ENCOUNTER POSTURING AND PETTINESS--
--OR PERHAPS JUST A MAN A LITTLE AFRAID.
HOLD, SUSAN RICHARDS.
MANY DEMONS RULE VICTOR VON DOOM--
BUT NOT THOSE OF PETTINESS OR FEAR! VERY WELL. I AM WITH YOU!
THEN LET'S HURRY!
19

THE JET CYCLE IS THE *FASTEST* WAY TO BEN AND JOHNNY.!

NO! *FIRST* TO THE LABORATORY OF REED RICHARDS--!

"IF STRENGTH OR NUMBERS *ALONE* MATTERED AGAINST THE *OVER-MIND*--

"--YOUR COMRADES WOULD NOT NOW BE FALLING *BEFORE* HIM.!"

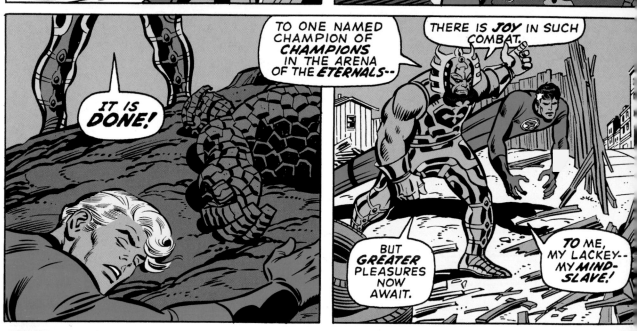

IT IS DONE!

TO ONE NAMED CHAMPION OF *CHAMPIONS* IN THE ARENA OF THE *ETERNALS*--

THERE IS *JOY* IN SUCH COMBAT.

BUT *GREATER* PLEASURES NOW AWAIT.

TO ME, MY LACKEY-- MY *MIND-SLAVE!*

THERE IS A *CITY* TO BE *CRUSHED*--

THERE IS A *WORLD* FOR THE *CONQUERING!*

20

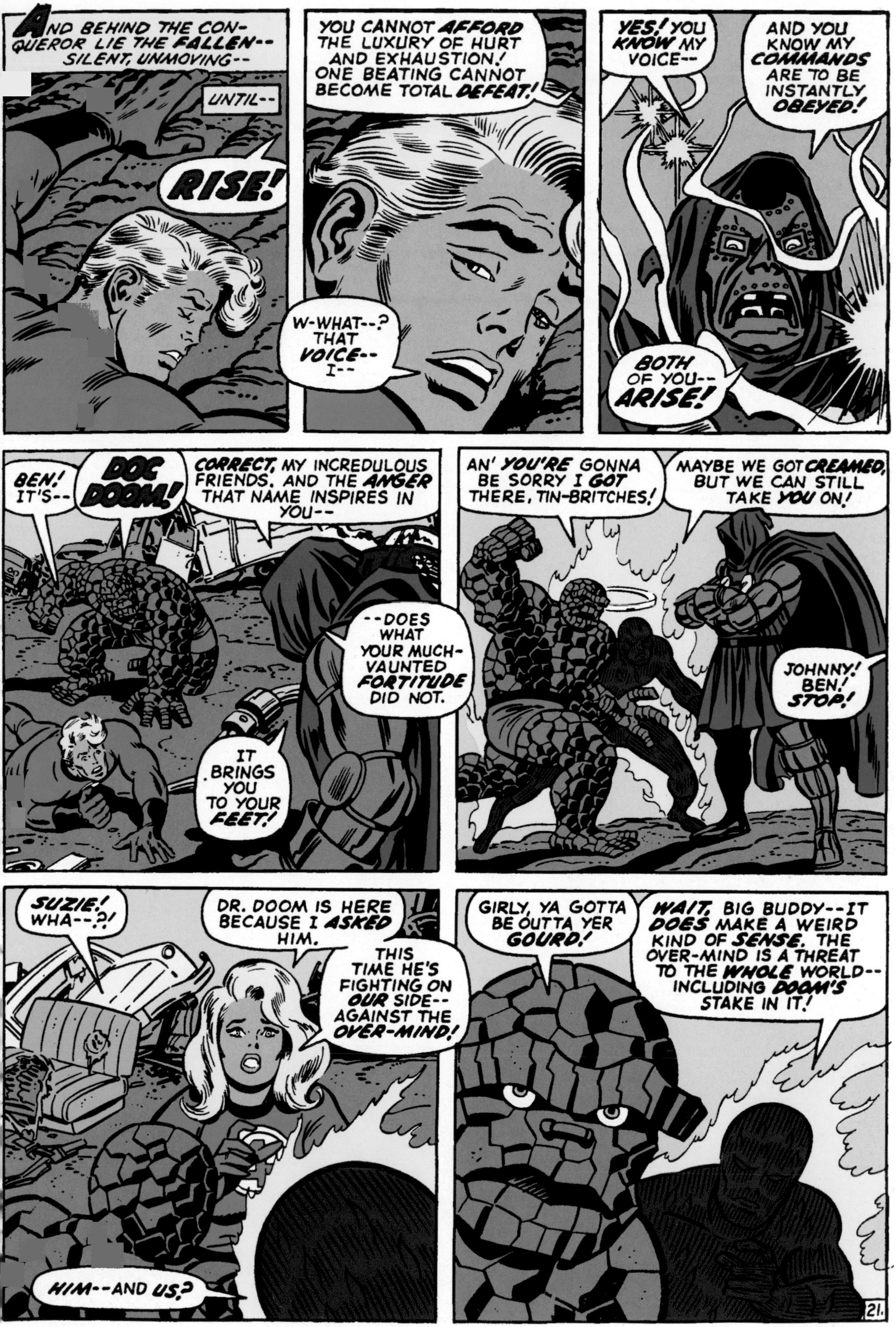
AND BEHIND THE CONQUEROR LIE THE FALLEN-- SILENT, UNMOVING--
UNTIL--
RISE!
YOU CANNOT AFFORD THE LUXURY OF HURT AND EXHAUSTION! ONE BEATING CANNOT BECOME TOTAL DEFEAT!
W-WHAT--? THAT VOICE-- I--
YES! YOU KNOW MY VOICE--
AND YOU KNOW MY COMMANDS ARE TO BE INSTANTLY OBEYED!
BOTH OF YOU-- ARISE!
BEN! IT'S--
DOC DOOM!
CORRECT, MY INCREDULOUS FRIENDS. AND THE ANGER THAT NAME INSPIRES IN YOU--
--DOES WHAT YOUR MUCH-VAUNTED FORTITUDE DID NOT.
IT BRINGS YOU TO YOUR FEET!
AN' YOU'RE GONNA BE SORRY I GOT THERE, TIN-BRITCHES!
MAYBE WE GOT CREAMED, BUT WE CAN STILL TAKE YOU ON!
JOHNNY! BEN! STOP!
SUZIE! WHA--?!
DR. DOOM IS HERE BECAUSE I ASKED HIM.
THIS TIME HE'S FIGHTING ON OUR SIDE-- AGAINST THE OVER-MIND!
HIM--AND US?
GIRLY, YA GOTTA BE OUTTA YER GOURD!
WAIT, BIG BUDDY--IT DOES MAKE A WEIRD KIND OF SENSE. THE OVER-MIND IS A THREAT TO THE WHOLE WORLD-- INCLUDING DOOM'S STAKE IN IT!
21.

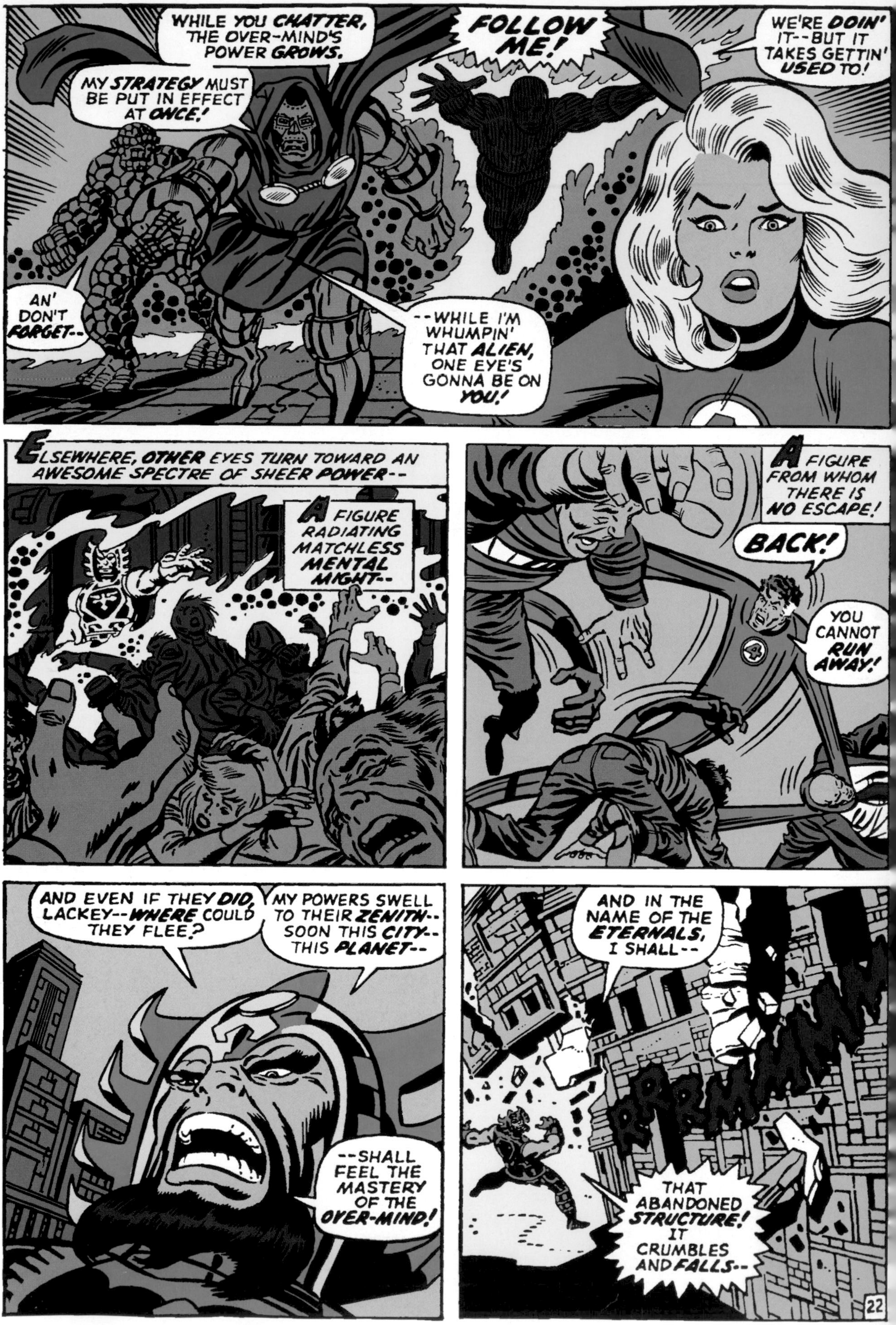
WHILE YOU CHATTER, THE OVER-MIND'S POWER GROWS.
MY STRATEGY MUST BE PUT IN EFFECT AT ONCE!
FOLLOW ME!
WE'RE DOIN' IT--BUT IT TAKES GETTIN' USED TO!
AN' DON'T FORGET--
--WHILE I'M WHUMPIN' THAT ALIEN, ONE EYE'S GONNA BE ON YOU!
ELSEWHERE, OTHER EYES TURN TOWARD AN AWESOME SPECTRE OF SHEER POWER--
A FIGURE RADIATING MATCHLESS MENTAL MIGHT--
A FIGURE FROM WHOM THERE IS NO ESCAPE!
BACK!
YOU CANNOT RUN AWAY!
AND EVEN IF THEY DID, LACKEY--WHERE COULD THEY FLEE?
MY POWERS SWELL TO THEIR ZENITH--SOON THIS CITY--THIS PLANET--
--SHALL FEEL THE MASTERY OF THE OVER-MIND!
AND IN THE NAME OF THE ETERNALS, I SHALL--
RRRMMMM
THAT ABANDONED STRUCTURE! IT CRUMBLES AND FALLS--
22

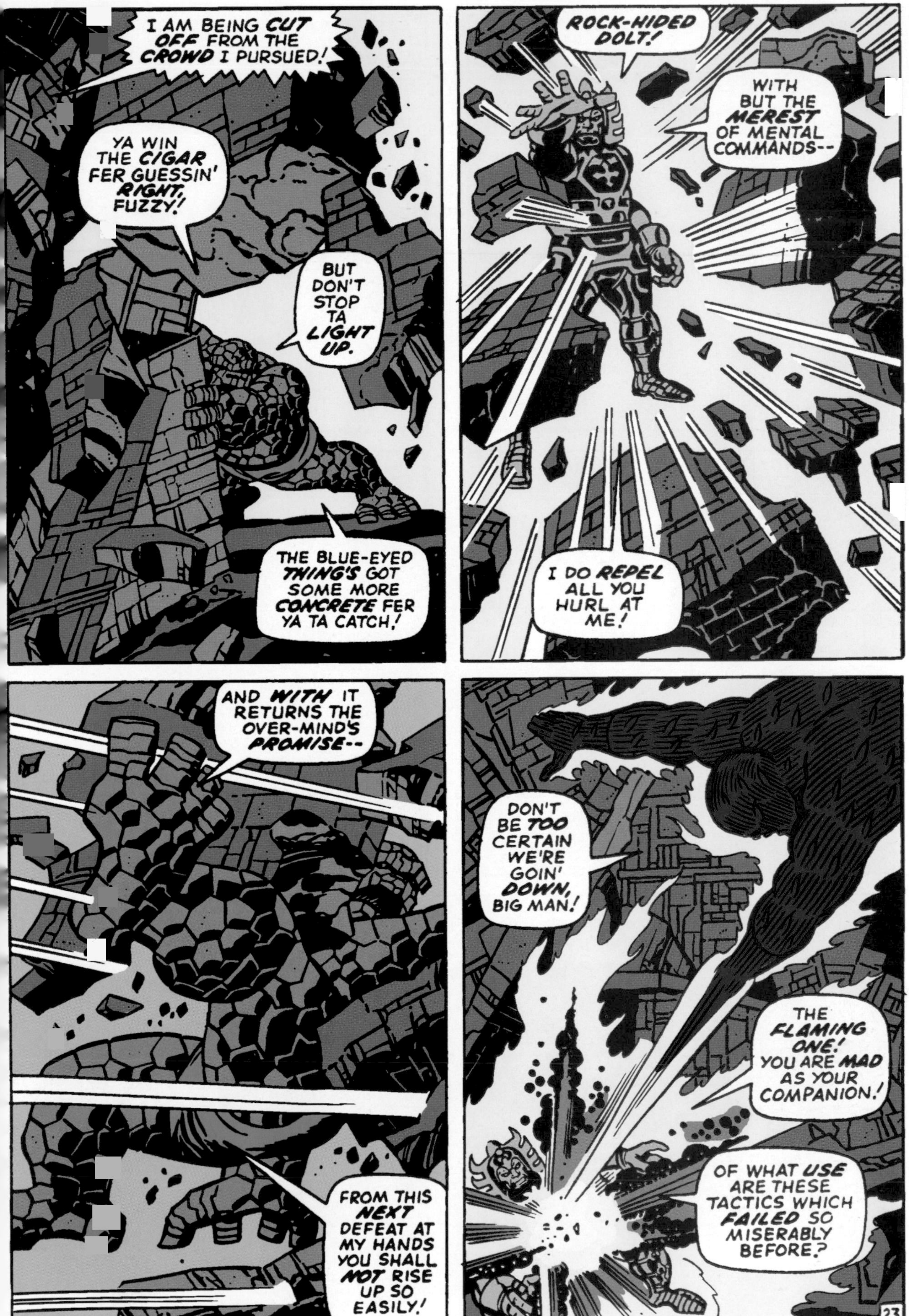
I AM BEING CUT OFF FROM THE CROWD I PURSUED!
YA WIN THE CIGAR FER GUESSIN' RIGHT, FUZZY!
BUT DON'T STOP TA LIGHT UP.
THE BLUE-EYED THING'S GOT SOME MORE CONCRETE FER YA TA CATCH!
ROCK-HIDED DOLT!
WITH BUT THE MEREST OF MENTAL COMMANDS--
I DO REPEL ALL YOU HURL AT ME!
AND WITH IT RETURNS THE OVER-MIND'S PROMISE--
FROM THIS NEXT DEFEAT AT MY HANDS YOU SHALL NOT RISE UP SO EASILY!
DON'T BE TOO CERTAIN WE'RE GOIN' DOWN, BIG MAN!
THE FLAMING ONE! YOU ARE MAD AS YOUR COMPANION!
OF WHAT USE ARE THESE TACTICS WHICH FAILED SO MISERABLY BEFORE?
23

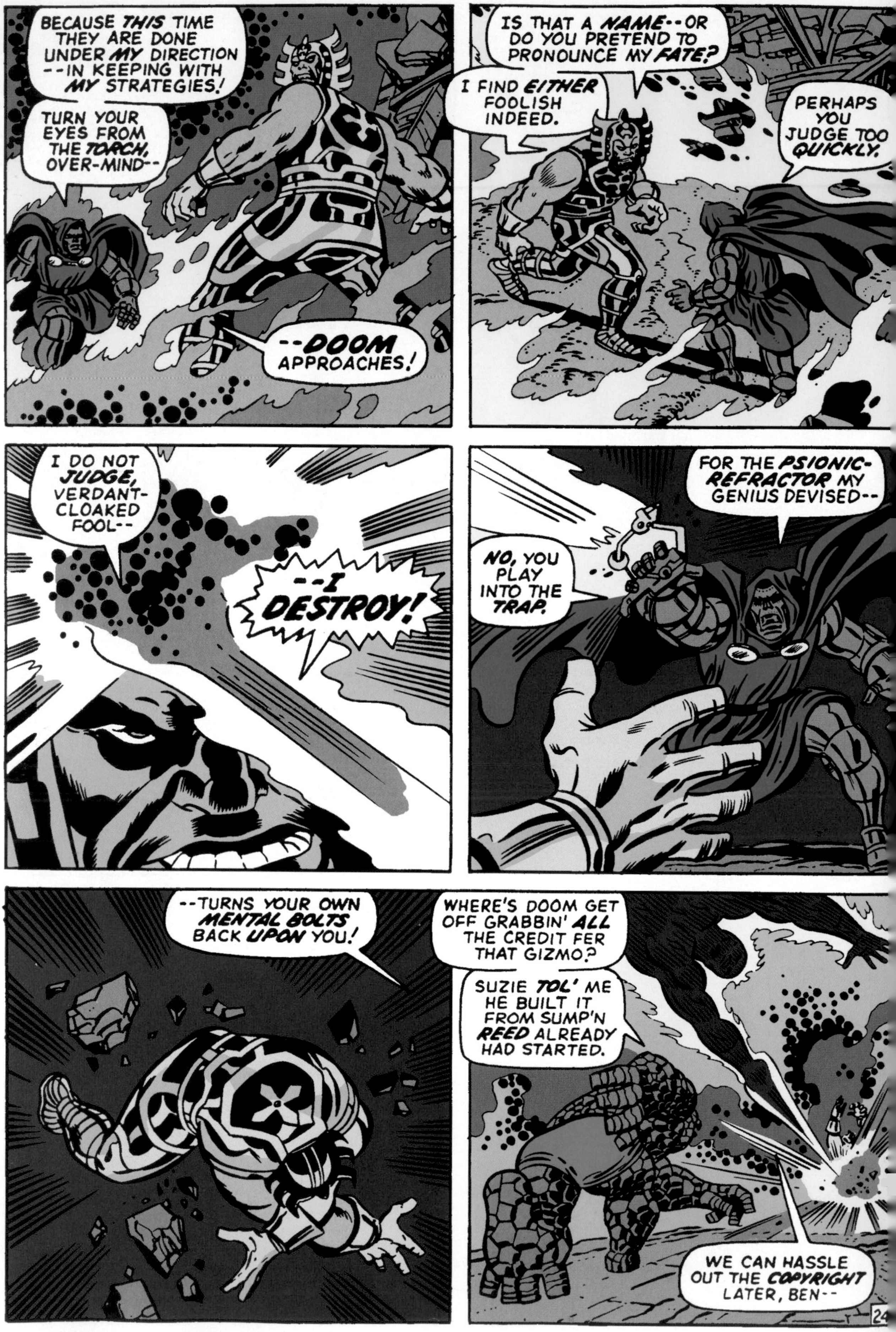
BECAUSE THIS TIME THEY ARE DONE UNDER MY DIRECTION --IN KEEPING WITH MY STRATEGIES!
TURN YOUR EYES FROM THE TORCH, OVER-MIND--
--DOOM APPROACHES!
IS THAT A NAME--OR DO YOU PRETEND TO PRONOUNCE MY FATE?
I FIND EITHER FOOLISH INDEED.
PERHAPS YOU JUDGE TOO QUICKLY.
I DO NOT JUDGE, VERDANT-CLOAKED FOOL--
--I DESTROY!
FOR THE PSIONIC-REFRACTOR MY GENIUS DEVISED--
NO, YOU PLAY INTO THE TRAP.
--TURNS YOUR OWN MENTAL BOLTS BACK UPON YOU!
WHERE'S DOOM GET OFF GRABBIN' ALL THE CREDIT FER THAT GIZMO?
SUZIE TOL' ME HE BUILT IT FROM SUMP'N REED ALREADY HAD STARTED.
WE CAN HASSLE OUT THE COPYRIGHT LATER, BEN--
24

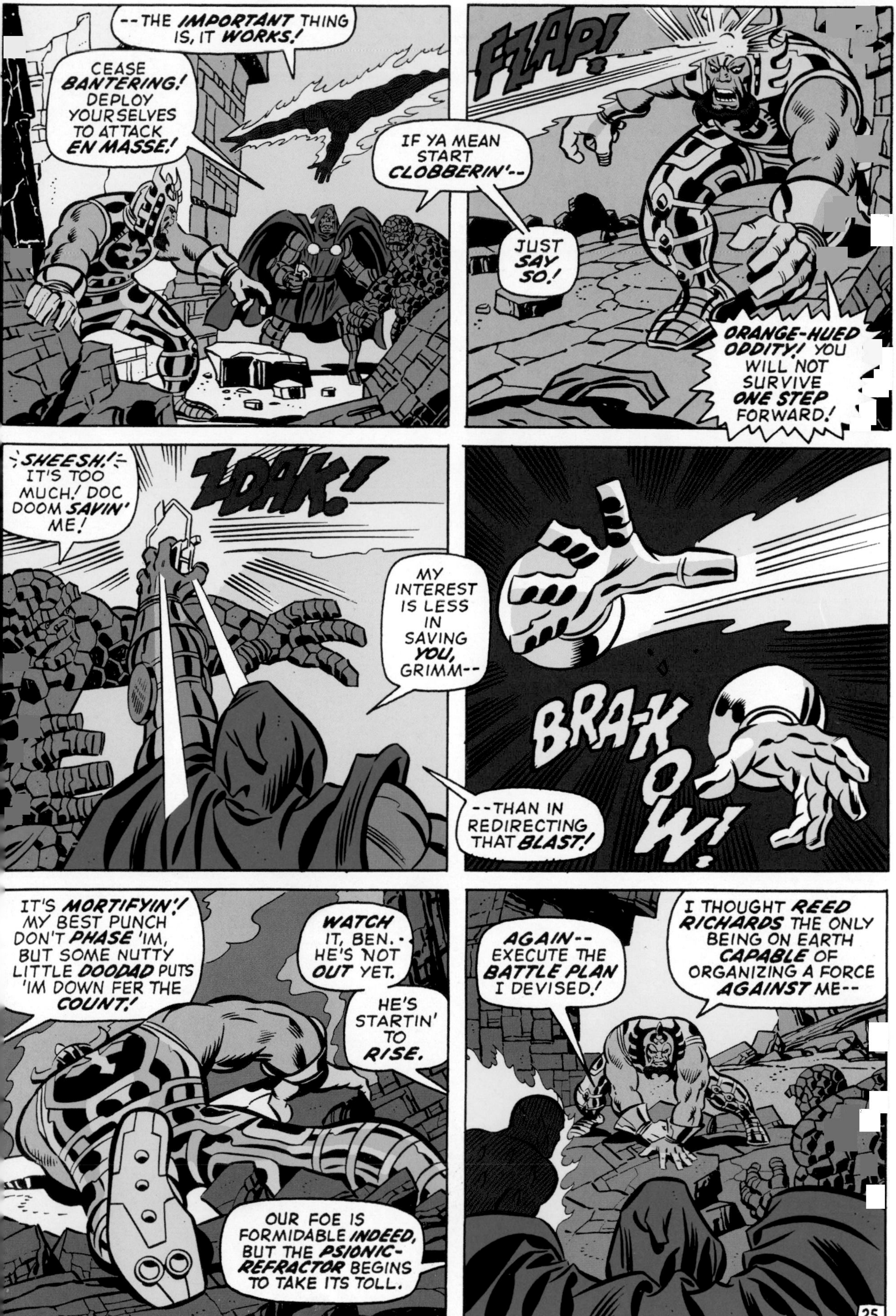
--THE IMPORTANT THING IS, IT WORKS!
CEASE BANTERING! DEPLOY YOURSELVES TO ATTACK EN MASSE!
IF YA MEAN START CLOBBERIN'--
JUST SAY SO!
FZAP!
ORANGE-HUED ODDITY! YOU WILL NOT SURVIVE ONE STEP FORWARD!
-SHEESH!- IT'S TOO MUCH! DOC DOOM SAVIN' ME!
ZDAK!
MY INTEREST IS LESS IN SAVING YOU, GRIMM--
--THAN IN REDIRECTING THAT BLAST!
BRA-KOW!
IT'S MORTIFYIN'! MY BEST PUNCH DON'T PHASE 'IM, BUT SOME NUTTY LITTLE DOODAD PUTS 'IM DOWN FER THE COUNT!
WATCH IT, BEN. HE'S NOT OUT YET.
HE'S STARTIN' TO RISE.
OUR FOE IS FORMIDABLE INDEED, BUT THE PSIONIC-REFRACTOR BEGINS TO TAKE ITS TOLL.
AGAIN-- EXECUTE THE BATTLE PLAN I DEVISED!
I THOUGHT REED RICHARDS THE ONLY BEING ON EARTH CAPABLE OF ORGANIZING A FORCE AGAINST ME--
25

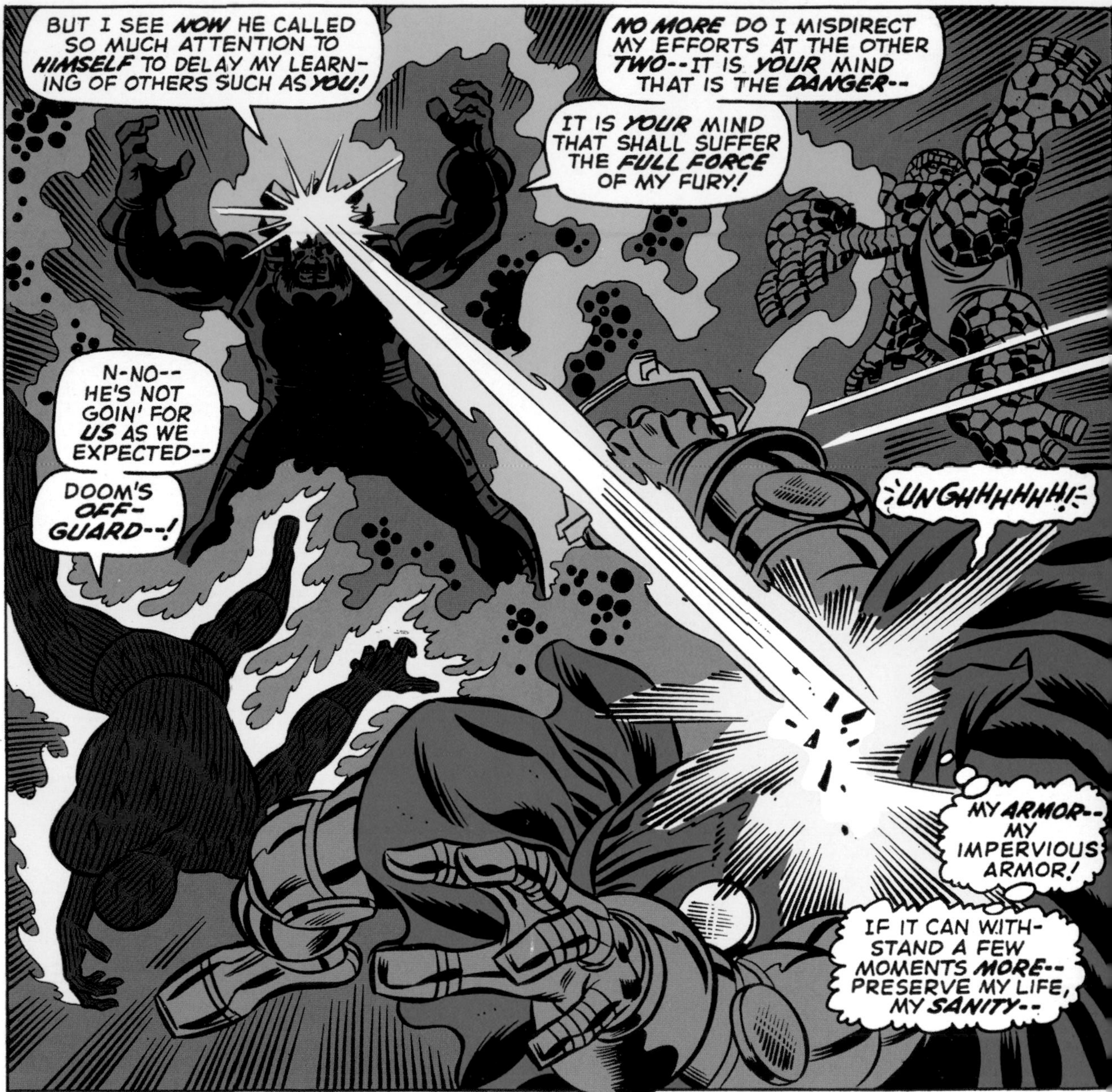
BUT I SEE NOW HE CALLED SO MUCH ATTENTION TO HIMSELF TO DELAY MY LEARNING OF OTHERS SUCH AS YOU!
NO MORE DO I MISDIRECT MY EFFORTS AT THE OTHER TWO--IT IS YOUR MIND THAT IS THE DANGER--
IT IS YOUR MIND THAT SHALL SUFFER THE FULL FORCE OF MY FURY!
N-NO-- HE'S NOT GOIN' FOR US AS WE EXPECTED--
DOOM'S OFF-GUARD--!
UNGHHHHHH!
MY ARMOR-- MY IMPERVIOUS ARMOR!
IF IT CAN WITHSTAND A FEW MOMENTS MORE-- PRESERVE MY LIFE, MY SANITY--
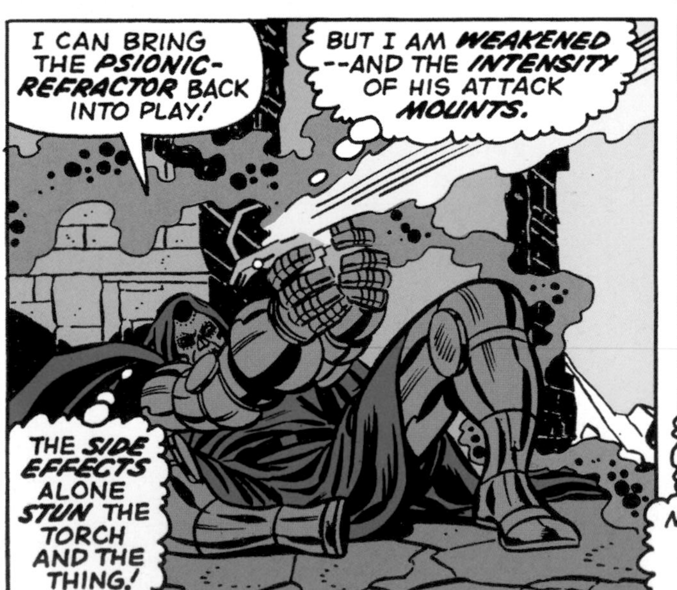
I CAN BRING THE PSIONIC-REFRACTOR BACK INTO PLAY!
BUT I AM WEAKENED --AND THE INTENSITY OF HIS ATTACK MOUNTS.
THE SIDE EFFECTS ALONE STUN THE TORCH AND THE THING!
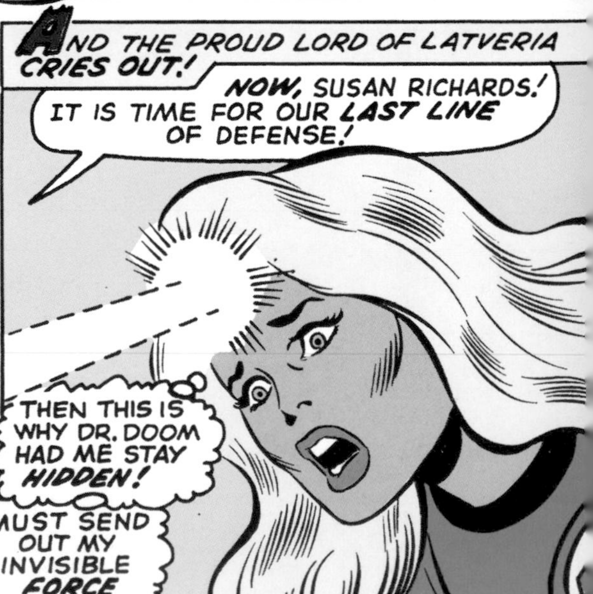
AND THE PROUD LORD OF LATVERIA CRIES OUT!
NOW, SUSAN RICHARDS! IT IS TIME FOR OUR LAST LINE OF DEFENSE!
THEN THIS IS WHY DR. DOOM HAD ME STAY HIDDEN!
MUST SEND OUT MY INVISIBLE FORCE FIELD--

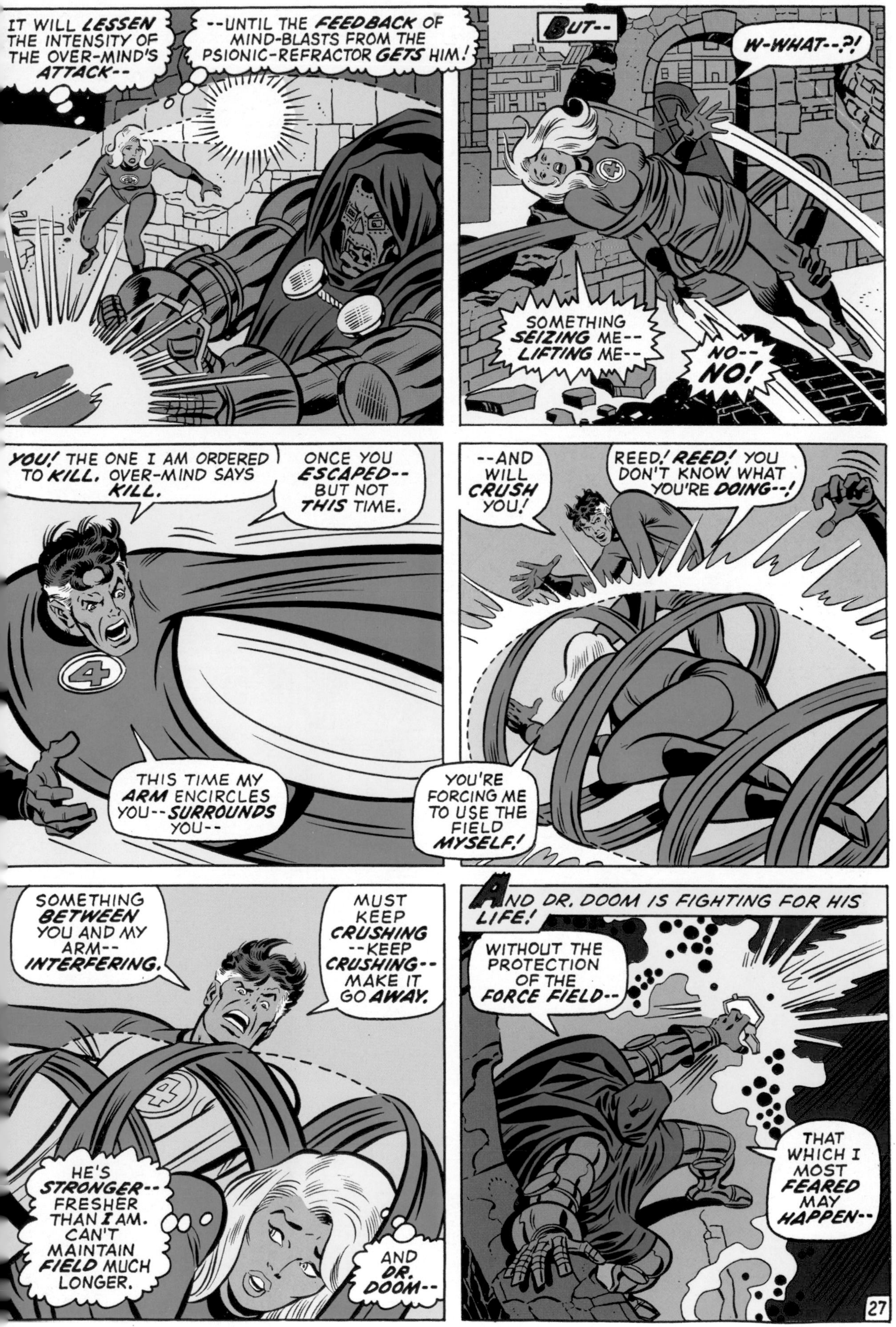
IT WILL LESSEN THE INTENSITY OF THE OVER-MIND'S ATTACK--
--UNTIL THE FEEDBACK OF MIND-BLASTS FROM THE PSIONIC-REFRACTOR GETS HIM!
BUT--
W-WHAT--?!
SOMETHING SEIZING ME-- LIFTING ME--
NO-- NO!
YOU! THE ONE I AM ORDERED TO KILL. OVER-MIND SAYS KILL.
ONCE YOU ESCAPED-- BUT NOT THIS TIME.
THIS TIME MY ARM ENCIRCLES YOU--SURROUNDS YOU--
--AND WILL CRUSH YOU!
REED! REED! YOU DON'T KNOW WHAT YOU'RE DOING--!
YOU'RE FORCING ME TO USE THE FIELD MYSELF!
SOMETHING BETWEEN YOU AND MY ARM-- INTERFERING.
MUST KEEP CRUSHING --KEEP CRUSHING-- MAKE IT GO AWAY.
HE'S STRONGER-- FRESHER THAN I AM. CAN'T MAINTAIN FIELD MUCH LONGER.
AND DR. DOOM--
AND DR. DOOM IS FIGHTING FOR HIS LIFE!
WITHOUT THE PROTECTION OF THE FORCE FIELD--
THAT WHICH I MOST FEARED MAY HAPPEN--
27

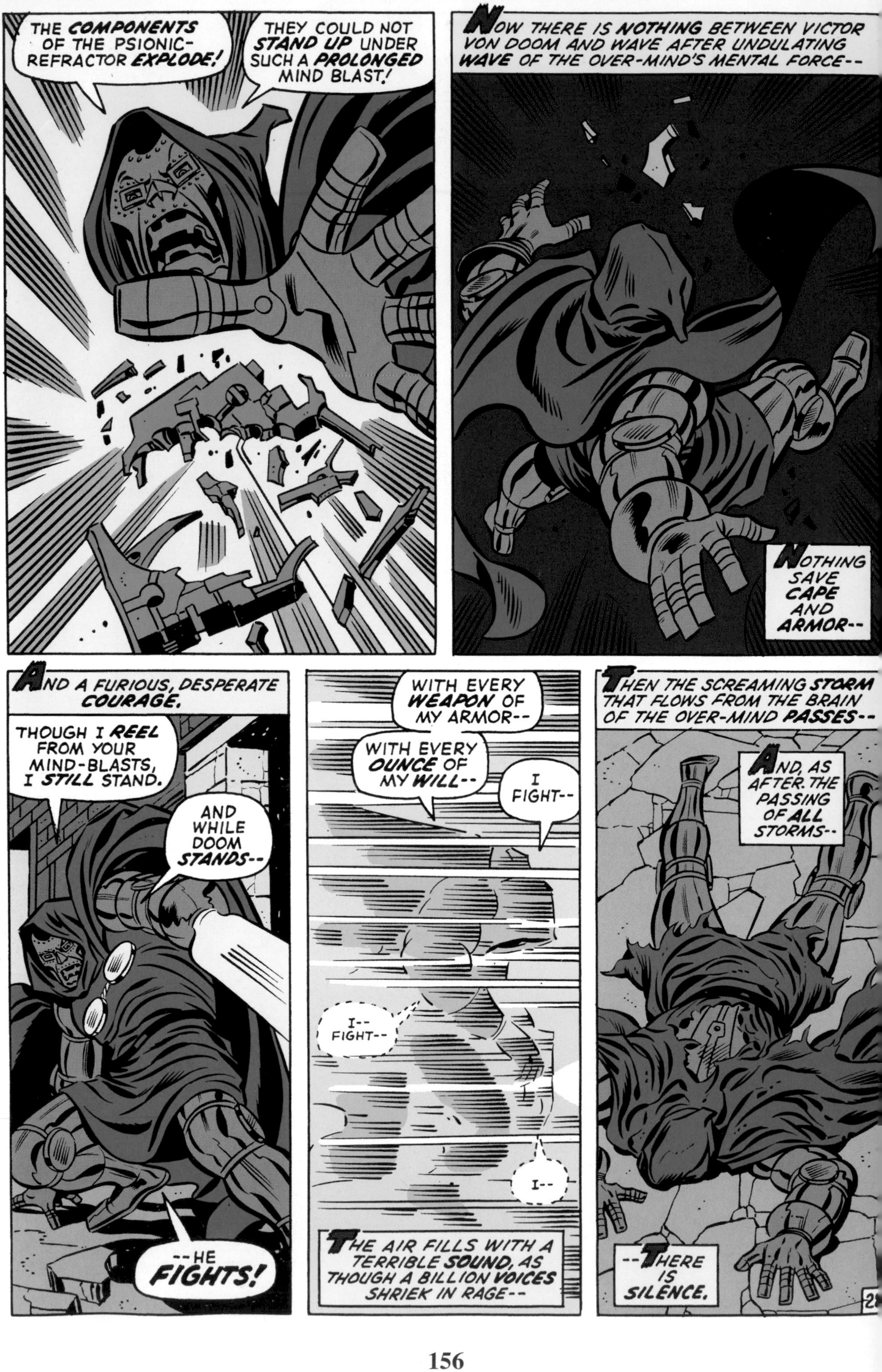
THE COMPONENTS OF THE PSIONIC-REFRACTOR EXPLODE!
THEY COULD NOT STAND UP UNDER SUCH A PROLONGED MIND BLAST!
NOW THERE IS NOTHING BETWEEN VICTOR VON DOOM AND WAVE AFTER UNDULATING WAVE OF THE OVER-MIND'S MENTAL FORCE--
NOTHING SAVE CAPE AND ARMOR--
AND A FURIOUS, DESPERATE COURAGE.
THOUGH I REEL FROM YOUR MIND-BLASTS, I STILL STAND.
AND WHILE DOOM STANDS--
--HE FIGHTS!
WITH EVERY WEAPON OF MY ARMOR--
WITH EVERY OUNCE OF MY WILL--
I FIGHT--
I-- FIGHT--
I--
THE AIR FILLS WITH A TERRIBLE SOUND, AS THOUGH A BILLION VOICES SHRIEK IN RAGE--
THEN THE SCREAMING STORM THAT FLOWS FROM THE BRAIN OF THE OVER-MIND PASSES--
AND, AS AFTER THE PASSING OF ALL STORMS--
--THERE IS SILENCE.

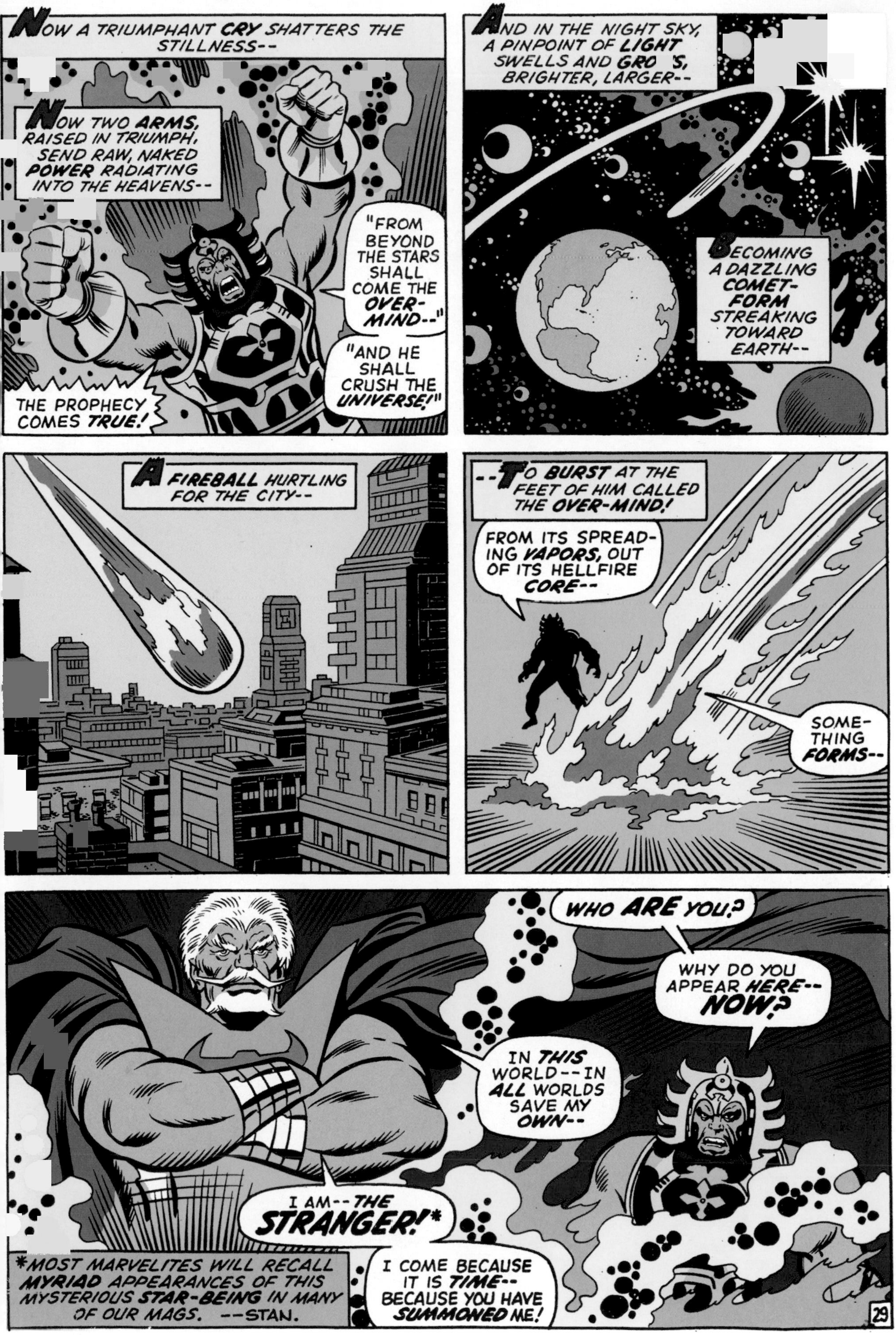
NOW A TRIUMPHANT CRY SHATTERS THE STILLNESS--
NOW TWO ARMS, RAISED IN TRIUMPH, SEND RAW, NAKED POWER RADIATING INTO THE HEAVENS--
THE PROPHECY COMES TRUE!
"FROM BEYOND THE STARS SHALL COME THE OVER-MIND--"
"AND HE SHALL CRUSH THE UNIVERSE!"
AND IN THE NIGHT SKY, A PINPOINT OF LIGHT SWELLS AND GROWS, BRIGHTER, LARGER--
BECOMING A DAZZLING COMET-FORM STREAKING TOWARD EARTH--
A FIREBALL HURTLING FOR THE CITY--
--TO BURST AT THE FEET OF HIM CALLED THE OVER-MIND!
FROM ITS SPREADING VAPORS, OUT OF ITS HELLFIRE CORE--
SOMETHING FORMS--
WHO ARE YOU?
WHY DO YOU APPEAR HERE-- NOW?
IN THIS WORLD--IN ALL WORLDS SAVE MY OWN--
I AM--THE STRANGER!*
I COME BECAUSE IT IS TIME-- BECAUSE YOU HAVE SUMMONED ME!
*MOST MARVELITES WILL RECALL MYRIAD APPEARANCES OF THIS MYSTERIOUS STAR-BEING IN MANY OF OUR MAGS. --STAN.
29

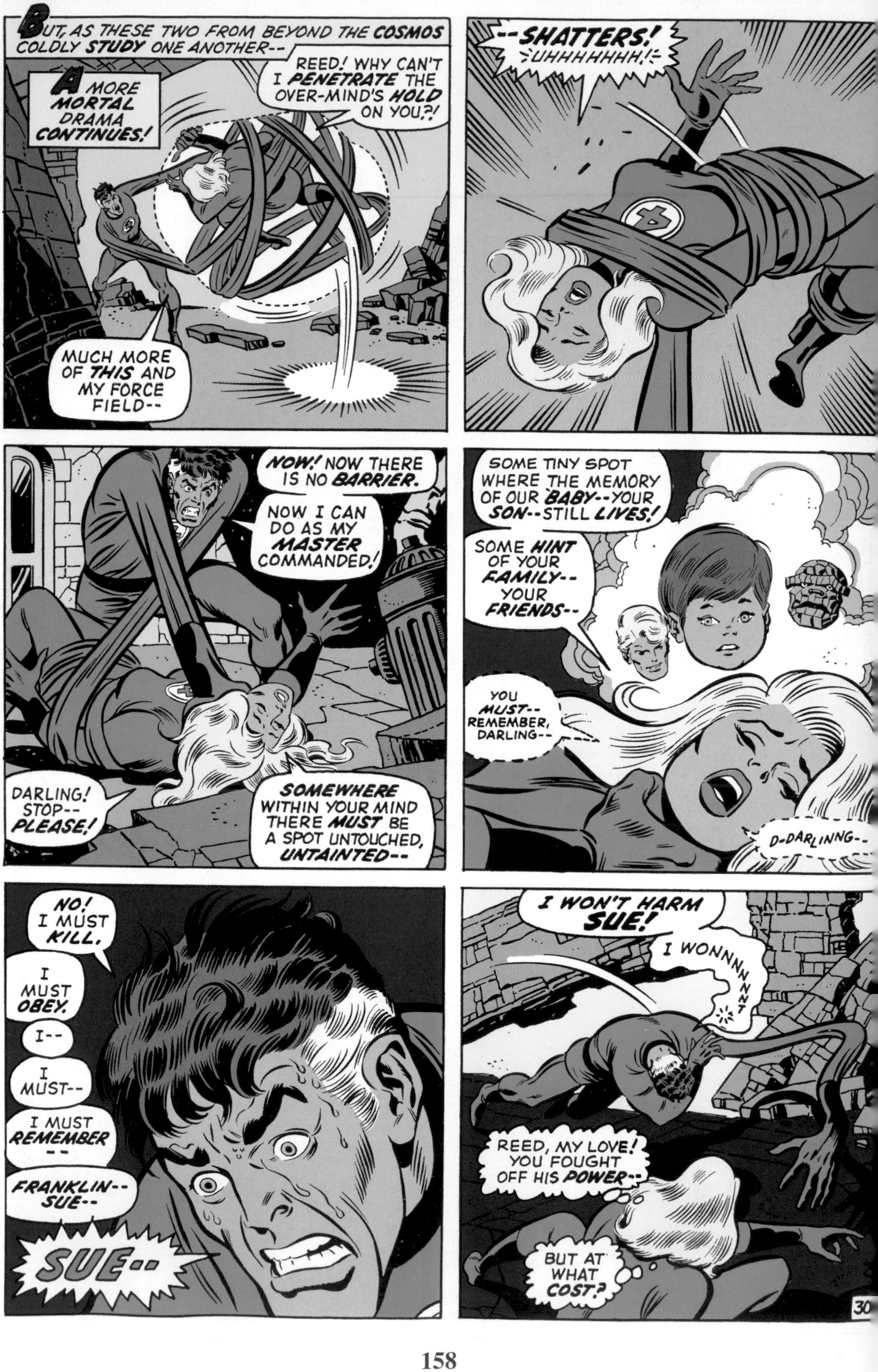

BUT, AS THESE TWO FROM BEYOND THE COSMOS COLDLY STUDY ONE ANOTHER--
A MORE MORTAL DRAMA CONTINUES!
REED! WHY CAN'T I PENETRATE THE OVER-MIND'S HOLD ON YOU?!
MUCH MORE OF THIS AND MY FORCE FIELD--
--SHATTERS!
UHHHHHHH!
NOW! NOW THERE IS NO BARRIER.
NOW I CAN DO AS MY MASTER COMMANDED!
DARLING! STOP-- PLEASE!
SOMEWHERE WITHIN YOUR MIND THERE MUST BE A SPOT UNTOUCHED, UNTAINTED--
SOME TINY SPOT WHERE THE MEMORY OF OUR BABY--YOUR SON--STILL LIVES!
SOME HINT OF YOUR FAMILY-- YOUR FRIENDS--
YOU MUST-- REMEMBER, DARLING--
D-DARLINNG--
NO! I MUST KILL.
I MUST OBEY.
I--
I MUST--
I MUST REMEMBER --
FRANKLIN-- SUE--
SUE--
I WON'T HARM SUE!
I WONNNNNNT
REED, MY LOVE! YOU FOUGHT OFF HIS POWER--
BUT AT WHAT COST?
30

UT, SUE RICHARDS' **SOBS**--HALF RELIEF, HALF ANXIETY-- ARE **LOST**--LOST IN THE THUNDER OF **GIANT'S** SPEAKING!

YOU **LIE**, STRANGER! THE OVER-MIND DID NOT **SUMMON** YOU.

BUT **WHOEVER** YOU ARE, **WHATEVER** YOUR PURPOSE--

MY POWER OF A **BILLION BRAINS** WILL--

WHAT?

IT DOES NOT **HARM**, DOES NOT **TOUCH** YOU! BUT--

BUT **YOU** ARE THE SUM TOTAL OF THE MIGHTY **ETERNALS?**

YET WERE THE ETERNALS NOT ONCE **DEFEATED?**

DEFEATED BY THE SURVIVORS OF **GIGANTUS**-- WORLD WHICH DWARFED **GALAXIES?**

KNOW THIS, OVER-MIND. AS **YOU** ARE ALL THE POWER OF THE **ETERNALS**--

SO THE STRANGER IS THE **SUM** OF THOSE OF **GIGANTUS!**

THE POWER OF A **BILLION BILLION** BRAINS-- AND **MORE!**

YOUR CREATION WAS DISCOVERED **TOO LATE**--BUT OUR RACE PREPARED **ME** AGAINST THE TIME OF YOUR **RETURN!**

AS **THAT** TIME HAS COME--

SO TOO HAS **YOURS!**

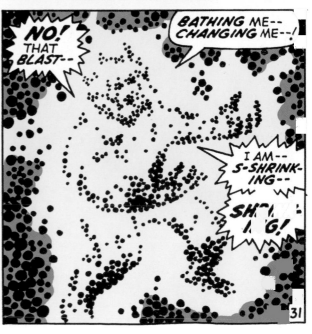

NO! THAT **BLAST**--

BATHING ME-- CHANGING ME--!

I AM-- S-SHRINK- ING--

SHR...ING!

31

AND THUS IT IS *DONE.*

THE EONS-OLD TRUST PLACED IN ME IS *FULFILLED.*

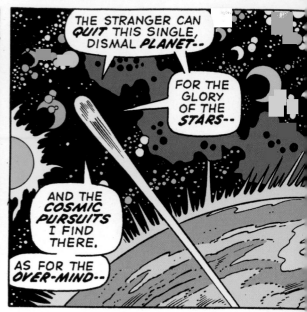

THE STRANGER CAN *QUIT* THIS SINGLE, DISMAL *PLANET--*

FOR THE GLORY OF THE *STARS--*

AND THE *COSMIC PURSUITS* I FIND THERE.

AS FOR THE *OVER-MIND--*

HE MAY *REVEL* IN AN ANCIENT PROPHECY COME *TRUE.*

HE WHO CAME FROM BEYOND THE STARS NOW *HAS* HIS UNIVERSE TO CRUSH--

A *DEAD* AND *LIFELESS* UNIVERSE--

--WITHIN A *MOTE* OF *DUST!*

*A*ND WITHIN THAT SUB-ATOMIC *VOID,* LOST AND DRIFTING IN A NAMELESS PARTICLE OF DUST, THERE IS A *SCREAM--*

32

160

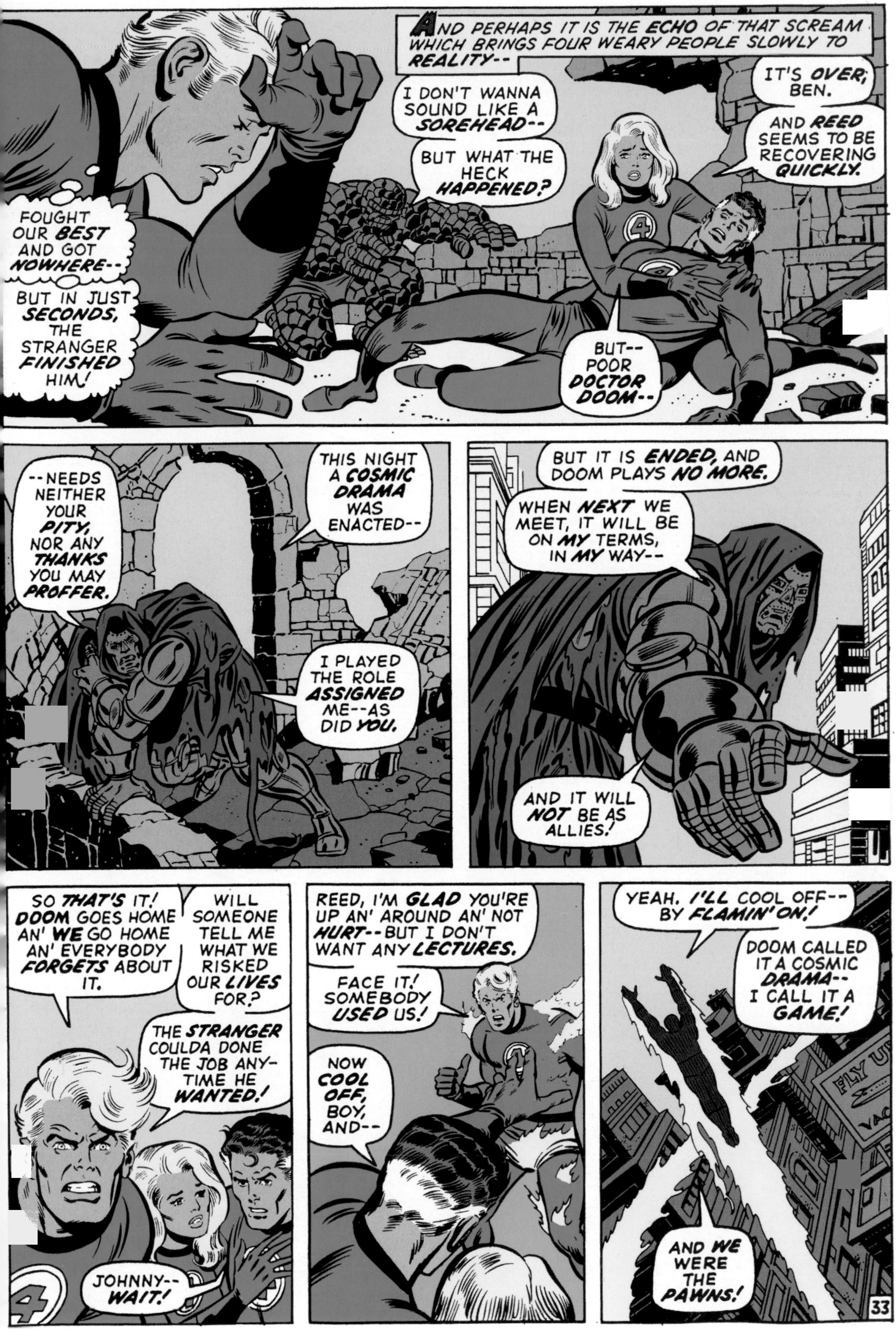
AND PERHAPS IT IS THE ECHO OF THAT SCREAM WHICH BRINGS FOUR WEARY PEOPLE SLOWLY TO REALITY--
I DON'T WANNA SOUND LIKE A SOREHEAD--
BUT WHAT THE HECK HAPPENED?
FOUGHT OUR BEST AND GOT NOWHERE--
BUT IN JUST SECONDS, THE STRANGER FINISHED HIM!
IT'S OVER, BEN.
AND REED SEEMS TO BE RECOVERING QUICKLY.
BUT--POOR DOCTOR DOOM--
--NEEDS NEITHER YOUR PITY, NOR ANY THANKS YOU MAY PROFFER.
THIS NIGHT A COSMIC DRAMA WAS ENACTED--
I PLAYED THE ROLE ASSIGNED ME--AS DID YOU.
BUT IT IS ENDED, AND DOOM PLAYS NO MORE.
WHEN NEXT WE MEET, IT WILL BE ON MY TERMS, IN MY WAY--
AND IT WILL NOT BE AS ALLIES!
SO THAT'S IT! DOOM GOES HOME AN' WE GO HOME AN' EVERYBODY FORGETS ABOUT IT.
WILL SOMEONE TELL ME WHAT WE RISKED OUR LIVES FOR?
THE STRANGER COULDA DONE THE JOB ANY-TIME HE WANTED!
JOHNNY--WAIT!
REED, I'M GLAD YOU'RE UP AN' AROUND AN' NOT HURT--BUT I DON'T WANT ANY LECTURES.
FACE IT! SOMEBODY USED US!
NOW COOL OFF, BOY, AND--
YEAH. I'LL COOL OFF--BY FLAMIN' ON!
DOOM CALLED IT A COSMIC DRAMA--I CALL IT A GAME!
AND WE WERE THE PAWNS!
33

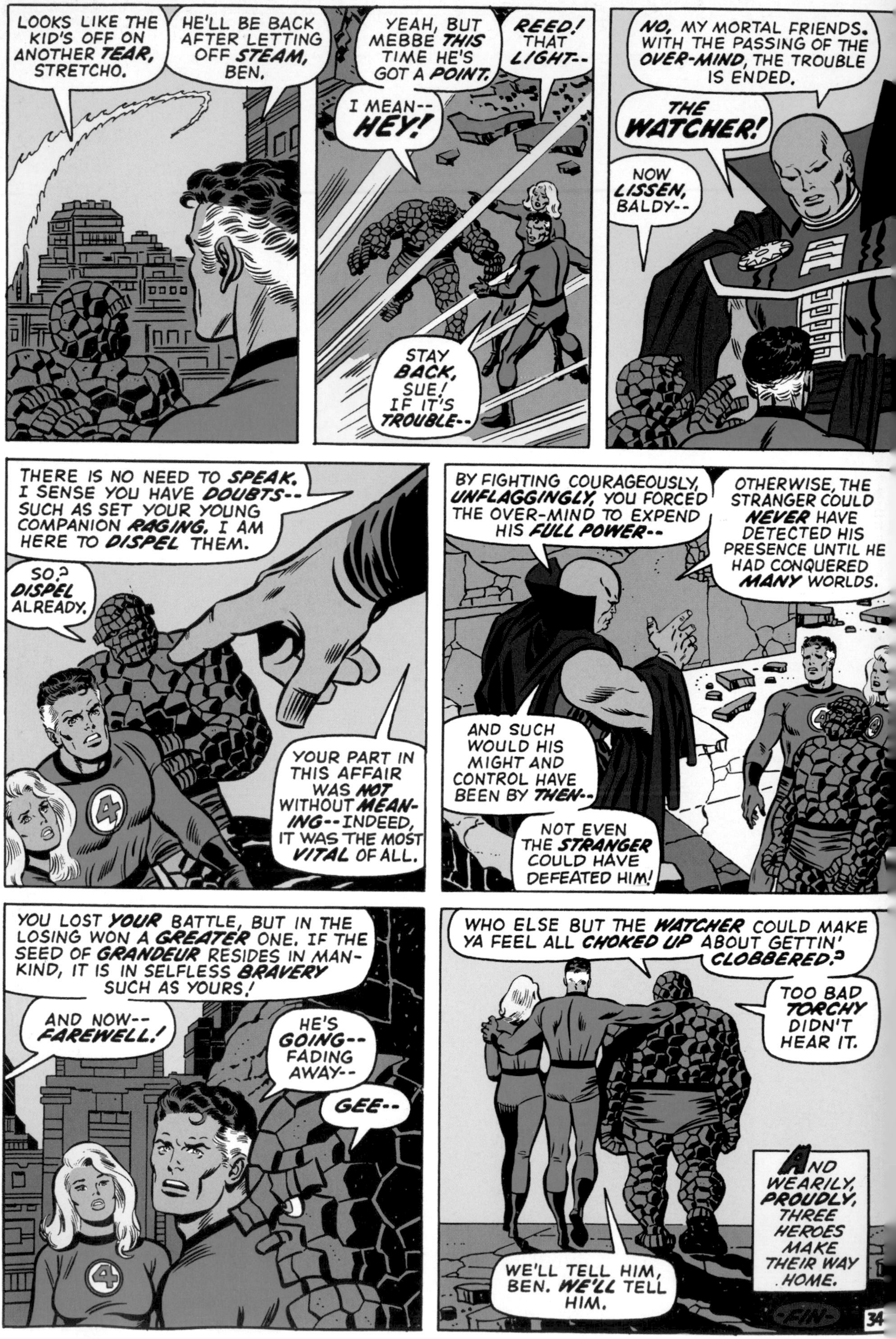
LOOKS LIKE THE KID'S OFF ON ANOTHER TEAR, STRETCHO.
HE'LL BE BACK AFTER LETTING OFF STEAM, BEN.
YEAH, BUT MEBBE THIS TIME HE'S GOT A POINT.
I MEAN-- HEY!
REED! THAT LIGHT--
STAY BACK, SUE! IF IT'S TROUBLE--
NO, MY MORTAL FRIENDS. WITH THE PASSING OF THE OVER-MIND, THE TROUBLE IS ENDED.
THE WATCHER!
NOW LISSEN, BALDY--
THERE IS NO NEED TO SPEAK. I SENSE YOU HAVE DOUBTS-- SUCH AS SET YOUR YOUNG COMPANION RAGING. I AM HERE TO DISPEL THEM.
SO? DISPEL ALREADY.
YOUR PART IN THIS AFFAIR WAS NOT WITHOUT MEANING--INDEED, IT WAS THE MOST VITAL OF ALL.
BY FIGHTING COURAGEOUSLY, UNFLAGGINGLY, YOU FORCED THE OVER-MIND TO EXPEND HIS FULL POWER--
OTHERWISE, THE STRANGER COULD NEVER HAVE DETECTED HIS PRESENCE UNTIL HE HAD CONQUERED MANY WORLDS.
AND SUCH WOULD HIS MIGHT AND CONTROL HAVE BEEN BY THEN--
NOT EVEN THE STRANGER COULD HAVE DEFEATED HIM!
YOU LOST YOUR BATTLE, BUT IN THE LOSING WON A GREATER ONE. IF THE SEED OF GRANDEUR RESIDES IN MANKIND, IT IS IN SELFLESS BRAVERY SUCH AS YOURS!
AND NOW-- FAREWELL!
HE'S GOING-- FADING AWAY--
GEE--
WHO ELSE BUT THE WATCHER COULD MAKE YA FEEL ALL CHOKED UP ABOUT GETTIN' CLOBBERED?
TOO BAD TORCHY DIDN'T HEAR IT.
WE'LL TELL HIM, BEN. WE'LL TELL HIM.
AND WEARILY, PROUDLY, THREE HEROES MAKE THEIR WAY HOME.
FIN
34

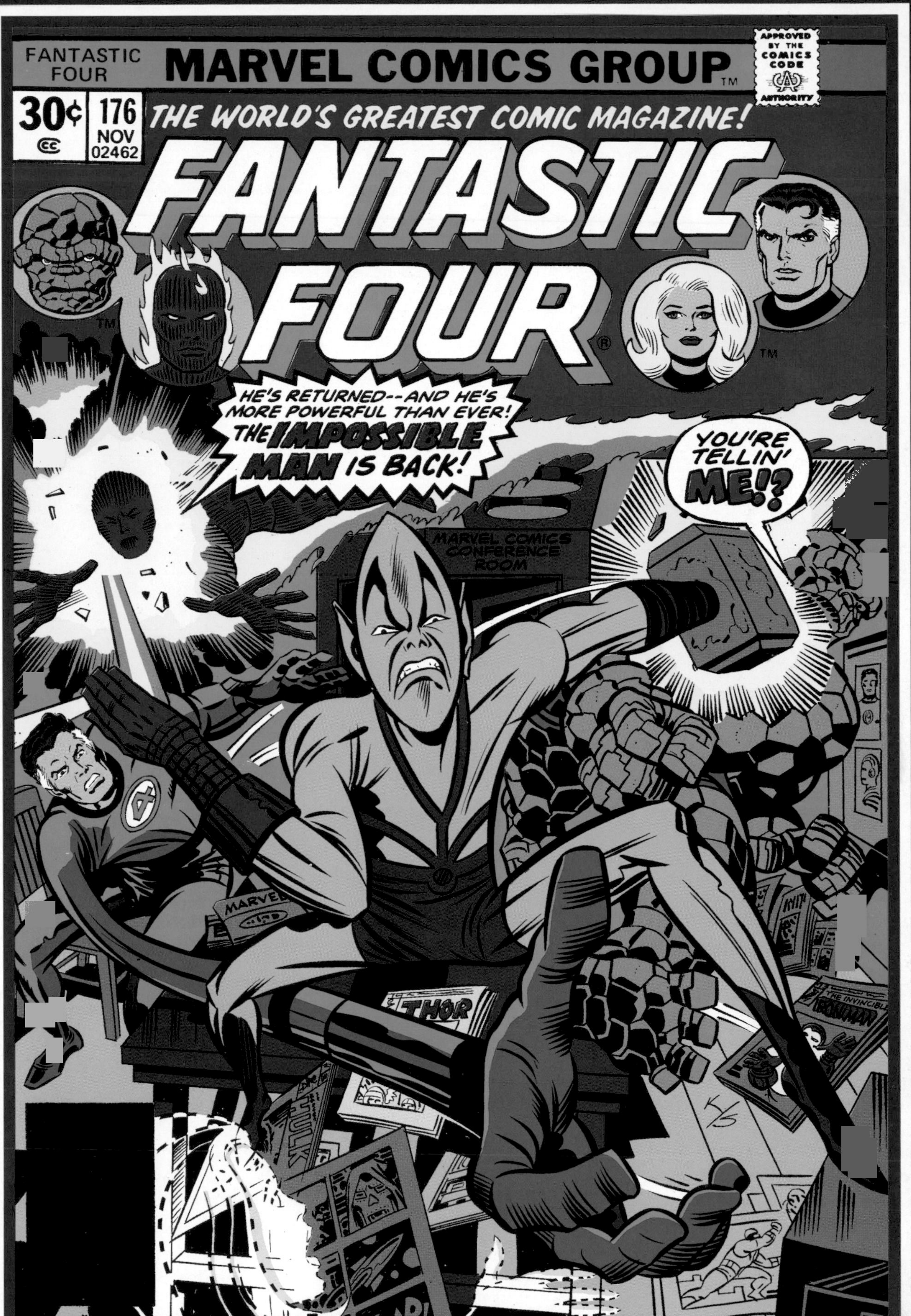
FANTASTIC FOUR
MARVEL COMICS GROUP
APPROVED BY THE COMICS CODE AUTHORITY
30¢
176
NOV
02462
THE WORLD'S GREATEST COMIC MAGAZINE!
FANTASTIC FOUR
HE'S RETURNED--AND HE'S MORE POWERFUL THAN EVER! THE IMPOSSIBLE MAN IS BACK!
YOU'RE TELLIN' ME!?
MARVEL COMICS CONFERENCE ROOM
MARVEL
THOR
HULK
THE INVINCIBLE IRON MAN

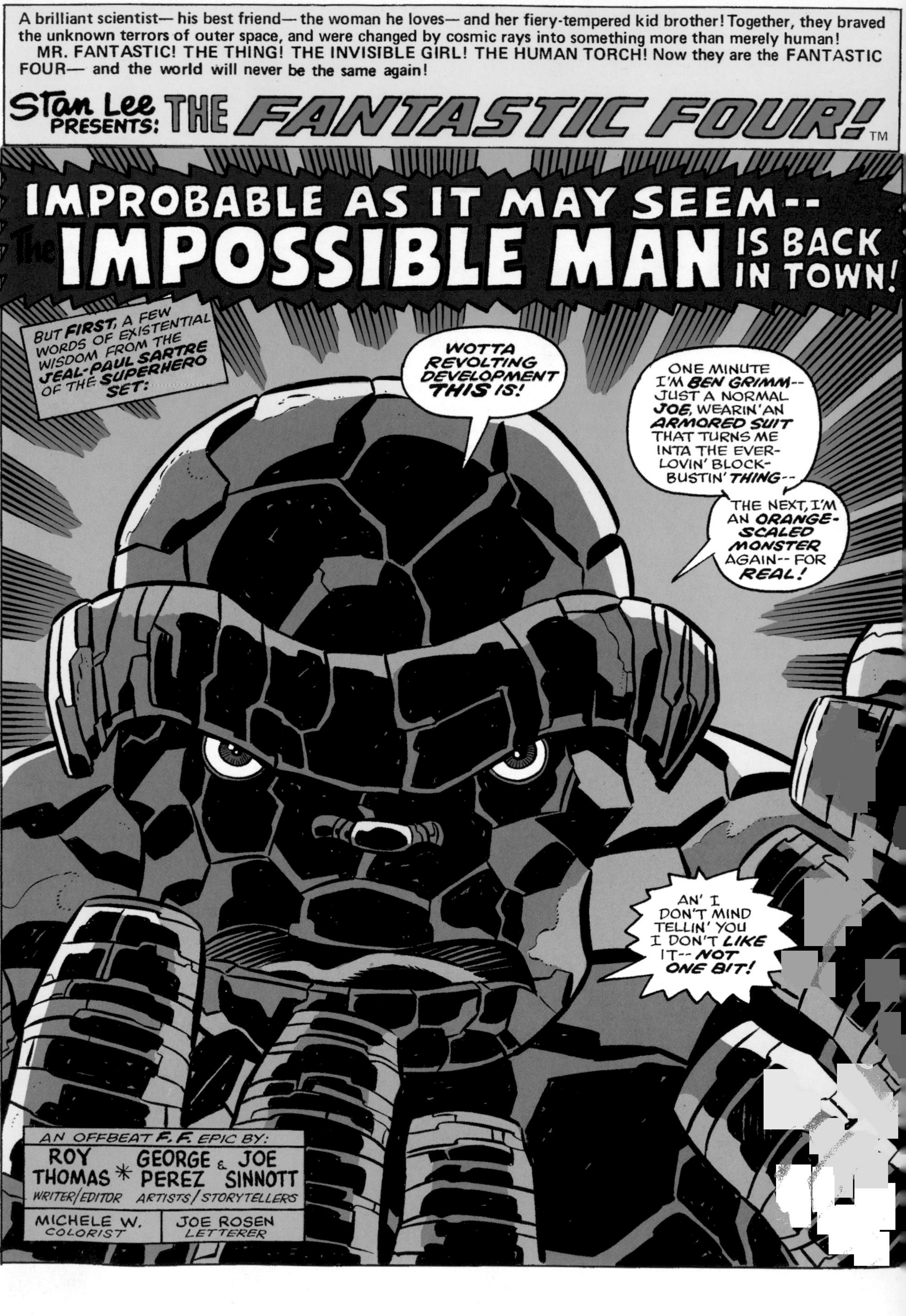
A brilliant scientist— his best friend— the woman he loves— and her fiery-tempered kid brother! Together, they braved the unknown terrors of outer space, and were changed by cosmic rays into something more than merely human!
MR. FANTASTIC! THE THING! THE INVISIBLE GIRL! THE HUMAN TORCH! Now they are the FANTASTIC FOUR— and the world will never be the same again!
Stan Lee PRESENTS: THE FANTASTIC FOUR! TM
IMPROBABLE AS IT MAY SEEM-- The IMPOSSIBLE MAN IS BACK IN TOWN!
BUT FIRST, A FEW WORDS OF EXISTENTIAL WISDOM FROM THE JEAL-PAUL SARTRE OF THE SUPERHERO SET:
WOTTA REVOLTING DEVELOPMENT THIS IS!
ONE MINUTE I'M BEN GRIMM-- JUST A NORMAL JOE, WEARIN' AN ARMORED SUIT THAT TURNS ME INTA THE EVER-LOVIN' BLOCK-BUSTIN' THING--
THE NEXT, I'M AN ORANGE-SCALED MONSTER AGAIN-- FOR REAL!
AN' I DON'T MIND TELLIN' YOU I DON'T LIKE IT-- NOT ONE BIT!
AN OFFBEAT F.F. EPIC BY:
ROY THOMAS WRITER/EDITOR
GEORGE PEREZ & JOE SINNOTT ARTISTS/STORYTELLERS
MICHELE W. COLORIST
JOE ROSEN LETTERER

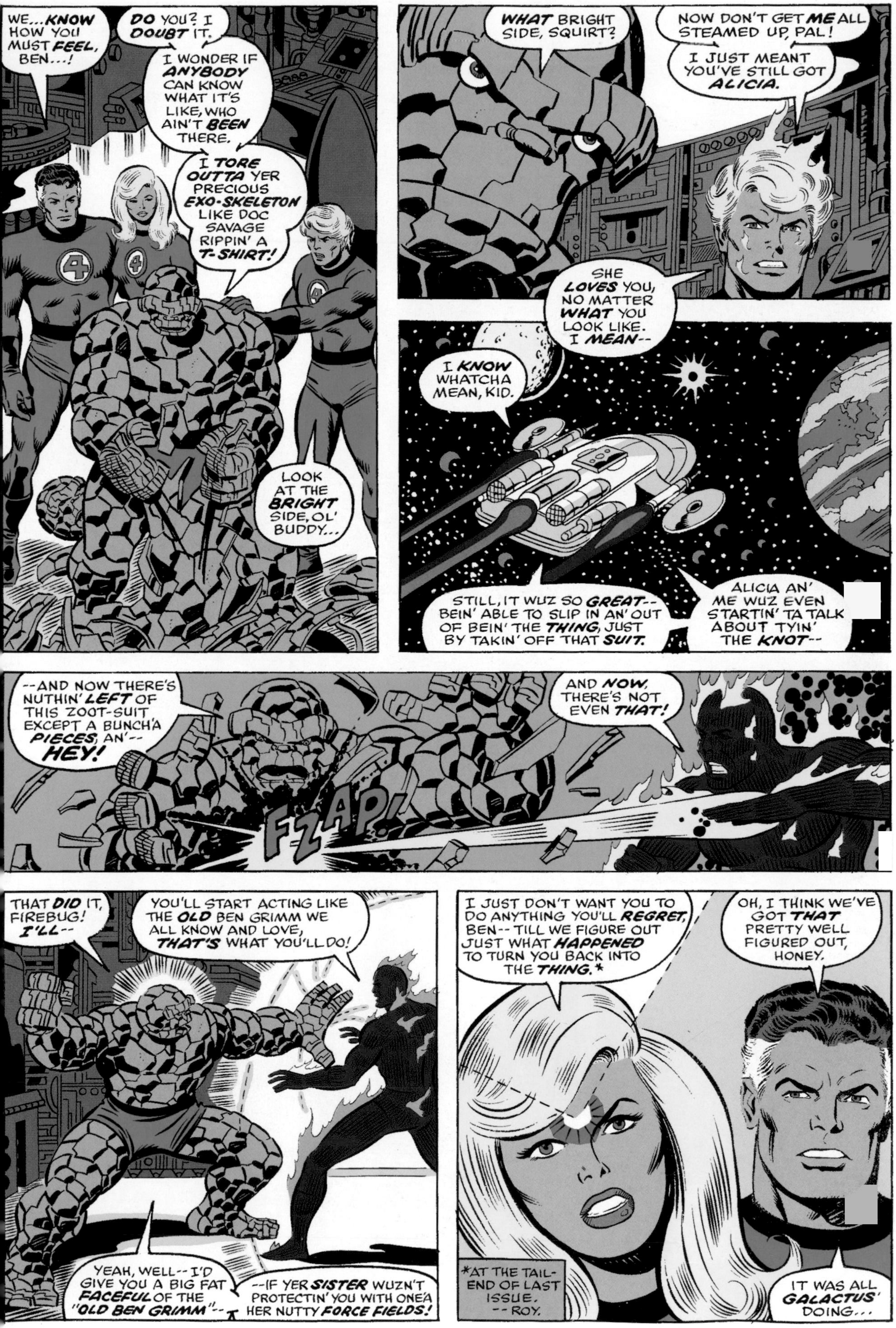
WE...KNOW HOW YOU MUST FEEL, BEN...!
DO YOU? I DOUBT IT.
I WONDER IF ANYBODY CAN KNOW WHAT IT'S LIKE, WHO AIN'T BEEN THERE.
I TORE OUTTA YER PRECIOUS EXO-SKELETON LIKE DOC SAVAGE RIPPIN' A T-SHIRT!
LOOK AT THE BRIGHT SIDE, OL' BUDDY...
WHAT BRIGHT SIDE, SQUIRT?
NOW DON'T GET ME ALL STEAMED UP, PAL!
I JUST MEANT YOU'VE STILL GOT ALICIA.
SHE LOVES YOU, NO MATTER WHAT YOU LOOK LIKE. I MEAN--
I KNOW WHATCHA MEAN, KID.
STILL, IT WUZ SO GREAT-- BEIN' ABLE TO SLIP IN AN' OUT OF BEIN' THE THING, JUST BY TAKIN' OFF THAT SUIT.
ALICIA AN' ME WUZ EVEN STARTIN' TA TALK ABOUT TYIN' THE KNOT--
--AND NOW THERE'S NUTHIN' LEFT OF THIS ZOOT-SUIT EXCEPT A BUNCH'A PIECES, AN'-- HEY!
AND NOW, THERE'S NOT EVEN THAT!
FZAP!
THAT DID IT, FIREBUG! I'LL--
YOU'LL START ACTING LIKE THE OLD BEN GRIMM WE ALL KNOW AND LOVE, THAT'S WHAT YOU'LL DO!
YEAH, WELL--I'D GIVE YOU A BIG FAT FACEFUL OF THE "OLD BEN GRIMM"--
--IF YER SISTER WUZN'T PROTECTIN' YOU WITH ONE'A HER NUTTY FORCE FIELDS!
I JUST DON'T WANT YOU TO DO ANYTHING YOU'LL REGRET, BEN-- TILL WE FIGURE OUT JUST WHAT HAPPENED TO TURN YOU BACK INTO THE THING.*
OH, I THINK WE'VE GOT THAT PRETTY WELL FIGURED OUT, HONEY.
*AT THE TAIL-END OF LAST ISSUE. --ROY.
IT WAS ALL GALACTUS' DOING...

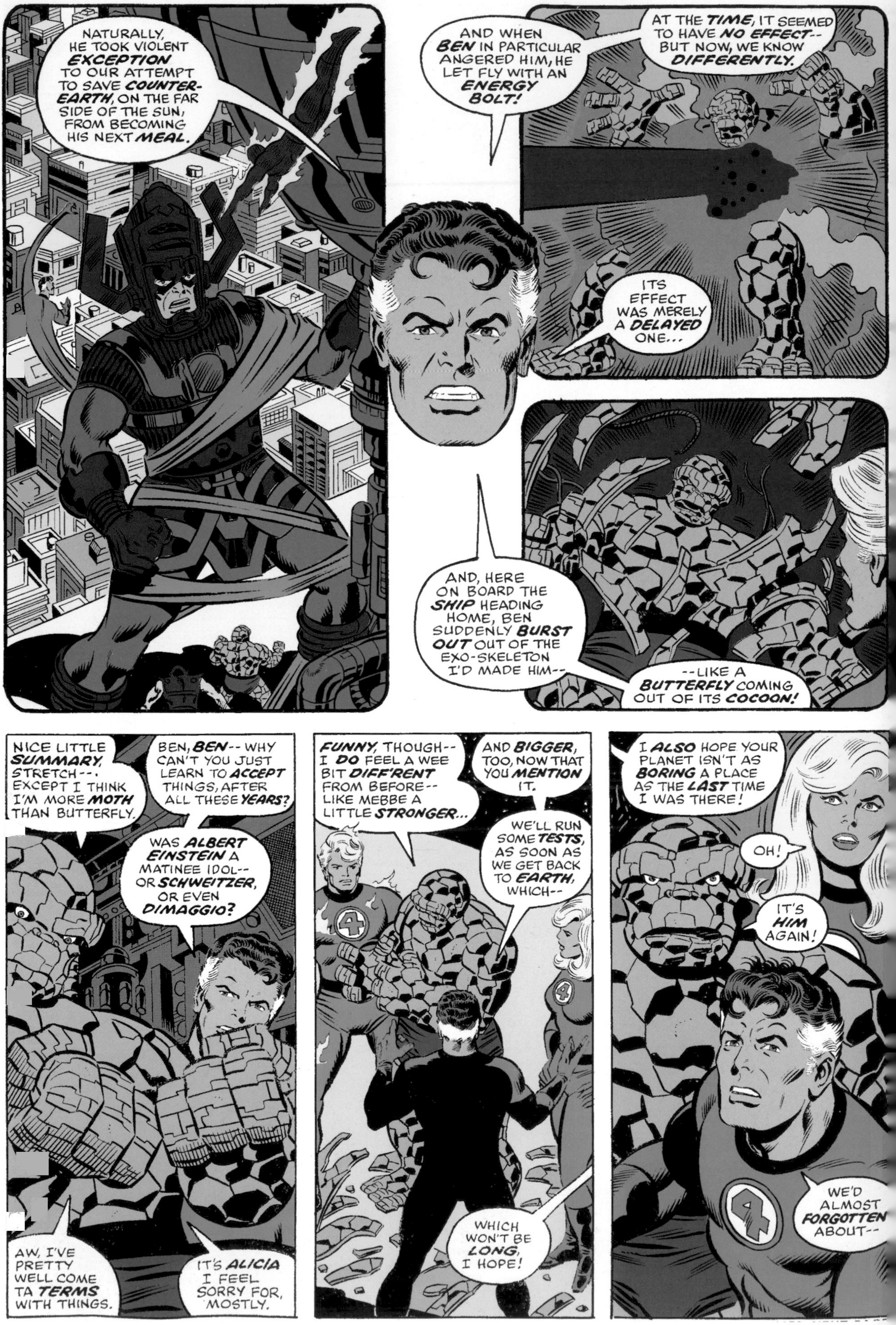
NATURALLY, HE TOOK VIOLENT EXCEPTION TO OUR ATTEMPT TO SAVE COUNTER-EARTH, ON THE FAR SIDE OF THE SUN, FROM BECOMING HIS NEXT MEAL.
AND WHEN BEN IN PARTICULAR ANGERED HIM, HE LET FLY WITH AN ENERGY BOLT!
AT THE TIME, IT SEEMED TO HAVE NO EFFECT-- BUT NOW, WE KNOW DIFFERENTLY.
ITS EFFECT WAS MERELY A DELAYED ONE...
AND, HERE ON BOARD THE SHIP HEADING HOME, BEN SUDDENLY BURST OUT OUT OF THE EXO-SKELETON I'D MADE HIM--
--LIKE A BUTTERFLY COMING OUT OF ITS COCOON!
NICE LITTLE SUMMARY, STRETCH--. EXCEPT I THINK I'M MORE MOTH THAN BUTTERFLY.
BEN, BEN-- WHY CAN'T YOU JUST LEARN TO ACCEPT THINGS, AFTER ALL THESE YEARS?
WAS ALBERT EINSTEIN A MATINEE IDOL-- OR SCHWEITZER, OR EVEN DIMAGGIO?
AW, I'VE PRETTY WELL COME TA TERMS WITH THINGS.
IT'S ALICIA I FEEL SORRY FOR, MOSTLY.
FUNNY, THOUGH-- I DO FEEL A WEE BIT DIFF'RENT FROM BEFORE-- LIKE MEBBE A LITTLE STRONGER...
AND BIGGER, TOO, NOW THAT YOU MENTION IT.
WE'LL RUN SOME TESTS, AS SOON AS WE GET BACK TO EARTH, WHICH--
WHICH WON'T BE LONG, I HOPE!
I ALSO HOPE YOUR PLANET ISN'T AS BORING A PLACE AS THE LAST TIME I WAS THERE!
OH!
IT'S HIM AGAIN!
WE'D ALMOST FORGOTTEN ABOUT--

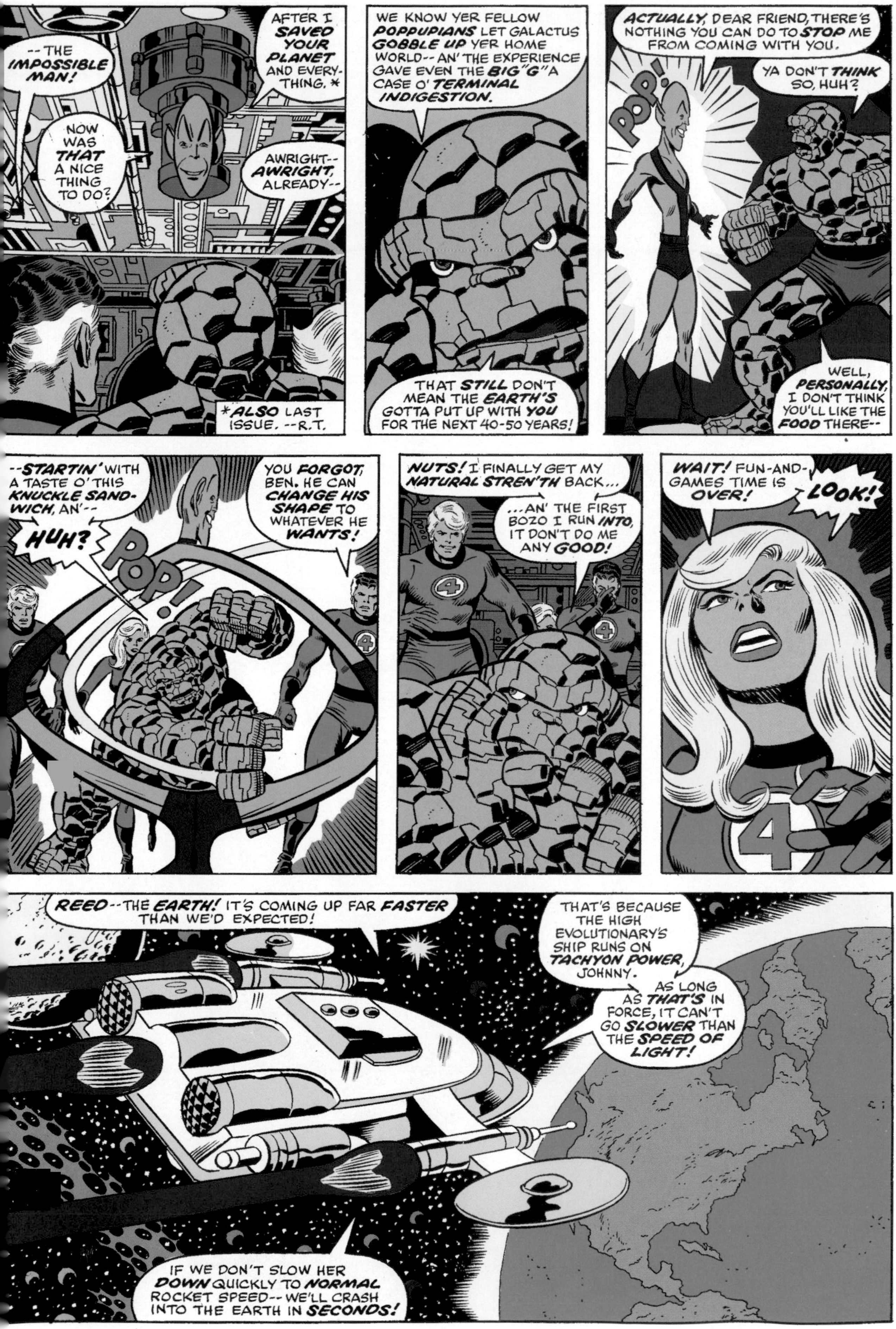
-- THE IMPOSSIBLE MAN!
AFTER I SAVED YOUR PLANET AND EVERY-THING. *
NOW WAS THAT A NICE THING TO DO?
AWRIGHT-- AWRIGHT, ALREADY--
*ALSO LAST ISSUE. --R.T.
WE KNOW YER FELLOW POPPUPIANS LET GALACTUS GOBBLE UP YER HOME WORLD-- AN' THE EXPERIENCE GAVE EVEN THE BIG "G" A CASE O' TERMINAL INDIGESTION.
THAT STILL DON'T MEAN THE EARTH'S GOTTA PUT UP WITH YOU FOR THE NEXT 40-50 YEARS!
ACTUALLY, DEAR FRIEND, THERE'S NOTHING YOU CAN DO TO STOP ME FROM COMING WITH YOU.
POP!
YA DON'T THINK SO, HUH?
WELL, PERSONALLY, I DON'T THINK YOU'LL LIKE THE FOOD THERE--
--STARTIN' WITH A TASTE O' THIS KNUCKLE SANDWICH, AN'--
HUH?
POP!
YOU FORGOT, BEN. HE CAN CHANGE HIS SHAPE TO WHATEVER HE WANTS!
NUTS! I FINALLY GET MY NATURAL STREN'TH BACK...
...AN' THE FIRST BOZO I RUN INTO, IT DON'T DO ME ANY GOOD!
WAIT! FUN-AND-GAMES TIME IS OVER!
LOOK!
REED--THE EARTH! IT'S COMING UP FAR FASTER THAN WE'D EXPECTED!
THAT'S BECAUSE THE HIGH EVOLUTIONARY'S SHIP RUNS ON TACHYON POWER, JOHNNY.
AS LONG AS THAT'S IN FORCE, IT CAN'T GO SLOWER THAN THE SPEED OF LIGHT!
IF WE DON'T SLOW HER DOWN QUICKLY TO NORMAL ROCKET SPEED-- WE'LL CRASH INTO THE EARTH IN SECONDS!

YEAH, WELL-- *I'M* SUPPOSEDTA BE THE HOT-SHOT *TEST PILOT* AROUND HERE, RIGHT?

AND *ONE* THING I KNOW WHEN I SEE IT-- IS A *BRAKE!*

WHOOPS!

SKRUNCH!

CORRECTION: *WAS* A BRAKE!

WE'VE *SLOWED* OUR DESCENT-- BUT NOW WE'RE GOING *OUT OF CONTROL!*

WHERE WILL WE *END UP?*

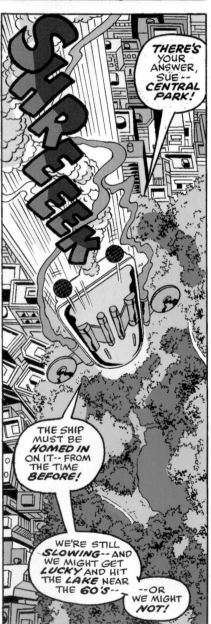

SHREEEK

THERE'S YOUR ANSWER, SUE-- *CENTRAL PARK!*

THE SHIP MUST BE *HOMED IN* ON IT-- FROM THE TIME *BEFORE!*

WE'RE STILL *SLOWING*-- AND WE MIGHT GET *LUCKY* AND HIT THE LAKE NEAR THE *60'S*--

--OR WE MIGHT *NOT!*

JOHNNY, DO YOU THINK *YOU* CAN-- ?

I KNOW WHAT YOU'RE *THINKING,* REED... AND I *DON'T KNOW.*

IT'S A *TALL ORDER,* BUT I'VE GOT TO *TRY!*

FLAME ON!

:YAWN:‹ NOT EVEN *THERE* YET, AND I'M *ALREADY* BORED.

YEAH? WELL, WE'LL *SEE* HOW BORED YA *STAY,* GREEN-GUY...

...IF WE WIND UP *SPLATTERED* CLEAN FROM THE *ZOO* TA *MORNING-SIDE HEIGHTS!*

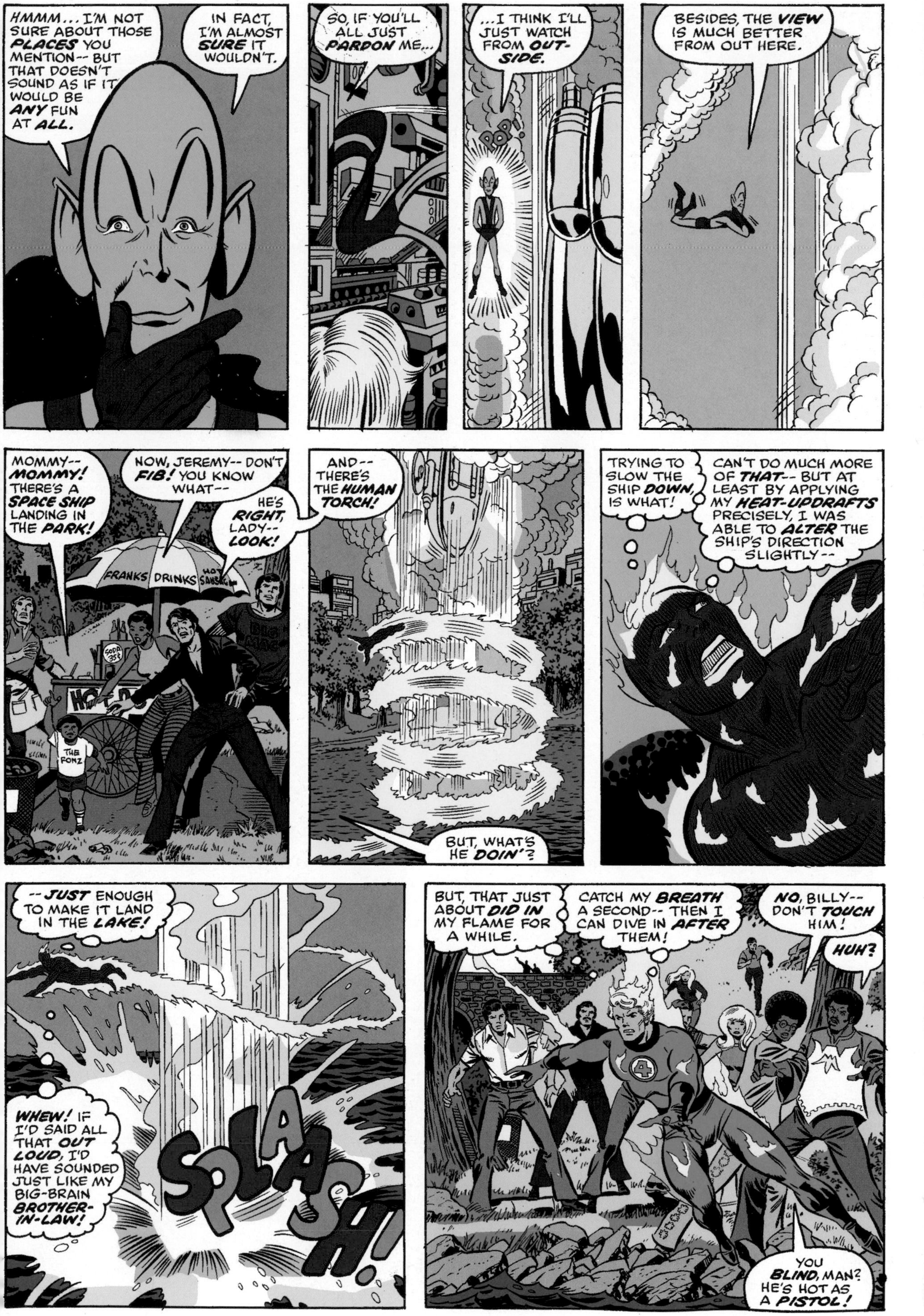
HMMM... I'M NOT SURE ABOUT THOSE PLACES YOU MENTION-- BUT THAT DOESN'T SOUND AS IF IT WOULD BE ANY FUN AT ALL.
IN FACT, I'M ALMOST SURE IT WOULDN'T.
SO, IF YOU'LL ALL JUST PARDON ME...
...I THINK I'LL JUST WATCH FROM OUT-SIDE.
BESIDES, THE VIEW IS MUCH BETTER FROM OUT HERE.
MOMMY-- MOMMY! THERE'S A SPACE SHIP LANDING IN THE PARK!
NOW, JEREMY-- DON'T FIB! YOU KNOW WHAT--
HE'S RIGHT, LADY-- LOOK!
FRANKS DRINKS
SODA 35¢
THE FONZ
AND-- THERE'S THE HUMAN TORCH!
BUT, WHAT'S HE DOIN'?
TRYING TO SLOW THE SHIP DOWN, IS WHAT!
CAN'T DO MUCH MORE OF THAT-- BUT AT LEAST BY APPLYING MY HEAT-UPDRAFTS PRECISELY, I WAS ABLE TO ALTER THE SHIP'S DIRECTION SLIGHTLY--
--JUST ENOUGH TO MAKE IT LAND IN THE LAKE!
WHEW! IF I'D SAID ALL THAT OUT LOUD, I'D HAVE SOUNDED JUST LIKE MY BIG-BRAIN BROTHER-IN-LAW!
SPLASH!
BUT, THAT JUST ABOUT DID IN MY FLAME FOR A WHILE.
CATCH MY BREATH A SECOND-- THEN I CAN DIVE IN AFTER THEM!
NO, BILLY-- DON'T TOUCH HIM!
HUH?
YOU BLIND, MAN? HE'S HOT AS A PISTOL!

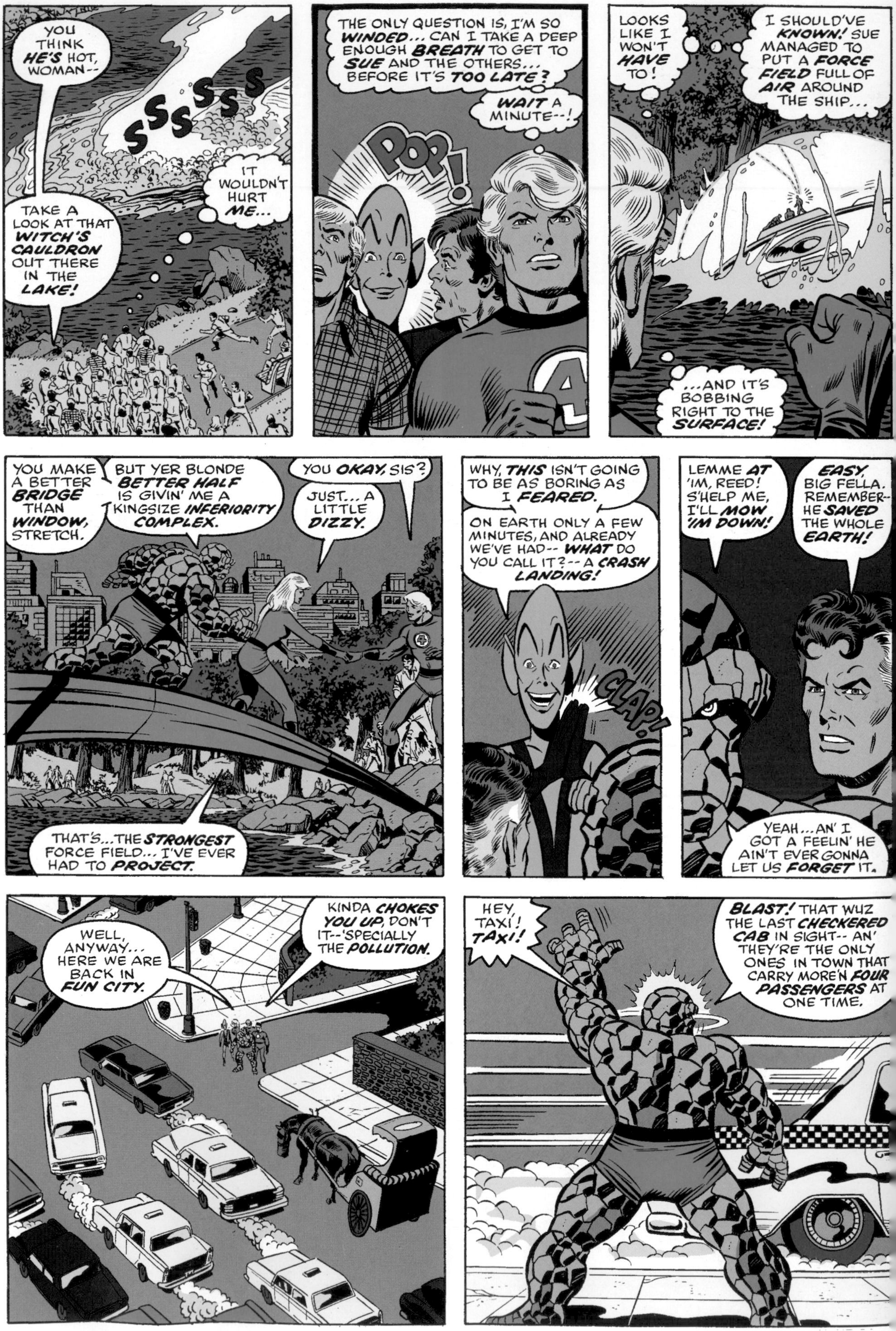
YOU THINK HE'S HOT, WOMAN--
SSSSSSS
IT WOULDN'T HURT ME...
TAKE A LOOK AT THAT WITCH'S CAULDRON OUT THERE IN THE LAKE!
THE ONLY QUESTION IS, I'M SO WINDED... CAN I TAKE A DEEP ENOUGH BREATH TO GET TO SUE AND THE OTHERS... BEFORE IT'S TOO LATE?
WAIT A MINUTE--!
POP!
LOOKS LIKE I WON'T HAVE TO!
I SHOULD'VE KNOWN! SUE MANAGED TO PUT A FORCE FIELD FULL OF AIR AROUND THE SHIP...
...AND IT'S BOBBING RIGHT TO THE SURFACE!
YOU MAKE A BETTER BRIDGE THAN WINDOW, STRETCH.
BUT YER BLONDE BETTER HALF IS GIVIN' ME A KINGSIZE INFERIORITY COMPLEX.
YOU OKAY, SIS?
JUST... A LITTLE DIZZY.
THAT'S... THE STRONGEST FORCE FIELD... I'VE EVER HAD TO PROJECT.
WHY, THIS ISN'T GOING TO BE AS BORING AS I FEARED.
ON EARTH ONLY A FEW MINUTES, AND ALREADY WE'VE HAD-- WHAT DO YOU CALL IT?-- A CRASH LANDING!
CLAP!
LEMME AT 'IM, REED! S'HELP ME, I'LL MOW 'IM DOWN!
EASY, BIG FELLA. REMEMBER-- HE SAVED THE WHOLE EARTH!
YEAH... AN' I GOT A FEELIN' HE AIN'T EVER GONNA LET US FORGET IT.
WELL, ANYWAY... HERE WE ARE BACK IN FUN CITY.
KINDA CHOKES YOU UP, DON'T IT--'SPECIALLY THE POLLUTION.
HEY, TAXI! TAXI!
BLAST! THAT WUZ THE LAST CHECKERED CAB IN SIGHT-- AN' THEY'RE THE ONLY ONES IN TOWN THAT CARRY MORE'N FOUR PASSENGERS AT ONE TIME.

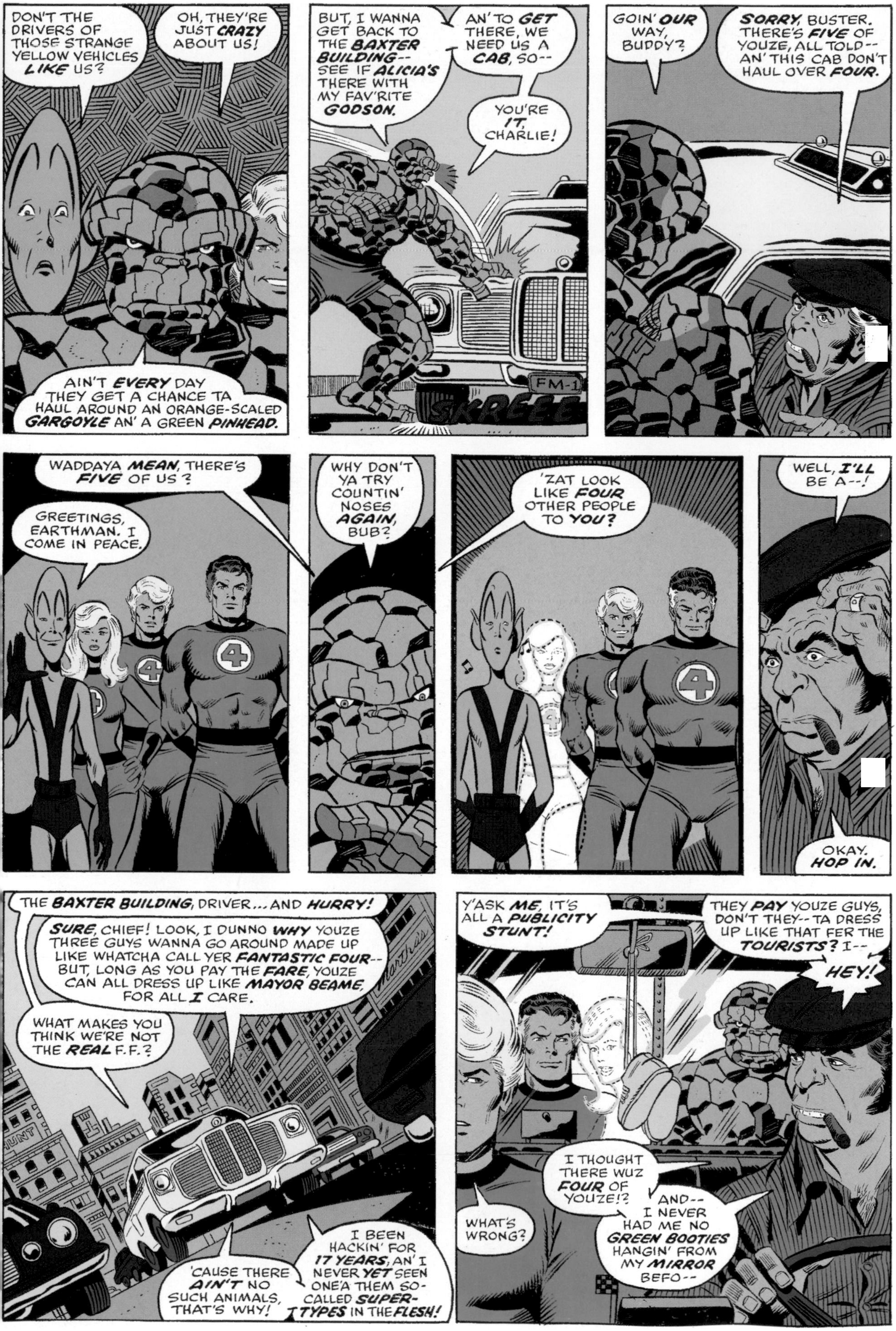

DON'T THE DRIVERS OF THOSE STRANGE YELLOW VEHICLES LIKE US?
OH, THEY'RE JUST CRAZY ABOUT US!
AIN'T EVERY DAY THEY GET A CHANCE TA HAUL AROUND AN ORANGE-SCALED GARGOYLE AN' A GREEN PINHEAD.
BUT, I WANNA GET BACK TO THE BAXTER BUILDING-- SEE IF ALICIA'S THERE WITH MY FAV'RITE GODSON.
AN' TO GET THERE, WE NEED US A CAB, SO--
YOU'RE IT, CHARLIE!
FM-1
SKREEE
GOIN' OUR WAY, BUDDY?
SORRY, BUSTER. THERE'S FIVE OF YOUZE, ALL TOLD-- AN' THIS CAB DON'T HAUL OVER FOUR.
WADDAYA MEAN, THERE'S FIVE OF US?
GREETINGS, EARTHMAN. I COME IN PEACE.
WHY DON'T YA TRY COUNTIN' NOSES AGAIN, BUB?
'ZAT LOOK LIKE FOUR OTHER PEOPLE TO YOU?
WELL, I'LL BE A--!
OKAY. HOP IN.
THE BAXTER BUILDING, DRIVER... AND HURRY!
SURE, CHIEF! LOOK, I DUNNO WHY YOUZE THREE GUYS WANNA GO AROUND MADE UP LIKE WHATCHA CALL YER FANTASTIC FOUR-- BUT, LONG AS YOU PAY THE FARE, YOUZE CAN ALL DRESS UP LIKE MAYOR BEAME, FOR ALL I CARE.
WHAT MAKES YOU THINK WE'RE NOT THE REAL F.F.?
'CAUSE THERE AIN'T NO SUCH ANIMALS, THAT'S WHY!
I BEEN HACKIN' FOR 17 YEARS, AN' I NEVER YET SEEN ONE'A THEM SO-CALLED SUPER-TYPES IN THE FLESH!
Y'ASK ME, IT'S ALL A PUBLICITY STUNT!
THEY PAY YOUZE GUYS, DON'T THEY-- TA DRESS UP LIKE THAT FER THE TOURISTS? I--
HEY!
WHAT'S WRONG?
I THOUGHT THERE WUZ FOUR OF YOUZE!?
AND-- I NEVER HAD ME NO GREEN BOOTIES HANGIN' FROM MY MIRROR BEFO--

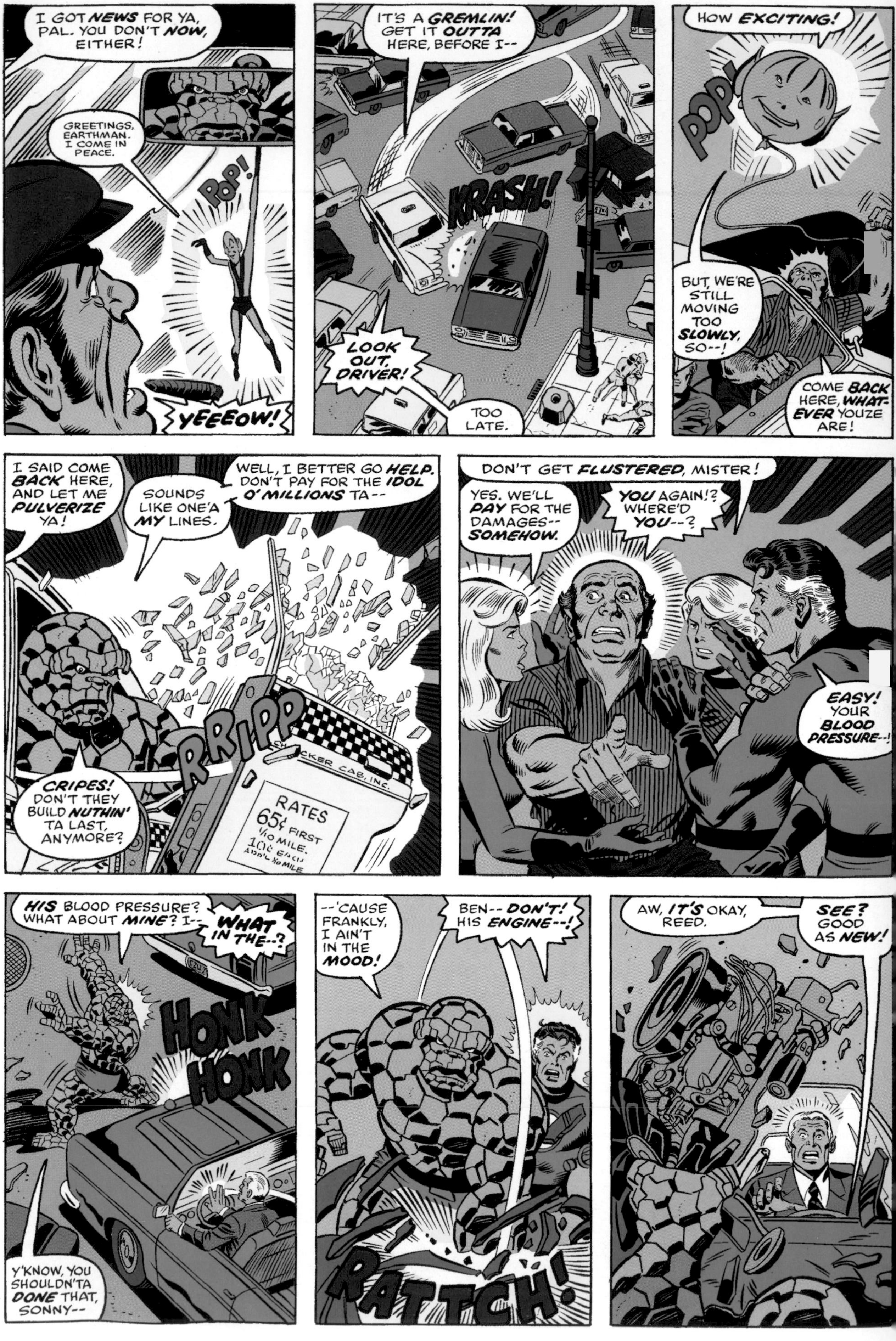
I GOT NEWS FOR YA, PAL. YOU DON'T NOW, EITHER!
GREETINGS, EARTHMAN. I COME IN PEACE.
POP!
YEEEOW!
IT'S A GREMLIN! GET IT OUTTA HERE, BEFORE I--
KRASH!
LOOK OUT, DRIVER!
TOO LATE.
HOW EXCITING!
POP!
BUT, WE'RE STILL MOVING TOO SLOWLY, SO--!
COME BACK HERE, WHAT-EVER YOUZE ARE!
I SAID COME BACK HERE, AND LET ME PULVERIZE YA!
SOUNDS LIKE ONE'A MY LINES.
WELL, I BETTER GO HELP. DON'T PAY FOR THE IDOL O' MILLIONS TA--
RRIPP
CRIPES! DON'T THEY BUILD NUTHIN' TA LAST, ANYMORE?
RATES 65¢ FIRST 1/10 MILE. 10¢ EACH ADD'L 1/10 MILE
DON'T GET FLUSTERED, MISTER!
YES. WE'LL PAY FOR THE DAMAGES-- SOMEHOW.
YOU AGAIN!? WHERE'D YOU--?
EASY! YOUR BLOOD PRESSURE--!
HIS BLOOD PRESSURE? WHAT ABOUT MINE? I--
WHAT IN THE--?
HONK HONK
Y'KNOW, YOU SHOULDN'TA DONE THAT, SONNY--
--'CAUSE FRANKLY, I AIN'T IN THE MOOD!
BEN-- DON'T! HIS ENGINE--!
RATTCH!
AW, IT'S OKAY, REED.
SEE? GOOD AS NEW!

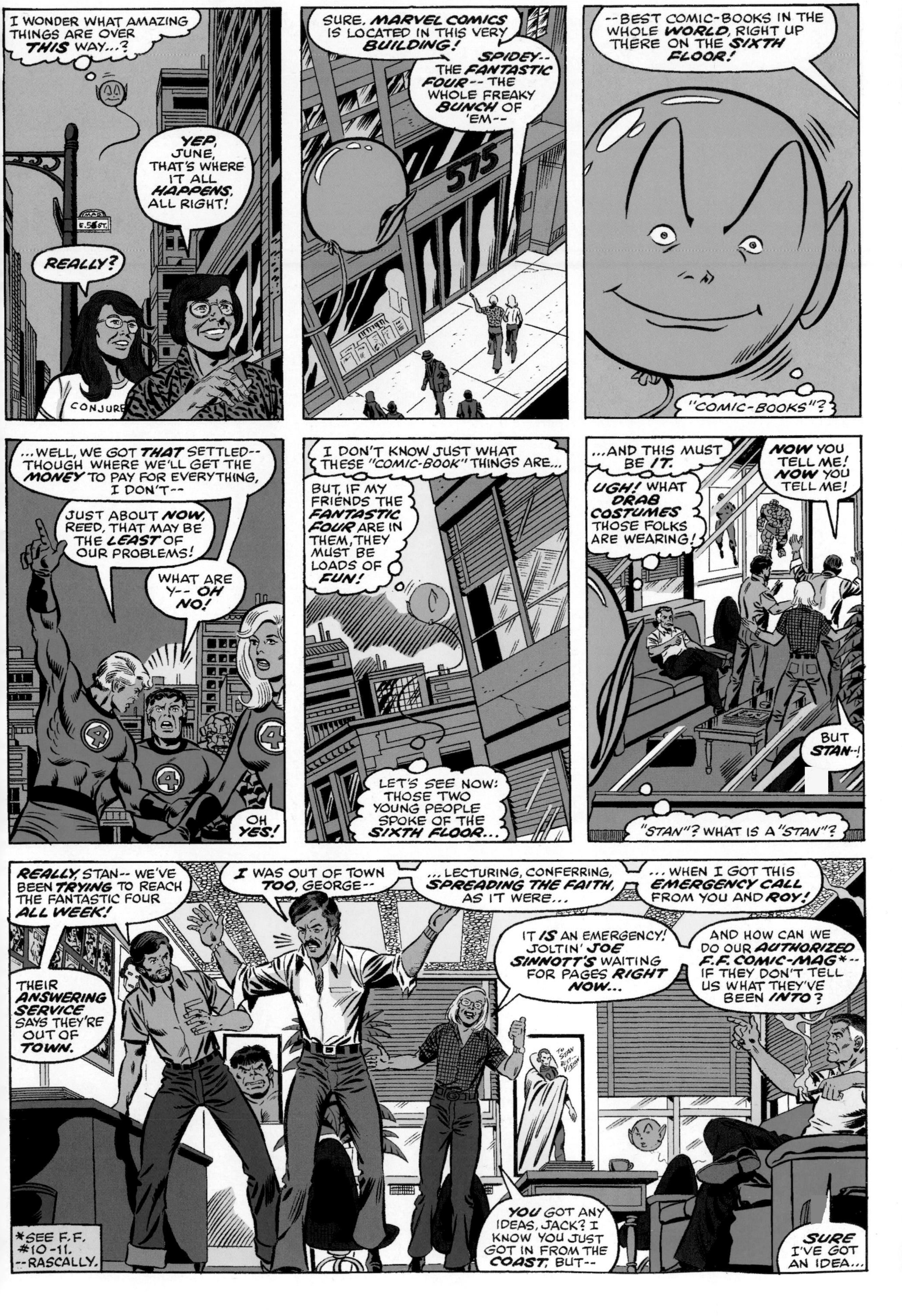

I WONDER WHAT AMAZING THINGS ARE OVER THIS WAY...?
YEP, JUNE, THAT'S WHERE IT ALL HAPPENS, ALL RIGHT!
REALLY?
CONJURE
SURE. MARVEL COMICS IS LOCATED IN THIS VERY BUILDING!
SPIDEY-- THE FANTASTIC FOUR-- THE WHOLE FREAKY BUNCH OF 'EM--
575
--BEST COMIC-BOOKS IN THE WHOLE WORLD, RIGHT UP THERE ON THE SIXTH FLOOR!
"COMIC-BOOKS"?
...WELL, WE GOT THAT SETTLED-- THOUGH WHERE WE'LL GET THE MONEY TO PAY FOR EVERYTHING, I DON'T--
JUST ABOUT NOW, REED, THAT MAY BE THE LEAST OF OUR PROBLEMS!
WHAT ARE Y-- OH NO!
OH YES!
I DON'T KNOW JUST WHAT THESE "COMIC-BOOK" THINGS ARE...
BUT, IF MY FRIENDS THE FANTASTIC FOUR ARE IN THEM, THEY MUST BE LOADS OF FUN!
LET'S SEE NOW: THOSE TWO YOUNG PEOPLE SPOKE OF THE SIXTH FLOOR...
...AND THIS MUST BE IT.
UGH! WHAT DRAB COSTUMES THOSE FOLKS ARE WEARING!
NOW YOU TELL ME! NOW YOU TELL ME!
BUT STAN--!
"STAN"? WHAT IS A "STAN"?
REALLY, STAN-- WE'VE BEEN TRYING TO REACH THE FANTASTIC FOUR ALL WEEK!
THEIR ANSWERING SERVICE SAYS THEY'RE OUT OF TOWN.
I WAS OUT OF TOWN TOO, GEORGE--
...LECTURING, CONFERRING, SPREADING THE FAITH, AS IT WERE...
...WHEN I GOT THIS EMERGENCY CALL FROM YOU AND ROY!
IT IS AN EMERGENCY! JOLTIN' JOE SINNOTT'S WAITING FOR PAGES RIGHT NOW...
AND HOW CAN WE DO OUR AUTHORIZED F.F. COMIC-MAG*-- IF THEY DON'T TELL US WHAT THEY'VE BEEN INTO?
YOU GOT ANY IDEAS, JACK? I KNOW YOU JUST GOT IN FROM THE COAST, BUT--
SURE I'VE GOT AN IDEA...
*SEE F.F. #10-11. --RASCALLY.

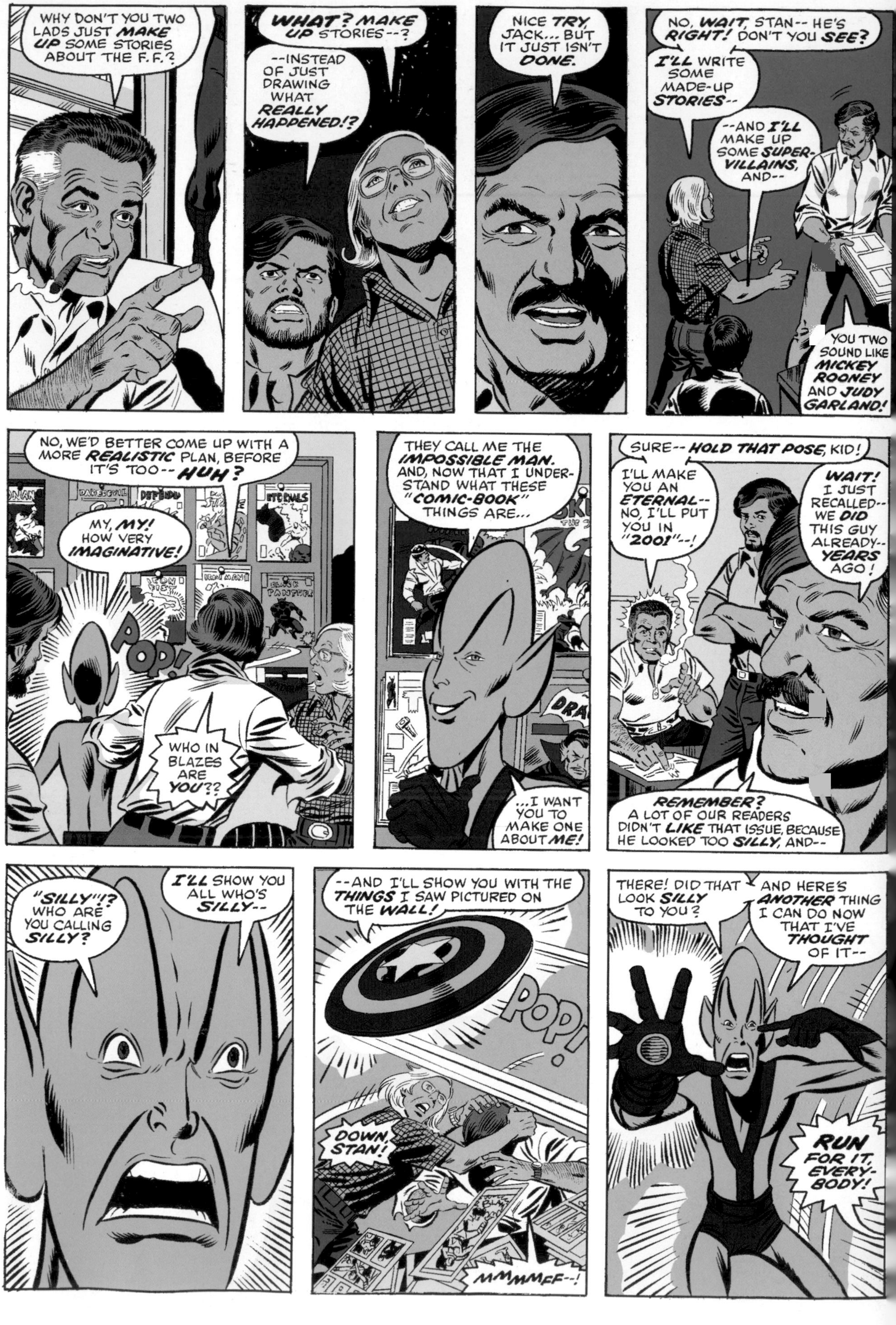
WHY DON'T YOU TWO LADS JUST MAKE UP SOME STORIES ABOUT THE F.F.?
WHAT? MAKE UP STORIES--?
--INSTEAD OF JUST DRAWING WHAT REALLY HAPPENED!?
NICE TRY, JACK... BUT IT JUST ISN'T DONE.
NO, WAIT, STAN-- HE'S RIGHT! DON'T YOU SEE?
I'LL WRITE SOME MADE-UP STORIES--
--AND I'LL MAKE UP SOME SUPER-VILLAINS, AND--
YOU TWO SOUND LIKE MICKEY ROONEY AND JUDY GARLAND!
NO, WE'D BETTER COME UP WITH A MORE REALISTIC PLAN, BEFORE IT'S TOO-- HUH?
MY, MY! HOW VERY IMAGINATIVE!
POP!
WHO IN BLAZES ARE YOU??
THEY CALL ME THE IMPOSSIBLE MAN. AND, NOW THAT I UNDERSTAND WHAT THESE "COMIC-BOOK" THINGS ARE...
...I WANT YOU TO MAKE ONE ABOUT ME!
SURE-- HOLD THAT POSE, KID!
I'LL MAKE YOU AN ETERNAL-- NO, I'LL PUT YOU IN "2001"--!
WAIT! I JUST RECALLED-- WE DID THIS GUY ALREADY-- YEARS AGO!
REMEMBER? A LOT OF OUR READERS DIDN'T LIKE THAT ISSUE, BECAUSE HE LOOKED TOO SILLY, AND--
"SILLY"!? WHO ARE YOU CALLING SILLY?
I'LL SHOW YOU ALL WHO'S SILLY--
--AND I'LL SHOW YOU WITH THE THINGS I SAW PICTURED ON THE WALL!
POP!
DOWN, STAN!
MMMMMF--!
THERE! DID THAT LOOK SILLY TO YOU?
AND HERE'S ANOTHER THING I CAN DO NOW THAT I'VE THOUGHT OF IT--
RUN FOR IT, EVERYBODY!

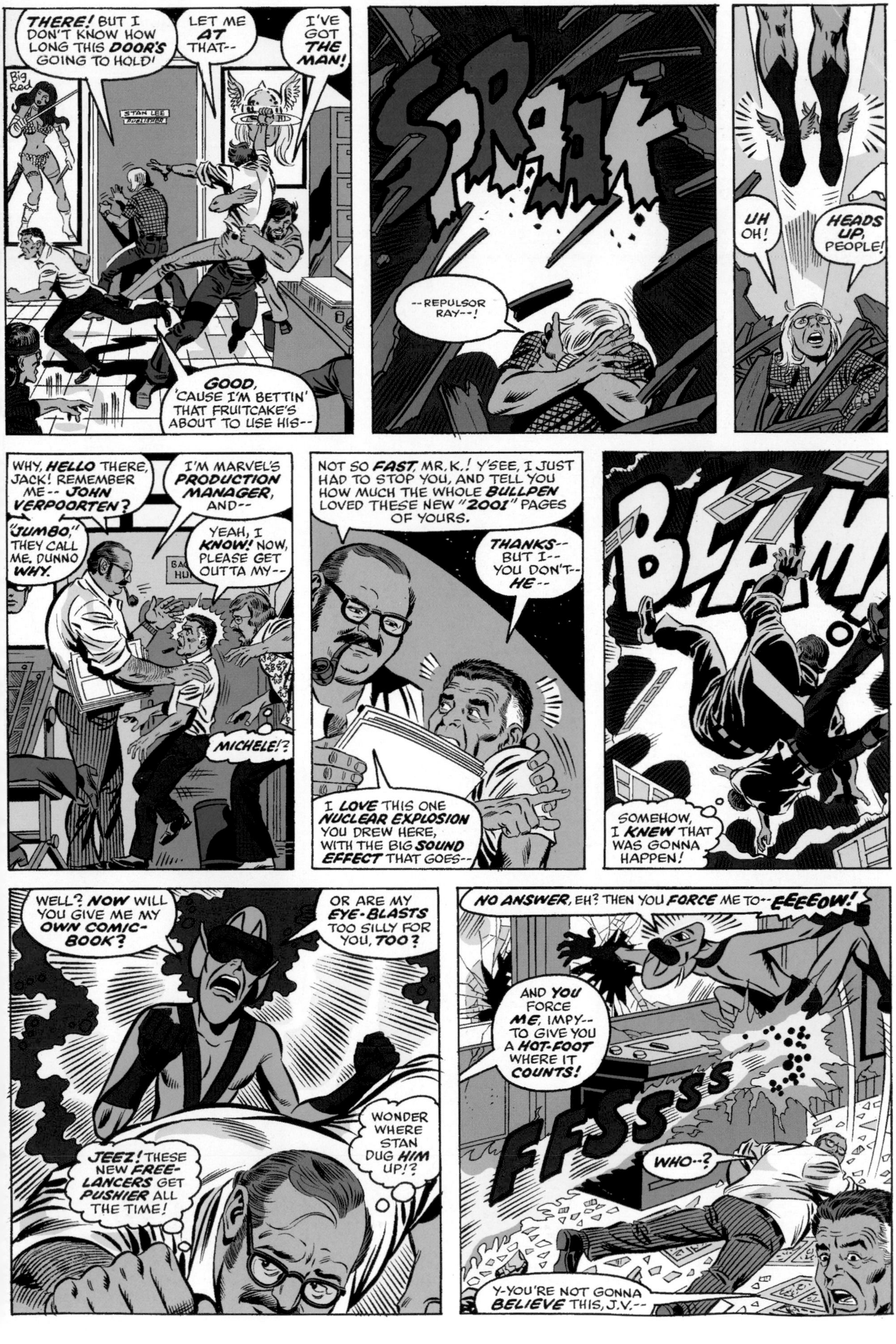

THERE! BUT I DON'T KNOW HOW LONG THIS DOOR'S GOING TO HOLD!
LET ME AT THAT--
I'VE GOT THE MAN!
Big Red
STAN LEE PUBLISHER
GOOD, 'CAUSE I'M BETTIN' THAT FRUITCAKE'S ABOUT TO USE HIS--
SPRAK
--REPULSOR RAY--!
UH OH!
HEADS UP, PEOPLE!
WHY, HELLO THERE, JACK! REMEMBER ME-- JOHN VERPOORTEN?
"JUMBO," THEY CALL ME. DUNNO WHY.
I'M MARVEL'S PRODUCTION MANAGER, AND--
YEAH, I KNOW! NOW, PLEASE GET OUTTA MY--
MICHELE!?
NOT SO FAST, MR. K.! Y'SEE, I JUST HAD TO STOP YOU, AND TELL YOU HOW MUCH THE WHOLE BULLPEN LOVED THESE NEW "2001" PAGES OF YOURS.
THANKS-- BUT I-- YOU DON'T-- HE--
I LOVE THIS ONE NUCLEAR EXPLOSION YOU DREW HERE, WITH THE BIG SOUND EFFECT THAT GOES--
BLAM!
SOMEHOW, I KNEW THAT WAS GONNA HAPPEN!
WELL? NOW WILL YOU GIVE ME MY OWN COMIC-BOOK?
OR ARE MY EYE-BLASTS TOO SILLY FOR YOU, TOO?
WONDER WHERE STAN DUG HIM UP!?
JEEZ! THESE NEW FREE-LANCERS GET PUSHIER ALL THE TIME!
NO ANSWER, EH? THEN YOU FORCE ME TO-- EEEEOW!
AND YOU FORCE ME, IMPY-- TO GIVE YOU A HOT-FOOT WHERE IT COUNTS!
FFSSSS
WHO--?
Y-YOU'RE NOT GONNA BELIEVE THIS, J.V.--

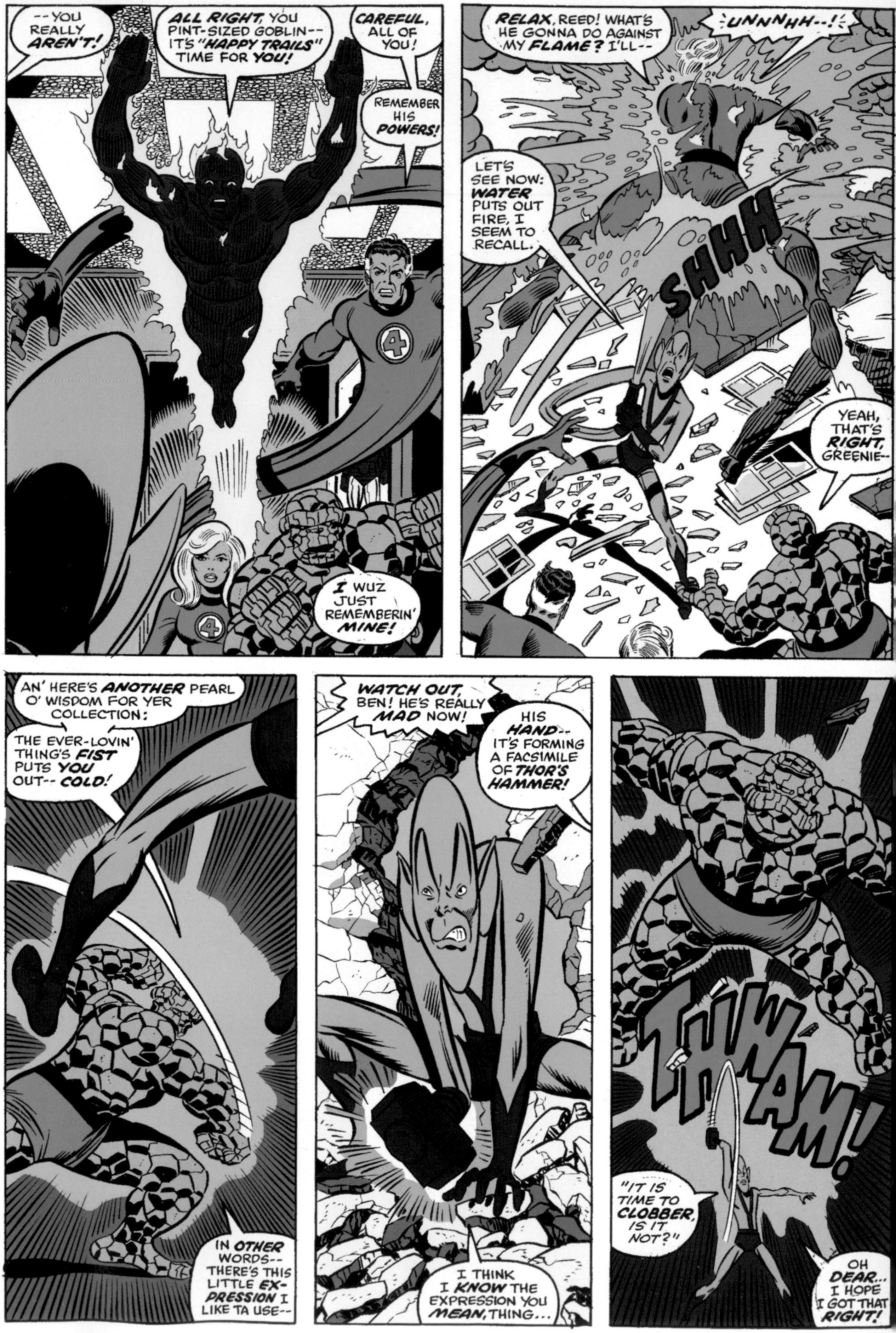
--YOU REALLY AREN'T!
ALL RIGHT, YOU PINT-SIZED GOBLIN-- IT'S "HAPPY TRAILS" TIME FOR YOU!
CAREFUL, ALL OF YOU!
REMEMBER HIS POWERS!
I WUZ JUST REMEMBERIN' MINE!
RELAX, REED! WHAT'S HE GONNA DO AGAINST MY FLAME? I'LL--
UNNNHH--!
LET'S SEE NOW: WATER PUTS OUT FIRE, I SEEM TO RECALL.
SHHH
YEAH, THAT'S RIGHT, GREENIE--
AN' HERE'S ANOTHER PEARL O' WISDOM FOR YER COLLECTION:
THE EVER-LOVIN' THING'S FIST PUTS YOU OUT-- COLD!
IN OTHER WORDS-- THERE'S THIS LITTLE EX-PRESSION I LIKE TA USE--
WATCH OUT, BEN! HE'S REALLY MAD NOW!
HIS HAND-- IT'S FORMING A FACSIMILE OF THOR'S HAMMER!
I THINK I KNOW THE EXPRESSION YOU MEAN, THING...
THWAM!
"IT IS TIME TO CLOBBER, IS IT NOT?"
OH DEAR... I HOPE I GOT THAT RIGHT!

FRAAKK'!

SEE, MARIE? I'VE BEEN *TELLING* 'EM THEY SHOULD GET THAT *WALL* FIXED!

WHAT *WALL*, JIM?

OKAY, "GREEN BOLT"-- THIS IS *IT!*

HERE'S WHERE WE FIND OUT WHICH ONE OF US IS *STRONGER* YOU OR *BENJY!*

EDITOR
STAN LEE
ROY THOMAS
LEN WEIN
MARV WOLFMAN
ROY THO~
GERRY CONWAY
ARCHIE GOODWIN
(YOUR NAME)

THAT IS IMPORTANT TO *YOU*, PERHAPS... BUT NOT TO *ME.*

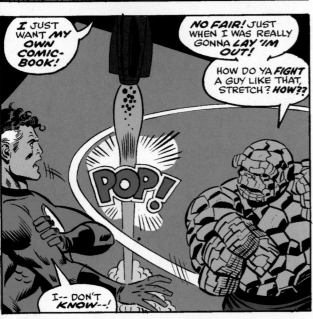

I JUST WANT *MY OWN* COMIC-BOOK!

NO *FAIR!* JUST WHEN I WAS REALLY GONNA *LAY 'IM OUT!*

HOW DO YA *FIGHT* A GUY LIKE THAT, STRETCH? *HOW??*

POP!

I-- DON'T *KNOW--!*

PARDON US, BUDDY! YOU SEE A *LITTLE GREEN GUY* COME THRU HERE?

ME? I'M STILL TRYING TO FIGURE OUT WHETHER I'M *ARTFUL* ARCHIE, OR *ARTICULATE* ARCHIE, OR--

THIS *EDITOR-IN-CHIEF* BUSINESS IS KIND-OF *TRICKY!*

BULLPEN BULLETINS

SOME-THING GREEN JUST *STREAKED* IN *THERE*--

--THAT OPEN DOOR MARKED *"ART DIRECTOR"!*

HEY, DID A *SHORT GREEN ALIEN* COME IN HERE?

YOU *KNOW* IT! WHY DO YOU THINK *I'M* GOING *OUT THERE?*

THE *F.F.--* AND THE *THING--* HERE??

I WONDER IF THEY'LL HELP ME OUT BY POSING FOR SOME *COVERS...!*

LOOK, *SIS--*

THAT'S THE *IMPOSSIBLE MAN*, ALL RIGHT--

BUT, HE'S *SHRUNK DOWN* AS SMALL AS *JOE ROSEN'S* LETTER-ING--OR A--

A *WASP*, PERHAPS?

JUST LEMME GET MY *MITTS* ON YA, AND YOU'LL BE *FLATTER'N* A *BUG* ON A *WINDSHIELD!*

NO NEED FOR FURTHER *THREATS*, BEN...

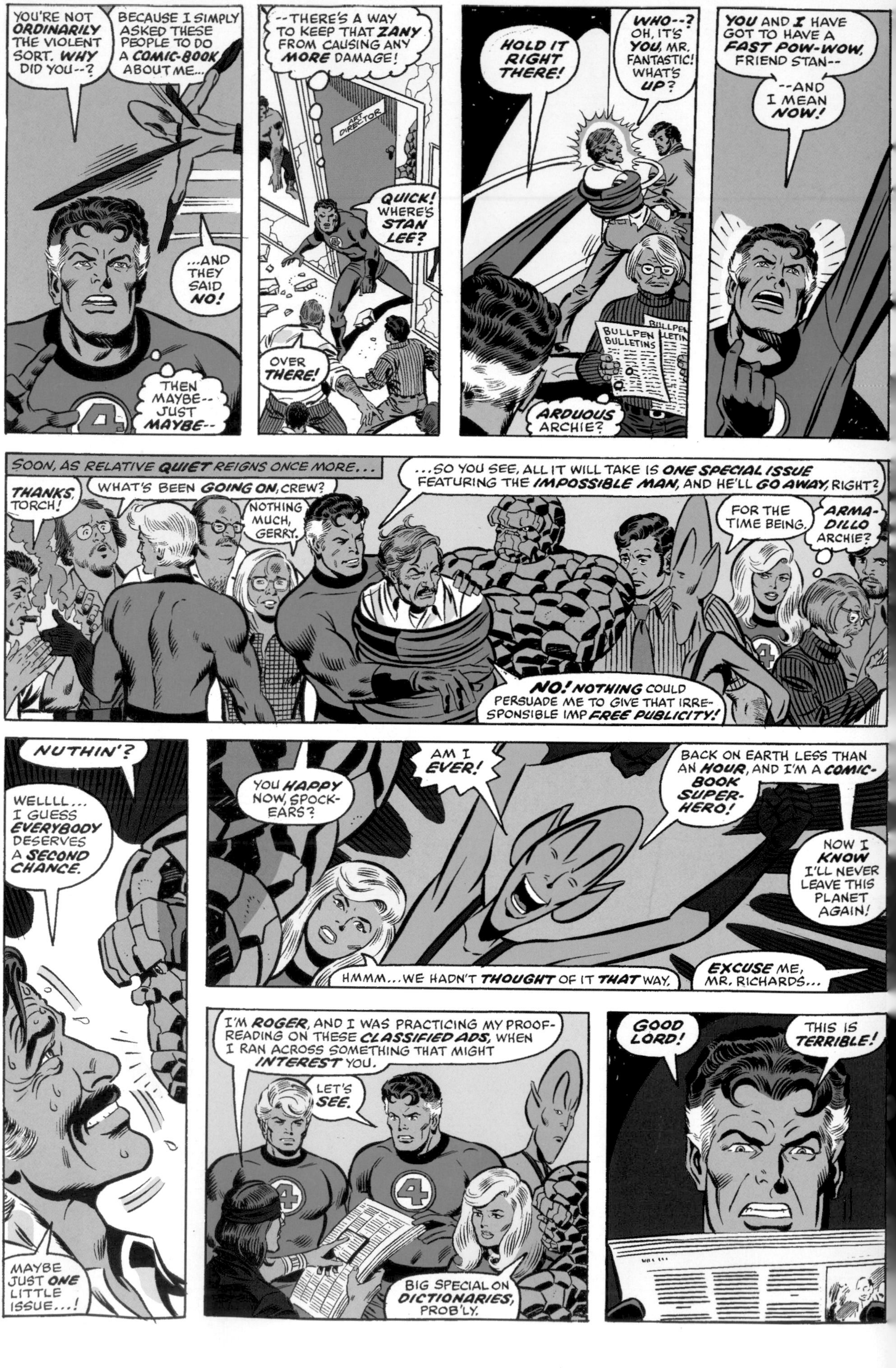

YOU'RE NOT ORDINARILY THE VIOLENT SORT. WHY DID YOU--?
BECAUSE I SIMPLY ASKED THESE PEOPLE TO DO A COMIC-BOOK ABOUT ME...
...AND THEY SAID NO!
THEN MAYBE-- JUST MAYBE--
--THERE'S A WAY TO KEEP THAT ZANY FROM CAUSING ANY MORE DAMAGE!
ART DIRECTOR
QUICK! WHERE'S STAN LEE?
OVER THERE!
HOLD IT RIGHT THERE!
WHO--? OH, IT'S YOU, MR. FANTASTIC! WHAT'S UP?
BULLPEN BULLETINS
ARDUOUS ARCHIE?
YOU AND I HAVE GOT TO HAVE A FAST POW-WOW, FRIEND STAN--
--AND I MEAN NOW!
SOON, AS RELATIVE QUIET REIGNS ONCE MORE...
THANKS, TORCH!
WHAT'S BEEN GOING ON, CREW?
NOTHING MUCH, GERRY.
...SO YOU SEE, ALL IT WILL TAKE IS ONE SPECIAL ISSUE FEATURING THE IMPOSSIBLE MAN, AND HE'LL GO AWAY, RIGHT?
FOR THE TIME BEING.
ARMA-DILLO ARCHIE?
NO! NOTHING COULD PERSUADE ME TO GIVE THAT IRRE-SPONSIBLE IMP FREE PUBLICITY!
NUTHIN'?
WELLLL... I GUESS EVERYBODY DESERVES A SECOND CHANCE.
MAYBE JUST ONE LITTLE ISSUE...!
YOU HAPPY NOW, SPOCK-EARS?
AM I EVER!
BACK ON EARTH LESS THAN AN HOUR, AND I'M A COMIC-BOOK SUPER-HERO!
NOW I KNOW I'LL NEVER LEAVE THIS PLANET AGAIN!
HMMM... WE HADN'T THOUGHT OF IT THAT WAY.
EXCUSE ME, MR. RICHARDS...
I'M ROGER, AND I WAS PRACTICING MY PROOF-READING ON THESE CLASSIFIED ADS, WHEN I RAN ACROSS SOMETHING THAT MIGHT INTEREST YOU.
LET'S SEE.
BIG SPECIAL ON DICTIONARIES, PROB'LY.
GOOD LORD!
THIS IS TERRIBLE!

LISTEN TO **THIS**, PEOPLE--!

CLASSIFIED ADS

ARE YOU A BONA FIDE SUPER-VILLAIN IN SEARCH OF **TOGETHERNESS?**

THE FRIGHTFUL FOUR ARE NOW ACCEPTING APPLICANTS FOR MEMBERSHIP AT THE **BAXTER BUILDING**, FORMER HEADQUARTERS OF THE **FANTASTIC FOUR.**

NO PREVIOUS SUPER-VILLAIN GROUP EXPERIENCE NECESSARY.

2:00 P.M. JULY 26, 1976

AND THAT'S **TODAY!**

SHEESH! THEY'RE NOT ONLY HAVIN' **TRY-OUTS**, BUT THEY'RE DOIN' IT IN **OUR** STOMPIN'-GROUNDS!

THEN **I** SAY, LET'S **US** GO DO SOME STOMPIN' OF OUR **OWN**-- RIGHT **NOW!**

WE'VE GOT TO GET THERE **FAST!**

SAY NO **MORE**, MR. RICHARDS!

I FOUND THIS **OLD COMIC-BOOK** IN THE **CLOSET** AS I ROCKETED THRU--

--AND IT GAVE ME THE MOST **MARVELOUS** IDEA!

THEN JUST FOLLOW THE WAY WE'RE **POINTING**, FRIEND--

YEAH! AND DON'T SPARE THE **HORSEFLIES!**

ACTUALLY, YOU KNOW, IT WAS KIND OF **NICE** TO SEE ALL THE **MARVEL BULLPEN** AGAIN, WASN'T IT?

I **GUESS** SO, SIS.... BUT **SOME** OF THOSE GUYS ARE DOWNRIGHT **WEIRD!**

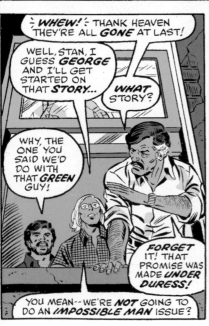

÷ **WHEW!** ÷ THANK HEAVEN THEY'RE ALL **GONE** AT LAST!

WELL, STAN, I GUESS **GEORGE** AND I'LL GET STARTED ON THAT **STORY**...

WHAT STORY?

WHY, THE ONE YOU SAID WE'D DO WITH THAT **GREEN** GUY!

FORGET IT! THAT PROMISE WAS MADE **UNDER DURESS!**

YOU MEAN--WE'RE **NOT** GOING TO DO AN **IMPOSSIBLE MAN** ISSUE?

NEVER!

To Stan & the Bullpen

MARVEL COMICS HASN'T GOT TIME TO WASTE ON **SILLY-LOOKING** CHARACTERS!

Howie

WELL, THERE IT **IS**, AMIGOS-- **HOME SWEET HOME!**

ONLY, RIGHT ABOUT **NOW**, IT MIGHT JUST BE INFESTED WITH **TERMITES!**

179

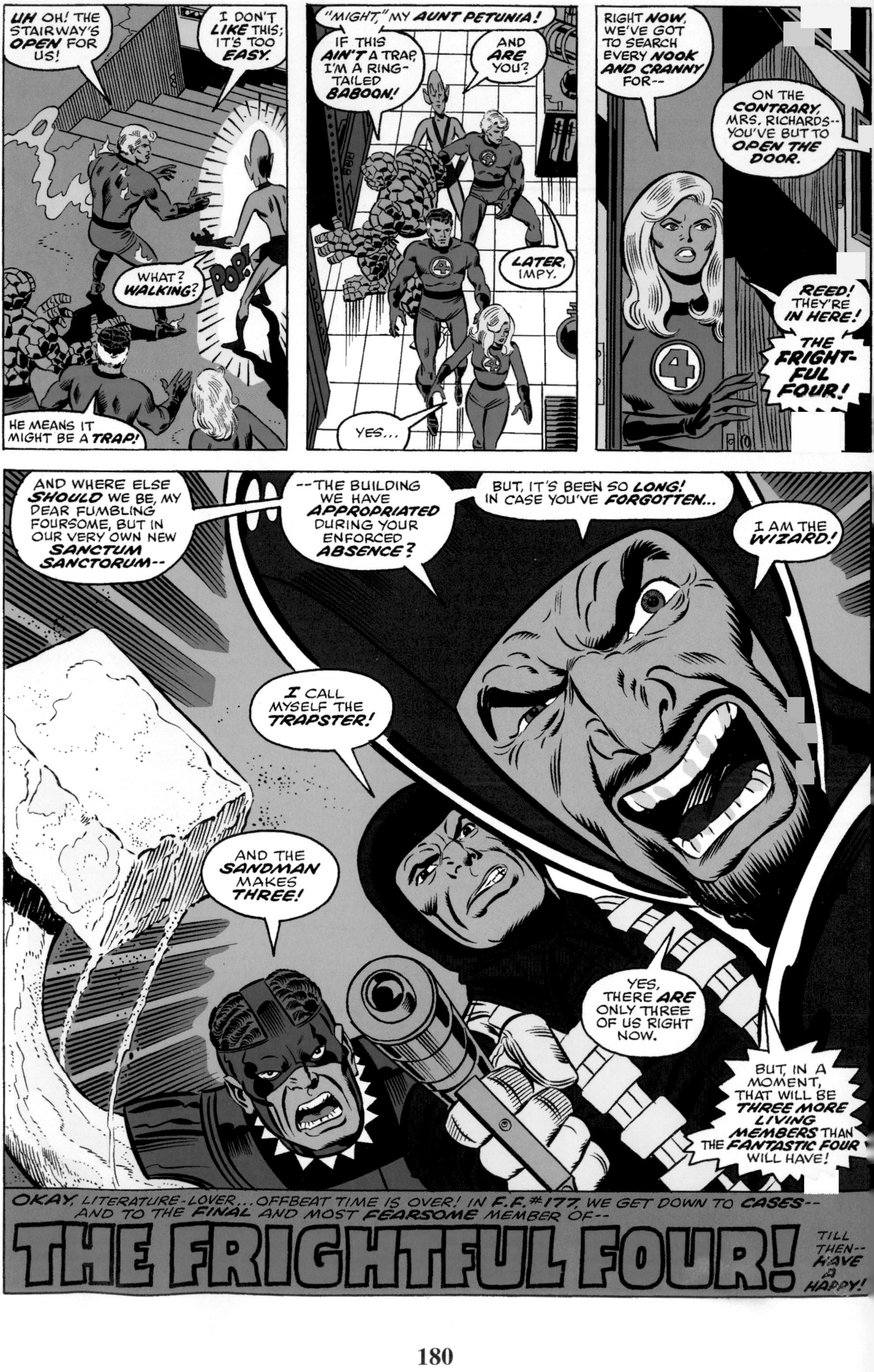
UH OH! THE STAIRWAY'S OPEN FOR US!
I DON'T LIKE THIS; IT'S TOO EASY.
WHAT? WALKING?
POP!
HE MEANS IT MIGHT BE A TRAP!
"MIGHT," MY AUNT PETUNIA!
IF THIS AIN'T A TRAP, I'M A RING-TAILED BABOON!
AND ARE YOU?
LATER, IMPY.
YES...
RIGHT NOW, WE'VE GOT TO SEARCH EVERY NOOK AND CRANNY FOR--
ON THE CONTRARY, MRS. RICHARDS-- YOU'VE BUT TO OPEN THE DOOR.
REED! THEY'RE IN HERE!
THE FRIGHT-FUL FOUR!
AND WHERE ELSE SHOULD WE BE, MY DEAR FUMBLING FOURSOME, BUT IN OUR VERY OWN NEW SANCTUM SANCTORUM--
--THE BUILDING WE HAVE APPROPRIATED DURING YOUR ENFORCED ABSENCE?
BUT, IT'S BEEN SO LONG! IN CASE YOU'VE FORGOTTEN...
I AM THE WIZARD!
I CALL MYSELF THE TRAPSTER!
AND THE SANDMAN MAKES THREE!
YES, THERE ARE ONLY THREE OF US RIGHT NOW.
BUT, IN A MOMENT, THERE WILL BE THREE MORE LIVING MEMBERS THAN THE FANTASTIC FOUR WILL HAVE!
OKAY, LITERATURE-LOVER... OFFBEAT TIME IS OVER! IN F.F. #177, WE GET DOWN TO CASES-- AND TO THE FINAL AND MOST FEARSOME MEMBER OF--
THE FRIGHTFUL FOUR!
TILL THEN-- HAVE A HAPPY!

BAXTER BUILDING BULLETINS

c/o MARVEL COMICS GROUP, 575 MADISON AVE. N.Y.C. 10022

THE STORY BEHIND THE STORY:
A Personal View by Roy Thomas

Every once in a while, a story comes along that, like it or don't, you just feel you want to do—no, *have* to do.

Once conceived, this issue of THE FANTASTIC FOUR was one of those stories for me. And, especially now that I've seen the fabulous artwork done for it by Let-George-Do-It Perez, and had a chance to add my own not-necessarily-deathless dialogue—well, I'm just glad my momentary obsession got the better of me.

For better or for worse, F.F. #176 is *also* one of those stories which had such a strange genesis that I'd like to share it with you, okay?

Anyway, I was--

No, wait a minute. Can't start yet. There's something I've got to do first.

Hey, all you sneaky types who read the letters pages of comic-mags before you peruse the stories themselves: Don't read this now, as it's meant to be read as an *afterthought* to the story, not as a *prologue* to it. All right, you have been warned!

Now, what was I saying? Oh, yes....

Anyway, I was up against this deadline, see? George needed a plot—and I was up to my ankles in pages for both the color and black-and-white CONAN books. I knew I wanted to do a story with the Frightful Four (see? We *told* you to read the story first!)—but it was going to be hard getting the F.F. back to earth *and* involved with the Frightful Four all in one tale, especially since I wanted to utilize the Impossible Man for a single issue as well.

So I decided that the only way to do it was to have Impy (as I call him, since he has no real name) go on a Manhattan, or perhaps earthwide, rampage. At first I toyed with having the F.F. battle him all over the world, simply trying to get him to stay put and stop causing trouble. But it was coming hard, and my heart wasn't in it.

Then I had this thought: Actually, it's not so hard getting around the world these days. The hard part is getting across town (and that goes for just about any city, not just NYC, right?).

So I figured, okay, we'll do a story in which the F.F. crash-land the High Evolutionary's space ship in Central Park and spend the whole issue trying to get to the Baxter Building. That'd be fun: bits with trying to get a taxi when there are five of them and New York taxis (except checkered ones, right?) can only take four, etc. Maybe even a colorful cabbie from the tradition which extends from FANTASTIC FOUR #1 thru, er, uh, Travis Bickle.

I even thought immediately of the scene in which the Thing tears the motor out of a guy's honking car—mainly because I've always wished *I* could do that to somebody who edged into the crosswalk at a stoplight.

And the Impossible Man, of course, would decide to strike out on his own, and he'd end up—where?

The Empire State Building? (It's been done, from King Kong to Gorr.) World Trade Center? (Ka-Zar—and King Kong, courtesy of Dino de Laurentiis.) Statue of Liberty? (Did that myself, years back, in THE HULK.) Chrysler Building? (Who ever *heard* of it?) The subway? (*Every*body does *that* one, me included.)

I decided to try another approach. Okay, now: the lake in which I wanted the ship to land is near the southeast end of Central Park, right? Right. I know that. *Why* do I know that? Because when I used to be editor-in-chief around here and flee my responsibilities for an hour at lunchtime, I'd often go walking there, because it's only a couple of blocks from--

Marvel Comics.

Yeah.

And so an idea was born. (Whether retroactive birth control should have been practiced is for someone else to decide, not me.)

I immediately called George to clue him in on the plot I was going to mail him, and, though he obviously thought I was out of my bird, he also got very enthusiastic about it. And this is as

good a place as any for me to say "Welcome back!" to Mr. P. on THE FANTASTIC FOUR—and that as far as Ye Editor/Writer is concerned, George has turned in one of the greatest art jobs ever done on this relatively offbeat (and very difficult) type of story. I couldn't have asked for better, pal!

Anyhow, even as I was plotting the tale, another problem: John Verpoorten and Romita informed me that if I wanted Jack "King" Kirby to pencil the cover for F.F. #176, I'd better give him a coast-to-coast phone-call right away and describe a cover scene to him.

And did I *ever* want Jack to do it! After all, he and Smilin' Stan Lee created the character, a decade and a half ago, in one-and-only story which, while it did not lead to fabulous sales or such-like, had become a cultish favorite among certain F.F. lovers (myself included, but definitely, since the night in late 1962 I first laid eyes on F.F. #11).

So I called Jack. Yes, he said, he vaguely remembered the Impossible Man. The thin green guy with the pinhead, right? I said right. And here's the important part: I asked Jack to have Impy, on the cover, using some of the gimmicks George and I had planned for the interior, such as hosing the Human Torch and hammering the Thing.

But, as Jazzy Johnny Romita always said: "Jack at his *worst* is better than most guys at their *best!*"

And not only is Jack seldom at his worst—but on this cover, he was definitely at his best!

A few days later, I got this strange penciled cover in the mail which was just what I'd asked, except that Impy was blasting the F.F. with hands shaped like Iron-Man's glove and Thor's magic hammer! And there was even a note suggesting he could have shaped a fist like Captain America's shield! Immediately I saw Jack's reasoning: this was the Marvel Comics office, right? So why not have him using Marvel-type gimmicks?

Ten minutes later I was on the phone describing the cover to George, and we instantly decided (since George was just beginning to draw the last half of the book) to utilize Jack's ideas.

And we just wanted you—and Jack—to know it, that's all.

So, there you have it. The offbeat story of an offbeat story. Answer #4579 in a series of answers to the question "Where do you get those nutty ideas?" Answer: From desperation, from perspiration, from inspiration—and sometimes we get by with a bit of help from our friends—guys like Jack Kirby and Stan Lee, who were out there 'way ahead of any of us.

Post scriptum: A couple of days after George finished the story and just as I was about to write it, I learned that—by the sheerest of coincidences—Marv (The) Wolfman had been up at the office taking photos for a Bullpen-oriented story *he* intended to do in his own brand-new action-packed NOVA mag. Panicky lest we accidentally tread on each other's toes, I gave him a call. Marv immediately (and very graciously, I might add) volunteered to scrap his story, but I said why? What he was planning to do, I saw as he outlined it, was wildly different from what I was doing—so, since THE FANTASTIC FOUR would come out first, I'd simply put a couple of lines into George's and my story to foreshadow what he and Sal were going to do in NOVA (and we'll let you guess which ones they were)—while Marv, for his part, could pick up where we left off and we'd all four be working together to strike another blow for Mighty Marvel Continuity!

All in all, the NOVA thing just made the whole thing more exciting to me, if that was possible.

One final note: For once, I think I even wrote a story faster than George can draw it! Namely, I had to sit up all night (from ten in the evening till seven in the morning, with alternate breaks for coffee and collapsing) to finish this critically-late issue. And why did I have to be done by seven? Because at 7:30 I had to go rent a car and drive down to Pennsylvania to meet Peerless Paul Lichter, founder of the Elvis Unique Record Club and one of the few guys around whose collection of Presley memorabilia dwarfs my own, *that's* why!

But, I digress. As is my wont.

Well, that's the story behind the Impossible Man's New York Adventure. We thought you might like to know. We hope we were right.

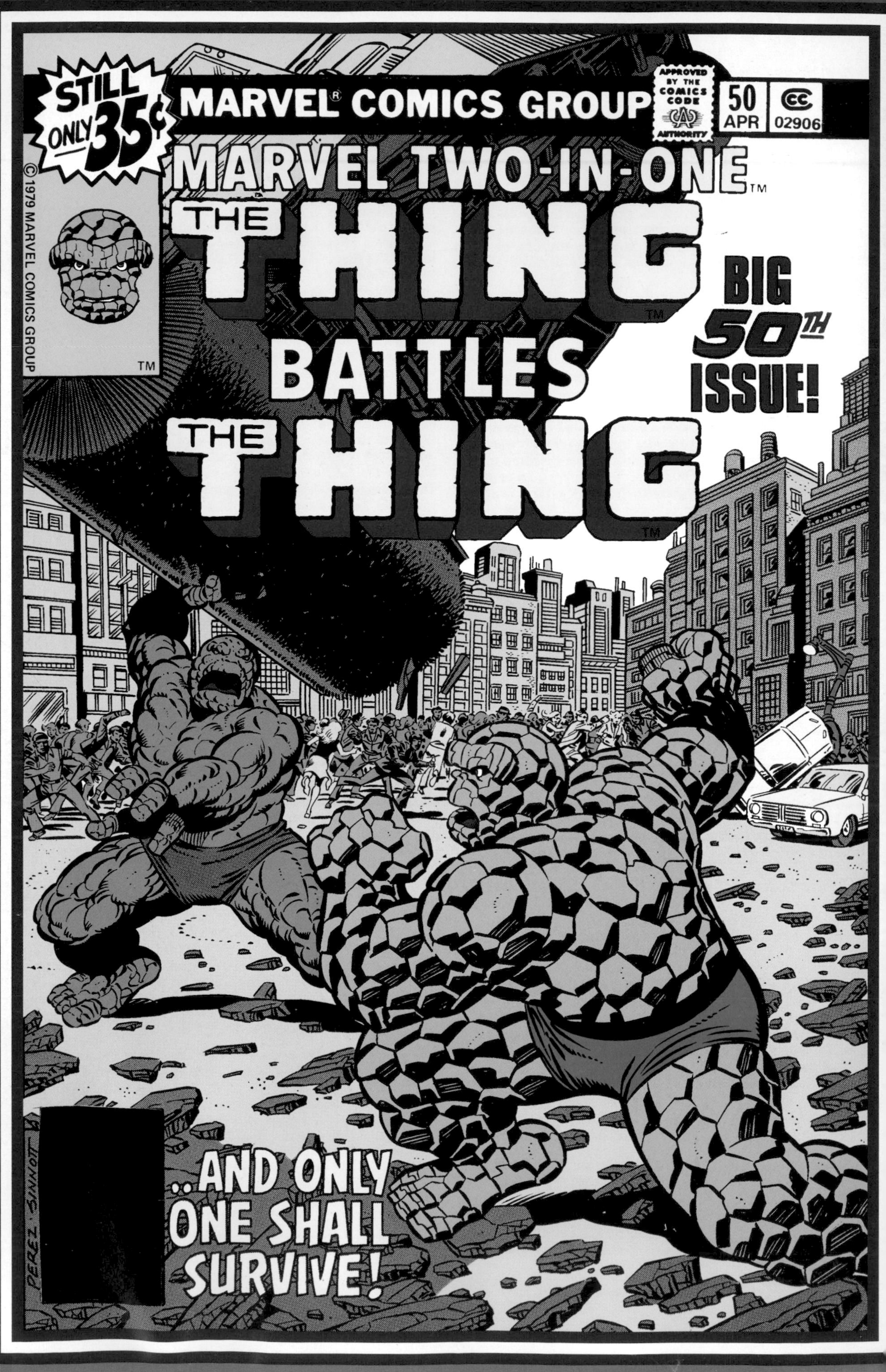
STILL ONLY 35¢
MARVEL® COMICS GROUP
APPROVED BY THE COMICS CODE AUTHORITY
50 APR
CC 02906
© 1979 MARVEL COMICS GROUP
MARVEL TWO-IN-ONE™
THE THING™
BATTLES
THE THING™
BIG 50TH ISSUE!
..AND ONLY ONE SHALL SURVIVE!
PEREZ SINNOTT

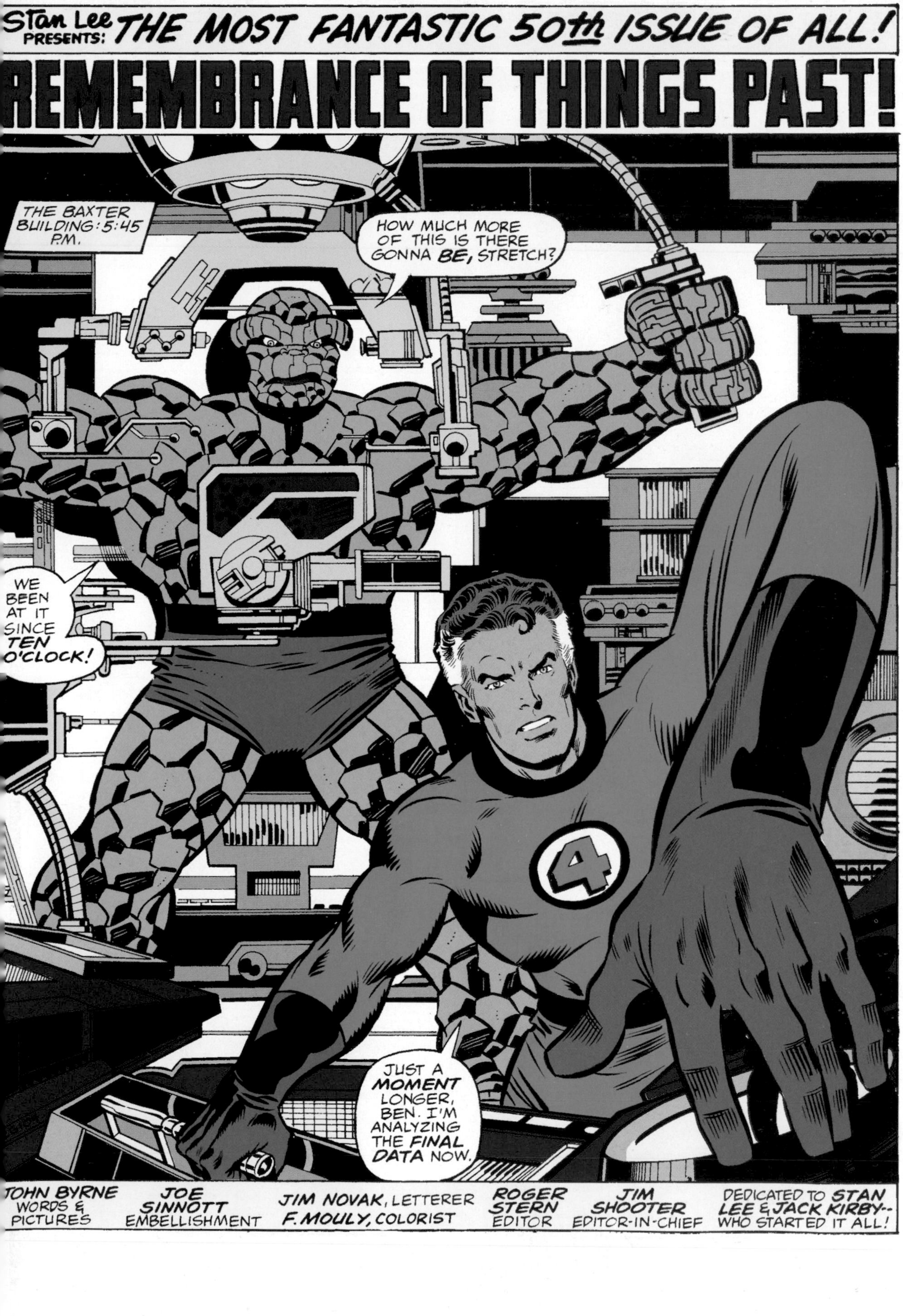
Stan Lee PRESENTS: THE MOST FANTASTIC 50th ISSUE OF ALL!
REMEMBRANCE OF THINGS PAST!
THE BAXTER BUILDING: 5:45 P.M.
HOW MUCH MORE OF THIS IS THERE GONNA BE, STRETCH?
WE BEEN AT IT SINCE TEN O'CLOCK!
JUST A MOMENT LONGER, BEN. I'M ANALYZING THE FINAL DATA NOW.
JOHN BYRNE WORDS & PICTURES
JOE SINNOTT EMBELLISHMENT
JIM NOVAK, LETTERER F. MOULY, COLORIST
ROGER STERN EDITOR
JIM SHOOTER EDITOR-IN-CHIEF
DEDICATED TO STAN LEE & JACK KIRBY-- WHO STARTED IT ALL!

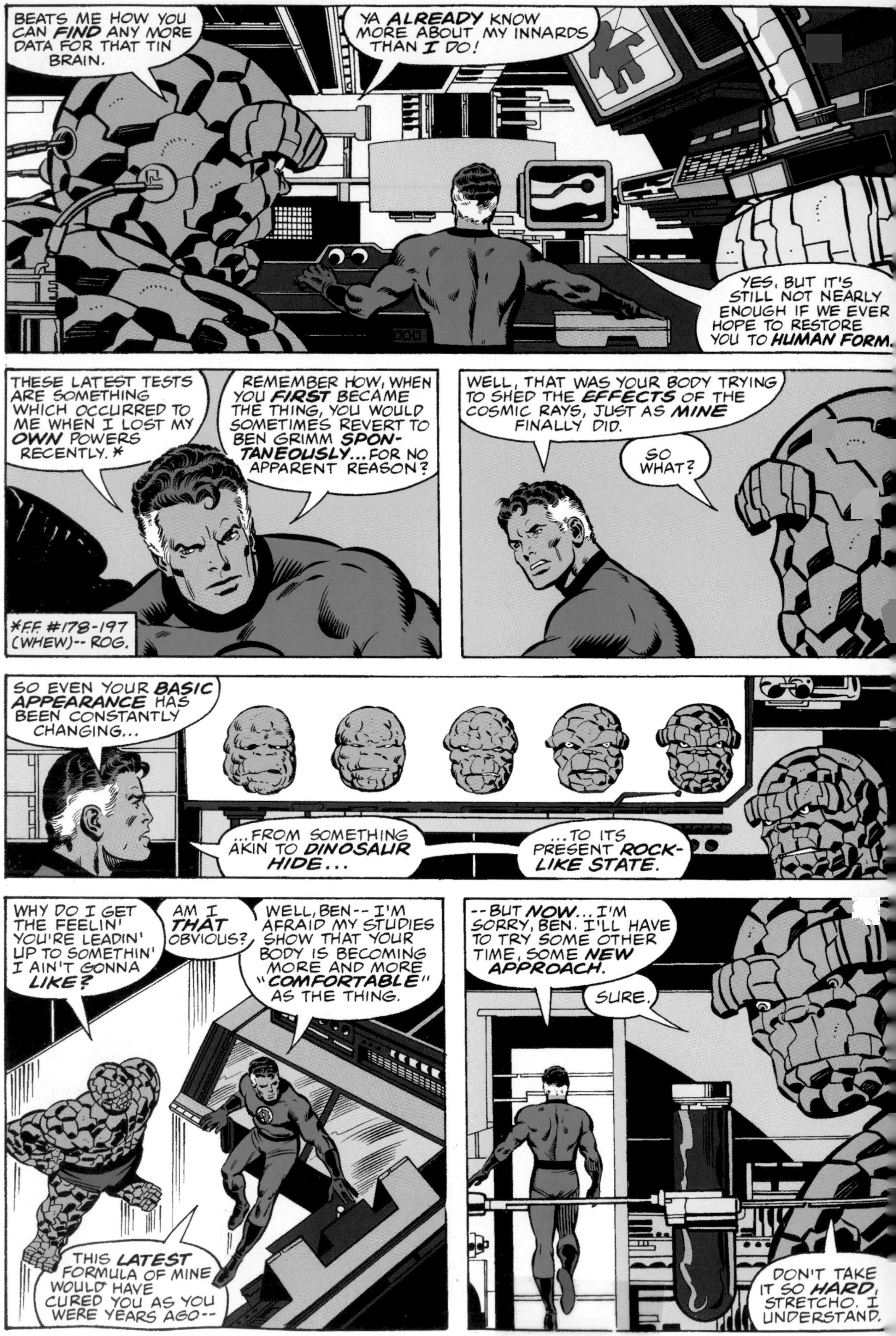
BEATS ME HOW YOU CAN FIND ANY MORE DATA FOR THAT TIN BRAIN.
YA ALREADY KNOW MORE ABOUT MY INNARDS THAN I DO!
YES, BUT IT'S STILL NOT NEARLY ENOUGH IF WE EVER HOPE TO RESTORE YOU TO HUMAN FORM.
THESE LATEST TESTS ARE SOMETHING WHICH OCCURRED TO ME WHEN I LOST MY OWN POWERS RECENTLY.*
REMEMBER HOW, WHEN YOU FIRST BECAME THE THING, YOU WOULD SOMETIMES REVERT TO BEN GRIMM SPONTANEOUSLY...FOR NO APPARENT REASON?
*F.F. #178-197 (WHEW)-- ROG.
WELL, THAT WAS YOUR BODY TRYING TO SHED THE EFFECTS OF THE COSMIC RAYS, JUST AS MINE FINALLY DID.
SO WHAT?
SO EVEN YOUR BASIC APPEARANCE HAS BEEN CONSTANTLY CHANGING...
...FROM SOMETHING AKIN TO DINOSAUR HIDE...
...TO ITS PRESENT ROCK-LIKE STATE.
WHY DO I GET THE FEELIN' YOU'RE LEADIN' UP TO SOMETHIN' I AIN'T GONNA LIKE?
AM I THAT OBVIOUS?
WELL, BEN-- I'M AFRAID MY STUDIES SHOW THAT YOUR BODY IS BECOMING MORE AND MORE "COMFORTABLE" AS THE THING.
THIS LATEST FORMULA OF MINE WOULD HAVE CURED YOU AS YOU WERE YEARS AGO--
--BUT NOW... I'M SORRY, BEN. I'LL HAVE TO TRY SOME OTHER TIME, SOME NEW APPROACH.
SURE.
DON'T TAKE IT SO HARD, STRETCHO. I UNDERSTAND.

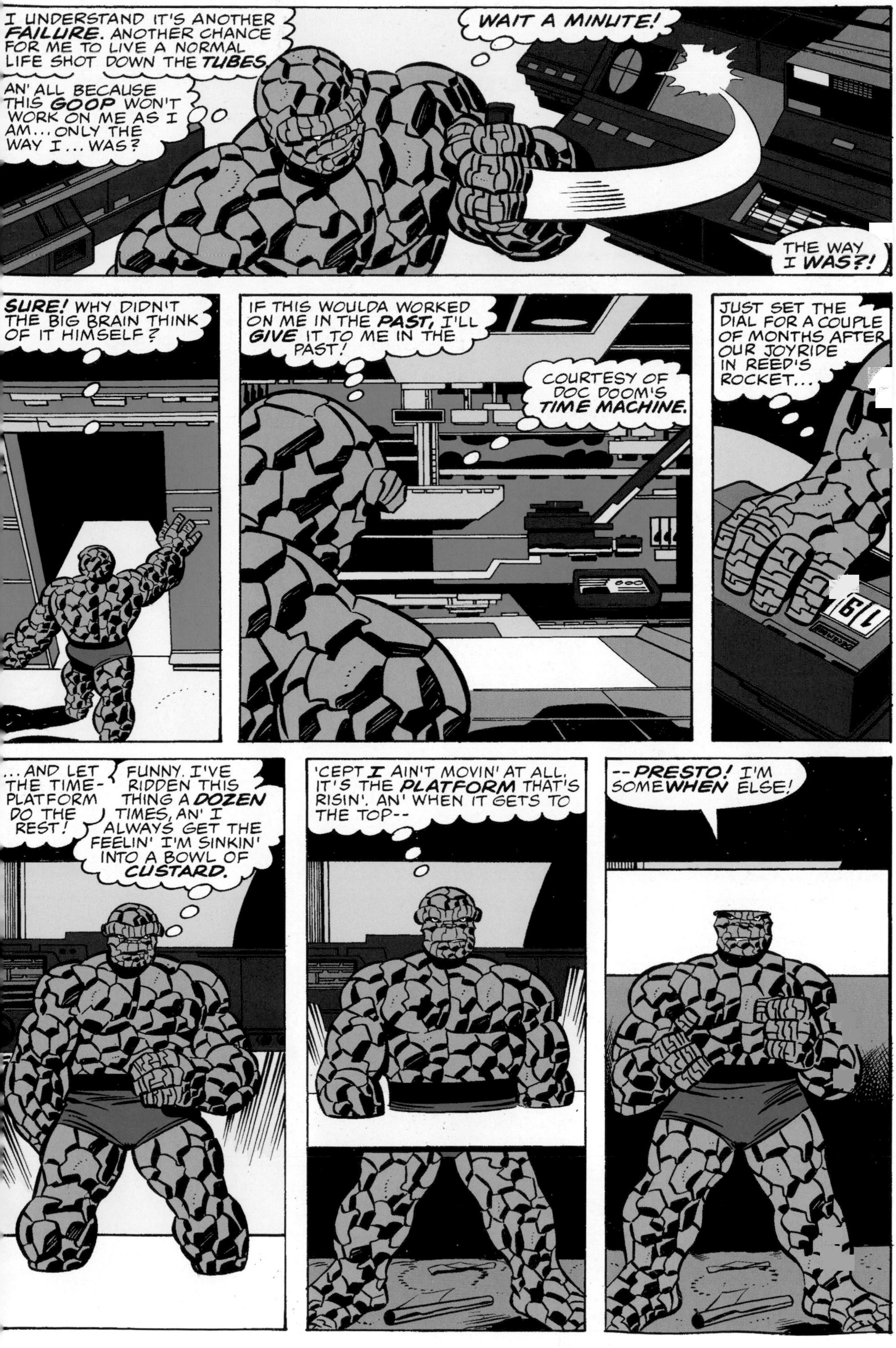
I UNDERSTAND IT'S ANOTHER FAILURE. ANOTHER CHANCE FOR ME TO LIVE A NORMAL LIFE SHOT DOWN THE TUBES.
AN' ALL BECAUSE THIS GOOP WON'T WORK ON ME AS I AM... ONLY THE WAY I... WAS?
WAIT A MINUTE!
THE WAY I WAS?!
SURE! WHY DIDN'T THE BIG BRAIN THINK OF IT HIMSELF?
IF THIS WOULDA WORKED ON ME IN THE PAST, I'LL GIVE IT TO ME IN THE PAST!
COURTESY OF DOC DOOM'S TIME MACHINE.
JUST SET THE DIAL FOR A COUPLE OF MONTHS AFTER OUR JOYRIDE IN REED'S ROCKET...
...AND LET THE TIME-PLATFORM DO THE REST!
FUNNY. I'VE RIDDEN THIS THING A DOZEN TIMES, AN' I ALWAYS GET THE FEELIN' I'M SINKIN' INTO A BOWL OF CUSTARD.
'CEPT I AIN'T MOVIN' AT ALL. IT'S THE PLATFORM THAT'S RISIN'. AN' WHEN IT GETS TO THE TOP--
--PRESTO! I'M SOMEWHEN ELSE!

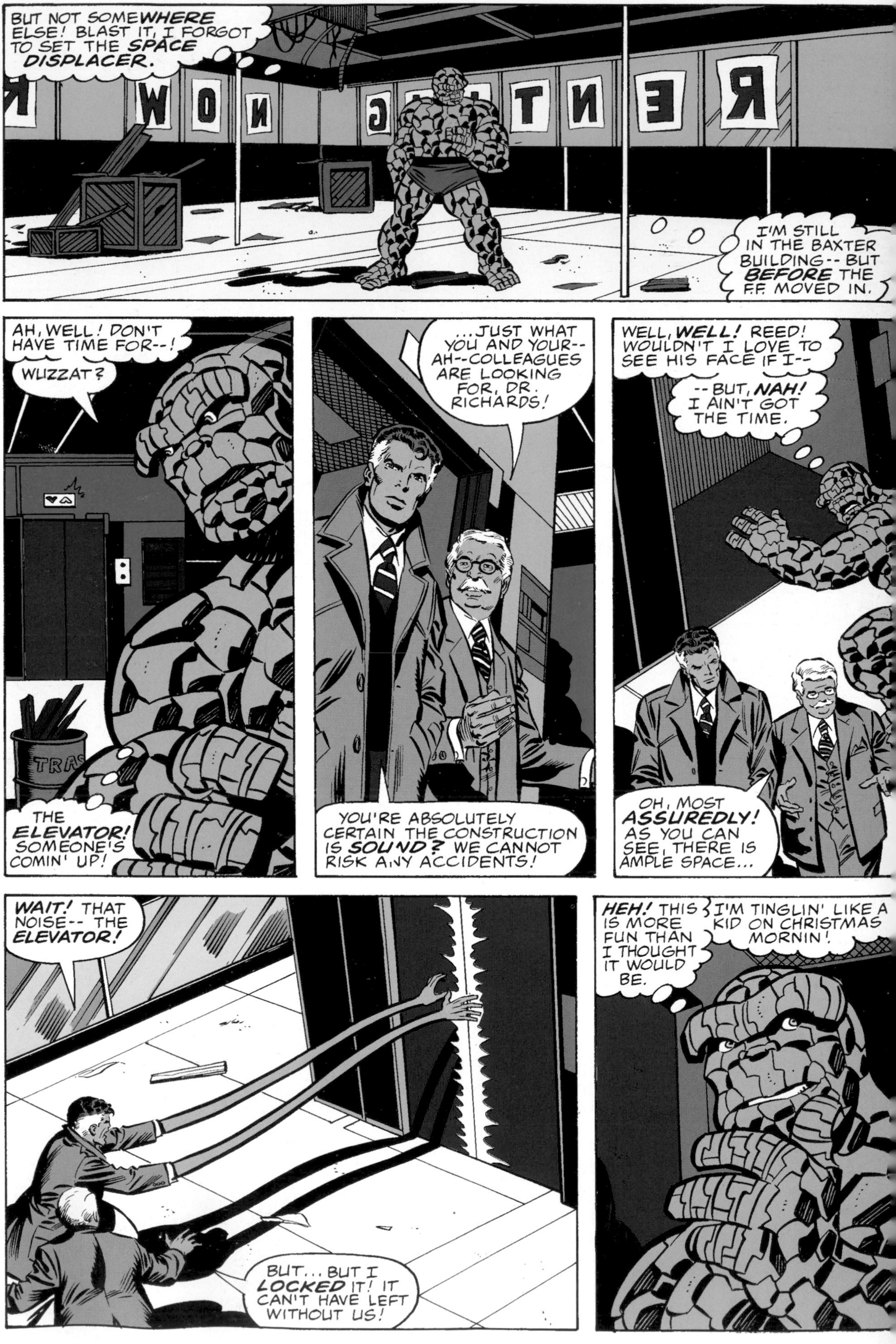
BUT NOT SOMEWHERE ELSE! BLAST IT, I FORGOT TO SET THE SPACE DISPLACER.
I'M STILL IN THE BAXTER BUILDING-- BUT BEFORE THE F.F. MOVED IN.
AH, WELL! DON'T HAVE TIME FOR--!
WUZZAT?
THE ELEVATOR! SOMEONE'S COMIN' UP!
...JUST WHAT YOU AND YOUR-- AH--COLLEAGUES ARE LOOKING FOR, DR. RICHARDS!
YOU'RE ABSOLUTELY CERTAIN THE CONSTRUCTION IS SOUND? WE CANNOT RISK ANY ACCIDENTS!
WELL, WELL! REED! WOULDN'T I LOVE TO SEE HIS FACE IF I--
--BUT, NAH! I AIN'T GOT THE TIME.
OH, MOST ASSUREDLY! AS YOU CAN SEE, THERE IS AMPLE SPACE...
WAIT! THAT NOISE-- THE ELEVATOR!
BUT... BUT I LOCKED IT! IT CAN'T HAVE LEFT WITHOUT US!
HEH! THIS IS MORE FUN THAN I THOUGHT IT WOULD BE.
I'M TINGLIN' LIKE A KID ON CHRISTMAS MORNIN'.

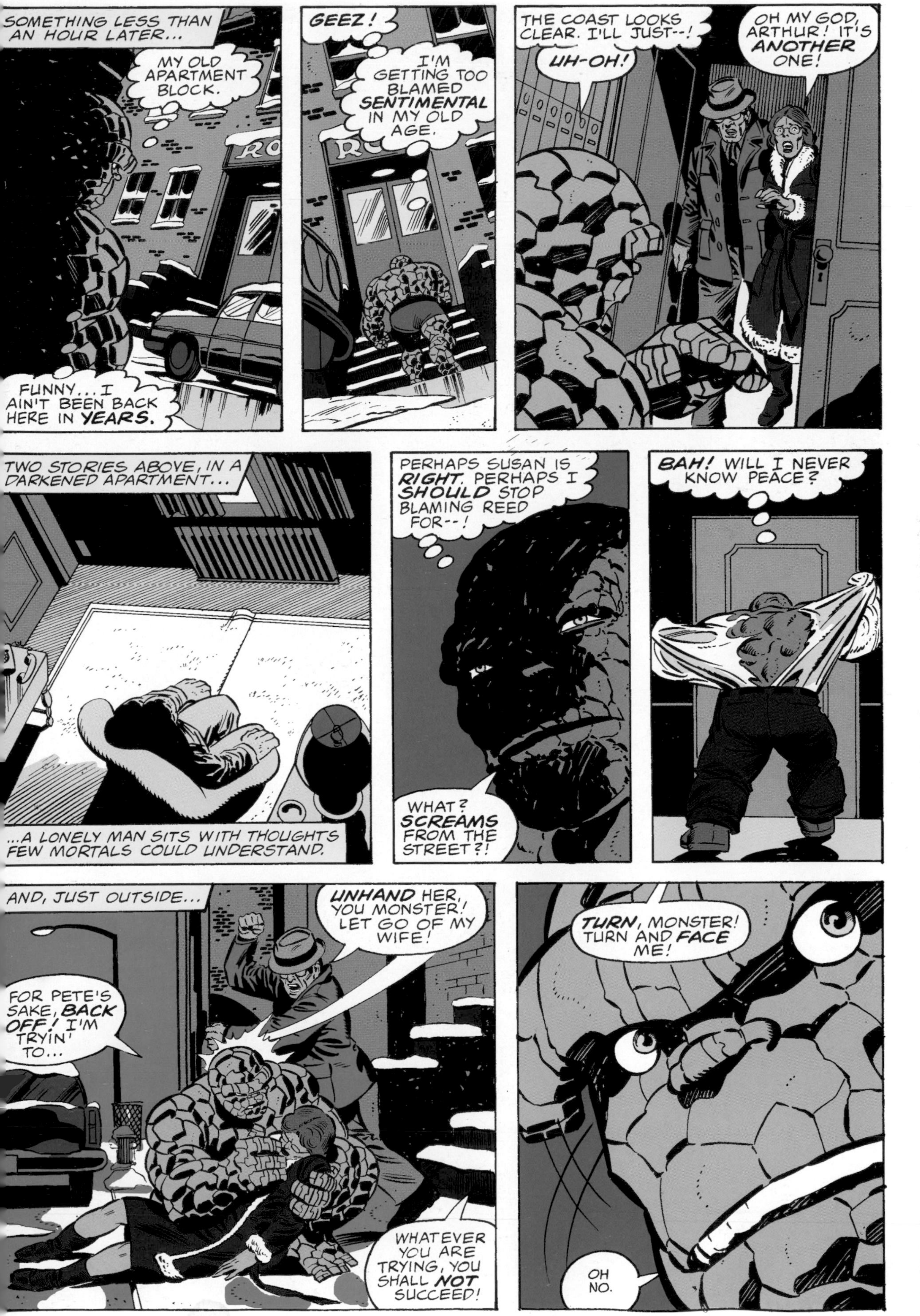
SOMETHING LESS THAN AN HOUR LATER...
MY OLD APARTMENT BLOCK.
FUNNY... I AIN'T BEEN BACK HERE IN YEARS.
GEEZ!
I'M GETTING TOO BLAMED SENTIMENTAL IN MY OLD AGE.
THE COAST LOOKS CLEAR. I'LL JUST--!
UH-OH!
OH MY GOD, ARTHUR! IT'S ANOTHER ONE!
TWO STORIES ABOVE, IN A DARKENED APARTMENT...
...A LONELY MAN SITS WITH THOUGHTS FEW MORTALS COULD UNDERSTAND.
PERHAPS SUSAN IS RIGHT. PERHAPS I SHOULD STOP BLAMING REED FOR--!
WHAT? SCREAMS FROM THE STREET?!
BAH! WILL I NEVER KNOW PEACE?
AND, JUST OUTSIDE...
UNHAND HER, YOU MONSTER! LET GO OF MY WIFE!
FOR PETE'S SAKE, BACK OFF! I'M TRYIN' TO...
WHATEVER YOU ARE TRYING, YOU SHALL NOT SUCCEED!
TURN, MONSTER! TURN AND FACE ME!
OH NO.

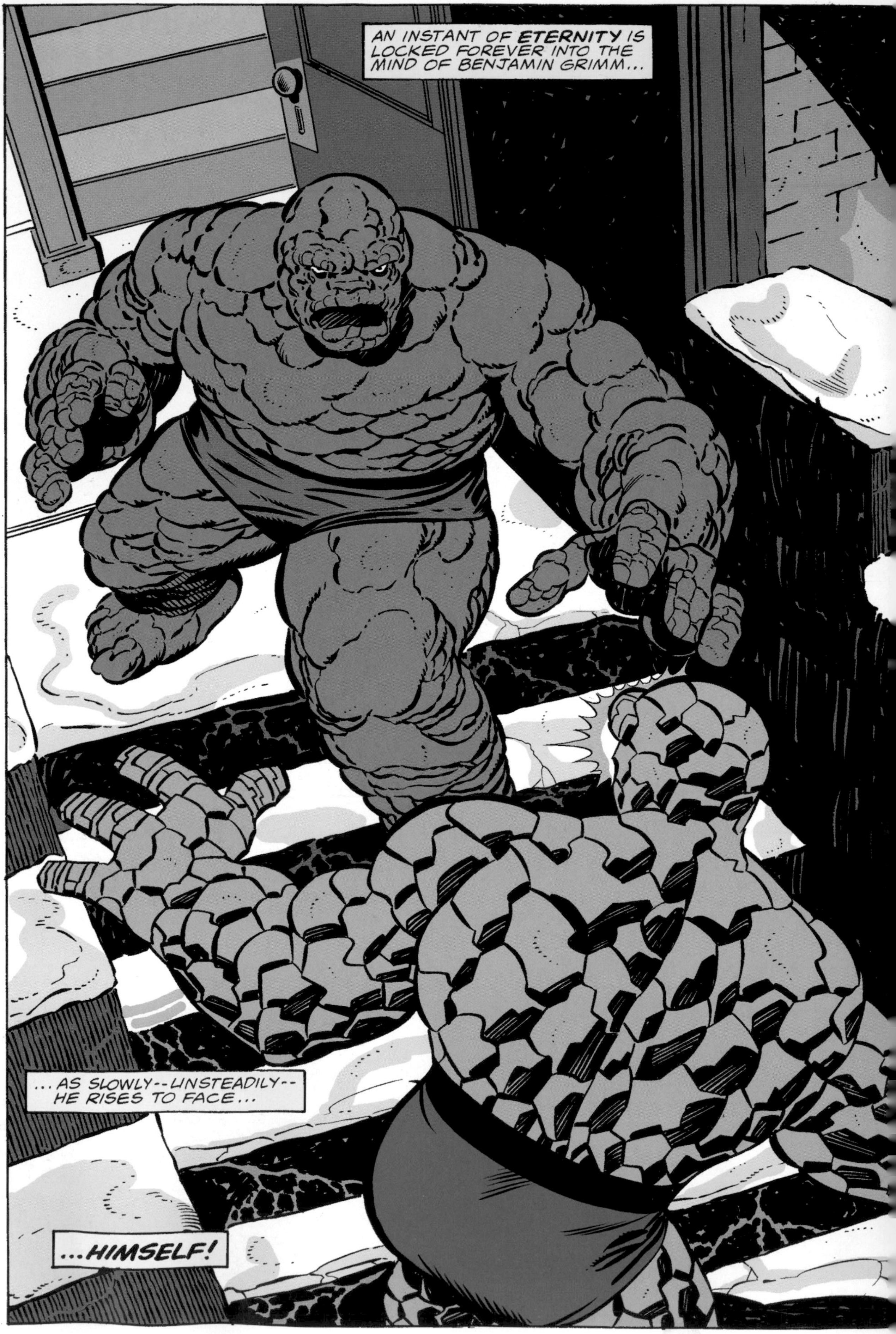
AN INSTANT OF ETERNITY IS LOCKED FOREVER INTO THE MIND OF BENJAMIN GRIMM...
...AS SLOWLY--UNSTEADILY--HE RISES TO FACE...
...HIMSELF!

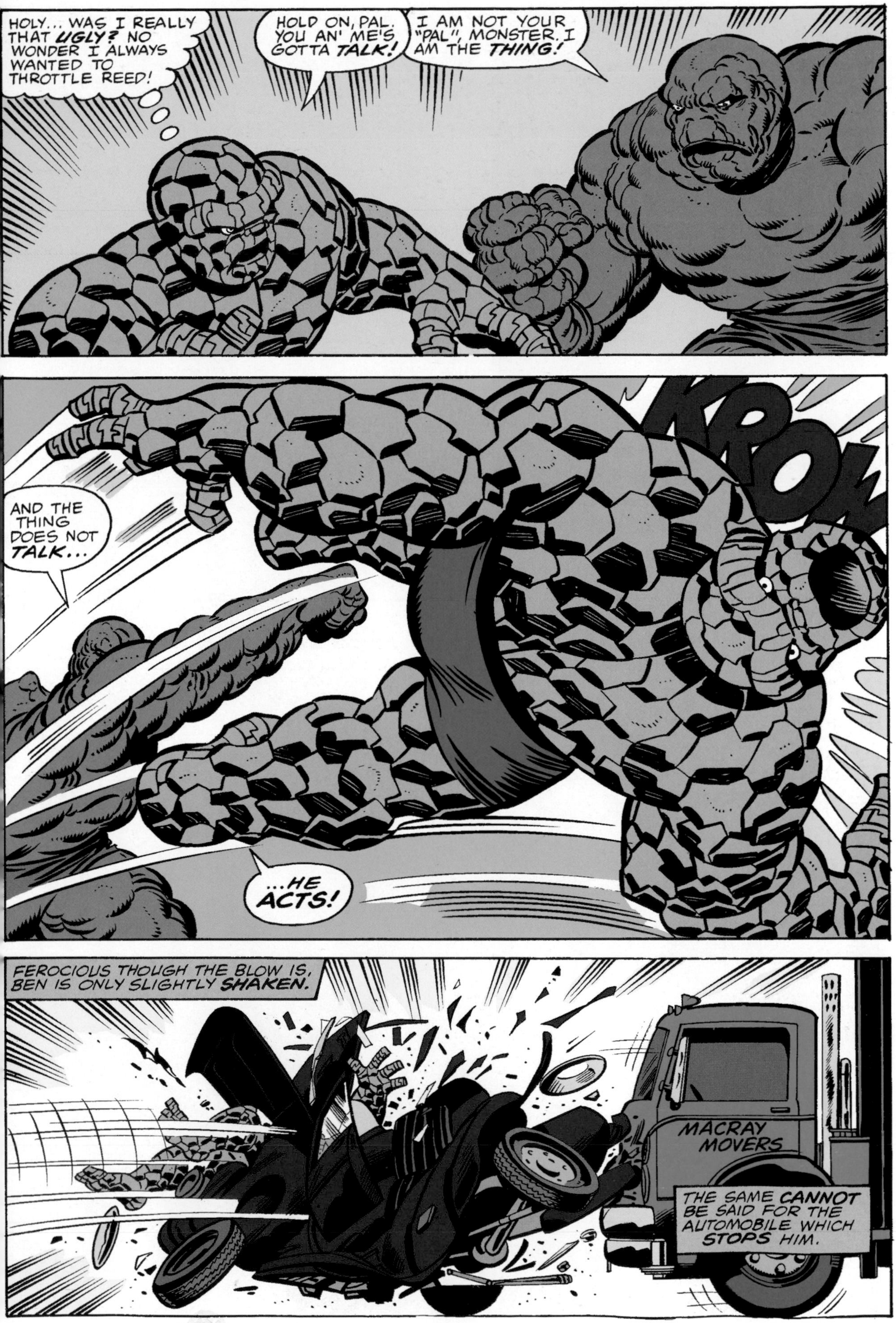
HOLY... WAS I REALLY THAT UGLY? NO WONDER I ALWAYS WANTED TO THROTTLE REED!
HOLD ON, PAL. YOU AN' ME'S GOTTA TALK!
I AM NOT YOUR "PAL", MONSTER. I AM THE THING!
AND THE THING DOES NOT TALK...
KROW
...HE ACTS!
FEROCIOUS THOUGH THE BLOW IS, BEN IS ONLY SLIGHTLY SHAKEN.
MACRAY MOVERS
THE SAME CANNOT BE SAID FOR THE AUTOMOBILE WHICH STOPS HIM.

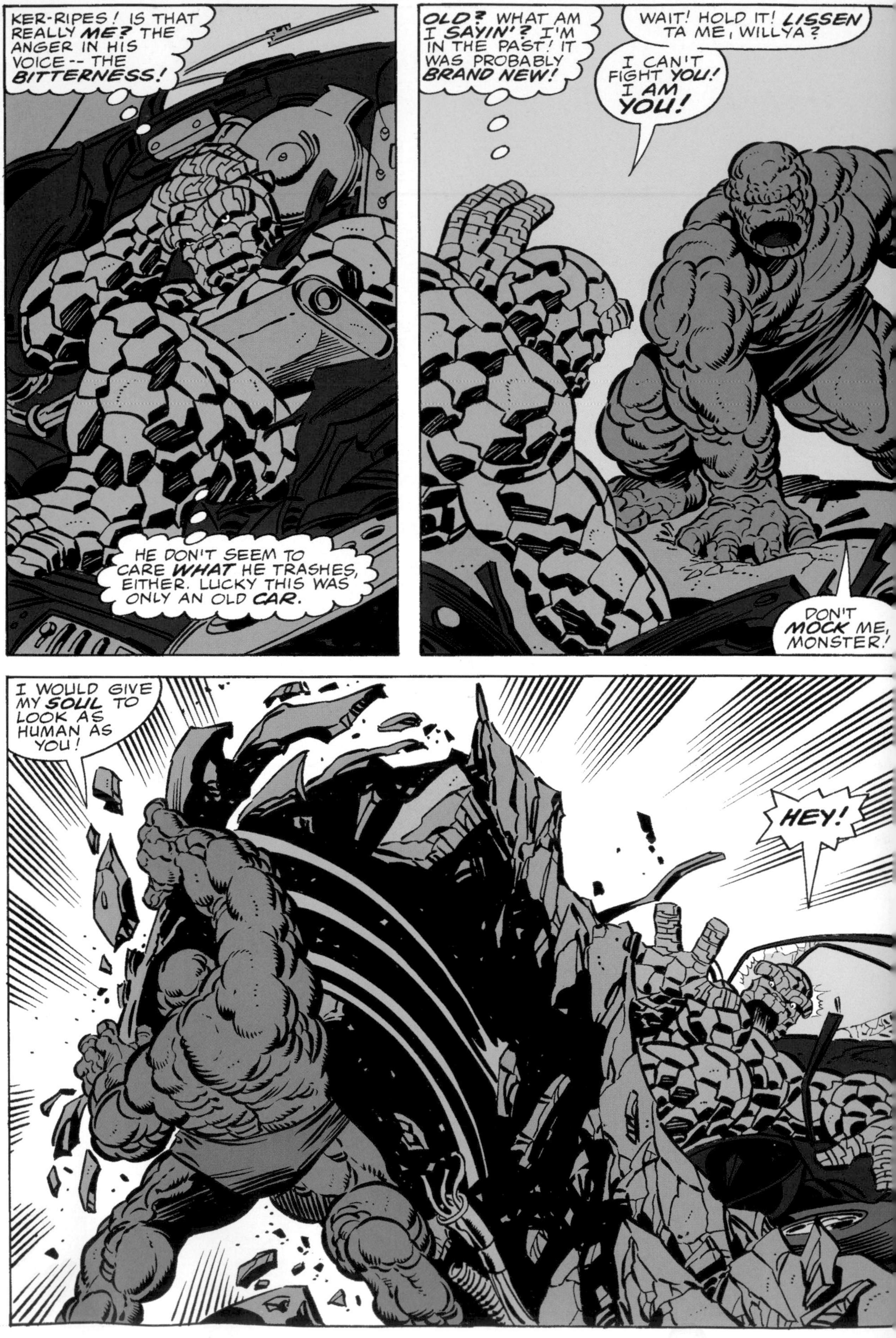
KER-RIPES! IS THAT REALLY ME? THE ANGER IN HIS VOICE -- THE BITTERNESS!
HE DON'T SEEM TO CARE WHAT HE TRASHES, EITHER. LUCKY THIS WAS ONLY AN OLD CAR.
OLD? WHAT AM I SAYIN'? I'M IN THE PAST! IT WAS PROBABLY BRAND NEW!
WAIT! HOLD IT! LISSEN TA ME, WILLYA?
I CAN'T FIGHT YOU! I AM YOU!
DON'T MOCK ME, MONSTER!
I WOULD GIVE MY SOUL TO LOOK AS HUMAN AS YOU!
HEY!

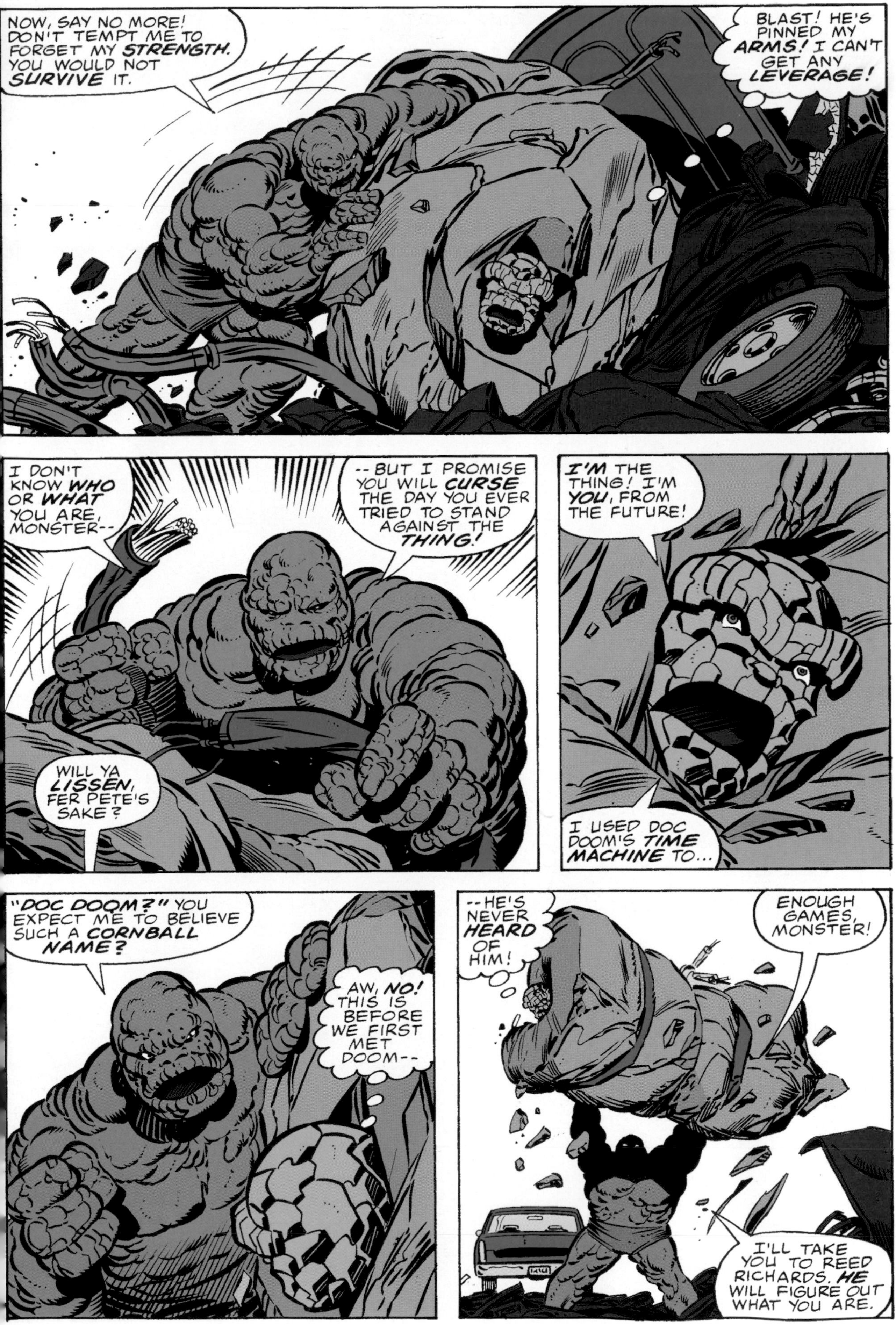
NOW, SAY NO MORE! DON'T TEMPT ME TO FORGET MY STRENGTH. YOU WOULD NOT SURVIVE IT.
BLAST! HE'S PINNED MY ARMS! I CAN'T GET ANY LEVERAGE!
I DON'T KNOW WHO OR WHAT YOU ARE, MONSTER--
--BUT I PROMISE YOU WILL CURSE THE DAY YOU EVER TRIED TO STAND AGAINST THE THING!
WILL YA LISSEN, FER PETE'S SAKE?
I'M THE THING! I'M YOU, FROM THE FUTURE!
I USED DOC DOOM'S TIME MACHINE TO...
"DOC DOOM?" YOU EXPECT ME TO BELIEVE SUCH A CORNBALL NAME?
AW, NO! THIS IS BEFORE WE FIRST MET DOOM--
--HE'S NEVER HEARD OF HIM!
ENOUGH GAMES, MONSTER!
I'LL TAKE YOU TO REED RICHARDS. HE WILL FIGURE OUT WHAT YOU ARE.

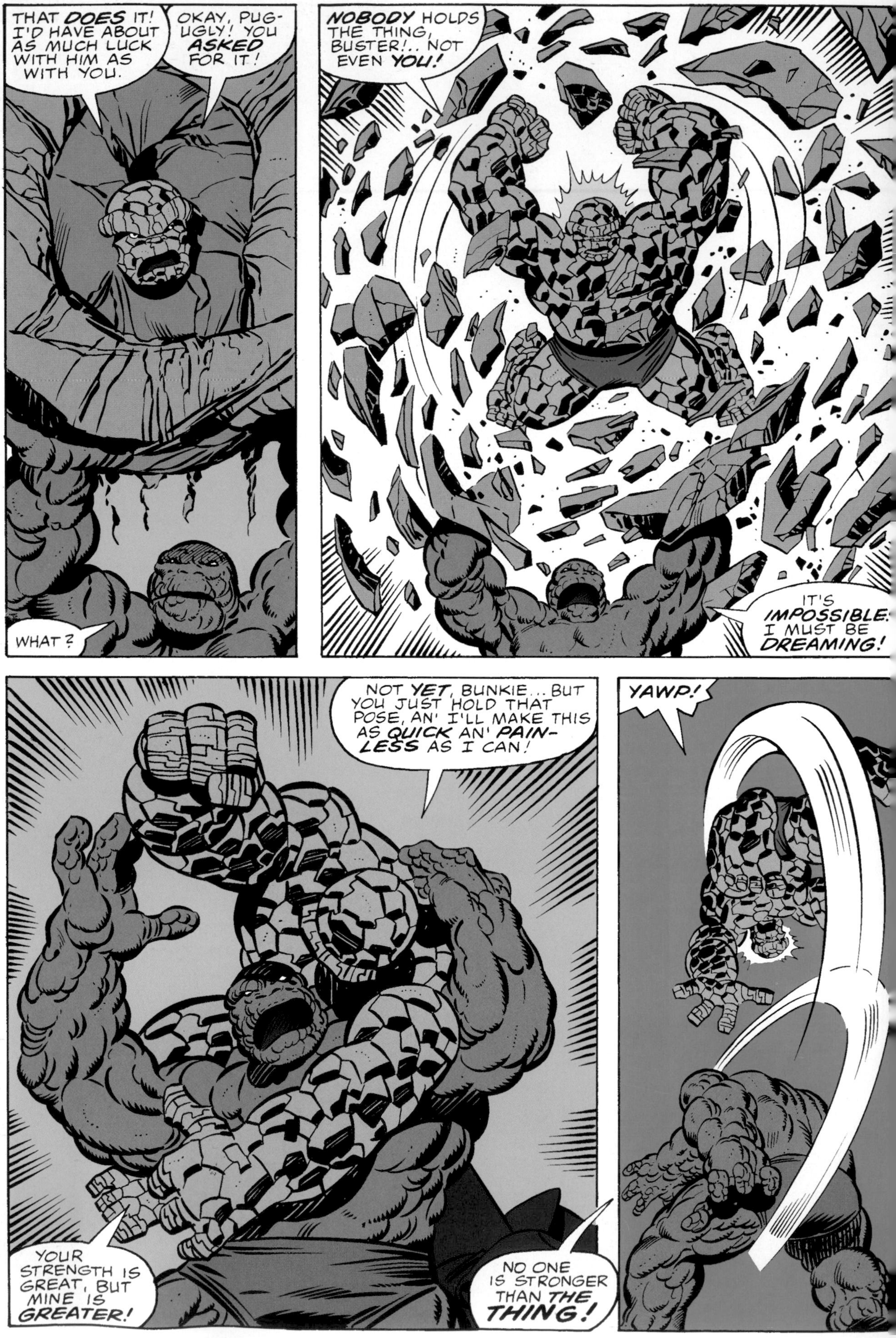
THAT DOES IT! I'D HAVE ABOUT AS MUCH LUCK WITH HIM AS WITH YOU.
OKAY, PUG-UGLY! YOU ASKED FOR IT!
WHAT?
NOBODY HOLDS THE THING, BUSTER!.. NOT EVEN YOU!
IT'S IMPOSSIBLE. I MUST BE DREAMING!
NOT YET, BUNKIE... BUT YOU JUST HOLD THAT POSE, AN' I'LL MAKE THIS AS QUICK AN' PAIN-LESS AS I CAN!
YOUR STRENGTH IS GREAT, BUT MINE IS GREATER!
NO ONE IS STRONGER THAN THE THING!
YAWP!

FOR A MOMENT BEN GRIMM SAILS THROUGH THE AIR AS GRACE- FULLY AS THISTLEDOWN...

BUT ONLY FOR A MOMENT.

THA-BOOOM

THE SHOCK OF IMPACT **SHATTERS** THE CONDEMNED BROWNSTONE AND FRACTURES WINDOWS FOR **BLOCKS** AROUND.

COMING SOON ON THIS RM SITE

ANOTHER SHMLESS GLAES AND STEEL MONSTROSITY WITH ABSOLUTELY NO ARCHITECTURAL MERITS

COURTESY OF RANDIMEACHUM

BLAST! I WASN'T WATCHING WHERE I **THREW** HIM! NOW REED WILL ONLY HAVE A **CORPSE** TO EXAMINE.

NOTHING COULD HAVE SURVIVED THAT COLLAPSE.

GUESS AGAIN, GONZO!

YOU JUST MADE A **BIG** MISTAKE, CHUCKLES. YA MADE ME LOSE MY EVER- LOVIN' **TEMPER!** AN' THAT'S SOMETHIN' I DON'T **NEVER** LIKE TO DO!

GET READY TO GET **BRUISED!**

193

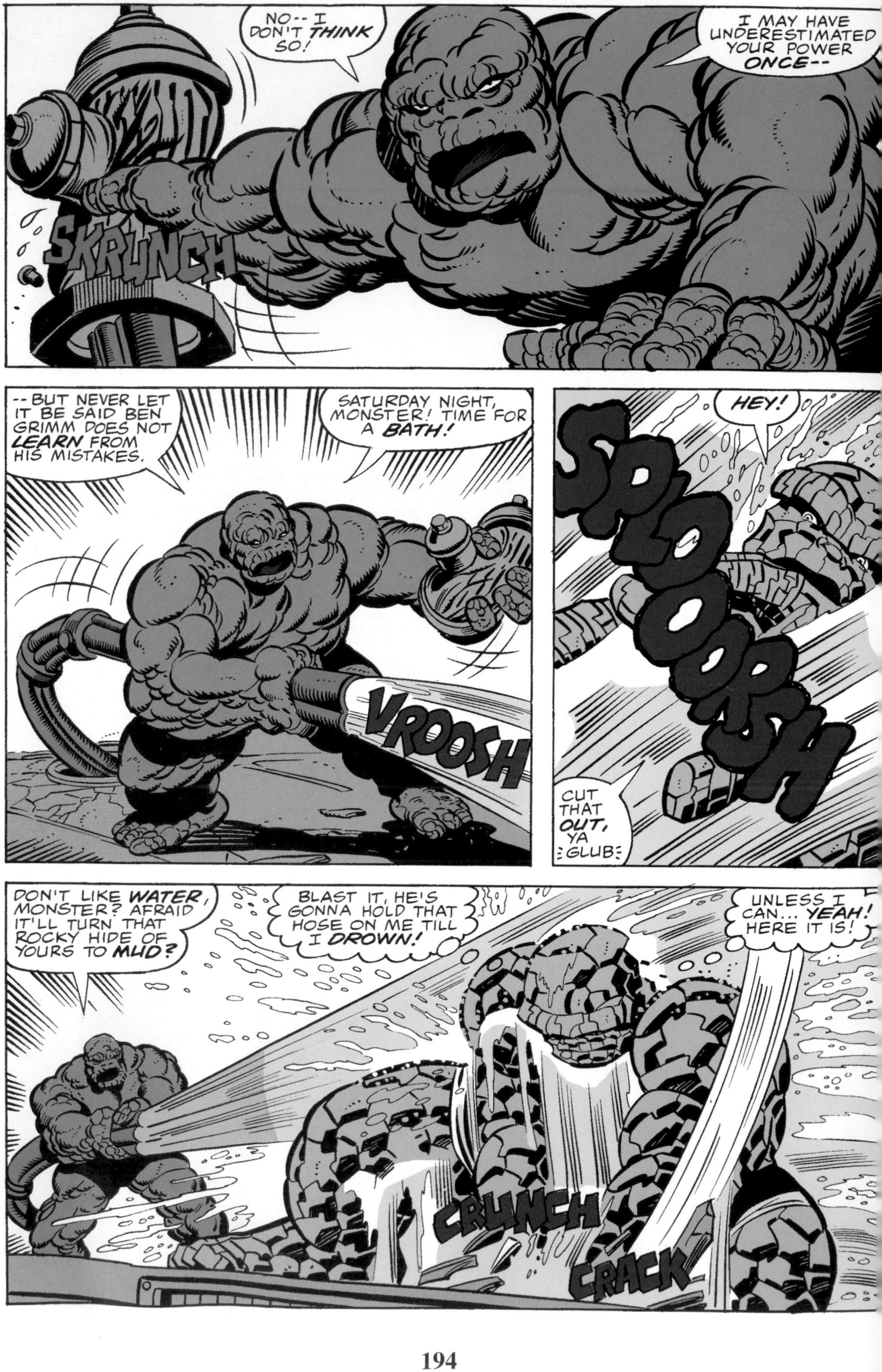
NO-- I DON'T THINK SO!
I MAY HAVE UNDERESTIMATED YOUR POWER ONCE--
SKRUNCH
--BUT NEVER LET IT BE SAID BEN GRIMM DOES NOT LEARN FROM HIS MISTAKES.
SATURDAY NIGHT, MONSTER! TIME FOR A BATH!
VROOSH
HEY!
SPLOOORSH
CUT THAT OUT, YA GLUB
DON'T LIKE WATER, MONSTER? AFRAID IT'LL TURN THAT ROCKY HIDE OF YOURS TO MUD?
BLAST IT, HE'S GONNA HOLD THAT HOSE ON ME TILL I DROWN!
UNLESS I CAN... YEAH! HERE IT IS!
CRUNCH
CRACK

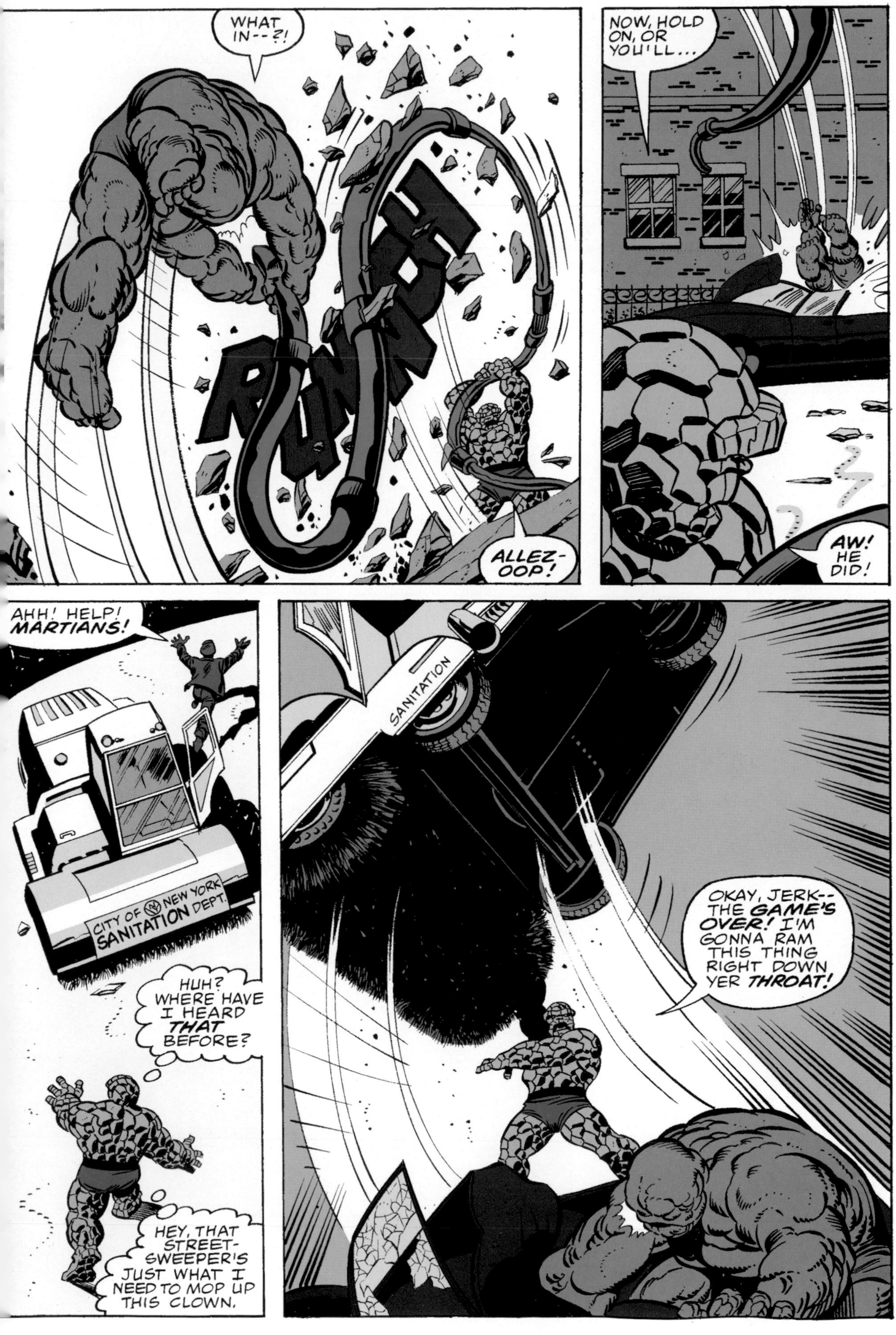
WHAT IN--?!
RUNCH
ALLEZ-OOP!
NOW, HOLD ON, OR YOU'LL...
AW! HE DID!
AHH! HELP! MARTIANS!
CITY OF NEW YORK SANITATION DEPT.
HUH? WHERE HAVE I HEARD THAT BEFORE?
HEY, THAT STREET-SWEEPER'S JUST WHAT I NEED TO MOP UP THIS CLOWN.
SANITATION
OKAY, JERK-- THE GAME'S OVER! I'M GONNA RAM THIS THING RIGHT DOWN YER THROAT!

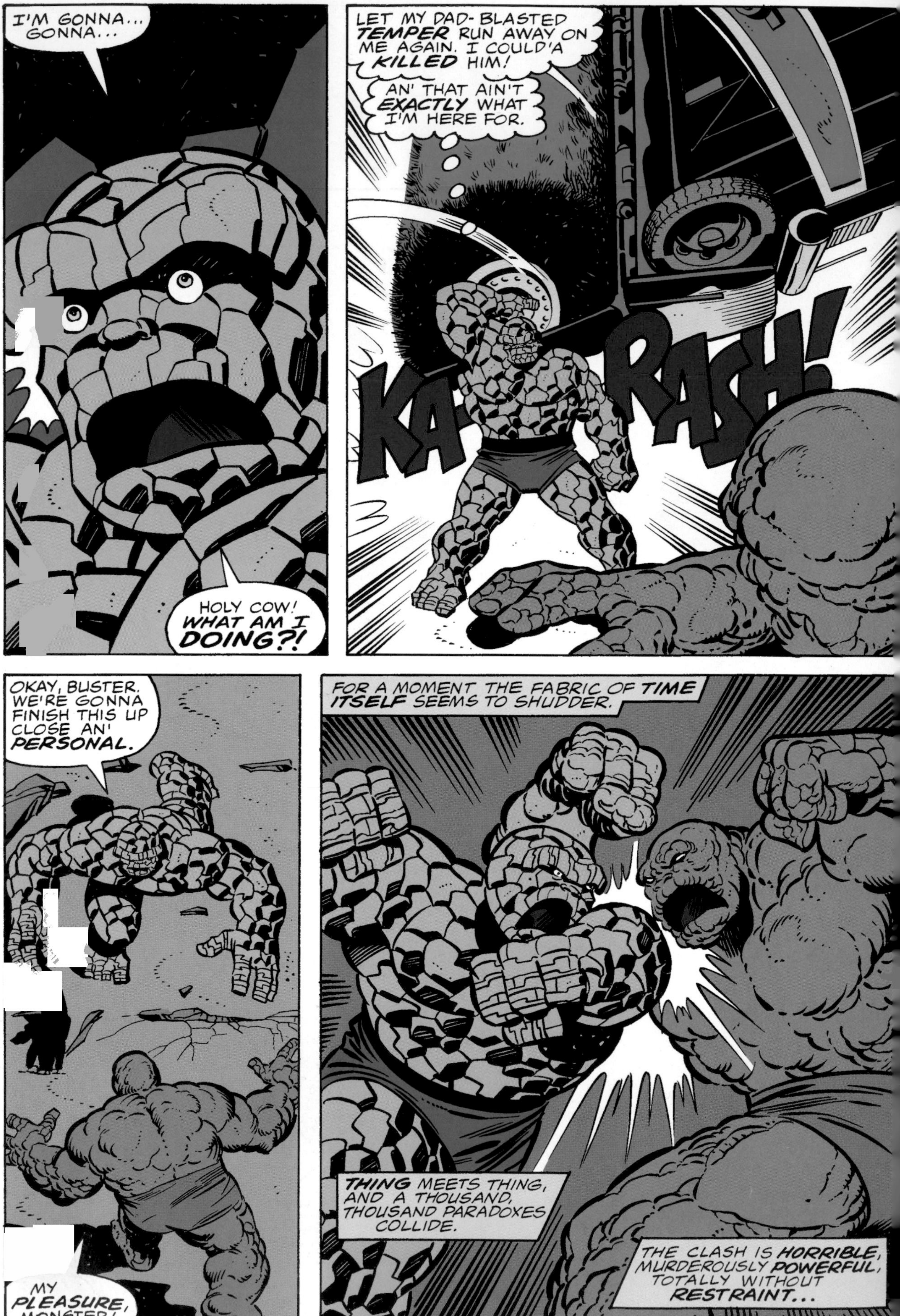
I'M GONNA... GONNA...
HOLY COW! WHAT AM I DOING?!
LET MY DAD-BLASTED TEMPER RUN AWAY ON ME AGAIN. I COULD'A KILLED HIM!
AN' THAT AIN'T EXACTLY WHAT I'M HERE FOR.
KA-RASH!
OKAY, BUSTER. WE'RE GONNA FINISH THIS UP CLOSE AN' PERSONAL.
MY PLEASURE, MONSTER!
FOR A MOMENT THE FABRIC OF TIME ITSELF SEEMS TO SHUDDER.
THING MEETS THING, AND A THOUSAND, THOUSAND PARADOXES COLLIDE.
THE CLASH IS HORRIBLE, MURDEROUSLY POWERFUL, TOTALLY WITHOUT RESTRAINT...

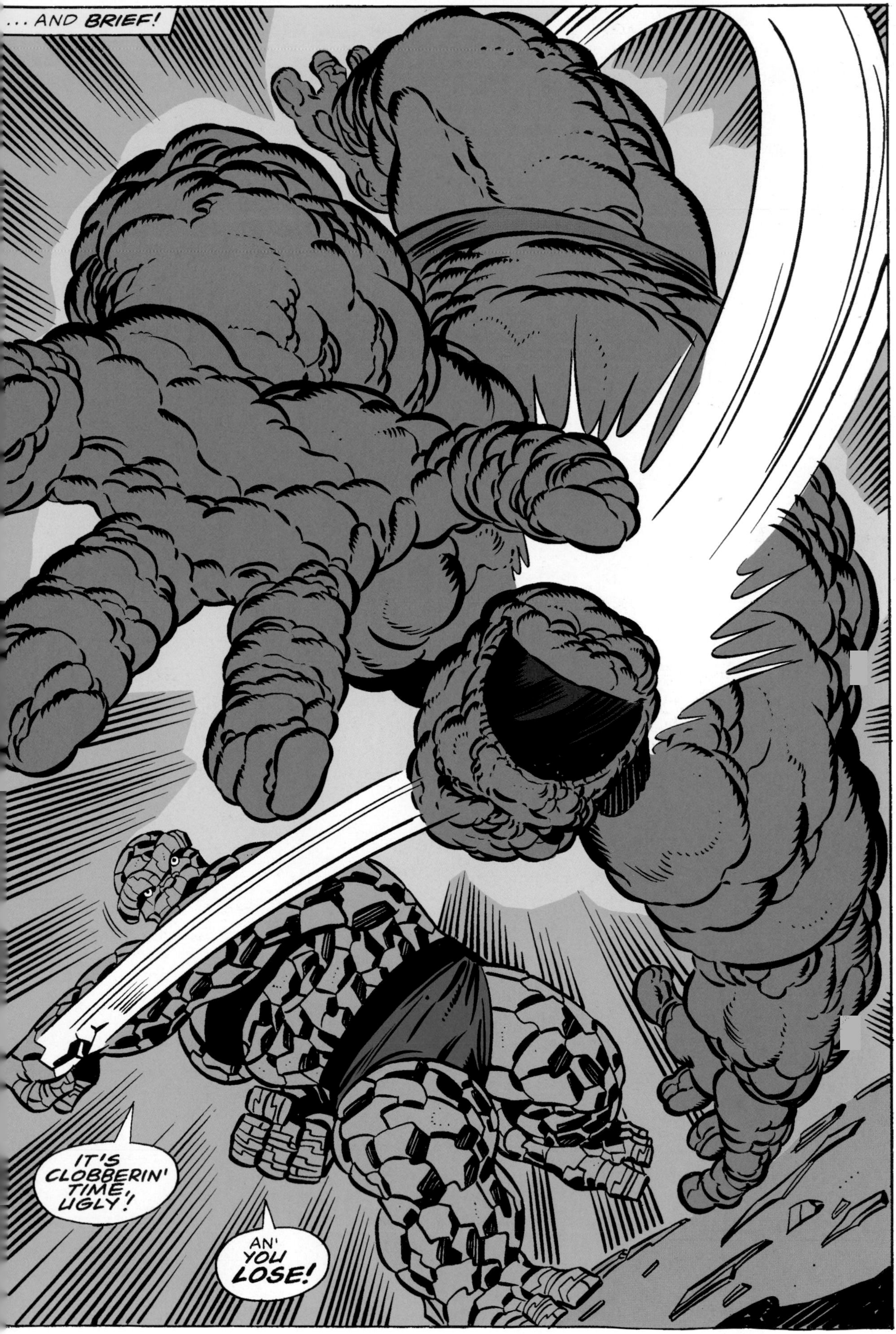
...AND BRIEF!
IT'S CLOBBERIN' TIME, UGLY!
AN' YOU LOSE!

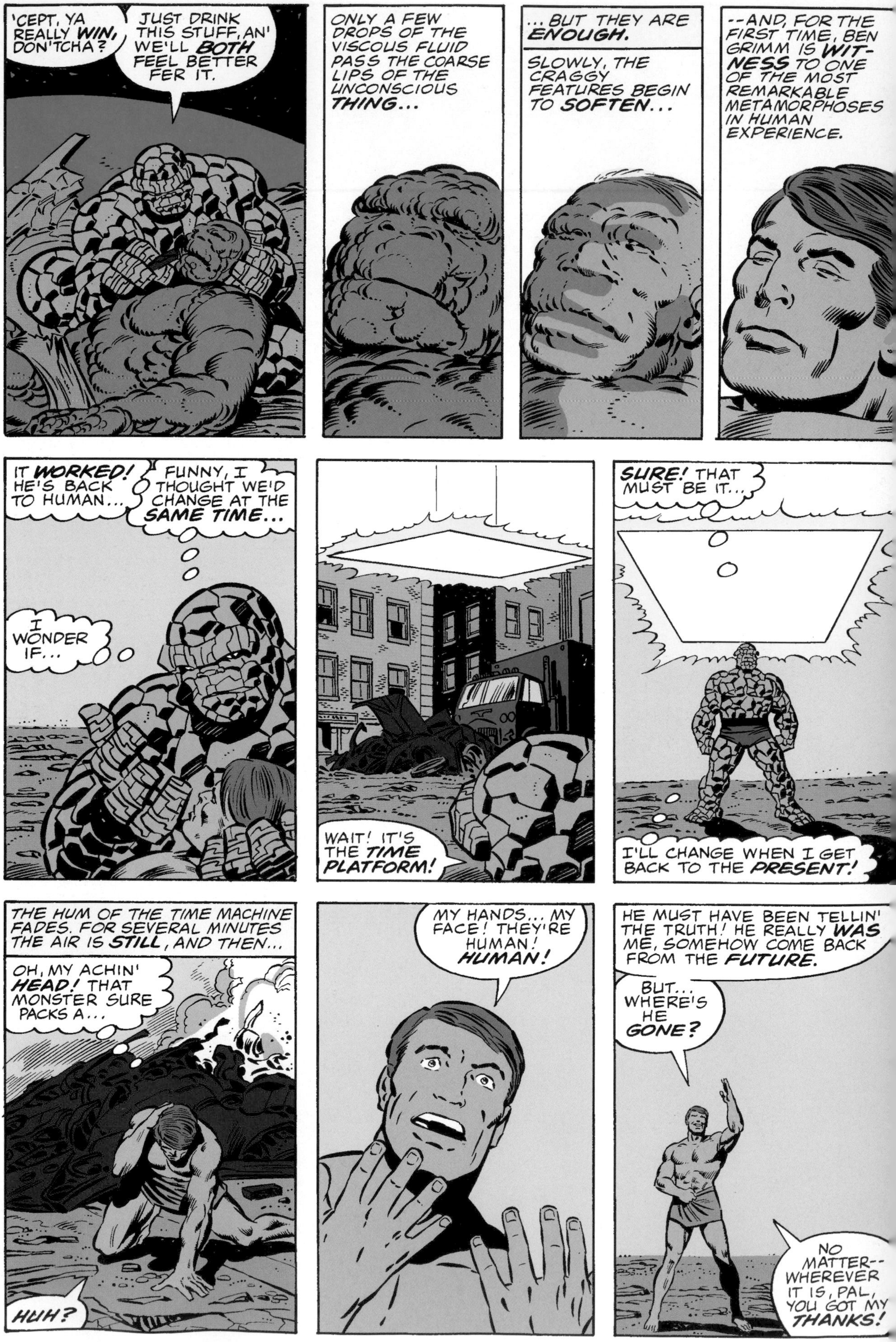
'CEPT, YA REALLY WIN, DON'TCHA?
JUST DRINK THIS STUFF, AN' WE'LL BOTH FEEL BETTER FER IT.
ONLY A FEW DROPS OF THE VISCOUS FLUID PASS THE COARSE LIPS OF THE UNCONSCIOUS THING...
...BUT THEY ARE ENOUGH.
SLOWLY, THE CRAGGY FEATURES BEGIN TO SOFTEN...
--AND, FOR THE FIRST TIME, BEN GRIMM IS WIT-NESS TO ONE OF THE MOST REMARKABLE METAMORPHOSES IN HUMAN EXPERIENCE.
IT WORKED! HE'S BACK TO HUMAN...
FUNNY, I THOUGHT WE'D CHANGE AT THE SAME TIME...
I WONDER IF...
WAIT! IT'S THE TIME PLATFORM!
SURE! THAT MUST BE IT...
I'LL CHANGE WHEN I GET BACK TO THE PRESENT!
THE HUM OF THE TIME MACHINE FADES. FOR SEVERAL MINUTES THE AIR IS STILL, AND THEN...
OH, MY ACHIN' HEAD! THAT MONSTER SURE PACKS A...
HUH?
MY HANDS... MY FACE! THEY'RE HUMAN! HUMAN!
HE MUST HAVE BEEN TELLIN' THE TRUTH! HE REALLY WAS ME, SOMEHOW COME BACK FROM THE FUTURE.
BUT... WHERE'S HE GONE?
NO MATTER-- WHEREVER IT IS, PAL, YOU GOT MY THANKS!

BEN! THANK GOD, I WAS ABLE TO FIND YOU!

DON'T YOU REALIZE WHAT YOUR PRESENCE IN YOUR OWN PAST COULD HAVE DONE TO THE *TIME-STREAM?*

NEVER MIND THE *LECTURE*, STRETCHO! HOW DO I *LOOK?*

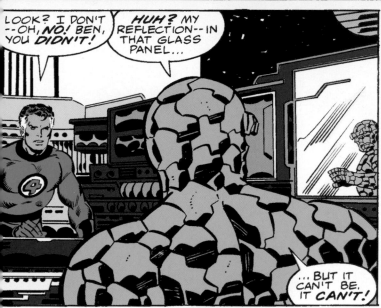

LOOK? I DON'T --OH, *NO!* BEN, YOU *DIDN'T!*

HUH? MY *REFLECTION*--IN THAT GLASS PANEL...

...BUT IT *CAN'T* BE, IT *CAN'T!*

MY HANDS...MY FACE! I'M STILL THE THING! THE *THING!*

YOU DON'T UNDER-STAND, *DO* YOU, OLD FRIEND? YOU DON'T REALIZE WHAT'S HAPPENED...

YOUR *PAST* IS IMMUTABLE, BEN. YOU ARE WHAT YOU ARE!

ANY CHANGE YOU MAKE IN THE PAST RESULTS IN *ANOTHER REALITY*--A *NEW* ONE CAUSED BY YOUR PRESENCE.

I'M SORRY, BEN...I THOUGHT YOU KNEW...

SKIP IT, REED. THE TRIP WASN'T A *TOTAL* WASTE.

AFTER SEEIN' MY OLD SELF FACE TO FACE LIKE THAT, I DON'T FEEL SO BAD ABOUT THE KISSER I GOT *NOW.*

HECK, COMPARED TO *HIM*, I'M A REG'LAR *ROBERT REDFORD!*

NEXT

AVENGERS ASSEMBLE!

THE BEST OF THE
FANTASTIC FOUR
VOLUME ONE

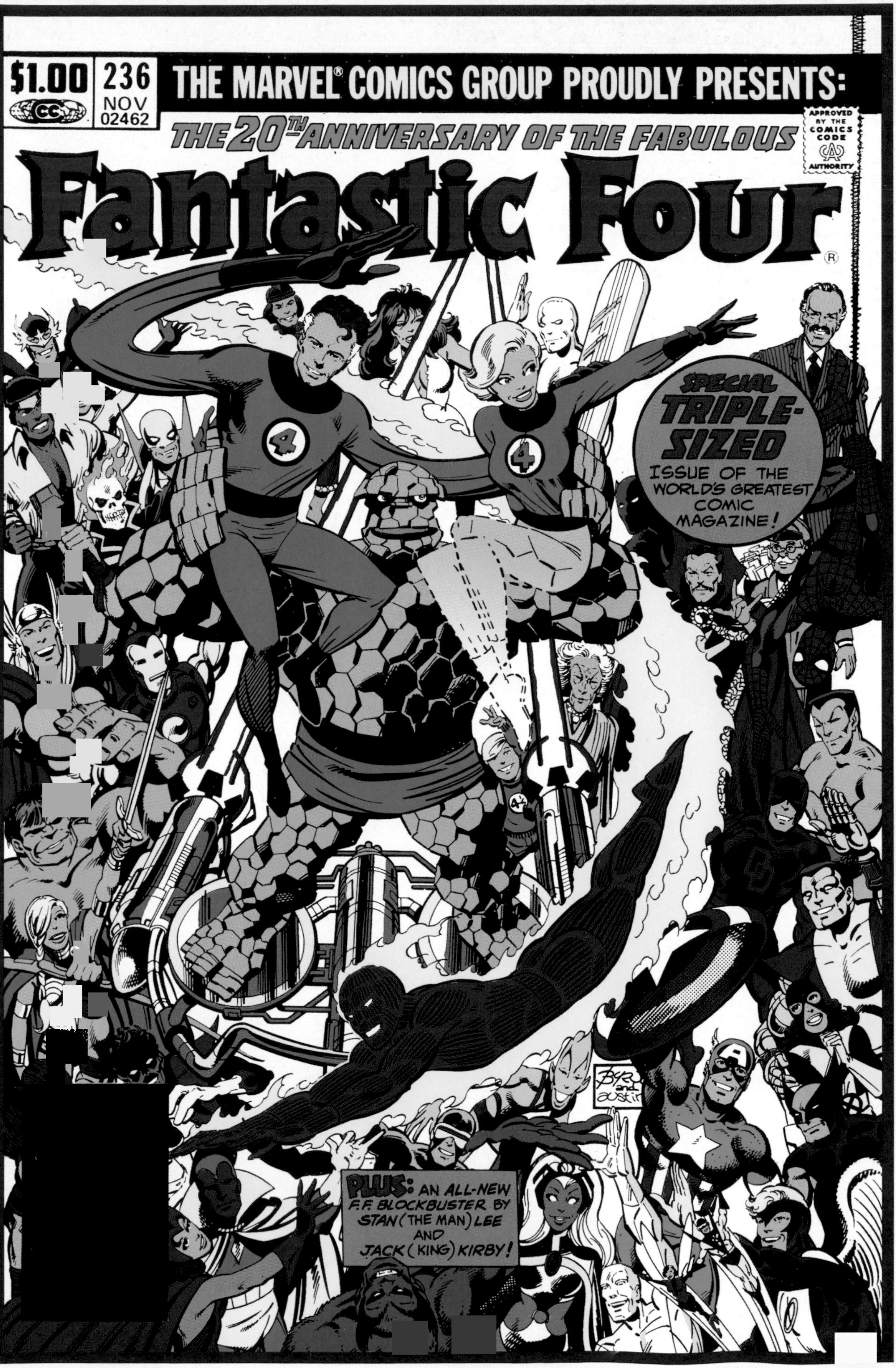
$1.00
236
NOV
02462
THE MARVEL® COMICS GROUP PROUDLY PRESENTS:
APPROVED BY THE COMICS CODE AUTHORITY
THE 20TH ANNIVERSARY OF THE FABULOUS
Fantastic Four®
SPECIAL TRIPLE-SIZED ISSUE OF THE WORLD'S GREATEST COMIC MAGAZINE!
PLUS: AN ALL-NEW F.F. BLOCKBUSTER BY STAN (THE MAN) LEE AND JACK (KING) KIRBY!

STAN LEE PRESENTS

THE FANTASTIC FOUR!

JOHN BYRNE | JIM NOVAK | GLYNIS WEIN | JIM SALICRUP | JIM SHOOTER
WORDS & PICTURES | LETTERS | COLORS | EDITOR | EDITOR-IN-CHIEF

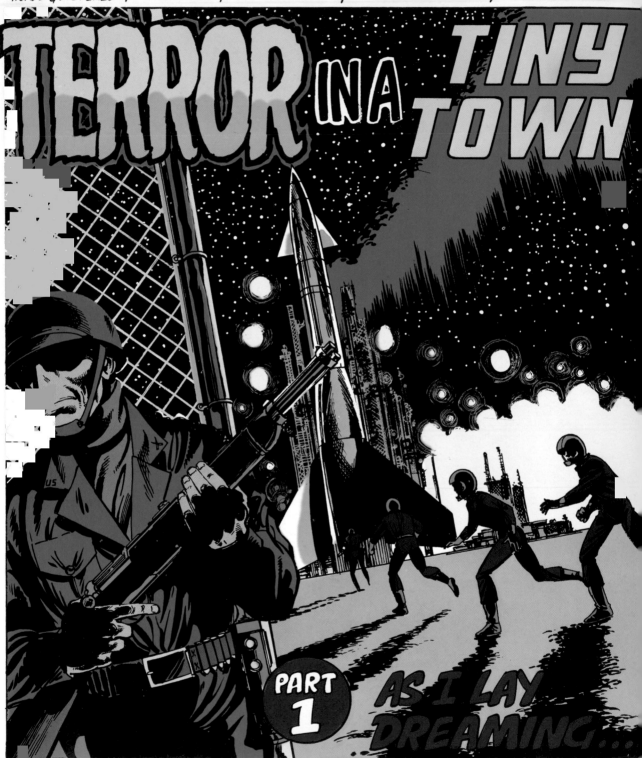

TERROR IN A TINY TOWN

PART 1

AS I LAY DREAMING...

THE THUNDER OF GIANT ROCKETS CRACKS WIDE THE EVENING STILLNESS OF A SECRET MISSILE BASE.

AN UNAUTHORIZED FLIGHT TO THE STARS IS UNDER-WAY...

THE COUNTDOWN OF HISTORY HAS BEGUN...

ABOARD THE HURTLING PROJECTILE FOUR VALIANT ADVENTURERS PLUNGE TOWARDS THE UNKNOWN...

PRIMARY CIRCUITS AT MAXIMUM FUNCTION. ALL SYSTEMS SHOW GREEN FOR FIRST STAGE JETTISON.

SHE'S BEHAVING LIKE A BABY. EVERYTHING IS PERFECT.

YEAH, EXCEPT FOR THE COSMIC RAYS. NO ONE KNOWS WHAT THEY'LL DO.

THE SOMBRE TONES OF TEST-PILOT BEN GRIMM ARE A HARD COUNTER-POINT TO THE ENTHUSIASM OF SCIENTIST REED RICHARDS.

THEN, AT AN ALTITUDE OF ONE HUNDRED MILES -- FIFTY MILES PAST THE OFFICIAL EDGE OF SPACE...

CHEMICAL ROCKETS EXHAUSTED.

FIRST STAGE JETTISON IS GO. WE HAD TO DO IT. WE HAD TO BE THE FIRST.

BUT WE'RE REACHING THE COSMIC STORM AREA ...HANG ON!

RAKTACTACTACTAC

HEAR THAT? IT'S THE COSMIC RAYS. I-- I WARNED YOU ABOUT 'EM!

BEN-- QUICKLY--YOU MUST ENGAGE THE EXPERIMENTAL STAR DRIVE NOW! GET US THROUGH THE RADIATION BELT BEFORE...

TOO LATE! THEY'RE PENE-TRATING THE SHIP! OUR SHIELDING ISN'T STRONG ENOUGH!

BUT, I DON'T FEEL ANYTHING...?

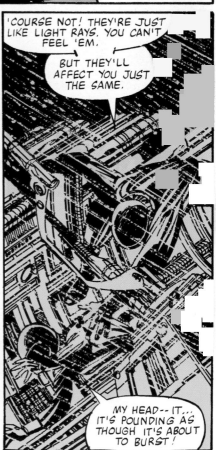

'COURSE NOT! THEY'RE JUST LIKE LIGHT RAYS. YOU CAN'T FEEL 'EM.

BUT THEY'LL AFFECT YOU JUST THE SAME.

MY HEAD-- IT... IT'S POUNDING AS THOUGH IT'S ABOUT TO BURST!

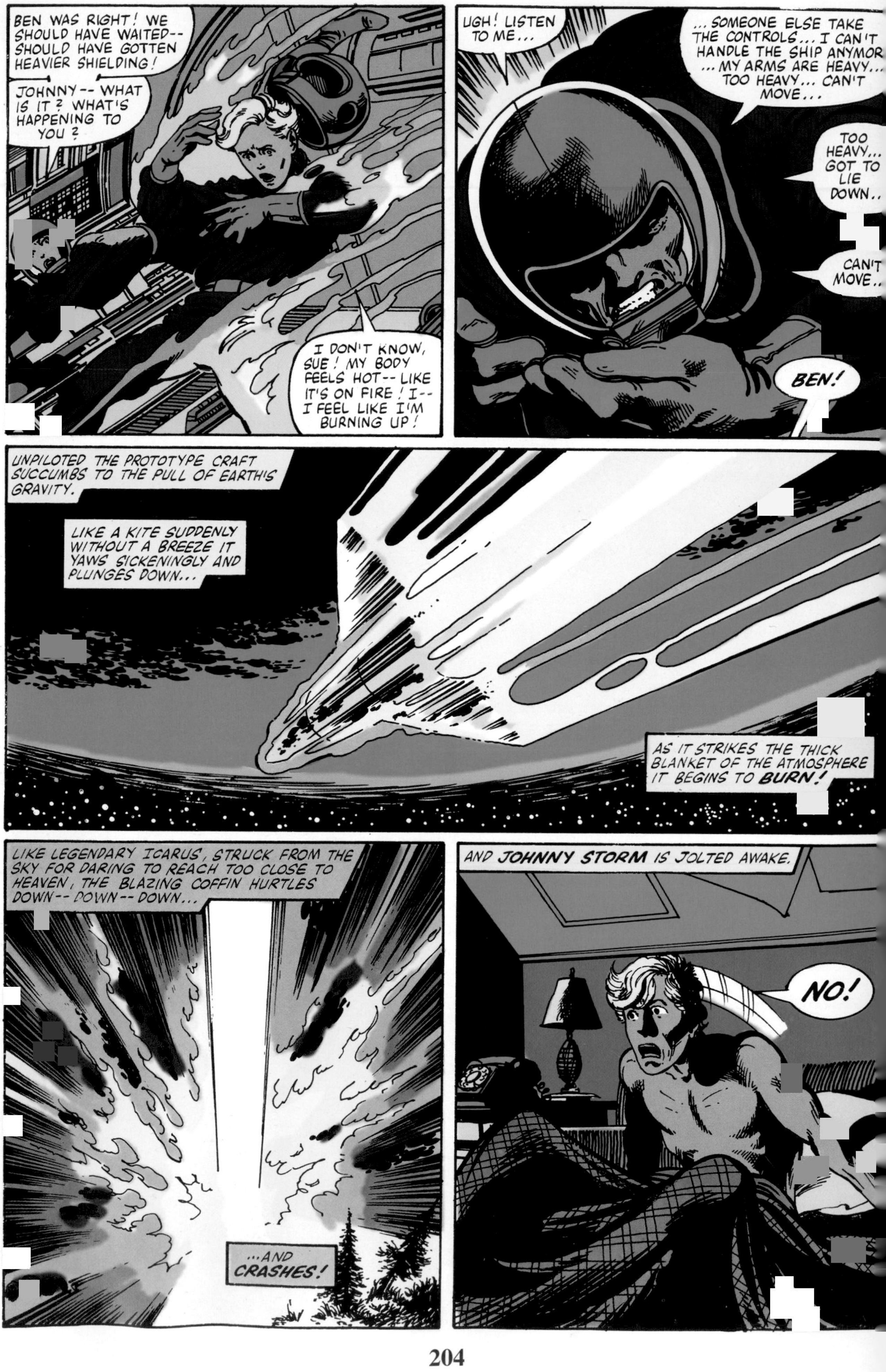
BEN WAS RIGHT! WE SHOULD HAVE WAITED-- SHOULD HAVE GOTTEN HEAVIER SHIELDING!
JOHNNY-- WHAT IS IT? WHAT'S HAPPENING TO YOU?
I DON'T KNOW, SUE! MY BODY FEELS HOT-- LIKE IT'S ON FIRE! I-- I FEEL LIKE I'M BURNING UP!
UGH! LISTEN TO ME...
... SOMEONE ELSE TAKE THE CONTROLS... I CAN'T HANDLE THE SHIP ANYMOR ... MY ARMS ARE HEAVY... TOO HEAVY... CAN'T MOVE...
TOO HEAVY... GOT TO LIE DOWN..
CAN'T MOVE..
BEN!
UNPILOTED THE PROTOTYPE CRAFT SUCCUMBS TO THE PULL OF EARTH'S GRAVITY.
LIKE A KITE SUDDENLY WITHOUT A BREEZE IT YAWS SICKENINGLY AND PLUNGES DOWN...
AS IT STRIKES THE THICK BLANKET OF THE ATMOSPHERE IT BEGINS TO BURN!
LIKE LEGENDARY ICARUS, STRUCK FROM THE SKY FOR DARING TO REACH TOO CLOSE TO HEAVEN, THE BLAZING COFFIN HURTLES DOWN-- DOWN-- DOWN...
...AND CRASHES!
AND JOHNNY STORM IS JOLTED AWAKE.
NO!

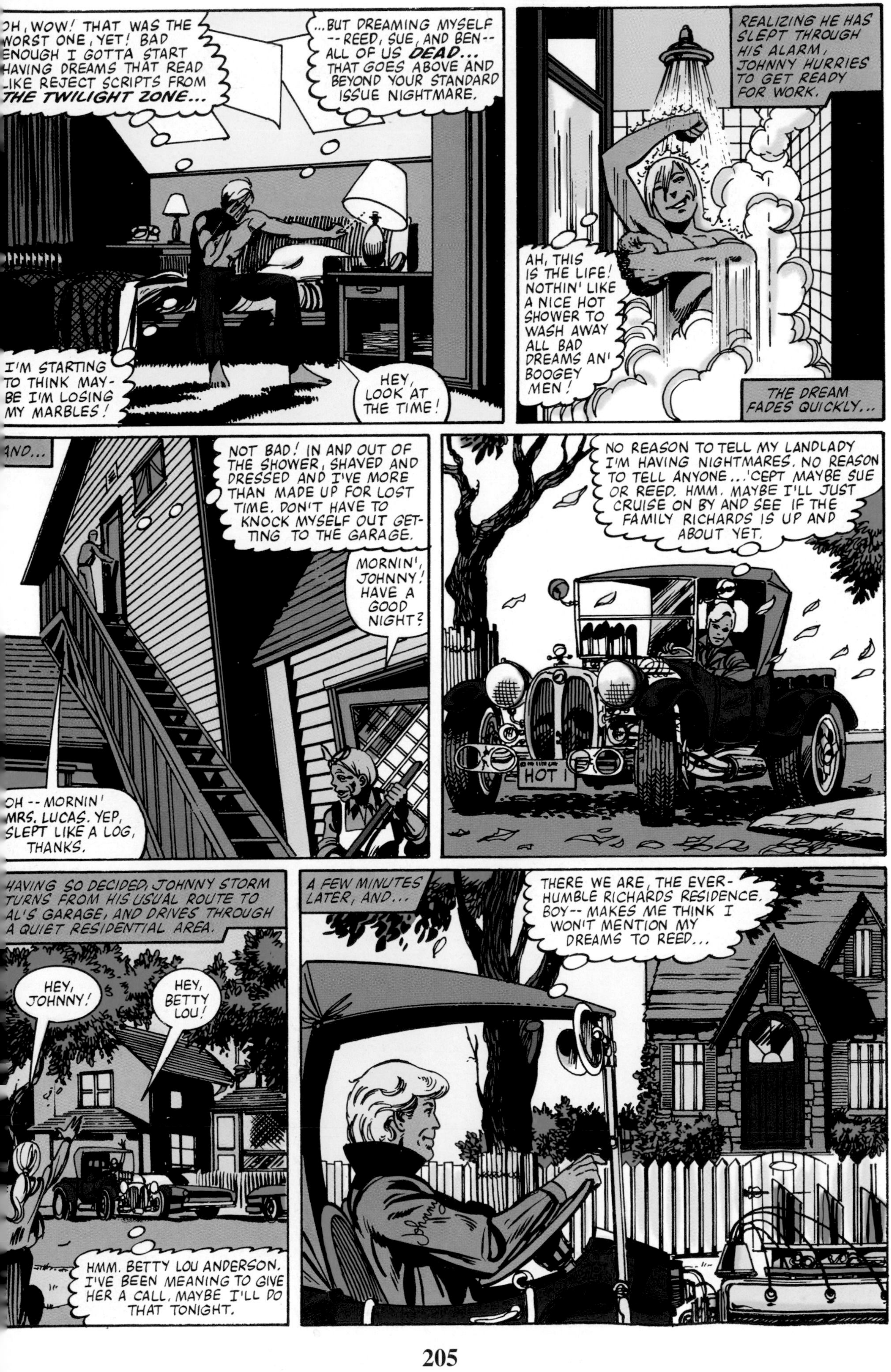
OH, WOW! THAT WAS THE WORST ONE, YET! BAD ENOUGH I GOTTA START HAVING DREAMS THAT READ LIKE REJECT SCRIPTS FROM THE TWILIGHT ZONE...
...BUT DREAMING MYSELF --REED, SUE, AND BEN-- ALL OF US DEAD... THAT GOES ABOVE AND BEYOND YOUR STANDARD ISSUE NIGHTMARE.
I'M STARTING TO THINK MAY-BE I'M LOSING MY MARBLES!
HEY, LOOK AT THE TIME!
REALIZING HE HAS SLEPT THROUGH HIS ALARM, JOHNNY HURRIES TO GET READY FOR WORK.
AH, THIS IS THE LIFE! NOTHIN' LIKE A NICE HOT SHOWER TO WASH AWAY ALL BAD DREAMS AN' BOOGEY MEN!
THE DREAM FADES QUICKLY...
AND...
NOT BAD! IN AND OUT OF THE SHOWER, SHAVED AND DRESSED AND I'VE MORE THAN MADE UP FOR LOST TIME. DON'T HAVE TO KNOCK MYSELF OUT GET-TING TO THE GARAGE.
MORNIN', JOHNNY! HAVE A GOOD NIGHT?
OH -- MORNIN' MRS. LUCAS. YEP, SLEPT LIKE A LOG, THANKS.
NO REASON TO TELL MY LANDLADY I'M HAVING NIGHTMARES. NO REASON TO TELL ANYONE...'CEPT MAYBE SUE OR REED. HMM. MAYBE I'LL JUST CRUISE ON BY AND SEE IF THE FAMILY RICHARDS IS UP AND ABOUT YET.
HOT 1
HAVING SO DECIDED, JOHNNY STORM TURNS FROM HIS USUAL ROUTE TO AL'S GARAGE, AND DRIVES THROUGH A QUIET RESIDENTIAL AREA.
HEY, JOHNNY!
HEY, BETTY LOU!
HMM. BETTY LOU ANDERSON. I'VE BEEN MEANING TO GIVE HER A CALL. MAYBE I'LL DO THAT TONIGHT.
A FEW MINUTES LATER, AND...
THERE WE ARE, THE EVER-HUMBLE RICHARDS RESIDENCE. BOY-- MAKES ME THINK I WON'T MENTION MY DREAMS TO REED...

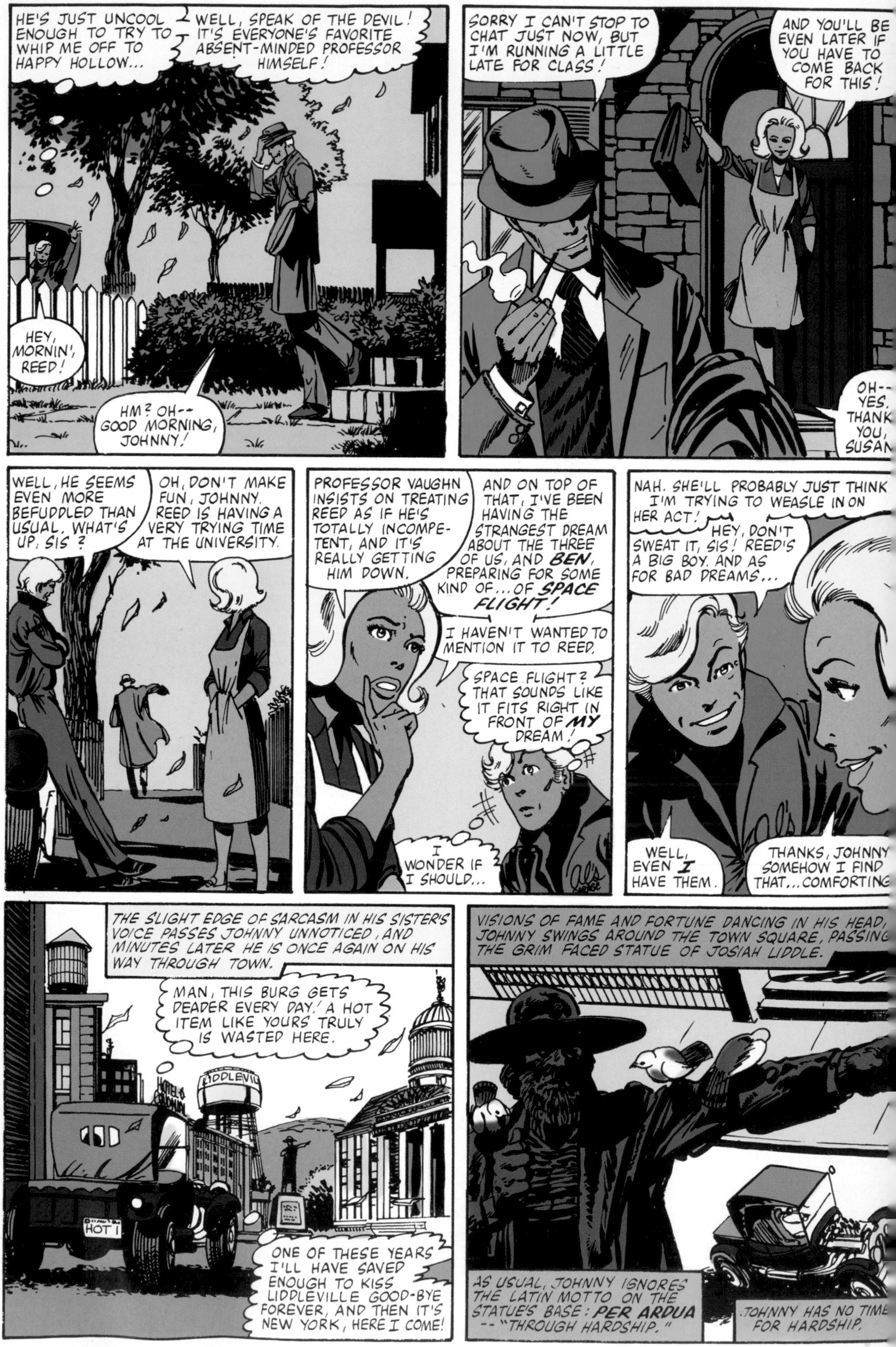

HE'S JUST UNCOOL ENOUGH TO TRY TO WHIP ME OFF TO HAPPY HOLLOW...
WELL, SPEAK OF THE DEVIL! IT'S EVERYONE'S FAVORITE ABSENT-MINDED PROFESSOR HIMSELF!
HEY, MORNIN', REED!
HM? OH-- GOOD MORNING, JOHNNY!
SORRY I CAN'T STOP TO CHAT JUST NOW, BUT I'M RUNNING A LITTLE LATE FOR CLASS!
AND YOU'LL BE EVEN LATER IF YOU HAVE TO COME BACK FOR THIS!
OH-- YES. THANK YOU, SUSAN
WELL, HE SEEMS EVEN MORE BEFUDDLED THAN USUAL. WHAT'S UP, SIS?
OH, DON'T MAKE FUN, JOHNNY. REED IS HAVING A VERY TRYING TIME AT THE UNIVERSITY.
PROFESSOR VAUGHN INSISTS ON TREATING REED AS IF HE'S TOTALLY INCOMPETENT, AND IT'S REALLY GETTING HIM DOWN.
AND ON TOP OF THAT, I'VE BEEN HAVING THE STRANGEST DREAM ABOUT THE THREE OF US, AND BEN, PREPARING FOR SOME KIND OF... OF SPACE FLIGHT!
I HAVEN'T WANTED TO MENTION IT TO REED.
SPACE FLIGHT? THAT SOUNDS LIKE IT FITS RIGHT IN FRONT OF MY DREAM!
I WONDER IF I SHOULD...
NAH. SHE'LL PROBABLY JUST THINK I'M TRYING TO WEASLE IN ON HER ACT!
HEY, DON'T SWEAT IT, SIS! REED'S A BIG BOY. AND AS FOR BAD DREAMS...
WELL, EVEN I HAVE THEM.
THANKS, JOHNNY SOMEHOW I FIND THAT... COMFORTING
THE SLIGHT EDGE OF SARCASM IN HIS SISTER'S VOICE PASSES JOHNNY UNNOTICED, AND MINUTES LATER HE IS ONCE AGAIN ON HIS WAY THROUGH TOWN.
MAN, THIS BURG GETS DEADER EVERY DAY! A HOT ITEM LIKE YOURS TRULY IS WASTED HERE.
HOT I
ONE OF THESE YEARS I'LL HAVE SAVED ENOUGH TO KISS LIDDLEVILLE GOOD-BYE FOREVER, AND THEN IT'S NEW YORK, HERE I COME!
VISIONS OF FAME AND FORTUNE DANCING IN HIS HEAD, JOHNNY SWINGS AROUND THE TOWN SQUARE, PASSING THE GRIM FACED STATUE OF JOSIAH LIDDLE.
AS USUAL, JOHNNY IGNORES THE LATIN MOTTO ON THE STATUE'S BASE: PER ARDUA -- "THROUGH HARDSHIP."
JOHNNY HAS NO TIME FOR HARDSHIP.

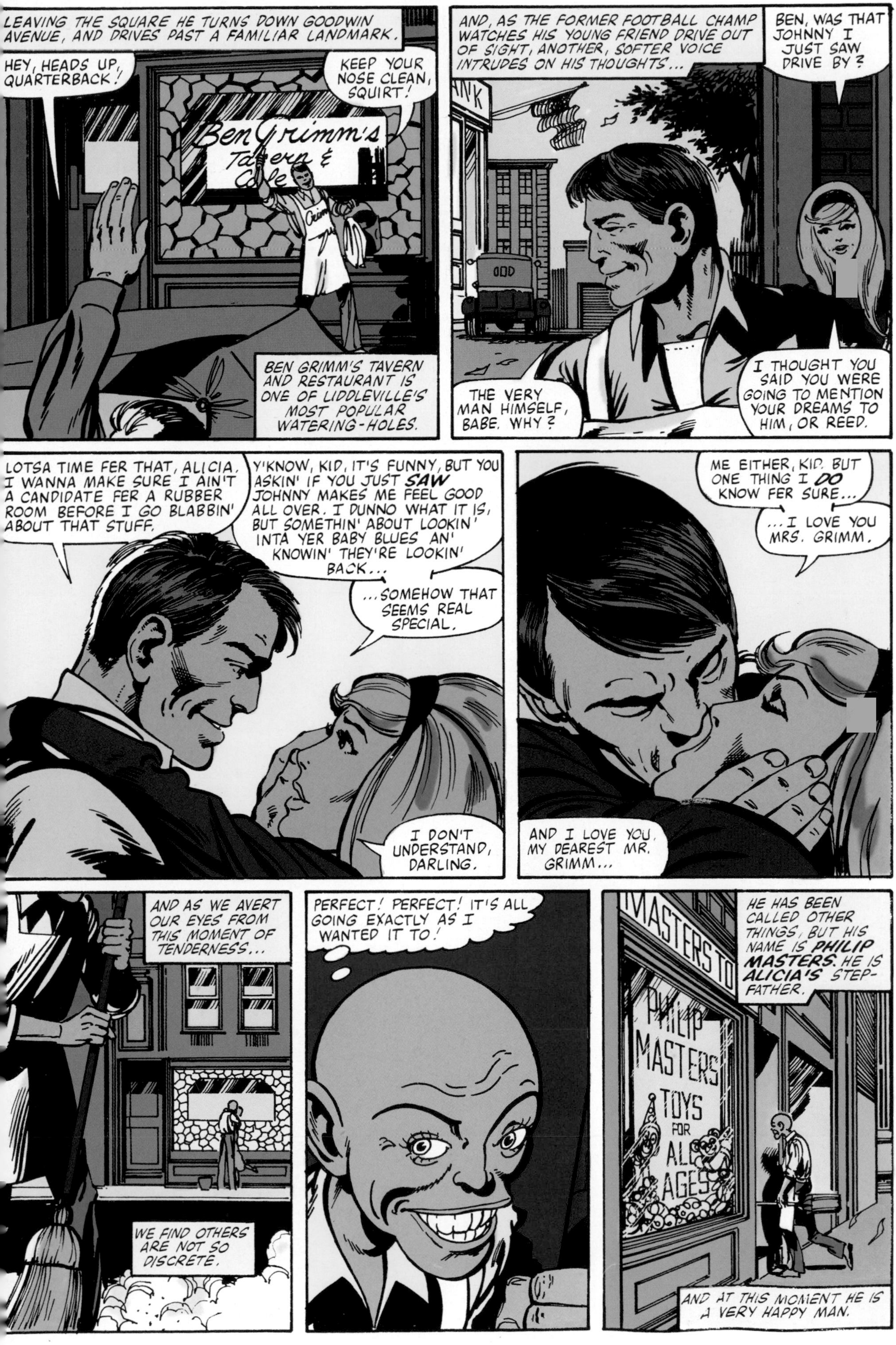
LEAVING THE SQUARE HE TURNS DOWN GOODWIN AVENUE, AND DRIVES PAST A FAMILIAR LANDMARK.
HEY, HEADS UP, QUARTERBACK!
KEEP YOUR NOSE CLEAN, SQUIRT!
Ben Grimm's Tavern & Cafe
BEN GRIMM'S TAVERN AND RESTAURANT IS ONE OF LIDDLEVILLE'S MOST POPULAR WATERING-HOLES.
AND, AS THE FORMER FOOTBALL CHAMP WATCHES HIS YOUNG FRIEND DRIVE OUT OF SIGHT, ANOTHER, SOFTER VOICE INTRUDES ON HIS THOUGHTS...
BEN, WAS THAT JOHNNY I JUST SAW DRIVE BY?
THE VERY MAN HIMSELF, BABE. WHY?
I THOUGHT YOU SAID YOU WERE GOING TO MENTION YOUR DREAMS TO HIM, OR REED.
LOTSA TIME FER THAT, ALICIA. I WANNA MAKE SURE I AIN'T A CANDIDATE FER A RUBBER ROOM BEFORE I GO BLABBIN' ABOUT THAT STUFF.
Y'KNOW, KID, IT'S FUNNY, BUT YOU ASKIN' IF YOU JUST SAW JOHNNY MAKES ME FEEL GOOD ALL OVER. I DUNNO WHAT IT IS, BUT SOMETHIN' ABOUT LOOKIN' INTA YER BABY BLUES AN' KNOWIN' THEY'RE LOOKIN' BACK...
...SOMEHOW THAT SEEMS REAL SPECIAL.
I DON'T UNDERSTAND, DARLING.
ME EITHER, KID. BUT ONE THING I DO KNOW FER SURE...
...I LOVE YOU MRS. GRIMM.
AND I LOVE YOU, MY DEAREST MR. GRIMM...
AND AS WE AVERT OUR EYES FROM THIS MOMENT OF TENDERNESS...
WE FIND OTHERS ARE NOT SO DISCRETE.
PERFECT! PERFECT! IT'S ALL GOING EXACTLY AS I WANTED IT TO!
MASTERS TO
HE HAS BEEN CALLED OTHER THINGS, BUT HIS NAME IS PHILIP MASTERS. HE IS ALICIA'S STEP-FATHER.
PHILIP MASTERS TOYS FOR ALL AGES
AND AT THIS MOMENT HE IS A VERY HAPPY MAN.

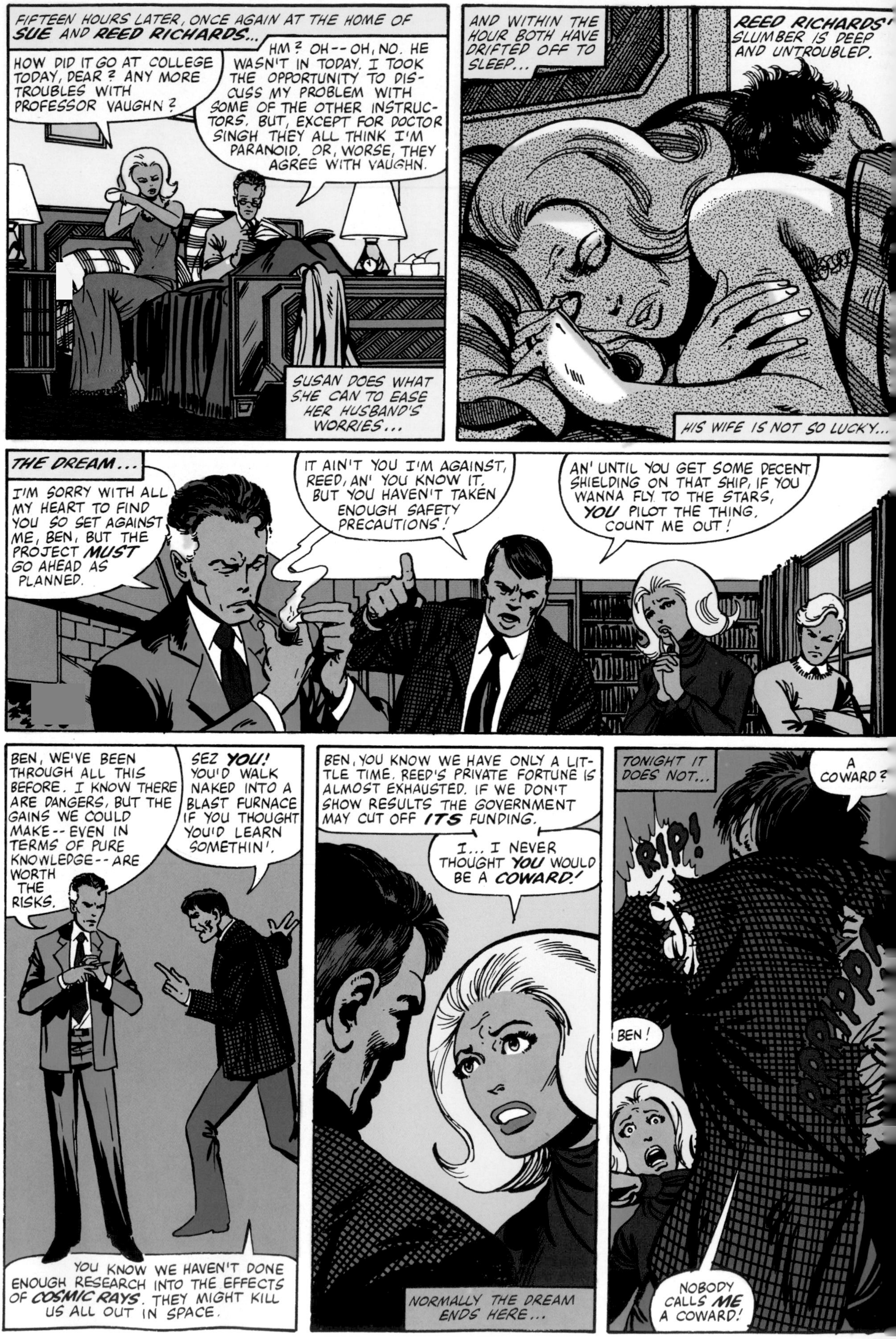

FIFTEEN HOURS LATER, ONCE AGAIN AT THE HOME OF SUE AND REED RICHARDS...
HOW DID IT GO AT COLLEGE TODAY, DEAR? ANY MORE TROUBLES WITH PROFESSOR VAUGHN?
HM? OH--OH, NO. HE WASN'T IN TODAY. I TOOK THE OPPORTUNITY TO DISCUSS MY PROBLEM WITH SOME OF THE OTHER INSTRUCTORS. BUT, EXCEPT FOR DOCTOR SINGH THEY ALL THINK I'M PARANOID. OR, WORSE, THEY AGREE WITH VAUGHN.
SUSAN DOES WHAT SHE CAN TO EASE HER HUSBAND'S WORRIES...
AND WITHIN THE HOUR BOTH HAVE DRIFTED OFF TO SLEEP...
REED RICHARDS' SLUMBER IS DEEP AND UNTROUBLED.
HIS WIFE IS NOT SO LUCKY...
THE DREAM...
I'M SORRY WITH ALL MY HEART TO FIND YOU SO SET AGAINST ME, BEN, BUT THE PROJECT MUST GO AHEAD AS PLANNED.
IT AIN'T YOU I'M AGAINST, REED, AN' YOU KNOW IT. BUT YOU HAVEN'T TAKEN ENOUGH SAFETY PRECAUTIONS!
AN' UNTIL YOU GET SOME DECENT SHIELDING ON THAT SHIP, IF YOU WANNA FLY TO THE STARS, YOU PILOT THE THING. COUNT ME OUT!
BEN, WE'VE BEEN THROUGH ALL THIS BEFORE. I KNOW THERE ARE DANGERS, BUT THE GAINS WE COULD MAKE--EVEN IN TERMS OF PURE KNOWLEDGE--ARE WORTH THE RISKS.
SEZ YOU! YOU'D WALK NAKED INTO A BLAST FURNACE IF YOU THOUGHT YOU'D LEARN SOMETHIN'.
YOU KNOW WE HAVEN'T DONE ENOUGH RESEARCH INTO THE EFFECTS OF COSMIC RAYS. THEY MIGHT KILL US ALL OUT IN SPACE.
BEN, YOU KNOW WE HAVE ONLY A LITTLE TIME. REED'S PRIVATE FORTUNE IS ALMOST EXHAUSTED. IF WE DON'T SHOW RESULTS THE GOVERNMENT MAY CUT OFF ITS FUNDING.
I... I NEVER THOUGHT YOU WOULD BE A COWARD!
NORMALLY THE DREAM ENDS HERE...
TONIGHT IT DOES NOT...
A COWARD?
RIP!
BEN!
NOBODY CALLS ME A COWARD!

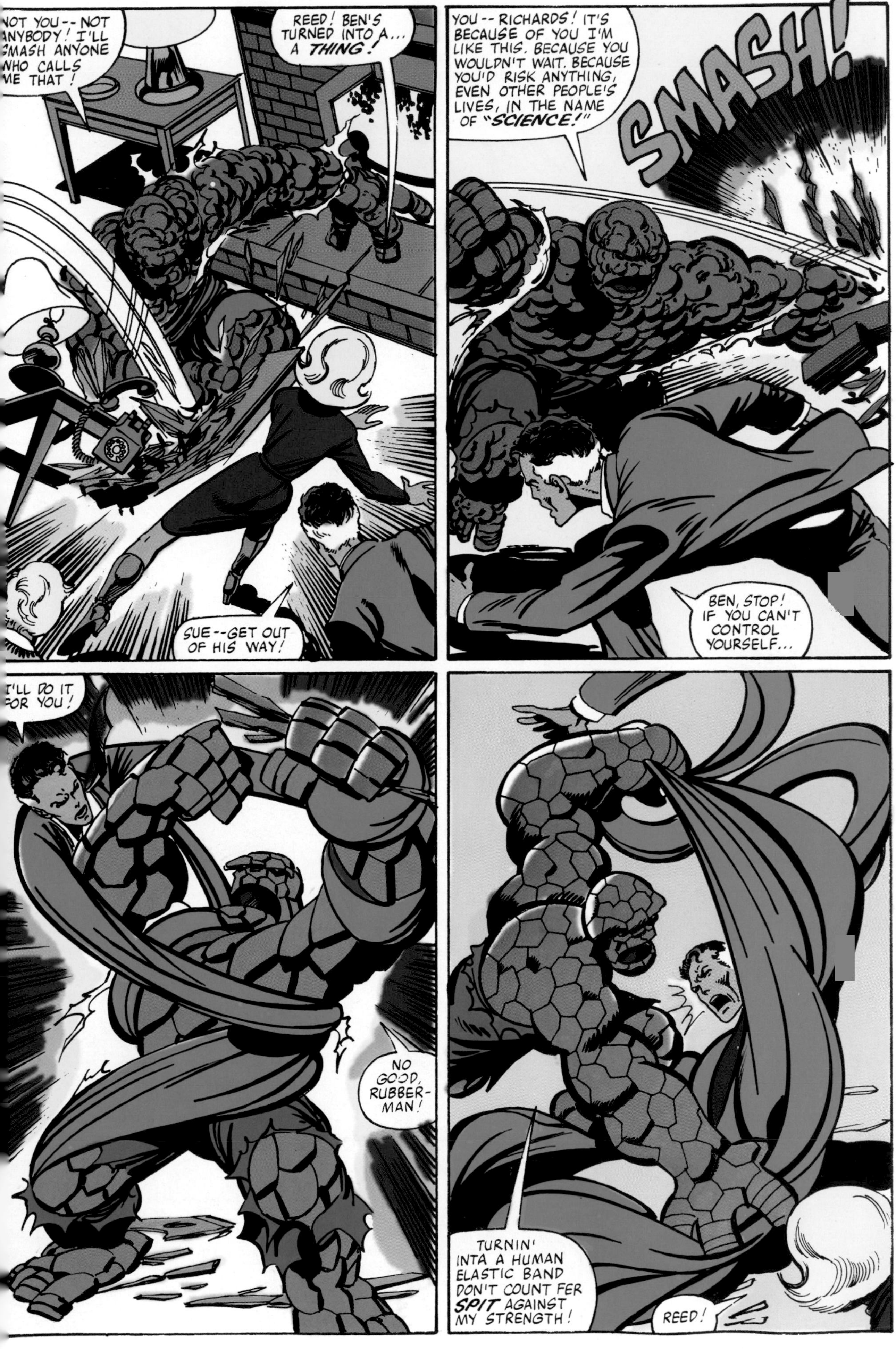

NOT YOU--NOT ANYBODY! I'LL SMASH ANYONE WHO CALLS ME THAT!
REED! BEN'S TURNED INTO A... A THING!
SUE--GET OUT OF HIS WAY!
YOU--RICHARDS! IT'S BECAUSE OF YOU I'M LIKE THIS. BECAUSE YOU WOULDN'T WAIT. BECAUSE YOU'D RISK ANYTHING, EVEN OTHER PEOPLE'S LIVES, IN THE NAME OF "SCIENCE!"
SMASH!
BEN, STOP! IF YOU CAN'T CONTROL YOURSELF...
I'LL DO IT FOR YOU!
NO GOOD, RUBBER-MAN!
TURNIN' INTA A HUMAN ELASTIC BAND DON'T COUNT FER SPIT AGAINST MY STRENGTH!
REED!

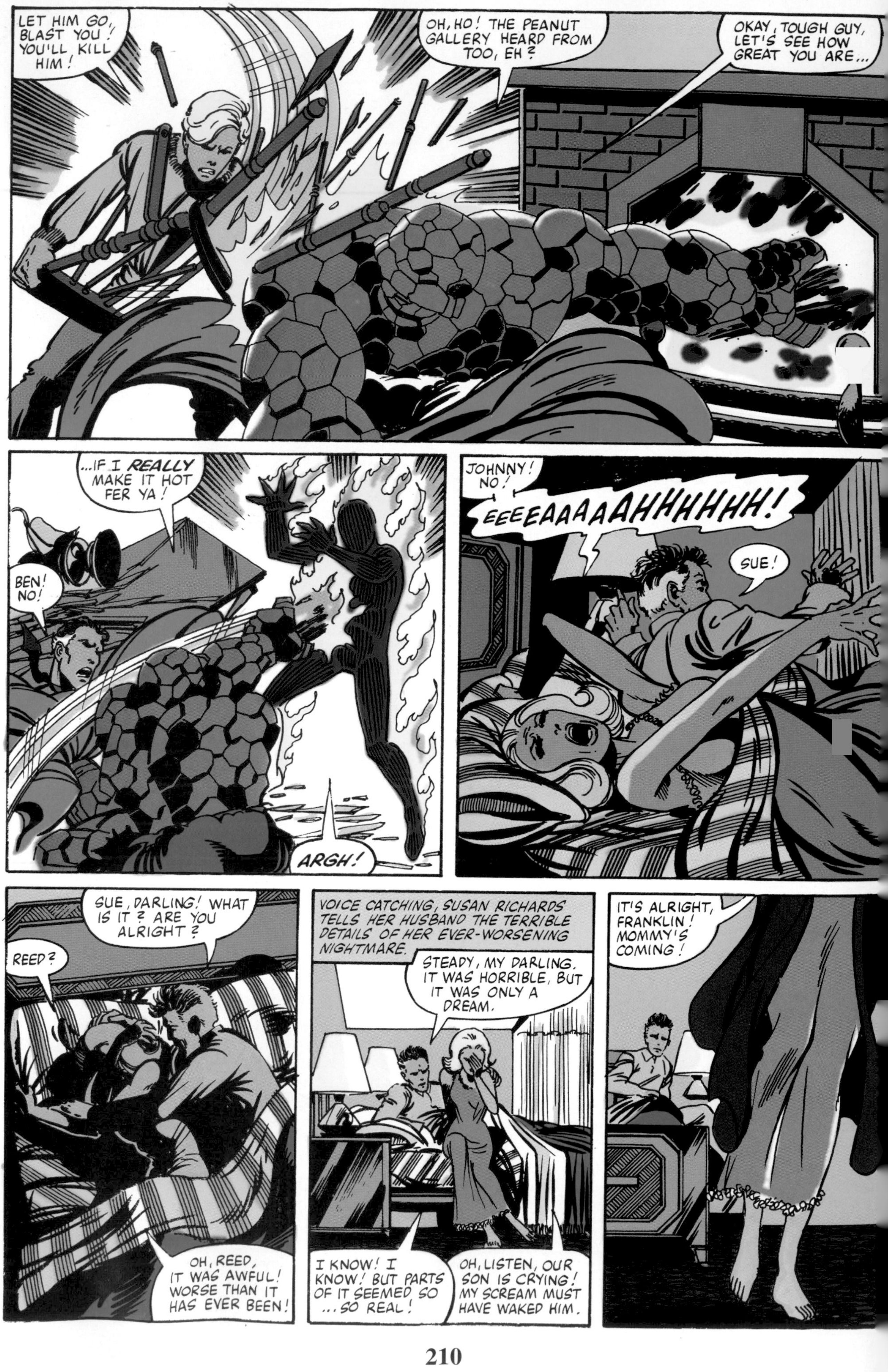
LET HIM GO, BLAST YOU! YOU'LL KILL HIM!
OH, HO! THE PEANUT GALLERY HEARD FROM TOO, EH?
OKAY, TOUGH GUY, LET'S SEE HOW GREAT YOU ARE...
...IF I REALLY MAKE IT HOT FER YA!
BEN! NO!
ARGH!
JOHNNY! NO!
EEEEAAAAAHHHHHHH!
SUE!
SUE, DARLING! WHAT IS IT? ARE YOU ALRIGHT?
REED?
OH, REED, IT WAS AWFUL! WORSE THAN IT HAS EVER BEEN!
VOICE CATCHING, SUSAN RICHARDS TELLS HER HUSBAND THE TERRIBLE DETAILS OF HER EVER-WORSENING NIGHTMARE.
STEADY, MY DARLING. IT WAS HORRIBLE, BUT IT WAS ONLY A DREAM.
I KNOW! I KNOW! BUT PARTS OF IT SEEMED SO ...SO REAL!
OH, LISTEN, OUR SON IS CRYING! MY SCREAM MUST HAVE WAKED HIM.
IT'S ALRIGHT, FRANKLIN! MOMMY'S COMING!

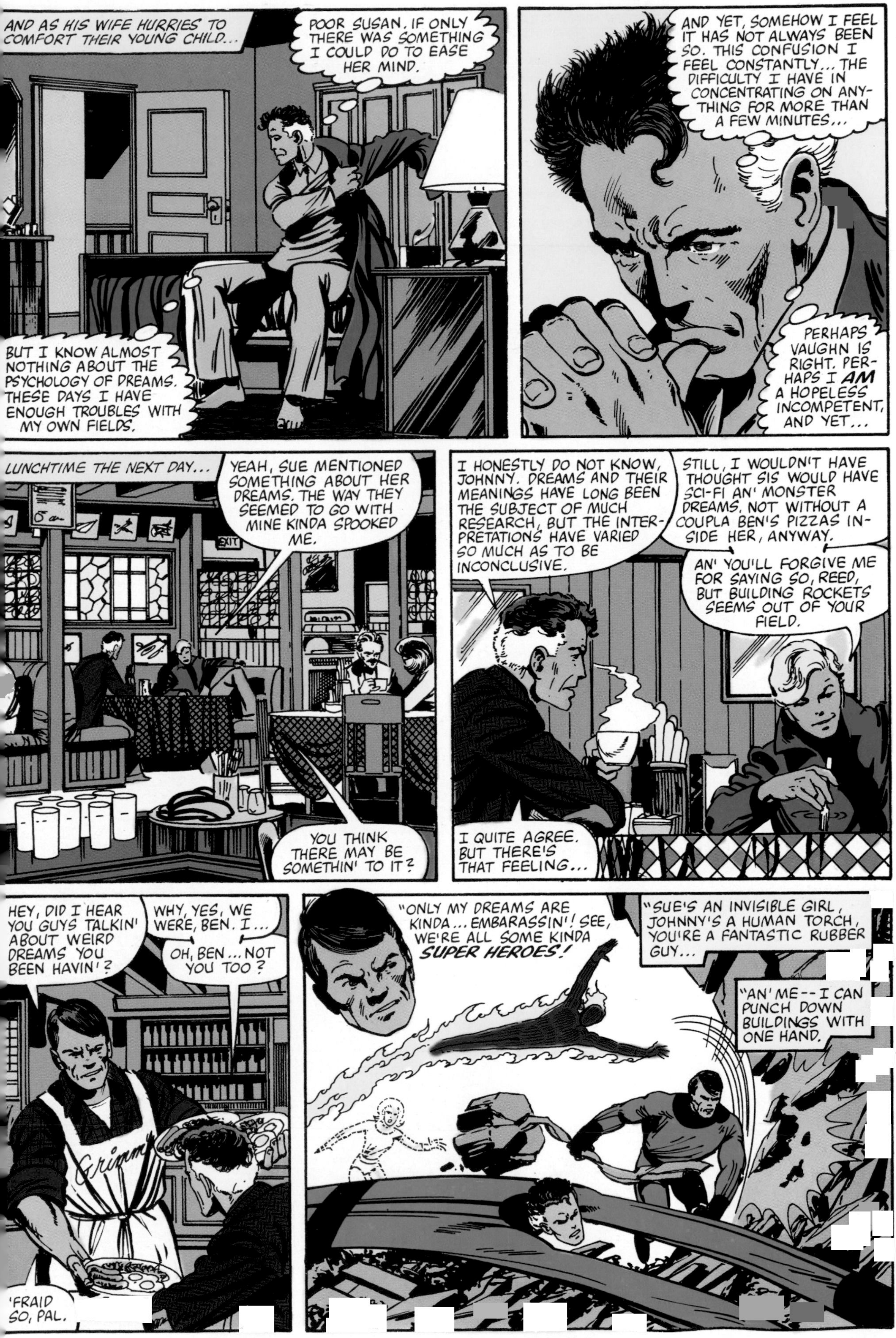
AND AS HIS WIFE HURRIES TO COMFORT THEIR YOUNG CHILD...
POOR SUSAN. IF ONLY THERE WAS SOMETHING I COULD DO TO EASE HER MIND.
BUT I KNOW ALMOST NOTHING ABOUT THE PSYCHOLOGY OF DREAMS. THESE DAYS I HAVE ENOUGH TROUBLES WITH MY OWN FIELDS.
AND YET, SOMEHOW I FEEL IT HAS NOT ALWAYS BEEN SO. THIS CONFUSION I FEEL CONSTANTLY... THE DIFFICULTY I HAVE IN CONCENTRATING ON ANY-THING FOR MORE THAN A FEW MINUTES...
PERHAPS VAUGHN IS RIGHT. PER-HAPS I AM A HOPELESS INCOMPETENT, AND YET...
LUNCHTIME THE NEXT DAY...
YEAH, SUE MENTIONED SOMETHING ABOUT HER DREAMS. THE WAY THEY SEEMED TO GO WITH MINE KINDA SPOOKED ME.
YOU THINK THERE MAY BE SOMETHIN' TO IT?
I HONESTLY DO NOT KNOW, JOHNNY. DREAMS AND THEIR MEANINGS HAVE LONG BEEN THE SUBJECT OF MUCH RESEARCH, BUT THE INTER-PRETATIONS HAVE VARIED SO MUCH AS TO BE INCONCLUSIVE.
STILL, I WOULDN'T HAVE THOUGHT SIS WOULD HAVE SCI-FI AN' MONSTER DREAMS, NOT WITHOUT A COUPLA BEN'S PIZZAS IN-SIDE HER, ANYWAY.
AN' YOU'LL FORGIVE ME FOR SAYING SO, REED, BUT BUILDING ROCKETS SEEMS OUT OF YOUR FIELD.
I QUITE AGREE. BUT THERE'S THAT FEELING...
HEY, DID I HEAR YOU GUYS TALKIN' ABOUT WEIRD DREAMS YOU BEEN HAVIN'?
WHY, YES, WE WERE, BEN. I...
OH, BEN... NOT YOU TOO?
'FRAID SO, PAL.
Grimm
"ONLY MY DREAMS ARE KINDA... EMBARASSIN'! SEE, WE'RE ALL SOME KINDA SUPER HEROES!
"SUE'S AN INVISIBLE GIRL, JOHNNY'S A HUMAN TORCH, YOU'RE A FANTASTIC RUBBER GUY...
"AN' ME-- I CAN PUNCH DOWN BUILDINGS WITH ONE HAND.

"ONLY-- ONLY THERE'S SOME STUFF EVEN STRANGER THAN THAT. ME AN' ALICIA AIN'T MARRIED IN MY DREAM.

"IN FACT, FER SOME REASON, I'M EVEN AFRAID TA ASK HER.

"AND... AND ALICIA IS... *BLIND!*"

I CAN'T MAKE NO SENSE OF IT.

IT'S DISTURBING. THE PARALLELS BETWEEN THE DIFFERENT DREAM SCENARIOS ARE SO EXACT, AND YET JUST DISSIMILAR ENOUGH.

JOHNNY'S DREAM HAS HIM BURNING UP IN THE COSMIC RAYS, SUE HAS HIM CATCHING FIRE. YOUR'S HAS HIM A HUMAN TORCH. YOUR STRENGTH IS COMMON TO YOURS AND SUE'S. MY STRETCHING ALSO.

IT'S CONFUSING, AND ANNOYING. I FEEL LIKE I SHOULD BE ABLE TO...

HEY, HEADS UP, GUYS. WE GOT COMPANY...

BEN, LOOK WHO'S COME TO JOIN US FOR LUNCH!

WELL, HEY, IF IT AIN'T MY FAVORITE FATHER-IN-LAW. HOW YA DOIN', PHIL?

VERY WELL, THANK YOU, BEN. I HOPE I'M NOT INTRUDING?

NOT A BIT. PULL UP A PEW AN' I'LL GETCHA A BURGER.

AND SO PHILLIP MASTERS JOINS THE OTHERS, AND TALK TURNS FROM THE STUFF OF DREAMS TO THE EVERYDAY GOINGS ON OF LIDDLE-VILLE.

BUT REED IS STILL TROUBLED...

AND HIS WORRIES HAVE NOT PASSED AN HOUR LATER WHEN HE RETURNS TO WORK...

RICHARDS, GOT A MOMENT?

HM? OH, SINGH. ER, YES, WHAT CAN I DO FOR YOU?

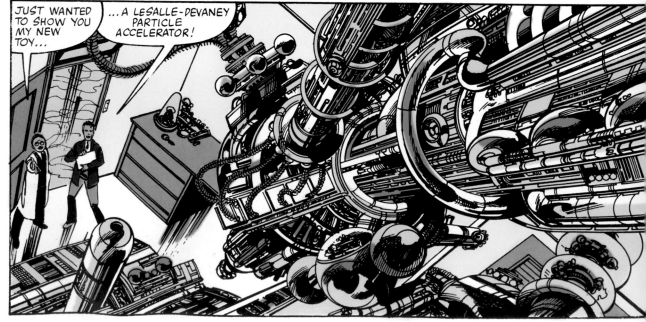

JUST WANTED TO SHOW YOU MY NEW TOY...

...A LESALLE-DEVANEY PARTICLE ACCELERATOR!

212

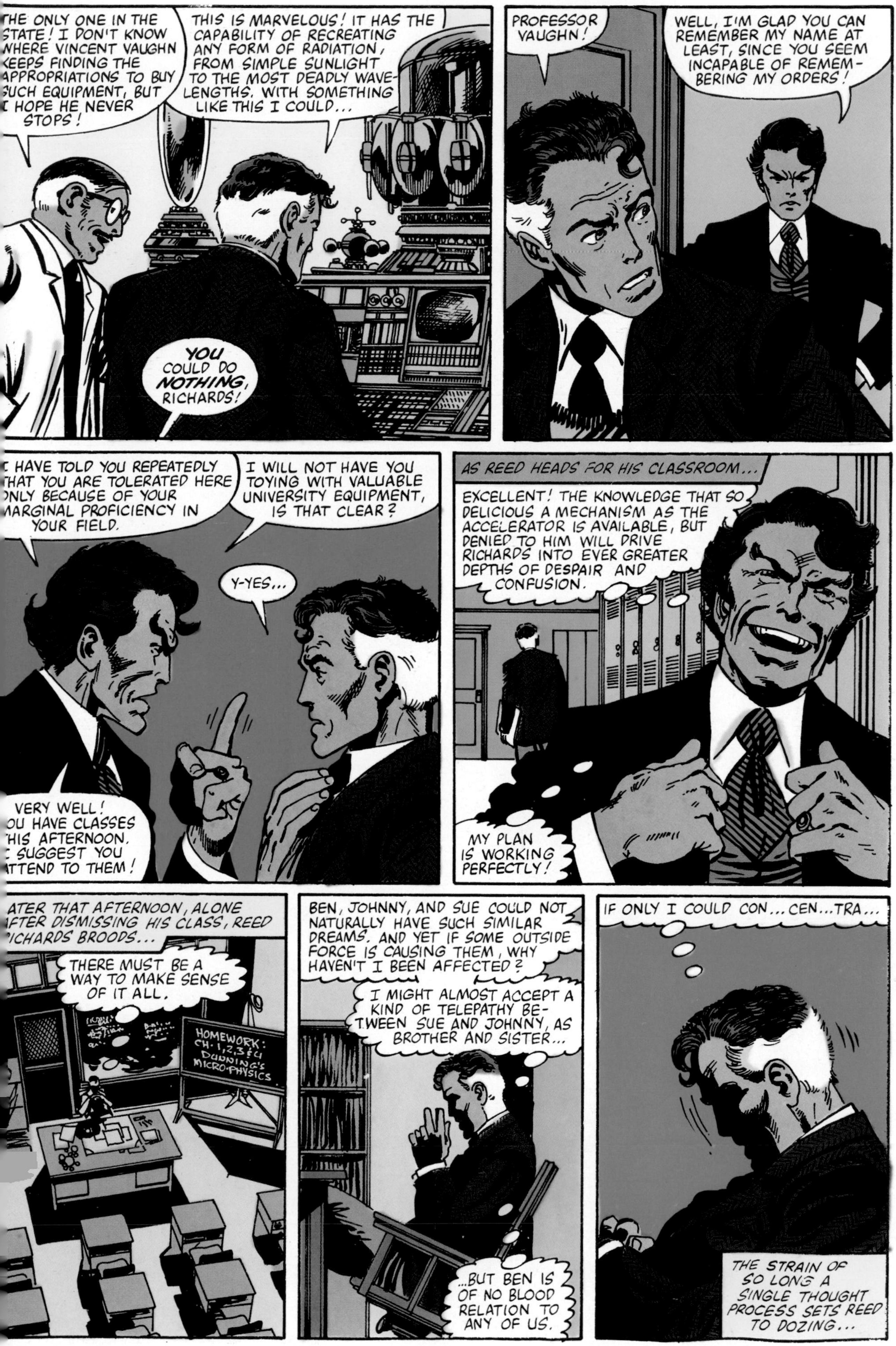
THE ONLY ONE IN THE STATE! I DON'T KNOW WHERE VINCENT VAUGHN KEEPS FINDING THE APPROPRIATIONS TO BUY SUCH EQUIPMENT, BUT I HOPE HE NEVER STOPS!
THIS IS MARVELOUS! IT HAS THE CAPABILITY OF RECREATING ANY FORM OF RADIATION, FROM SIMPLE SUNLIGHT TO THE MOST DEADLY WAVE-LENGTHS. WITH SOMETHING LIKE THIS I COULD...
YOU COULD DO NOTHING, RICHARDS!
PROFESSOR VAUGHN!
WELL, I'M GLAD YOU CAN REMEMBER MY NAME AT LEAST, SINCE YOU SEEM INCAPABLE OF REMEMBERING MY ORDERS!
I HAVE TOLD YOU REPEATEDLY THAT YOU ARE TOLERATED HERE ONLY BECAUSE OF YOUR MARGINAL PROFICIENCY IN YOUR FIELD.
I WILL NOT HAVE YOU TOYING WITH VALUABLE UNIVERSITY EQUIPMENT, IS THAT CLEAR?
Y-YES...
VERY WELL! YOU HAVE CLASSES THIS AFTERNOON. I SUGGEST YOU ATTEND TO THEM!
AS REED HEADS FOR HIS CLASSROOM...
EXCELLENT! THE KNOWLEDGE THAT SO DELICIOUS A MECHANISM AS THE ACCELERATOR IS AVAILABLE, BUT DENIED TO HIM WILL DRIVE RICHARDS INTO EVER GREATER DEPTHS OF DESPAIR AND CONFUSION.
MY PLAN IS WORKING PERFECTLY!
LATER THAT AFTERNOON, ALONE AFTER DISMISSING HIS CLASS, REED RICHARDS BROODS...
THERE MUST BE A WAY TO MAKE SENSE OF IT ALL.
HOMEWORK: CH. 1,2,3 & 4 DUNNING'S MICRO-PHYSICS
BEN, JOHNNY, AND SUE COULD NOT NATURALLY HAVE SUCH SIMILAR DREAMS. AND YET IF SOME OUTSIDE FORCE IS CAUSING THEM, WHY HAVEN'T I BEEN AFFECTED?
I MIGHT ALMOST ACCEPT A KIND OF TELEPATHY BETWEEN SUE AND JOHNNY, AS BROTHER AND SISTER...
...BUT BEN IS OF NO BLOOD RELATION TO ANY OF US.
IF ONLY I COULD CON... CEN... TRA...
THE STRAIN OF SO LONG A SINGLE THOUGHT PROCESS SETS REED TO DOZING...

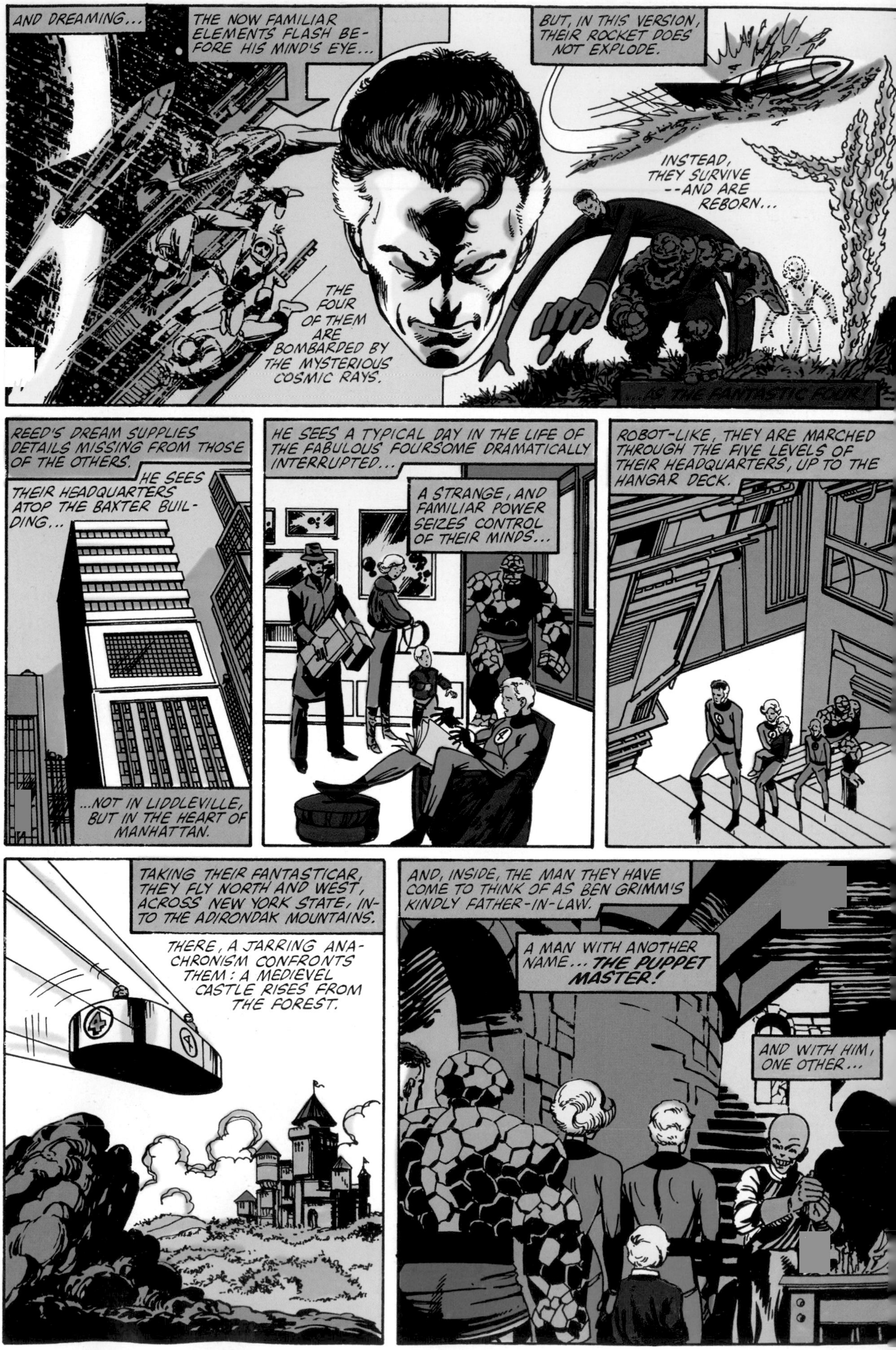
AND DREAMING...
THE NOW FAMILIAR ELEMENTS FLASH BEFORE HIS MIND'S EYE...
THE FOUR OF THEM ARE BOMBARDED BY THE MYSTERIOUS COSMIC RAYS.
BUT, IN THIS VERSION, THEIR ROCKET DOES NOT EXPLODE.
INSTEAD, THEY SURVIVE --AND ARE REBORN...
...AS THE FANTASTIC FOUR!
REED'S DREAM SUPPLIES DETAILS MISSING FROM THOSE OF THE OTHERS.
HE SEES THEIR HEADQUARTERS ATOP THE BAXTER BUILDING...
...NOT IN LIDDLEVILLE, BUT IN THE HEART OF MANHATTAN.
HE SEES A TYPICAL DAY IN THE LIFE OF THE FABULOUS FOURSOME DRAMATICALLY INTERRUPTED...
A STRANGE, AND FAMILIAR POWER SEIZES CONTROL OF THEIR MINDS...
ROBOT-LIKE, THEY ARE MARCHED THROUGH THE FIVE LEVELS OF THEIR HEADQUARTERS, UP TO THE HANGAR DECK.
TAKING THEIR FANTASTICAR, THEY FLY NORTH AND WEST, ACROSS NEW YORK STATE, INTO THE ADIRONDAK MOUNTAINS.
THERE, A JARRING ANACHRONISM CONFRONTS THEM: A MEDIEVEL CASTLE RISES FROM THE FOREST.
AND, INSIDE, THE MAN THEY HAVE COME TO THINK OF AS BEN GRIMM'S KINDLY FATHER-IN-LAW.
A MAN WITH ANOTHER NAME... THE PUPPET MASTER!
AND WITH HIM, ONE OTHER...

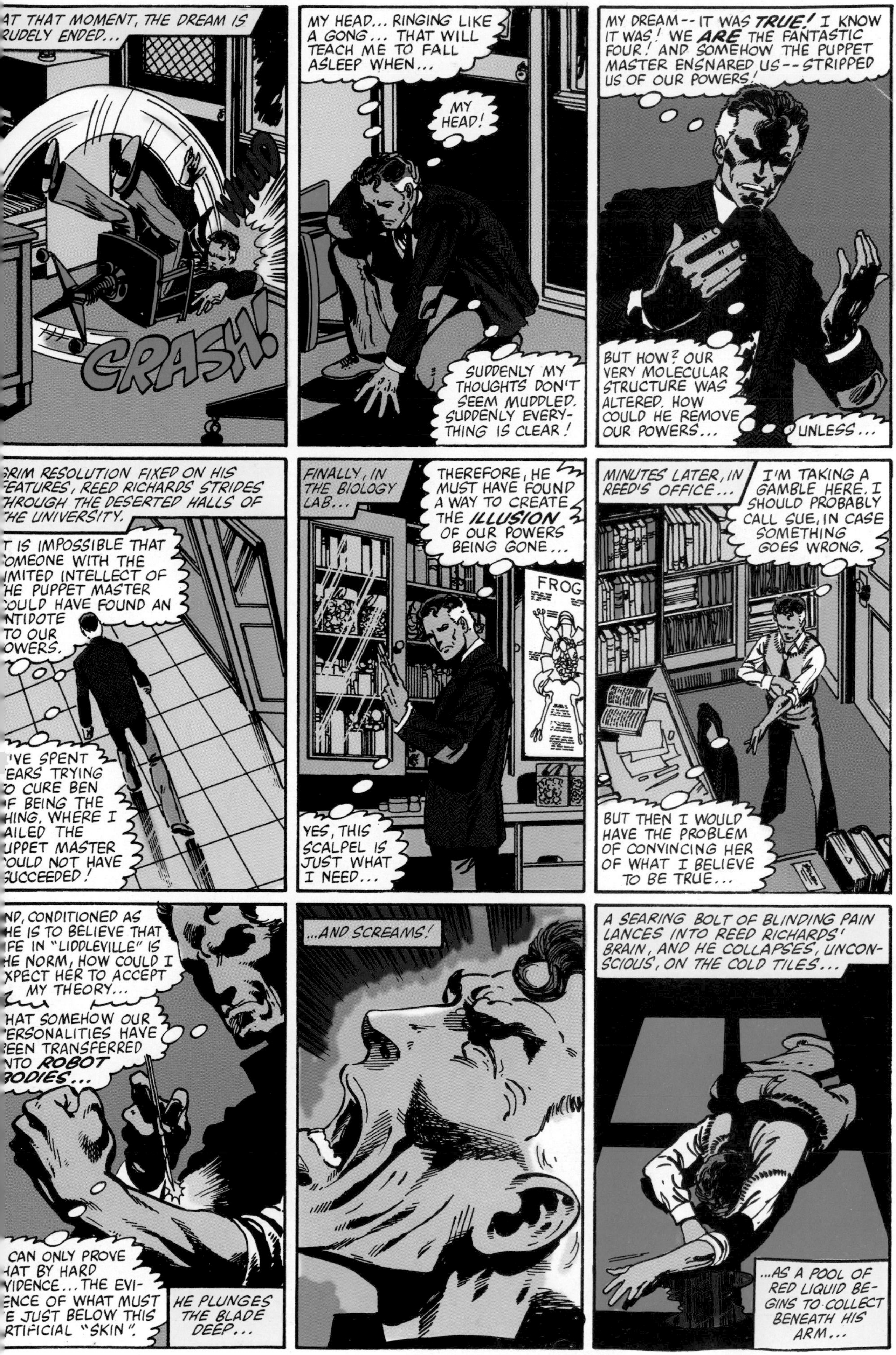
AT THAT MOMENT, THE DREAM IS RUDELY ENDED...
WHUD
CRASH!
MY HEAD... RINGING LIKE A GONG... THAT WILL TEACH ME TO FALL ASLEEP WHEN...
MY HEAD!
SUDDENLY MY THOUGHTS DON'T SEEM MUDDLED. SUDDENLY EVERYTHING IS CLEAR!
MY DREAM--IT WAS TRUE! I KNOW IT WAS! WE ARE THE FANTASTIC FOUR! AND SOMEHOW THE PUPPET MASTER ENSNARED US--STRIPPED US OF OUR POWERS!
BUT HOW? OUR VERY MOLECULAR STRUCTURE WAS ALTERED. HOW COULD HE REMOVE OUR POWERS...
UNLESS...
GRIM RESOLUTION FIXED ON HIS FEATURES, REED RICHARDS STRIDES THROUGH THE DESERTED HALLS OF THE UNIVERSITY.
IT IS IMPOSSIBLE THAT SOMEONE WITH THE LIMITED INTELLECT OF THE PUPPET MASTER COULD HAVE FOUND AN ANTIDOTE TO OUR POWERS.
I'VE SPENT YEARS TRYING TO CURE BEN OF BEING THE THING. WHERE I FAILED THE PUPPET MASTER COULD NOT HAVE SUCCEEDED!
FINALLY, IN THE BIOLOGY LAB...
THEREFORE, HE MUST HAVE FOUND A WAY TO CREATE THE ILLUSION OF OUR POWERS BEING GONE...
FROG
YES, THIS SCALPEL IS JUST WHAT I NEED...
MINUTES LATER, IN REED'S OFFICE...
I'M TAKING A GAMBLE HERE. I SHOULD PROBABLY CALL SUE, IN CASE SOMETHING GOES WRONG.
BUT THEN I WOULD HAVE THE PROBLEM OF CONVINCING HER OF WHAT I BELIEVE TO BE TRUE...
AND, CONDITIONED AS SHE IS TO BELIEVE THAT LIFE IN "LIDDLEVILLE" IS THE NORM, HOW COULD I EXPECT HER TO ACCEPT MY THEORY...
THAT SOMEHOW OUR PERSONALITIES HAVE BEEN TRANSFERRED INTO ROBOT BODIES...
I CAN ONLY PROVE THAT BY HARD EVIDENCE... THE EVIDENCE OF WHAT MUST BE JUST BELOW THIS ARTIFICIAL "SKIN".
HE PLUNGES THE BLADE DEEP...
...AND SCREAMS!
A SEARING BOLT OF BLINDING PAIN LANCES INTO REED RICHARDS' BRAIN, AND HE COLLAPSES, UNCONSCIOUS, ON THE COLD TILES...
...AS A POOL OF RED LIQUID BEGINS TO COLLECT BENEATH HIS ARM...

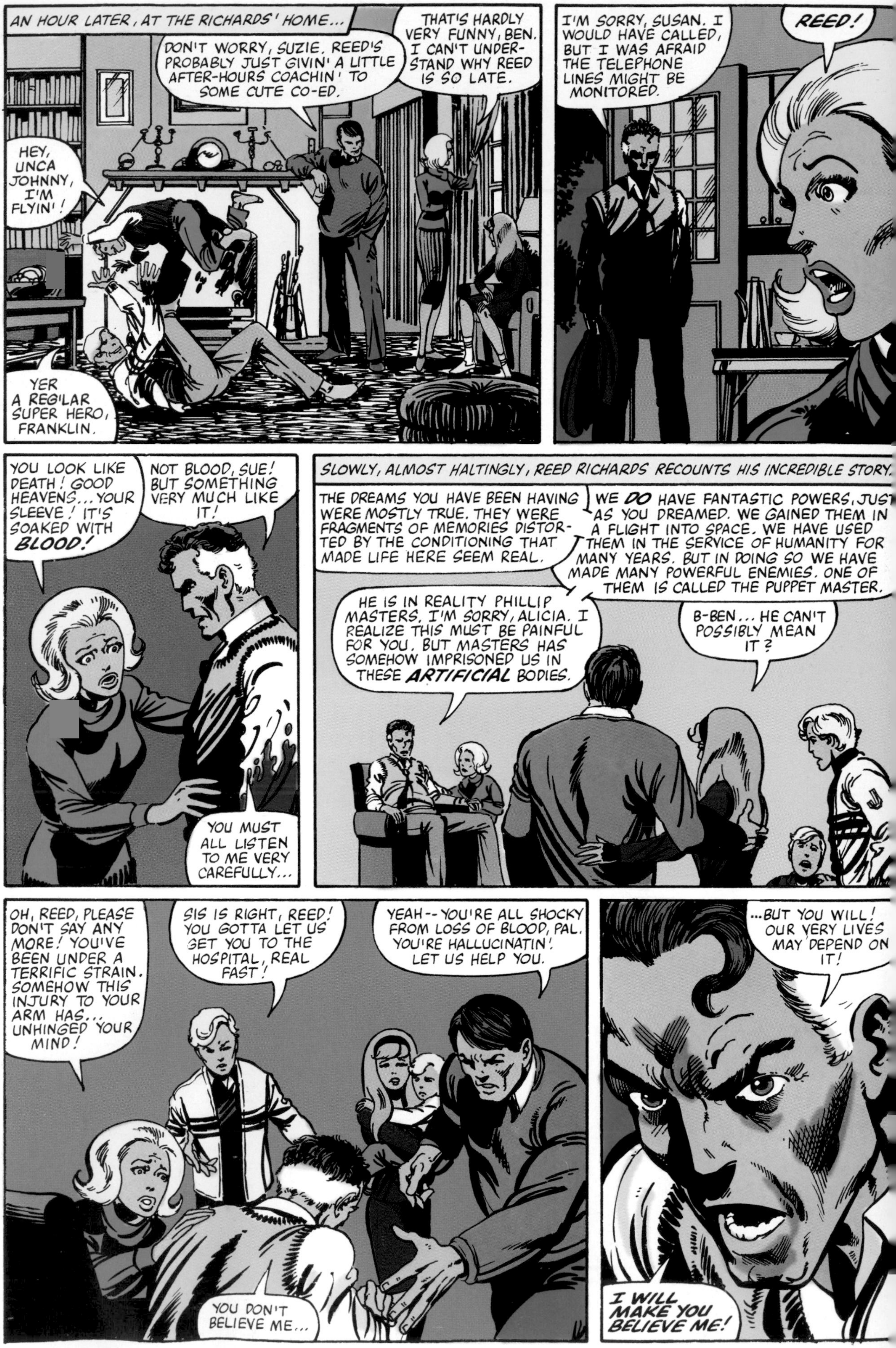

AN HOUR LATER, AT THE RICHARDS' HOME...
DON'T WORRY, SUZIE. REED'S PROBABLY JUST GIVIN' A LITTLE AFTER-HOURS COACHIN' TO SOME CUTE CO-ED.
THAT'S HARDLY VERY FUNNY, BEN. I CAN'T UNDERSTAND WHY REED IS SO LATE.
HEY, UNCA JOHNNY, I'M FLYIN'!
YER A REG'LAR SUPER HERO, FRANKLIN.
I'M SORRY, SUSAN. I WOULD HAVE CALLED, BUT I WAS AFRAID THE TELEPHONE LINES MIGHT BE MONITORED.
REED!
YOU LOOK LIKE DEATH! GOOD HEAVENS... YOUR SLEEVE! IT'S SOAKED WITH BLOOD!
NOT BLOOD, SUE! BUT SOMETHING VERY MUCH LIKE IT!
YOU MUST ALL LISTEN TO ME VERY CAREFULLY...
SLOWLY, ALMOST HALTINGLY, REED RICHARDS RECOUNTS HIS INCREDIBLE STORY.
THE DREAMS YOU HAVE BEEN HAVING WERE MOSTLY TRUE. THEY WERE FRAGMENTS OF MEMORIES DISTORTED BY THE CONDITIONING THAT MADE LIFE HERE SEEM REAL.
WE DO HAVE FANTASTIC POWERS, JUST AS YOU DREAMED. WE GAINED THEM IN A FLIGHT INTO SPACE. WE HAVE USED THEM IN THE SERVICE OF HUMANITY FOR MANY YEARS. BUT IN DOING SO WE HAVE MADE MANY POWERFUL ENEMIES. ONE OF THEM IS CALLED THE PUPPET MASTER.
HE IS IN REALITY PHILLIP MASTERS, I'M SORRY, ALICIA. I REALIZE THIS MUST BE PAINFUL FOR YOU, BUT MASTERS HAS SOMEHOW IMPRISONED US IN THESE ARTIFICIAL BODIES.
B-BEN... HE CAN'T POSSIBLY MEAN IT?
OH, REED, PLEASE DON'T SAY ANY MORE! YOU'VE BEEN UNDER A TERRIFIC STRAIN. SOMEHOW THIS INJURY TO YOUR ARM HAS... UNHINGED YOUR MIND!
SIS IS RIGHT, REED! YOU GOTTA LET US GET YOU TO THE HOSPITAL, REAL FAST!
YEAH -- YOU'RE ALL SHOCKY FROM LOSS OF BLOOD, PAL. YOU'RE HALLUCINATIN'! LET US HELP YOU.
YOU DON'T BELIEVE ME...
...BUT YOU WILL! OUR VERY LIVES MAY DEPEND ON IT!
I WILL MAKE YOU BELIEVE ME!

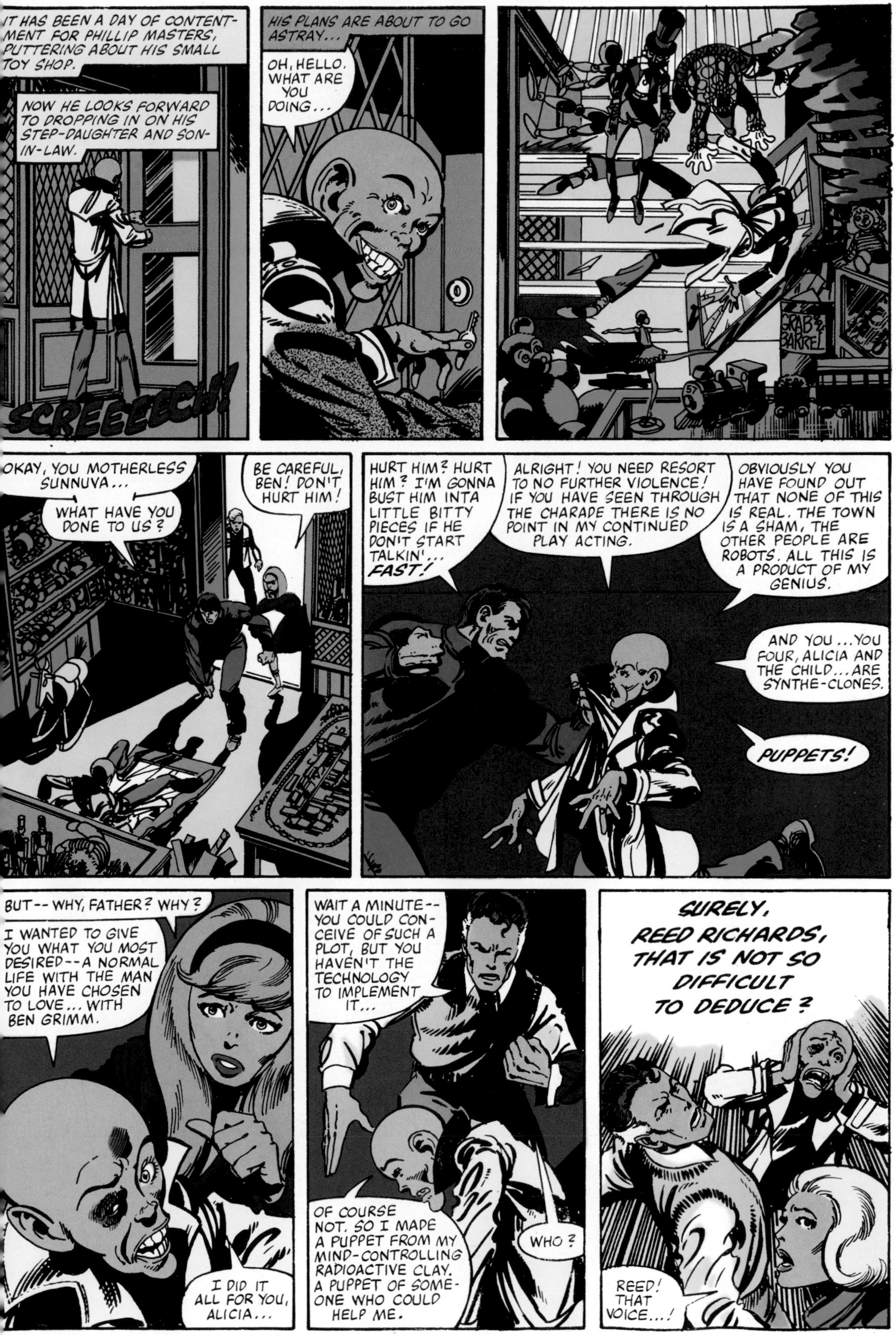
IT HAS BEEN A DAY OF CONTENTMENT FOR PHILLIP MASTERS, PUTTERING ABOUT HIS SMALL TOY SHOP.
NOW HE LOOKS FORWARD TO DROPPING IN ON HIS STEP-DAUGHTER AND SON-IN-LAW.
SCREEEEECH!
HIS PLANS ARE ABOUT TO GO ASTRAY...
OH, HELLO. WHAT ARE YOU DOING...
WHAM
GRAB BARREL
OKAY, YOU MOTHERLESS SUNNUVA...
WHAT HAVE YOU DONE TO US?
BE CAREFUL, BEN! DON'T HURT HIM!
HURT HIM? HURT HIM? I'M GONNA BUST HIM INTA LITTLE BITTY PIECES IF HE DON'T START TALKIN'... FAST!
ALRIGHT! YOU NEED RESORT TO NO FURTHER VIOLENCE! IF YOU HAVE SEEN THROUGH THE CHARADE THERE IS NO POINT IN MY CONTINUED PLAY ACTING.
OBVIOUSLY YOU HAVE FOUND OUT THAT NONE OF THIS IS REAL. THE TOWN IS A SHAM, THE OTHER PEOPLE ARE ROBOTS. ALL THIS IS A PRODUCT OF MY GENIUS.
AND YOU... YOU FOUR, ALICIA AND THE CHILD... ARE SYNTHE-CLONES.
PUPPETS!
BUT-- WHY, FATHER? WHY?
I WANTED TO GIVE YOU WHAT YOU MOST DESIRED--A NORMAL LIFE WITH THE MAN YOU HAVE CHOSEN TO LOVE... WITH BEN GRIMM.
I DID IT ALL FOR YOU, ALICIA...
WAIT A MINUTE-- YOU COULD CONCEIVE OF SUCH A PLOT, BUT YOU HAVEN'T THE TECHNOLOGY TO IMPLEMENT IT...
OF COURSE NOT. SO I MADE A PUPPET FROM MY MIND-CONTROLLING RADIOACTIVE CLAY. A PUPPET OF SOMEONE WHO COULD HELP ME.
WHO?
SURELY, REED RICHARDS, THAT IS NOT SO DIFFICULT TO DEDUCE?
REED! THAT VOICE...!

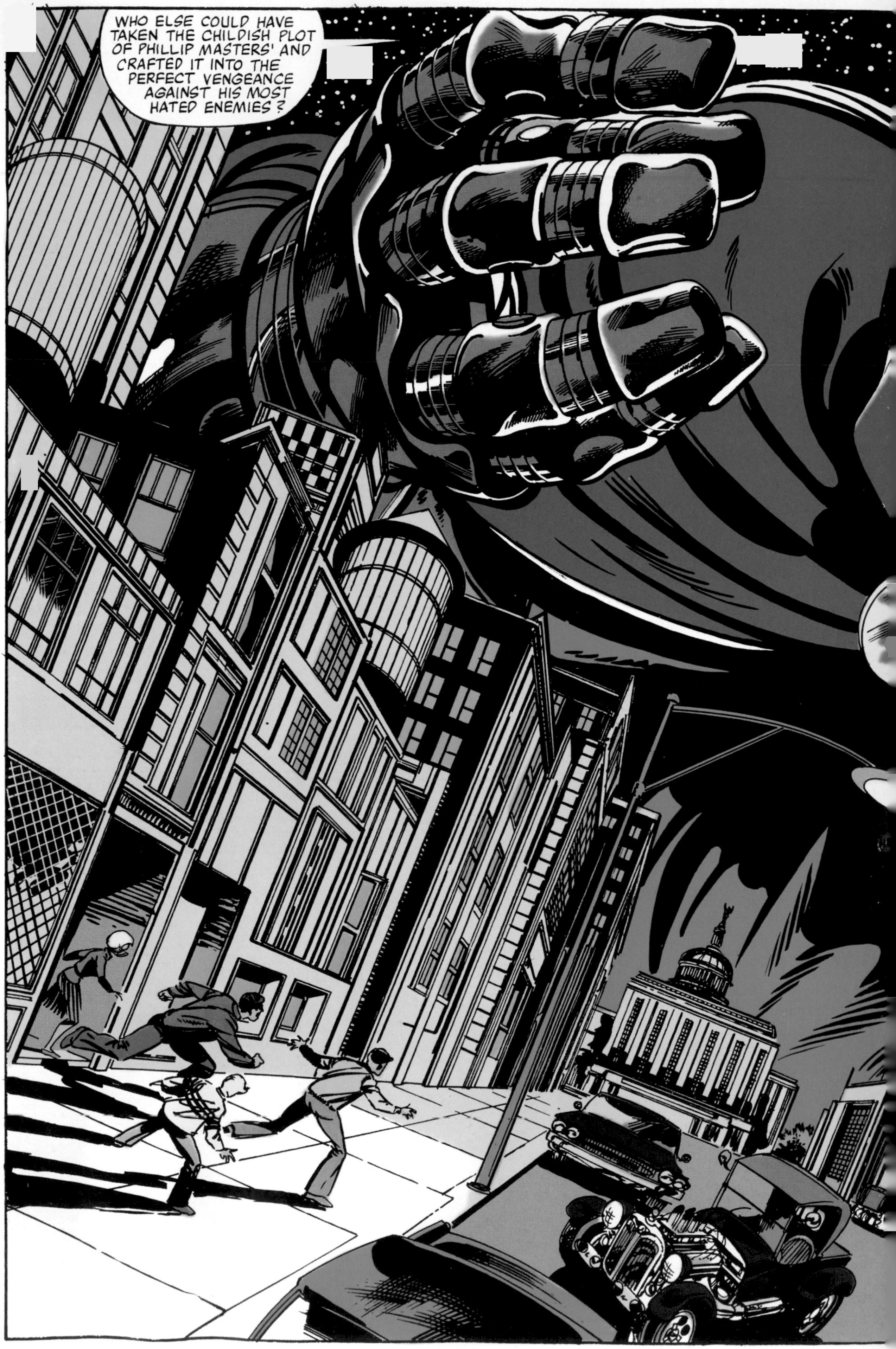
WHO ELSE COULD HAVE TAKEN THE CHILDISH PLOT OF PHILLIP MASTERS' AND CRAFTED IT INTO THE PERFECT VENGEANCE AGAINST HIS MOST HATED ENEMIES?

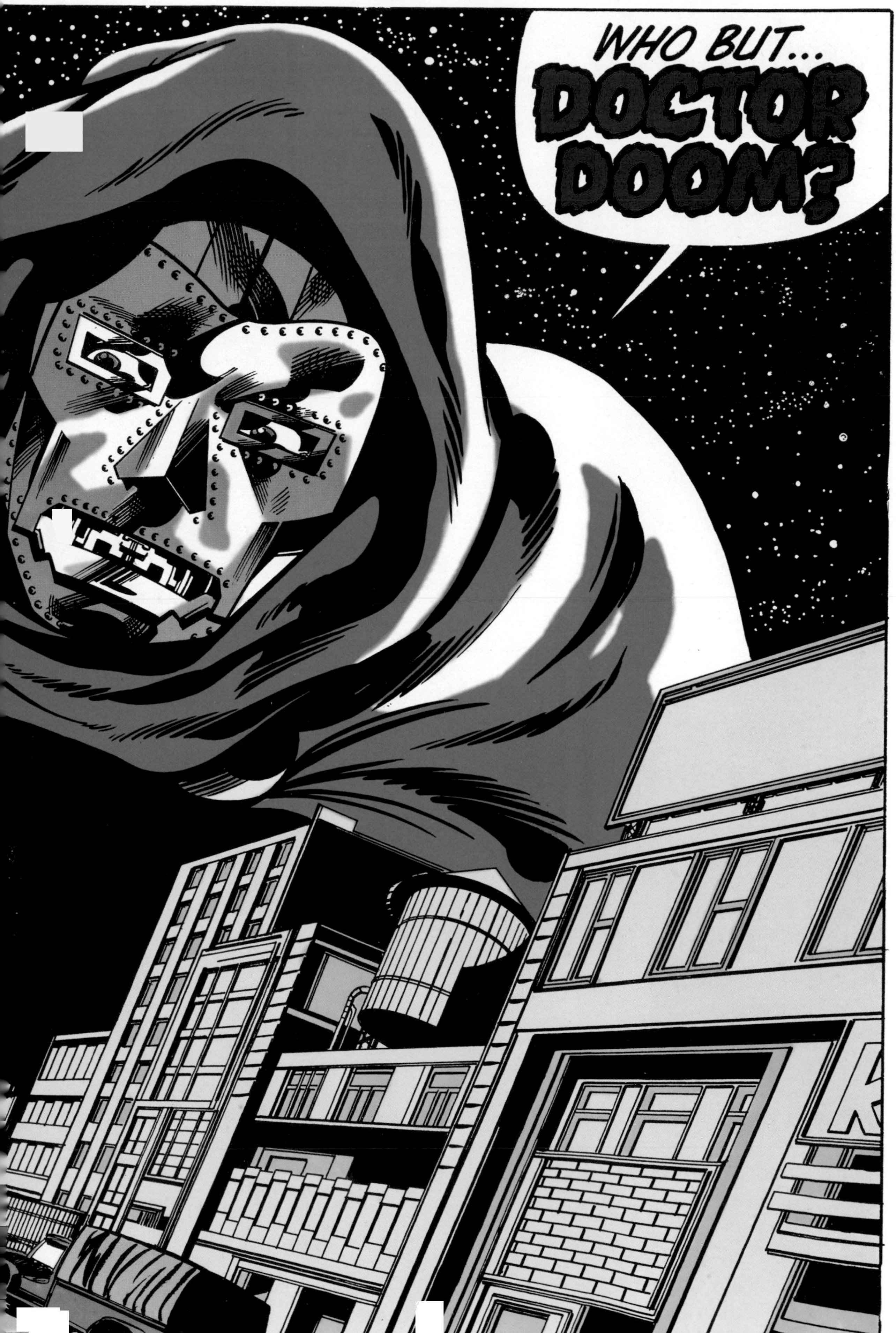
WHO BUT... DOCTOR DOOM?

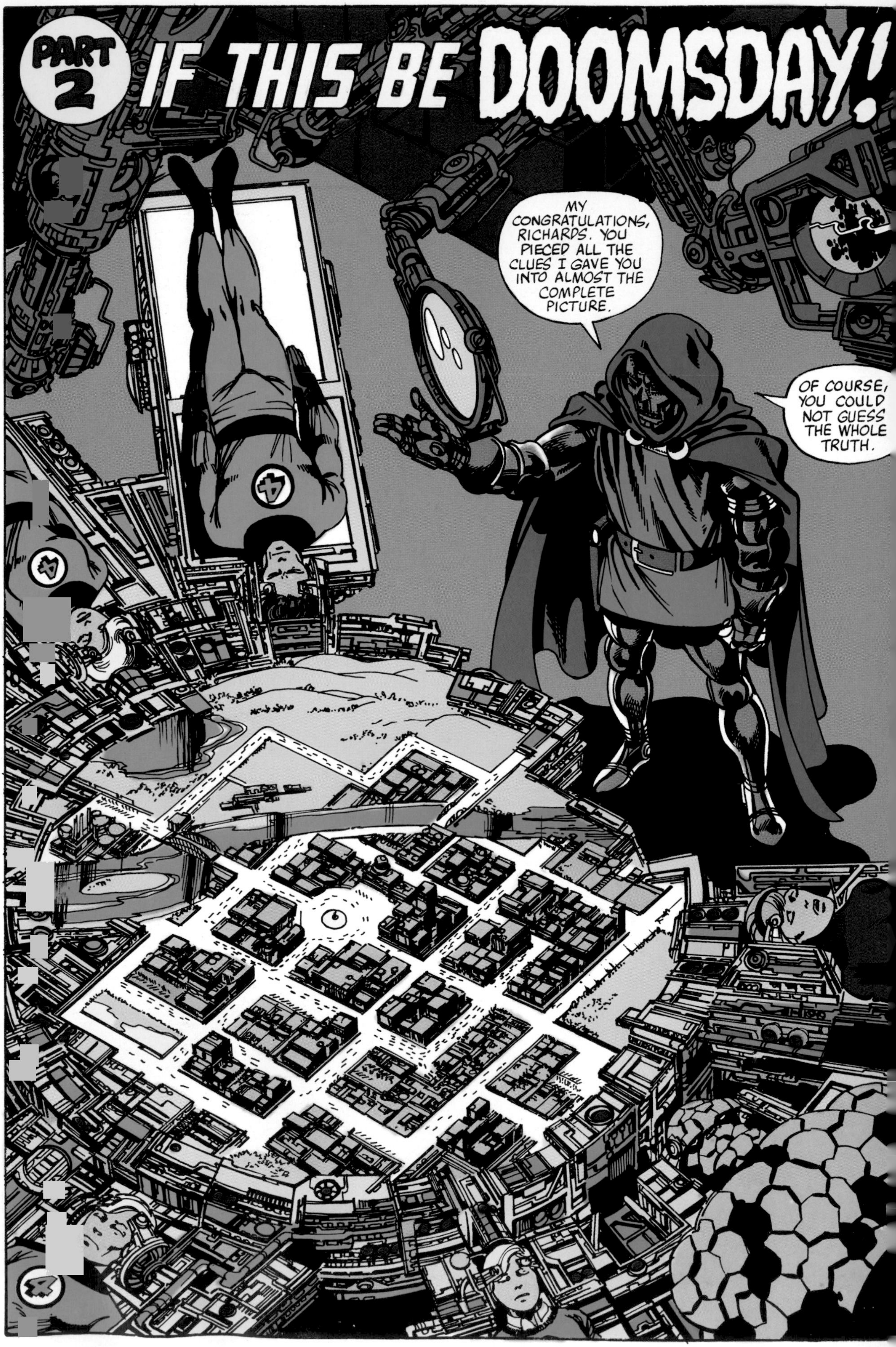
PART 2
IF THIS BE DOOMSDAY!
MY CONGRATULATIONS, RICHARDS. YOU PIECED ALL THE CLUES I GAVE YOU INTO ALMOST THE COMPLETE PICTURE.
OF COURSE, YOU COULD NOT GUESS THE WHOLE TRUTH.

HOW COULD YOU GUESS THAT ALL OF "LIDDLEVILLE" WAS BUT A CONSTRUCT, A SCALE MODEL BUILT BY THE PUPPET MASTER, TO MY SPECIFICATIONS.

YOUR TRUE BODIES LIE HELPLESS, THEIR MINDS TRANSMITTED INTO THE MINIATURE SYNTHE-CLONES I CREATED OF YOU.

AND YOU! YOU WERE VINCENT VAUGHN!

OF COURSE. IT OCCASIONALLY AMUSED ME TO ENTER A ROBOT FACSIMILE OF MYSELF--TO OBSERVE YOU FIRST HAND.

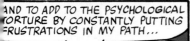

AND TO ADD TO THE PSYCHOLOGICAL TORTURE BY CONSTANTLY PUTTING FRUSTRATIONS IN MY PATH...

..AND SOMEHOW CAUSING MY THOUGHT PROCESSES TO BE ADDLED--TO FURTHER FRUSTRATE ME--AND KEEP ME FROM RECOGNIZING VINCENT VAUGHN.

ALRIGHT, DOOM, THE BALL IS CLEARLY IN YOUR COURT. WHAT DO YOU INTEND TO DO NOW?

DO?

WHY, MY DEAR RICHARDS, I HAVE DONE ALL I NEED TO DO.

THE PUPPET MASTER'S CLAY CAPTURED YOU-- MY GENIUS REDUCED YOU TO MERE PLAYTHINGS.

AS SUCH, YOU ARE OF NO FURTHER INTEREST TO ME.

THEREFORE, I SHALL LEAVE YOU ALL TO LIVE OUT THE REST OF YOUR LIVES IN THE QUITE PLEASANT SURROUNDINGS OF "LIDDLEVILLE."

WHILST I-- I GO TO CONCLUDE THE EXERCISES WHICH WILL SEE ME RESTORED TO THE THRONE OF LATVERIA-- AS IS MY RIGHT!

"RIGHT?" YOU FORFEITED ANY "RIGHT" YOU MIGHT HAVE HAD YEARS AGO!

THE FANTASTIC FOUR WILL FIND A WAY TO STOP YOU DOOM. I SWEAR IT!

SAVE YOUR BREATH, PAL. HE'S TURNED OFF THE MONITORS. HE AIN'T INTERESTED IN US ANYMORE.

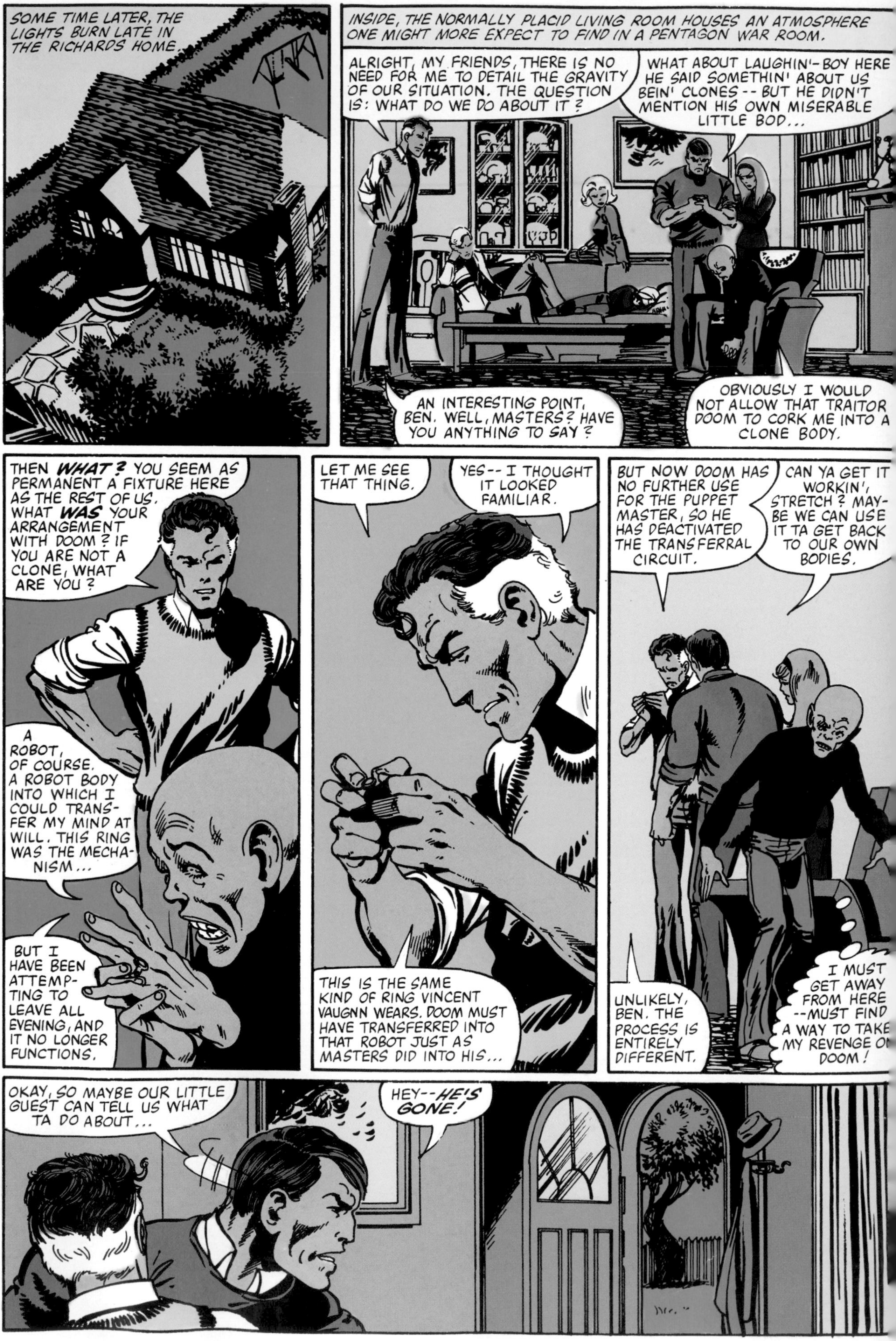
SOME TIME LATER, THE LIGHTS BURN LATE IN THE RICHARDS HOME.
INSIDE, THE NORMALLY PLACID LIVING ROOM HOUSES AN ATMOSPHERE ONE MIGHT MORE EXPECT TO FIND IN A PENTAGON WAR ROOM.
ALRIGHT, MY FRIENDS, THERE IS NO NEED FOR ME TO DETAIL THE GRAVITY OF OUR SITUATION. THE QUESTION IS: WHAT DO WE DO ABOUT IT?
WHAT ABOUT LAUGHIN'-BOY HERE HE SAID SOMETHIN' ABOUT US BEIN' CLONES -- BUT HE DIDN'T MENTION HIS OWN MISERABLE LITTLE BOD...
AN INTERESTING POINT, BEN. WELL, MASTERS? HAVE YOU ANYTHING TO SAY?
OBVIOUSLY I WOULD NOT ALLOW THAT TRAITOR DOOM TO CORK ME INTO A CLONE BODY.
THEN WHAT? YOU SEEM AS PERMANENT A FIXTURE HERE AS THE REST OF US. WHAT WAS YOUR ARRANGEMENT WITH DOOM? IF YOU ARE NOT A CLONE, WHAT ARE YOU?
A ROBOT, OF COURSE. A ROBOT BODY INTO WHICH I COULD TRANSFER MY MIND AT WILL. THIS RING WAS THE MECHANISM...
BUT I HAVE BEEN ATTEMPTING TO LEAVE ALL EVENING, AND IT NO LONGER FUNCTIONS.
LET ME SEE THAT THING.
YES-- I THOUGHT IT LOOKED FAMILIAR.
THIS IS THE SAME KIND OF RING VINCENT VAUGNN WEARS. DOOM MUST HAVE TRANSFERRED INTO THAT ROBOT JUST AS MASTERS DID INTO HIS...
BUT NOW DOOM HAS NO FURTHER USE FOR THE PUPPET MASTER, SO HE HAS DEACTIVATED THE TRANSFERRAL CIRCUIT.
CAN YA GET IT WORKIN', STRETCH? MAYBE WE CAN USE IT TA GET BACK TO OUR OWN BODIES.
UNLIKELY, BEN. THE PROCESS IS ENTIRELY DIFFERENT.
I MUST GET AWAY FROM HERE --MUST FIND A WAY TO TAKE MY REVENGE ON DOOM!
OKAY, SO MAYBE OUR LITTLE GUEST CAN TELL US WHAT TA DO ABOUT...
HEY--HE'S GONE!

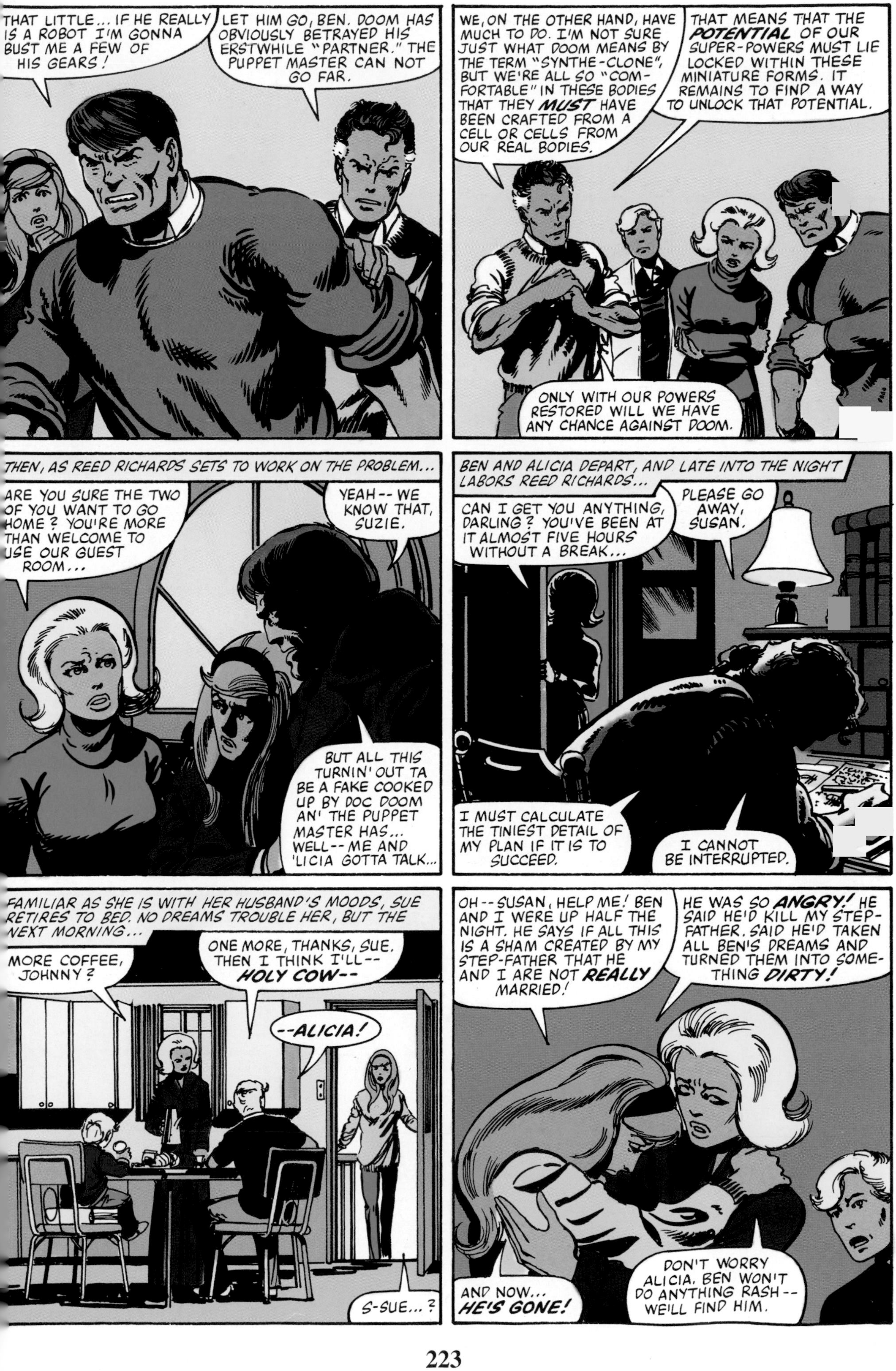
THAT LITTLE... IF HE REALLY IS A ROBOT I'M GONNA BUST ME A FEW OF HIS GEARS!
LET HIM GO, BEN. DOOM HAS OBVIOUSLY BETRAYED HIS ERSTWHILE "PARTNER." THE PUPPET MASTER CAN NOT GO FAR.
WE, ON THE OTHER HAND, HAVE MUCH TO DO. I'M NOT SURE JUST WHAT DOOM MEANS BY THE TERM "SYNTHE-CLONE", BUT WE'RE ALL SO "COM-FORTABLE" IN THESE BODIES THAT THEY MUST HAVE BEEN CRAFTED FROM A CELL OR CELLS FROM OUR REAL BODIES.
THAT MEANS THAT THE POTENTIAL OF OUR SUPER-POWERS MUST LIE LOCKED WITHIN THESE MINIATURE FORMS. IT REMAINS TO FIND A WAY TO UNLOCK THAT POTENTIAL.
ONLY WITH OUR POWERS RESTORED WILL WE HAVE ANY CHANCE AGAINST DOOM.
THEN, AS REED RICHARDS SETS TO WORK ON THE PROBLEM...
ARE YOU SURE THE TWO OF YOU WANT TO GO HOME? YOU'RE MORE THAN WELCOME TO USE OUR GUEST ROOM...
YEAH -- WE KNOW THAT, SUZIE.
BUT ALL THIS TURNIN' OUT TA BE A FAKE COOKED UP BY DOC DOOM AN' THE PUPPET MASTER HAS... WELL -- ME AND 'LICIA GOTTA TALK...
BEN AND ALICIA DEPART, AND LATE INTO THE NIGHT LABORS REED RICHARDS...
CAN I GET YOU ANYTHING, DARLING? YOU'VE BEEN AT IT ALMOST FIVE HOURS WITHOUT A BREAK...
PLEASE GO AWAY, SUSAN.
I MUST CALCULATE THE TINIEST DETAIL OF MY PLAN IF IT IS TO SUCCEED.
I CANNOT BE INTERRUPTED.
FAMILIAR AS SHE IS WITH HER HUSBAND'S MOODS, SUE RETIRES TO BED. NO DREAMS TROUBLE HER, BUT THE NEXT MORNING...
MORE COFFEE, JOHNNY?
ONE MORE, THANKS, SUE. THEN I THINK I'LL -- HOLY COW --
-- ALICIA!
S-SUE...?
OH -- SUSAN, HELP ME! BEN AND I WERE UP HALF THE NIGHT. HE SAYS IF ALL THIS IS A SHAM CREATED BY MY STEP-FATHER THAT HE AND I ARE NOT REALLY MARRIED!
HE WAS SO ANGRY! HE SAID HE'D KILL MY STEP-FATHER. SAID HE'D TAKEN ALL BEN'S DREAMS AND TURNED THEM INTO SOME-THING DIRTY!
AND NOW... HE'S GONE!
DON'T WORRY ALICIA. BEN WON'T DO ANYTHING RASH -- WE'LL FIND HIM.

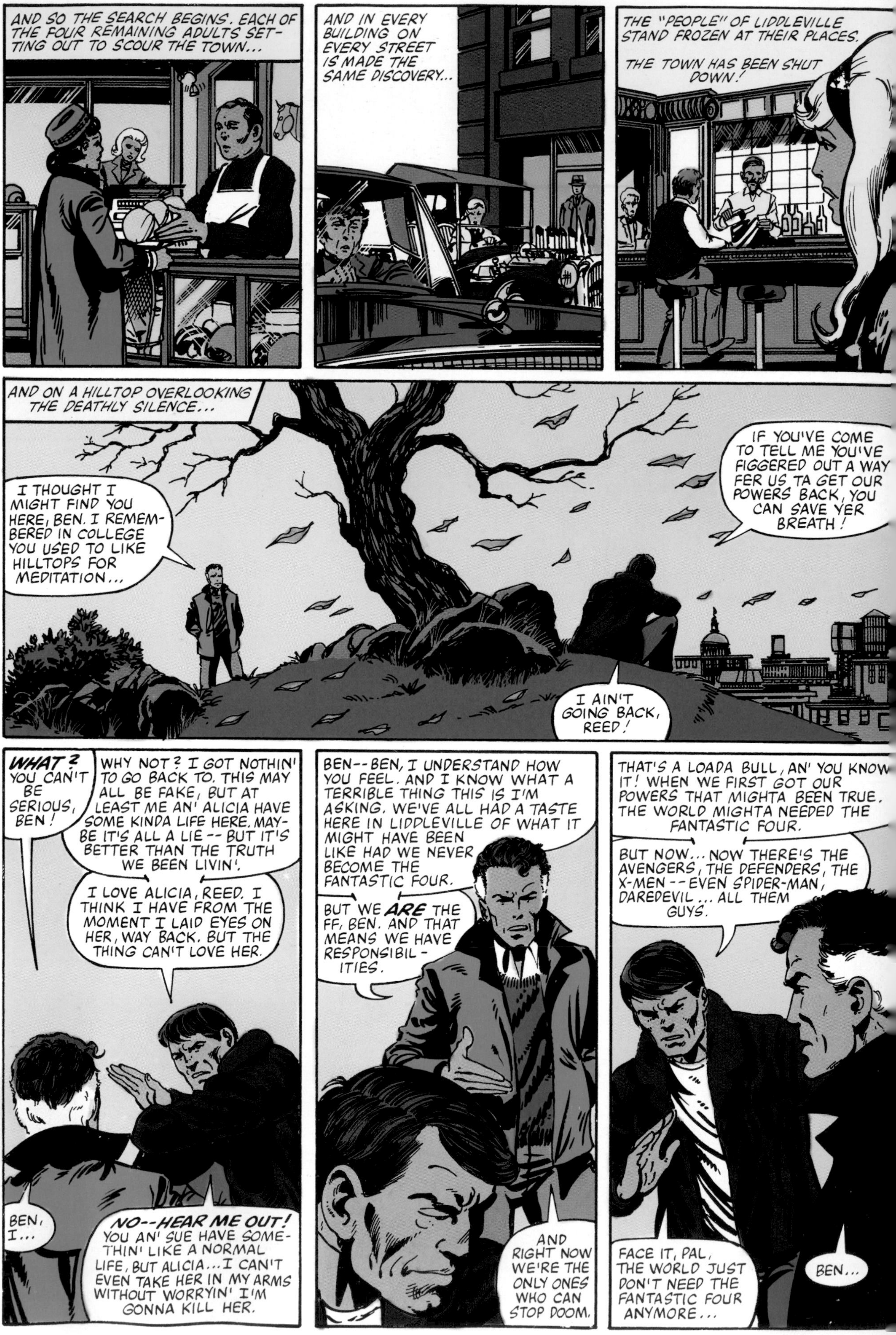
AND SO THE SEARCH BEGINS. EACH OF THE FOUR REMAINING ADULTS SETTING OUT TO SCOUR THE TOWN...
AND IN EVERY BUILDING ON EVERY STREET IS MADE THE SAME DISCOVERY...
THE "PEOPLE" OF LIDDLEVILLE STAND FROZEN AT THEIR PLACES.
THE TOWN HAS BEEN SHUT DOWN!
AND ON A HILLTOP OVERLOOKING THE DEATHLY SILENCE...
I THOUGHT I MIGHT FIND YOU HERE, BEN. I REMEMBERED IN COLLEGE YOU USED TO LIKE HILLTOPS FOR MEDITATION...
IF YOU'VE COME TO TELL ME YOU'VE FIGGERED OUT A WAY FER US TA GET OUR POWERS BACK, YOU CAN SAVE YER BREATH!
I AIN'T GOING BACK, REED!
WHAT? YOU CAN'T BE SERIOUS, BEN!
WHY NOT? I GOT NOTHIN' TO GO BACK TO. THIS MAY ALL BE FAKE, BUT AT LEAST ME AN' ALICIA HAVE SOME KINDA LIFE HERE. MAYBE IT'S ALL A LIE -- BUT IT'S BETTER THAN THE TRUTH WE BEEN LIVIN'.
I LOVE ALICIA, REED. I THINK I HAVE FROM THE MOMENT I LAID EYES ON HER, WAY BACK. BUT THE THING CAN'T LOVE HER.
BEN, I...
NO--HEAR ME OUT! YOU AN' SUE HAVE SOMETHIN' LIKE A NORMAL LIFE, BUT ALICIA... I CAN'T EVEN TAKE HER IN MY ARMS WITHOUT WORRYIN' I'M GONNA KILL HER.
BEN--BEN, I UNDERSTAND HOW YOU FEEL. AND I KNOW WHAT A TERRIBLE THING THIS IS I'M ASKING. WE'VE ALL HAD A TASTE HERE IN LIDDLEVILLE OF WHAT IT MIGHT HAVE BEEN LIKE HAD WE NEVER BECOME THE FANTASTIC FOUR.
BUT WE ARE THE FF, BEN. AND THAT MEANS WE HAVE RESPONSIBILITIES.
AND RIGHT NOW WE'RE THE ONLY ONES WHO CAN STOP DOOM.
THAT'S A LOADA BULL, AN' YOU KNOW IT! WHEN WE FIRST GOT OUR POWERS THAT MIGHTA BEEN TRUE. THE WORLD MIGHTA NEEDED THE FANTASTIC FOUR.
BUT NOW... NOW THERE'S THE AVENGERS, THE DEFENDERS, THE X-MEN -- EVEN SPIDER-MAN, DAREDEVIL... ALL THEM GUYS.
FACE IT, PAL, THE WORLD JUST DON'T NEED THE FANTASTIC FOUR ANYMORE...
BEN...

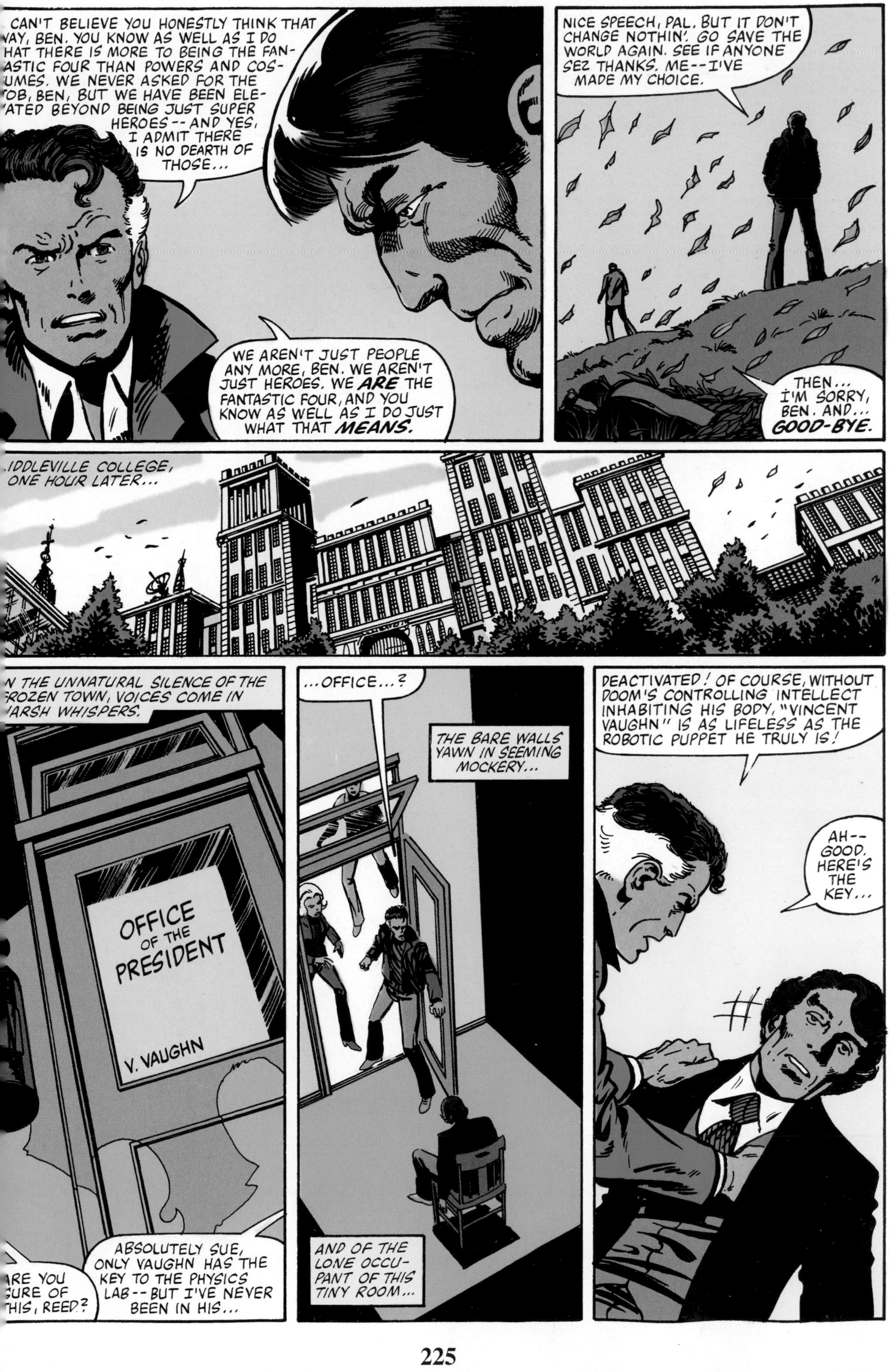

CAN'T BELIEVE YOU HONESTLY THINK THAT WAY, BEN. YOU KNOW AS WELL AS I DO THAT THERE IS MORE TO BEING THE FANTASTIC FOUR THAN POWERS AND COSTUMES. WE NEVER ASKED FOR THE JOB, BEN, BUT WE HAVE BEEN ELEVATED BEYOND BEING JUST SUPER HEROES--AND YES, I ADMIT THERE IS NO DEARTH OF THOSE...
WE AREN'T JUST PEOPLE ANY MORE, BEN. WE AREN'T JUST HEROES. WE ARE THE FANTASTIC FOUR, AND YOU KNOW AS WELL AS I DO JUST WHAT THAT MEANS.
NICE SPEECH, PAL. BUT IT DON'T CHANGE NOTHIN'. GO SAVE THE WORLD AGAIN. SEE IF ANYONE SEZ THANKS. ME--I'VE MADE MY CHOICE.
THEN... I'M SORRY, BEN. AND... GOOD-BYE.
IDDLEVILLE COLLEGE, ONE HOUR LATER...
N THE UNNATURAL SILENCE OF THE FROZEN TOWN, VOICES COME IN HARSH WHISPERS.
OFFICE OF THE PRESIDENT
V. VAUGHN
ARE YOU SURE OF THIS, REED?
ABSOLUTELY SUE, ONLY VAUGHN HAS THE KEY TO THE PHYSICS LAB--BUT I'VE NEVER BEEN IN HIS...
...OFFICE...?
THE BARE WALLS YAWN IN SEEMING MOCKERY...
AND OF THE LONE OCCUPANT OF THIS TINY ROOM...
DEACTIVATED! OF COURSE, WITHOUT DOOM'S CONTROLLING INTELLECT INHABITING HIS BODY, "VINCENT VAUGHN" IS AS LIFELESS AS THE ROBOTIC PUPPET HE TRULY IS!
AH--GOOD. HERE'S THE KEY...

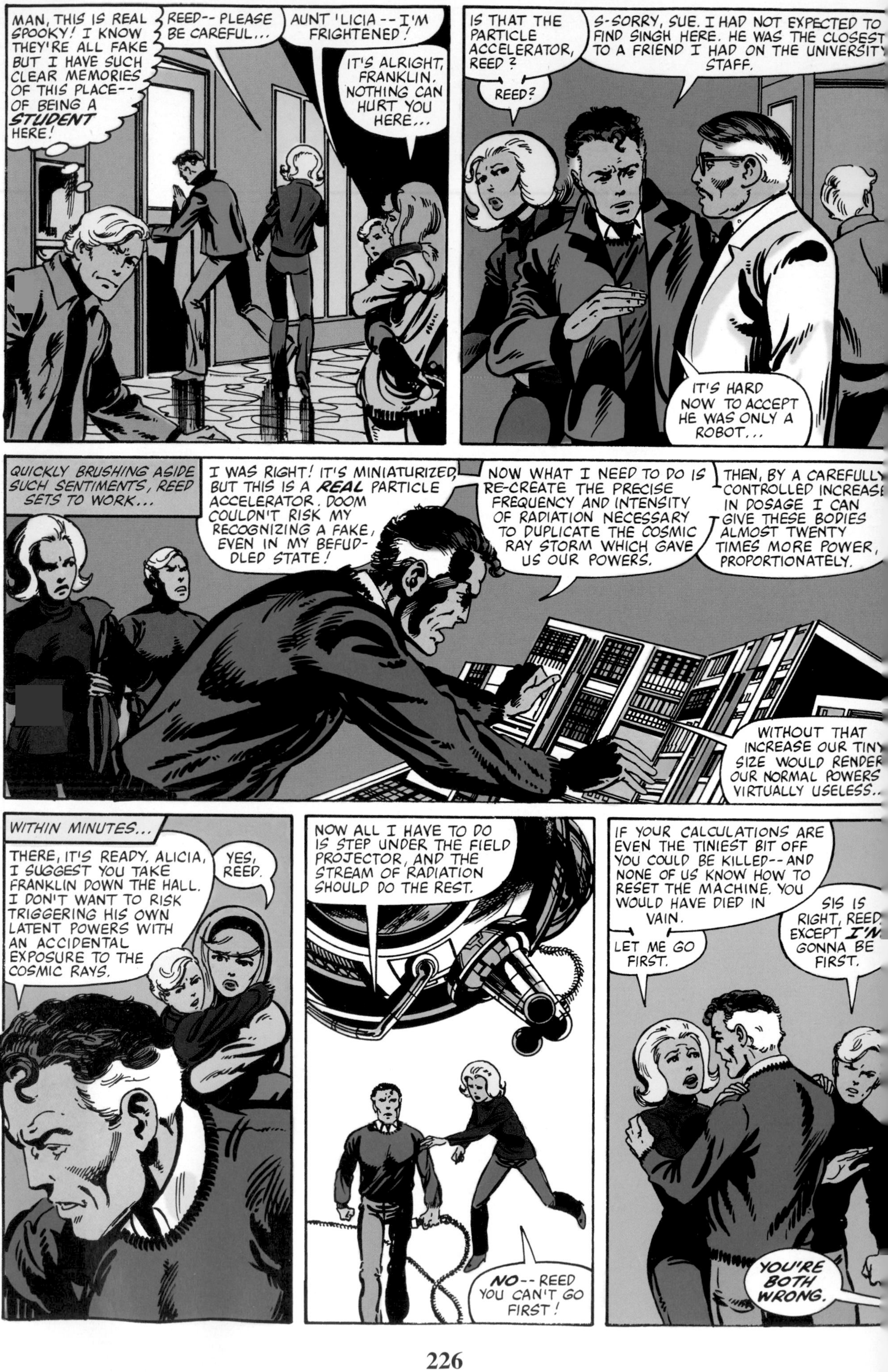
MAN, THIS IS REAL SPOOKY! I KNOW THEY'RE ALL FAKE BUT I HAVE SUCH CLEAR MEMORIES OF THIS PLACE-- OF BEING A STUDENT HERE!
REED-- PLEASE BE CAREFUL...
AUNT 'LICIA -- I'M FRIGHTENED!
IT'S ALRIGHT, FRANKLIN. NOTHING CAN HURT YOU HERE...
IS THAT THE PARTICLE ACCELERATOR, REED?
REED?
S-SORRY, SUE. I HAD NOT EXPECTED TO FIND SINGH HERE. HE WAS THE CLOSEST TO A FRIEND I HAD ON THE UNIVERSITY STAFF.
IT'S HARD NOW TO ACCEPT HE WAS ONLY A ROBOT...
QUICKLY BRUSHING ASIDE SUCH SENTIMENTS, REED SETS TO WORK...
I WAS RIGHT! IT'S MINIATURIZED, BUT THIS IS A REAL PARTICLE ACCELERATOR. DOOM COULDN'T RISK MY RECOGNIZING A FAKE, EVEN IN MY BEFUDDLED STATE!
NOW WHAT I NEED TO DO IS RE-CREATE THE PRECISE FREQUENCY AND INTENSITY OF RADIATION NECESSARY TO DUPLICATE THE COSMIC RAY STORM WHICH GAVE US OUR POWERS.
THEN, BY A CAREFULLY CONTROLLED INCREASE IN DOSAGE I CAN GIVE THESE BODIES ALMOST TWENTY TIMES MORE POWER, PROPORTIONATELY.
WITHOUT THAT INCREASE OUR TINY SIZE WOULD RENDER OUR NORMAL POWERS VIRTUALLY USELESS...
WITHIN MINUTES...
THERE, IT'S READY, ALICIA. I SUGGEST YOU TAKE FRANKLIN DOWN THE HALL. I DON'T WANT TO RISK TRIGGERING HIS OWN LATENT POWERS WITH AN ACCIDENTAL EXPOSURE TO THE COSMIC RAYS.
YES, REED.
NOW ALL I HAVE TO DO IS STEP UNDER THE FIELD PROJECTOR, AND THE STREAM OF RADIATION SHOULD DO THE REST.
NO-- REED YOU CAN'T GO FIRST!
IF YOUR CALCULATIONS ARE EVEN THE TINIEST BIT OFF YOU COULD BE KILLED-- AND NONE OF US KNOW HOW TO RESET THE MACHINE. YOU WOULD HAVE DIED IN VAIN.
LET ME GO FIRST.
SIS IS RIGHT, REED. EXCEPT I'M GONNA BE FIRST.
YOU'RE BOTH WRONG.

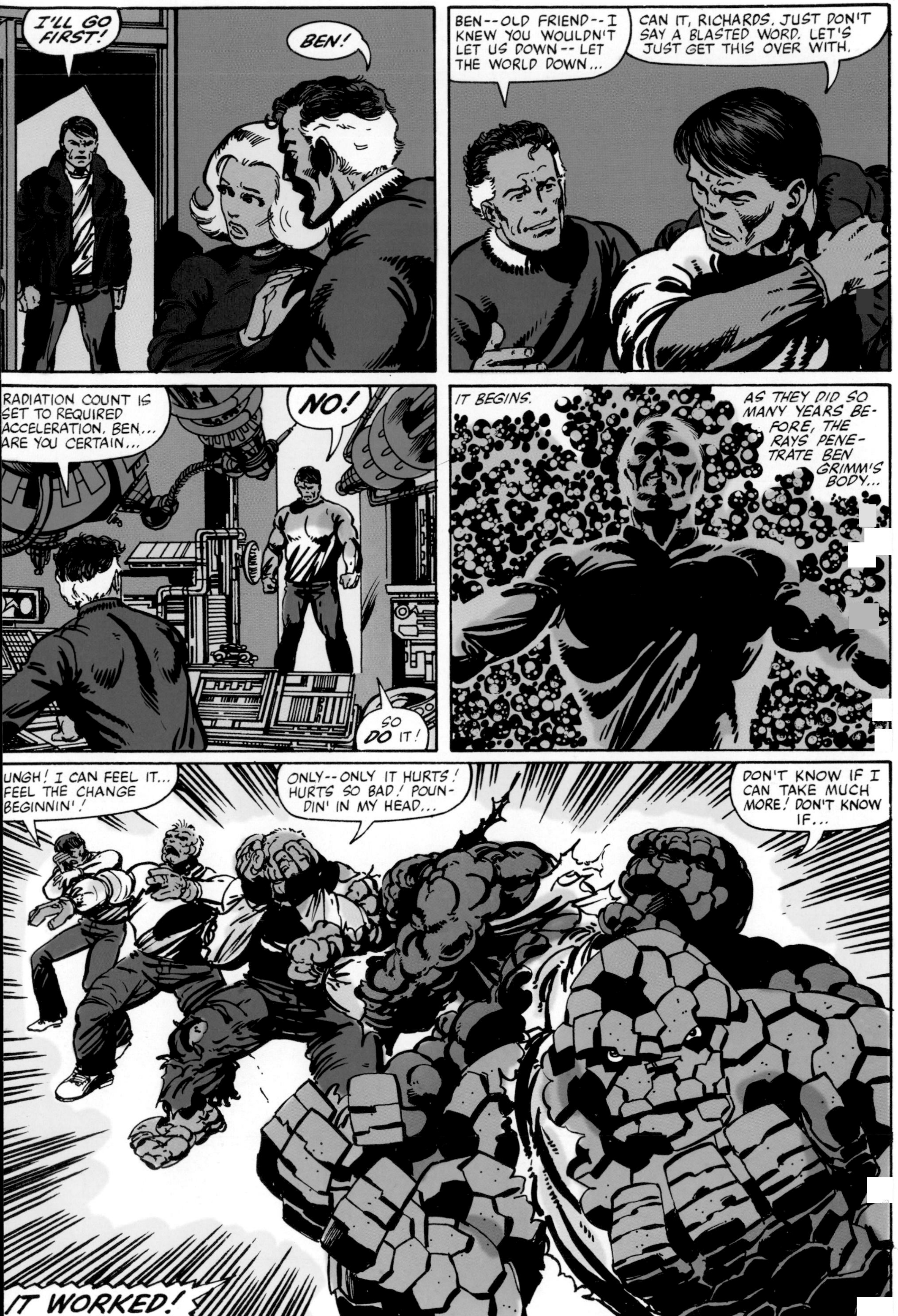
I'LL GO FIRST!
BEN!
BEN--OLD FRIEND--I KNEW YOU WOULDN'T LET US DOWN--LET THE WORLD DOWN...
CAN IT, RICHARDS. JUST DON'T SAY A BLASTED WORD. LET'S JUST GET THIS OVER WITH.
RADIATION COUNT IS SET TO REQUIRED ACCELERATION, BEN... ARE YOU CERTAIN...
NO!
SO DO IT!
IT BEGINS.
AS THEY DID SO MANY YEARS BEFORE, THE RAYS PENETRATE BEN GRIMM'S BODY...
UNGH! I CAN FEEL IT... FEEL THE CHANGE BEGINNIN'!
ONLY--ONLY IT HURTS! HURTS SO BAD! POUNDIN' IN MY HEAD...
DON'T KNOW IF I CAN TAKE MUCH MORE! DON'T KNOW IF...
IT WORKED!

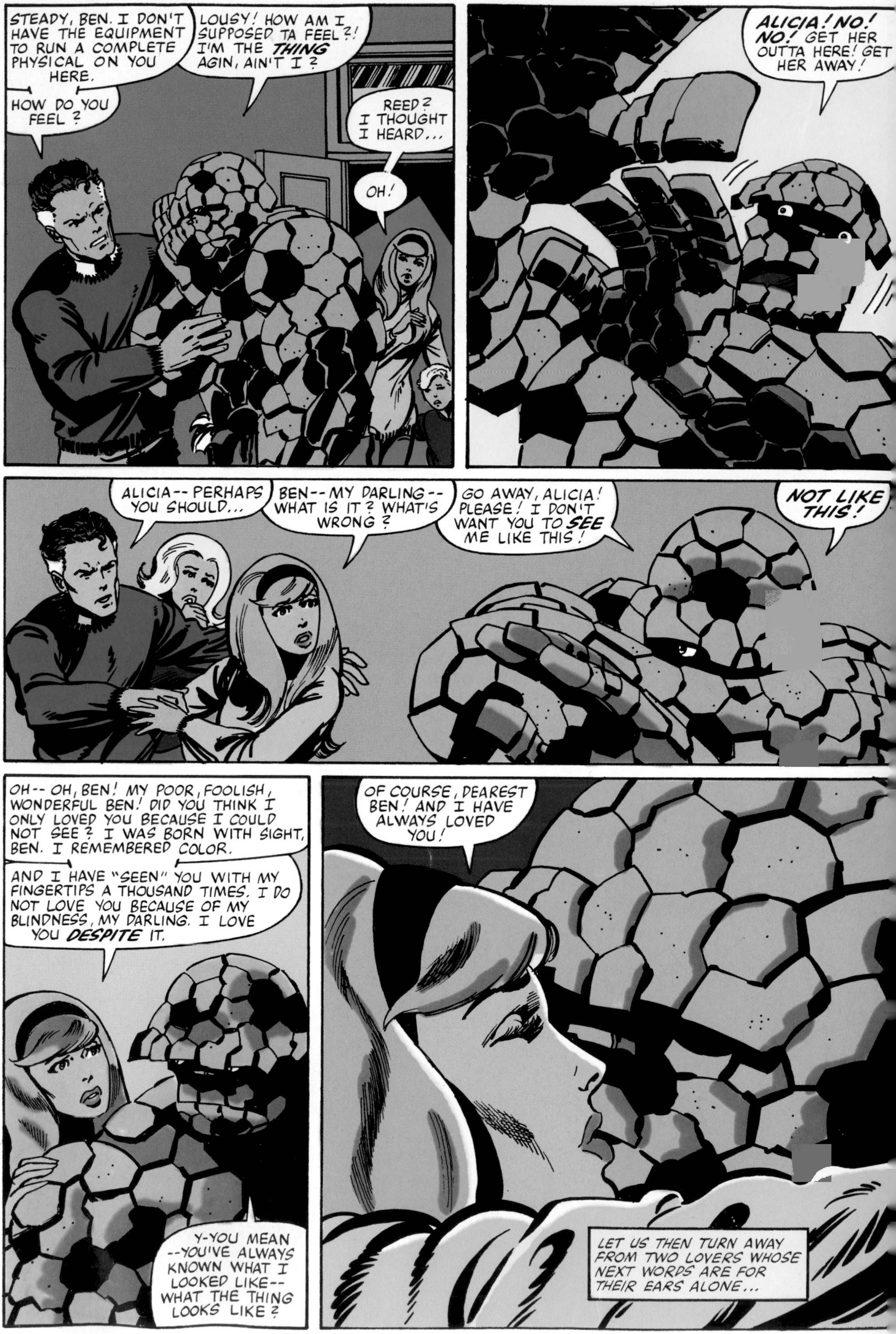
STEADY, BEN. I DON'T HAVE THE EQUIPMENT TO RUN A COMPLETE PHYSICAL ON YOU HERE.
HOW DO YOU FEEL?
LOUSY! HOW AM I SUPPOSED TA FEEL?! I'M THE THING AGIN, AIN'T I?
REED? I THOUGHT I HEARD...
OH!
ALICIA! NO! NO! GET HER OUTTA HERE! GET HER AWAY!
ALICIA-- PERHAPS YOU SHOULD...
BEN-- MY DARLING-- WHAT IS IT? WHAT'S WRONG?
GO AWAY, ALICIA! PLEASE! I DON'T WANT YOU TO SEE ME LIKE THIS!
NOT LIKE THIS!
OH-- OH, BEN! MY POOR, FOOLISH, WONDERFUL BEN! DID YOU THINK I ONLY LOVED YOU BECAUSE I COULD NOT SEE? I WAS BORN WITH SIGHT, BEN. I REMEMBERED COLOR.
AND I HAVE "SEEN" YOU WITH MY FINGERTIPS A THOUSAND TIMES. I DO NOT LOVE YOU BECAUSE OF MY BLINDNESS, MY DARLING. I LOVE YOU DESPITE IT.
Y-YOU MEAN --YOU'VE ALWAYS KNOWN WHAT I LOOKED LIKE-- WHAT THE THING LOOKS LIKE?
OF COURSE, DEAREST BEN! AND I HAVE ALWAYS LOVED YOU!
LET US THEN TURN AWAY FROM TWO LOVERS WHOSE NEXT WORDS ARE FOR THEIR EARS ALONE...

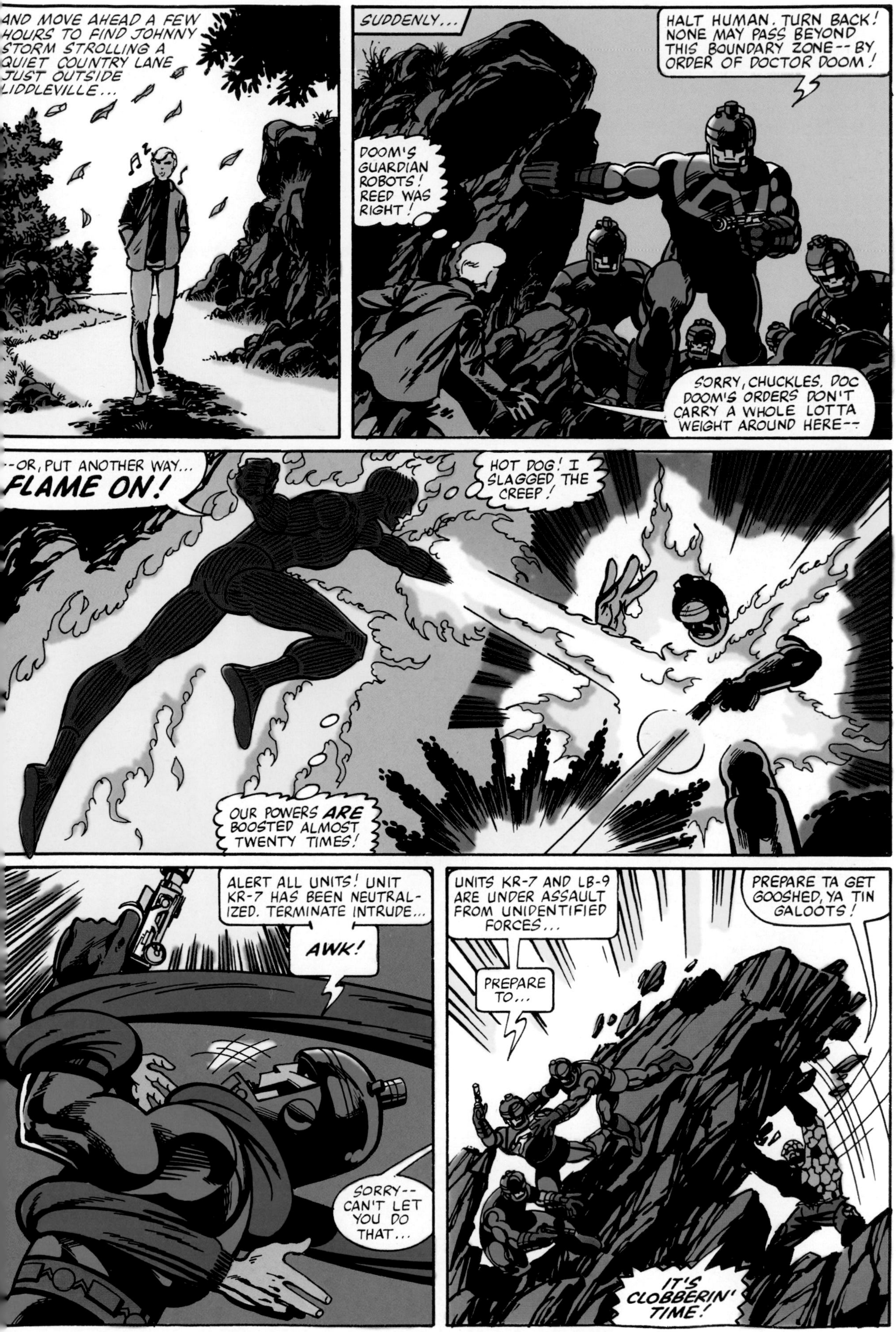
AND MOVE AHEAD A FEW HOURS TO FIND JOHNNY STORM STROLLING A QUIET COUNTRY LANE JUST OUTSIDE LIDDLEVILLE...
SUDDENLY...
HALT HUMAN. TURN BACK! NONE MAY PASS BEYOND THIS BOUNDARY ZONE--BY ORDER OF DOCTOR DOOM!
DOOM'S GUARDIAN ROBOTS! REED WAS RIGHT!
SORRY, CHUCKLES. DOC DOOM'S ORDERS DON'T CARRY A WHOLE LOTTA WEIGHT AROUND HERE--
--OR, PUT ANOTHER WAY... FLAME ON!
HOT DOG! I SLAGGED THE CREEP!
OUR POWERS ARE BOOSTED ALMOST TWENTY TIMES!
ALERT ALL UNITS! UNIT KR-7 HAS BEEN NEUTRALIZED. TERMINATE INTRUDE...
AWK!
SORRY-- CAN'T LET YOU DO THAT...
UNITS KR-7 AND LB-9 ARE UNDER ASSAULT FROM UNIDENTIFIED FORCES...
PREPARE TO...
PREPARE TA GET GOOSHED, YA TIN GALOOTS!
IT'S CLOBBERIN' TIME!

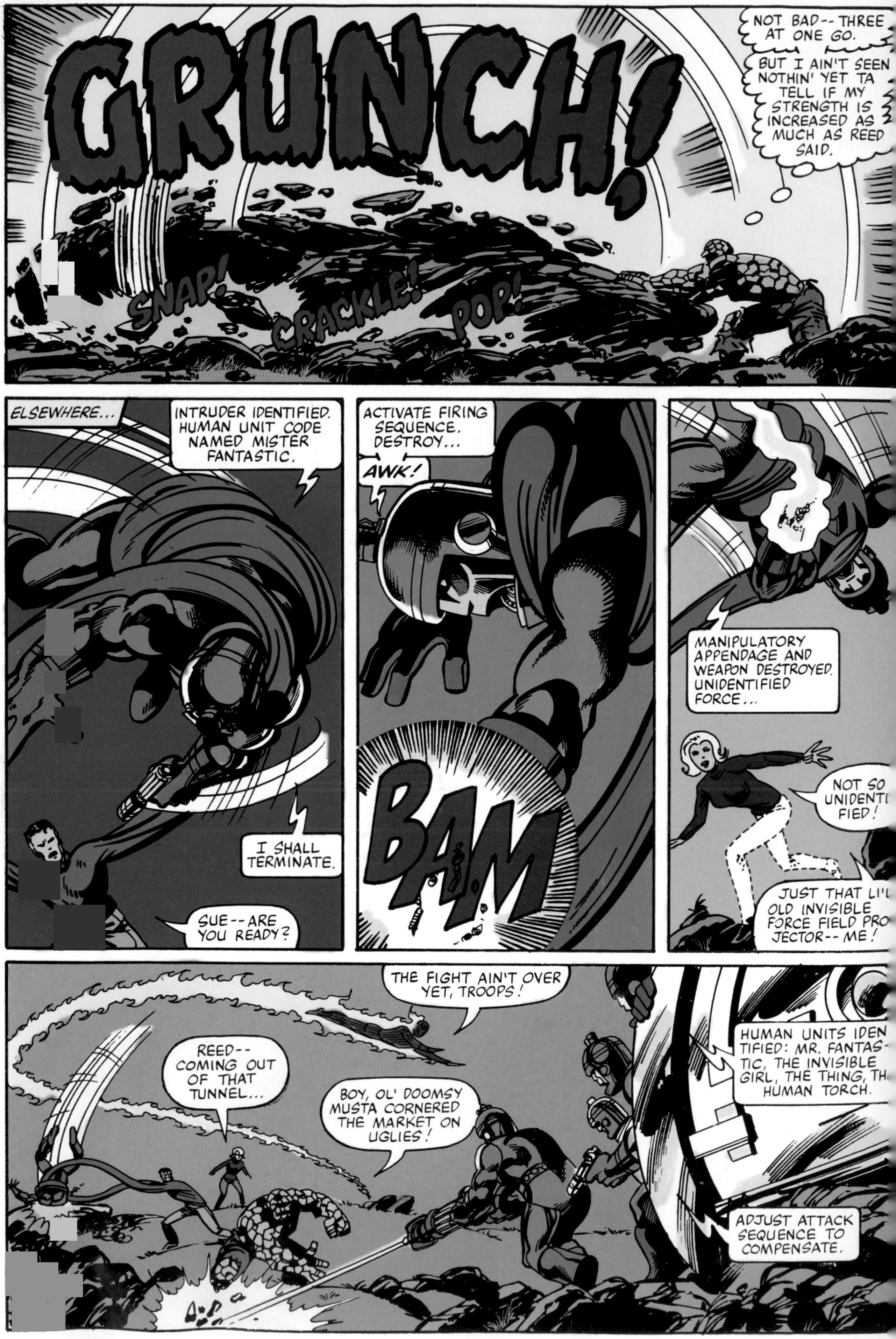
GRUNCH!
NOT BAD-- THREE AT ONE GO.
BUT I AIN'T SEEN NOTHIN' YET TA TELL IF MY STRENGTH IS INCREASED AS MUCH AS REED SAID.
SNAP! CRACKLE! POP!
ELSEWHERE...
INTRUDER IDENTIFIED. HUMAN UNIT CODE NAMED MISTER FANTASTIC.
I SHALL TERMINATE.
SUE--ARE YOU READY?
ACTIVATE FIRING SEQUENCE. DESTROY...
AWK!
BAM
MANIPULATORY APPENDAGE AND WEAPON DESTROYED. UNIDENTIFIED FORCE...
NOT SO UNIDENTI FIED!
JUST THAT LI'L OLD INVISIBLE FORCE FIELD PRO JECTOR-- ME!
THE FIGHT AIN'T OVER YET, TROOPS!
REED-- COMING OUT OF THAT TUNNEL...
BOY, OL' DOOMSY MUSTA CORNERED THE MARKET ON UGLIES!
HUMAN UNITS IDEN TIFIED: MR. FANTAS- TIC, THE INVISIBLE GIRL, THE THING, TH HUMAN TORCH.
ADJUST ATTACK SEQUENCE TO COMPENSATE.

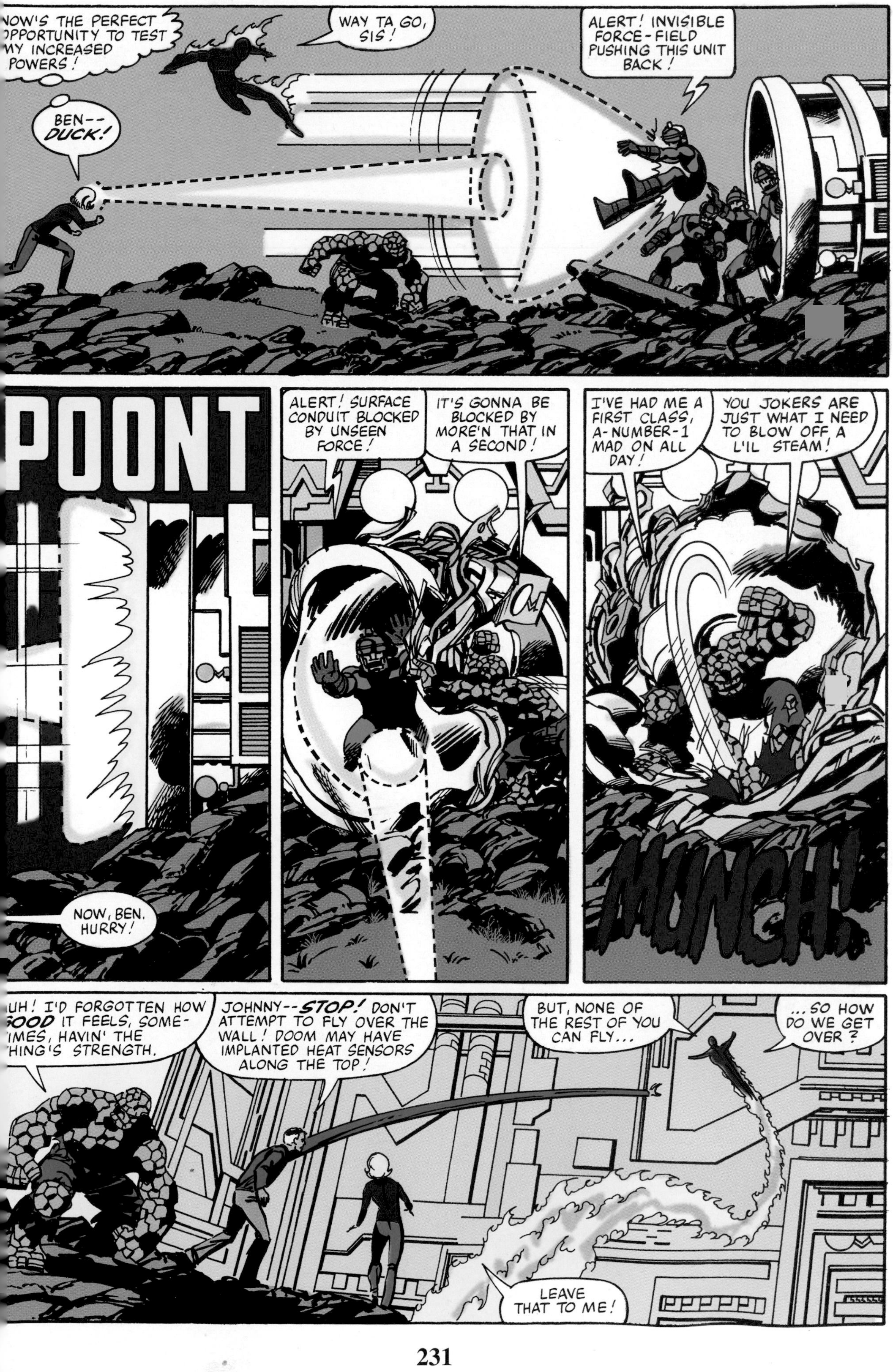
NOW'S THE PERFECT OPPORTUNITY TO TEST MY INCREASED POWERS!
WAY TA GO, SIS!
ALERT! INVISIBLE FORCE-FIELD PUSHING THIS UNIT BACK!
BEN-- DUCK!
POONT
NOW, BEN. HURRY!
ALERT! SURFACE CONDUIT BLOCKED BY UNSEEN FORCE!
IT'S GONNA BE BLOCKED BY MORE'N THAT IN A SECOND!
I'VE HAD ME A FIRST CLASS, A-NUMBER-1 MAD ON ALL DAY!
YOU JOKERS ARE JUST WHAT I NEED TO BLOW OFF A L'IL STEAM!
MUNCH!
UH! I'D FORGOTTEN HOW GOOD IT FEELS, SOMETIMES, HAVIN' THE THING'S STRENGTH.
JOHNNY--STOP! DON'T ATTEMPT TO FLY OVER THE WALL! DOOM MAY HAVE IMPLANTED HEAT SENSORS ALONG THE TOP!
BUT, NONE OF THE REST OF YOU CAN FLY...
...SO HOW DO WE GET OVER?
LEAVE THAT TO ME!

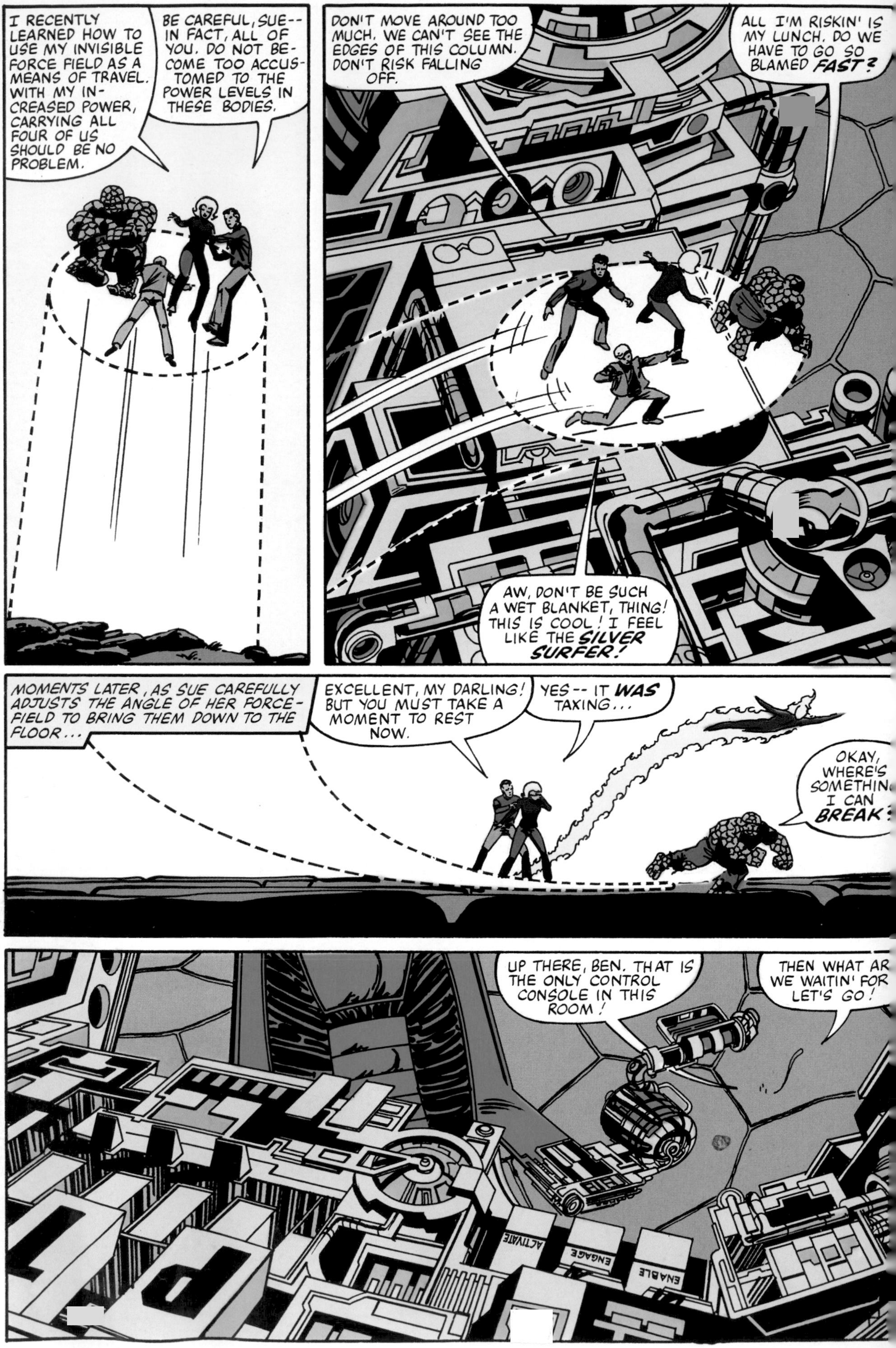

I RECENTLY LEARNED HOW TO USE MY INVISIBLE FORCE FIELD AS A MEANS OF TRAVEL. WITH MY INCREASED POWER, CARRYING ALL FOUR OF US SHOULD BE NO PROBLEM.
BE CAREFUL, SUE-- IN FACT, ALL OF YOU. DO NOT BECOME TOO ACCUSTOMED TO THE POWER LEVELS IN THESE BODIES.
DON'T MOVE AROUND TOO MUCH. WE CAN'T SEE THE EDGES OF THIS COLUMN. DON'T RISK FALLING OFF.
ALL I'M RISKIN' IS MY LUNCH. DO WE HAVE TO GO SO BLAMED FAST?
AW, DON'T BE SUCH A WET BLANKET, THING! THIS IS COOL! I FEEL LIKE THE SILVER SURFER!
MOMENTS LATER, AS SUE CAREFULLY ADJUSTS THE ANGLE OF HER FORCE-FIELD TO BRING THEM DOWN TO THE FLOOR...
EXCELLENT, MY DARLING! BUT YOU MUST TAKE A MOMENT TO REST NOW.
YES -- IT WAS TAXING...
OKAY, WHERE'S SOMETHIN I CAN BREAK?
UP THERE, BEN. THAT IS THE ONLY CONTROL CONSOLE IN THIS ROOM!
THEN WHAT AR WE WAITIN' FOR LET'S GO!
ACTIVATE
ENGAGE
ENABLE

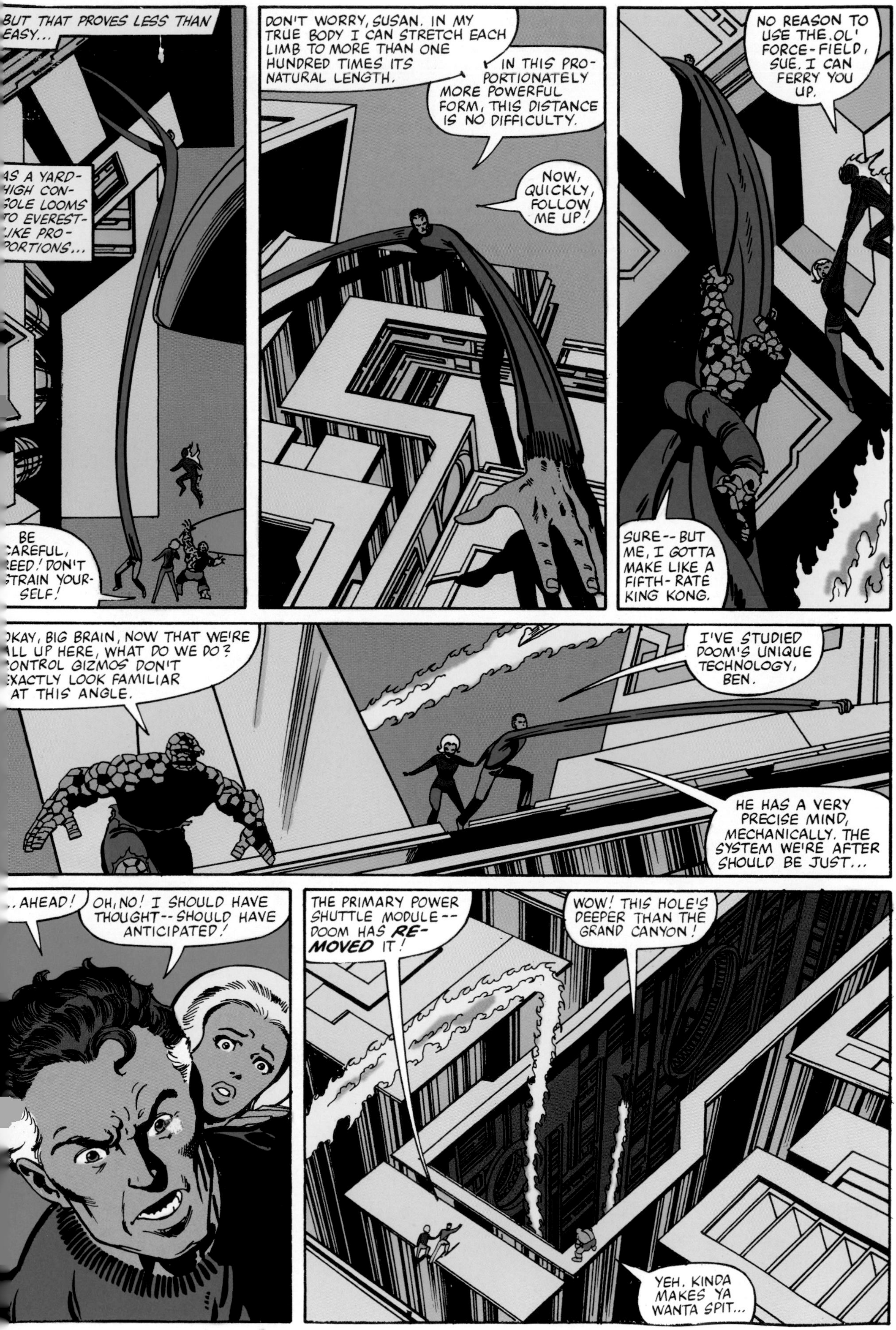
BUT THAT PROVES LESS THAN EASY...
AS A YARD-HIGH CONSOLE LOOMS TO EVEREST-LIKE PROPORTIONS...
BE CAREFUL, REED! DON'T STRAIN YOURSELF!
DON'T WORRY, SUSAN. IN MY TRUE BODY I CAN STRETCH EACH LIMB TO MORE THAN ONE HUNDRED TIMES ITS NATURAL LENGTH.
IN THIS PROPORTIONATELY MORE POWERFUL FORM, THIS DISTANCE IS NO DIFFICULTY.
NOW, QUICKLY, FOLLOW ME UP!
NO REASON TO USE THE OL' FORCE-FIELD, SUE. I CAN FERRY YOU UP.
SURE--BUT ME, I GOTTA MAKE LIKE A FIFTH-RATE KING KONG.
OKAY, BIG BRAIN, NOW THAT WE'RE ALL UP HERE, WHAT DO WE DO? CONTROL GIZMOS DON'T EXACTLY LOOK FAMILIAR AT THIS ANGLE.
I'VE STUDIED DOOM'S UNIQUE TECHNOLOGY, BEN.
HE HAS A VERY PRECISE MIND, MECHANICALLY. THE SYSTEM WE'RE AFTER SHOULD BE JUST...
...AHEAD!
OH, NO! I SHOULD HAVE THOUGHT--SHOULD HAVE ANTICIPATED!
THE PRIMARY POWER SHUTTLE MODULE--DOOM HAS REMOVED IT!
WOW! THIS HOLE'S DEEPER THAN THE GRAND CANYON!
YEH. KINDA MAKES YA WANTA SPIT...

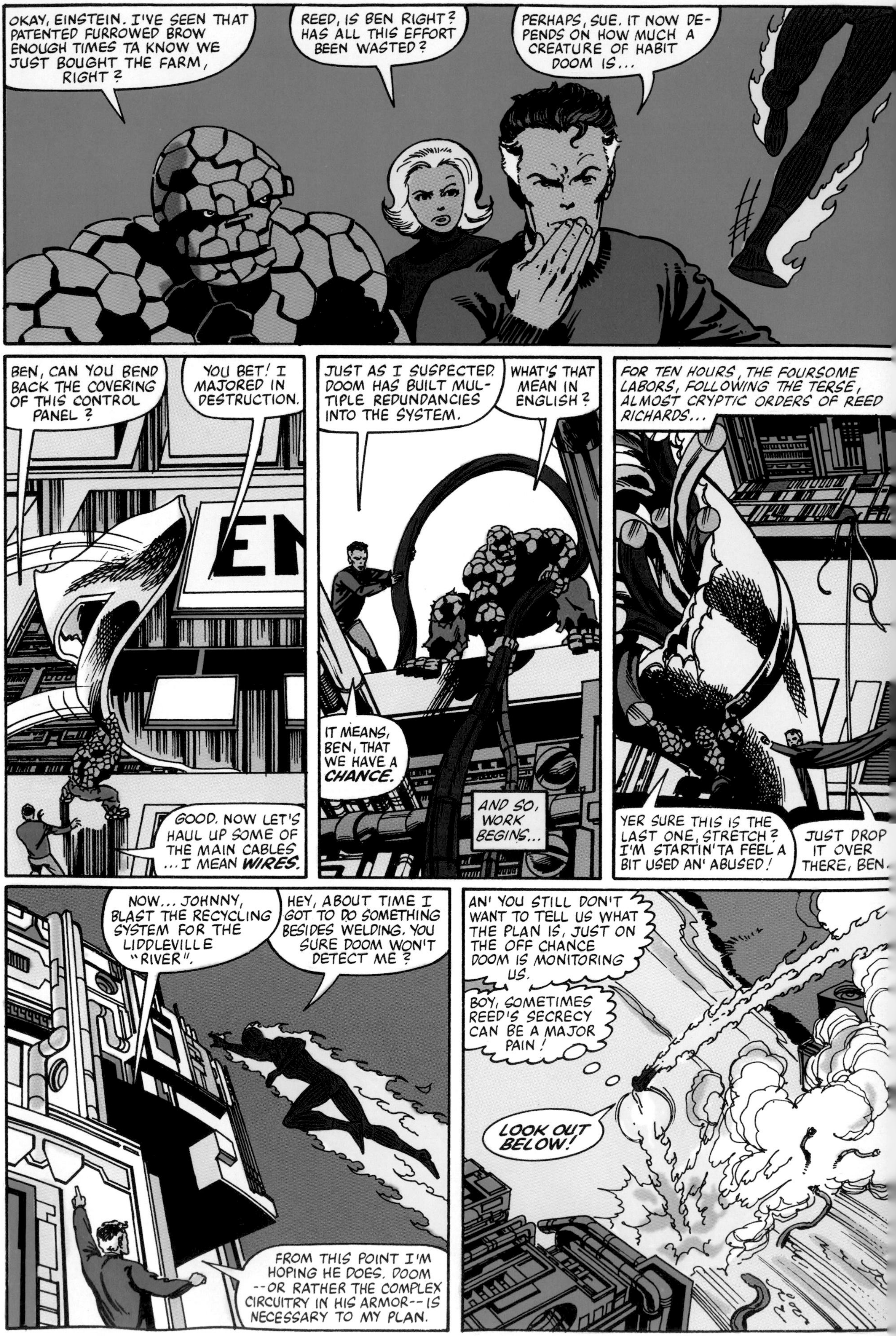
OKAY, EINSTEIN. I'VE SEEN THAT PATENTED FURROWED BROW ENOUGH TIMES TA KNOW WE JUST BOUGHT THE FARM, RIGHT?
REED, IS BEN RIGHT? HAS ALL THIS EFFORT BEEN WASTED?
PERHAPS, SUE. IT NOW DEPENDS ON HOW MUCH A CREATURE OF HABIT DOOM IS...
BEN, CAN YOU BEND BACK THE COVERING OF THIS CONTROL PANEL?
YOU BET! I MAJORED IN DESTRUCTION.
GOOD. NOW LET'S HAUL UP SOME OF THE MAIN CABLES ...I MEAN WIRES.
JUST AS I SUSPECTED. DOOM HAS BUILT MULTIPLE REDUNDANCIES INTO THE SYSTEM.
WHAT'S THAT MEAN IN ENGLISH?
IT MEANS, BEN, THAT WE HAVE A CHANCE.
AND SO, WORK BEGINS...
FOR TEN HOURS, THE FOURSOME LABORS, FOLLOWING THE TERSE, ALMOST CRYPTIC ORDERS OF REED RICHARDS...
YER SURE THIS IS THE LAST ONE, STRETCH? I'M STARTIN' TA FEEL A BIT USED AN' ABUSED!
JUST DROP IT OVER THERE, BEN.
NOW... JOHNNY, BLAST THE RECYCLING SYSTEM FOR THE LIDDLEVILLE "RIVER".
HEY, ABOUT TIME I GOT TO DO SOMETHING BESIDES WELDING. YOU SURE DOOM WON'T DETECT ME?
FROM THIS POINT I'M HOPING HE DOES. DOOM --OR RATHER THE COMPLEX CIRCUITRY IN HIS ARMOR--IS NECESSARY TO MY PLAN.
AN' YOU STILL DON'T WANT TO TELL US WHAT THE PLAN IS, JUST ON THE OFF CHANCE DOOM IS MONITORING US.
BOY, SOMETIMES REED'S SECRECY CAN BE A MAJOR PAIN!
LOOK OUT BELOW!

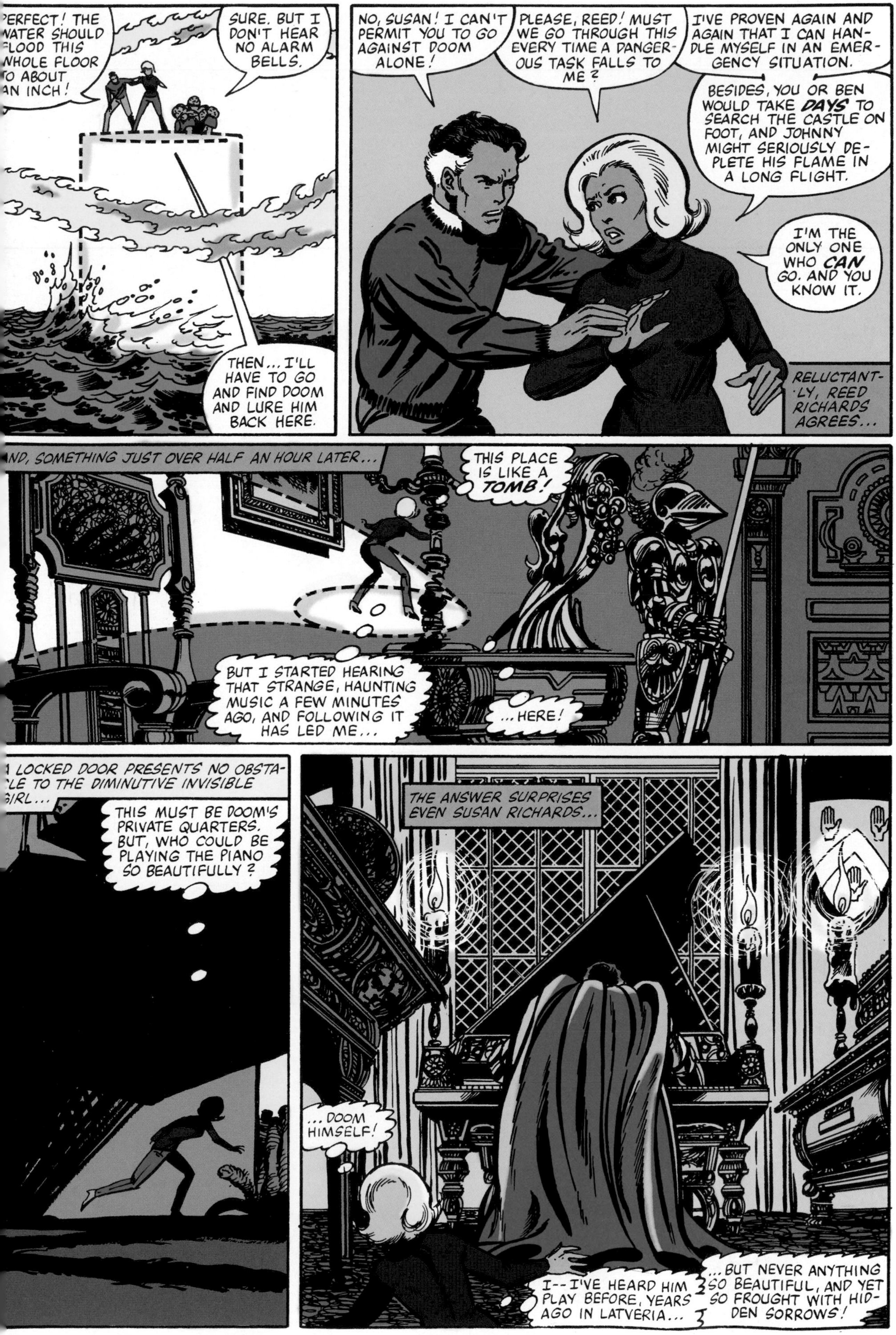
ERFECT! THE WATER SHOULD FLOOD THIS WHOLE FLOOR TO ABOUT AN INCH!
SURE. BUT I DON'T HEAR NO ALARM BELLS.
THEN... I'LL HAVE TO GO AND FIND DOOM AND LURE HIM BACK HERE.
NO, SUSAN! I CAN'T PERMIT YOU TO GO AGAINST DOOM ALONE!
PLEASE, REED! MUST WE GO THROUGH THIS EVERY TIME A DANGEROUS TASK FALLS TO ME?
I'VE PROVEN AGAIN AND AGAIN THAT I CAN HANDLE MYSELF IN AN EMERGENCY SITUATION.
BESIDES, YOU OR BEN WOULD TAKE DAYS TO SEARCH THE CASTLE ON FOOT, AND JOHNNY MIGHT SERIOUSLY DEPLETE HIS FLAME IN A LONG FLIGHT.
I'M THE ONLY ONE WHO CAN GO. AND YOU KNOW IT.
RELUCTANTLY, REED RICHARDS AGREES...
ND, SOMETHING JUST OVER HALF AN HOUR LATER...
THIS PLACE IS LIKE A TOMB!
BUT I STARTED HEARING THAT STRANGE, HAUNTING MUSIC A FEW MINUTES AGO, AND FOLLOWING IT HAS LED ME...
...HERE!
A LOCKED DOOR PRESENTS NO OBSTACLE TO THE DIMINUTIVE INVISIBLE GIRL...
THIS MUST BE DOOM'S PRIVATE QUARTERS. BUT, WHO COULD BE PLAYING THE PIANO SO BEAUTIFULLY?
THE ANSWER SURPRISES EVEN SUSAN RICHARDS...
...DOOM HIMSELF!
I--I'VE HEARD HIM PLAY BEFORE, YEARS AGO IN LATVERIA...
...BUT NEVER ANYTHING SO BEAUTIFUL, AND YET SO FROUGHT WITH HIDDEN SORROWS!

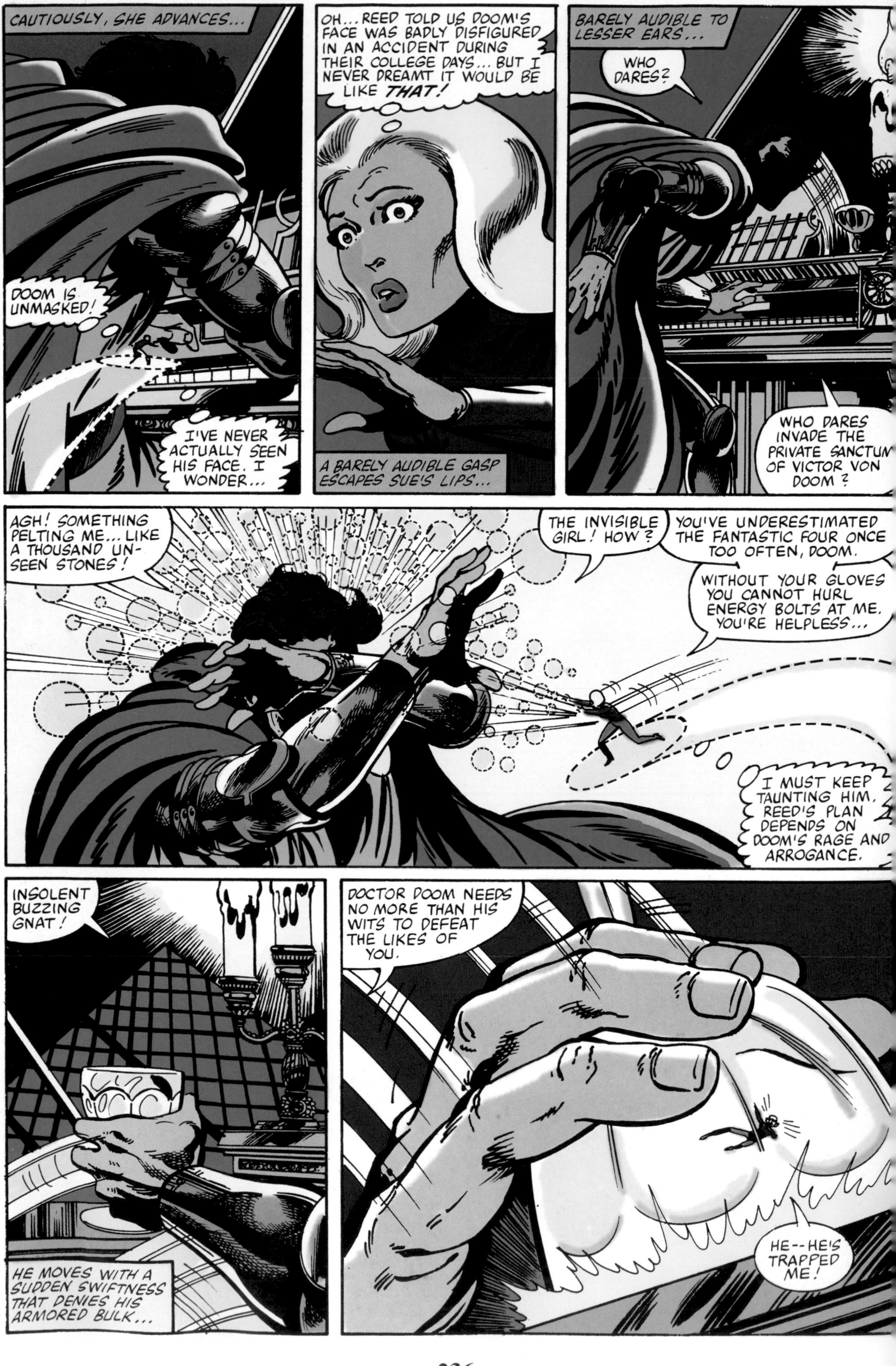
CAUTIOUSLY, SHE ADVANCES...
DOOM IS UNMASKED!
I'VE NEVER ACTUALLY SEEN HIS FACE. I WONDER...
OH... REED TOLD US DOOM'S FACE WAS BADLY DISFIGURED IN AN ACCIDENT DURING THEIR COLLEGE DAYS... BUT I NEVER DREAMT IT WOULD BE LIKE THAT!
A BARELY AUDIBLE GASP ESCAPES SUE'S LIPS...
BARELY AUDIBLE TO LESSER EARS...
WHO DARES?
WHO DARES INVADE THE PRIVATE SANCTUM OF VICTOR VON DOOM?
AGH! SOMETHING PELTING ME... LIKE A THOUSAND UN-SEEN STONES!
THE INVISIBLE GIRL! HOW?
YOU'VE UNDERESTIMATED THE FANTASTIC FOUR ONCE TOO OFTEN, DOOM.
WITHOUT YOUR GLOVES YOU CANNOT HURL ENERGY BOLTS AT ME. YOU'RE HELPLESS...
I MUST KEEP TAUNTING HIM. REED'S PLAN DEPENDS ON DOOM'S RAGE AND ARROGANCE.
INSOLENT BUZZING GNAT!
HE MOVES WITH A SUDDEN SWIFTNESS THAT DENIES HIS ARMORED BULK...
DOCTOR DOOM NEEDS NO MORE THAN HIS WITS TO DEFEAT THE LIKES OF YOU.
HE--HE'S TRAPPED ME!

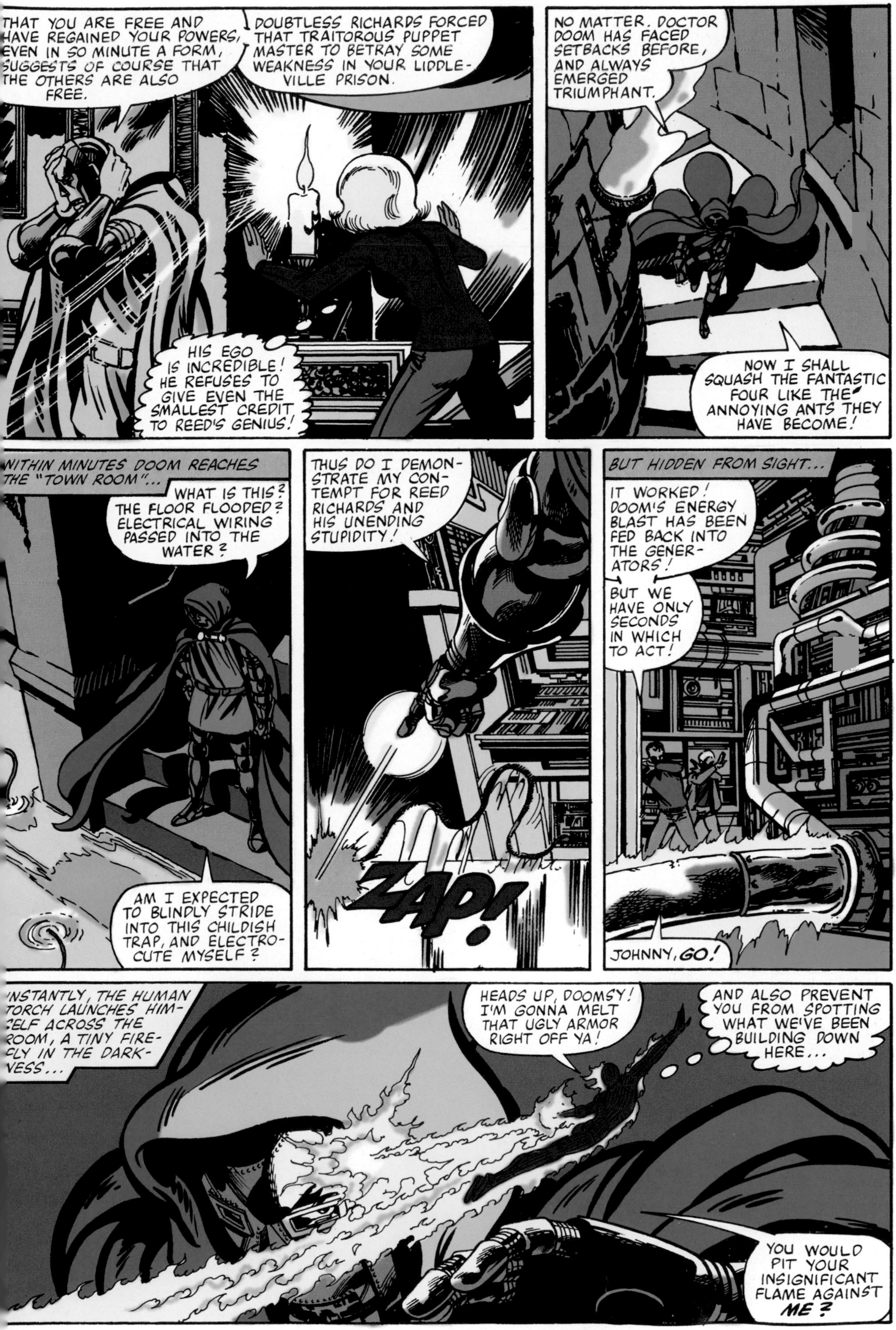
THAT YOU ARE FREE AND HAVE REGAINED YOUR POWERS, EVEN IN SO MINUTE A FORM, SUGGESTS OF COURSE THAT THE OTHERS ARE ALSO FREE.
DOUBTLESS RICHARDS FORCED THAT TRAITOROUS PUPPET MASTER TO BETRAY SOME WEAKNESS IN YOUR LIDDLEVILLE PRISON.
HIS EGO IS INCREDIBLE! HE REFUSES TO GIVE EVEN THE SMALLEST CREDIT TO REED'S GENIUS!
NO MATTER. DOCTOR DOOM HAS FACED SETBACKS BEFORE, AND ALWAYS EMERGED TRIUMPHANT.
NOW I SHALL SQUASH THE FANTASTIC FOUR LIKE THE ANNOYING ANTS THEY HAVE BECOME!
WITHIN MINUTES DOOM REACHES THE "TOWN ROOM"...
WHAT IS THIS? THE FLOOR FLOODED? ELECTRICAL WIRING PASSED INTO THE WATER?
AM I EXPECTED TO BLINDLY STRIDE INTO THIS CHILDISH TRAP, AND ELECTROCUTE MYSELF?
THUS DO I DEMONSTRATE MY CONTEMPT FOR REED RICHARDS AND HIS UNENDING STUPIDITY!
ZAP!
BUT HIDDEN FROM SIGHT...
IT WORKED! DOOM'S ENERGY BLAST HAS BEEN FED BACK INTO THE GENERATORS!
BUT WE HAVE ONLY SECONDS IN WHICH TO ACT!
JOHNNY, GO!
INSTANTLY, THE HUMAN TORCH LAUNCHES HIMSELF ACROSS THE ROOM, A TINY FIREFLY IN THE DARKNESS...
HEADS UP, DOOMSY! I'M GONNA MELT THAT UGLY ARMOR RIGHT OFF YA!
AND ALSO PREVENT YOU FROM SPOTTING WHAT WE'VE BEEN BUILDING DOWN HERE...
YOU WOULD PIT YOUR INSIGNIFICANT FLAME AGAINST ME?

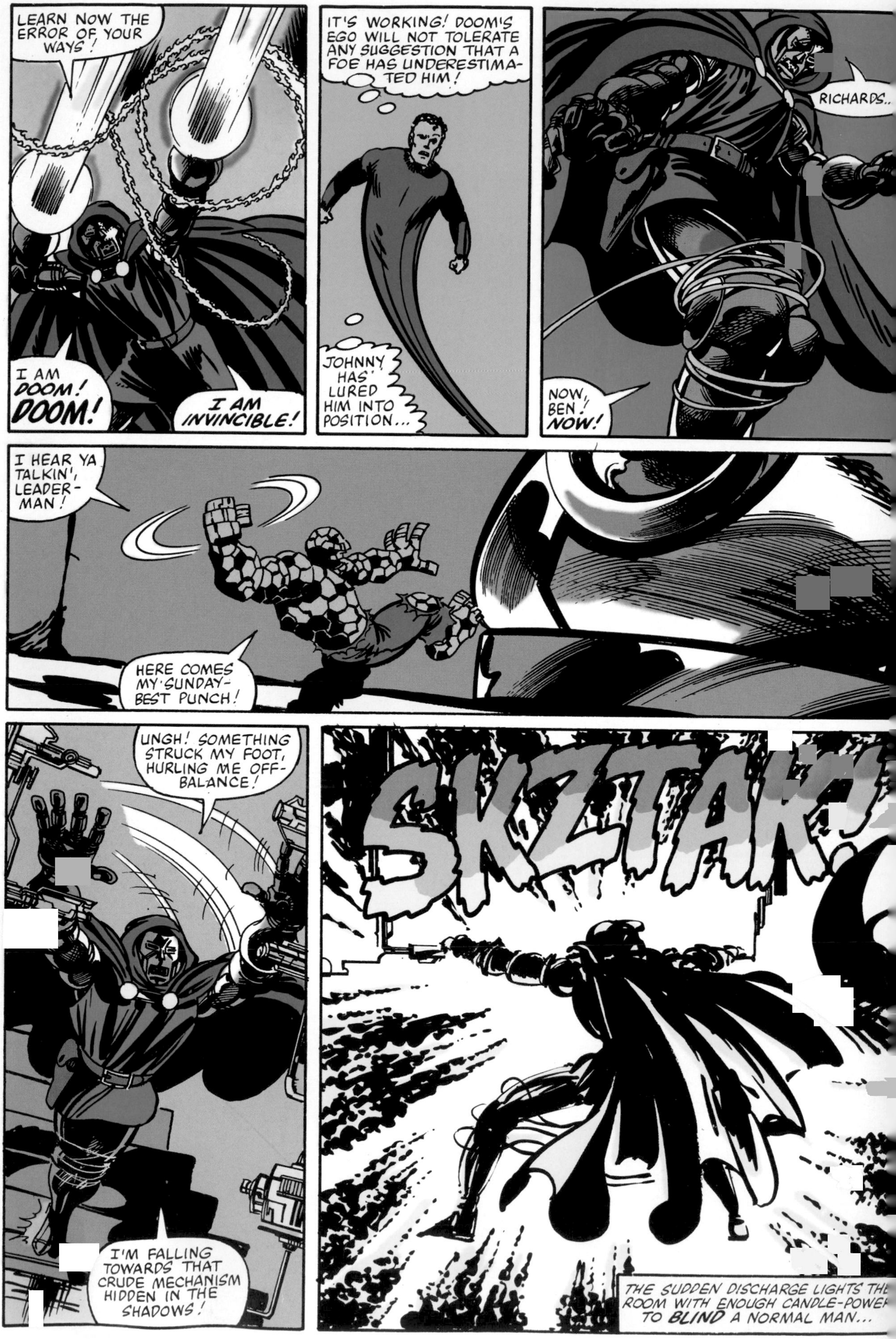

LEARN NOW THE ERROR OF YOUR WAYS!
I AM DOOM! DOOM!
I AM INVINCIBLE!
IT'S WORKING! DOOM'S EGO WILL NOT TOLERATE ANY SUGGESTION THAT A FOE HAS UNDERESTIMATED HIM!
JOHNNY HAS LURED HIM INTO POSITION...
RICHARDS..
NOW, BEN! NOW!
I HEAR YA TALKIN', LEADER-MAN!
HERE COMES MY SUNDAY-BEST PUNCH!
UNGH! SOMETHING STRUCK MY FOOT, HURLING ME OFF-BALANCE!
I'M FALLING TOWARDS THAT CRUDE MECHANISM HIDDEN IN THE SHADOWS!
SKZTAK!
THE SUDDEN DISCHARGE LIGHTS THE ROOM WITH ENOUGH CANDLE-POWER TO BLIND A NORMAL MAN...

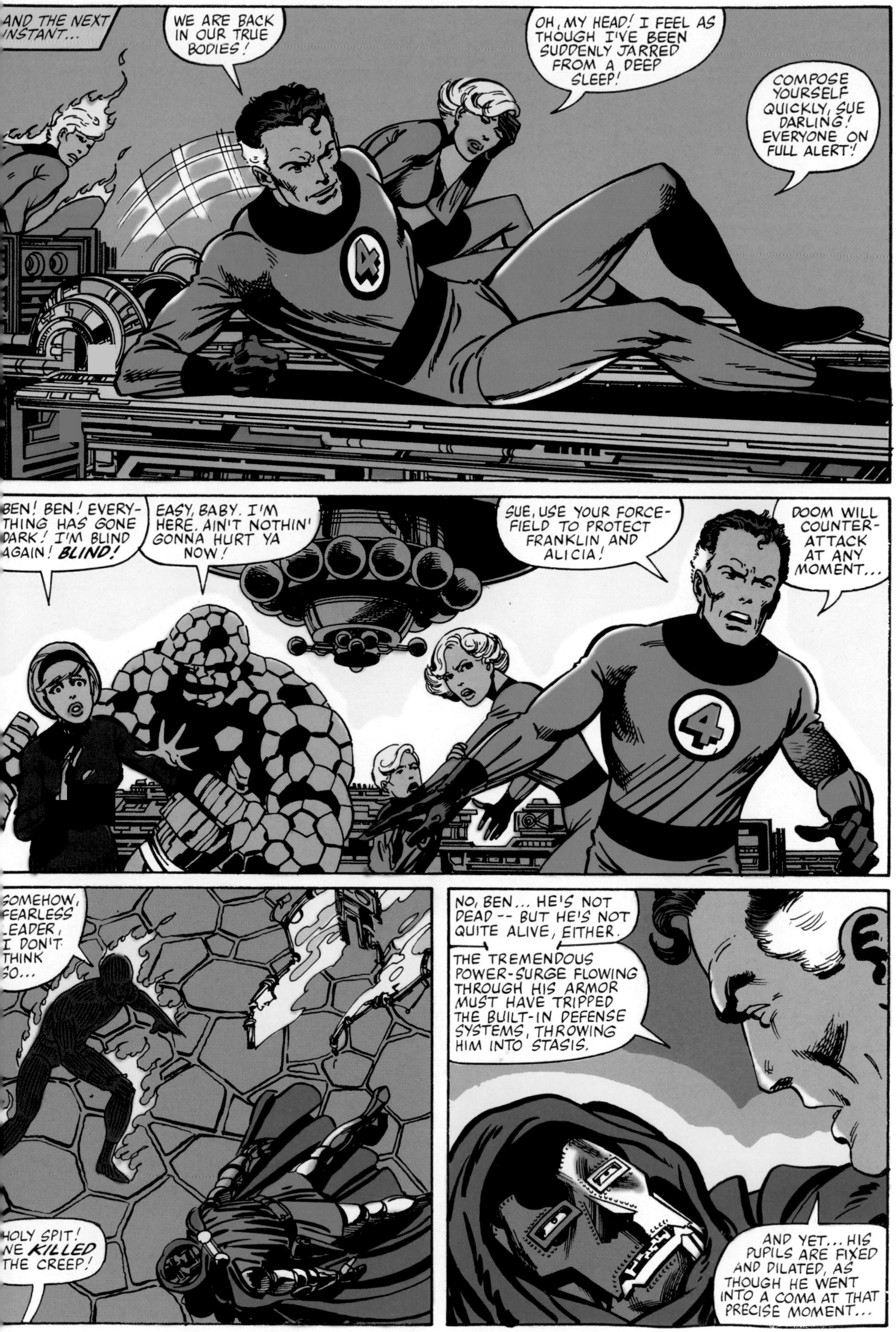
AND THE NEXT INSTANT...
WE ARE BACK IN OUR TRUE BODIES!
OH, MY HEAD! I FEEL AS THOUGH I'VE BEEN SUDDENLY JARRED FROM A DEEP SLEEP!
COMPOSE YOURSELF QUICKLY, SUE DARLING! EVERYONE ON FULL ALERT!
BEN! BEN! EVERYTHING HAS GONE DARK! I'M BLIND AGAIN! BLIND!
EASY, BABY. I'M HERE. AIN'T NOTHIN' GONNA HURT YA NOW!
SUE, USE YOUR FORCE-FIELD TO PROTECT FRANKLIN AND ALICIA!
DOOM WILL COUNTER-ATTACK AT ANY MOMENT...
SOMEHOW, FEARLESS LEADER, I DON'T THINK SO...
HOLY SPIT! WE KILLED THE CREEP!
NO, BEN... HE'S NOT DEAD -- BUT HE'S NOT QUITE ALIVE, EITHER.
THE TREMENDOUS POWER-SURGE FLOWING THROUGH HIS ARMOR MUST HAVE TRIPPED THE BUILT-IN DEFENSE SYSTEMS, THROWING HIM INTO STASIS.
AND YET... HIS PUPILS ARE FIXED AND DILATED, AS THOUGH HE WENT INTO A COMA AT THAT PRECISE MOMENT...

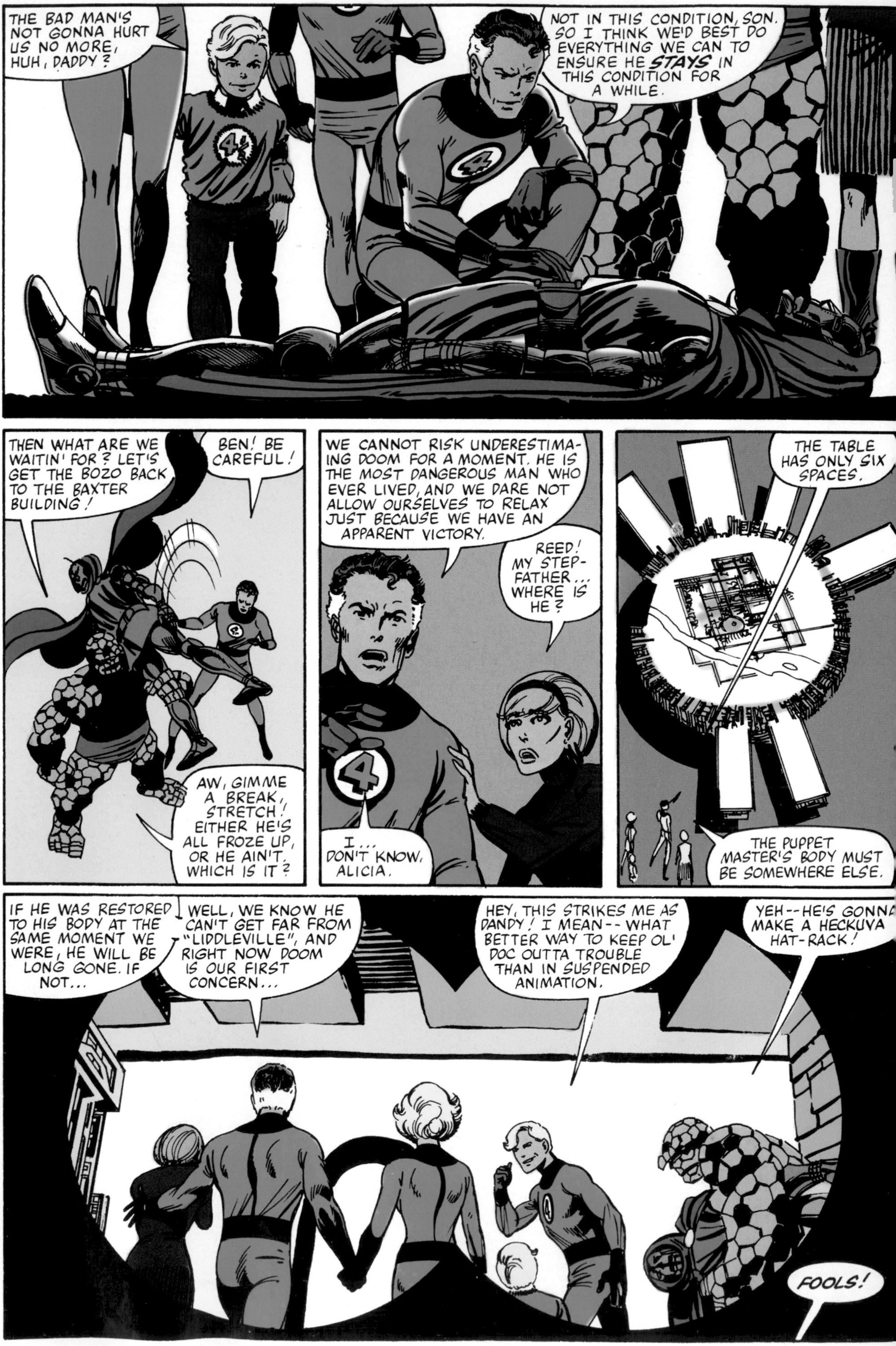
THE BAD MAN'S NOT GONNA HURT US NO MORE, HUH, DADDY?
NOT IN THIS CONDITION, SON. SO I THINK WE'D BEST DO EVERYTHING WE CAN TO ENSURE HE STAYS IN THIS CONDITION FOR A WHILE.
THEN WHAT ARE WE WAITIN' FOR? LET'S GET THE BOZO BACK TO THE BAXTER BUILDING!
BEN! BE CAREFUL!
AW, GIMME A BREAK, STRETCH! EITHER HE'S ALL FROZE UP, OR HE AIN'T. WHICH IS IT?
WE CANNOT RISK UNDERESTIMATING DOOM FOR A MOMENT. HE IS THE MOST DANGEROUS MAN WHO EVER LIVED, AND WE DARE NOT ALLOW OURSELVES TO RELAX JUST BECAUSE WE HAVE AN APPARENT VICTORY.
REED! MY STEP-FATHER... WHERE IS HE?
I... DON'T KNOW, ALICIA.
THE TABLE HAS ONLY SIX SPACES.
THE PUPPET MASTER'S BODY MUST BE SOMEWHERE ELSE.
IF HE WAS RESTORED TO HIS BODY AT THE SAME MOMENT WE WERE, HE WILL BE LONG GONE. IF NOT...
WELL, WE KNOW HE CAN'T GET FAR FROM "LIDDLEVILLE", AND RIGHT NOW DOOM IS OUR FIRST CONCERN...
HEY, THIS STRIKES ME AS DANDY! I MEAN--WHAT BETTER WAY TO KEEP OL' DOC OUTTA TROUBLE THAN IN SUSPENDED ANIMATION.
YEH--HE'S GONNA MAKE A HECKUVA HAT-RACK!
FOOLS!

JUST OUTSIDE LIDDLEVILLE COLLEGE...

ONCE AGAIN THEY SOW THE SEED OF THEIR OWN UNDOING BY UNDERESTIMATING DOOM!

RICHARDS IS TOO STUPID TO REALIZE THAT USING MY ARMOR TO TRIGGER HIS CRUDE TRANSFERAL SYSTEM...

...SERVED ALSO TO TRANSMIT MY MIND INTO THE ROBOTIC BODY OF "VINCENT VAUGHN."

NOW I HAVE BUT TO WAIT UNTIL THEY ARE OFF-GUARD...

AND A SIMPLE TWIST OF THIS RING WILL RESTORE ME TO MY TRUE BODY.

AND THEN I SHALL DESTROY...

WHAT!?!

CRACK!

YOU HAVE DESTROYED ENOUGH, VON DOOM. YOU HAVE TWISTED AND PERVERTED MY DREAMS OF HAPPINESS FOR ALICIA. YOU TURNED MY LIDDLEVILLE INTO A STAGE FOR YOUR TRIVIAL VENGEANCE SCHEME.

WHAT IS YOUR HATRED FOR THE FANTASTIC FOUR COMPARED TO MY HOPES FOR MY STEP-DAUGHTER?

I HAVE REPROGRAMMED THE ROBOTS TO SERVE MY WILL. AND MINE ALONE.

MASTERS... YOU CANNOT...

NO!

I CAN DO ANYTHING, DOOM!

THERE IS YOUR ENEMY, MY PUPPETS! THERE IS THE DESPOILER, THE CORRUPTOR!

DESTROY HIM!

DOOM FLEES, KNOWING THAT SHOULD THIS ROBOT BODY "DIE", HIS MIND, HIS SOUL WILL PERISH WITH IT.

HE RUNS, KNOWING THAT HE CAN DO SO FOREVER, FOR AS A ROBOT HE WILL NOT TIRE, WILL NOT NEED TO PAUSE FOR REST...

BUT, THEN, NEITHER WILL THEY...

NEITHER WILL THEY...

241

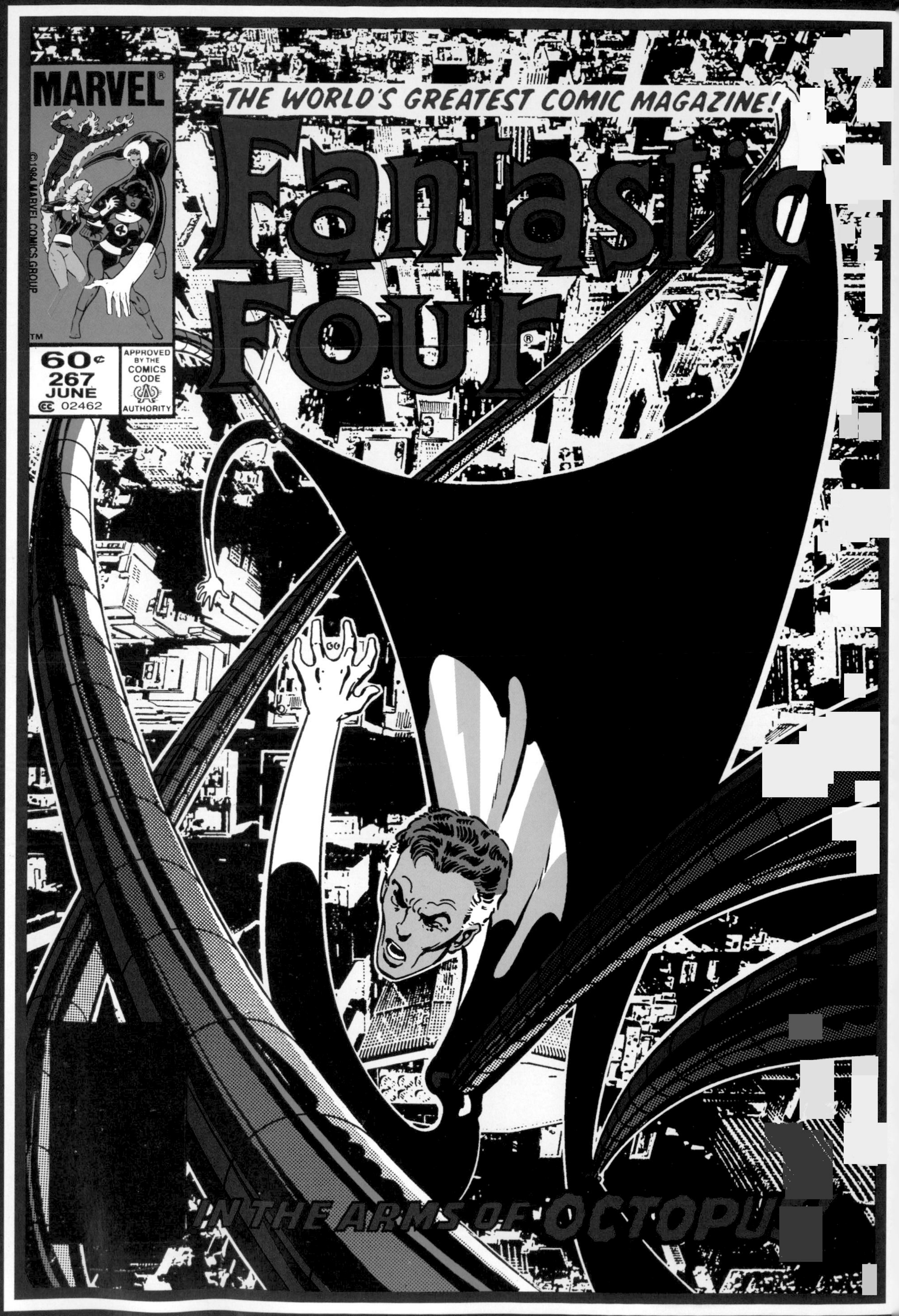
MARVEL
60¢
267
JUNE
02462
APPROVED BY THE COMICS CODE AUTHORITY
©1984 MARVEL COMICS GROUP
THE WORLD'S GREATEST COMIC MAGAZINE!
Fantastic Four
IN THE ARMS OF OCTOPU

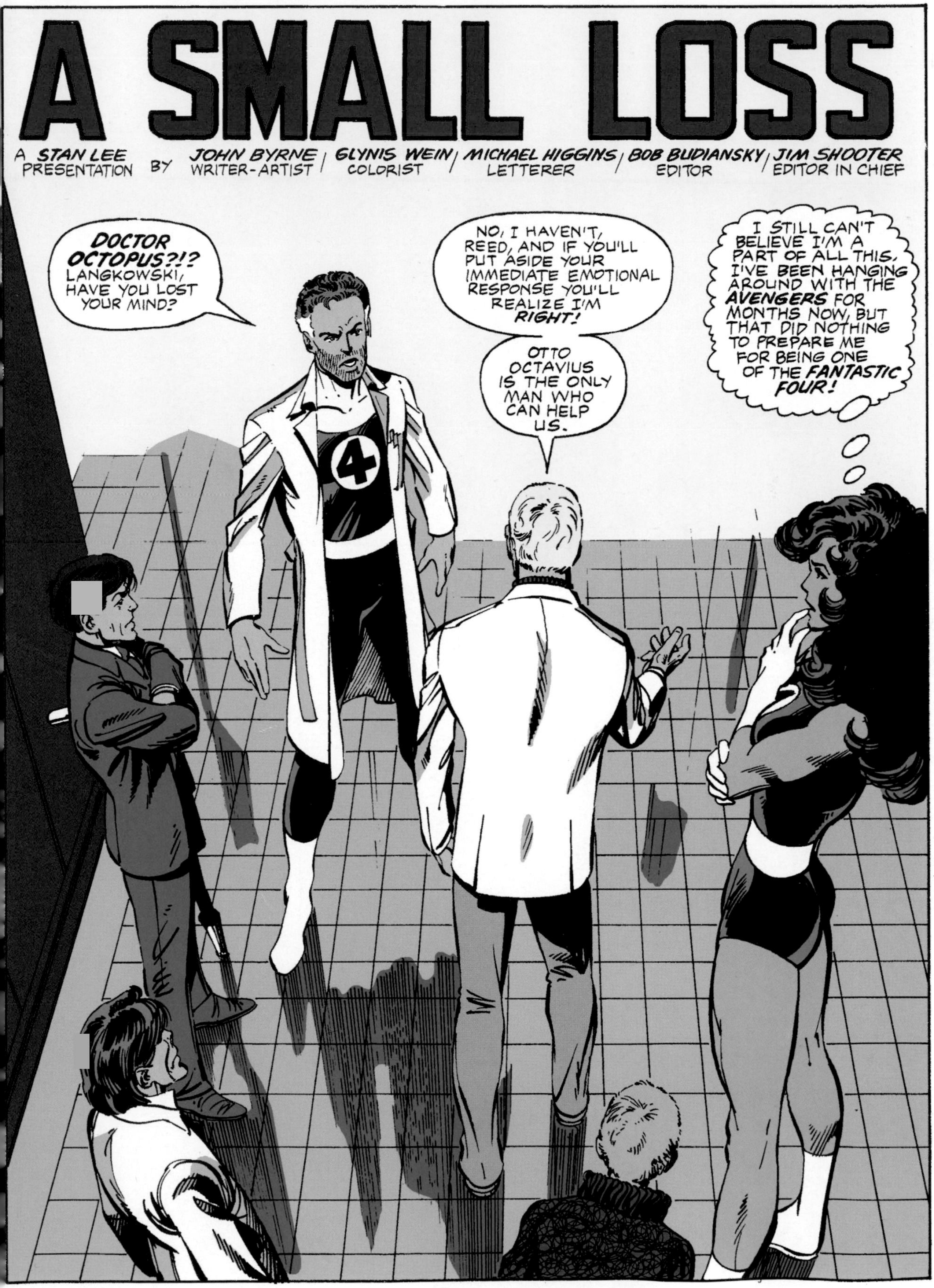

A SMALL LOSS
A STAN LEE PRESENTATION BY JOHN BYRNE WRITER-ARTIST / GLYNIS WEIN COLORIST / MICHAEL HIGGINS LETTERER / BOB BUDIANSKY EDITOR / JIM SHOOTER EDITOR IN CHIEF
DOCTOR OCTOPUS?!? LANGKOWSKI, HAVE YOU LOST YOUR MIND?
NO, I HAVEN'T, REED, AND IF YOU'LL PUT ASIDE YOUR IMMEDIATE EMOTIONAL RESPONSE YOU'LL REALIZE I'M RIGHT!
OTTO OCTAVIUS IS THE ONLY MAN WHO CAN HELP US.
I STILL CAN'T BELIEVE I'M A PART OF ALL THIS. I'VE BEEN HANGING AROUND WITH THE AVENGERS FOR MONTHS NOW, BUT THAT DID NOTHING TO PREPARE ME FOR BEING ONE OF THE FANTASTIC FOUR!

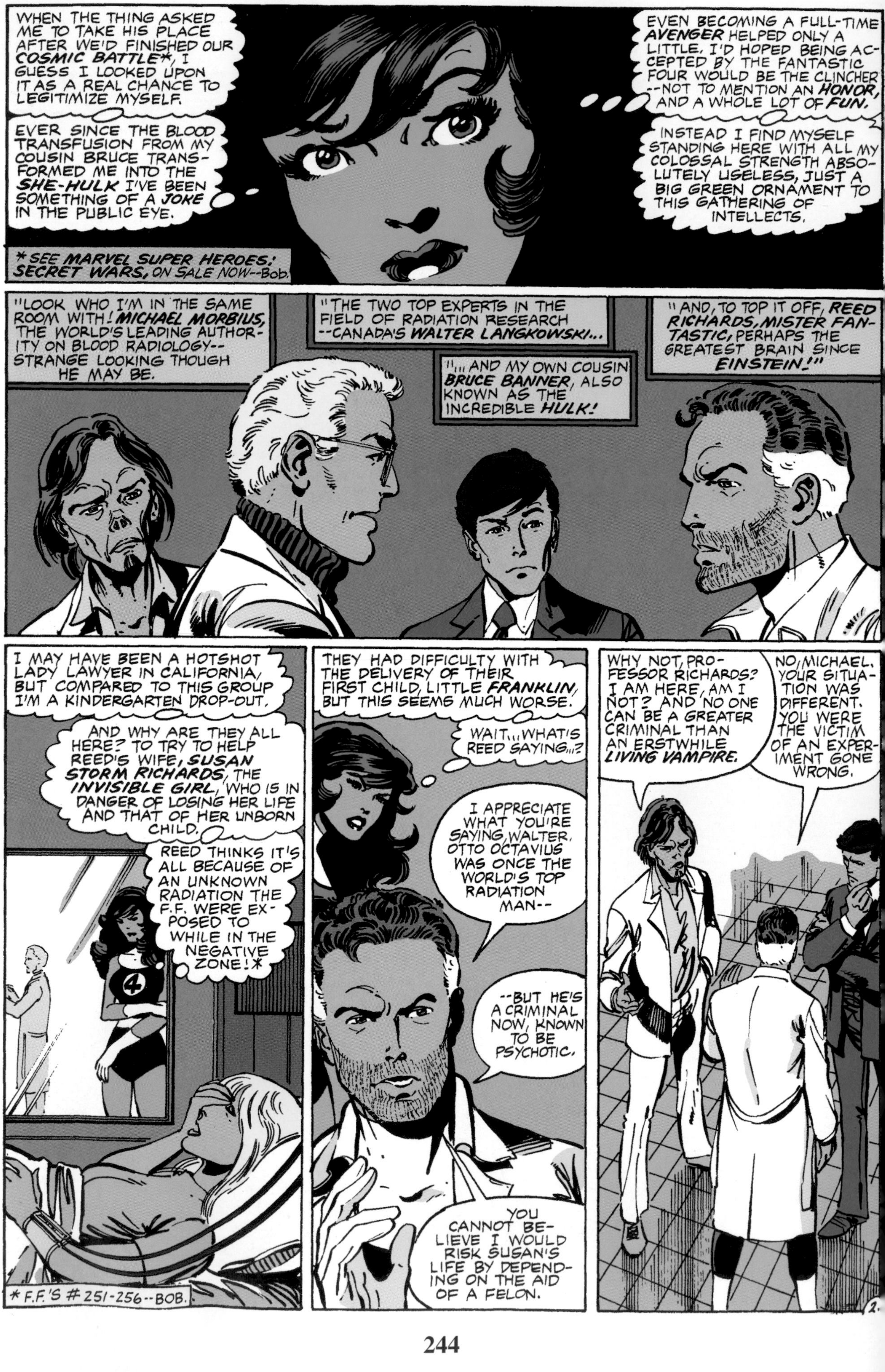
WHEN THE THING ASKED ME TO TAKE HIS PLACE AFTER WE'D FINISHED OUR COSMIC BATTLE*, I GUESS I LOOKED UPON IT AS A REAL CHANCE TO LEGITIMIZE MYSELF.
EVER SINCE THE BLOOD TRANSFUSION FROM MY COUSIN BRUCE TRANSFORMED ME INTO THE SHE-HULK I'VE BEEN SOMETHING OF A JOKE IN THE PUBLIC EYE.
EVEN BECOMING A FULL-TIME AVENGER HELPED ONLY A LITTLE. I'D HOPED BEING ACCEPTED BY THE FANTASTIC FOUR WOULD BE THE CLINCHER --NOT TO MENTION AN HONOR, AND A WHOLE LOT OF FUN.
INSTEAD I FIND MYSELF STANDING HERE WITH ALL MY COLOSSAL STRENGTH ABSOLUTELY USELESS, JUST A BIG GREEN ORNAMENT TO THIS GATHERING OF INTELLECTS.
*SEE MARVEL SUPER HEROES: SECRET WARS, ON SALE NOW--Bob.
"LOOK WHO I'M IN THE SAME ROOM WITH! MICHAEL MORBIUS, THE WORLD'S LEADING AUTHORITY ON BLOOD RADIOLOGY-- STRANGE LOOKING THOUGH HE MAY BE.
"THE TWO TOP EXPERTS IN THE FIELD OF RADIATION RESEARCH --CANADA'S WALTER LANGKOWSKI...
"...AND MY OWN COUSIN BRUCE BANNER, ALSO KNOWN AS THE INCREDIBLE HULK!
"AND, TO TOP IT OFF, REED RICHARDS, MISTER FANTASTIC, PERHAPS THE GREATEST BRAIN SINCE EINSTEIN!"
I MAY HAVE BEEN A HOTSHOT LADY LAWYER IN CALIFORNIA, BUT COMPARED TO THIS GROUP I'M A KINDERGARTEN DROP-OUT.
AND WHY ARE THEY ALL HERE? TO TRY TO HELP REED'S WIFE, SUSAN STORM RICHARDS, THE INVISIBLE GIRL, WHO IS IN DANGER OF LOSING HER LIFE AND THAT OF HER UNBORN CHILD.
REED THINKS IT'S ALL BECAUSE OF AN UNKNOWN RADIATION THE F.F. WERE EXPOSED TO WHILE IN THE NEGATIVE ZONE!*
*F.F.'S #251-256--BOB.
THEY HAD DIFFICULTY WITH THE DELIVERY OF THEIR FIRST CHILD, LITTLE FRANKLIN, BUT THIS SEEMS MUCH WORSE.
WAIT...WHAT'S REED SAYING...?
I APPRECIATE WHAT YOU'RE SAYING, WALTER. OTTO OCTAVIUS WAS ONCE THE WORLD'S TOP RADIATION MAN--
--BUT HE'S A CRIMINAL NOW, KNOWN TO BE PSYCHOTIC.
YOU CANNOT BELIEVE I WOULD RISK SUSAN'S LIFE BY DEPENDING ON THE AID OF A FELON.
WHY NOT, PROFESSOR RICHARDS? I AM HERE, AM I NOT? AND NO ONE CAN BE A GREATER CRIMINAL THAN AN ERSTWHILE LIVING VAMPIRE.
NO, MICHAEL. YOUR SITUATION WAS DIFFERENT. YOU WERE THE VICTIM OF AN EXPERIMENT GONE WRONG.
2.

NO, MORBIUS IS RIGHT, REED, WE CAN'T DISMISS OCTAVIUS BECAUSE HE'S ON THE SHADOW SIDE OF THE LAW, WE'VE ALL SEEN THAT SIDE OF THE STREET.

CONSIDER MY OWN SITUATION BEFORE I LEARNED TO CONTROL MY HULKING ALTER-EGO.

"ONCE OTTO OCTAVIUS WAS A SCIENTIST, A MAN MUCH LIKE YOU OR ME, SEEKING TO UNLOCK THE SECRETS OF NATURE.

"HIS CHOSEN FIELD WAS *RADIOACTIVITY*, AND HE WAS THE VERY BEST.

"HE'D CREATED A SET OF ROBOT ARMS, TO DO THE DANGEROUS WORK AT LONG DISTANCE.

"IT WAS THOSE ARMS WHICH HAD HIS CO-WORKERS CALLING HIM *DOCTOR OCTOPUS*.

"THEN, ONE DAY TRAGEDY STRUCK.

"A SMALL SCALE CHAIN-REACTION BLASTED HIM AND HIS ARMS WITH UNKNOWN RADIATION WAVELENGTHS.

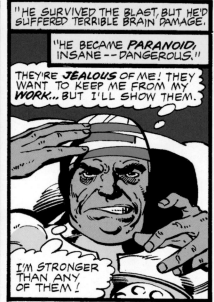

"HE SURVIVED THE BLAST, BUT HE'D SUFFERED TERRIBLE BRAIN DAMAGE.

"HE BECAME *PARANOID*, INSANE -- DANGEROUS."

THEY'RE *JEALOUS* OF ME! THEY WANT TO KEEP ME FROM MY *WORK*... BUT I'LL SHOW THEM.

I'M STRONGER THAN ANY OF THEM!

"SOMEHOW HIS ARMS HAD BEEN PSIONICALLY LINKED TO HIS BRAIN.

"THEY NOW OBEYED HIS EVERY THOUGHT."

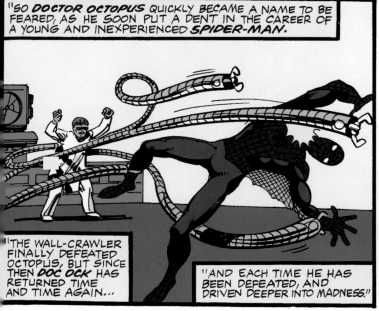

"SO *DOCTOR OCTOPUS* QUICKLY BECAME A NAME TO BE FEARED, AS HE SOON PUT A DENT IN THE CAREER OF A YOUNG AND INEXPERIENCED *SPIDER-MAN*.

"THE WALL-CRAWLER FINALLY DEFEATED OCTOPUS, BUT SINCE THEN *DOC OCK* HAS RETURNED TIME AND TIME AGAIN...

"AND EACH TIME HE HAS BEEN DEFEATED, AND DRIVEN DEEPER INTO MADNESS."

BUT HOW DIFFERENT IS HIS STORY FROM THAT OF YOURS OR MINE, REED? WE MIGHT ALSO HAVE LOST EVERYTHING TO OUR OWN EXPERIENCES WITH RADIATION, MINE WITH THE *GAMMA BOMB*, YOURS WITH *COSMIC RAYS*.

PERHAPS ALL OCTAVIUS NEEDS IS, JUST ONCE, FOR SOMEONE TO APPEAL TO THE MAN HE USED TO BE,

AND, REED, I THINK *YOU'RE* JUST THE ONE TO DO IT!

3.

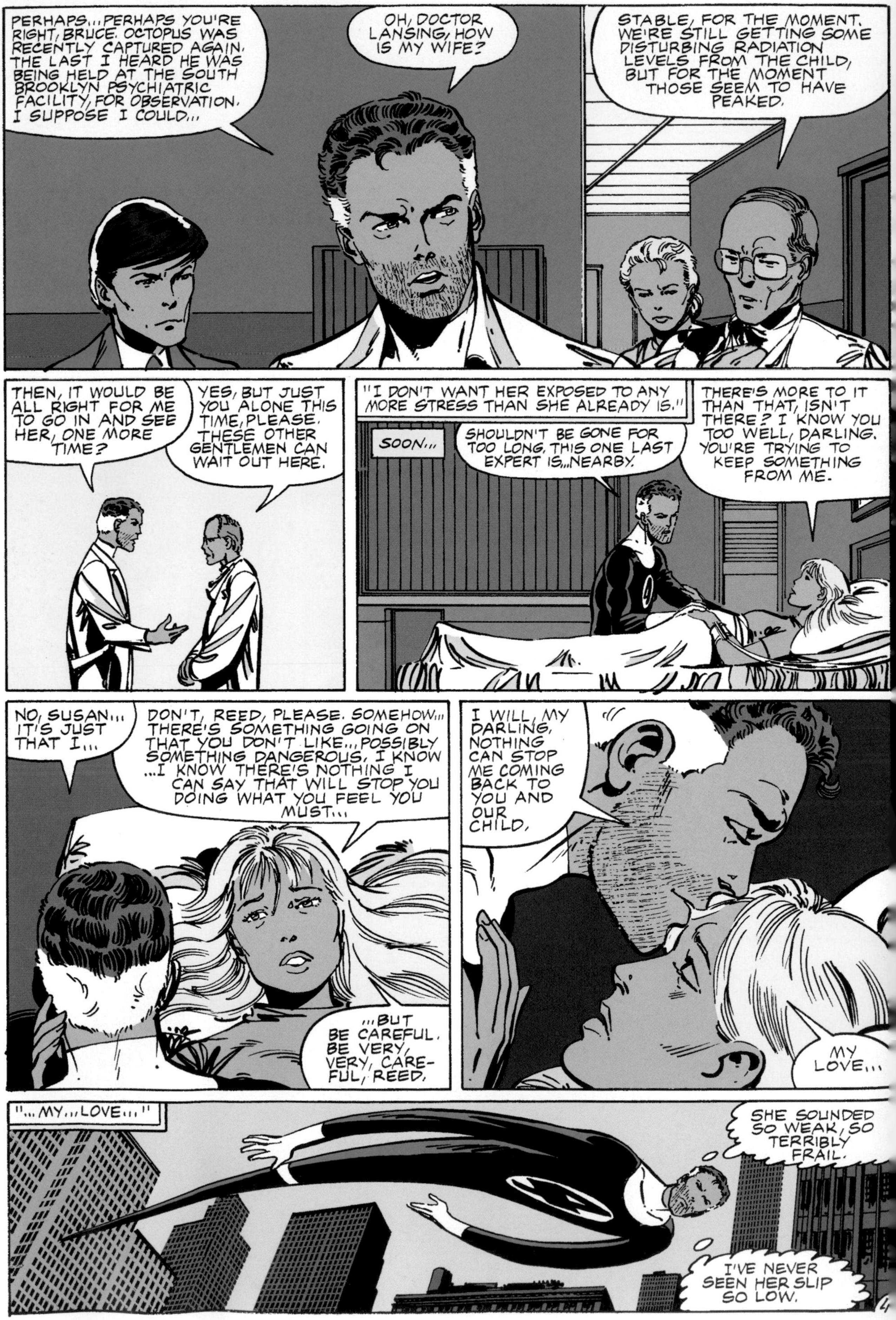

PERHAPS... PERHAPS YOU'RE RIGHT, BRUCE. OCTOPUS WAS RECENTLY CAPTURED AGAIN. THE LAST I HEARD HE WAS BEING HELD AT THE SOUTH BROOKLYN PSYCHIATRIC FACILITY, FOR OBSERVATION. I SUPPOSE I COULD...
OH, DOCTOR LANSING, HOW IS MY WIFE?
STABLE, FOR THE MOMENT. WE'RE STILL GETTING SOME DISTURBING RADIATION LEVELS FROM THE CHILD, BUT FOR THE MOMENT THOSE SEEM TO HAVE PEAKED.
THEN, IT WOULD BE ALL RIGHT FOR ME TO GO IN AND SEE HER, ONE MORE TIME?
YES, BUT JUST YOU ALONE THIS TIME, PLEASE. THESE OTHER GENTLEMEN CAN WAIT OUT HERE.
"I DON'T WANT HER EXPOSED TO ANY MORE STRESS THAN SHE ALREADY IS."
SOON...
SHOULDN'T BE GONE FOR TOO LONG. THIS ONE LAST EXPERT IS...NEARBY.
THERE'S MORE TO IT THAN THAT, ISN'T THERE? I KNOW YOU TOO WELL, DARLING. YOU'RE TRYING TO KEEP SOMETHING FROM ME.
NO, SUSAN... IT'S JUST THAT I...
DON'T, REED, PLEASE. SOMEHOW... THERE'S SOMETHING GOING ON THAT YOU DON'T LIKE... POSSIBLY SOMETHING DANGEROUS. I KNOW ...I KNOW THERE'S NOTHING I CAN SAY THAT WILL STOP YOU DOING WHAT YOU FEEL YOU MUST...
...BUT BE CAREFUL. BE VERY, VERY, CARE-FUL, REED.
I WILL, MY DARLING. NOTHING CAN STOP ME COMING BACK TO YOU AND OUR CHILD.
MY LOVE...
"...MY...LOVE..."
SHE SOUNDED SO WEAK, SO TERRIBLY FRAIL.
I'VE NEVER SEEN HER SLIP SO LOW.
4

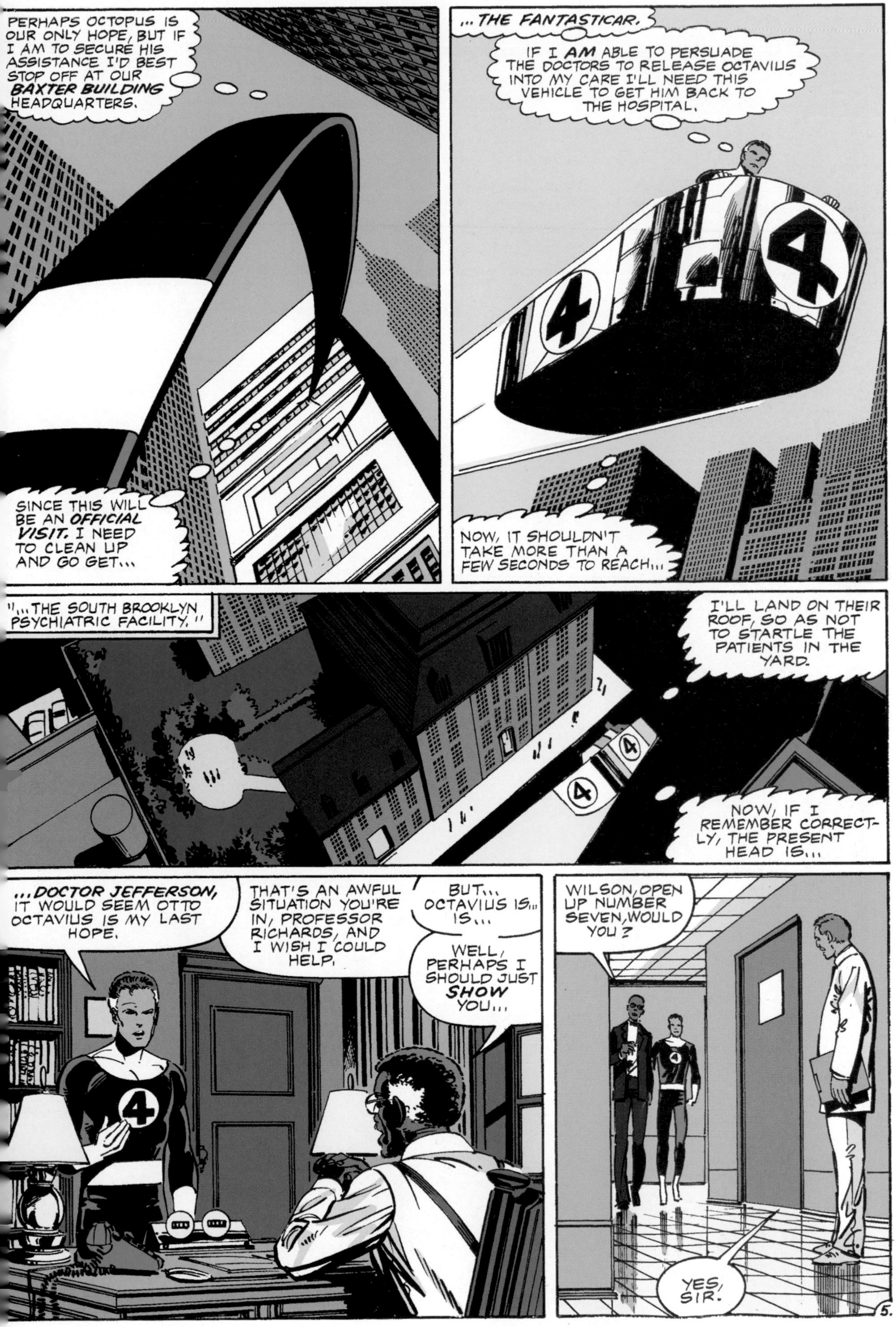
PERHAPS OCTOPUS IS OUR ONLY HOPE, BUT IF I AM TO SECURE HIS ASSISTANCE I'D BEST STOP OFF AT OUR BAXTER BUILDING HEADQUARTERS.
SINCE THIS WILL BE AN OFFICIAL VISIT, I NEED TO CLEAN UP AND GO GET...
...THE FANTASTICAR.
IF I AM ABLE TO PERSUADE THE DOCTORS TO RELEASE OCTAVIUS INTO MY CARE I'LL NEED THIS VEHICLE TO GET HIM BACK TO THE HOSPITAL.
NOW, IT SHOULDN'T TAKE MORE THAN A FEW SECONDS TO REACH...
"...THE SOUTH BROOKLYN PSYCHIATRIC FACILITY."
I'LL LAND ON THEIR ROOF, SO AS NOT TO STARTLE THE PATIENTS IN THE YARD.
NOW, IF I REMEMBER CORRECTLY, THE PRESENT HEAD IS...
...DOCTOR JEFFERSON, IT WOULD SEEM OTTO OCTAVIUS IS MY LAST HOPE.
THAT'S AN AWFUL SITUATION YOU'RE IN, PROFESSOR RICHARDS, AND I WISH I COULD HELP.
BUT... OCTAVIUS IS... IS...
WELL, PERHAPS I SHOULD JUST SHOW YOU...
WILSON, OPEN UP NUMBER SEVEN, WOULD YOU?
YES, SIR.
5.

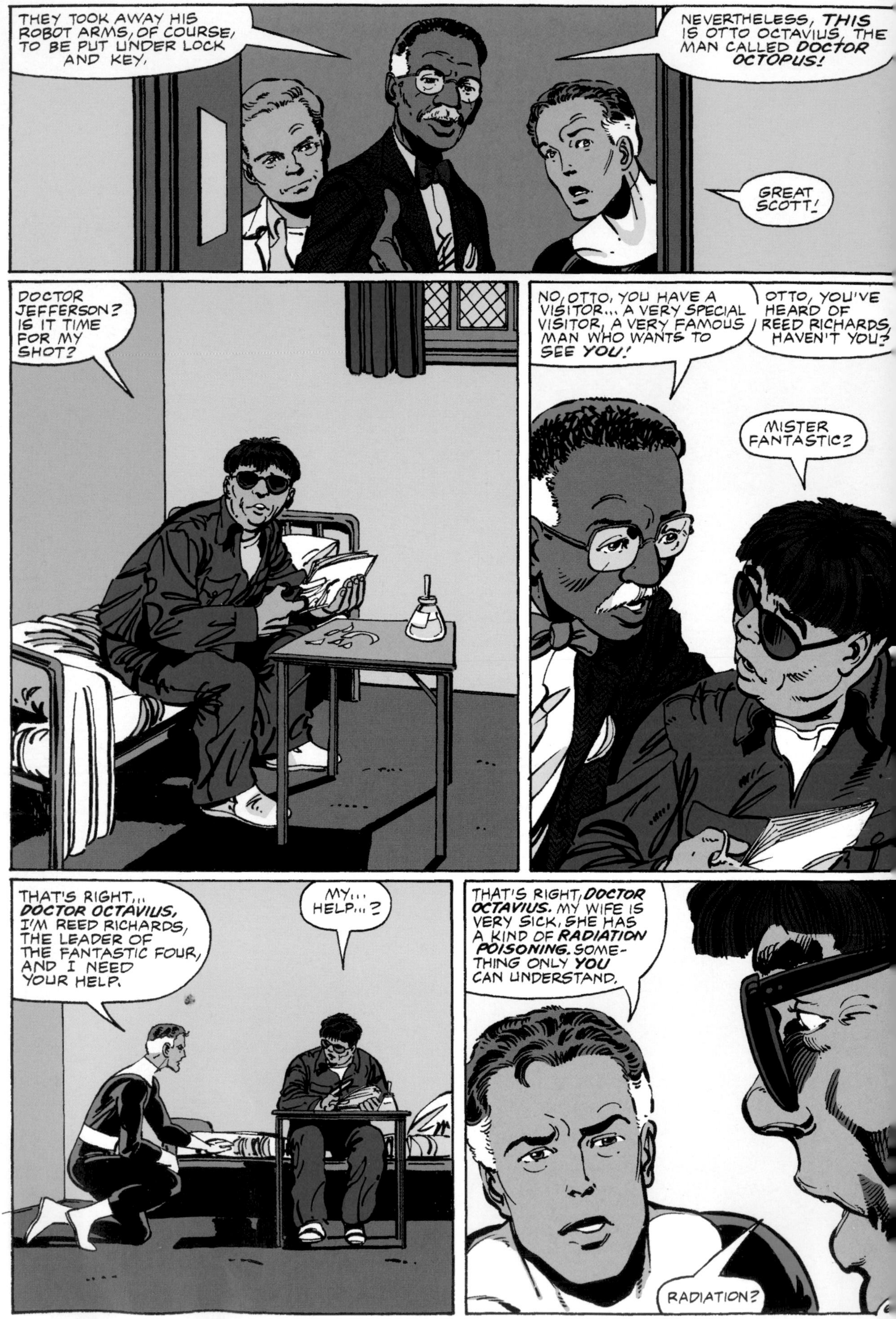
THEY TOOK AWAY HIS ROBOT ARMS, OF COURSE, TO BE PUT UNDER LOCK AND KEY.
NEVERTHELESS, THIS IS OTTO OCTAVIUS, THE MAN CALLED DOCTOR OCTOPUS!
GREAT SCOTT!
DOCTOR JEFFERSON? IS IT TIME FOR MY SHOT?
NO, OTTO, YOU HAVE A VISITOR... A VERY SPECIAL VISITOR, A VERY FAMOUS MAN WHO WANTS TO SEE YOU!
OTTO, YOU'VE HEARD OF REED RICHARDS, HAVEN'T YOU?
MISTER FANTASTIC?
THAT'S RIGHT... DOCTOR OCTAVIUS, I'M REED RICHARDS, THE LEADER OF THE FANTASTIC FOUR, AND I NEED YOUR HELP.
MY... HELP...?
THAT'S RIGHT, DOCTOR OCTAVIUS. MY WIFE IS VERY SICK, SHE HAS A KIND OF RADIATION POISONING. SOMETHING ONLY YOU CAN UNDERSTAND.
RADIATION?

YES, *DOCTOR OCTAVIUS,* YOU ARE ACKNOWLEDGED AS THE LEADING EXPERT IN THE FIELD, YOU ARE THE ONLY ONE WHO CAN HELP ME SAVE MY WIFE, THE ONLY ONE!

REMARKABLE! I WAS NOT AWARE OF RICHARDS HAVING HAD ANY PSYCHIATRIC TRAINING, YET HE IS TAKING *PRECISELY* THE CORRECT APPROACH, REINFORCING THROUGH REPETITION OCTAVIUS'S *TRUE* IDENTITY,

IT'S AN ABSOLUTELY *BRILLIANT* STRATEGY, AND, UNLESS I'M VERY MUCH MISTAKEN...

"...I BELIEVE...,

"...IT'S GOING...,

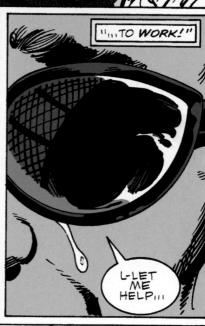

"...TO *WORK!*"

L-LET ME HELP...,

OH, PLEASE, PLEASE LET ME HELP, LET ME GET BACK TO MY WORK... BACK TO *HELPING* PEOPLE, IT'S BEEN SO *LONG,* SO VERY, VERY LONG...,

YES, DOCTOR OCTAVIUS, YOU CAN HELP, YOU *MUST* HELP,

CONGRATULATIONS, PROFESSOR RICHARDS, YOU'VE DONE WEEKS-- PERHAPS MONTHS--OF WORK IN *MINUTES!*

I HOPE SO, DOCTOR JEFFERSON, NOW, IF WE CAN GET THE RELEASE PAPERS TAKEN CARE OF...,

7.

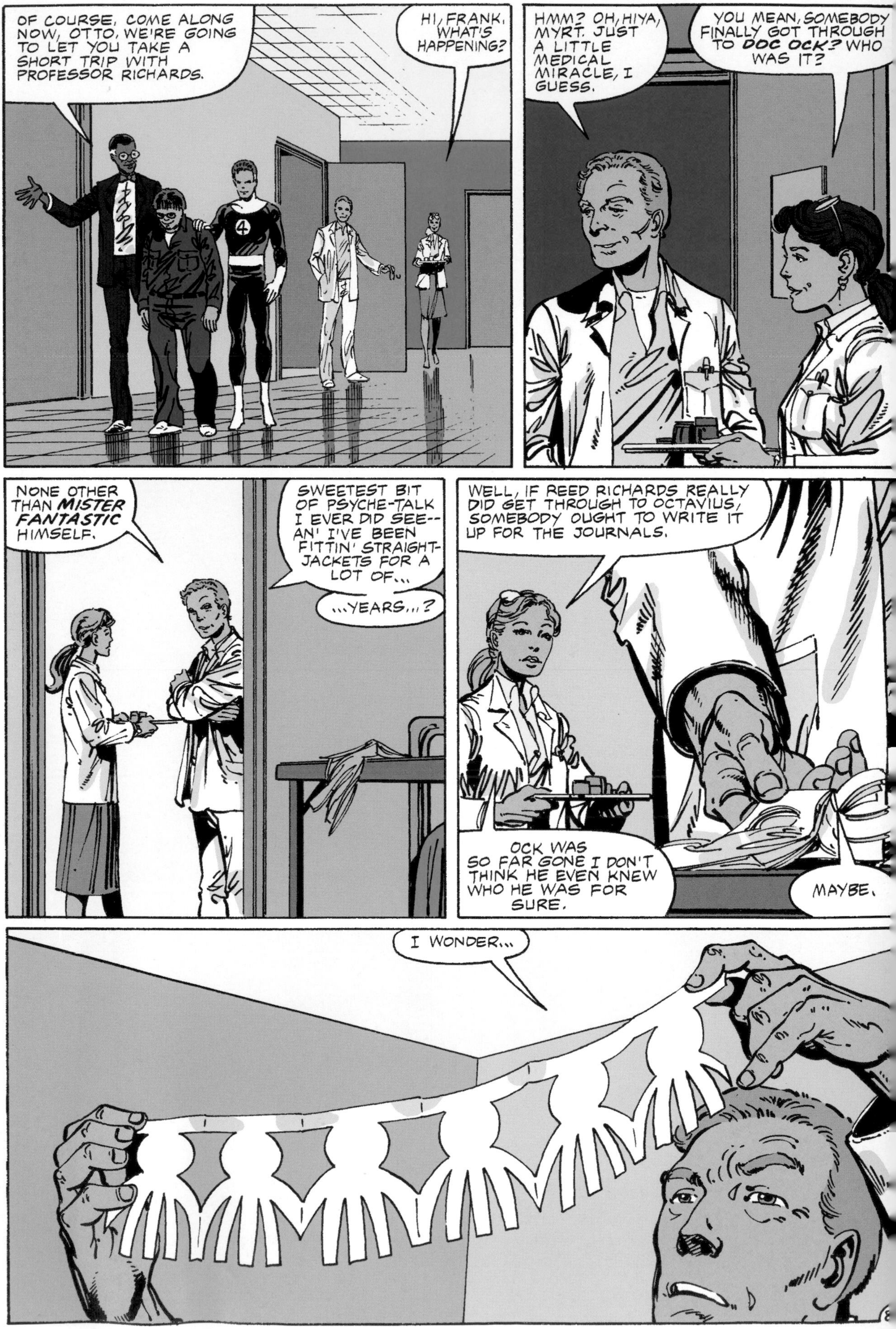
OF COURSE. COME ALONG NOW, OTTO. WE'RE GOING TO LET YOU TAKE A SHORT TRIP WITH PROFESSOR RICHARDS.
HI, FRANK. WHAT'S HAPPENING?
HMM? OH, HIYA, MYRT. JUST A LITTLE MEDICAL MIRACLE, I GUESS.
YOU MEAN, SOMEBODY FINALLY GOT THROUGH TO DOC OCK? WHO WAS IT?
NONE OTHER THAN MISTER FANTASTIC HIMSELF.
SWEETEST BIT OF PSYCHE-TALK I EVER DID SEE-- AN' I'VE BEEN FITTIN' STRAIGHT-JACKETS FOR A LOT OF...
...YEARS...?
WELL, IF REED RICHARDS REALLY DID GET THROUGH TO OCTAVIUS, SOMEBODY OUGHT TO WRITE IT UP FOR THE JOURNALS.
OCK WAS SO FAR GONE I DON'T THINK HE EVEN KNEW WHO HE WAS FOR SURE.
MAYBE.
I WONDER...

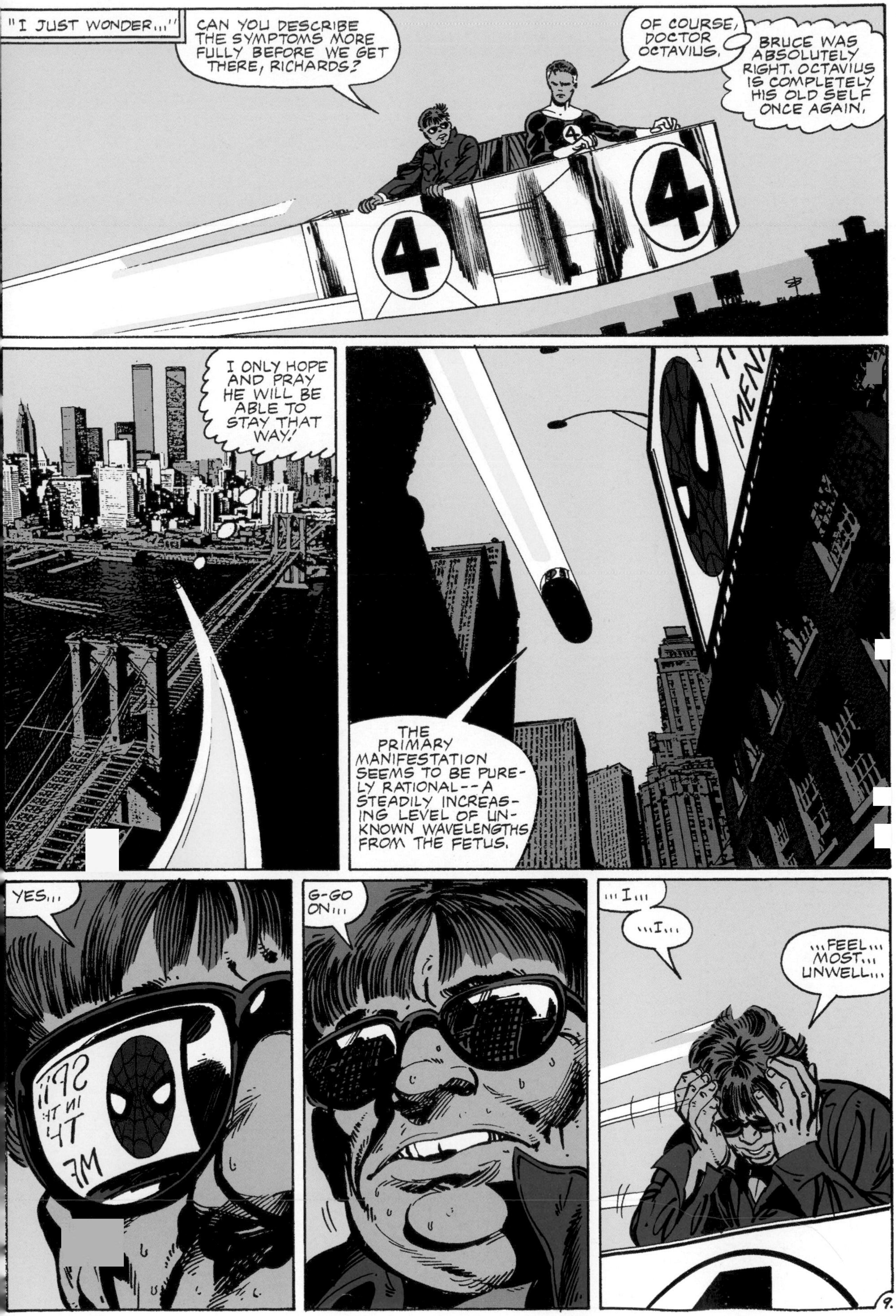
"I JUST WONDER..."
CAN YOU DESCRIBE THE SYMPTOMS MORE FULLY BEFORE WE GET THERE, RICHARDS?
OF COURSE, DOCTOR OCTAVIUS.
BRUCE WAS ABSOLUTELY RIGHT. OCTAVIUS IS COMPLETELY HIS OLD SELF ONCE AGAIN.
I ONLY HOPE AND PRAY HE WILL BE ABLE TO STAY THAT WAY!
THE PRIMARY MANIFESTATION SEEMS TO BE PURELY RATIONAL-- A STEADILY INCREASING LEVEL OF UNKNOWN WAVELENGTHS FROM THE FETUS.
YES...
G-GO ON...
...I...
...I...
...FEEL... MOST... UNWELL...
9.

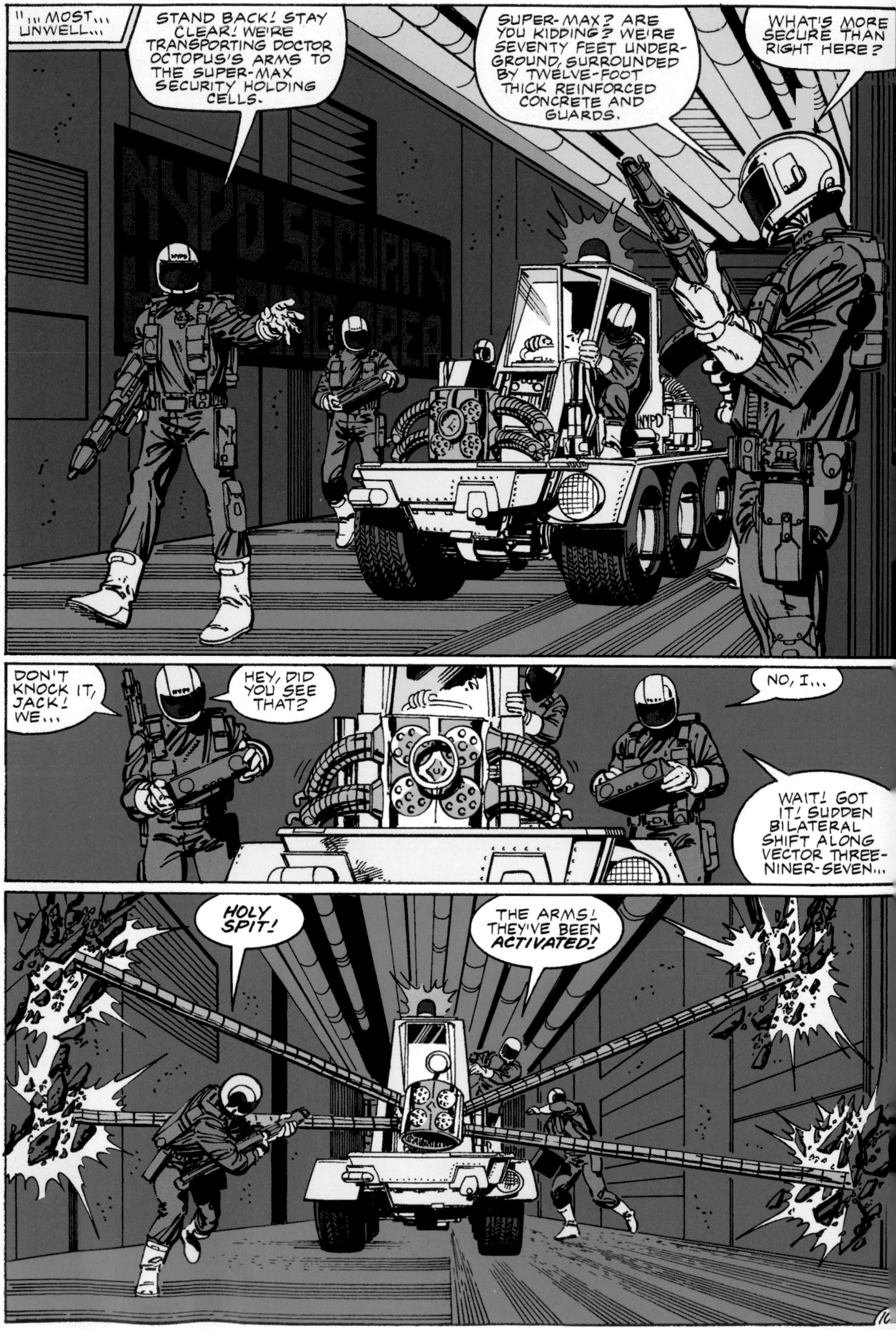
"...MOST... UNWELL...
STAND BACK! STAY CLEAR! WE'RE TRANSPORTING DOCTOR OCTOPUS'S ARMS TO THE SUPER-MAX SECURITY HOLDING CELLS.
SUPER-MAX? ARE YOU KIDDING? WE'RE SEVENTY FEET UNDER-GROUND, SURROUNDED BY TWELVE-FOOT THICK REINFORCED CONCRETE AND GUARDS.
WHAT'S MORE SECURE THAN RIGHT HERE?
NYPD SECURITY
NYPD
DON'T KNOCK IT, JACK! WE...
HEY, DID YOU SEE THAT?
NO, I...
WAIT! GOT IT! SUDDEN BILATERAL SHIFT ALONG VECTOR THREE-NINER-SEVEN...
HOLY SPIT!
THE ARMS! THEY'VE BEEN ACTIVATED!

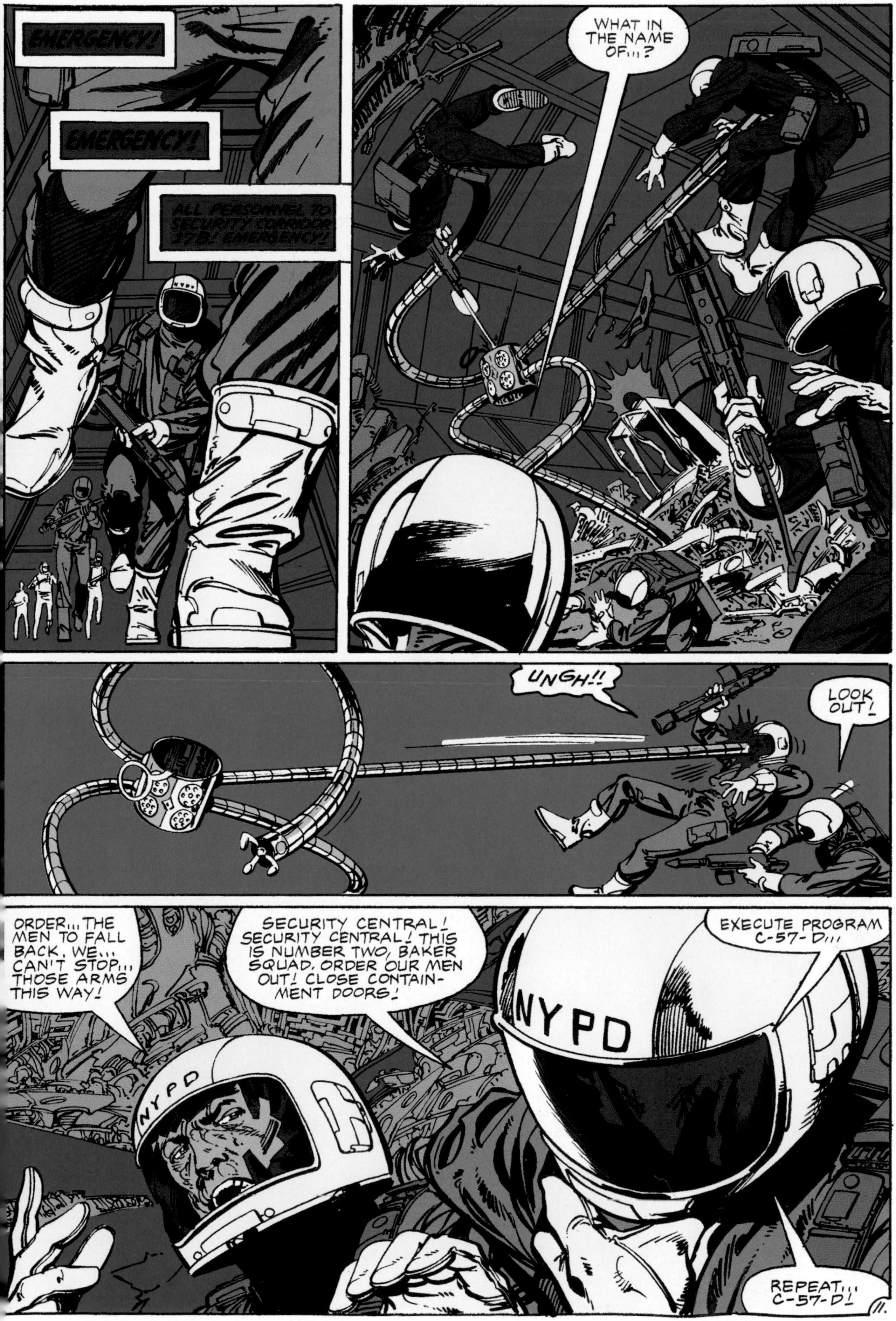
EMERGENCY!
EMERGENCY!
ALL PERSONNEL TO SECURITY CORRIDOR 17B! EMERGENCY!
WHAT IN THE NAME OF...?
UNGH!!
LOOK OUT!
ORDER... THE MEN TO FALL BACK. WE... CAN'T STOP... THOSE ARMS THIS WAY!
SECURITY CENTRAL! SECURITY CENTRAL! THIS IS NUMBER TWO, BAKER SQUAD. ORDER OUR MEN OUT! CLOSE CONTAINMENT DOORS!
NYPD
NYPD
EXECUTE PROGRAM C-57-D...
REPEAT... C-57-D!
11.

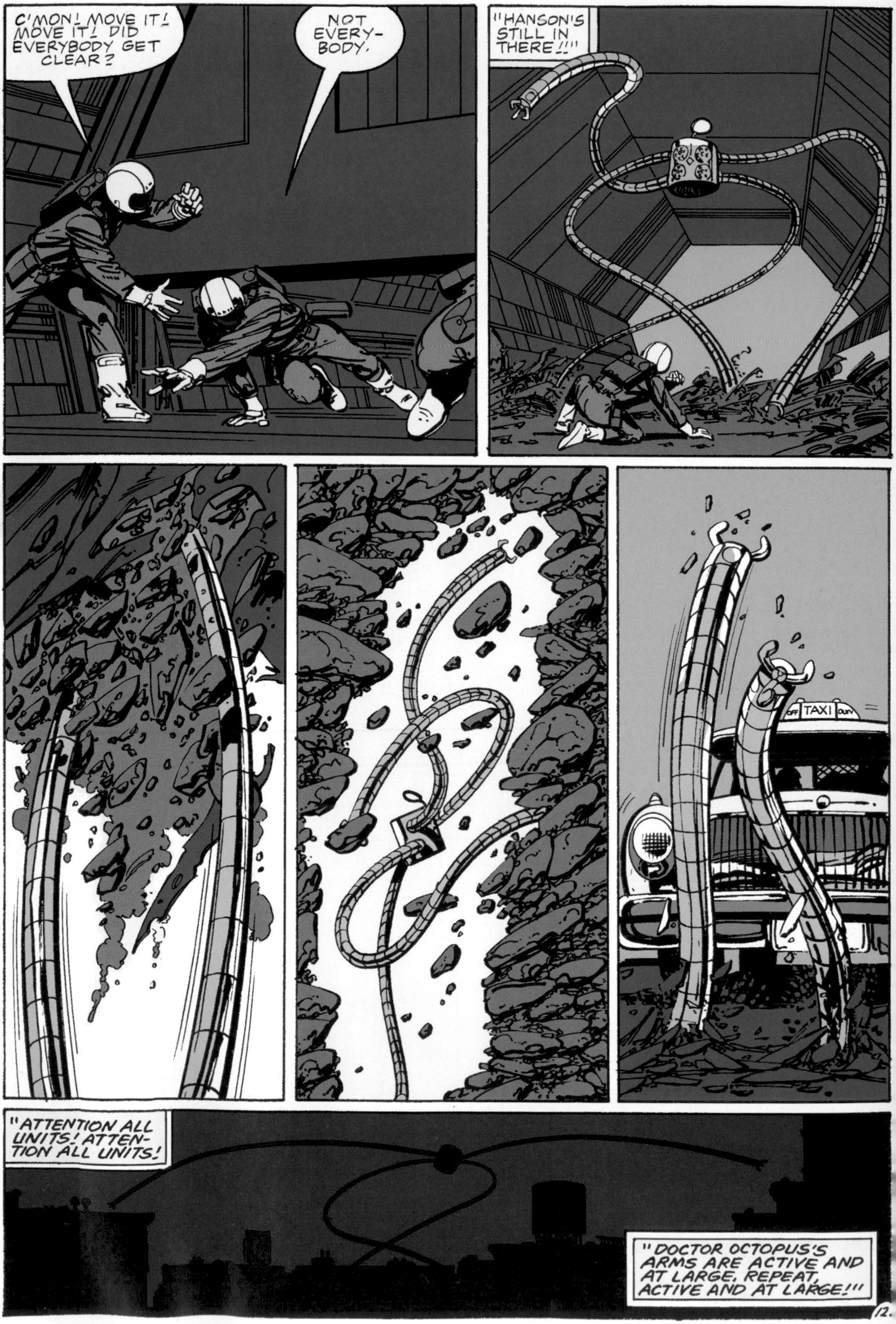
C'MON! MOVE IT! MOVE IT! DID EVERYBODY GET CLEAR?
NOT EVERY-BODY.
"HANSON'S STILL IN THERE!!"
TAXI
"ATTENTION ALL UNITS! ATTEN-TION ALL UNITS!
"DOCTOR OCTOPUS'S ARMS ARE ACTIVE AND AT LARGE. REPEAT, ACTIVE AND AT LARGE!"
12.

...MOST UNWELL...

OCTAVIUS... WHAT IS IT? WHAT'S...?

...WRONGGHH!!

HIS ARMS! GREAT SCOTT! IT'S OCTOPUS'S ROBOT ARMS!!

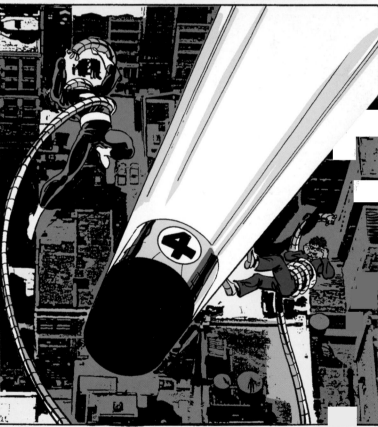

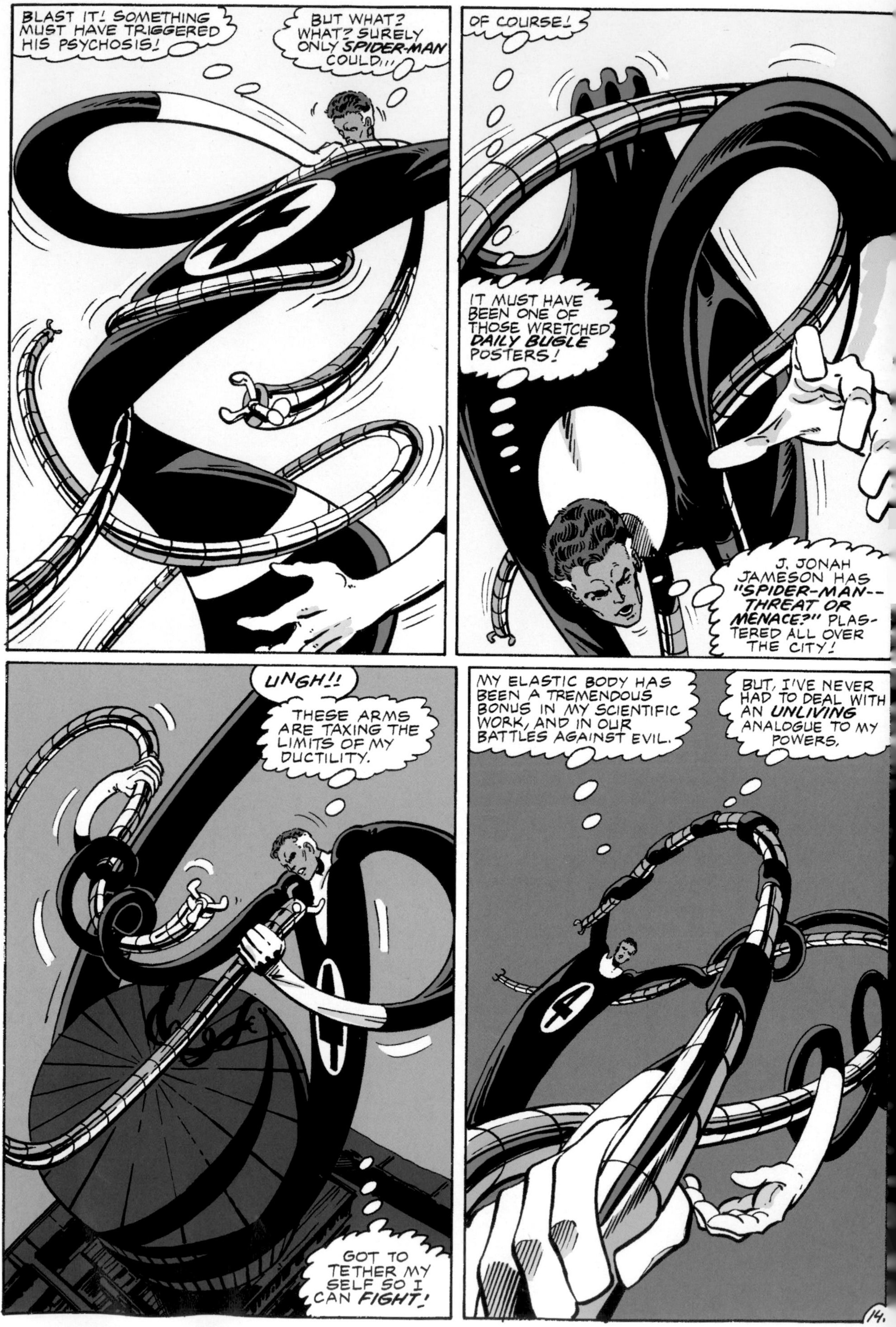
BLAST IT! SOMETHING MUST HAVE TRIGGERED HIS PSYCHOSIS!
BUT WHAT? WHAT? SURELY ONLY SPIDER-MAN COULD...
OF COURSE!
IT MUST HAVE BEEN ONE OF THOSE WRETCHED DAILY BUGLE POSTERS!
J. JONAH JAMESON HAS "SPIDER-MAN-- THREAT OR MENACE?" PLASTERED ALL OVER THE CITY!
UNGH!!
THESE ARMS ARE TAXING THE LIMITS OF MY DUCTILITY.
GOT TO TETHER MY SELF SO I CAN FIGHT!
MY ELASTIC BODY HAS BEEN A TREMENDOUS BONUS IN MY SCIENTIFIC WORK, AND IN OUR BATTLES AGAINST EVIL.
BUT, I'VE NEVER HAD TO DEAL WITH AN UNLIVING ANALOGUE TO MY POWERS.
14.

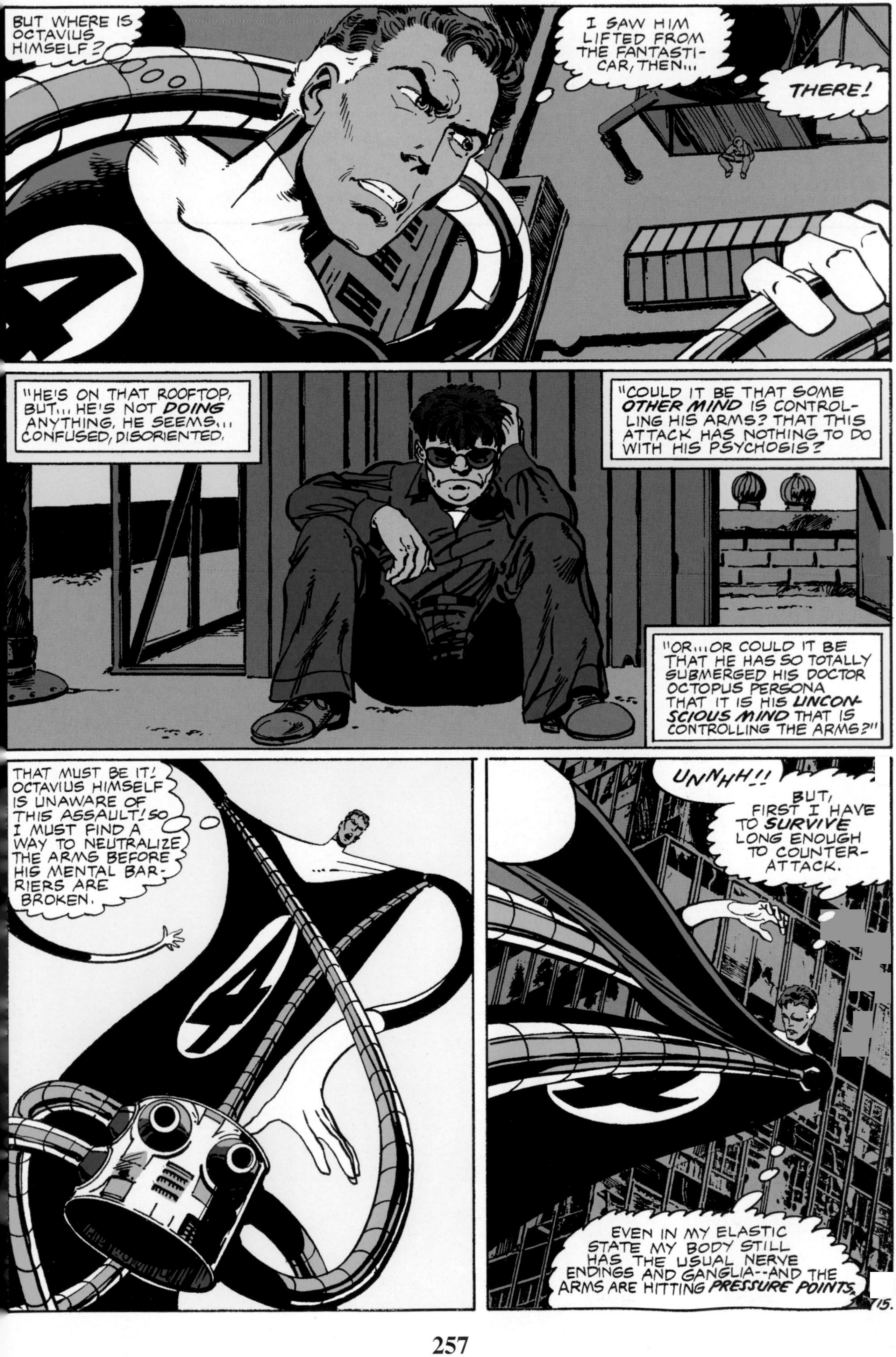

BUT WHERE IS OCTAVIUS HIMSELF?
I SAW HIM LIFTED FROM THE FANTASTI-CAR, THEN...
THERE!
"HE'S ON THAT ROOFTOP, BUT... HE'S NOT *DOING* ANYTHING. HE SEEMS... CONFUSED, DISORIENTED.
"COULD IT BE THAT SOME *OTHER MIND* IS CONTROLLING HIS ARMS? THAT THIS ATTACK HAS NOTHING TO DO WITH HIS PSYCHOSIS?
"OR... OR COULD IT BE THAT HE HAS SO TOTALLY SUBMERGED HIS DOCTOR OCTOPUS PERSONA THAT IT IS HIS *UNCONSCIOUS MIND* THAT IS CONTROLLING THE ARMS?"
THAT MUST BE IT! OCTAVIUS HIMSELF IS UNAWARE OF THIS ASSAULT! SO I MUST FIND A WAY TO NEUTRALIZE THE ARMS BEFORE HIS MENTAL BARRIERS ARE BROKEN.
UNNHH!!
BUT, FIRST I HAVE TO *SURVIVE* LONG ENOUGH TO COUNTER-ATTACK.
EVEN IN MY ELASTIC STATE MY BODY STILL HAS THE USUAL NERVE ENDINGS AND GANGLIA--AND THE ARMS ARE HITTING *PRESSURE POINTS*.
15.

THE ARMS SEEM TO HAVE "DECIDED" TO CARRY THE BATTLE INDOORS.

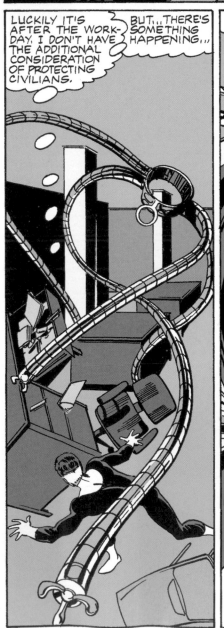

LUCKILY IT'S AFTER THE WORK-DAY, I DON'T HAVE THE ADDITIONAL CONSIDERATION OF PROTECTING CIVILIANS.

BUT...THERE'S SOMETHING HAPPENING...

YES. IT'S...UNGH...SUBTLE, BUT THE ARMS ARE ALTERING THEIR ATTACK...

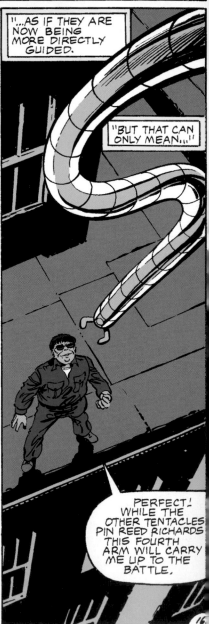

"...AS IF THEY ARE NOW BEING MORE DIRECTLY GUIDED.

"BUT THAT CAN ONLY MEAN...."

PERFECT! WHILE THE OTHER TENTACLES PIN REED RICHARDS THIS FOURTH ARM WILL CARRY ME UP TO THE BATTLE.

16.

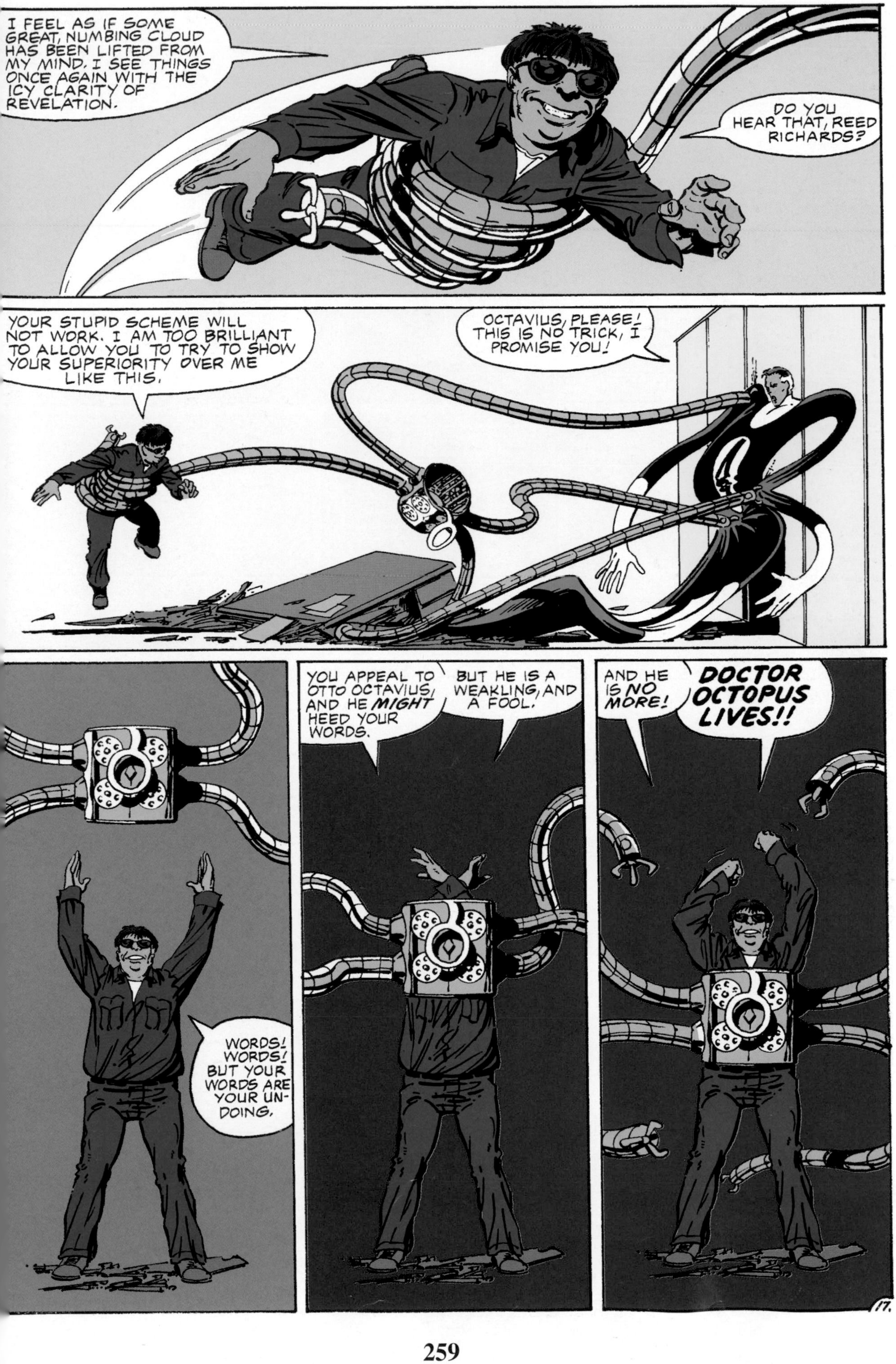
I FEEL AS IF SOME GREAT, NUMBING CLOUD HAS BEEN LIFTED FROM MY MIND. I SEE THINGS ONCE AGAIN WITH THE ICY CLARITY OF REVELATION.
DO YOU HEAR THAT, REED RICHARDS?
YOUR STUPID SCHEME WILL NOT WORK. I AM TOO BRILLIANT TO ALLOW YOU TO TRY TO SHOW YOUR SUPERIORITY OVER ME LIKE THIS.
OCTAVIUS, PLEASE! THIS IS NO TRICK, I PROMISE YOU!
WORDS! WORDS! BUT YOUR WORDS ARE YOUR UNDOING.
YOU APPEAL TO OTTO OCTAVIUS, AND HE MIGHT HEED YOUR WORDS.
BUT HE IS A WEAKLING, AND A FOOL.
AND HE IS NO MORE!
DOCTOR OCTOPUS LIVES!!
17.

AND DOCTOR OCTOPUS **KILLS!**

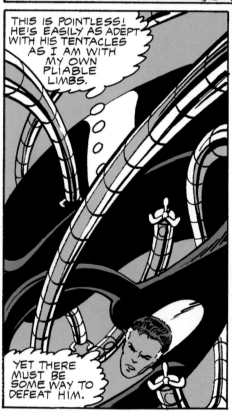

THIS IS POINTLESS! HE'S EASILY AS ADEPT WITH HIS TENTACLES AS I AM WITH MY OWN PLIABLE LIMBS.

YET THERE MUST BE SOME WAY TO DEFEAT HIM.

"SOMETHING I'M OVERLOOKING...

"OF COURSE! THE MANUAL CONTROLS ON THE CHEST PLATE!

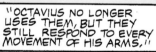

"OCTAVIUS NO LONGER USES THEM, BUT THEY STILL RESPOND TO EVERY MOVEMENT OF HIS ARMS."

IF I CAN JUST REACH THEM...

"I DID IT!"

WHAT...

...THE...

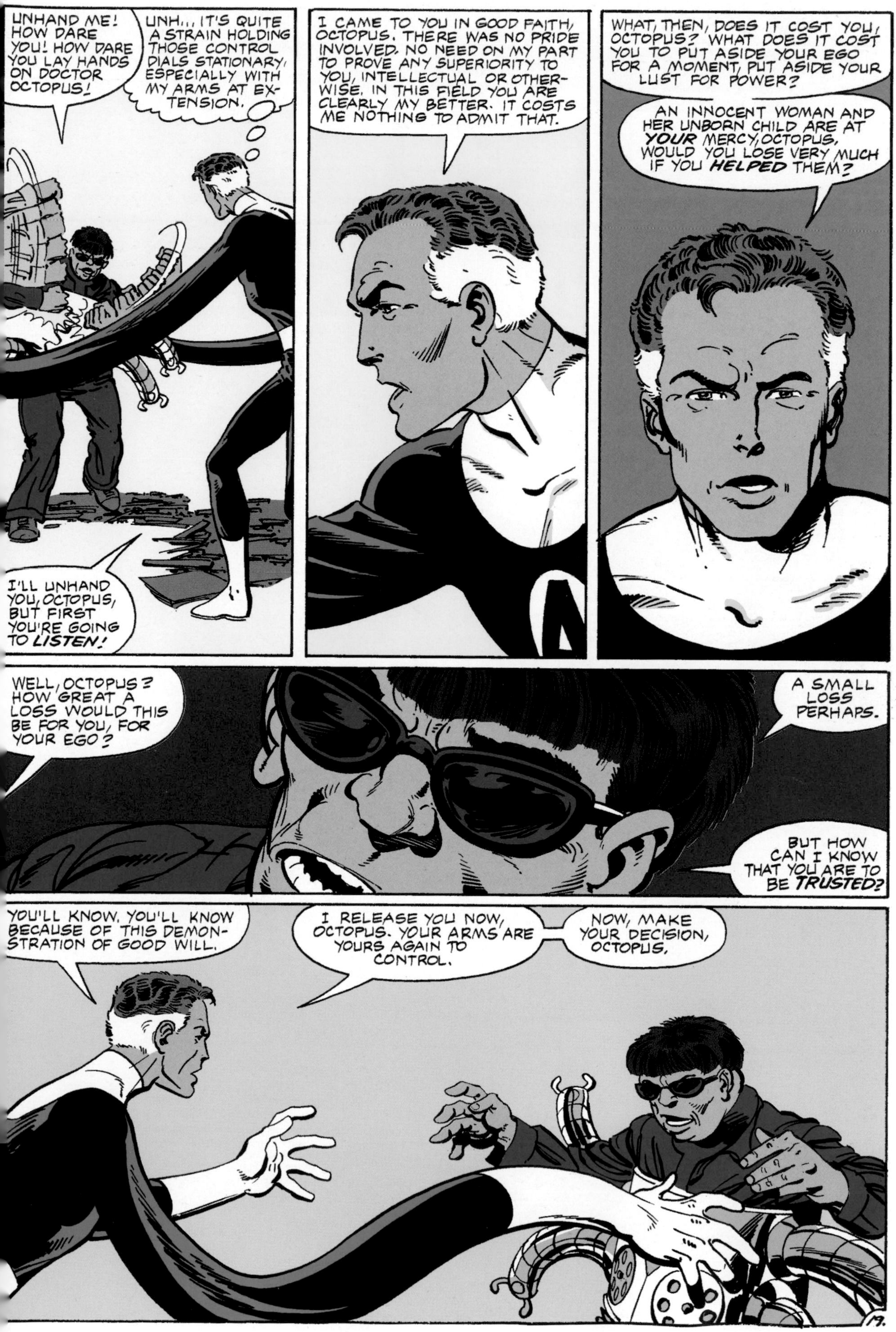
UNHAND ME! HOW DARE YOU! HOW DARE YOU LAY HANDS ON DOCTOR OCTOPUS!
UNH... IT'S QUITE A STRAIN HOLDING THOSE CONTROL DIALS STATIONARY, ESPECIALLY WITH MY ARMS AT EXTENSION.
I'LL UNHAND YOU, OCTOPUS, BUT FIRST YOU'RE GOING TO LISTEN!
I CAME TO YOU IN GOOD FAITH, OCTOPUS. THERE WAS NO PRIDE INVOLVED, NO NEED ON MY PART TO PROVE ANY SUPERIORITY TO YOU, INTELLECTUAL OR OTHERWISE. IN THIS FIELD YOU ARE CLEARLY MY BETTER. IT COSTS ME NOTHING TO ADMIT THAT.
WHAT, THEN, DOES IT COST YOU, OCTOPUS? WHAT DOES IT COST YOU TO PUT ASIDE YOUR EGO FOR A MOMENT, PUT ASIDE YOUR LUST FOR POWER?
AN INNOCENT WOMAN AND HER UNBORN CHILD ARE AT YOUR MERCY, OCTOPUS, WOULD YOU LOSE VERY MUCH IF YOU HELPED THEM?
WELL, OCTOPUS? HOW GREAT A LOSS WOULD THIS BE FOR YOU, FOR YOUR EGO?
A SMALL LOSS PERHAPS.
BUT HOW CAN I KNOW THAT YOU ARE TO BE TRUSTED?
YOU'LL KNOW. YOU'LL KNOW BECAUSE OF THIS DEMONSTRATION OF GOOD WILL.
I RELEASE YOU NOW, OCTOPUS. YOUR ARMS ARE YOURS AGAIN TO CONTROL.
NOW, MAKE YOUR DECISION, OCTOPUS.
19.

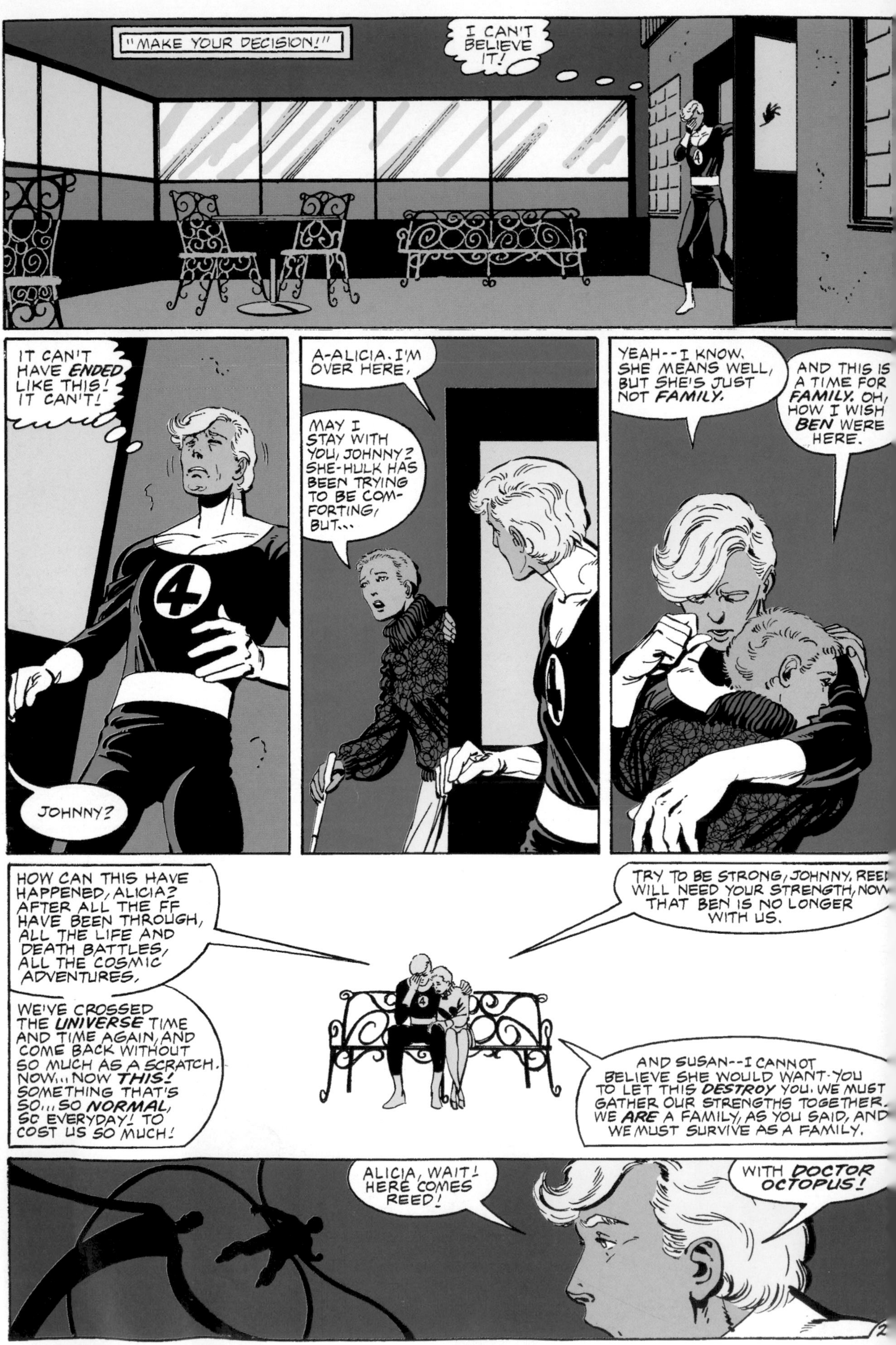
"MAKE YOUR DECISION!"
I CAN'T BELIEVE IT!
IT CAN'T HAVE ENDED LIKE THIS! IT CAN'T!
JOHNNY?
A-ALICIA. I'M OVER HERE.
MAY I STAY WITH YOU, JOHNNY? SHE-HULK HAS BEEN TRYING TO BE COMFORTING, BUT...
YEAH--I KNOW. SHE MEANS WELL, BUT SHE'S JUST NOT FAMILY.
AND THIS IS A TIME FOR FAMILY. OH, HOW I WISH BEN WERE HERE.
HOW CAN THIS HAVE HAPPENED, ALICIA? AFTER ALL THE FF HAVE BEEN THROUGH, ALL THE LIFE AND DEATH BATTLES, ALL THE COSMIC ADVENTURES.
WE'VE CROSSED THE UNIVERSE TIME AND TIME AGAIN, AND COME BACK WITHOUT SO MUCH AS A SCRATCH. NOW... NOW THIS! SOMETHING THAT'S SO... SO NORMAL, SO EVERYDAY! TO COST US SO MUCH!
TRY TO BE STRONG, JOHNNY. REED WILL NEED YOUR STRENGTH, NOW THAT BEN IS NO LONGER WITH US.
AND SUSAN--I CANNOT BELIEVE SHE WOULD WANT YOU TO LET THIS DESTROY YOU. WE MUST GATHER OUR STRENGTHS TOGETHER. WE ARE A FAMILY, AS YOU SAID, AND WE MUST SURVIVE AS A FAMILY.
ALICIA, WAIT! HERE COMES REED!
WITH DOCTOR OCTOPUS!

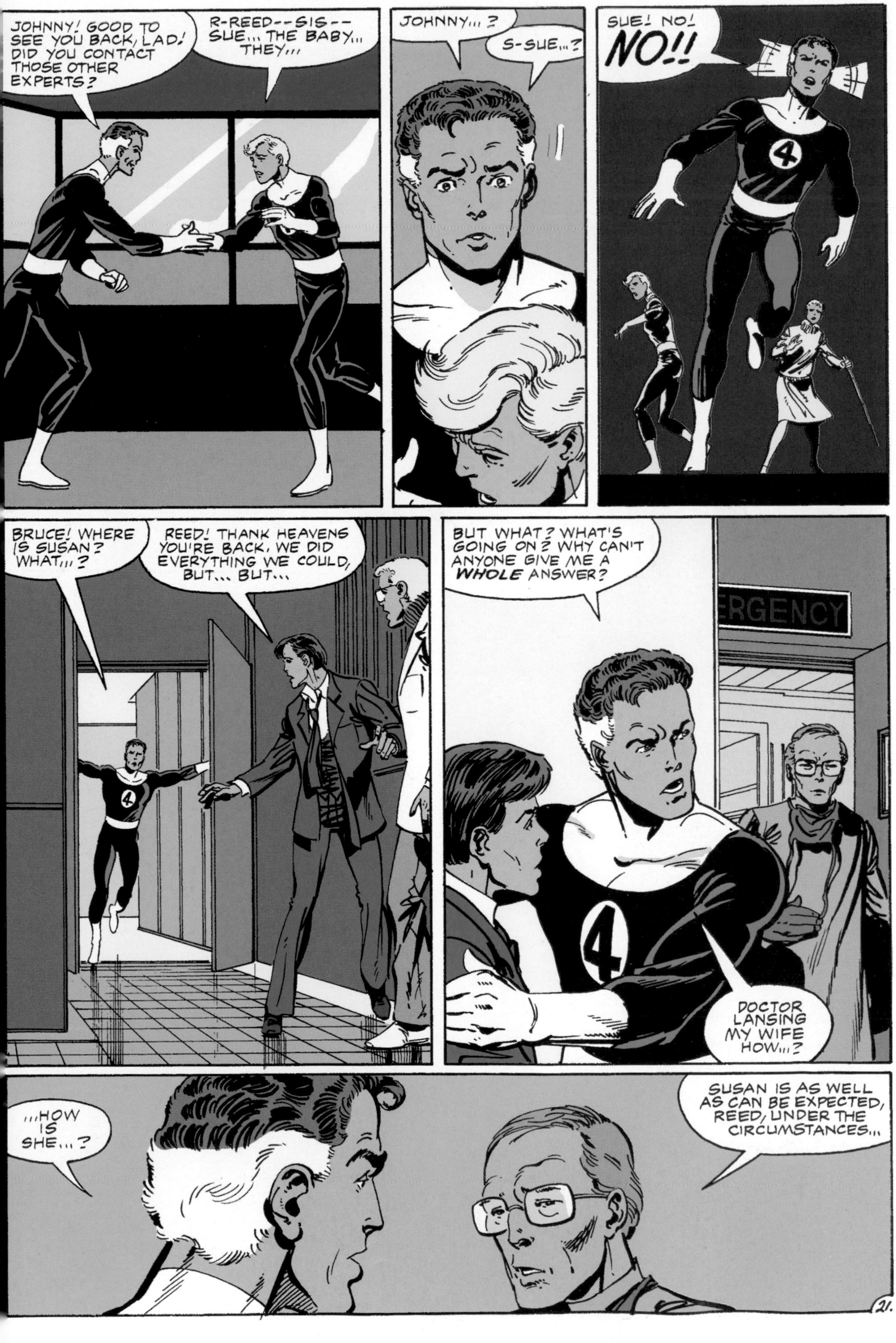
JOHNNY! GOOD TO SEE YOU BACK, LAD! DID YOU CONTACT THOSE OTHER EXPERTS?
R-REED--SIS--SUE... THE BABY... THEY...
JOHNNY...?
S-SUE...?
SUE! NO! NO!!
BRUCE! WHERE IS SUSAN? WHAT...?
REED! THANK HEAVENS YOU'RE BACK. WE DID EVERYTHING WE COULD, BUT... BUT...
BUT WHAT? WHAT'S GOING ON? WHY CAN'T ANYONE GIVE ME A WHOLE ANSWER?
ERGENCY
DOCTOR LANSING MY WIFE HOW...?
...HOW IS SHE...?
SUSAN IS AS WELL AS CAN BE EXPECTED, REED, UNDER THE CIRCUMSTANCES...
21.

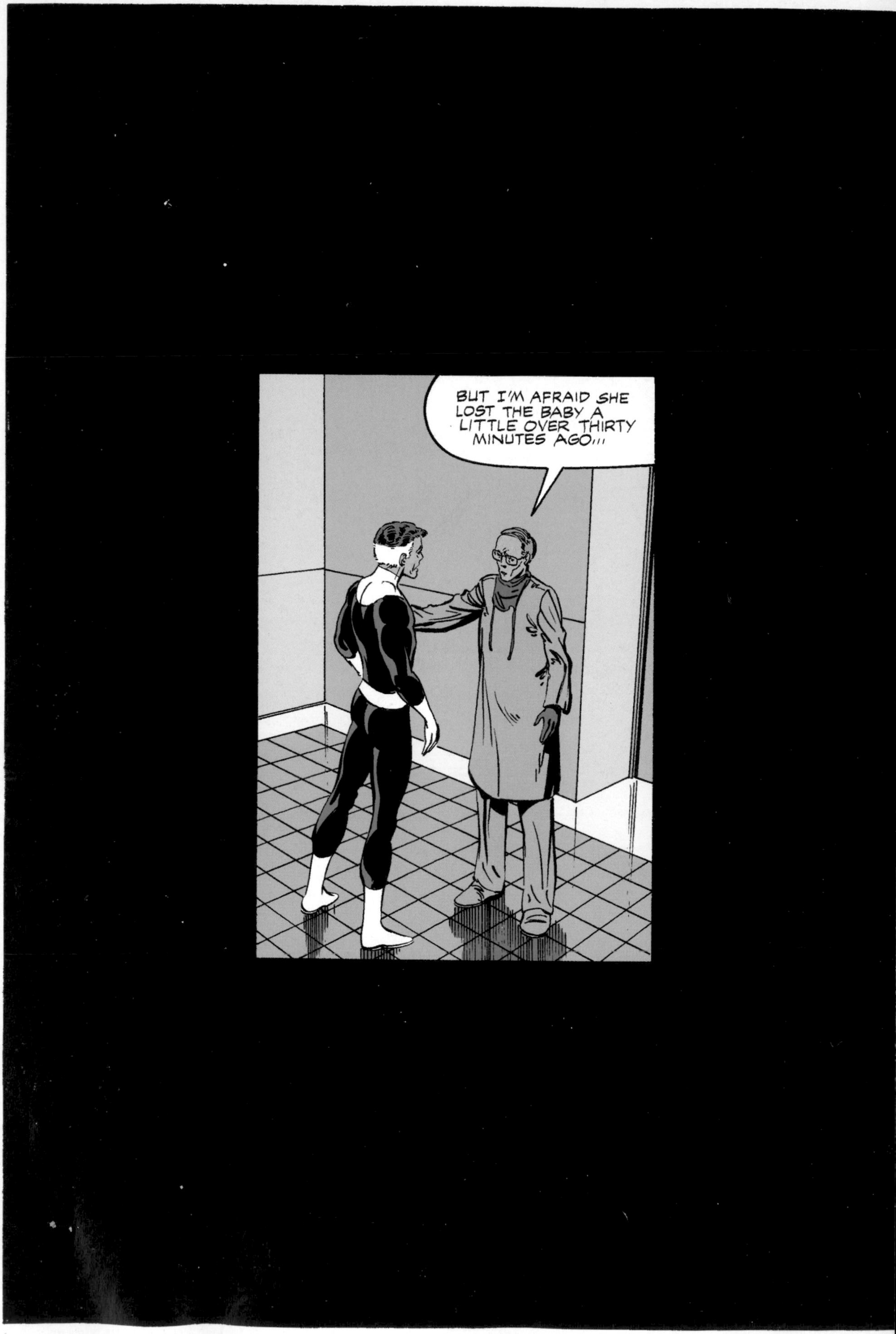
BUT I'M AFRAID SHE LOST THE BABY A LITTLE OVER THIRTY MINUTES AGO...

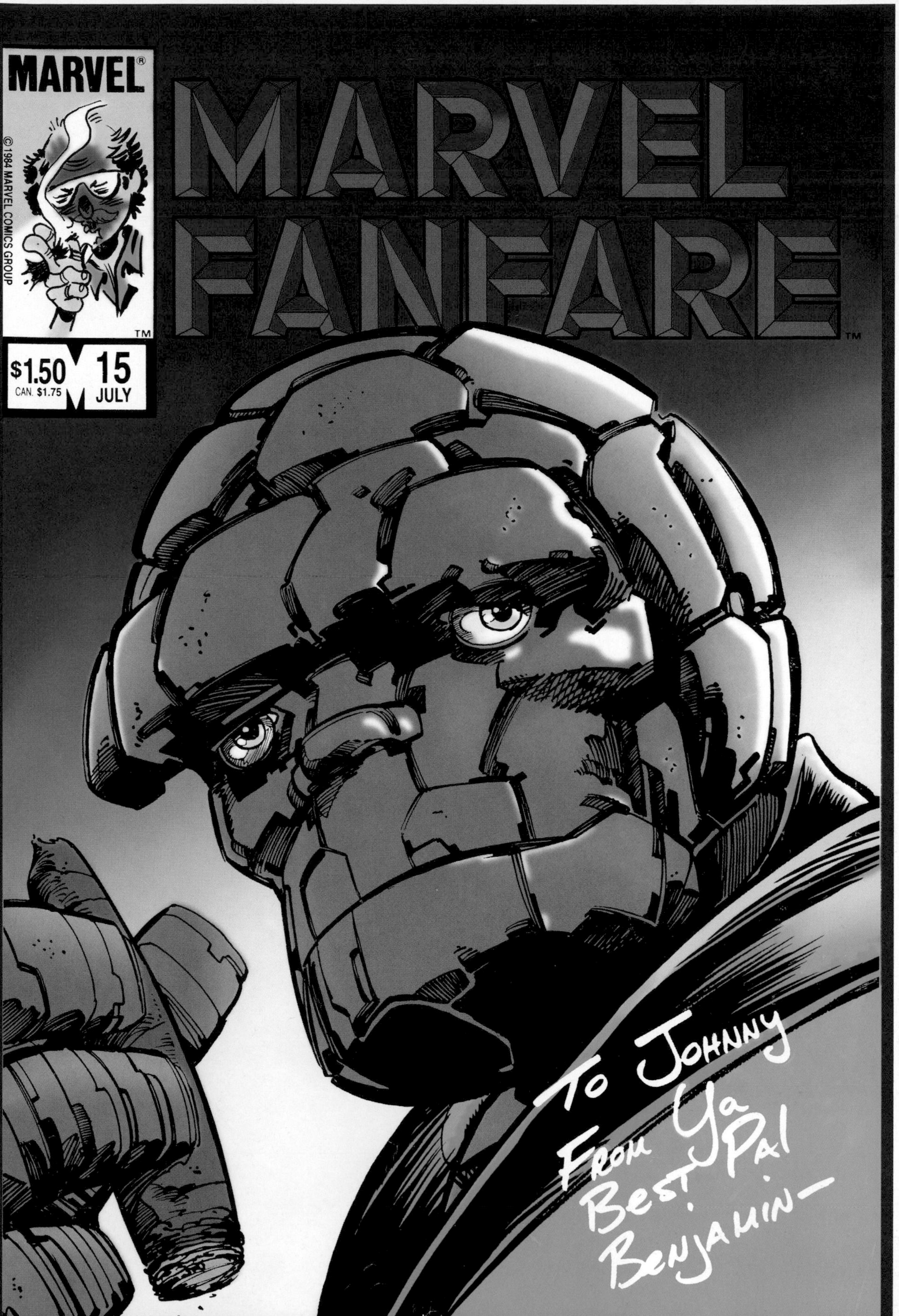

MARVEL
© 1984 MARVEL COMICS GROUP
MARVEL FANFARE
$1.50
CAN. $1.75
15
JULY
To Johnny
From Ya
Best Pal
Benjamin—

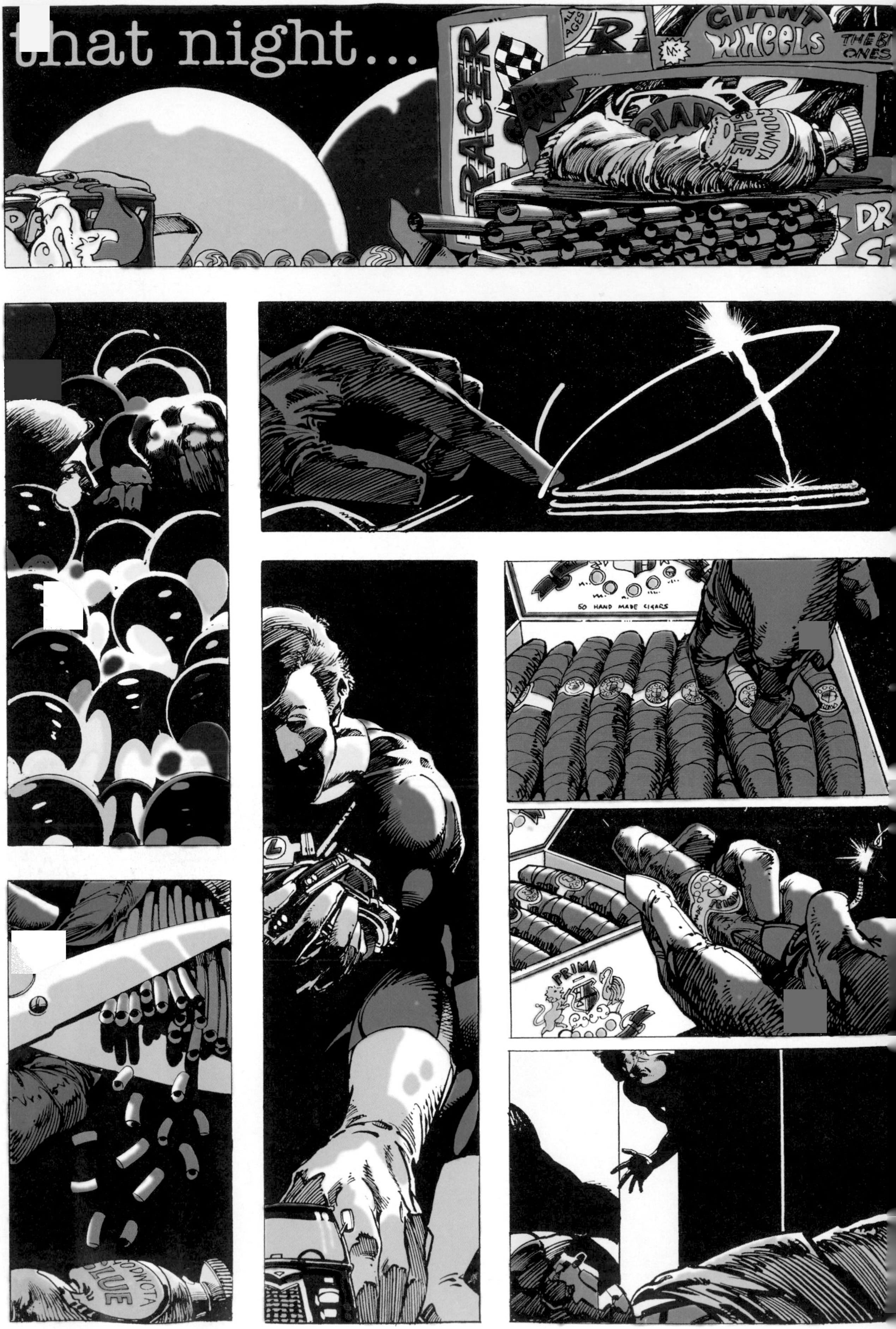
that night...
RACER
ALL AGES
GIANT WHEELS
DIE CAST
GODWOTA GLUE
50 HAND MADE CIGARS
PRIMA
GODWOTA GLUE

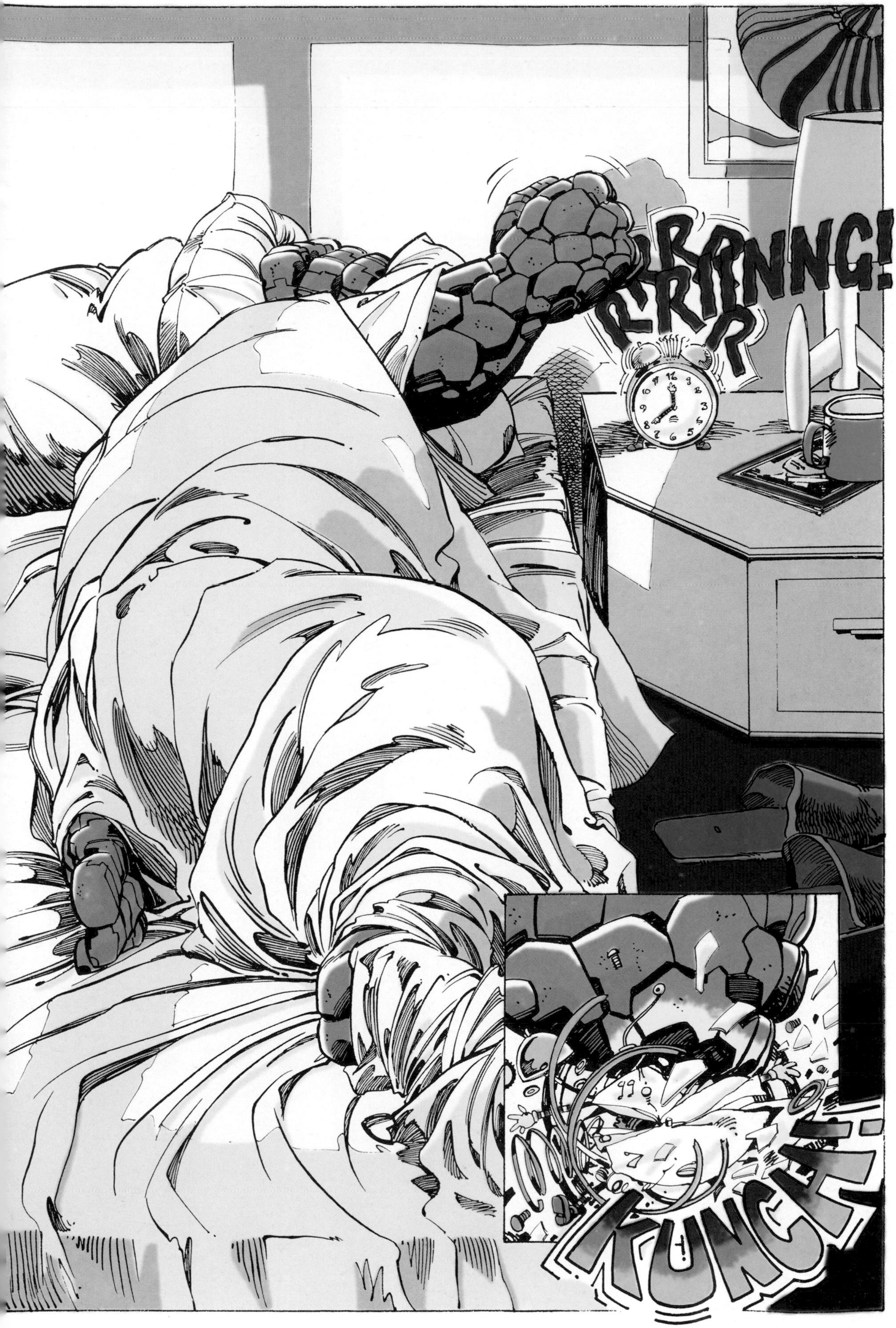
RRRRIINNG!
KUNCH!

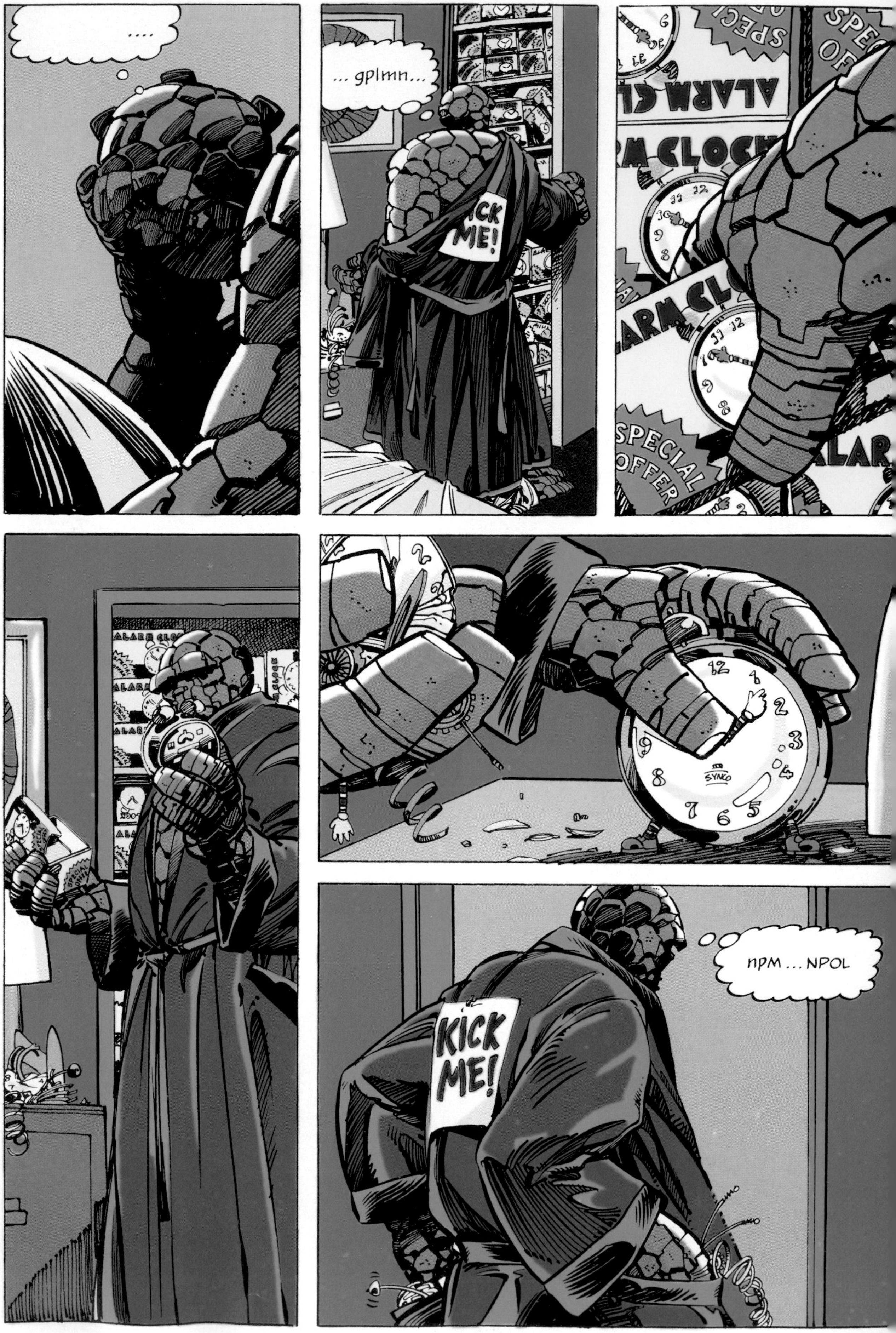
....
... gplmn...
KICK ME!
ALARM CLOCK
SPECIAL OFFER
SYNKO
KICK ME!
npm ... NPOL

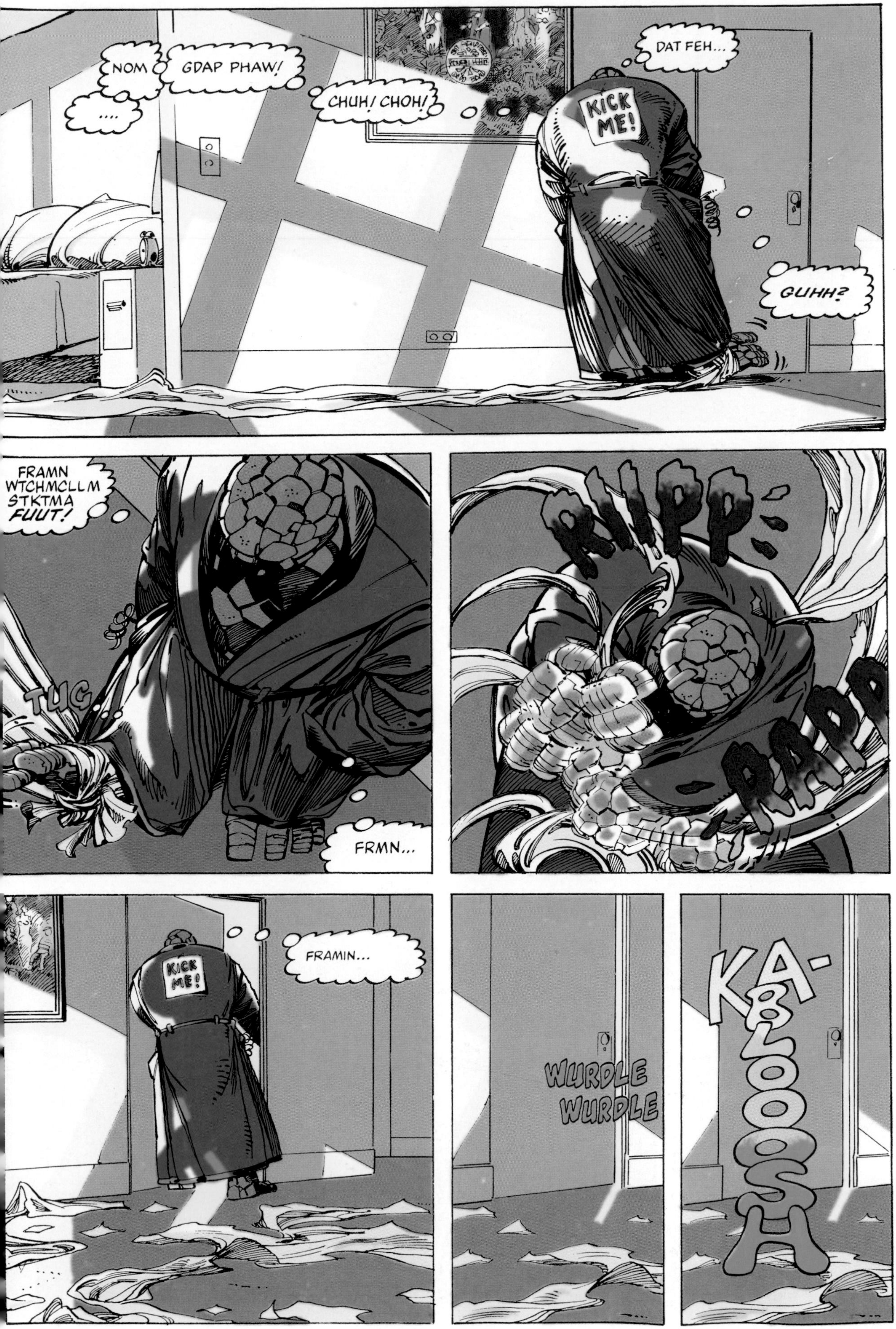

NOM
....
GDAP PHAW!
CHUH! CHOH!
DAT FEH...
KICK ME!
GUHH?
FRAMN WTCHMCLLM STKTMA FUUT!
TUG
FRMN...
RIIPP
RAPP
FRAMIN...
KICK ME!
WURDLE WURDLE
KA-BLOOOSH

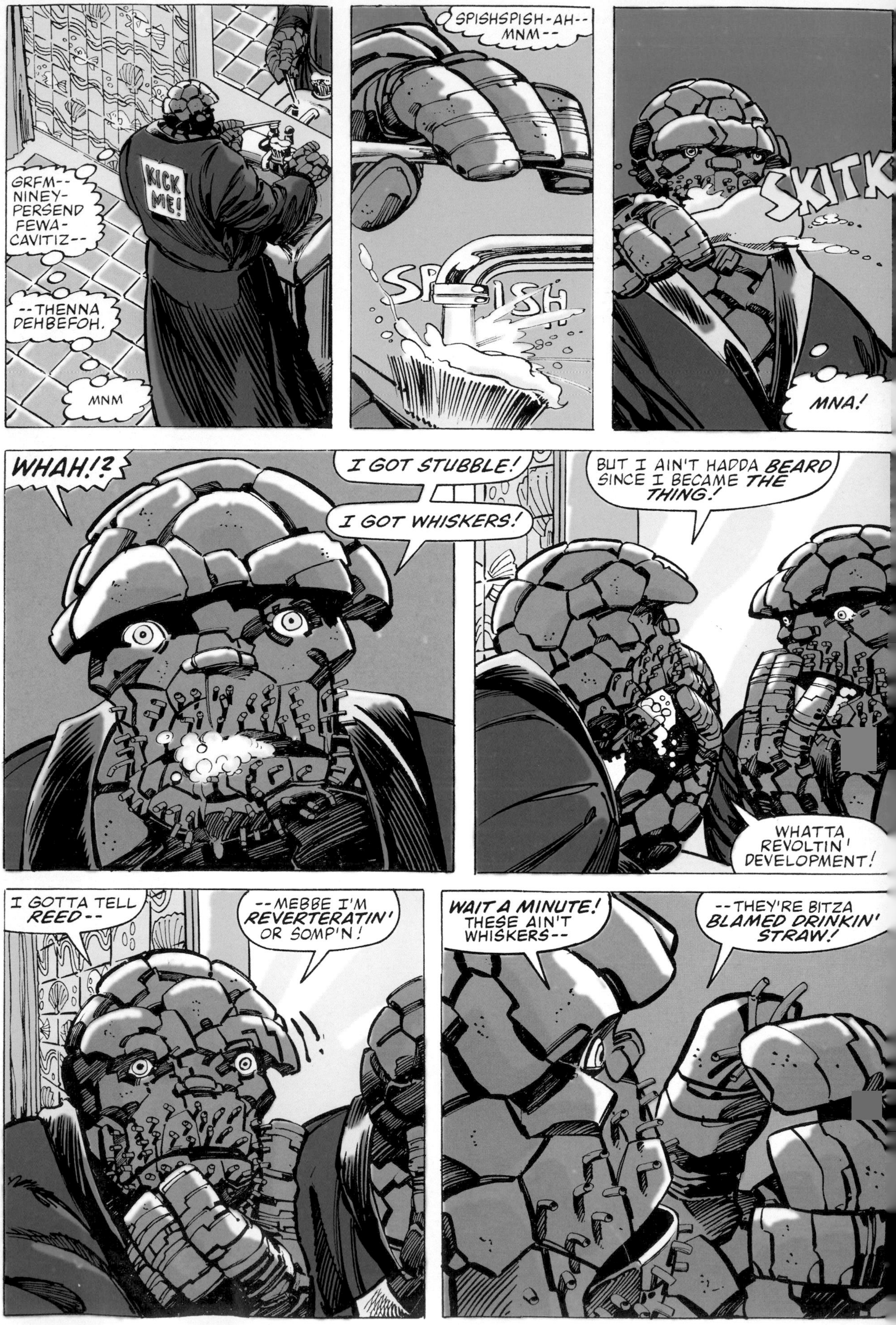
GRFM--
NINEY-
PERSEND
FEWA-
CAVITIZ--
--THENNA
DEHBEFOH.
MNM
KICK ME!
SPISHSPISH-AH--
MNM--
SPISH
SKITK
MNA!
WHAH!?
I GOT STUBBLE!
I GOT WHISKERS!
BUT I AIN'T HADDA BEARD SINCE I BECAME THE THING!
WHATTA REVOLTIN' DEVELOPMENT!
I GOTTA TELL REED--
--MEBBE I'M REVERTERATIN' OR SOMP'N!
WAIT A MINUTE! THESE AIN'T WHISKERS--
--THEY'RE BITZA BLAMED DRINKIN' STRAW!

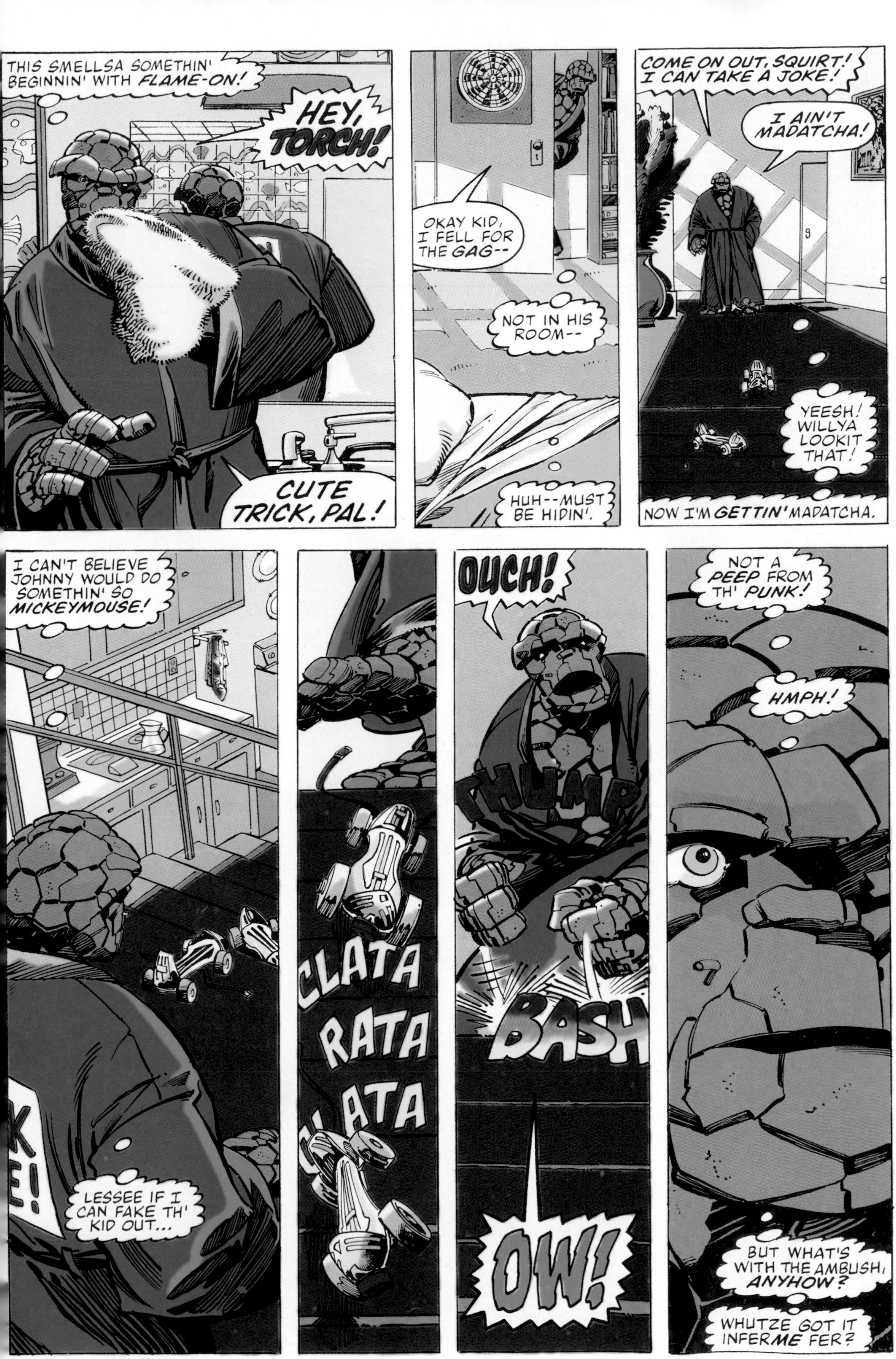

THIS SMELLSA SOMETHIN' BEGINNIN' WITH FLAME-ON!
HEY, TORCH!
CUTE TRICK, PAL!
OKAY KID, I FELL FOR THE GAG--
NOT IN HIS ROOM--
HUH--MUST BE HIDIN'.
COME ON OUT, SQUIRT! I CAN TAKE A JOKE!
I AIN'T MADATCHA!
YEESH! WILLYA LOOKIT THAT!
NOW I'M GETTIN' MADATCHA.
I CAN'T BELIEVE JOHNNY WOULD DO SOMETHIN' SO MICKEYMOUSE!
LESSEE IF I CAN FAKE TH' KID OUT...
CLATA
RATA
ATA
OUCH!
THUMP
BASH
OW!
NOT A PEEP FROM TH' PUNK!
HMPH!
BUT WHAT'S WITH THE AMBUSH, ANYHOW?
WHUTZE GOT IT INFERME FER?

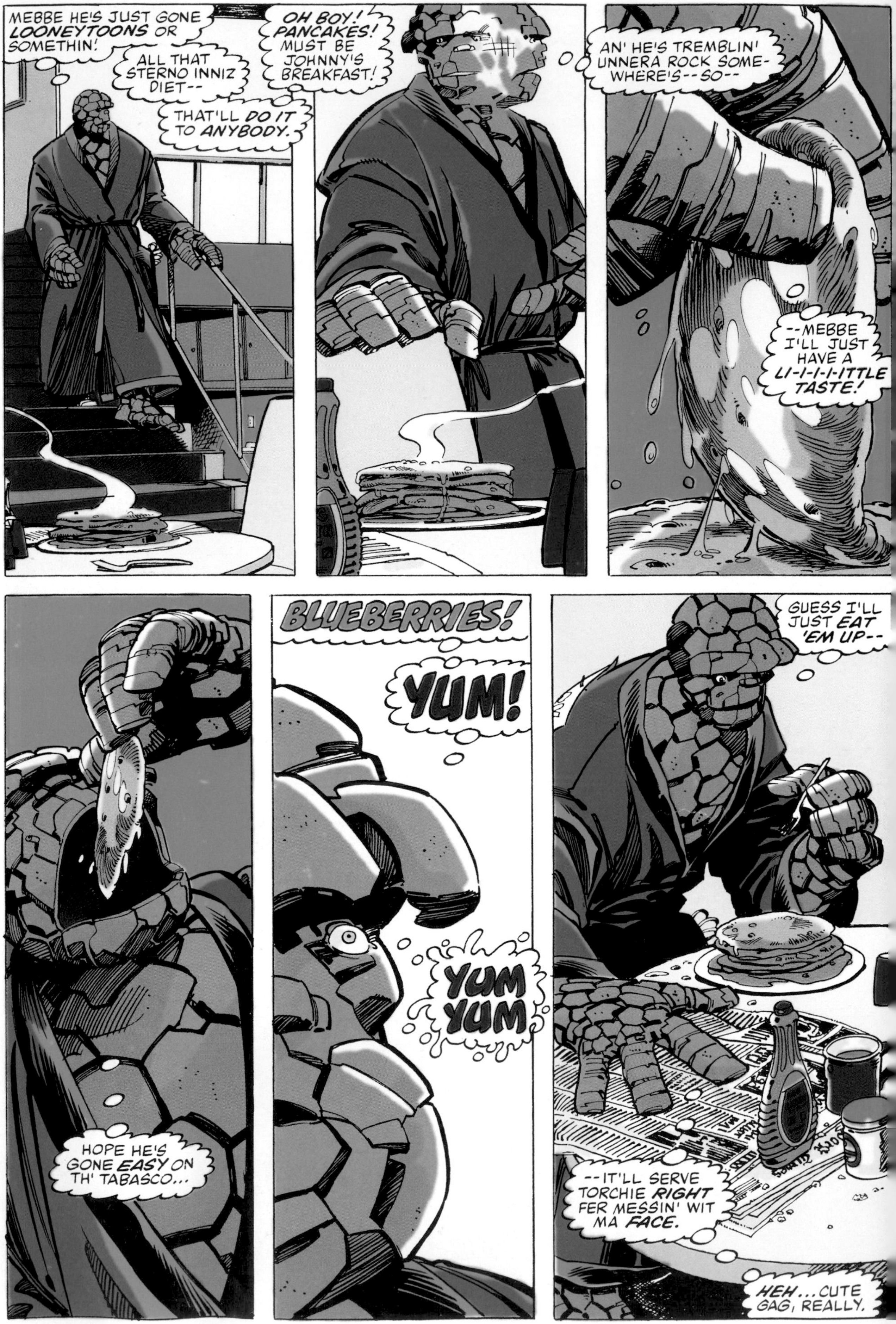
MEBBE HE'S JUST GONE LOONEYTOONS OR SOMETHIN!
ALL THAT STERNO INNIZ DIET--
THAT'LL DO IT TO ANYBODY.
OH BOY! PANCAKES! MUST BE JOHNNY'S BREAKFAST!
AN' HE'S TREMBLIN' UNNERA ROCK SOME-WHERE'S--SO--
--MEBBE I'LL JUST HAVE A LI-I-I-I-ITTLE TASTE!
HOPE HE'S GONE EASY ON TH' TABASCO...
BLUEBERRIES!
YUM!
YUM YUM
GUESS I'LL JUST EAT 'EM UP--
--IT'LL SERVE TORCHIE RIGHT FER MESSIN' WIT MA FACE.
HEH...CUTE GAG, REALLY.

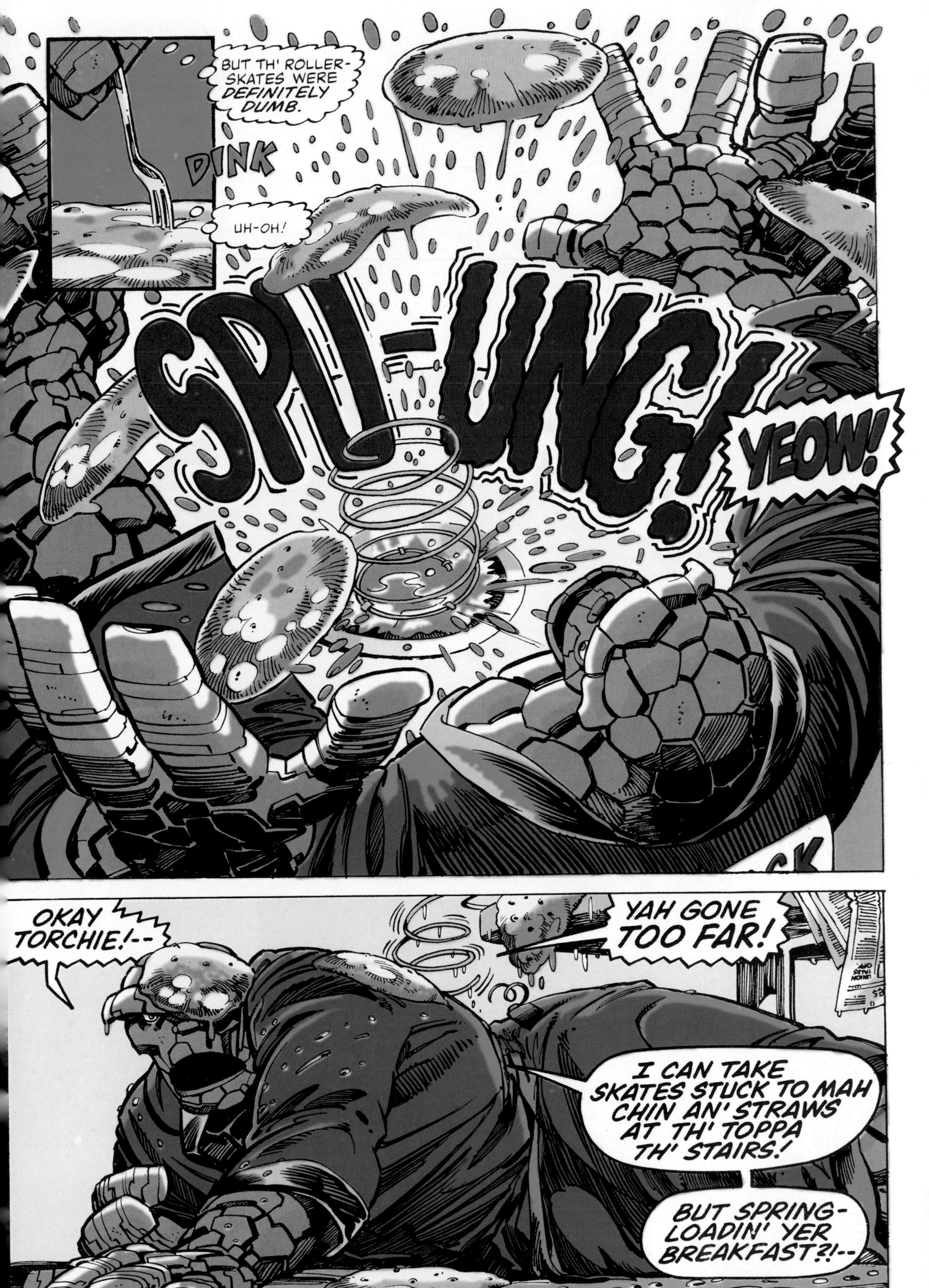
BUT TH' ROLLER-SKATES WERE DEFINITELY DUMB.
DINK
UH-OH!
SPLI-UNG!
YEOW!
OKAY TORCHIE!--
YAH GONE TOO FAR!
I CAN TAKE SKATES STUCK TO MAH CHIN AN' STRAWS AT TH' TOPPA TH' STAIRS!
BUT SPRING-LOADIN' YER BREAKFAST?!--

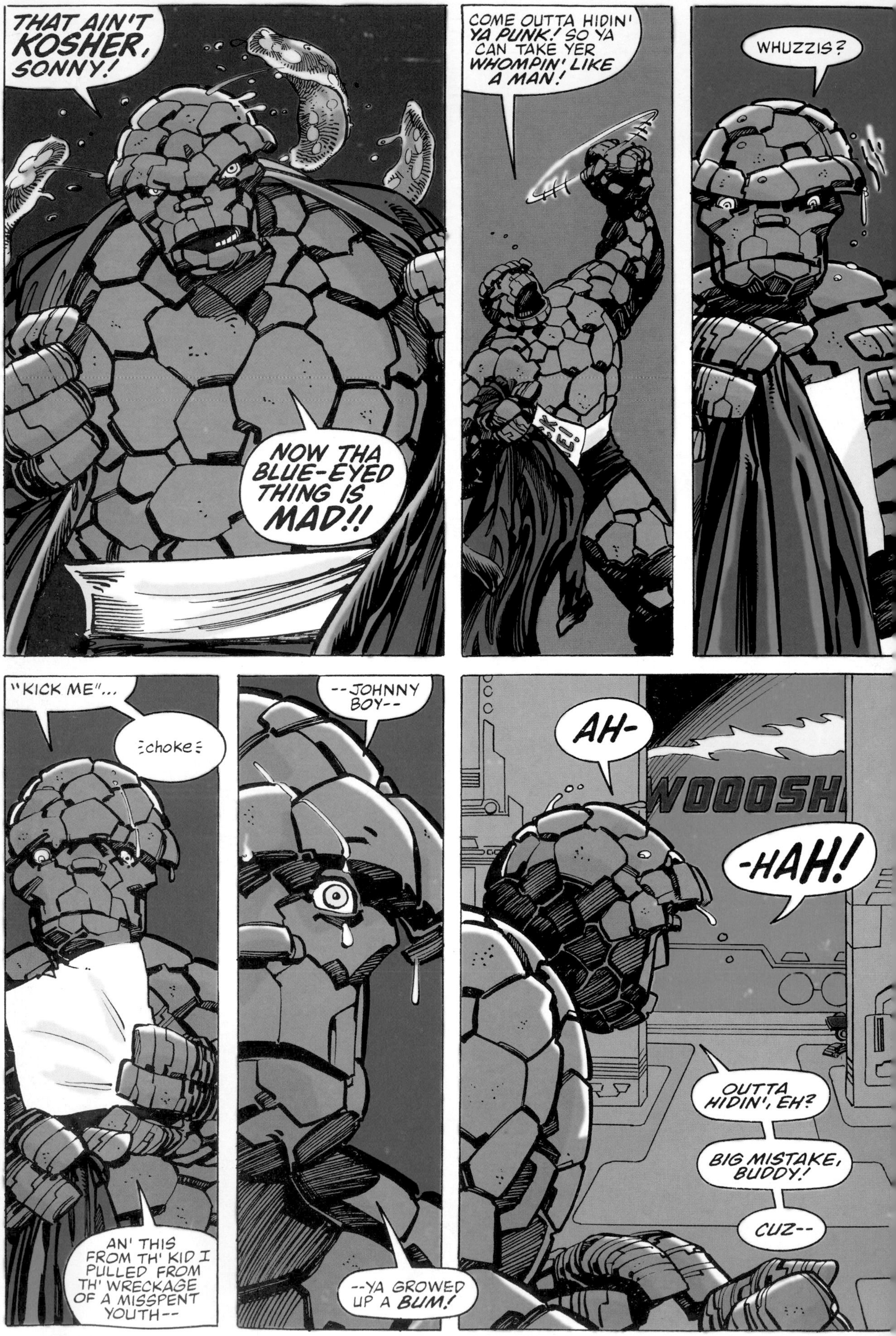
THAT AIN'T KOSHER, SONNY!
NOW THA BLUE-EYED THING IS MAD!!
COME OUTTA HIDIN' YA PUNK! SO YA CAN TAKE YER WHOMPIN' LIKE A MAN!
WHUZZIS?
"KICK ME"...
choke
AN' THIS FROM TH' KID I PULLED FROM TH' WRECKAGE OF A MISSPENT YOUTH--
--JOHNNY BOY--
--YA GROWED UP A BUM!
AH-
WOOOSH
-HAH!
OUTTA HIDIN', EH?
BIG MISTAKE, BUDDY!
CUZ--

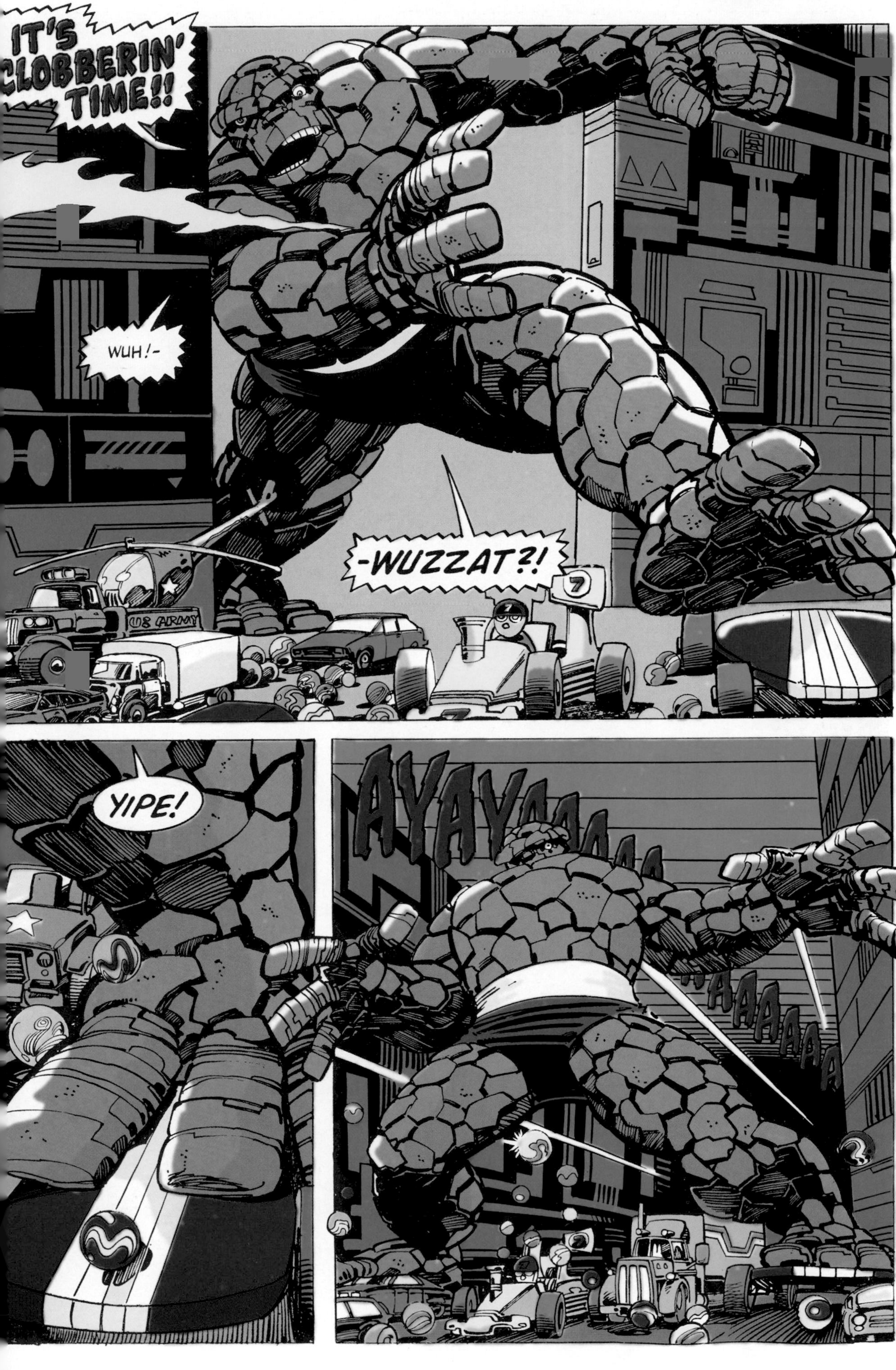
IT'S CLOBBERIN' TIME!!
WUH!-
-WUZZAT?!
YIPE!
AYAYAAAAAA
AAAAAAA

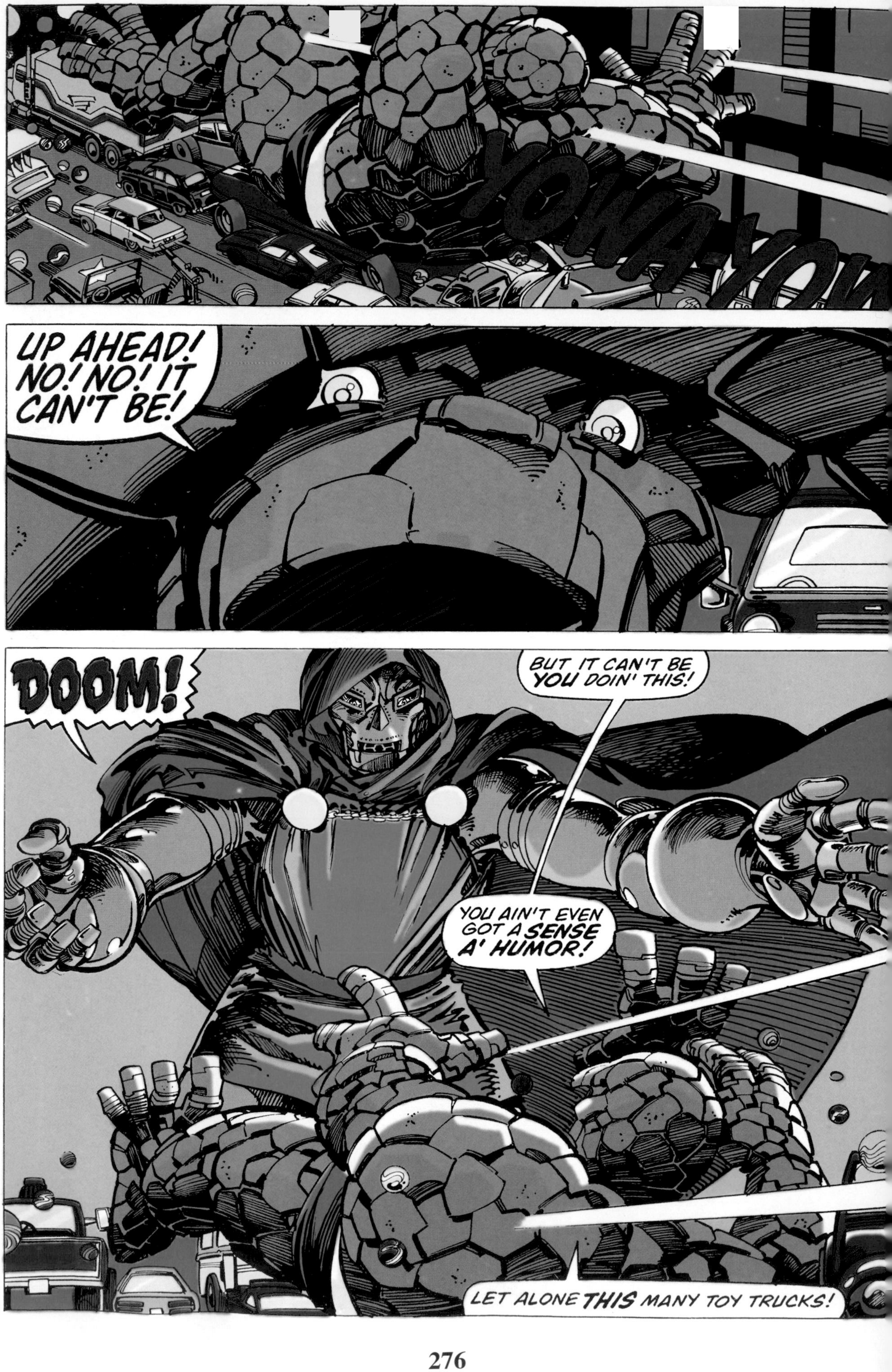
YOWA-YOW
UP AHEAD! NO! NO! IT CAN'T BE!
DOOM!
BUT IT CAN'T BE YOU DOIN' THIS!
YOU AIN'T EVEN GOT A SENSE A' HUMOR!
LET ALONE THIS MANY TOY TRUCKS!

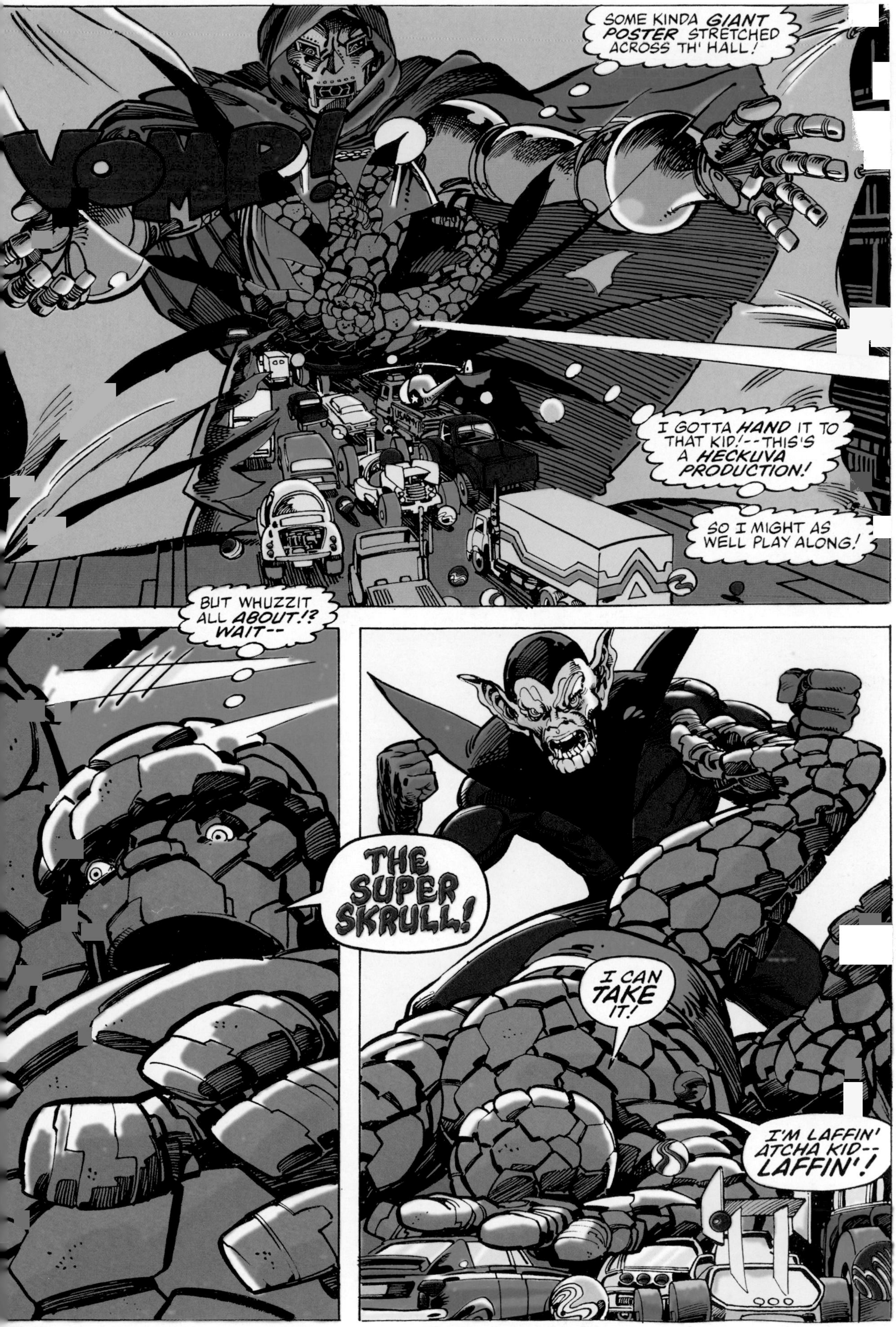
SOME KINDA GIANT POSTER STRETCHED ACROSS TH' HALL!
VOMP!
I GOTTA HAND IT TO THAT KID!--THIS'S A HECKUVA PRODUCTION!
SO I MIGHT AS WELL PLAY ALONG!
BUT WHUZZIT ALL ABOUT!? WAIT--
THE SUPER SKRULL!
I CAN TAKE IT!
I'M LAFFIN' ATCHA KID--LAFFIN'!

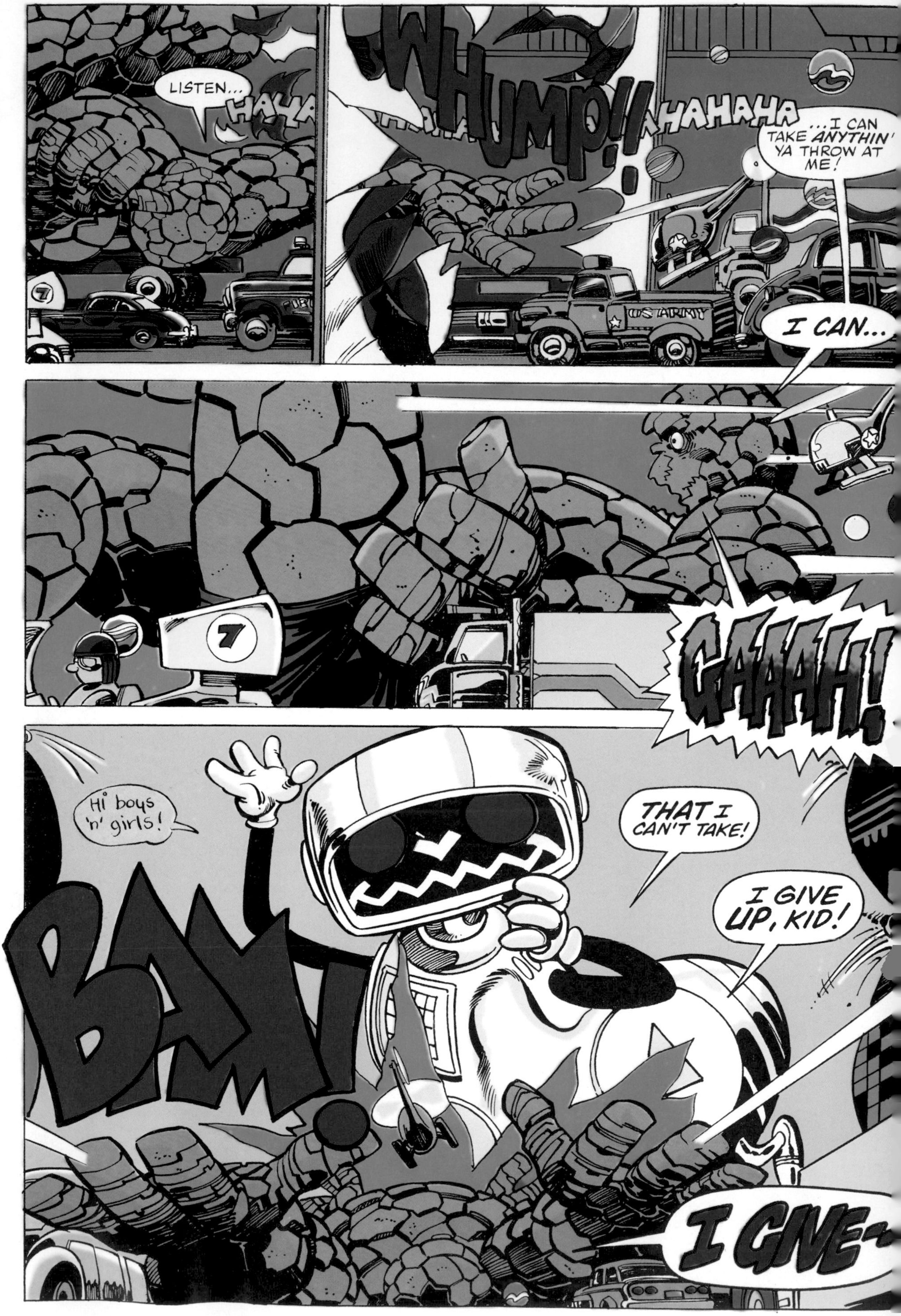
LISTEN...
HAHA
WHUMP!!
HAHAHAHA
...I CAN TAKE ANYTHIN' YA THROW AT ME!
I CAN...
GAAAH!
Hi boys 'n' girls!
BAM!
THAT I CAN'T TAKE!
I GIVE UP, KID!
I GIVE--

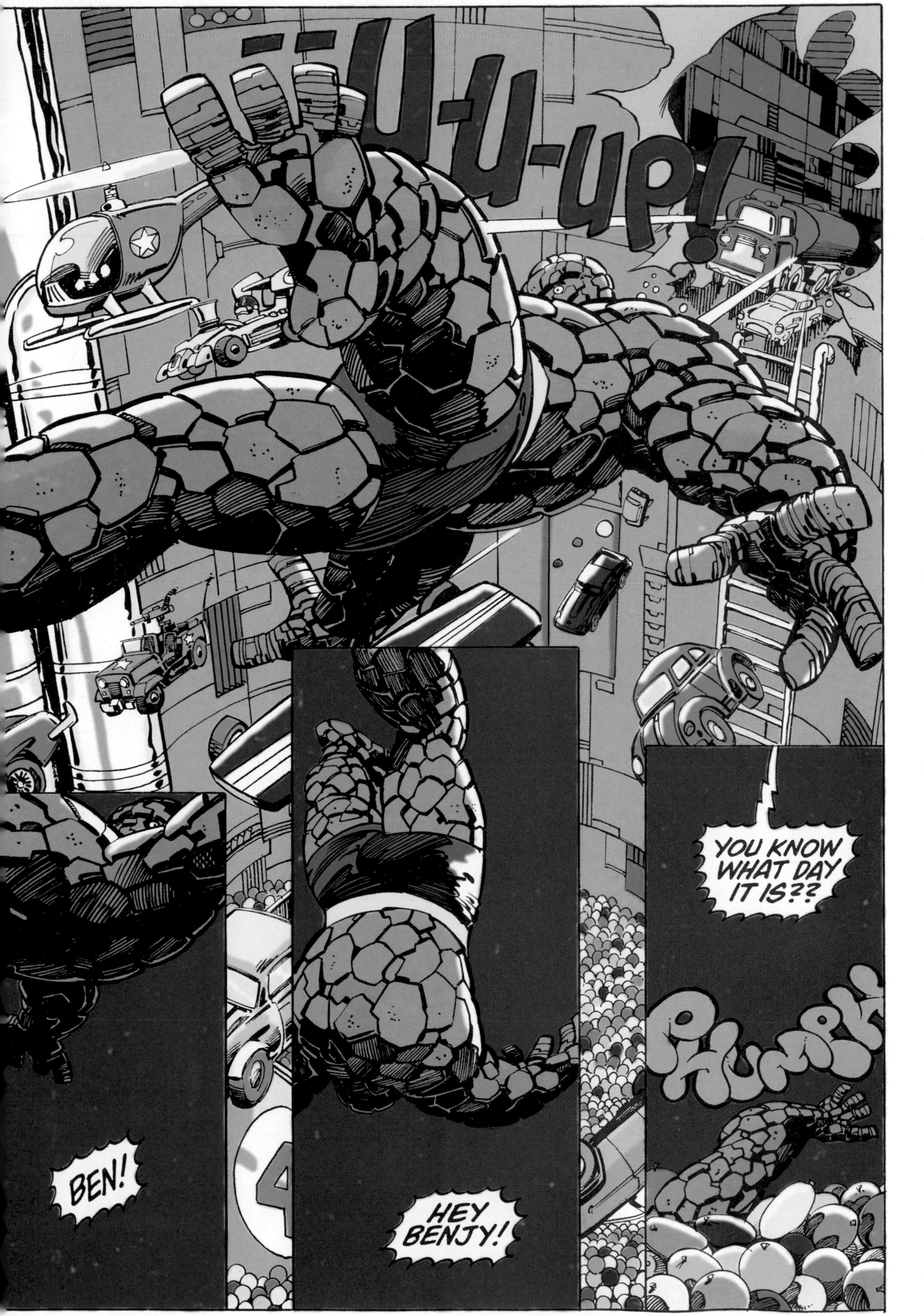

--U-U-U-UP!
BEN!
HEY BENJY!
YOU KNOW WHAT DAY IT IS??
PHUMPF

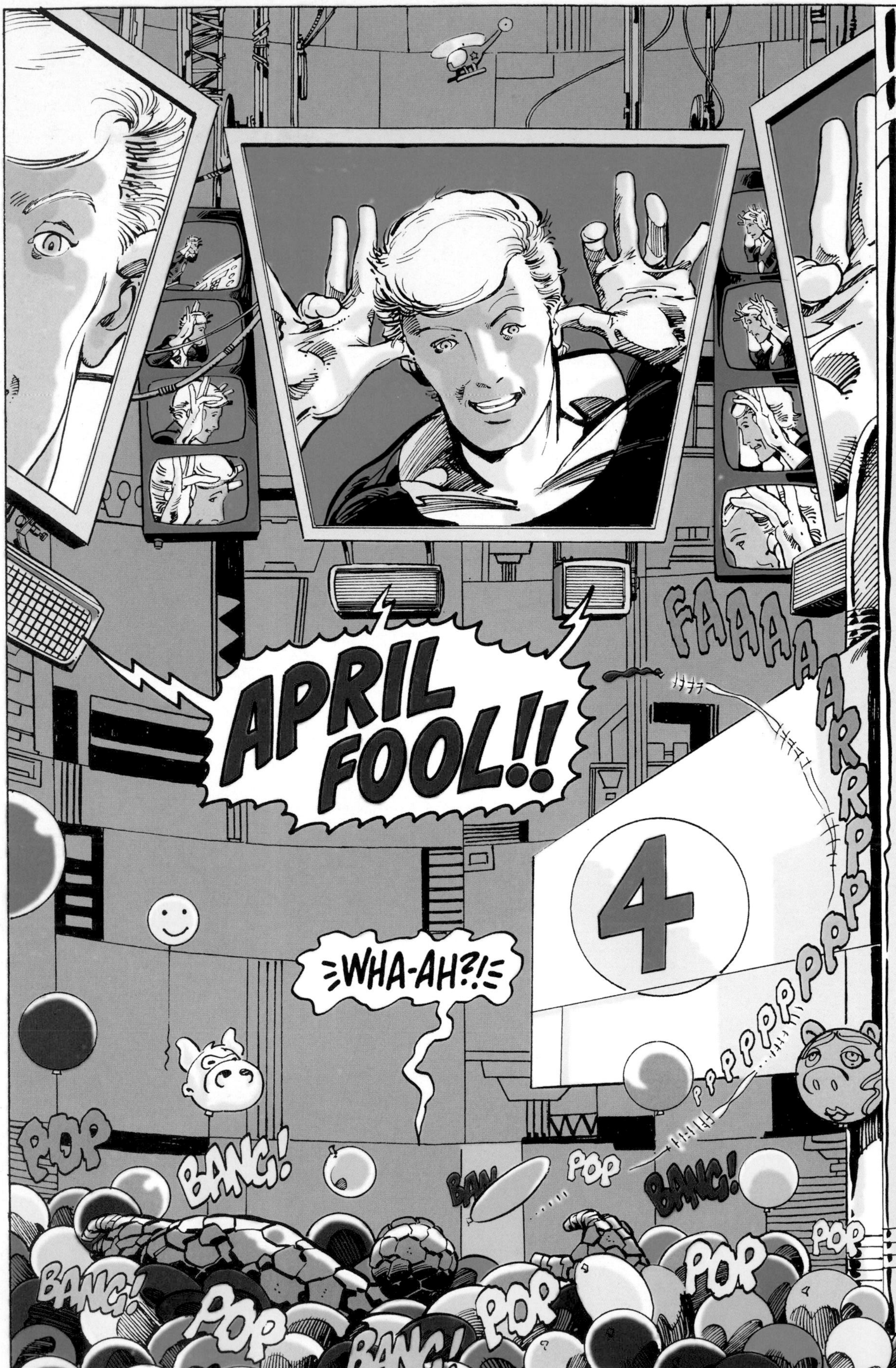
APRIL FOOL!!
FAAAAARRRPPPPPPPPPPPP
WHA-AH?!
POP
BANG!
BANG!
POP
BANG!
POP
BANG!
POP
POP
POP
BANG!
POP

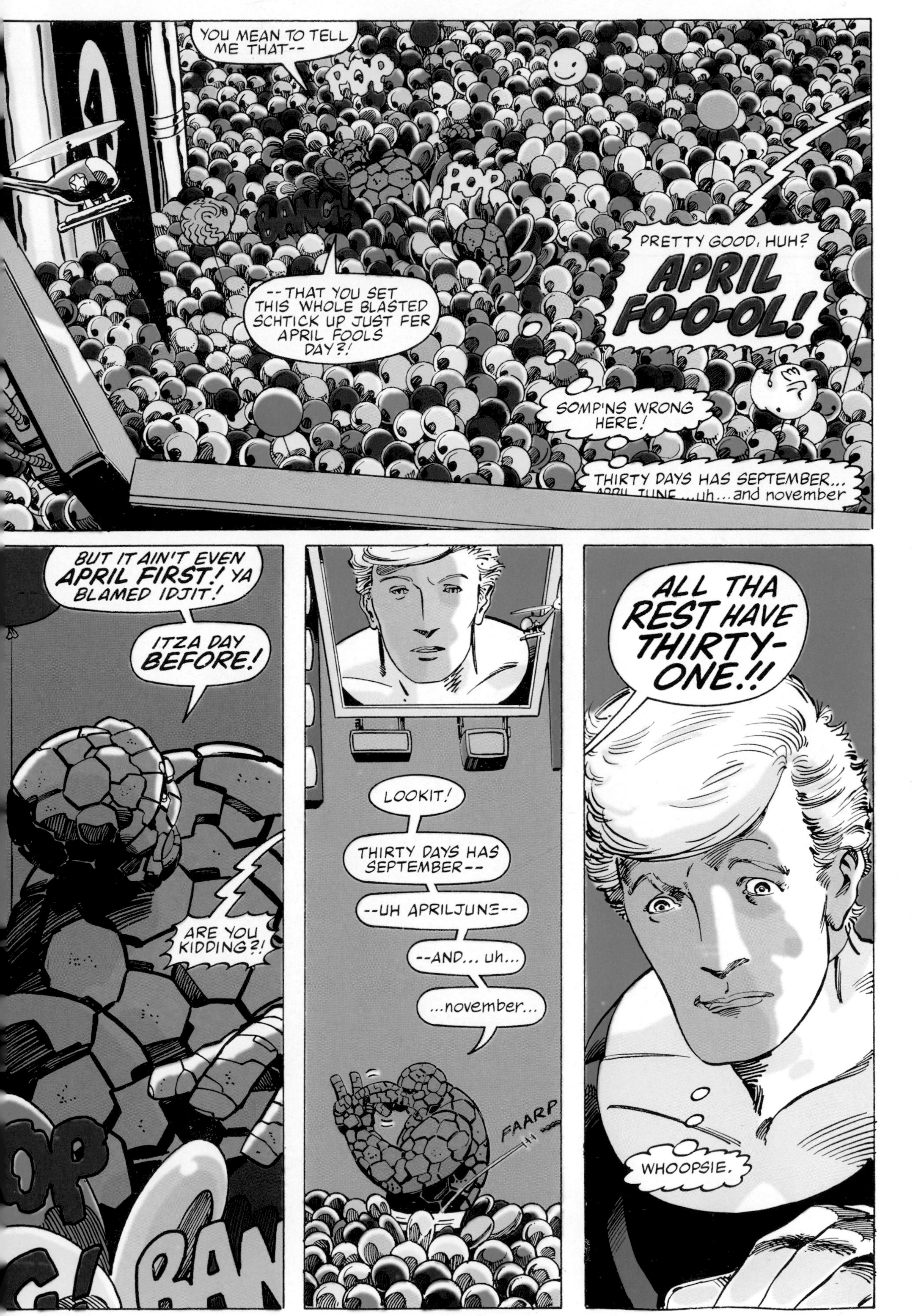
YOU MEAN TO TELL ME THAT--
POP
POP
BANG!
--THAT YOU SET THIS WHOLE BLASTED SCHTICK UP JUST FER APRIL FOOLS DAY?!
PRETTY GOOD, HUH? APRIL FO-O-OL!
SOMP'NS WRONG HERE!
THIRTY DAYS HAS SEPTEMBER...
...uh...and november
BUT IT AIN'T EVEN APRIL FIRST! YA BLAMED IDJIT!
ITZA DAY BEFORE!
ARE YOU KIDDING?!
LOOKIT!
THIRTY DAYS HAS SEPTEMBER--
--UH APRILJUNE--
--AND... uh...
...november...
FAARP
ALL THA REST HAVE THIRTY-ONE.!!
WHOOPSIE.

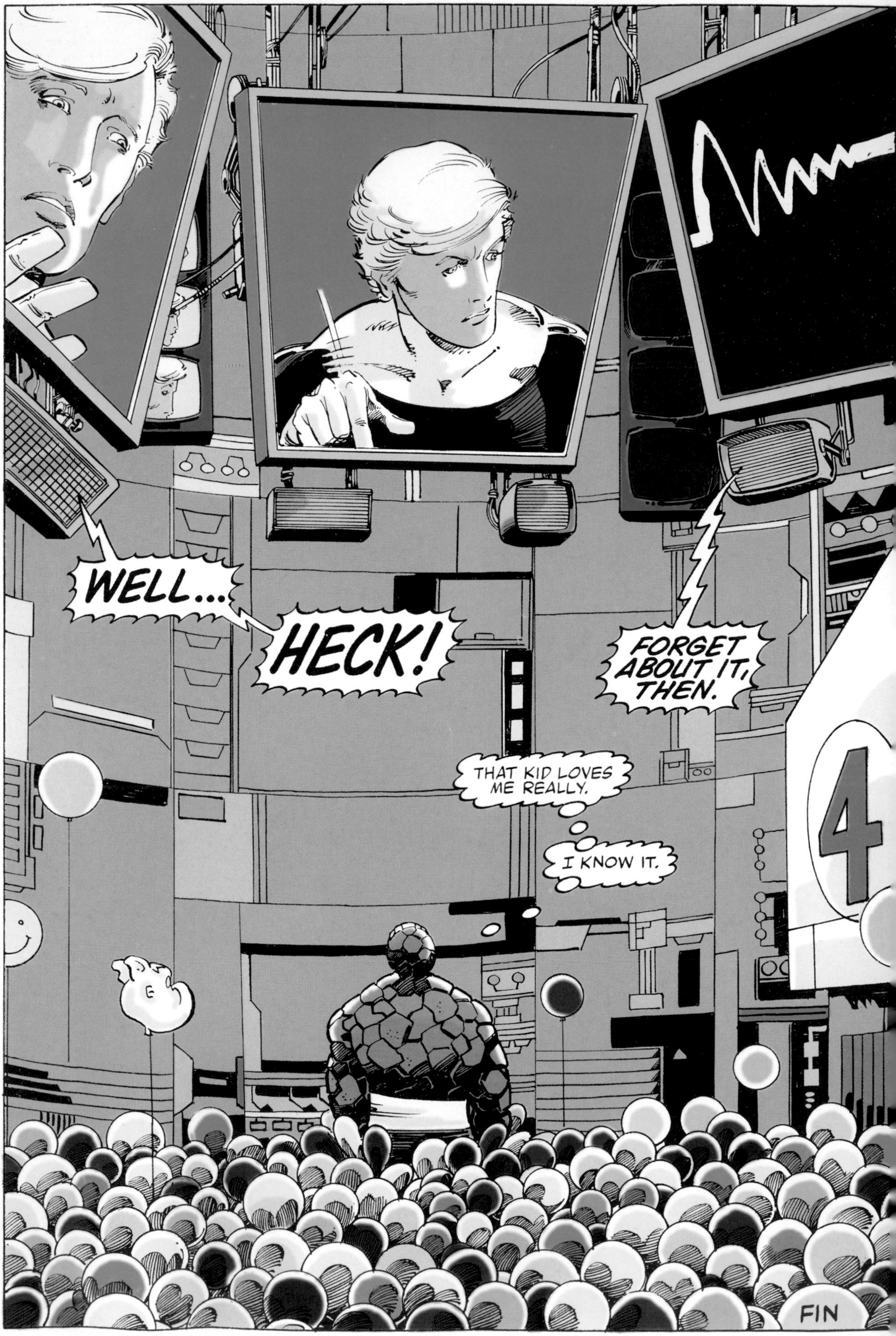
WELL...
HECK!
FORGET ABOUT IT, THEN.
THAT KID LOVES ME REALLY.
I KNOW IT.
4
FIN

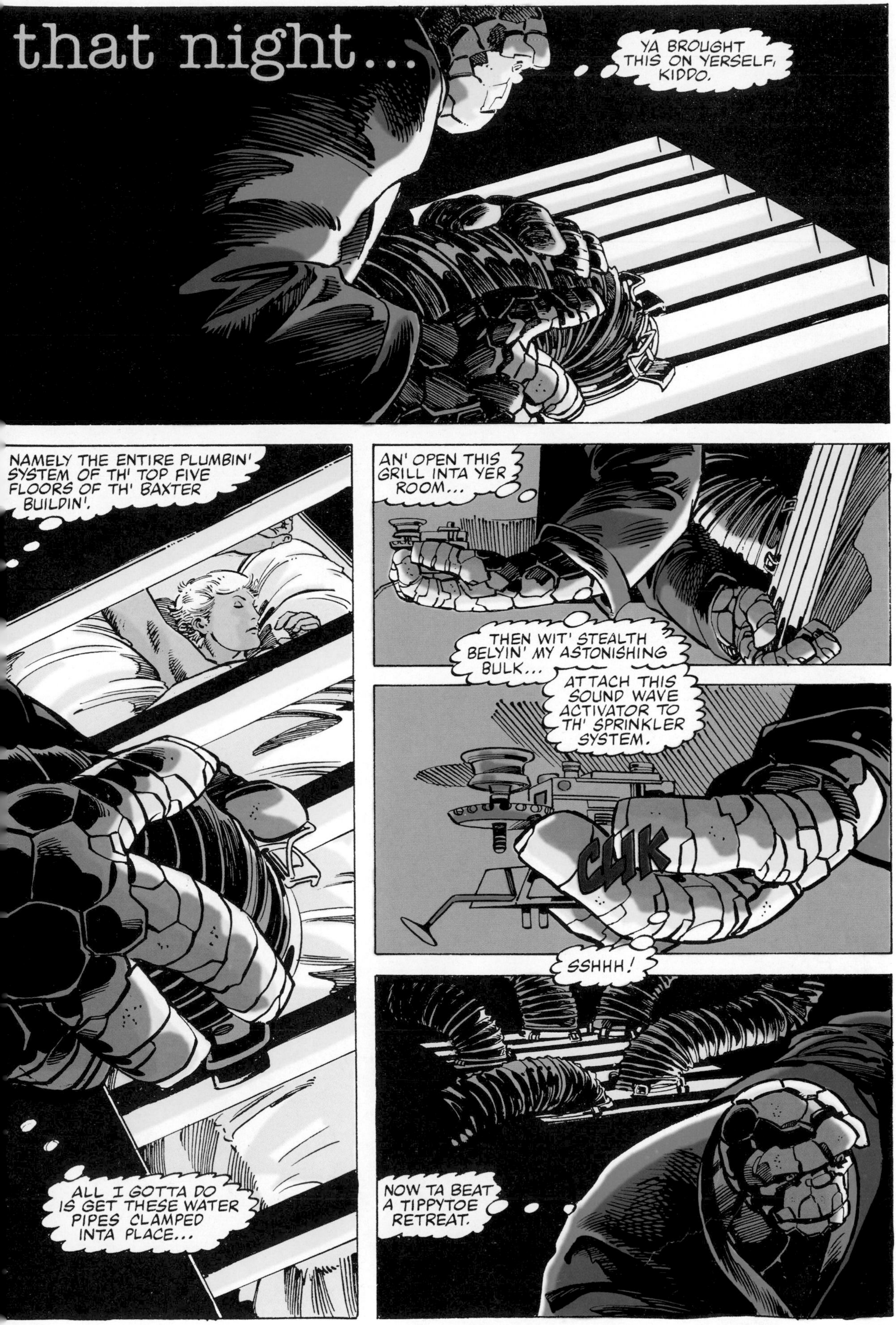
that night...
YA BROUGHT THIS ON YERSELF, KIDDO.
NAMELY THE ENTIRE PLUMBIN' SYSTEM OF TH' TOP FIVE FLOORS OF TH' BAXTER BUILDIN'.
ALL I GOTTA DO IS GET THESE WATER PIPES CLAMPED INTA PLACE...
AN' OPEN THIS GRILL INTA YER ROOM...
THEN WIT' STEALTH BELYIN' MY ASTONISHING BULK...
ATTACH THIS SOUND WAVE ACTIVATOR TO TH' SPRINKLER SYSTEM.
CLIK
SSHHH!
NOW TA BEAT A TIPPYTOE RETREAT.

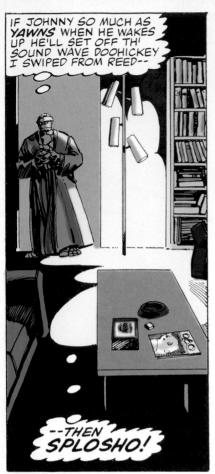

IF JOHNNY SO MUCH AS *YAWNS* WHEN HE WAKES UP HE'LL SET OFF TH' SOUND WAVE DOOHICKEY I SWIPED FROM REED--

--THEN *SPLOSHO!*

APRIL FOOL, HOTSHOT!

H'YOK H'YOK ≈snorf≈

NOW ALL I GOTTA DO IS RELAX...

...HAVE A CIGAR...

CLICK

...SIT BACK, AN' WAIT FOR TH' FIREWORKS TO BEGIN!

THE END

PRODUCED BY BARRY WINDSOR-SMITH • LETTERED BY JIM NOVAK • ALLEN MILGROM, EDITOR • JIM SHOOTER, EDITOR-IN-CHIEF.

FANTASTIC FOUR VOL.3 #56

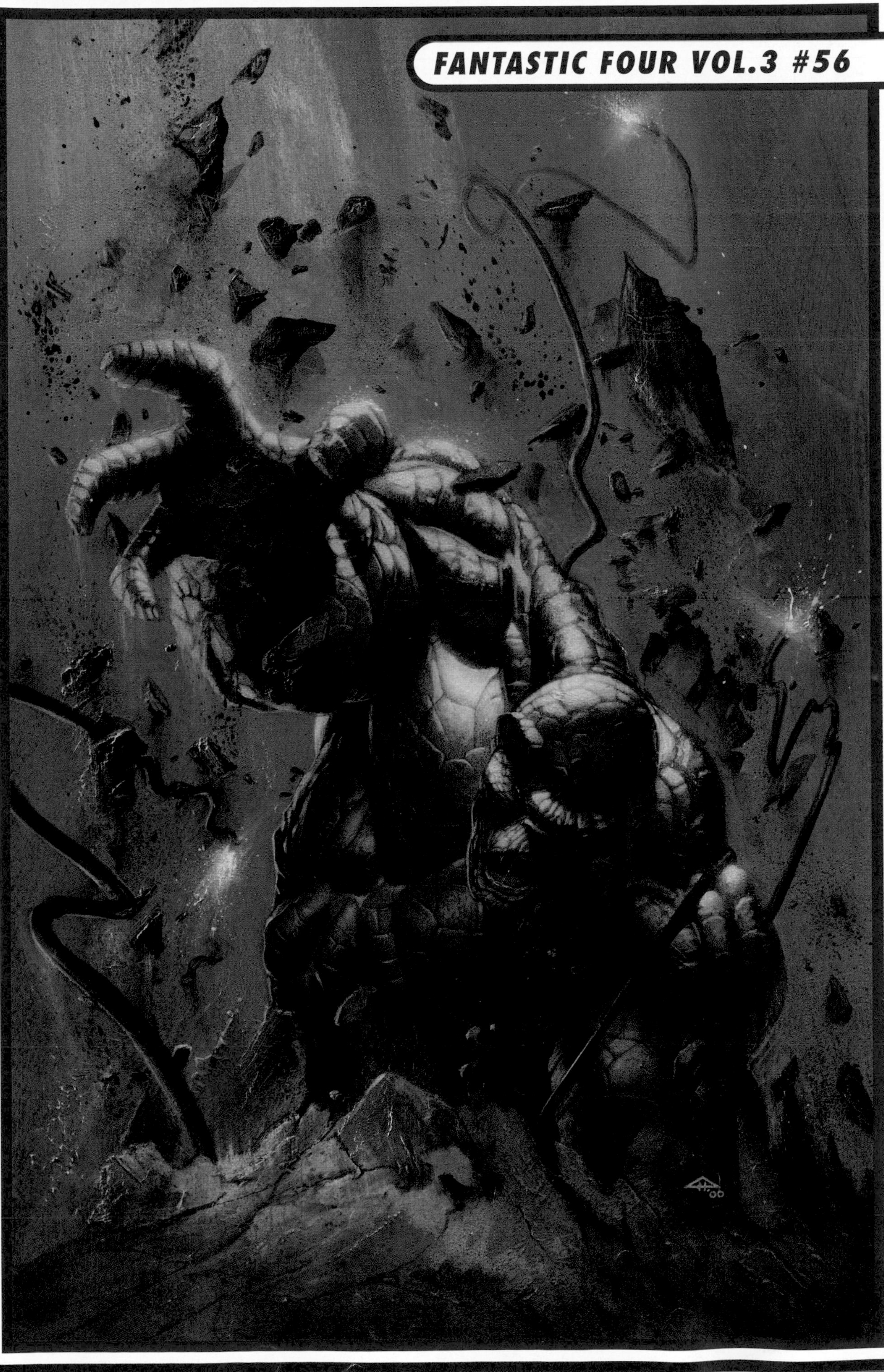

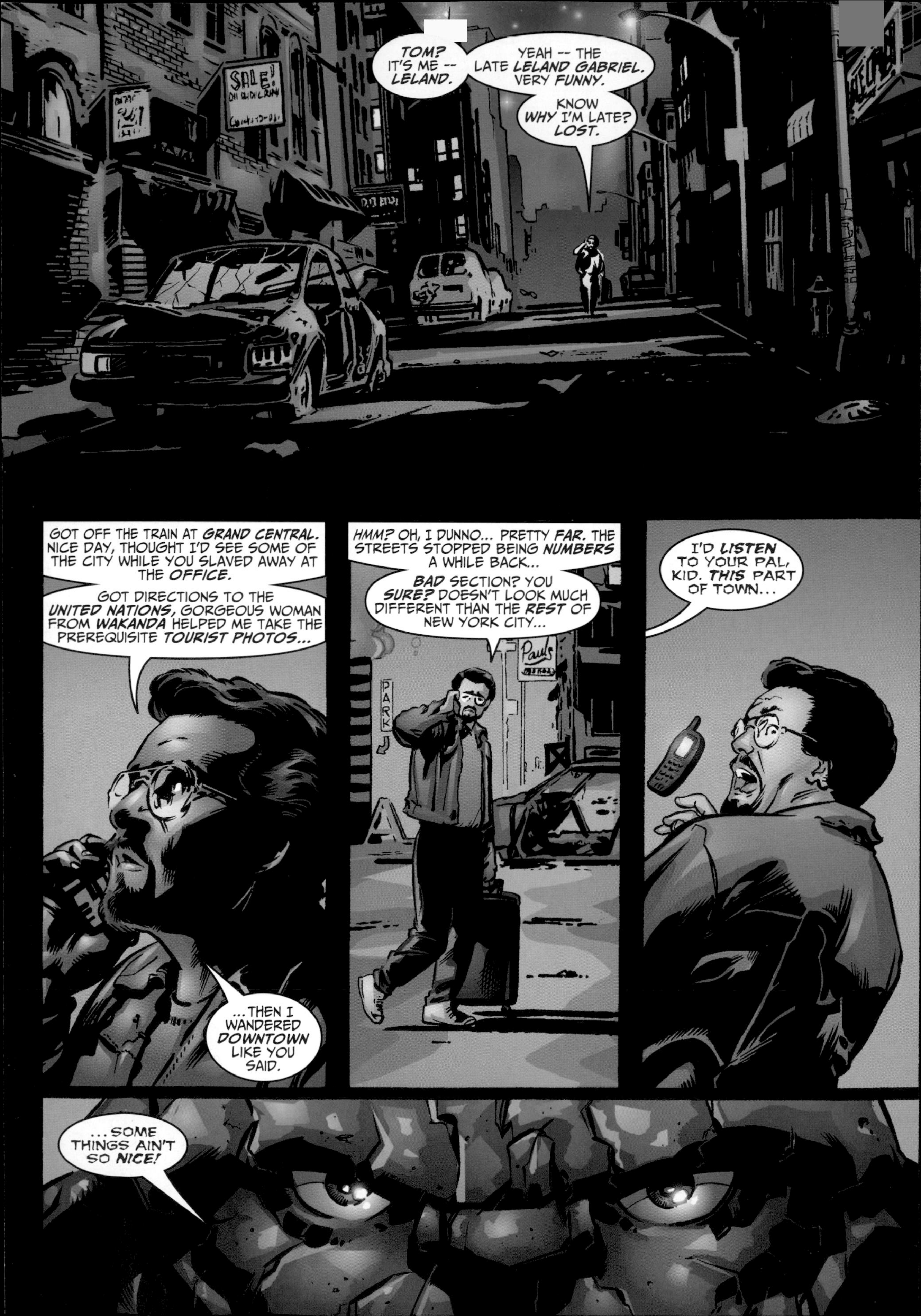

TOM? IT'S ME -- LELAND.
YEAH -- THE LATE LELAND GABRIEL. VERY FUNNY.
KNOW WHY I'M LATE? LOST.
SALE!
GOT OFF THE TRAIN AT GRAND CENTRAL. NICE DAY, THOUGHT I'D SEE SOME OF THE CITY WHILE YOU SLAVED AWAY AT THE OFFICE.
GOT DIRECTIONS TO THE UNITED NATIONS, GORGEOUS WOMAN FROM WAKANDA HELPED ME TAKE THE PREREQUISITE TOURIST PHOTOS...
...THEN I WANDERED DOWNTOWN LIKE YOU SAID.
HMM? OH, I DUNNO... PRETTY FAR. THE STREETS STOPPED BEING NUMBERS A WHILE BACK...
BAD SECTION? YOU SURE? DOESN'T LOOK MUCH DIFFERENT THAN THE REST OF NEW YORK CITY...
PARK
Paul's
I'D LISTEN TO YOUR PAL, KID. THIS PART OF TOWN...
...SOME THINGS AIN'T SO NICE!

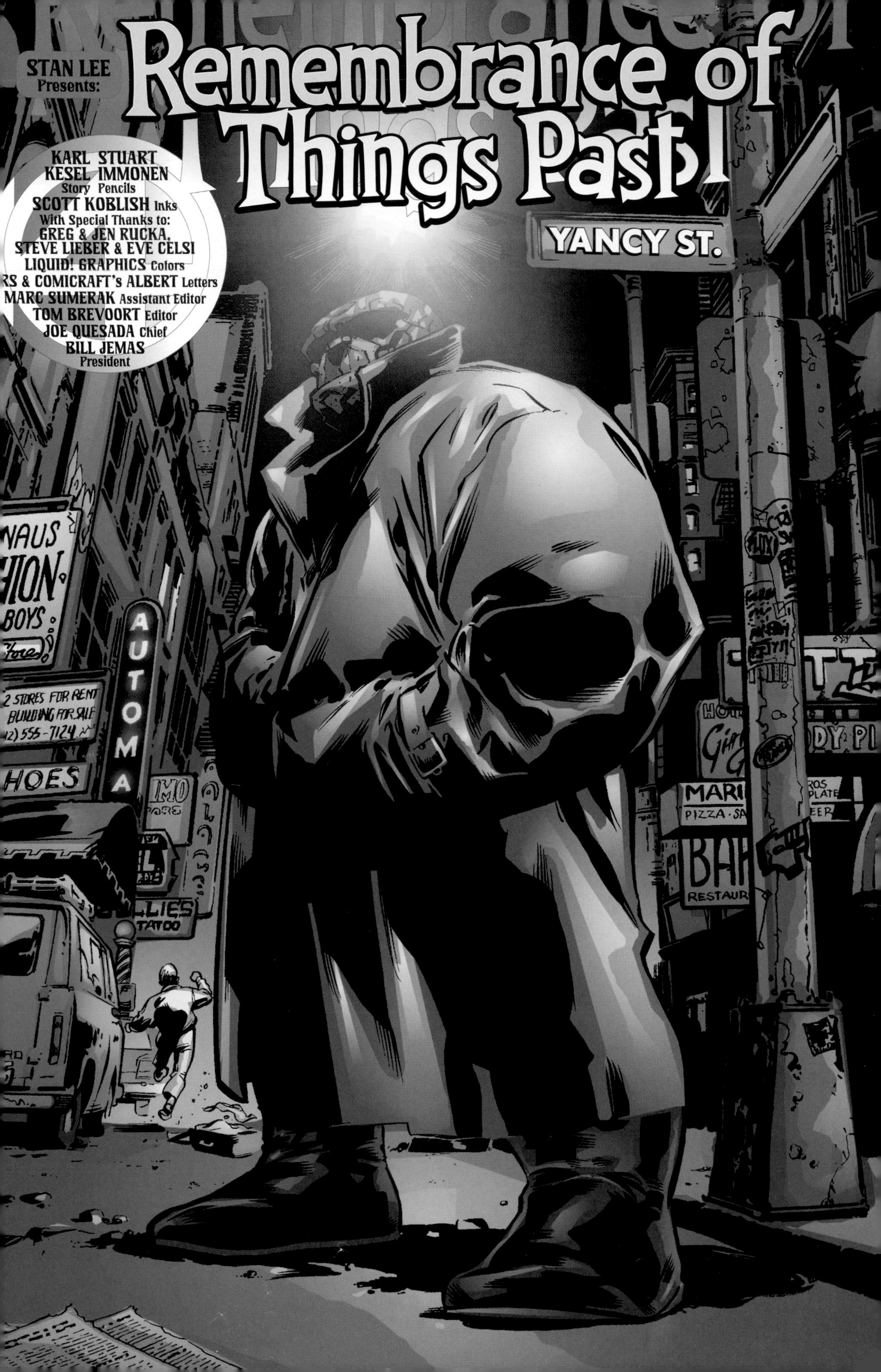
STAN LEE Presents:
Remembrance of Things Past
KARL KESEL Story
STUART IMMONEN Pencils
SCOTT KOBLISH Inks
With Special Thanks to:
GREG & JEN RUCKA,
STEVE LIEBER & EVE CELSI
LIQUID! GRAPHICS Colors
RS & COMICRAFT's ALBERT Letters
MARC SUMERAK Assistant Editor
TOM BREVOORT Editor
JOE QUESADA Chief
BILL JEMAS President
YANCY ST.
AUTOMA
2 STORES FOR RENT
BUILDING FOR SALE
HOES
PIZZA
RESTAUR

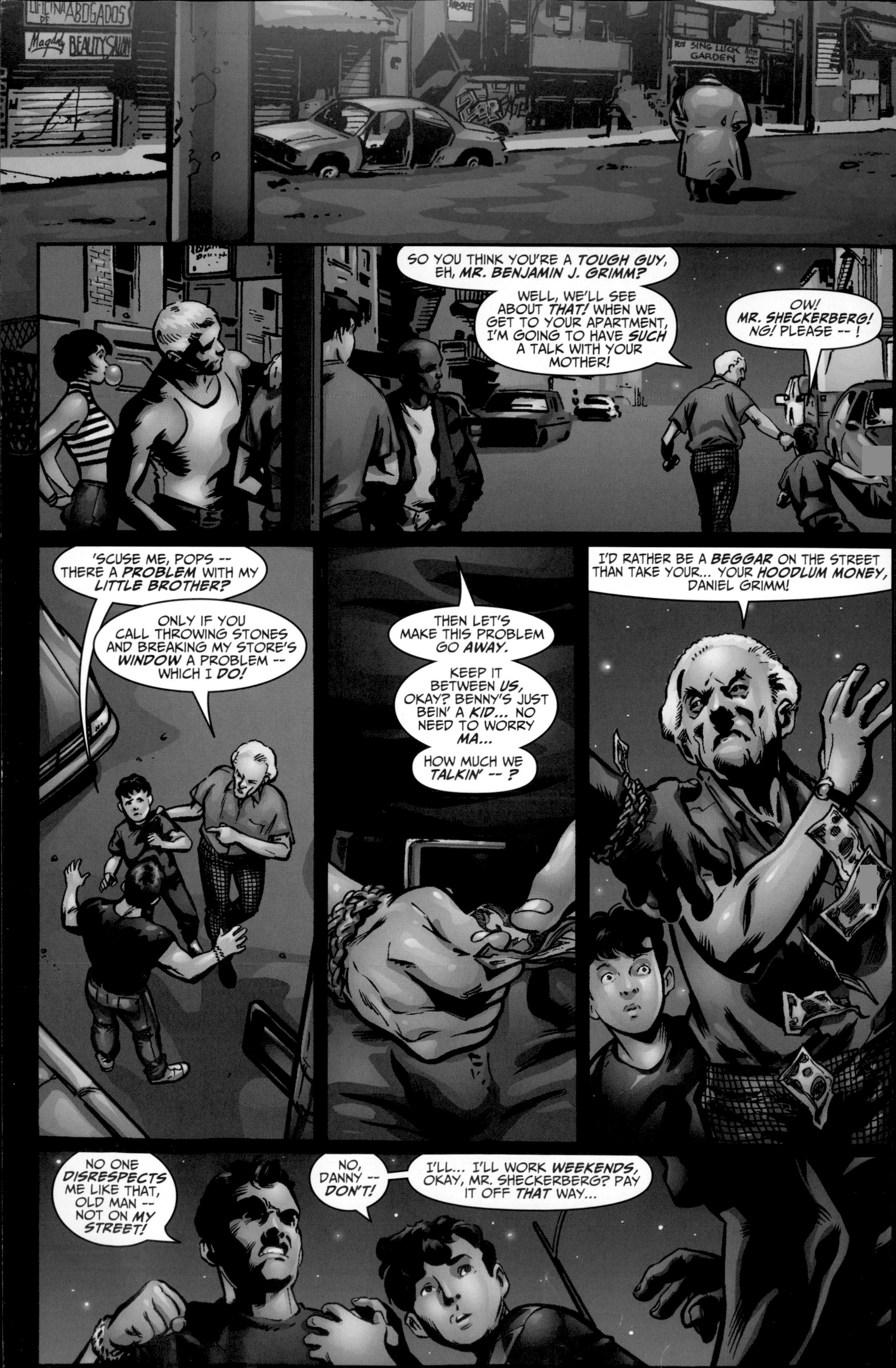
SING LUCK GARDEN
SO YOU THINK YOU'RE A TOUGH GUY, EH, MR. BENJAMIN J. GRIMM?
WELL, WE'LL SEE ABOUT THAT! WHEN WE GET TO YOUR APARTMENT, I'M GOING TO HAVE SUCH A TALK WITH YOUR MOTHER!
OW! MR. SHECKERBERG! NG! PLEASE -- !
'SCUSE ME, POPS -- THERE A PROBLEM WITH MY LITTLE BROTHER?
ONLY IF YOU CALL THROWING STONES AND BREAKING MY STORE'S WINDOW A PROBLEM -- WHICH I DO!
THEN LET'S MAKE THIS PROBLEM GO AWAY.
KEEP IT BETWEEN US, OKAY? BENNY'S JUST BEIN' A KID... NO NEED TO WORRY MA...
HOW MUCH WE TALKIN' -- ?
I'D RATHER BE A BEGGAR ON THE STREET THAN TAKE YOUR... YOUR HOODLUM MONEY, DANIEL GRIMM!
NO ONE DISRESPECTS ME LIKE THAT, OLD MAN -- NOT ON MY STREET!
NO, DANNY -- DON'T!
I'LL... I'LL WORK WEEKENDS, OKAY, MR. SHECKERBERG? PAY IT OFF THAT WAY...

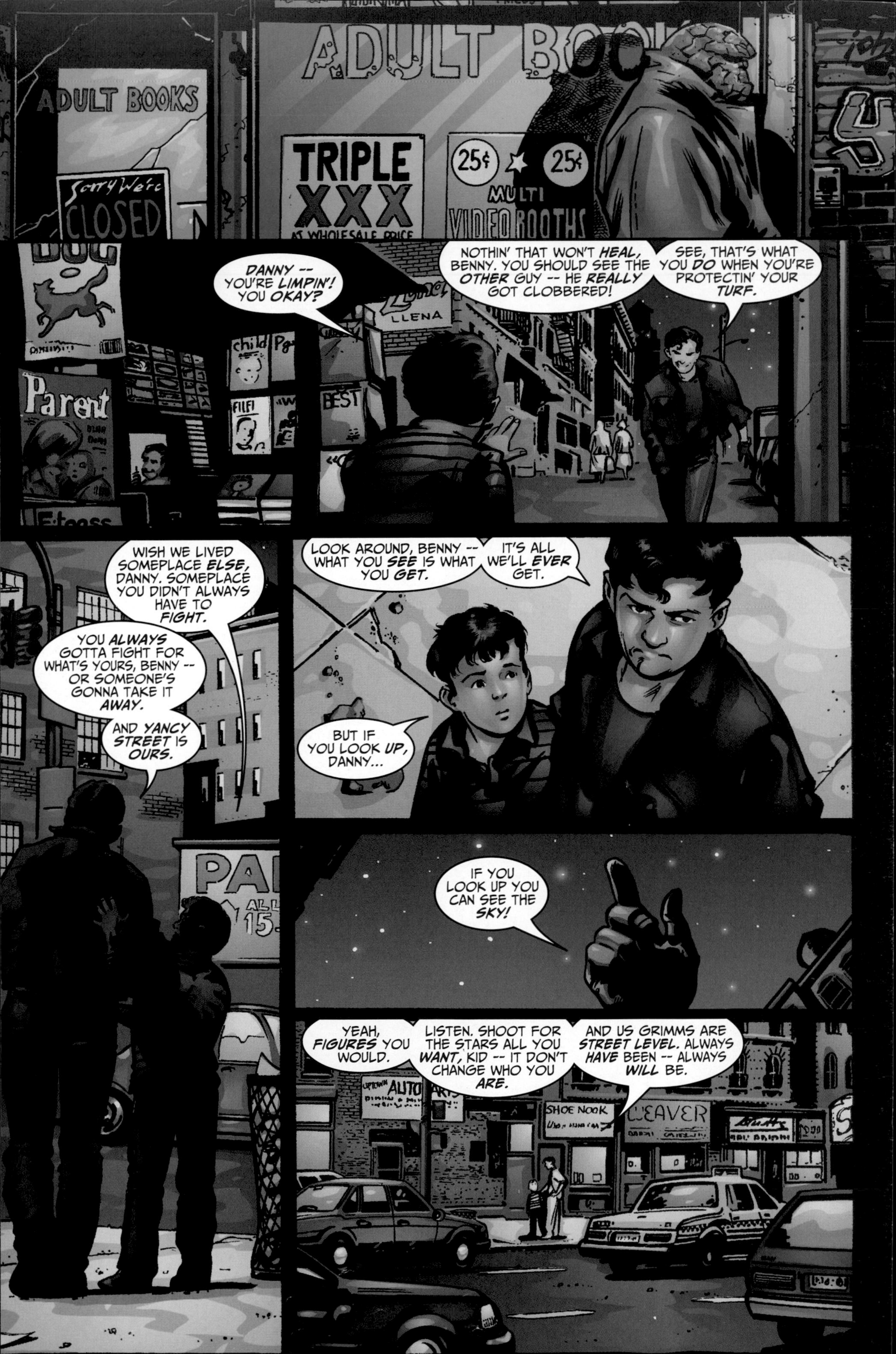
ADULT BOOKS
ADULT BOOKS
Sorry We're CLOSED
TRIPLE XXX AT WHOLESALE PRICE
25¢ 25¢ MULTI VIDEO BOOTHS
DANNY -- YOU'RE LIMPIN'! YOU OKAY?
NOTHIN' THAT WON'T HEAL, BENNY. YOU SHOULD SEE THE OTHER GUY -- HE REALLY GOT CLOBBERED!
SEE, THAT'S WHAT YOU DO WHEN YOU'RE PROTECTIN' YOUR TURF.
LLENA
Parent
WISH WE LIVED SOMEPLACE ELSE, DANNY. SOMEPLACE YOU DIDN'T ALWAYS HAVE TO FIGHT.
YOU ALWAYS GOTTA FIGHT FOR WHAT'S YOURS, BENNY -- OR SOMEONE'S GONNA TAKE IT AWAY.
AND YANCY STREET IS OURS.
LOOK AROUND, BENNY -- WHAT YOU SEE IS WHAT YOU GET.
IT'S ALL WE'LL EVER GET.
BUT IF YOU LOOK UP, DANNY...
IF YOU LOOK UP YOU CAN SEE THE SKY!
YEAH, FIGURES YOU WOULD.
LISTEN. SHOOT FOR THE STARS ALL YOU WANT, KID -- IT DON'T CHANGE WHO YOU ARE.
AND US GRIMMS ARE STREET LEVEL. ALWAYS HAVE BEEN -- ALWAYS WILL BE.
SHOE NOOK
WEAVER

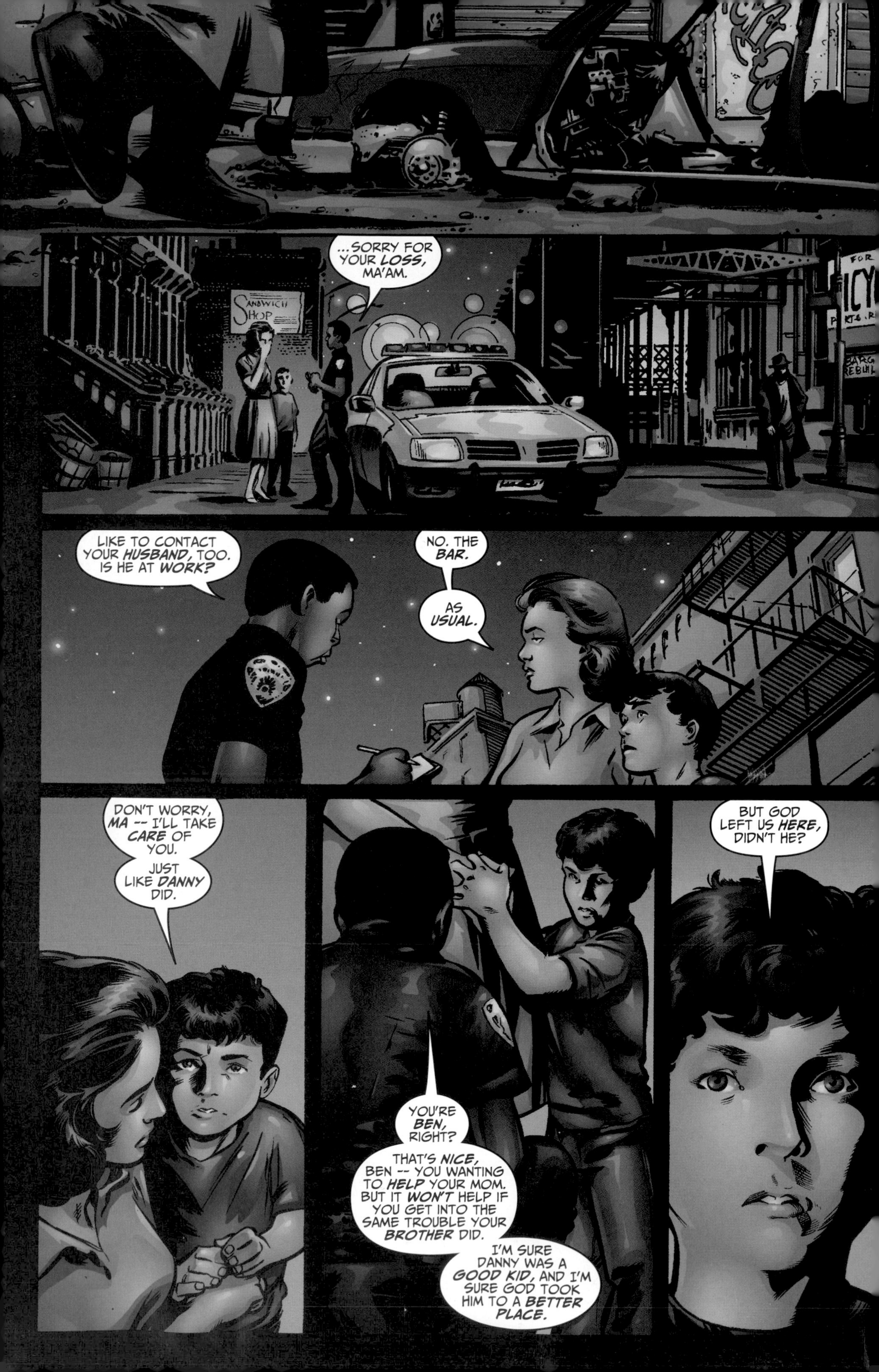
SANDWICH SHOP
...SORRY FOR YOUR LOSS, MA'AM.
LIKE TO CONTACT YOUR HUSBAND, TOO. IS HE AT WORK?
NO. THE BAR.
AS USUAL.
DON'T WORRY, MA -- I'LL TAKE CARE OF YOU.
JUST LIKE DANNY DID.
YOU'RE BEN, RIGHT?
THAT'S NICE, BEN -- YOU WANTING TO HELP YOUR MOM. BUT IT WON'T HELP IF YOU GET INTO THE SAME TROUBLE YOUR BROTHER DID.
I'M SURE DANNY WAS A GOOD KID, AND I'M SURE GOD TOOK HIM TO A BETTER PLACE.
BUT GOD LEFT US HERE, DIDN'T HE?

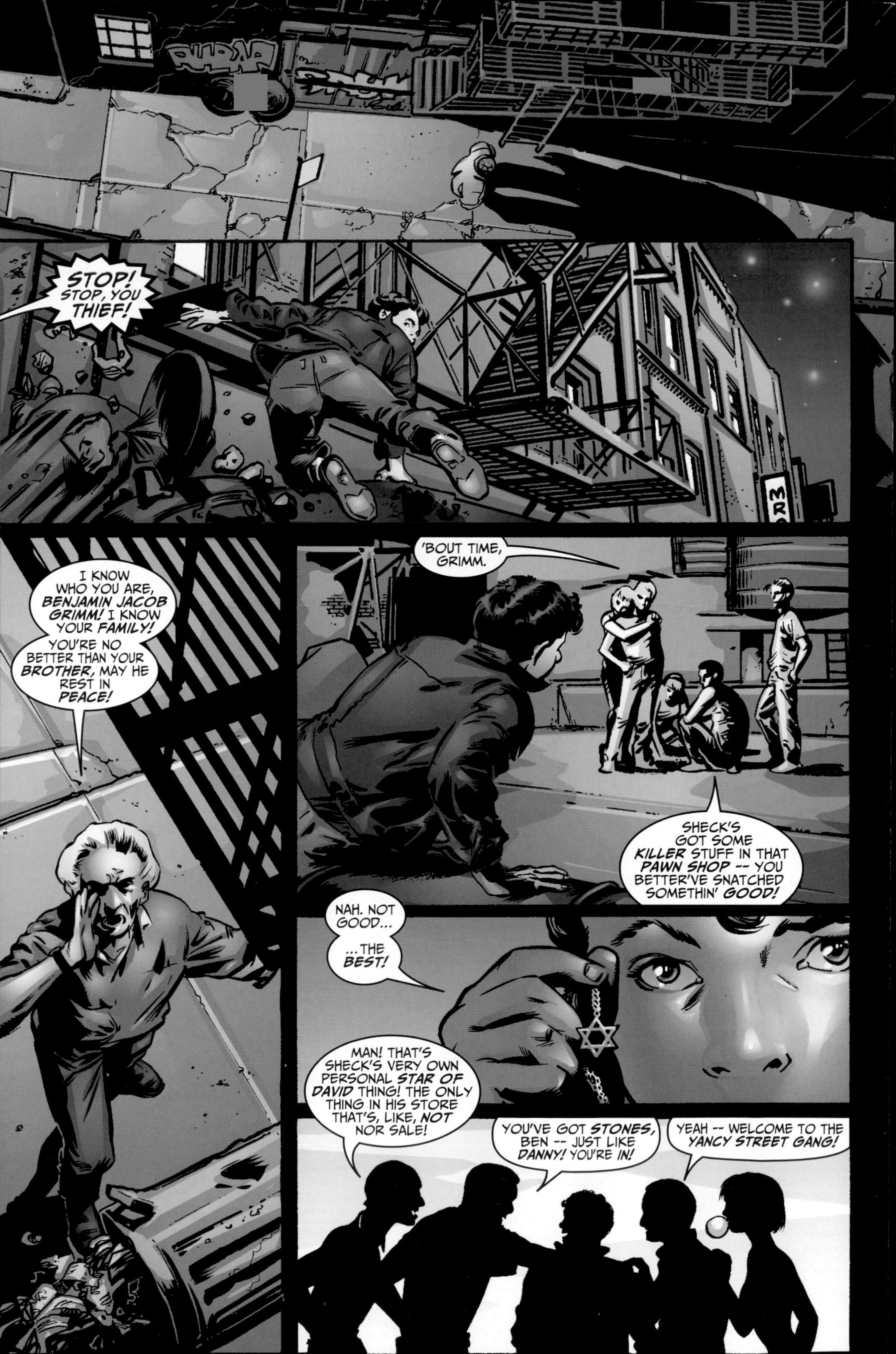
STOP! STOP, YOU THIEF!
I KNOW WHO YOU ARE, BENJAMIN JACOB GRIMM! I KNOW YOUR FAMILY! YOU'RE NO BETTER THAN YOUR BROTHER, MAY HE REST IN PEACE!
'BOUT TIME, GRIMM.
SHECK'S GOT SOME KILLER STUFF IN THAT PAWN SHOP -- YOU BETTER'VE SNATCHED SOMETHIN' GOOD!
NAH. NOT GOOD...
...THE BEST!
MAN! THAT'S SHECK'S VERY OWN PERSONAL STAR OF DAVID THING! THE ONLY THING IN HIS STORE THAT'S, LIKE, NOT NOR SALE!
YOU'VE GOT STONES, BEN -- JUST LIKE DANNY! YOU'RE IN!
YEAH -- WELCOME TO THE YANCY STREET GANG!

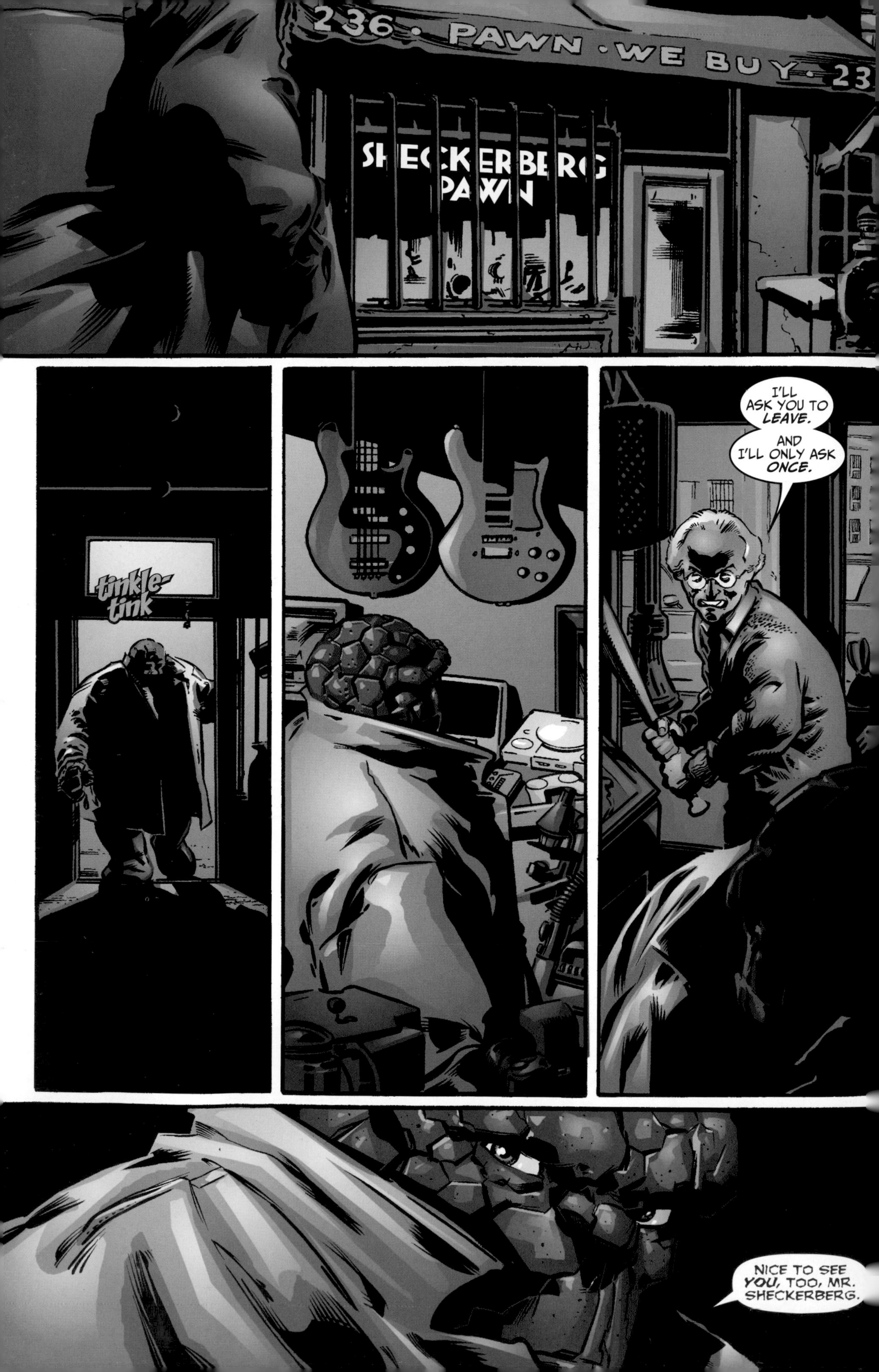
236 · PAWN · WE BUY · 23
SHECKERBERG PAWN
tinkle-tink
I'LL ASK YOU TO LEAVE.
AND I'LL ONLY ASK ONCE.
NICE TO SEE YOU, TOO, MR. SHECKERBERG.

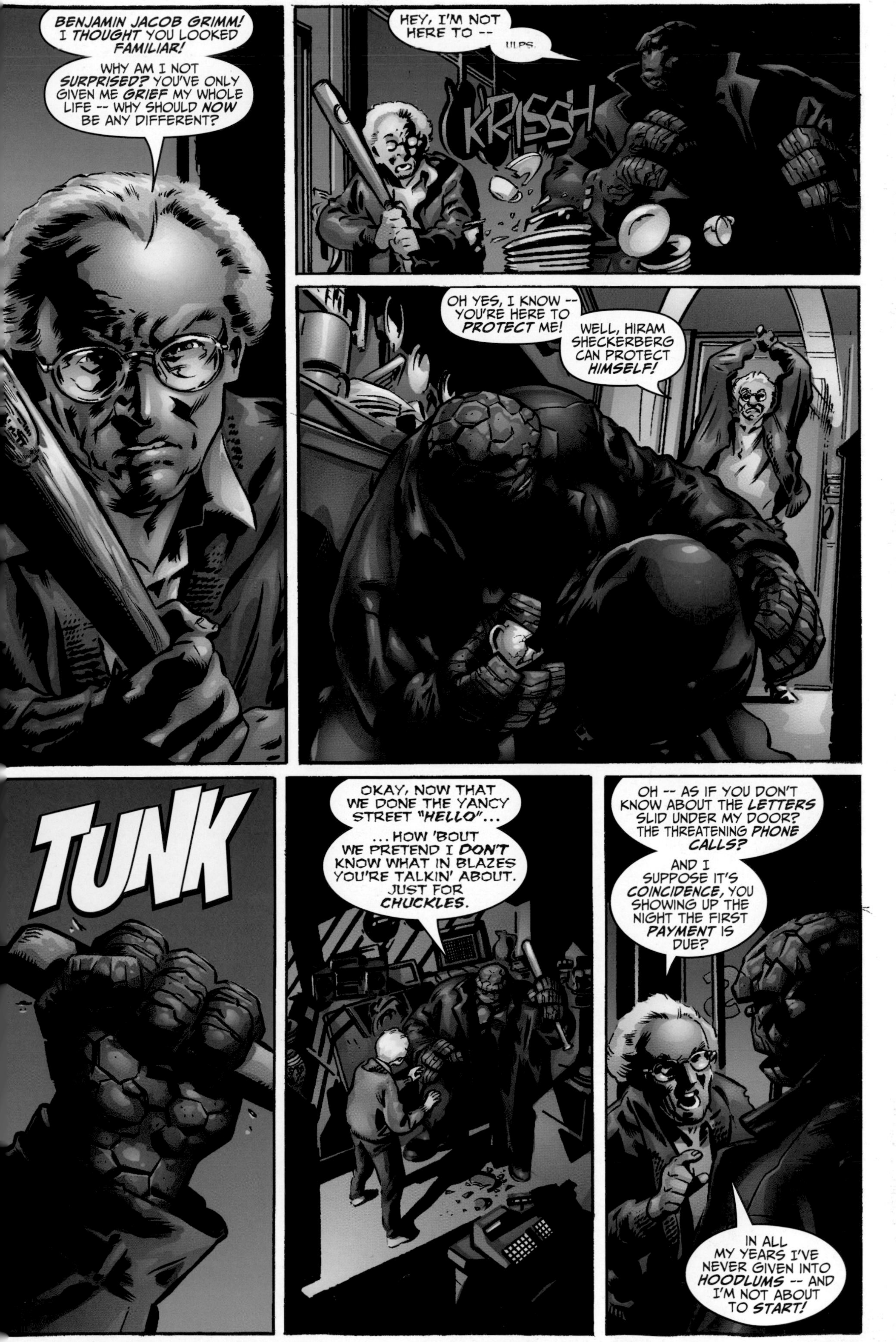
BENJAMIN JACOB GRIMM! I THOUGHT YOU LOOKED FAMILIAR!
WHY AM I NOT SURPRISED? YOU'VE ONLY GIVEN ME GRIEF MY WHOLE LIFE -- WHY SHOULD NOW BE ANY DIFFERENT?
HEY, I'M NOT HERE TO --
ULPS.
KRISSH
OH YES, I KNOW -- YOU'RE HERE TO PROTECT ME!
WELL, HIRAM SHECKERBERG CAN PROTECT HIMSELF!
TUNK
OKAY, NOW THAT WE DONE THE YANCY STREET "HELLO"...
...HOW 'BOUT WE PRETEND I DON'T KNOW WHAT IN BLAZES YOU'RE TALKIN' ABOUT. JUST FOR CHUCKLES.
OH -- AS IF YOU DON'T KNOW ABOUT THE LETTERS SLID UNDER MY DOOR? THE THREATENING PHONE CALLS?
AND I SUPPOSE IT'S COINCIDENCE, YOU SHOWING UP THE NIGHT THE FIRST PAYMENT IS DUE?
IN ALL MY YEARS I'VE NEVER GIVEN INTO HOODLUMS -- AND I'M NOT ABOUT TO START!

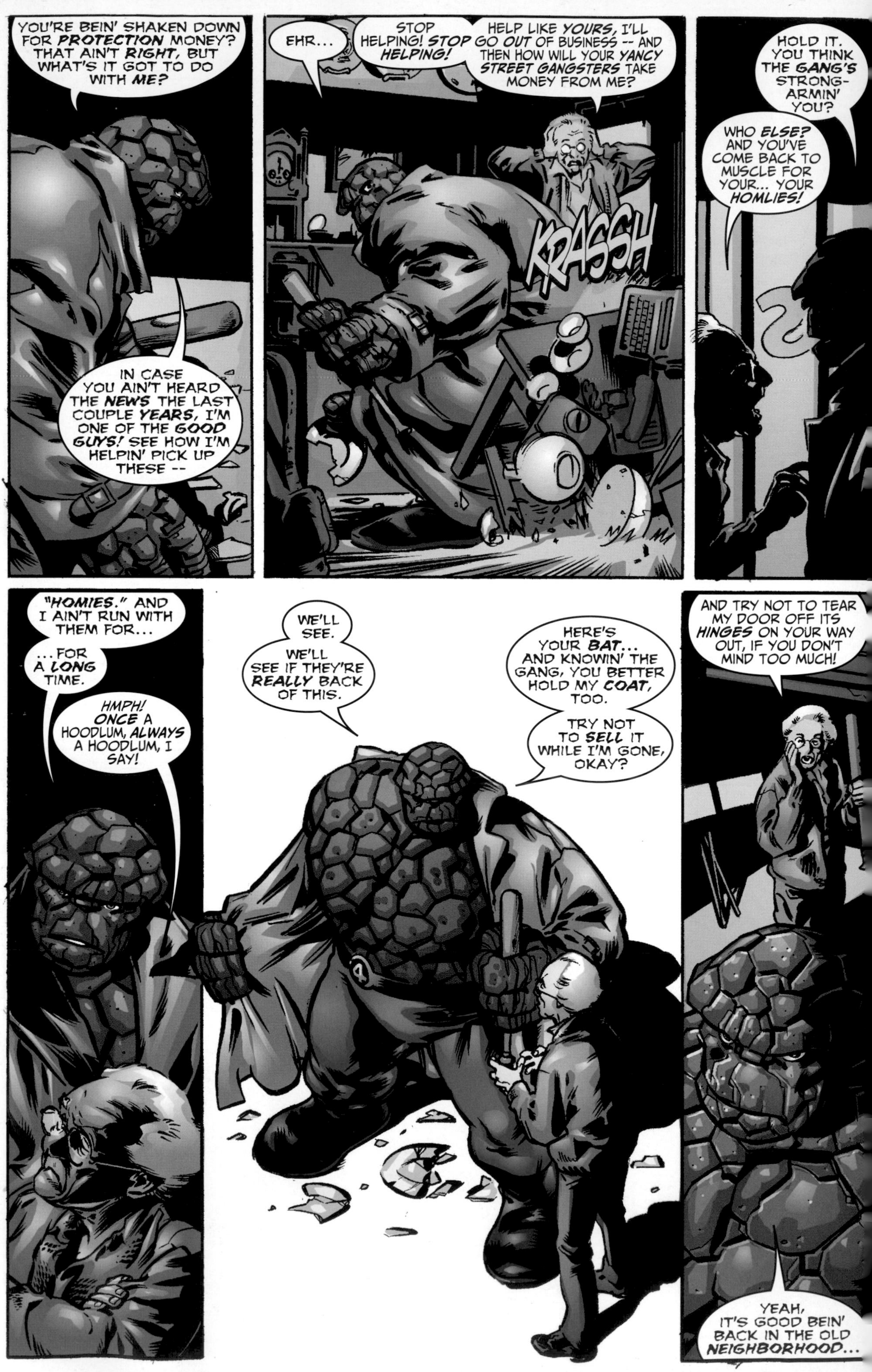
YOU'RE BEIN' SHAKEN DOWN FOR PROTECTION MONEY? THAT AIN'T RIGHT, BUT WHAT'S IT GOT TO DO WITH ME?
IN CASE YOU AIN'T HEARD THE NEWS THE LAST COUPLE YEARS, I'M ONE OF THE GOOD GUYS! SEE HOW I'M HELPIN' PICK UP THESE --
EHR...
STOP HELPING! STOP HELPING!
HELP LIKE YOURS, I'LL GO OUT OF BUSINESS -- AND THEN HOW WILL YOUR YANCY STREET GANGSTERS TAKE MONEY FROM ME?
KRASSH
HOLD IT. YOU THINK THE GANG'S STRONG-ARMIN' YOU?
WHO ELSE? AND YOU'VE COME BACK TO MUSCLE FOR YOUR... YOUR HOMLIES!
"HOMIES." AND I AIN'T RUN WITH THEM FOR...
...FOR A LONG TIME.
HMPH! ONCE A HOODLUM, ALWAYS A HOODLUM, I SAY!
WE'LL SEE.
WE'LL SEE IF THEY'RE REALLY BACK OF THIS.
HERE'S YOUR BAT... AND KNOWIN' THE GANG, YOU BETTER HOLD MY COAT, TOO.
TRY NOT TO SELL IT WHILE I'M GONE, OKAY?
AND TRY NOT TO TEAR MY DOOR OFF ITS HINGES ON YOUR WAY OUT, IF YOU DON'T MIND TOO MUCH!
YEAH, IT'S GOOD BEIN' BACK IN THE OLD NEIGHBORHOOD...

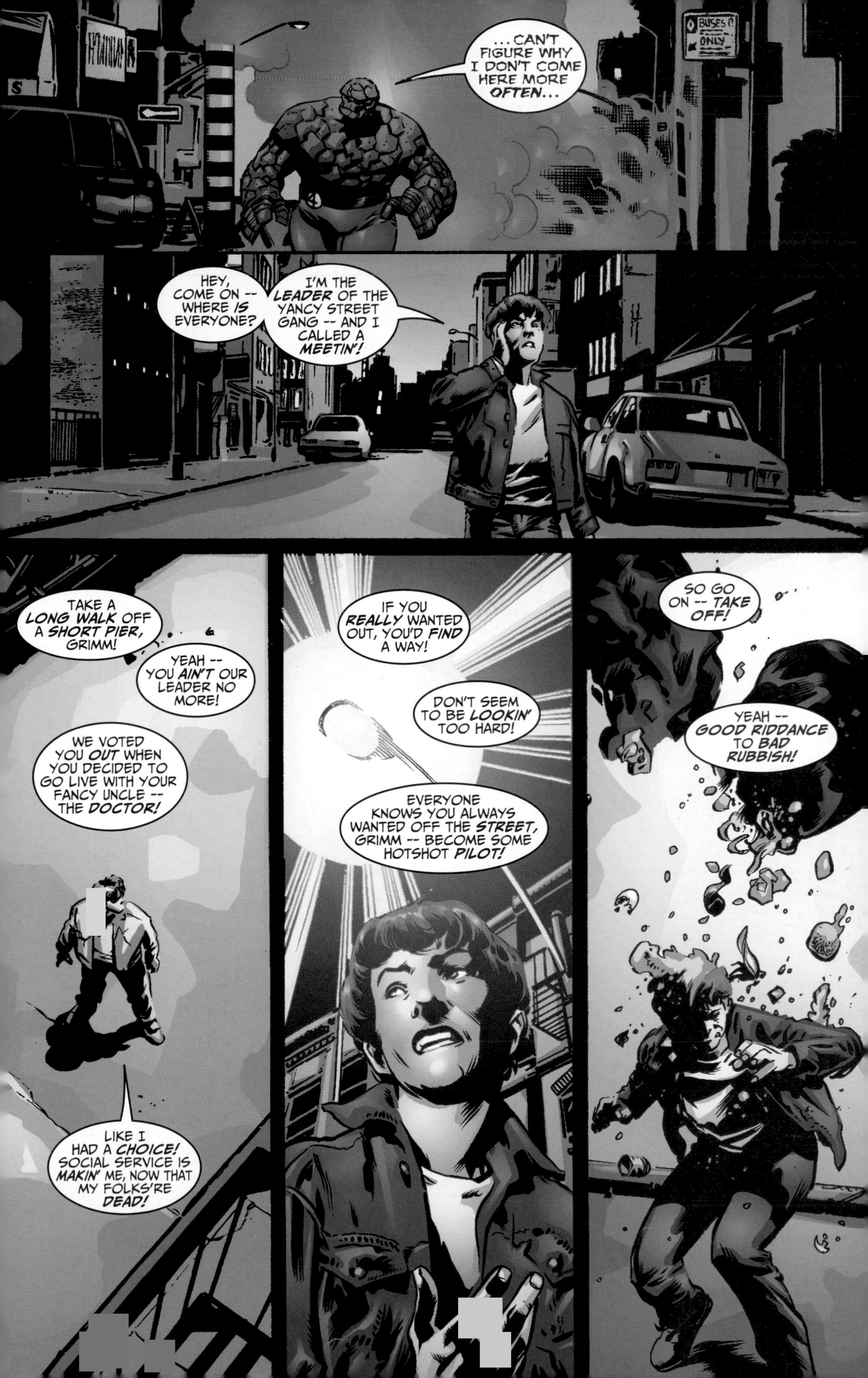

... CAN'T FIGURE WHY I DON'T COME HERE MORE OFTEN...
BUSES ONLY
HEY, COME ON -- WHERE IS EVERYONE?
I'M THE LEADER OF THE YANCY STREET GANG -- AND I CALLED A MEETIN'!
TAKE A LONG WALK OFF A SHORT PIER, GRIMM!
YEAH -- YOU AIN'T OUR LEADER NO MORE!
WE VOTED YOU OUT WHEN YOU DECIDED TO GO LIVE WITH YOUR FANCY UNCLE -- THE DOCTOR!
LIKE I HAD A CHOICE! SOCIAL SERVICE IS MAKIN' ME, NOW THAT MY FOLKS'RE DEAD!
IF YOU REALLY WANTED OUT, YOU'D FIND A WAY!
DON'T SEEM TO BE LOOKIN' TOO HARD!
EVERYONE KNOWS YOU ALWAYS WANTED OFF THE STREET, GRIMM -- BECOME SOME HOTSHOT PILOT!
SO GO ON -- TAKE OFF!
YEAH -- GOOD RIDDANCE TO BAD RUBBISH!

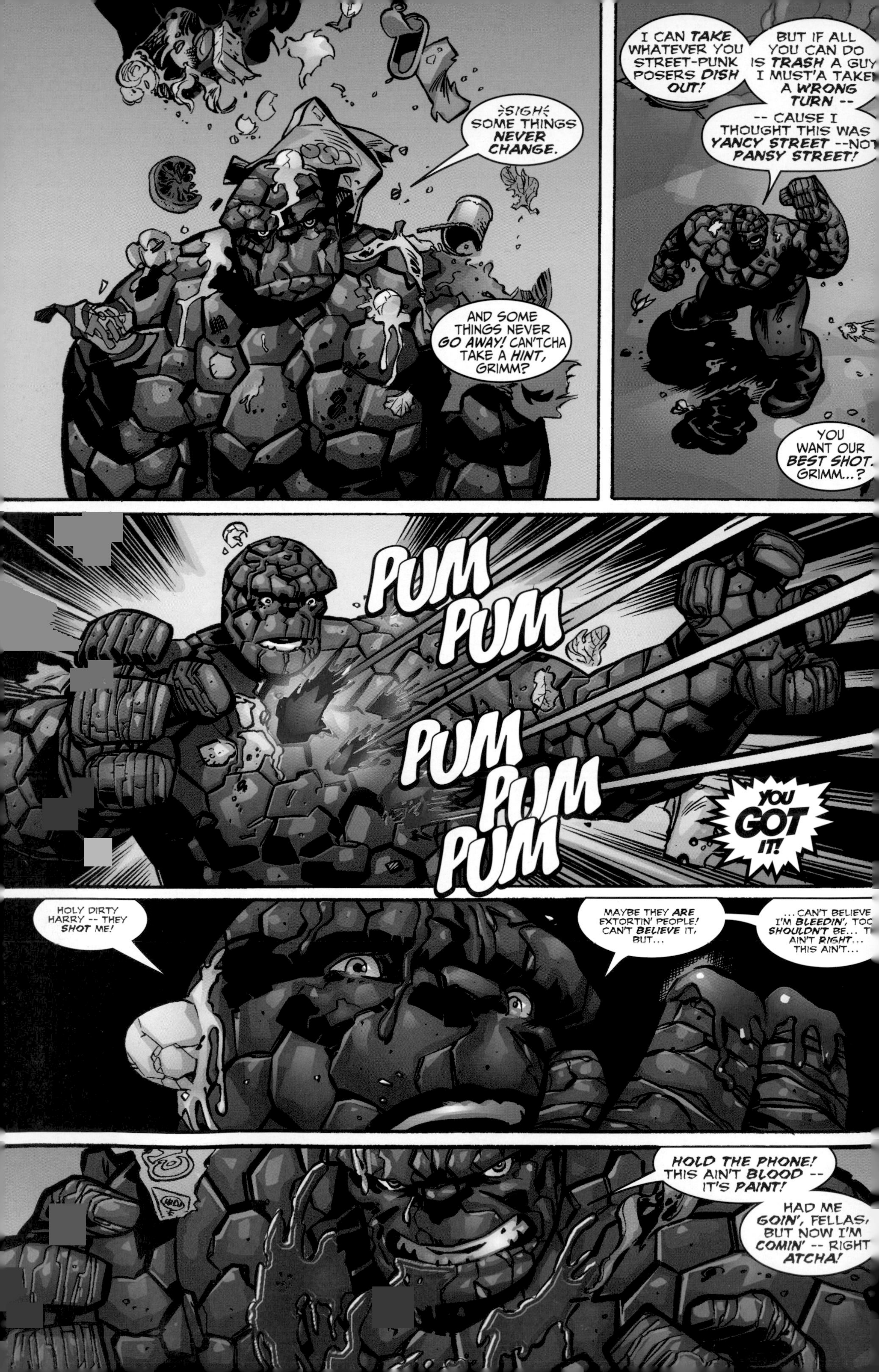
SIGH
SOME THINGS NEVER CHANGE.
AND SOME THINGS NEVER GO AWAY! CAN'TCHA TAKE A HINT, GRIMM?
I CAN TAKE WHATEVER YOU STREET-PUNK POSERS DISH OUT!
BUT IF ALL YOU CAN DO IS TRASH A GUY I MUST'A TAKE A WRONG TURN --
-- CAUSE I THOUGHT THIS WAS YANCY STREET --NOT PANSY STREET!
YOU WANT OUR BEST SHOT, GRIMM...?
PUM PUM
PUM PUM PUM
YOU GOT IT!
HOLY DIRTY HARRY -- THEY SHOT ME!
MAYBE THEY ARE EXTORTIN' PEOPLE! CAN'T BELIEVE IT, BUT...
...CAN'T BELIEVE I'M BLEEDIN', TOO SHOULDN'T BE... AIN'T RIGHT... THIS AIN'T...
HOLD THE PHONE! THIS AIN'T BLOOD -- IT'S PAINT!
HAD ME GOIN', FELLAS, BUT NOW I'M COMIN' -- RIGHT ATCHA!

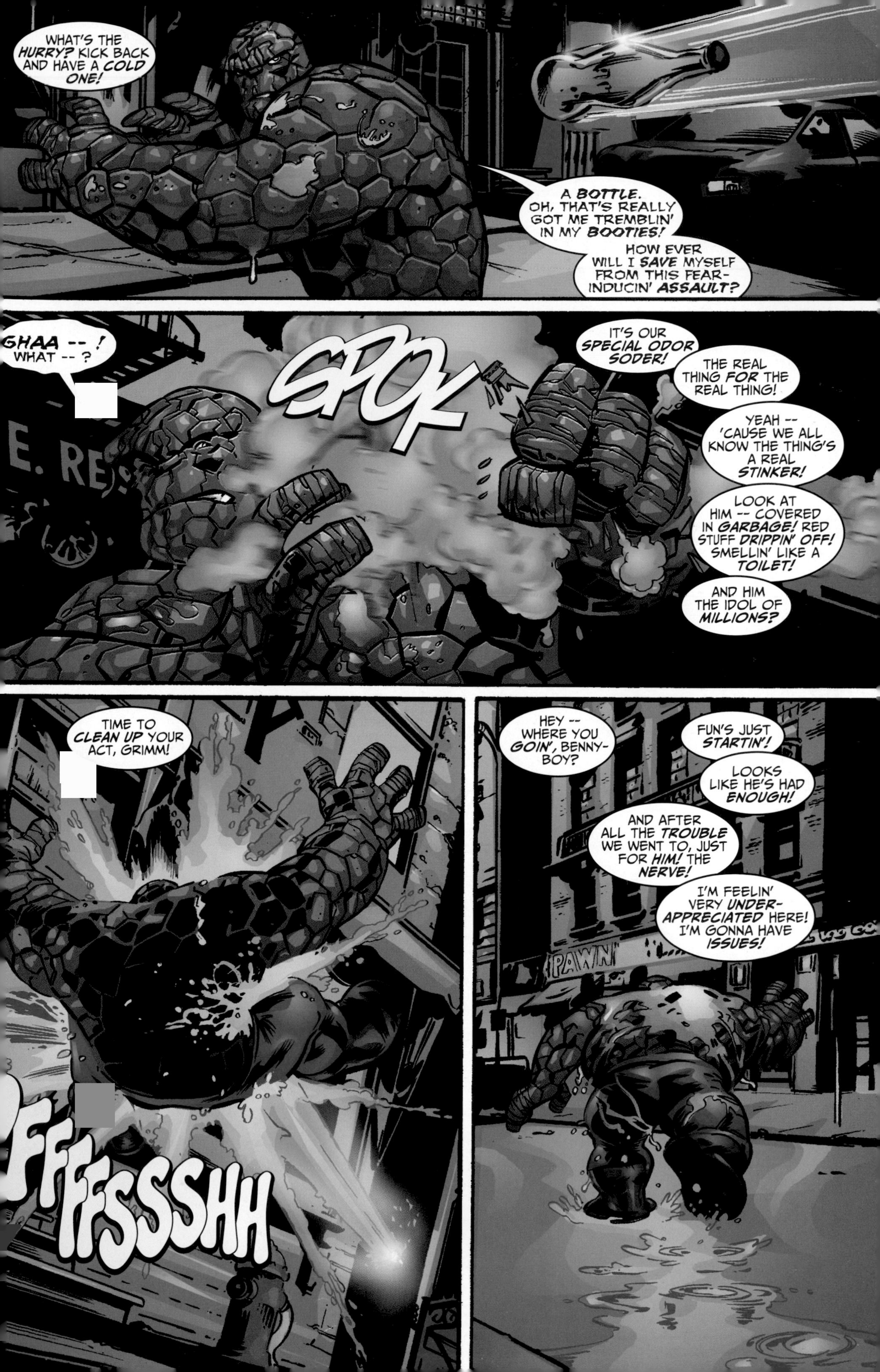
WHAT'S THE HURRY? KICK BACK AND HAVE A COLD ONE!
A BOTTLE. OH, THAT'S REALLY GOT ME TREMBLIN' IN MY BOOTIES!
HOW EVER WILL I SAVE MYSELF FROM THIS FEAR-INDUCIN' ASSAULT?
GHAA -- ! WHAT -- ?
SPOK
IT'S OUR SPECIAL ODOR SODER!
THE REAL THING FOR THE REAL THING!
YEAH -- 'CAUSE WE ALL KNOW THE THING'S A REAL STINKER!
LOOK AT HIM -- COVERED IN GARBAGE! RED STUFF DRIPPIN' OFF! SMELLIN' LIKE A TOILET!
AND HIM THE IDOL OF MILLIONS?
TIME TO CLEAN UP YOUR ACT, GRIMM!
FFFFSSSHH
HEY -- WHERE YOU GOIN', BENNY-BOY?
FUN'S JUST STARTIN'!
LOOKS LIKE HE'S HAD ENOUGH!
AND AFTER ALL THE TROUBLE WE WENT TO, JUST FOR HIM! THE NERVE!
I'M FEELIN' VERY UNDER-APPRECIATED HERE! I'M GONNA HAVE ISSUES!
PAWN

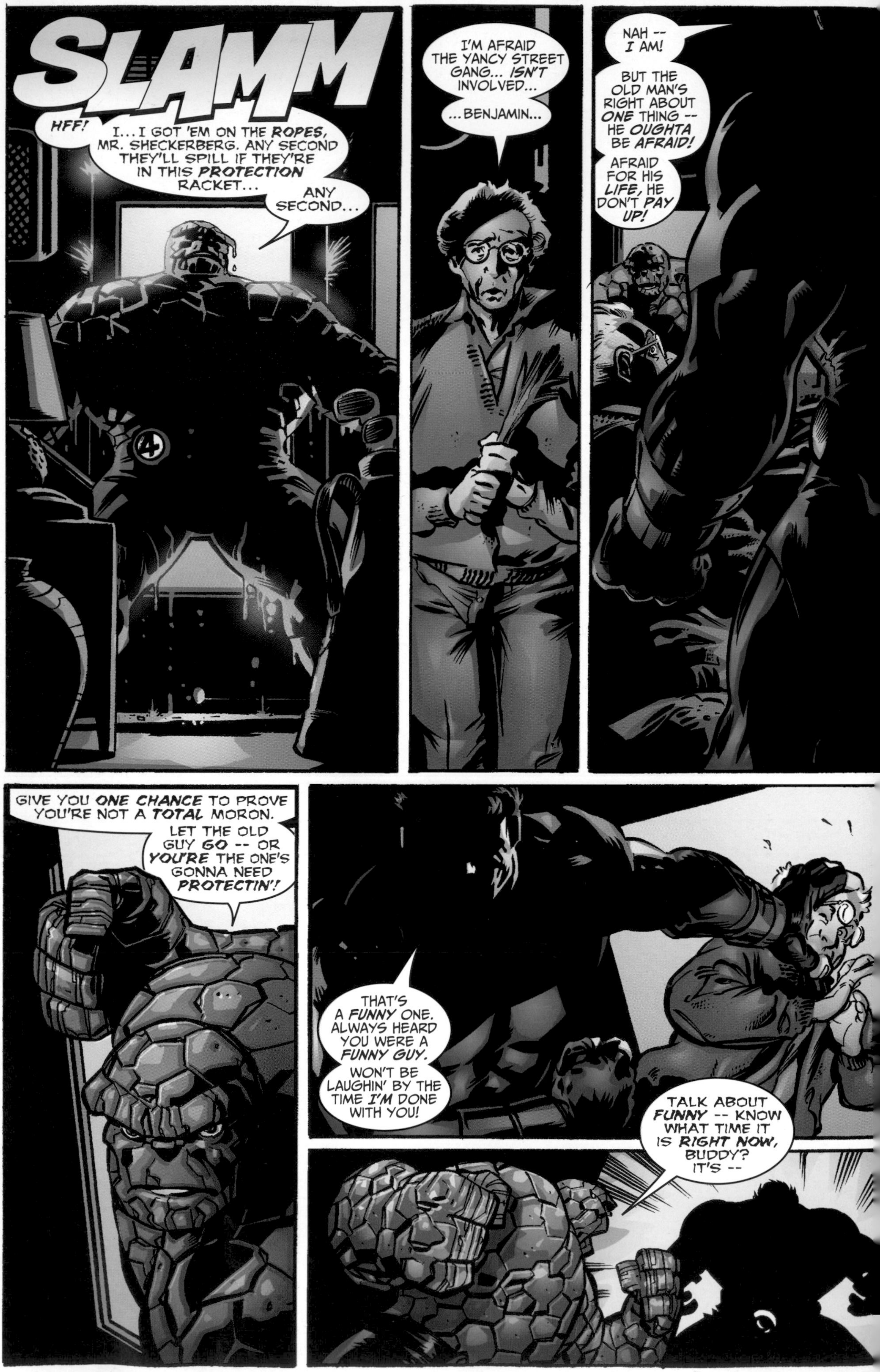

SLAMM
HFF!
I... I GOT 'EM ON THE ROPES, MR. SHECKERBERG. ANY SECOND THEY'LL SPILL IF THEY'RE IN THIS PROTECTION RACKET...
ANY SECOND...
I'M AFRAID THE YANCY STREET GANG... ISN'T INVOLVED...
...BENJAMIN...
NAH -- I AM!
BUT THE OLD MAN'S RIGHT ABOUT ONE THING -- HE OUGHTA BE AFRAID!
AFRAID FOR HIS LIFE, HE DON'T PAY UP!
GIVE YOU ONE CHANCE TO PROVE YOU'RE NOT A TOTAL MORON.
LET THE OLD GUY GO -- OR YOU'RE THE ONE'S GONNA NEED PROTECTIN'!
THAT'S A FUNNY ONE. ALWAYS HEARD YOU WERE A FUNNY GUY.
WON'T BE LAUGHIN' BY THE TIME I'M DONE WITH YOU!
TALK ABOUT FUNNY -- KNOW WHAT TIME IT IS RIGHT NOW, BUDDY? IT'S --

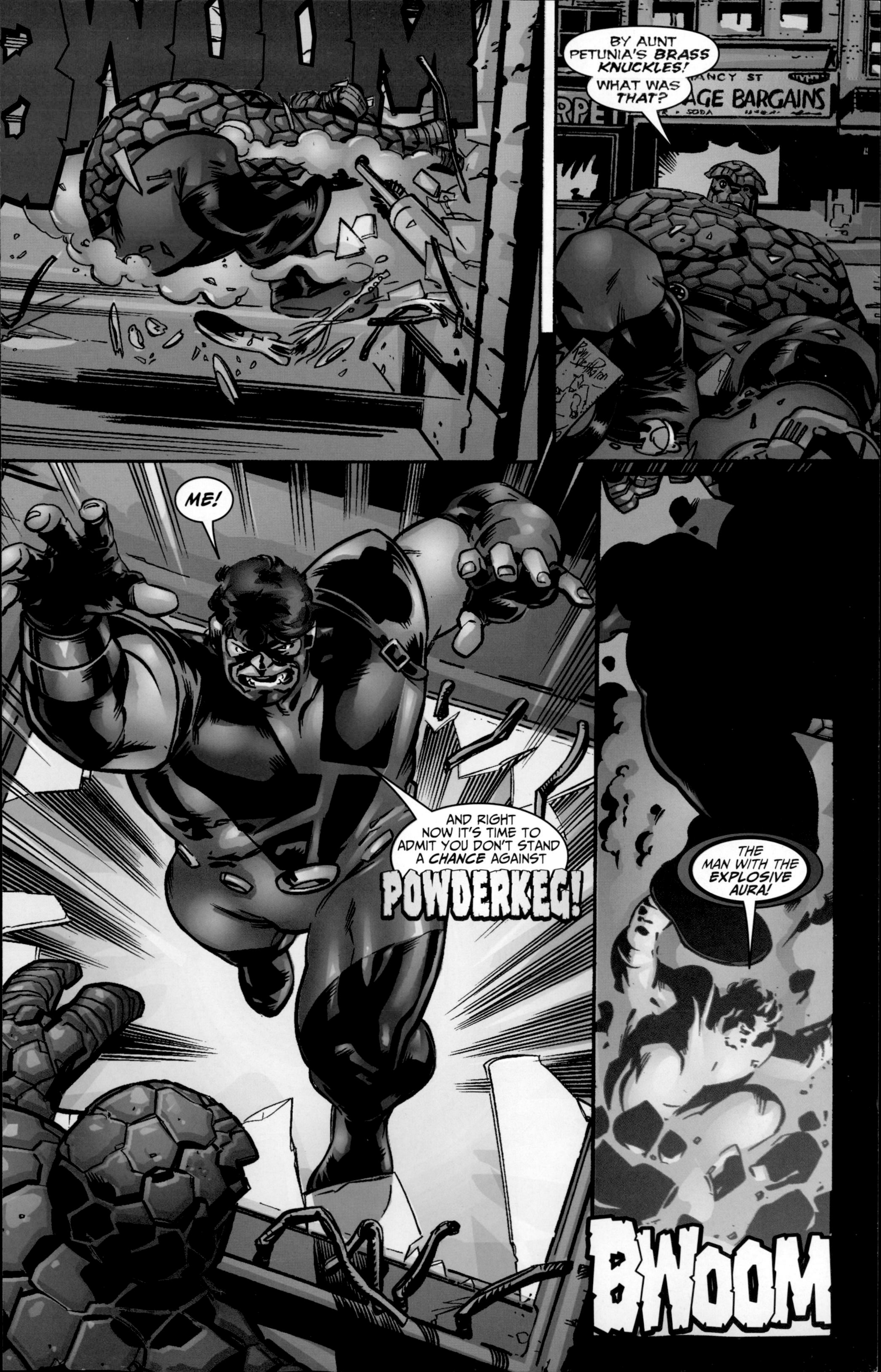
BY AUNT PETUNIA'S BRASS KNUCKLES! WHAT WAS THAT?
ME!
AND RIGHT NOW IT'S TIME TO ADMIT YOU DON'T STAND A CHANCE AGAINST
POWDERKEG!
THE MAN WITH THE EXPLOSIVE AURA!
BWOOM

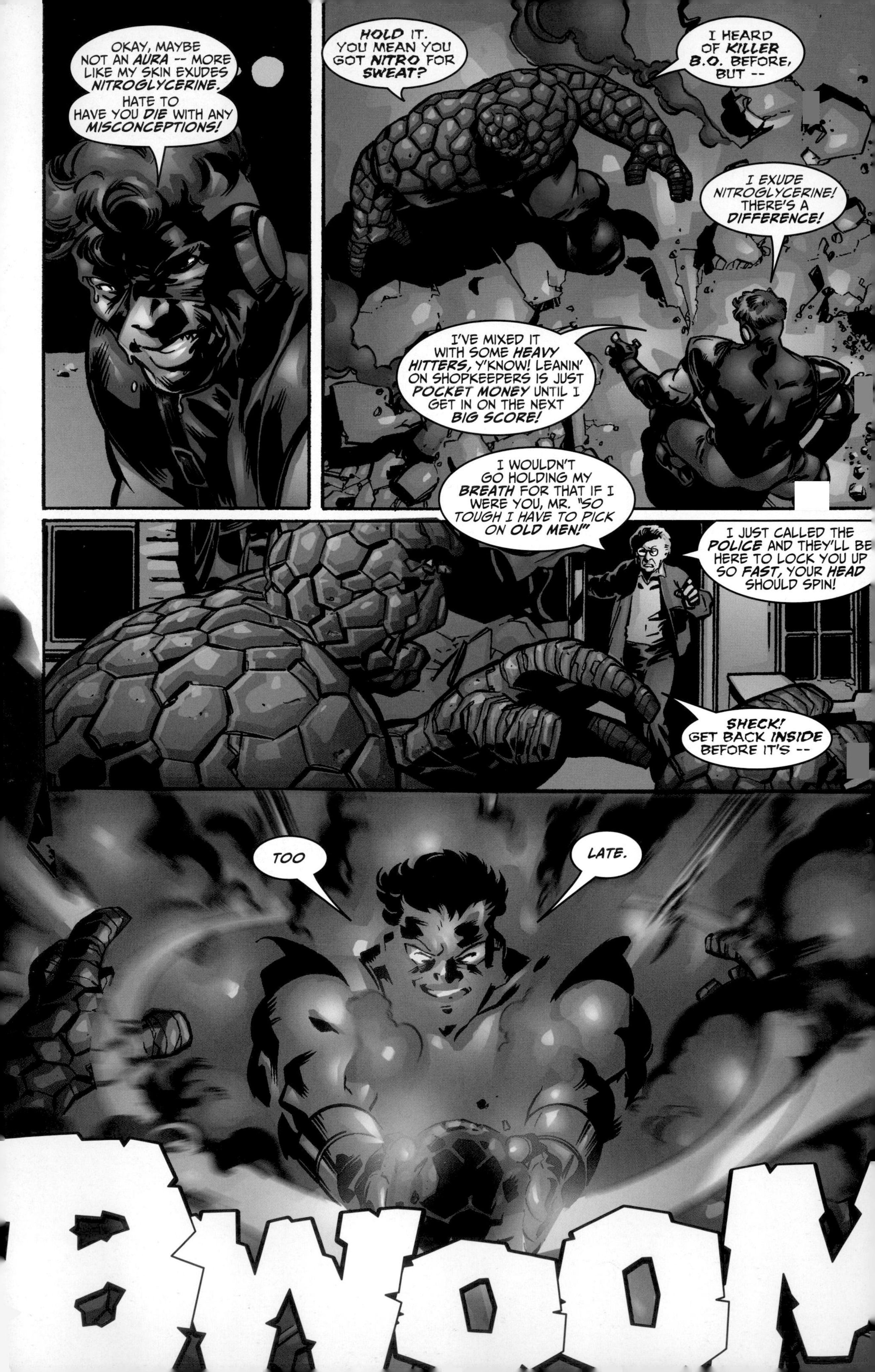
OKAY, MAYBE NOT AN AURA -- MORE LIKE MY SKIN EXUDES NITROGLYCERINE.
HATE TO HAVE YOU DIE WITH ANY MISCONCEPTIONS!
HOLD IT. YOU MEAN YOU GOT NITRO FOR SWEAT?
I HEARD OF KILLER B.O. BEFORE, BUT --
I EXUDE NITROGLYCERINE! THERE'S A DIFFERENCE!
I'VE MIXED IT WITH SOME HEAVY HITTERS, Y'KNOW! LEANIN' ON SHOPKEEPERS IS JUST POCKET MONEY UNTIL I GET IN ON THE NEXT BIG SCORE!
I WOULDN'T GO HOLDING MY BREATH FOR THAT IF I WERE YOU, MR. "SO TOUGH I HAVE TO PICK ON OLD MEN!"
I JUST CALLED THE POLICE AND THEY'LL BE HERE TO LOCK YOU UP SO FAST, YOUR HEAD SHOULD SPIN!
SHECK! GET BACK INSIDE BEFORE IT'S --
TOO
LATE.

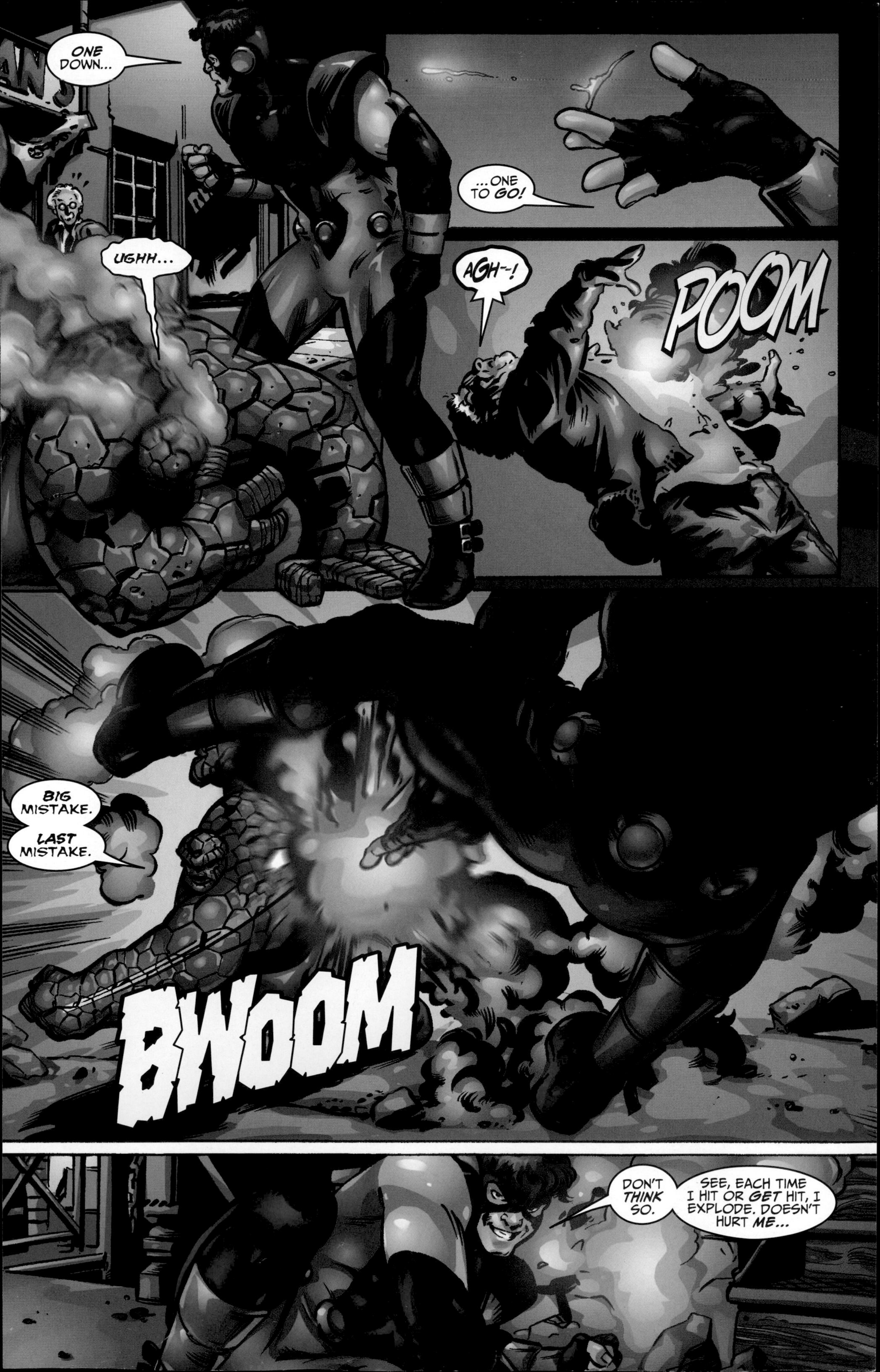
ONE DOWN...
...ONE TO GO!
UGHH...
AGH--!
POOM
BIG MISTAKE.
LAST MISTAKE.
BWOOM
DON'T THINK SO.
SEE, EACH TIME I HIT OR GET HIT, I EXPLODE. DOESN'T HURT ME...

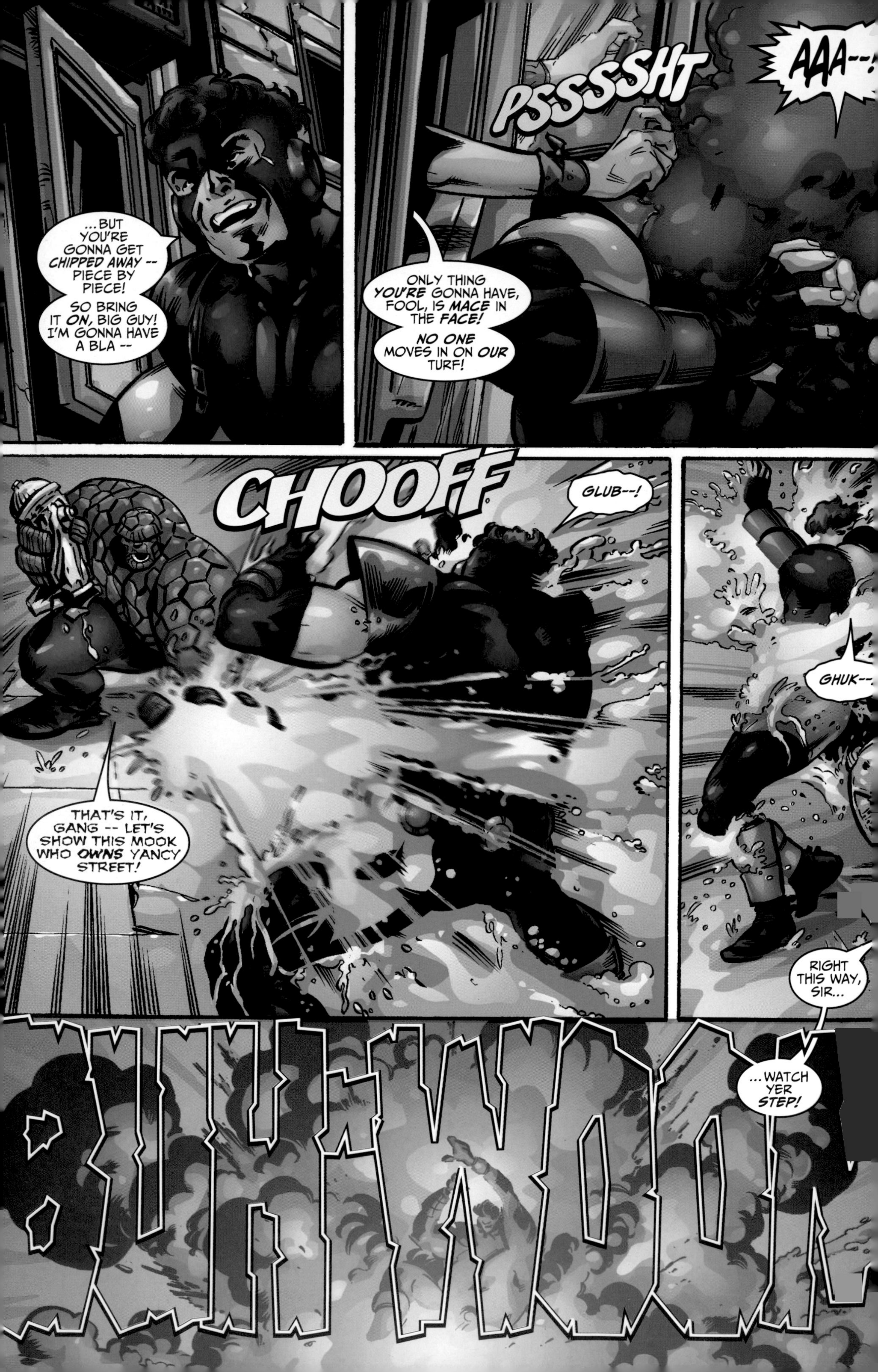
...BUT YOU'RE GONNA GET CHIPPED AWAY -- PIECE BY PIECE!
SO BRING IT ON, BIG GUY! I'M GONNA HAVE A BLA --
PSSSSHT
AAA--!
ONLY THING YOU'RE GONNA HAVE, FOOL, IS MACE IN THE FACE!
NO ONE MOVES IN ON OUR TURF!
CHOOFF
GLUB--!
THAT'S IT, GANG -- LET'S SHOW THIS MOOK WHO OWNS YANCY STREET!
GHUK--
RIGHT THIS WAY, SIR...
...WATCH YER STEP!

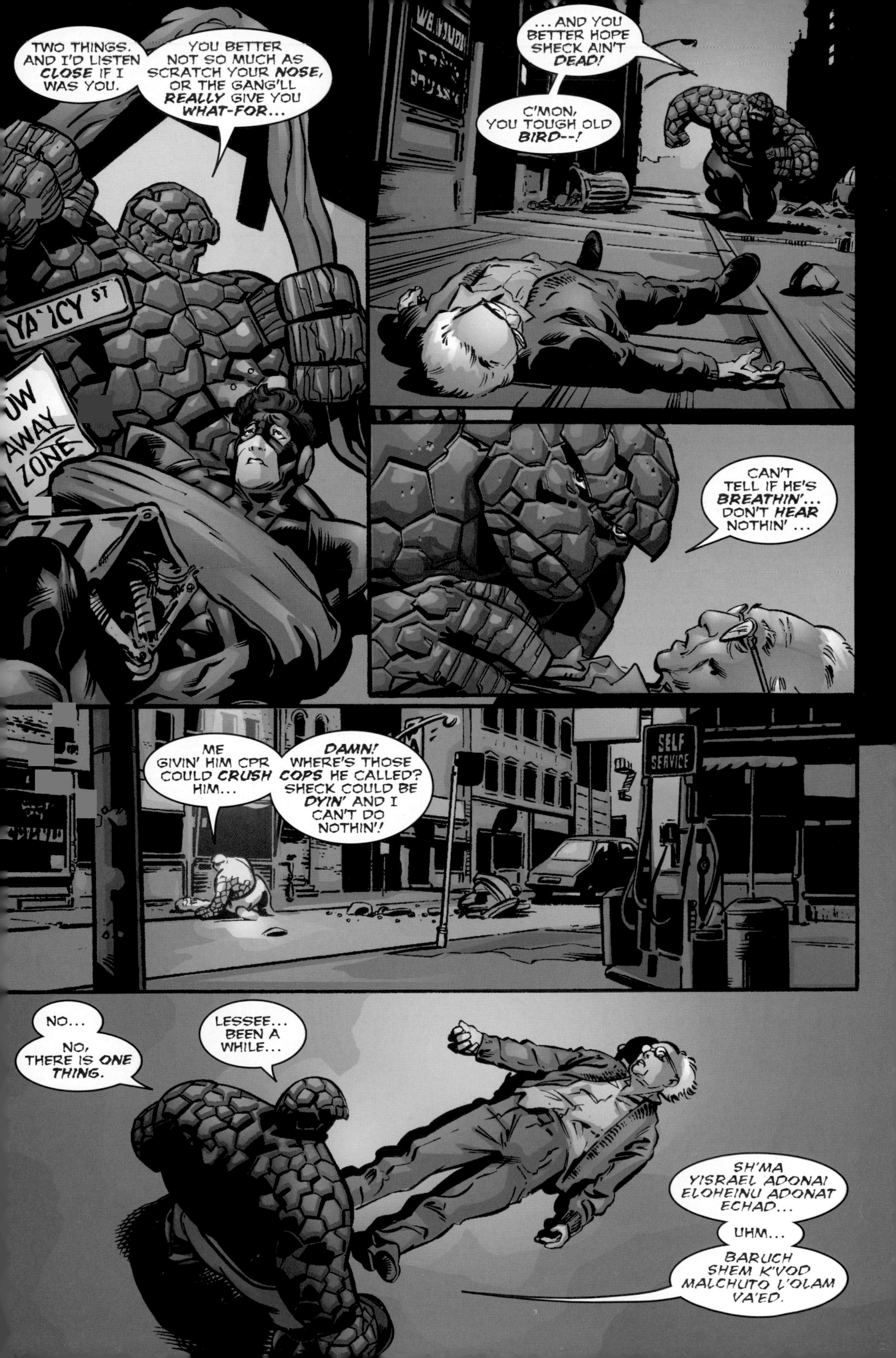
TWO THINGS. AND I'D LISTEN CLOSE IF I WAS YOU.
YOU BETTER NOT SO MUCH AS SCRATCH YOUR NOSE, OR THE GANG'LL REALLY GIVE YOU WHAT-FOR...
AWAY ZONE
...AND YOU BETTER HOPE SHECK AIN'T DEAD!
C'MON, YOU TOUGH OLD BIRD--!
CAN'T TELL IF HE'S BREATHIN'... DON'T HEAR NOTHIN'...
ME GIVIN' HIM CPR COULD CRUSH HIM...
DAMN! WHERE'S THOSE COPS HE CALLED? SHECK COULD BE DYIN' AND I CAN'T DO NOTHIN'!
SELF SERVICE
NO...
NO, THERE IS ONE THING.
LESSEE... BEEN A WHILE...
SH'MA YISRAEL ADONAI ELOHEINU ADONAI ECHAD...
UHM...
BARUCH SHEM K'VOD MALCHUTO L'OLAM VA'ED.

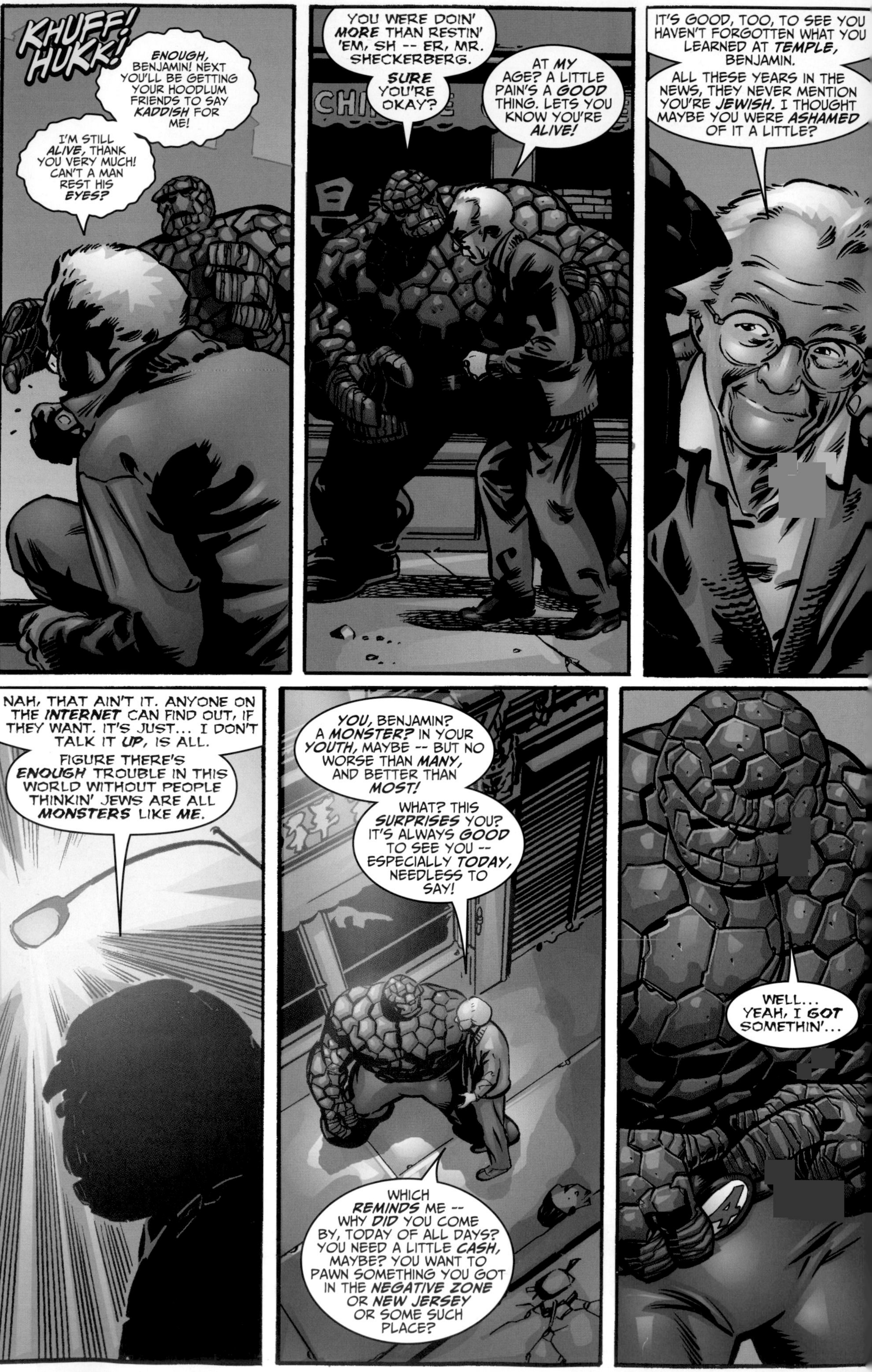
KHUFF! HUKK!
ENOUGH, BENJAMIN! NEXT YOU'LL BE GETTING YOUR HOODLUM FRIENDS TO SAY KADDISH FOR ME!
I'M STILL ALIVE, THANK YOU VERY MUCH! CAN'T A MAN REST HIS EYES?
YOU WERE DOIN' MORE THAN RESTIN' 'EM, SH -- ER, MR. SHECKERBERG.
SURE YOU'RE OKAY?
AT MY AGE? A LITTLE PAIN'S A GOOD THING. LETS YOU KNOW YOU'RE ALIVE!
IT'S GOOD, TOO, TO SEE YOU HAVEN'T FORGOTTEN WHAT YOU LEARNED AT TEMPLE, BENJAMIN.
ALL THESE YEARS IN THE NEWS, THEY NEVER MENTION YOU'RE JEWISH. I THOUGHT MAYBE YOU WERE ASHAMED OF IT A LITTLE?
NAH, THAT AIN'T IT. ANYONE ON THE INTERNET CAN FIND OUT, IF THEY WANT. IT'S JUST... I DON'T TALK IT UP, IS ALL.
FIGURE THERE'S ENOUGH TROUBLE IN THIS WORLD WITHOUT PEOPLE THINKIN' JEWS ARE ALL MONSTERS LIKE ME.
YOU, BENJAMIN? A MONSTER? IN YOUR YOUTH, MAYBE -- BUT NO WORSE THAN MANY, AND BETTER THAN MOST!
WHAT? THIS SURPRISES YOU? IT'S ALWAYS GOOD TO SEE YOU -- ESPECIALLY TODAY, NEEDLESS TO SAY!
WHICH REMINDS ME -- WHY DID YOU COME BY, TODAY OF ALL DAYS? YOU NEED A LITTLE CASH, MAYBE? YOU WANT TO PAWN SOMETHING YOU GOT IN THE NEGATIVE ZONE OR NEW JERSEY OR SOME SUCH PLACE?
WELL... YEAH, I GOT SOMETHIN'...

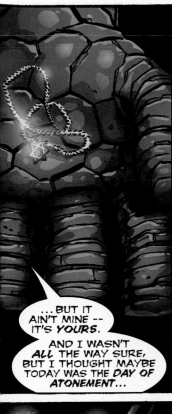

...BUT IT AIN'T MINE -- IT'S *YOURS.*

AND I WASN'T *ALL* THE WAY SURE, BUT I THOUGHT MAYBE TODAY WAS THE *DAY OF ATONEMENT...*

...AND ON THAT DAY, PAST TRANSGRESSIONS SHALL BE *FORGIVEN.*

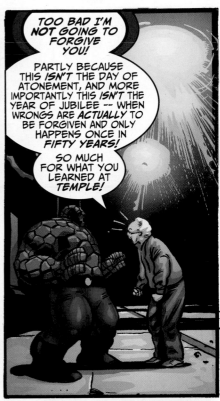

TOO BAD I'M *NOT GOING TO FORGIVE* YOU!

PARTLY BECAUSE THIS *ISN'T* THE DAY OF ATONEMENT, AND MORE IMPORTANTLY THIS *ISN'T* THE YEAR OF JUBILEE -- WHEN WRONGS ARE *ACTUALLY* TO BE FORGIVEN AND ONLY HAPPENS ONCE IN *FIFTY YEARS!*

SO MUCH FOR WHAT YOU LEARNED AT *TEMPLE!*

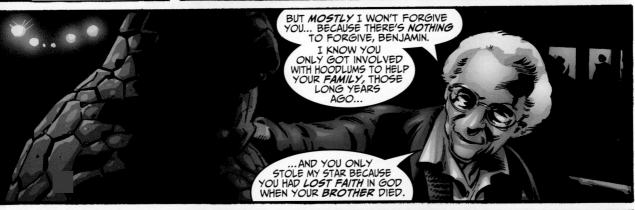

BUT *MOSTLY* I WON'T FORGIVE YOU... BECAUSE THERE'S *NOTHING* TO FORGIVE, BENJAMIN.

I KNOW YOU ONLY GOT INVOLVED WITH HOODLUMS TO HELP YOUR *FAMILY,* THOSE LONG YEARS AGO...

...AND YOU ONLY STOLE MY STAR BECAUSE YOU HAD *LOST FAITH* IN GOD WHEN YOUR *BROTHER* DIED.

NOW *TELL* ME SOMETHING. MR. SWVITZ-KABOOM OVER THERE -- HE CAN BRING DOWN *BUILDINGS* WITH HIS BARE HANDS, YET YOU *STAND UP* TO HIM. *STOP* HIM.

BUT WHEN THE YANCY STREET GANG THROWS *TOMATOES* -- YOU *RUN?*

WELL, Y'KNOW... THEY'RE JUST *KIDS.*

I COULD *HURT* 'EM.

AND I SUPPOSE THAT'S WHY YOU KEEP COMING *BACK* AND KEEP LETTING THEM *ABUSE* YOU, TIME AFTER TIME? SO YOU *WON'T* HURT THEM?

UHM...

KNOW WHAT I THINK, MR. *COLLEGE-BOY?* MR. *ACE PILOT?* MR. *FANTASTIC FOUR SAVES THE WORLD?*

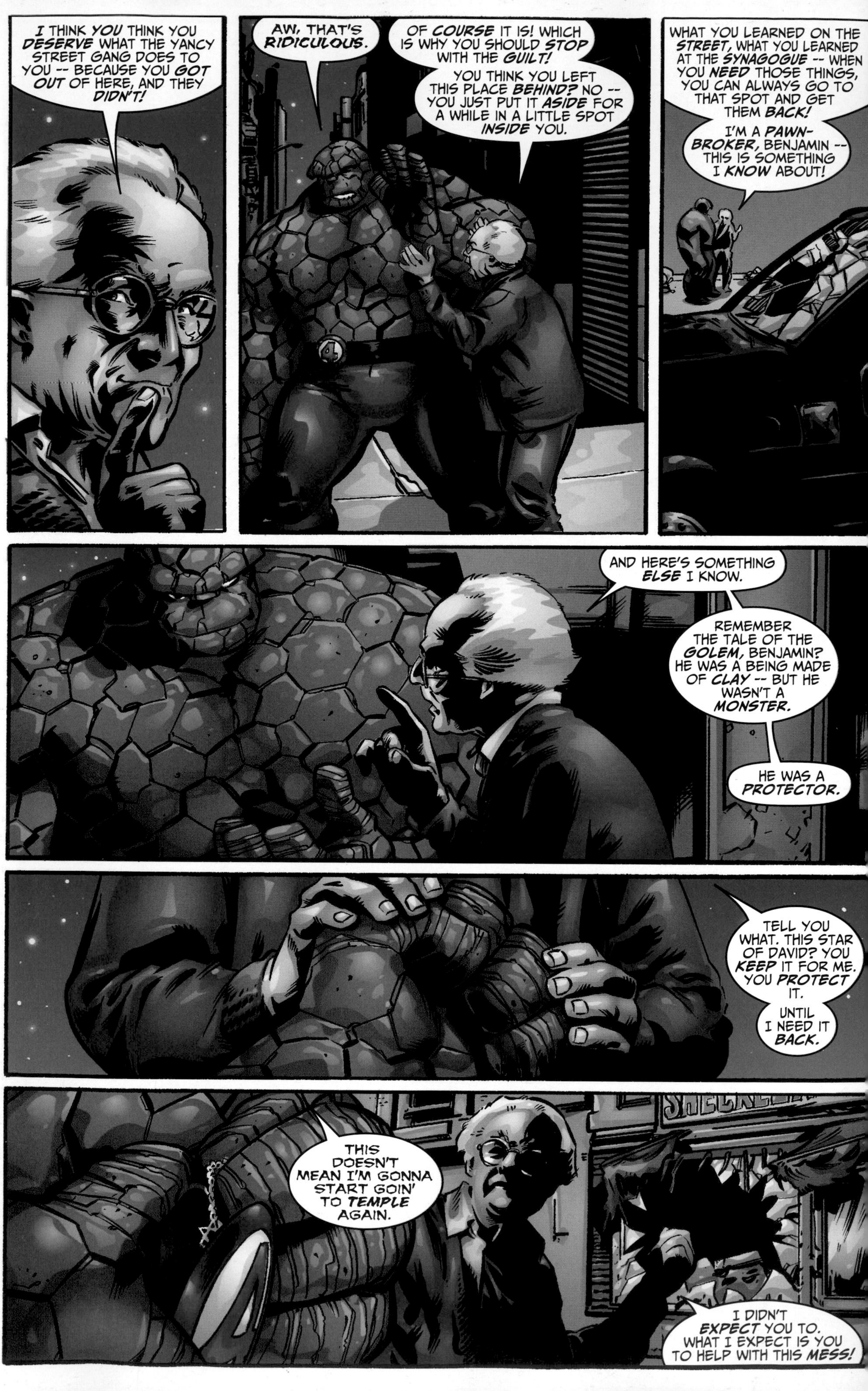
I THINK YOU THINK YOU DESERVE WHAT THE YANCY STREET GANG DOES TO YOU -- BECAUSE YOU GOT OUT OF HERE, AND THEY DIDN'T!
AW, THAT'S RIDICULOUS.
OF COURSE IT IS! WHICH IS WHY YOU SHOULD STOP WITH THE GUILT!
YOU THINK YOU LEFT THIS PLACE BEHIND? NO -- YOU JUST PUT IT ASIDE FOR A WHILE IN A LITTLE SPOT INSIDE YOU.
WHAT YOU LEARNED ON THE STREET, WHAT YOU LEARNED AT THE SYNAGOGUE -- WHEN YOU NEED THOSE THINGS, YOU CAN ALWAYS GO TO THAT SPOT AND GET THEM BACK!
I'M A PAWN-BROKER, BENJAMIN -- THIS IS SOMETHING I KNOW ABOUT!
AND HERE'S SOMETHING ELSE I KNOW.
REMEMBER THE TALE OF THE GOLEM, BENJAMIN? HE WAS A BEING MADE OF CLAY -- BUT HE WASN'T A MONSTER.
HE WAS A PROTECTOR.
TELL YOU WHAT. THIS STAR OF DAVID? YOU KEEP IT FOR ME. YOU PROTECT IT.
UNTIL I NEED IT BACK.
THIS DOESN'T MEAN I'M GONNA START GOIN' TO TEMPLE AGAIN.
I DIDN'T EXPECT YOU TO. WHAT I EXPECT IS YOU TO HELP WITH THIS MESS!

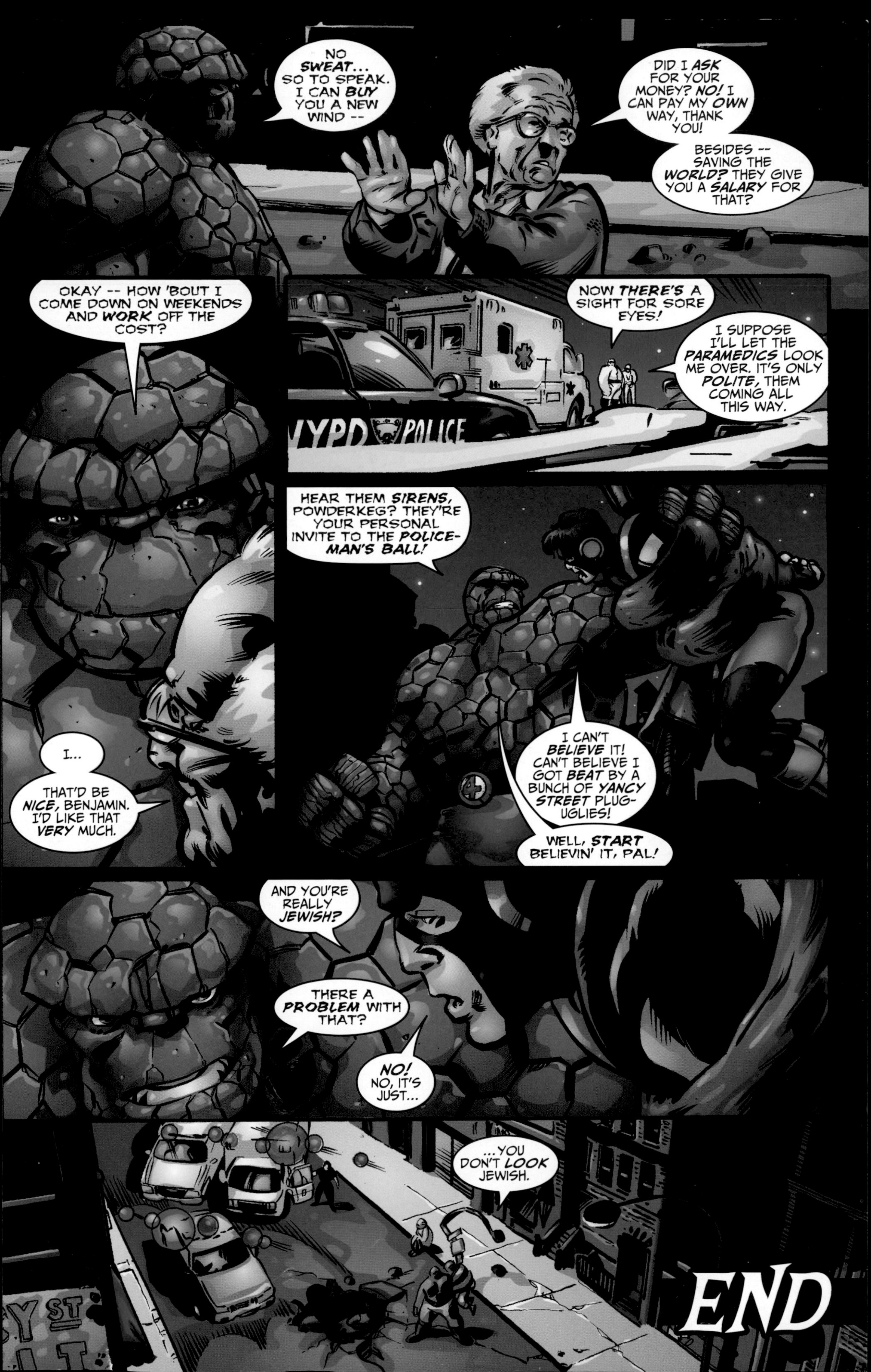
NO SWEAT... SO TO SPEAK. I CAN BUY YOU A NEW WIND --
DID I ASK FOR YOUR MONEY? NO! I CAN PAY MY OWN WAY, THANK YOU!
BESIDES -- SAVING THE WORLD? THEY GIVE YOU A SALARY FOR THAT?
OKAY -- HOW 'BOUT I COME DOWN ON WEEKENDS AND WORK OFF THE COST?
I...
THAT'D BE NICE, BENJAMIN. I'D LIKE THAT VERY MUCH.
NYPD POLICE
NOW THERE'S A SIGHT FOR SORE EYES!
I SUPPOSE I'LL LET THE PARAMEDICS LOOK ME OVER. IT'S ONLY POLITE, THEM COMING ALL THIS WAY.
HEAR THEM SIRENS, POWDERKEG? THEY'RE YOUR PERSONAL INVITE TO THE POLICE-MAN'S BALL!
I CAN'T BELIEVE IT! CAN'T BELIEVE I GOT BEAT BY A BUNCH OF YANCY STREET PLUG-UGLIES!
WELL, START BELIEVIN' IT, PAL!
AND YOU'RE REALLY JEWISH?
THERE A PROBLEM WITH THAT?
NO! NO, IT'S JUST...
...YOU DON'T LOOK JEWISH.
END

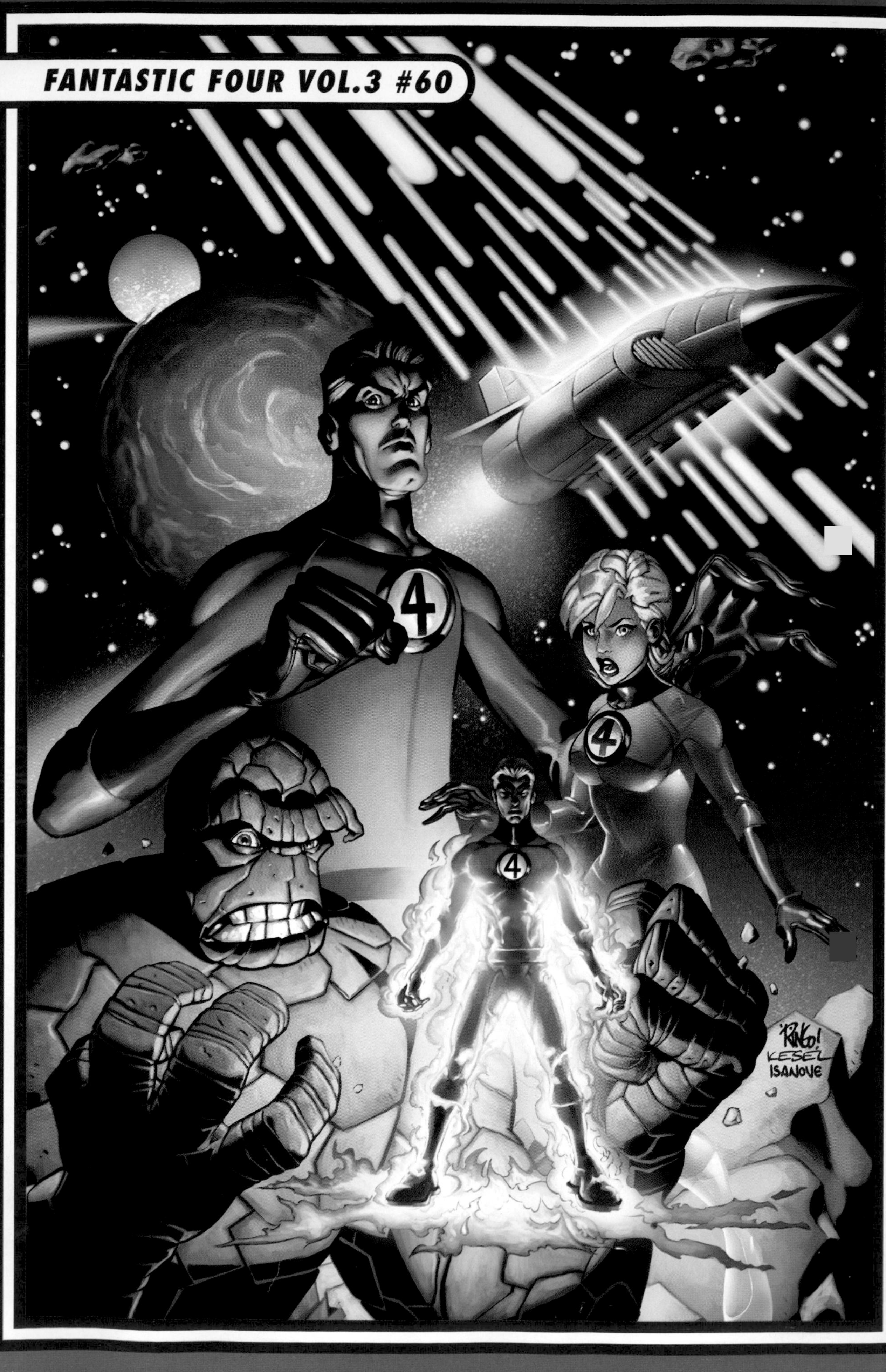
FANTASTIC FOUR VOL.3 #60
4
4
4
RINGO!
KESEL
ISANOVE

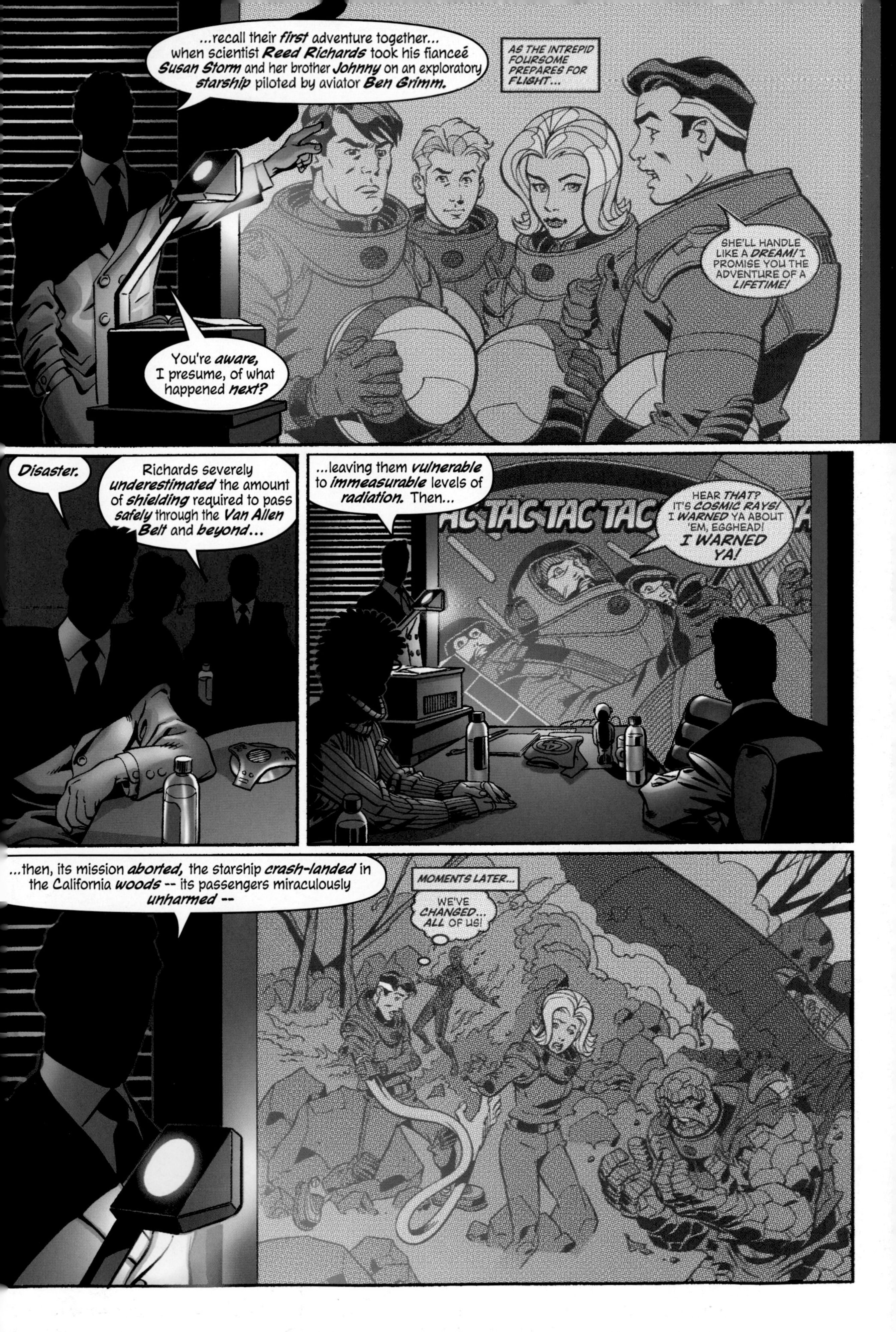
...recall their first adventure together... when scientist Reed Richards took his fianceé Susan Storm and her brother Johnny on an exploratory starship piloted by aviator Ben Grimm.
AS THE INTREPID FOURSOME PREPARES FOR FLIGHT...
SHE'LL HANDLE LIKE A DREAM! I PROMISE YOU THE ADVENTURE OF A LIFETIME!
You're aware, I presume, of what happened next?
Disaster.
Richards severely underestimated the amount of shielding required to pass safely through the Van Allen Belt and beyond...
...leaving them vulnerable to immeasurable levels of radiation. Then...
TAC TAC TAC TAC
HEAR THAT? IT'S COSMIC RAYS! I WARNED YA ABOUT 'EM, EGGHEAD! I WARNED YA!
...then, its mission aborted, the starship crash-landed in the California woods -- its passengers miraculously unharmed --
MOMENTS LATER...
WE'VE CHANGED... ALL OF US!

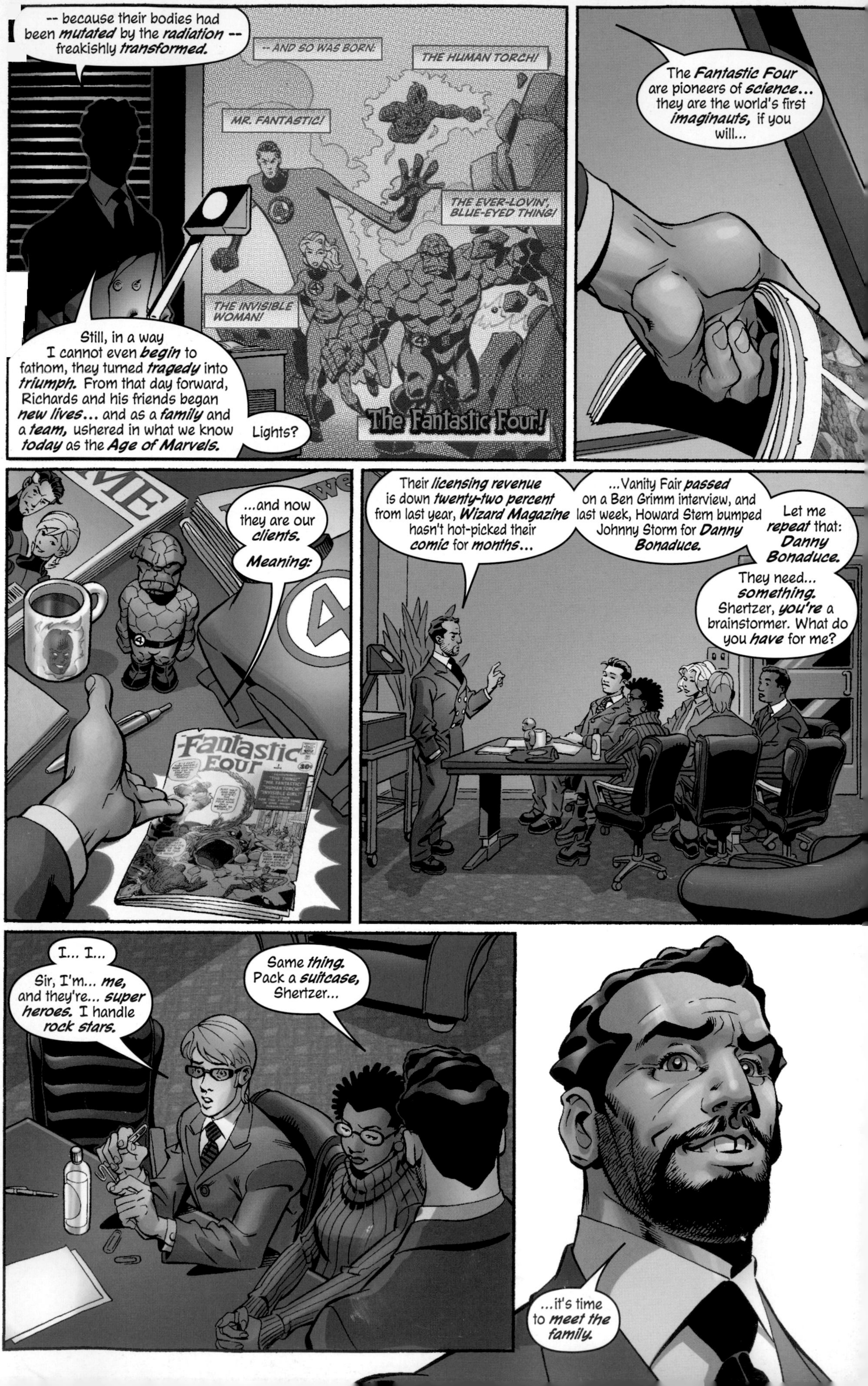

-- because their bodies had been mutated by the radiation -- freakishly transformed.
-- AND SO WAS BORN:
THE HUMAN TORCH!
MR. FANTASTIC!
THE EVER-LOVIN', BLUE-EYED THING!
THE INVISIBLE WOMAN!
The Fantastic Four!
Still, in a way I cannot even begin to fathom, they turned tragedy into triumph. From that day forward, Richards and his friends began new lives... and as a family and a team, ushered in what we know today as the Age of Marvels.
Lights?
The Fantastic Four are pioneers of science... they are the world's first imaginauts, if you will...
...and now they are our clients.
Meaning:
Fantastic Four
Their licensing revenue is down twenty-two percent from last year, Wizard Magazine hasn't hot-picked their comic for months...
...Vanity Fair passed on a Ben Grimm interview, and last week, Howard Stern bumped Johnny Storm for Danny Bonaduce.
Let me repeat that: Danny Bonaduce.
They need... something. Shertzer, you're a brainstormer. What do you have for me?
I... I...
Sir, I'm... me, and they're... super heroes. I handle rock stars.
Same thing. Pack a suitcase, Shertzer...
...it's time to meet the family.

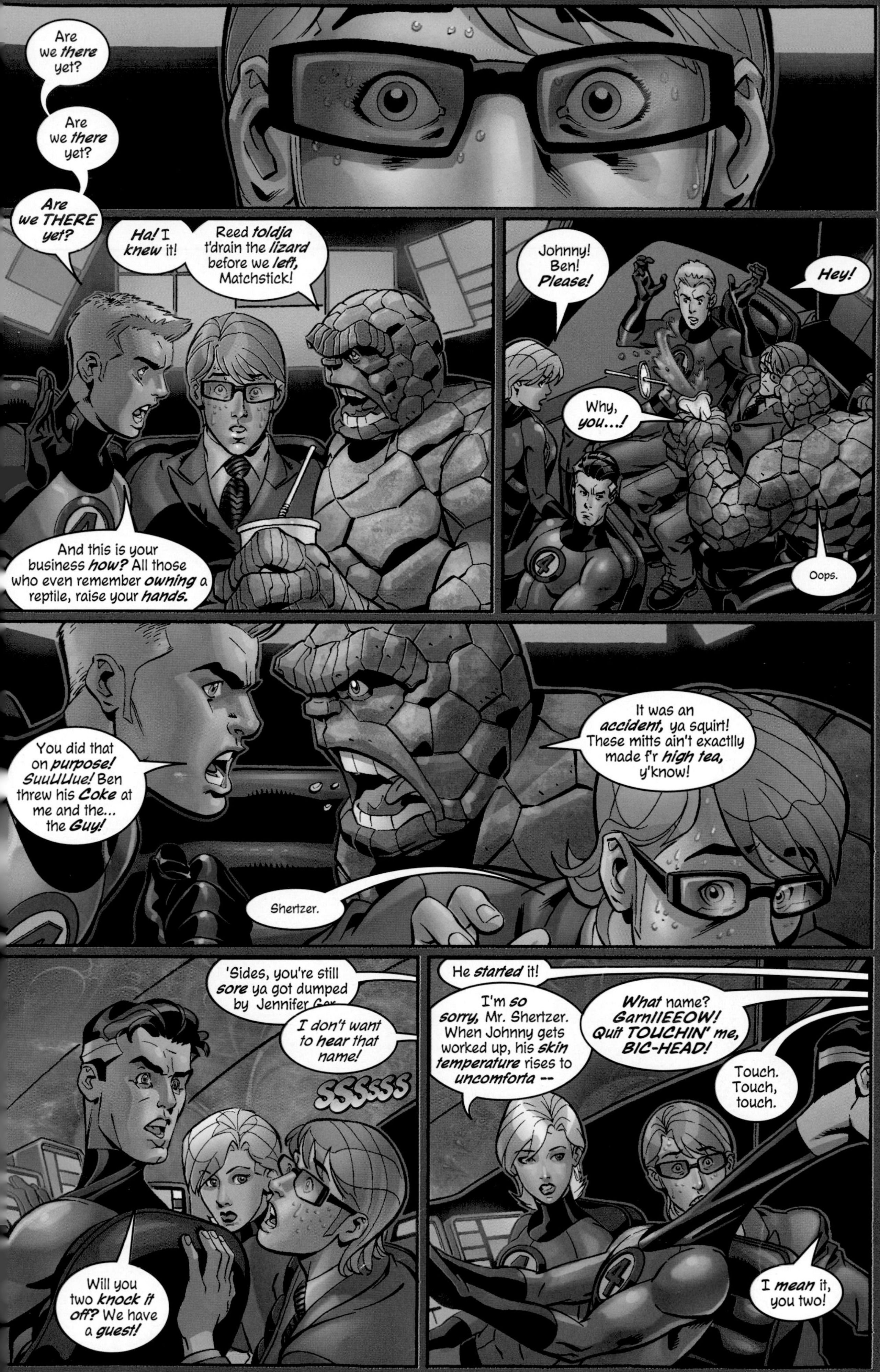
Are we *there* yet?
Are we *there* yet?
Are we THERE yet?
Ha! I *knew* it!
Reed *toldja* t'drain the *lizard* before we *left,* Matchstick!
And this is your business *how?* All those who even remember *owning* a reptile, raise your *hands.*
Johnny! Ben! *Please!*
Hey!
Why, *you...!*
Oops.
It was an *accident,* ya squirt! These mitts ain't exactlly made f'r *high tea,* y'know!
You did that on *purpose! SuuUUue!* Ben threw his *Coke* at me and the... the *Guy!*
Shertzer.
'Sides, you're still *sore* ya got dumped by Jennifer Gar
I don't want to hear that name!
SSSSSS
Will you two *knock it off?* We have a *guest!*
He *started* it!
I'm *so sorry,* Mr. Shertzer. When Johnny gets worked up, his *skin temperature* rises to *uncomforta --*
What name? *GarnIIEEOW! Quit TOUCHIN' me, BIG-HEAD!*
Touch. Touch, touch.
I *mean* it, you two!

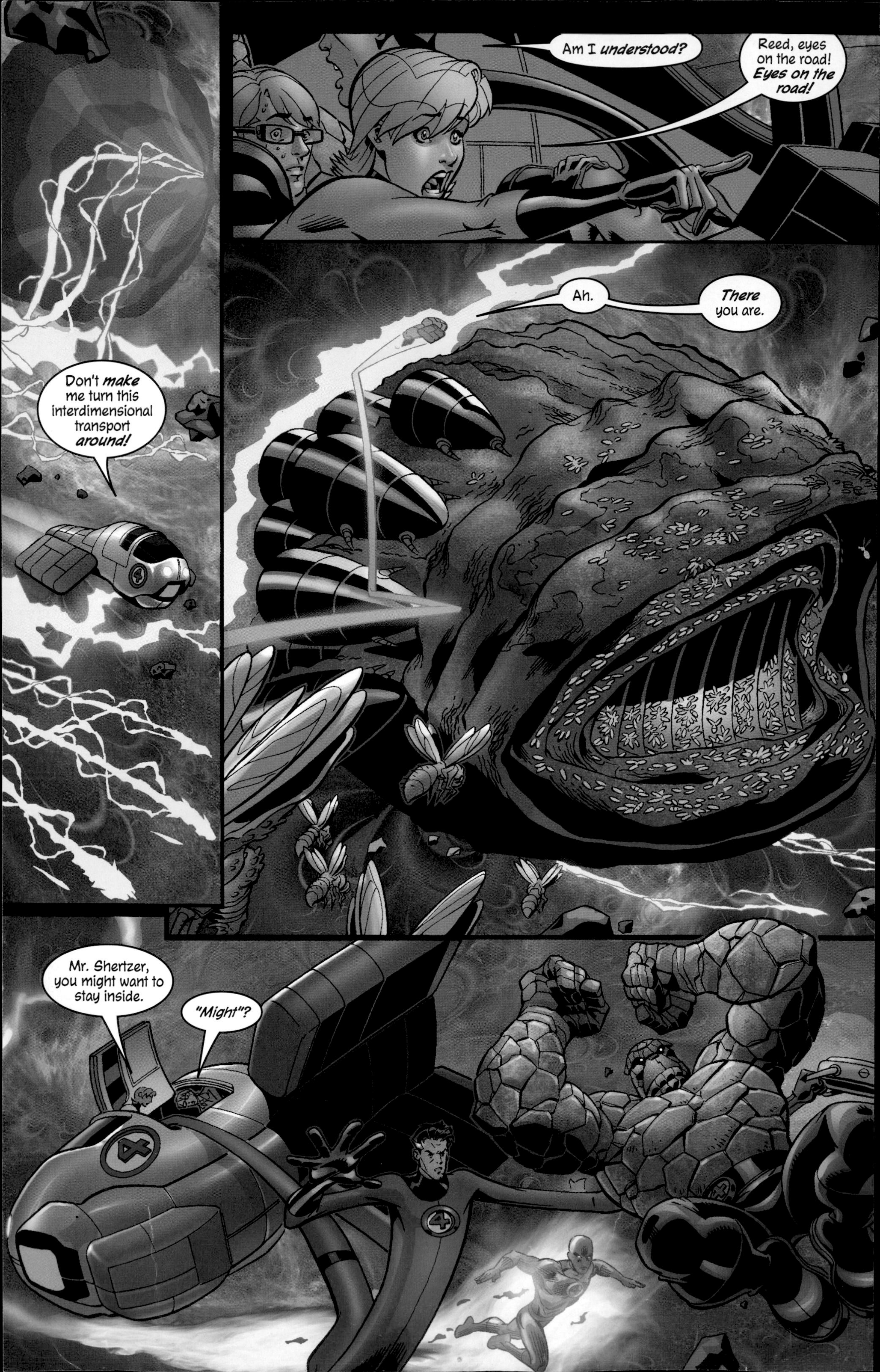
Am I *understood?*
Reed, eyes on the road! ***Eyes on the road!***
Don't ***make*** me turn this interdimensional transport ***around!***
Ah.
There you are.
Mr. Shertzer, you might want to stay inside.
"Might"?

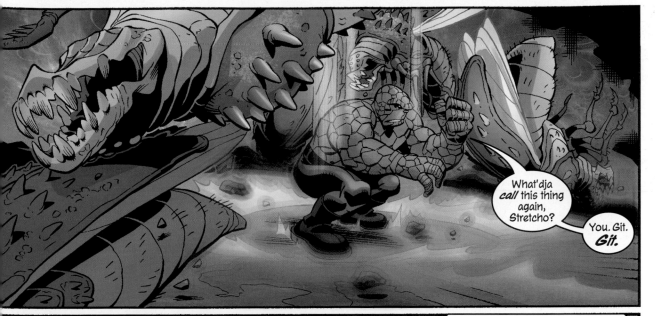

What'dja *call* this thing again, Stretcho?

You. Git. *Git*.

The *Datavore*, Ben! I concluded that the best way to gather information from the *Leviaverse* was to bioengineer a self-sustaining *dimensional probe* that could convert *ingested matter* into *fuel* and—

Datavore. *Got* it.

Your husband sure has some *cool* hobbies, sis.

What can I *say?* Guess a big brain really *does* it for me.

I was being *sarcastic* and, oh yeah, EEEWWWWW.

Digging the *invisible force field* work, though. Need a *hand?*

I'm fine, sweetie. Just thinking about how sexy *big brains* are... mmMMMmm...

Oh, God, *please* stop.

Heh.

By *swarming* the *Datavore*, these *indigenous lifeforms* are *killing* it -- ruining *months* of research!

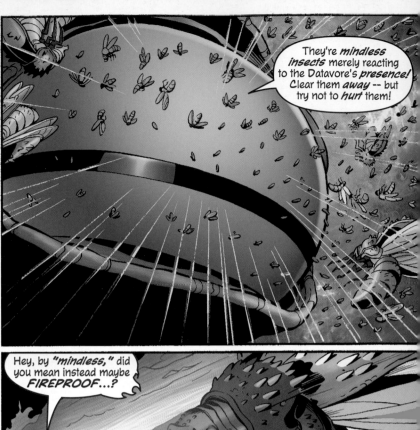

They're *mindless insects* merely reacting to the Datavore's *presence!* Clear them *away* -- but try not to *hurt* them!

Hey, by *"mindless,"* did you mean instead maybe *FIREPROOF...?*

heat blood
life warm
hunger hurt
taste fire

I said *GIT!*

You *okay,* kid?

Yeah. Just...

Yeah.

There. This should repel any further *attacks.* We're *done* here.

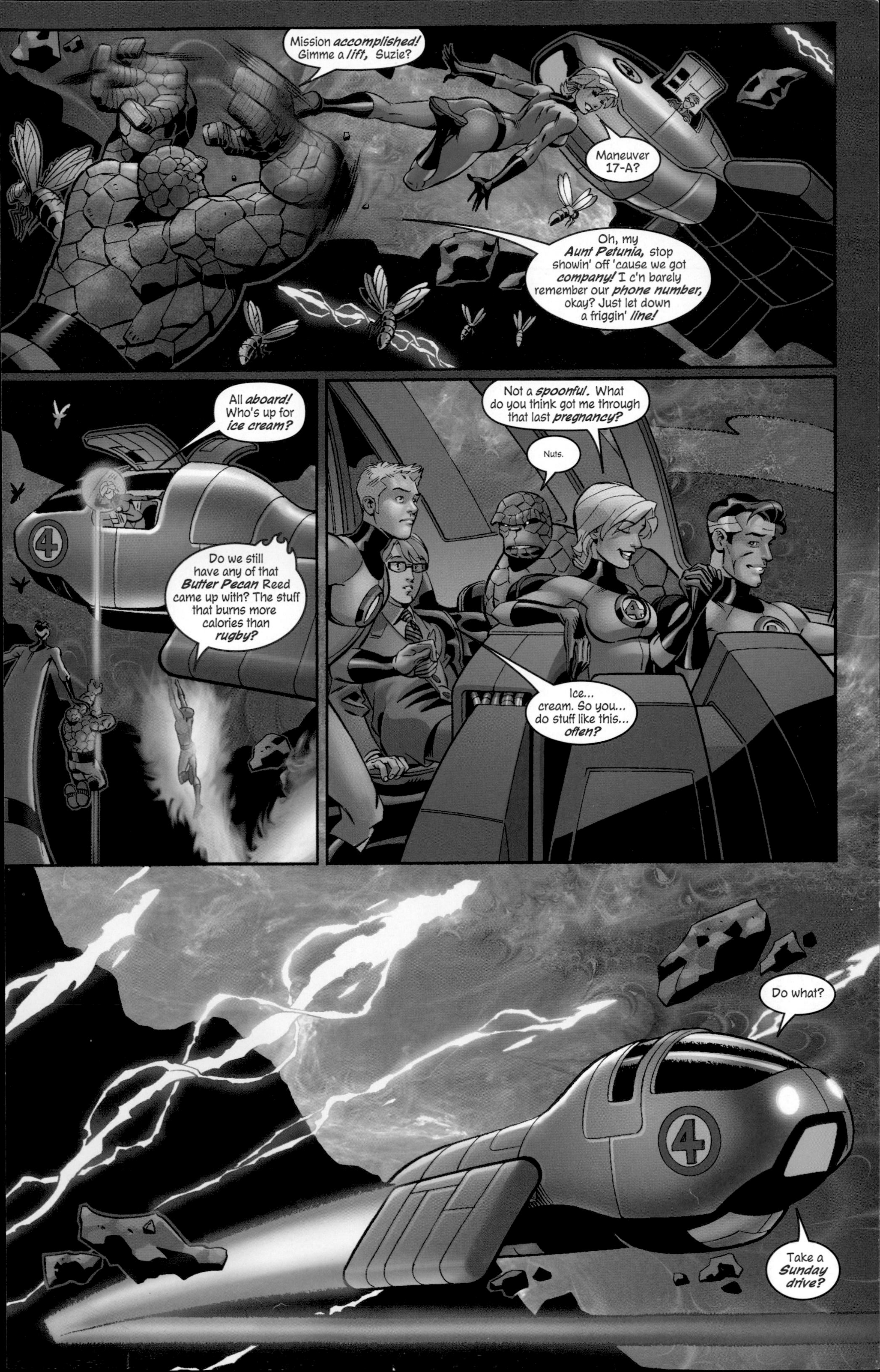
Mission accomplished! Gimme a lift, Suzie?
Maneuver 17-A?
Oh, my Aunt Petunia, stop showin' off 'cause we got company! I c'n barely remember our phone number, okay? Just let down a friggin' line!
All aboard! Who's up for ice cream?
Do we still have any of that Butter Pecan Reed came up with? The stuff that burns more calories than rugby?
Not a spoonful. What do you think got me through that last pregnancy?
Nuts.
Ice... cream. So you... do stuff like this... often?
Do what?
Take a Sunday drive?

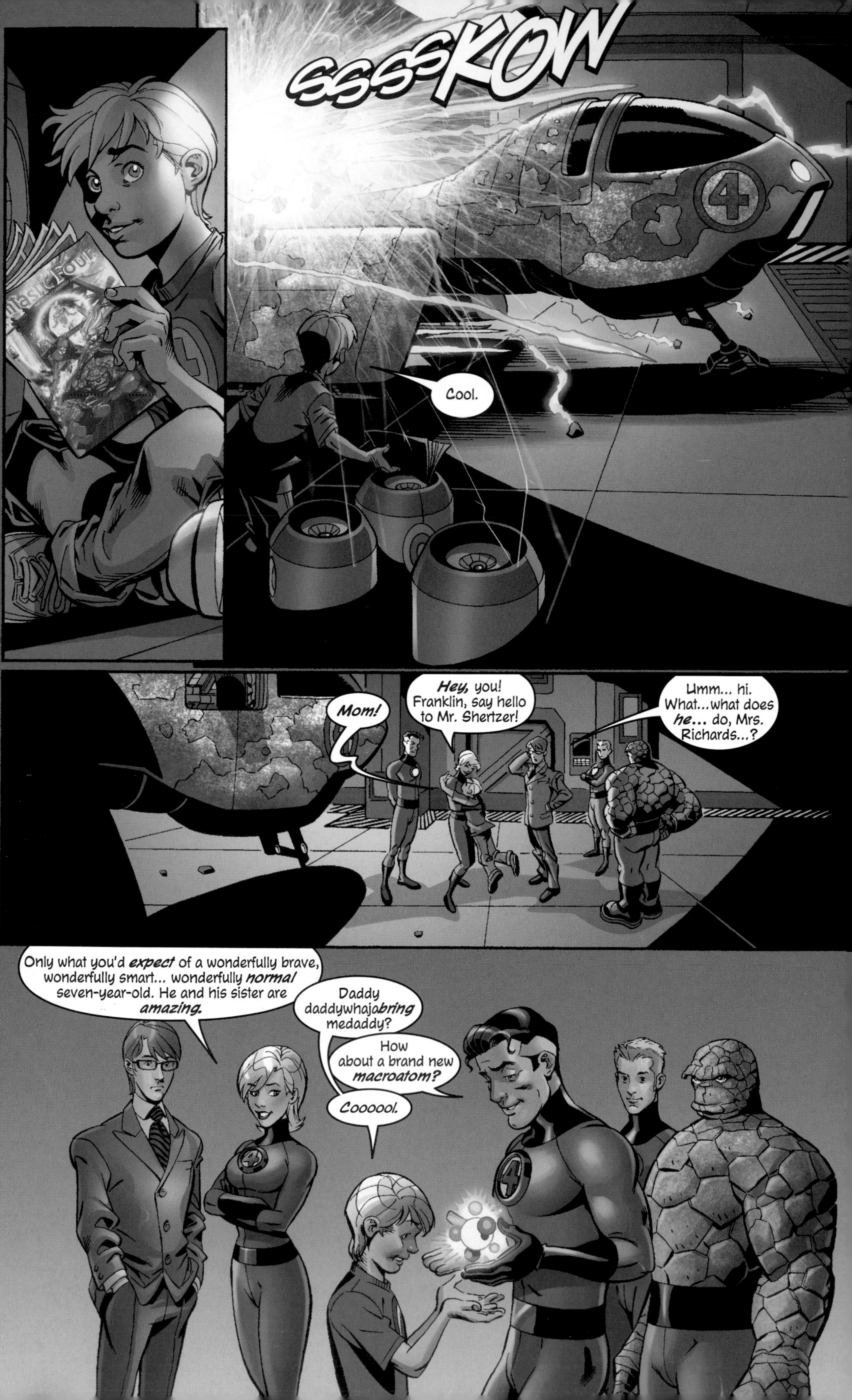
SSSSKOW
Cool.
Mom!
Hey, you! Franklin, say hello to Mr. Shertzer!
Umm... hi. What...what does he... do, Mrs. Richards...?
Only what you'd expect of a wonderfully brave, wonderfully smart... wonderfully normal seven-year-old. He and his sister are amazing.
Daddy daddywhajabring medaddy?
How about a brand new macroatom?
Coooool.

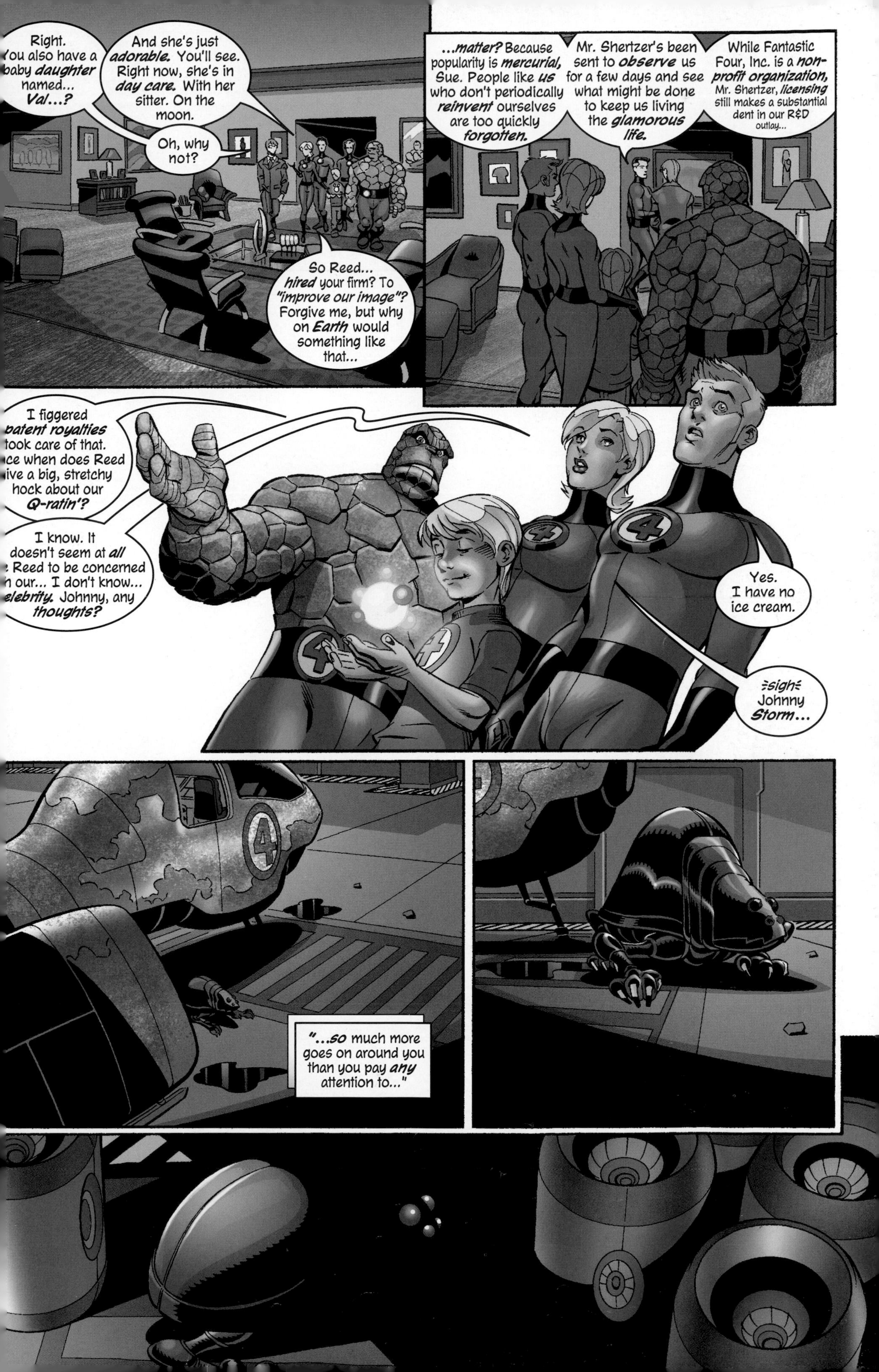

Right. You also have a baby daughter named... Val...?
And she's just adorable. You'll see. Right now, she's in day care. With her sitter. On the moon.
Oh, why not?
So Reed... hired your firm? To "improve our image"? Forgive me, but why on Earth would something like that...
...matter? Because popularity is mercurial, Sue. People like us who don't periodically reinvent ourselves are too quickly forgotten.
Mr. Shertzer's been sent to observe us for a few days and see what might be done to keep us living the glamorous life.
While Fantastic Four, Inc. is a non-profit organization, Mr. Shertzer, licensing still makes a substantial dent in our R&D outlay...
I figgered patent royalties took care of that. ...ce when does Reed ...ive a big, stretchy ...hock about our Q-ratin'?
I know. It doesn't seem at all ... Reed to be concerned ...n our... I don't know... ...elebrity. Johnny, any thoughts?
Yes. I have no ice cream.
=sigh= Johnny Storm...
"...so much more goes on around you than you pay any attention to..."

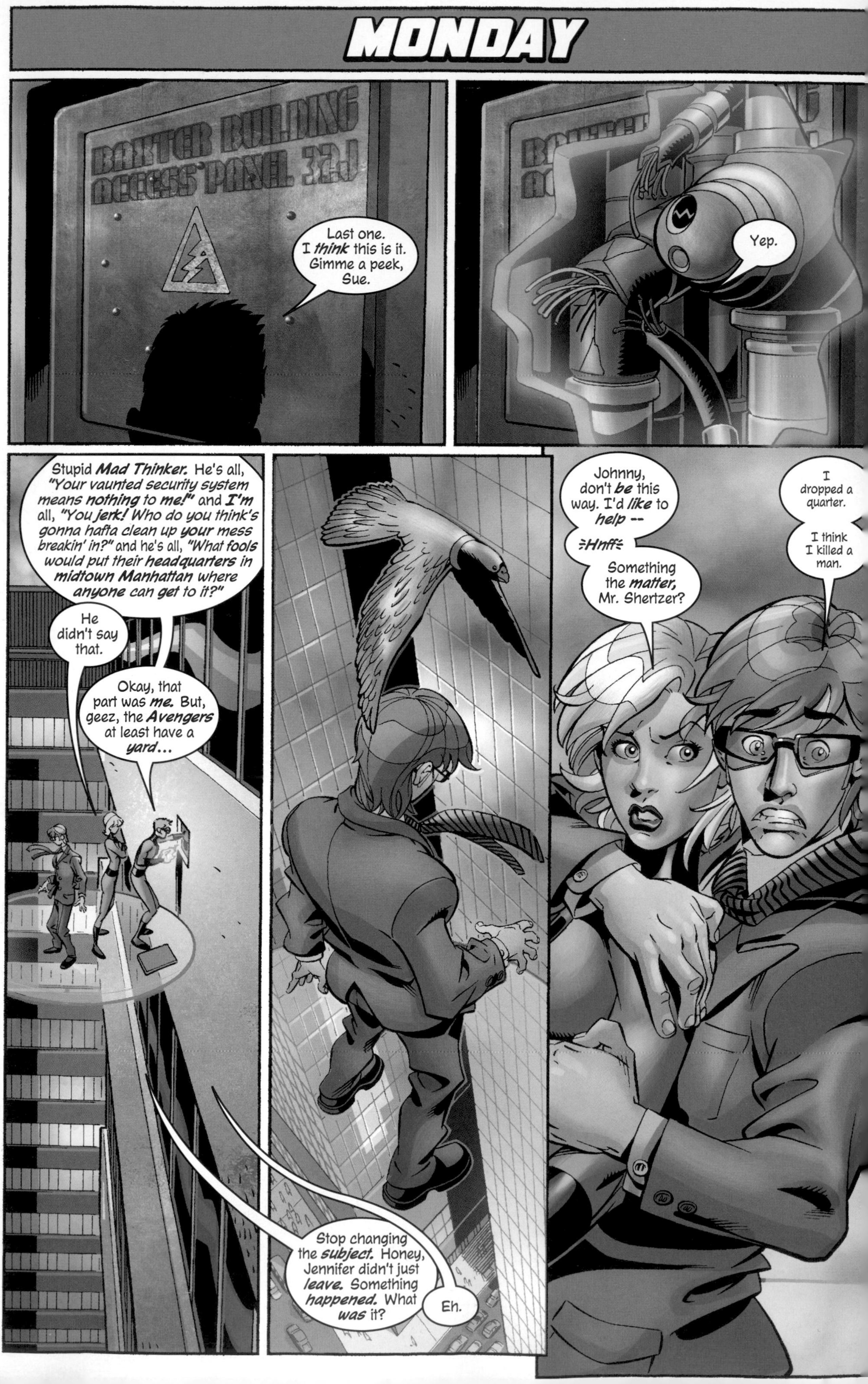
MONDAY
BAXTER BUILDING ACCESS PANEL 32J
Last one. I *think* this is it. Gimme a peek, Sue.
Yep.
Stupid *Mad Thinker.* He's all, *"Your vaunted security system means **nothing** to me!"* and ***I'm*** all, *"You **jerk!** Who do you think's gonna hafta clean up **your** mess breakin' in?"* and he's all, *"What **fools** would put their **headquarters** in **midtown Manhattan** where **anyone** can get to it?"*
He didn't say that.
Okay, that part was ***me.*** But, geez, the ***Avengers*** at least have a ***yard...***
Stop changing the ***subject.*** Honey, Jennifer didn't just ***leave.*** Something ***happened.*** What ***was*** it?
Eh.
Johnny, don't ***be*** this way. I'd ***like*** to ***help --***
Hnff
Something the ***matter,*** Mr. Shertzer?
I dropped a quarter.
I think I killed a man.

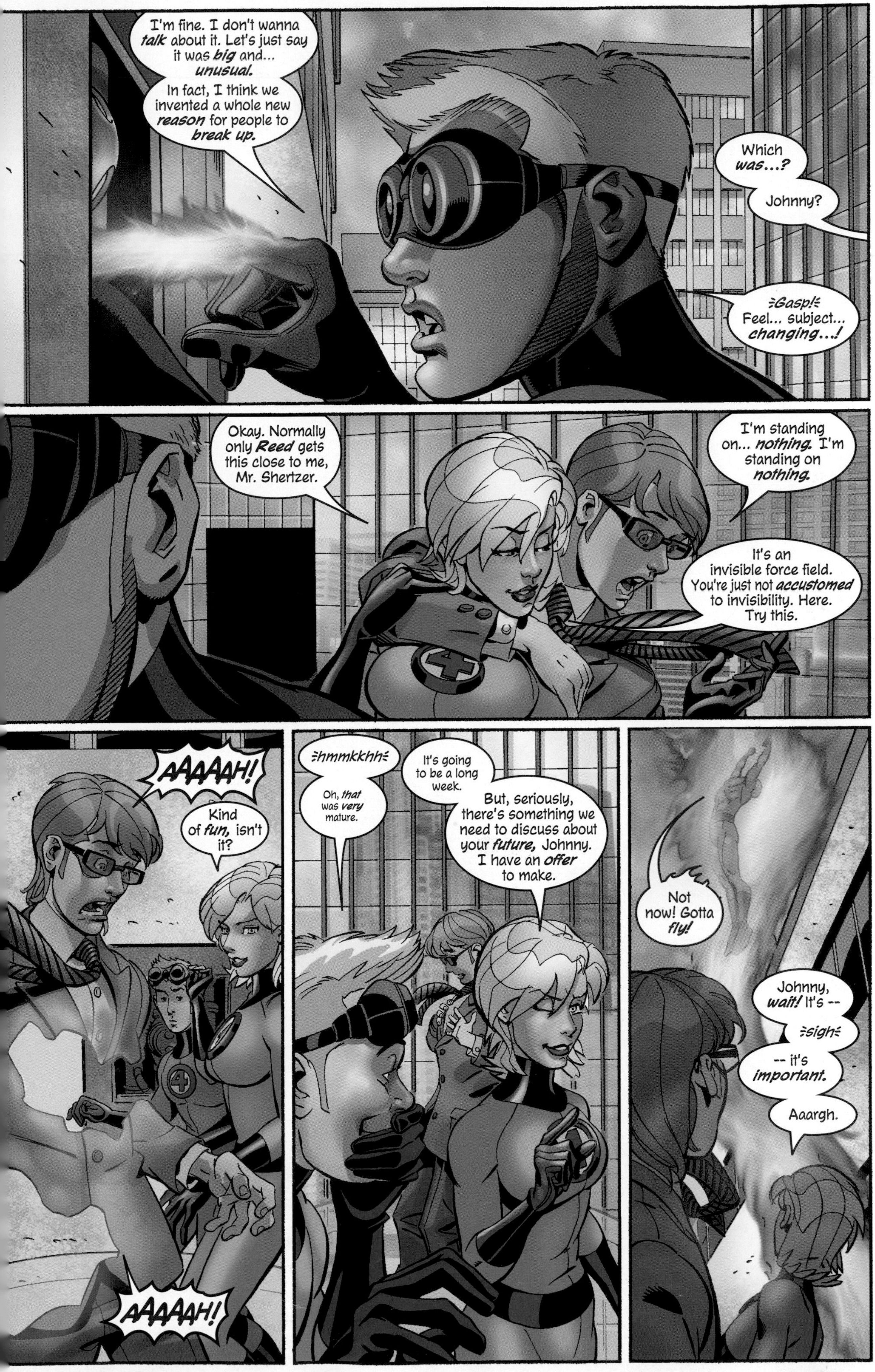
I'm fine. I don't wanna *talk* about it. Let's just say it was *big* and... *unusual.*
In fact, I think we invented a whole new *reason* for people to *break up.*
Which *was...?*
Johnny?
=Gasp!= Feel... subject... *changing...!*
Okay. Normally only *Reed* gets this close to me, Mr. Shertzer.
I'm standing on... *nothing.* I'm standing on *nothing.*
It's an invisible force field. You're just not *accustomed* to invisibility. Here. Try this.
AAAAAH!
Kind of *fun,* isn't it?
AAAAAH!
=hmmkkhh=
Oh, *that* was *very* mature.
It's going to be a long week.
But, seriously, there's something we need to discuss about your *future,* Johnny. I have an *offer* to make.
Not now! Gotta *fly!*
Johnny, *wait!* It's --
=sigh=
-- it's *important.*
Aaargh.

TUESDAY

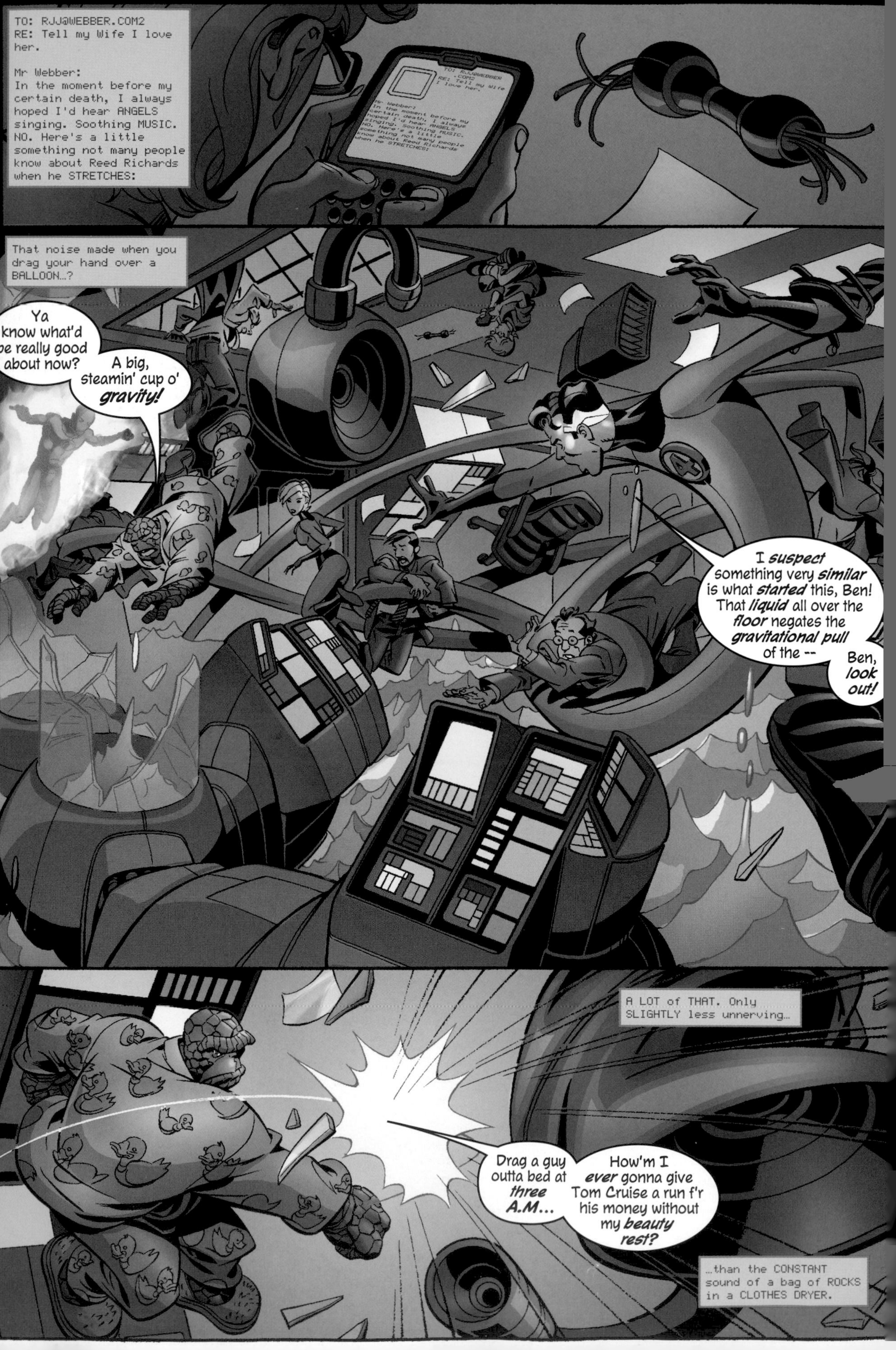

TO: RJJ@WEBBER.COM2
RE: Tell my Wife I love her.
Mr Webber:
In the moment before my certain death, I always hoped I'd hear ANGELS singing. Soothing MUSIC. NO. Here's a little something not many people know about Reed Richards when he STRETCHES:
That noise made when you drag your hand over a BALLOON...?
Ya know what'd be really good about now?
A big, steamin' cup o' *gravity!*
I *suspect* something very *similar* is what *started* this, Ben! That *liquid* all over the *floor* negates the *gravitational pull* of the --
Ben, *look out!*
A LOT of THAT. Only SLIGHTLY less unnerving...
Drag a guy outta bed at *three A.M...*
How'm I *ever* gonna give Tom Cruise a run f'r his money without my *beauty rest?*
...than the CONSTANT sound of a bag of ROCKS in a CLOTHES DRYER.

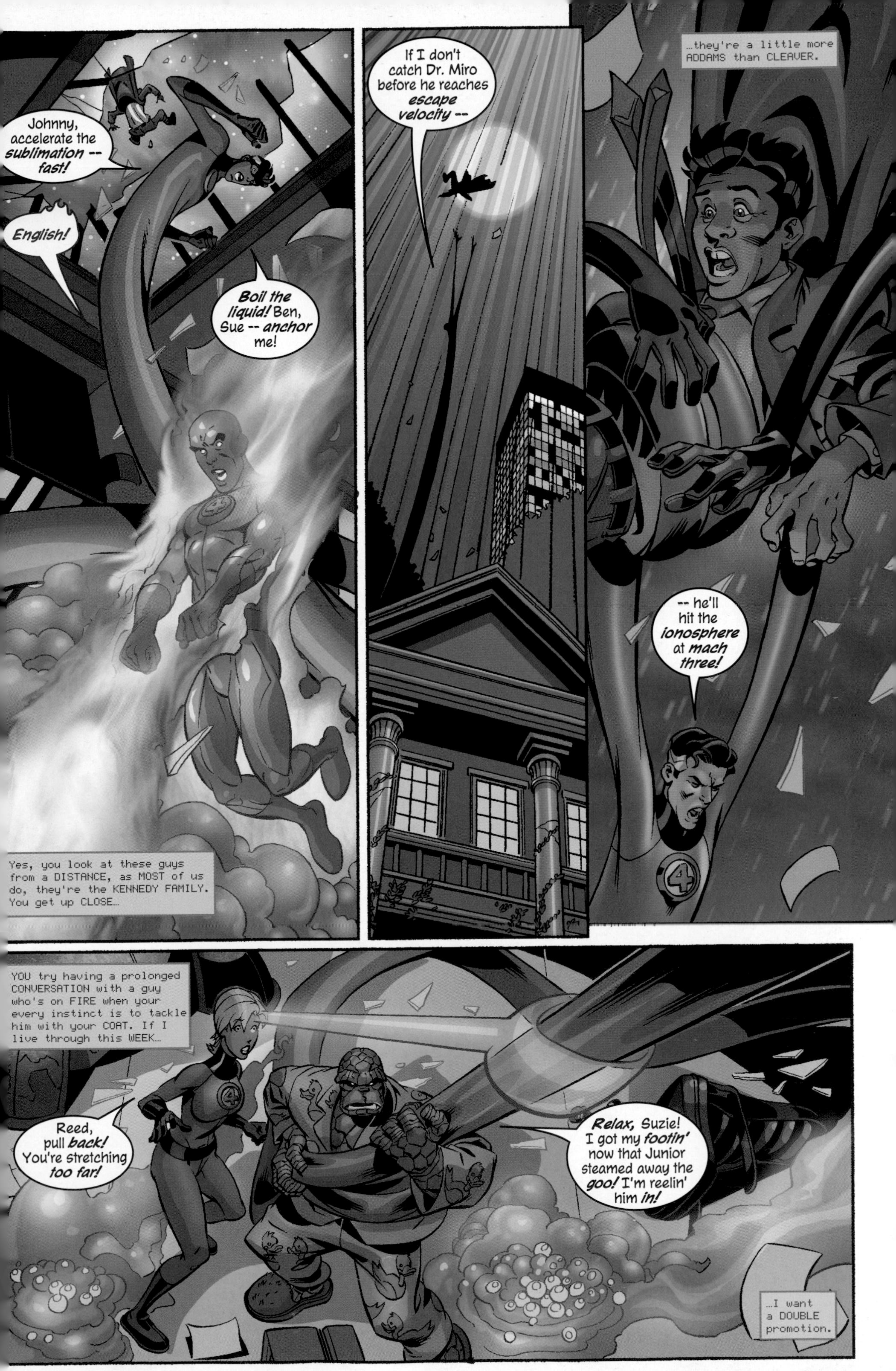

Johnny, accelerate the *sublimation* -- *fast!*
English!
Boil the liquid! Ben, Sue -- ***anchor*** me!
Yes, you look at these guys from a DISTANCE, as MOST of us do, they're the KENNEDY FAMILY. You get up CLOSE...
If I don't catch Dr. Miro before he reaches *escape velocity* --
...they're a little more ADDAMS than CLEAVER.
-- he'll hit the *ionosphere* at *mach three!*
YOU try having a prolonged CONVERSATION with a guy who's on FIRE when your every instinct is to tackle him with your COAT. If I live through this WEEK...
Reed, pull *back!* You're stretching *too far!*
Relax, Suzie! I got my *footin'* now that Junior steamed away the *goo!* I'm reelin' him *in!*
...I want a DOUBLE promotion.

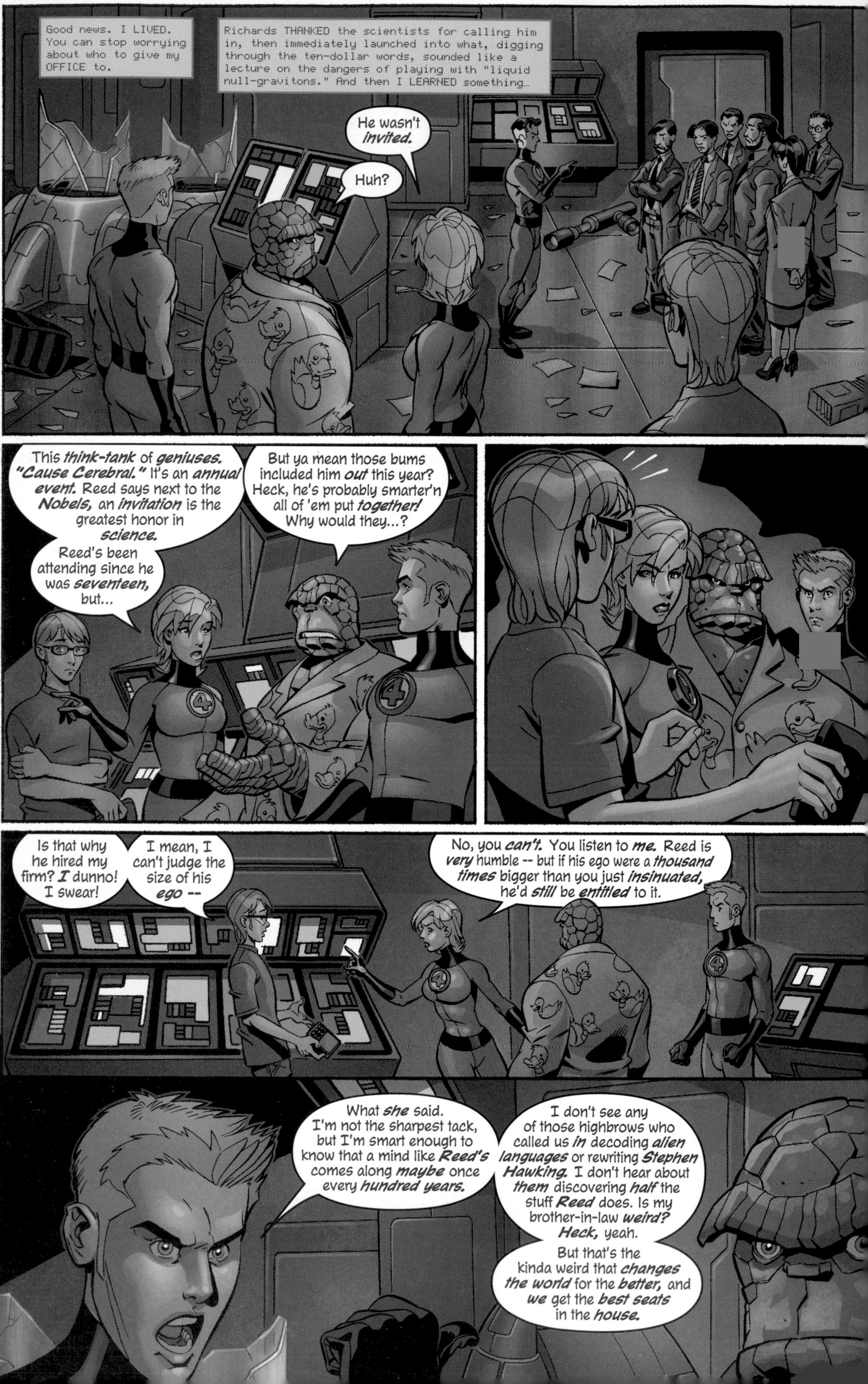
Good news. I LIVED. You can stop worrying about who to give my OFFICE to.
Richards THANKED the scientists for calling him in, then immediately launched into what, digging through the ten-dollar words, sounded like a lecture on the dangers of playing with "liquid null-gravitons." And then I LEARNED something...
He wasn't *invited.*
Huh?
This *think-tank* of *geniuses. "Cause Cerebral."* It's an *annual event.* Reed says next to the *Nobels,* an *invitation* is the greatest honor in *science.*
Reed's been attending since he was *seventeen,* but...
But ya mean those bums included him *out* this year? Heck, he's probably smarter'n all of 'em put *together!* Why would they...?
Is that why he hired my firm? *I* dunno! I swear!
I mean, I can't judge the size of his *ego* --
No, you *can't.* You listen to *me.* Reed is *very* humble -- but if his ego were a *thousand times* bigger than you just *insinuated,* he'd *still* be *entitled* to it.
What *she* said. I'm not the sharpest tack, but I'm smart enough to know that a mind like *Reed's* comes along *maybe* once every *hundred years.*
I don't see any of those highbrows who called us *in* decoding *alien languages* or rewriting *Stephen Hawking.* I don't hear about *them* discovering *half* the stuff *Reed* does. Is my brother-in-law *weird? Heck,* yeah.
But that's the kinda weird that *changes the world* for the *better,* and *we* get the *best seats* in the *house.*

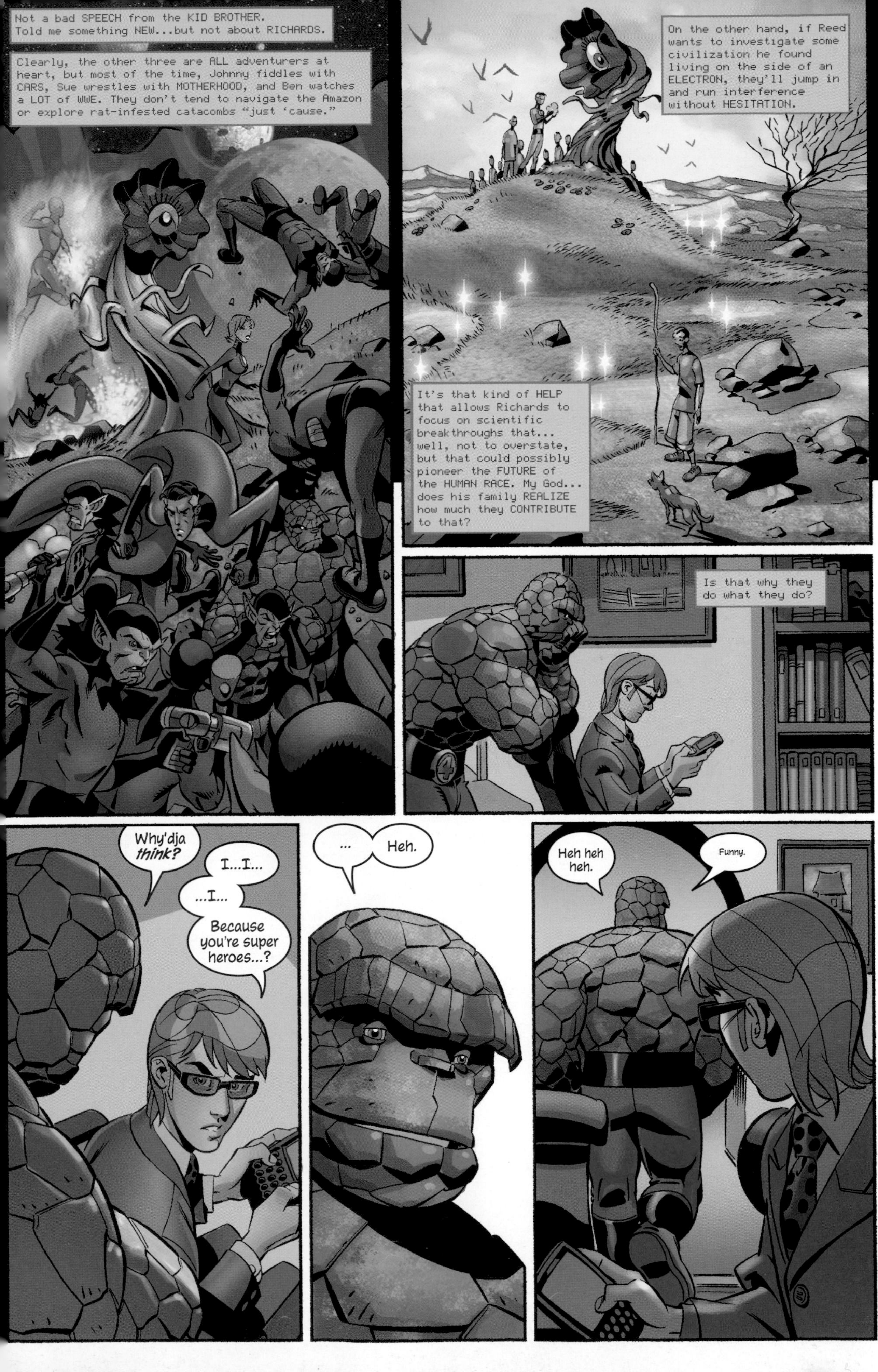
Not a bad SPEECH from the KID BROTHER. Told me something NEW...but not about RICHARDS.
Clearly, the other three are ALL adventurers at heart, but most of the time, Johnny fiddles with CARS, Sue wrestles with MOTHERHOOD, and Ben watches a LOT of WWE. They don't tend to navigate the Amazon or explore rat-infested catacombs "just 'cause."
On the other hand, if Reed wants to investigate some civilization he found living on the side of an ELECTRON, they'll jump in and run interference without HESITATION.
It's that kind of HELP that allows Richards to focus on scientific breakthroughs that... well, not to overstate, but that could possibly pioneer the FUTURE of the HUMAN RACE. My God... does his family REALIZE how much they CONTRIBUTE to that?
Is that why they do what they do?
Why'dja *think?*
I...I...
...I...
Because you're super heroes...?
...
Heh.
Heh heh heh.
Funny.

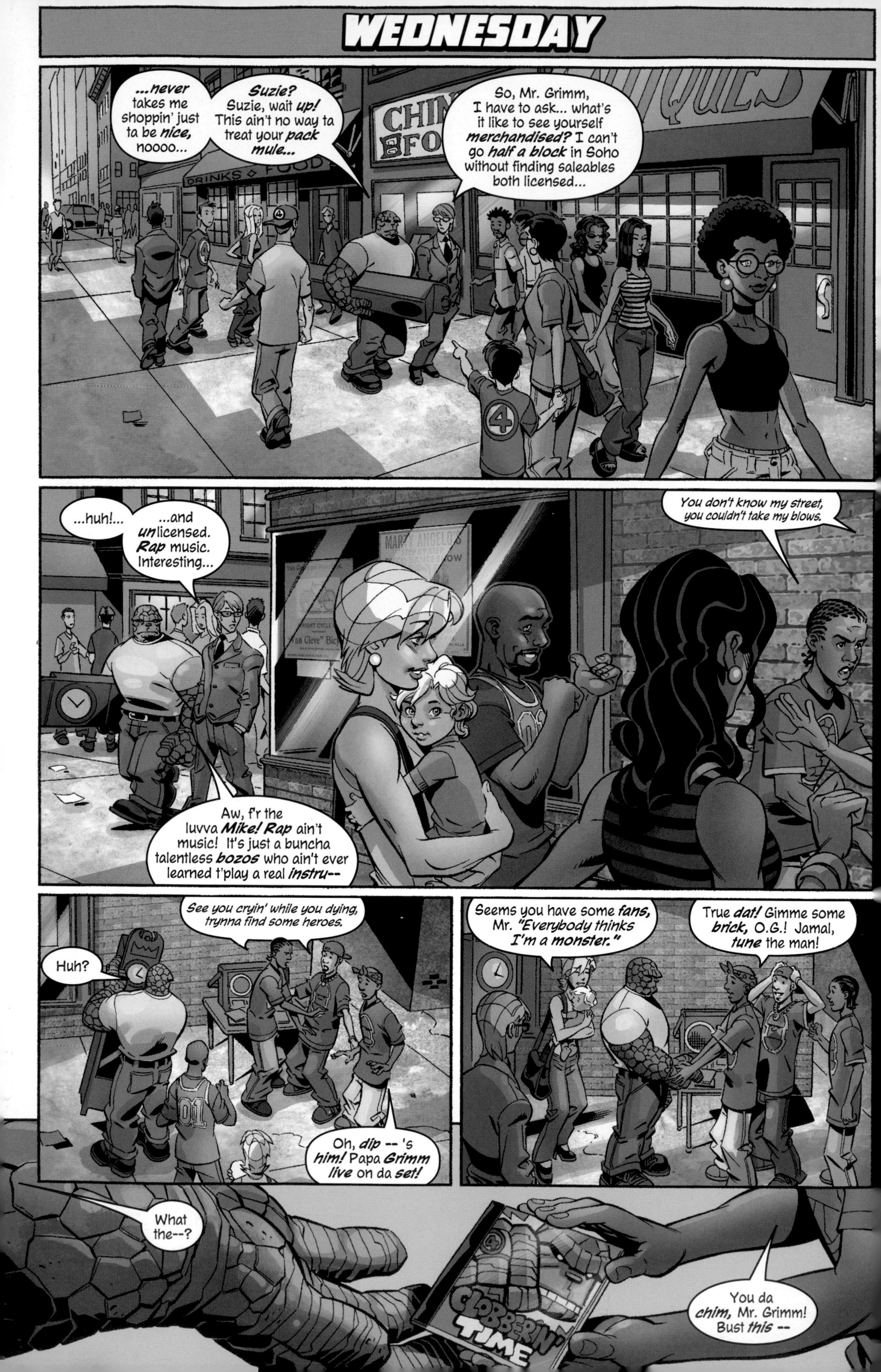
WEDNESDAY
...never takes me shoppin' just ta be nice, noooo...
Suzie? Suzie, wait up! This ain't no way ta treat your pack mule...
So, Mr. Grimm, I have to ask... what's it like to see yourself merchandised? I can't go half a block in Soho without finding saleables both licensed...
...huh!...
...and unlicensed. Rap music. Interesting...
You don't know my street, you couldn't take my blows.
Aw, f'r the luvva Mike! Rap ain't music! It's just a buncha talentless bozos who ain't ever learned t'play a real instru--
See you cryin' while you dying, trynna find some heroes.
Huh?
Oh, dip -- 's him! Papa Grimm live on da set!
Seems you have some fans, Mr. "Everybody thinks I'm a monster."
True dat! Gimme some brick, O.G.! Jamal, tune the man!
What the--?
CLOBBERIN' TIME
You da chim, Mr. Grimm! Bust this --

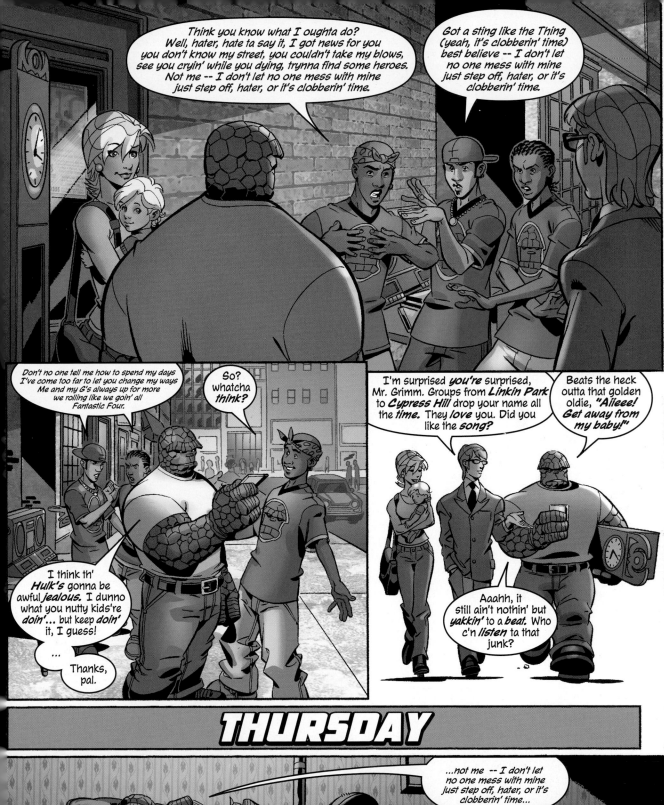

Think you know what I oughta do? Well, hater, hate ta say it, I got news for you you don't know my street, you couldn't take my blows, see you cryin' while you dying, trynna find some heroes. Not me -- I don't let no one mess with mine just step off, hater, or it's clobberin' time.

Got a sting like the Thing (yeah, it's clobberin' time) best believe -- I don't let no one mess with mine just step off, hater, or it's clobberin' time.

Don't no one tell me how to spend my days I've come too far to let you change my ways Me and my G's always up for more we rolling like we goin' all Fantastic Four.

So? whatcha think?

I think th' Hulk's gonna be awful jealous. I dunno what you nutty kids're doin'... but keep doin' it, I guess!

...

Thanks, pal.

I'm surprised you're surprised, Mr. Grimm. Groups from Linkin Park to Cypress Hill drop your name all the time. They love you. Did you like the song?

Beats the heck outta that golden oldie, "Aiieee! Get away from my baby!"

Aaahh, it still ain't nothin' but yakkin' to a beat. Who c'n listen ta that junk?

THURSDAY

...not me -- I don't let no one mess with mine just step off, hater, or it's clobberin' time...

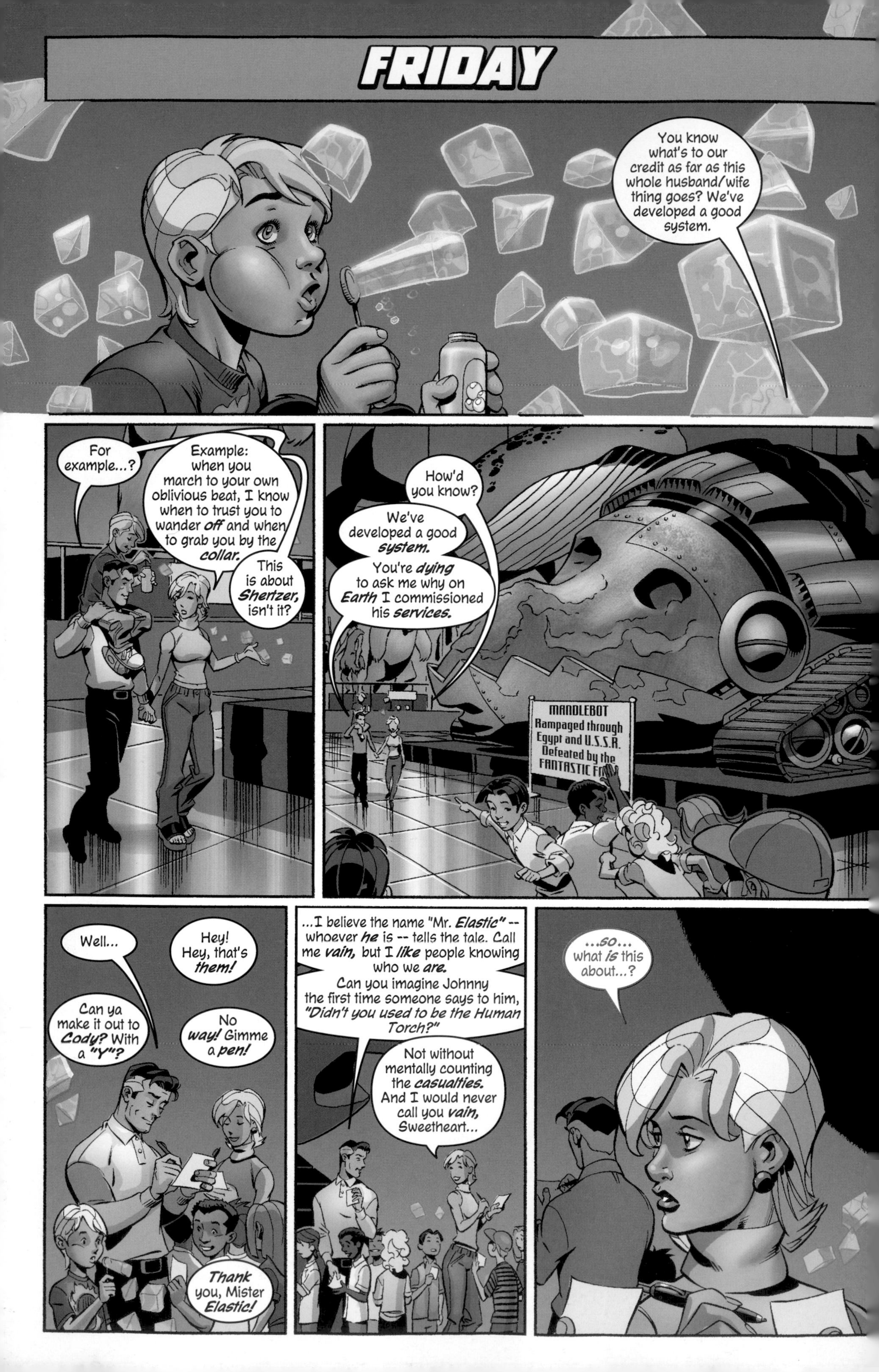
FRIDAY
You know what's to our credit as far as this whole husband/wife thing goes? We've developed a good system.
For example...?
Example: when you march to your own oblivious beat, I know when to trust you to wander *off* and when to grab you by the *collar.*
This is about *Shertzer,* isn't it?
How'd you know?
We've developed a good *system.*
You're *dying* to ask me why on *Earth* I commissioned his *services.*
MANDLEBOT Rampaged through Egypt and U.S.S.R. Defeated by the FANTASTIC F
Well...
Hey! Hey, that's *them!*
Can ya make it out to *Cody?* With a *"Y"?*
No *way!* Gimme a *pen!*
Thank you, Mister *Elastic!*
...I believe the name "Mr. *Elastic*" -- whoever *he* is -- tells the tale. Call me *vain,* but I *like* people knowing who we *are.*
Can you imagine Johnny the first time someone says to him, *"Didn't you used to be the Human Torch?"*
Not without mentally counting the *casualties.* And I would never call you *vain,* Sweetheart...
...so... what *is* this about...?

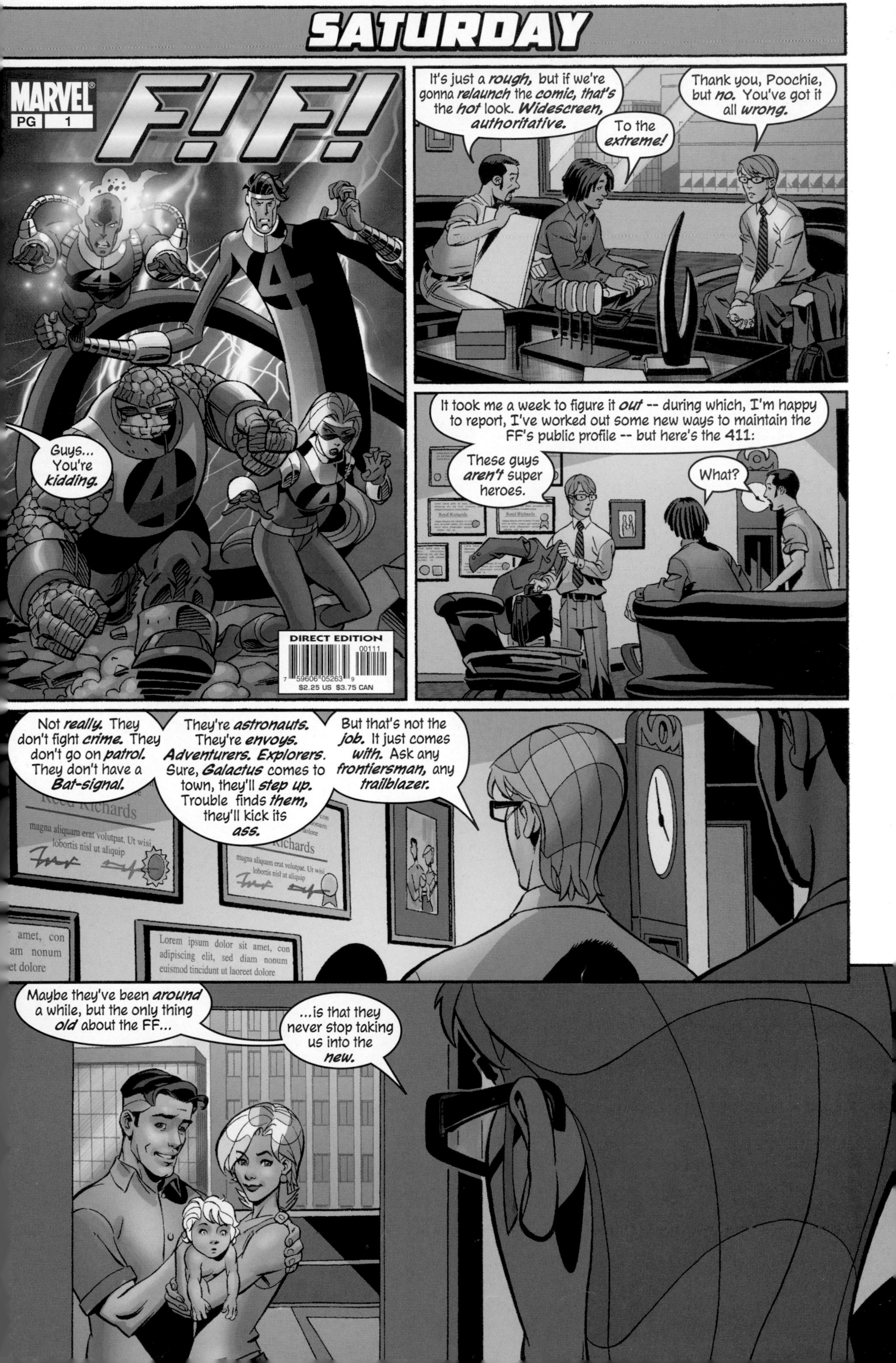
SATURDAY
MARVEL
PG 1
F!F!
Guys... You're *kidding.*
DIRECT EDITION
$2.25 US $3.75 CAN
It's just a *rough,* but if we're gonna *relaunch* the *comic, that's* the *hot* look. *Widescreen, authoritative.*
To the *extreme!*
Thank you, Poochie, but *no.* You've got it all *wrong.*
It took me a week to figure it *out* -- during which, I'm happy to report, I've worked out some new ways to maintain the FF's public profile -- but here's the 411:
These guys *aren't* super heroes.
What?
Not *really.* They don't fight *crime.* They don't go on *patrol.* They don't have a *Bat-signal.*
They're *astronauts.* They're *envoys. Adventurers. Explorers.* Sure, *Galactus* comes to town, they'll *step up.* Trouble finds *them,* they'll kick its *ass.*
But that's not the *job.* It just comes *with.* Ask any *frontiersman,* any *trailblazer.*
Maybe they've been *around* a while, but the only thing *old* about the FF...
...is that they never stop taking us into the *new.*

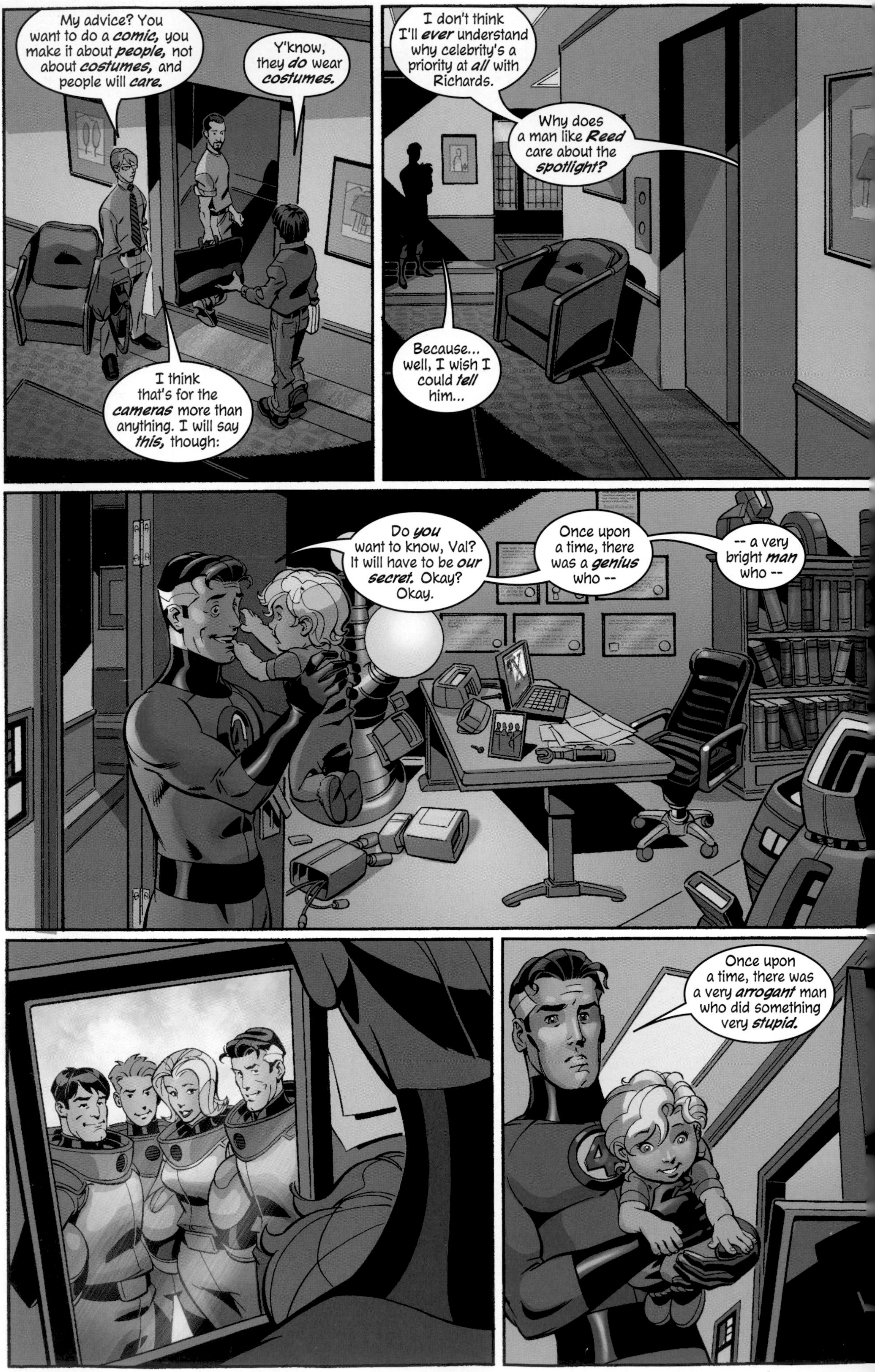
My advice? You want to do a comic, you make it about people, not about costumes, and people will care.
Y'know, they do wear costumes.
I think that's for the cameras more than anything. I will say this, though:
I don't think I'll ever understand why celebrity's a priority at all with Richards.
Why does a man like Reed care about the spotlight?
Because... well, I wish I could tell him...
Do you want to know, Val? It will have to be our secret. Okay? Okay.
Once upon a time, there was a genius who --
-- a very bright man who --
Once upon a time, there was a very arrogant man who did something very stupid.

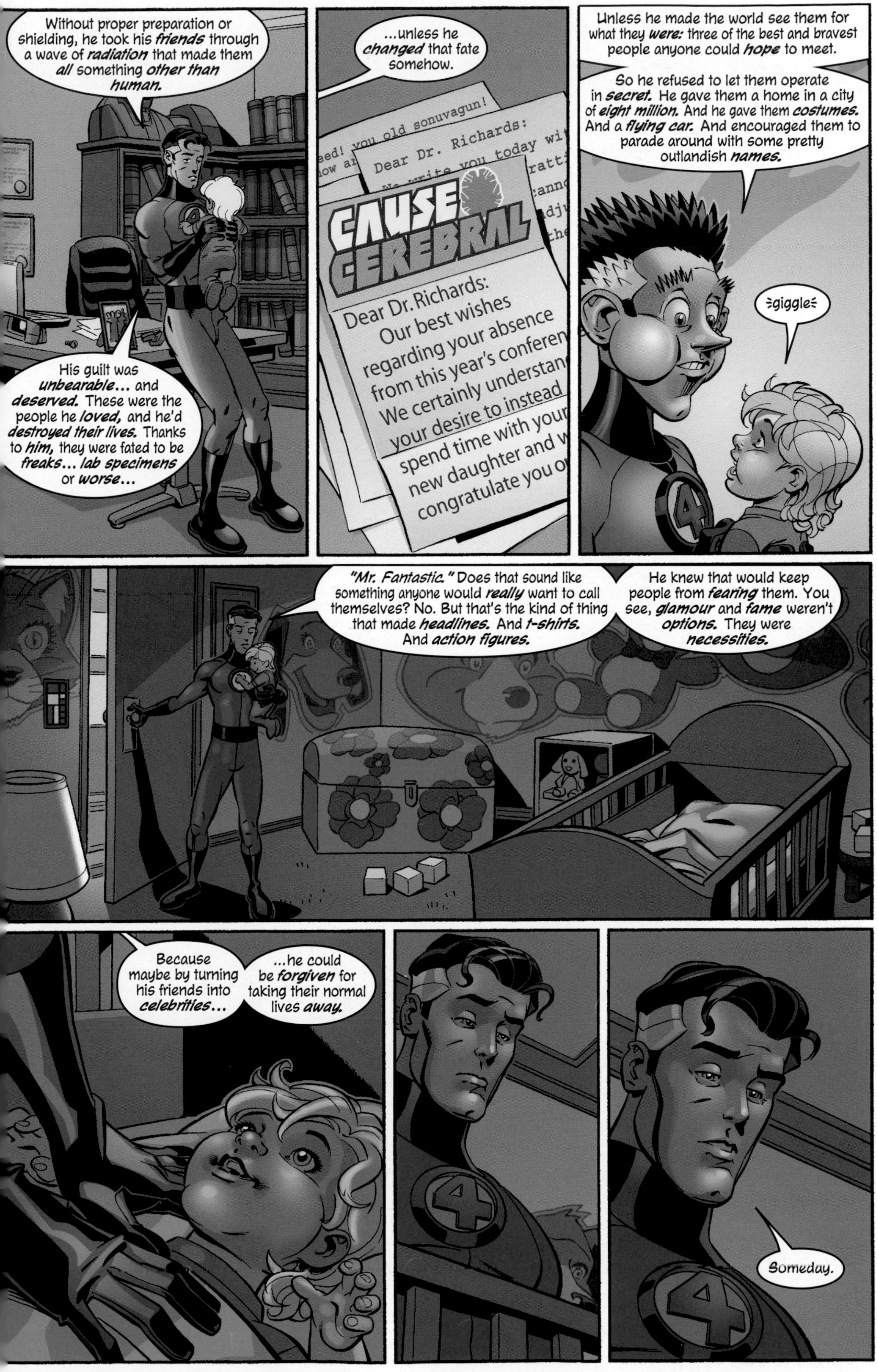
Without proper preparation or shielding, he took his *friends* through a wave of *radiation* that made them *all* something *other than human.*
His guilt was *unbearable*... and *deserved.* These were the people he *loved,* and he'd *destroyed their lives.* Thanks to *him,* they were fated to be *freaks*... *lab specimens* or *worse*...
...unless he *changed* that fate somehow.
CAUSE CEREBRAL
Dear Dr. Richards:
Our best wishes regarding your absence from this year's conferen
We certainly understan
your desire to instead
spend time with your
new daughter and w
congratulate you o
Unless he made the world see them for what they *were:* three of the best and bravest people anyone could *hope* to meet.
So he refused to let them operate in *secret.* He gave them a home in a city of *eight million.* And he gave them *costumes.* And a *flying car.* And encouraged them to parade around with some pretty outlandish *names.*
giggle
"*Mr. Fantastic.*" Does that sound like something anyone would *really* want to call themselves? No. But that's the kind of thing that made *headlines.* And *t-shirts.* And *action figures.*
He knew that would keep people from *fearing* them. You see, *glamour* and *fame* weren't *options.* They were *necessities.*
Because maybe by turning his friends into *celebrities*...
...he could be *forgiven* for taking their normal lives *away.*
Someday.

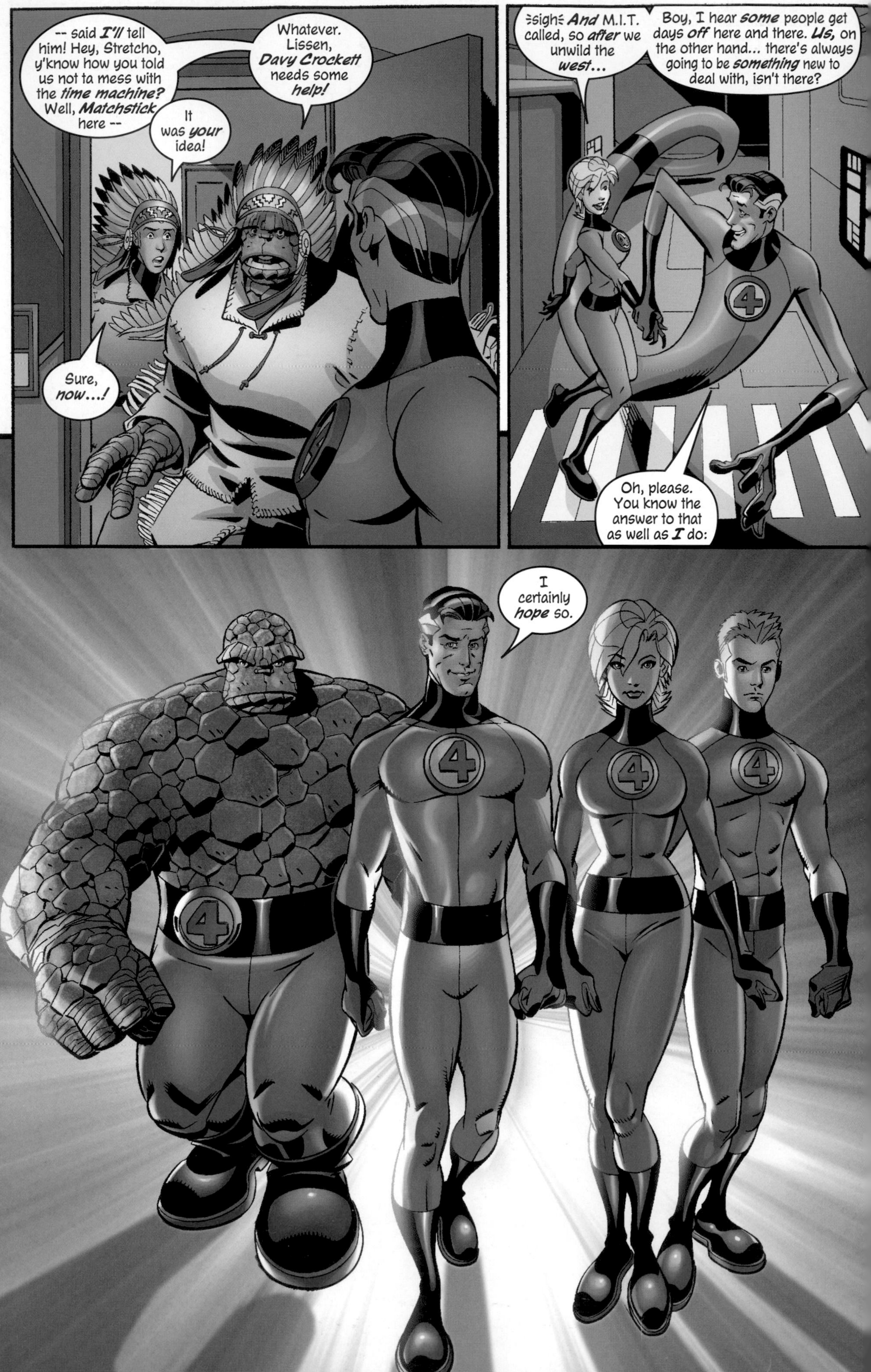
-- said I'll tell him! Hey, Stretcho, y'know how you told us not ta mess with the time machine? Well, Matchstick here --
Whatever. Lissen, Davy Crockett needs some help!
It was your idea!
Sure, now...!
=sigh= And M.I.T. called, so after we unwild the west...
Boy, I hear some people get days off here and there. Us, on the other hand... there's always going to be something new to deal with, isn't there?
Oh, please. You know the answer to that as well as I do:
I certainly hope so.

MARVEL KNIGHTS 4 #4

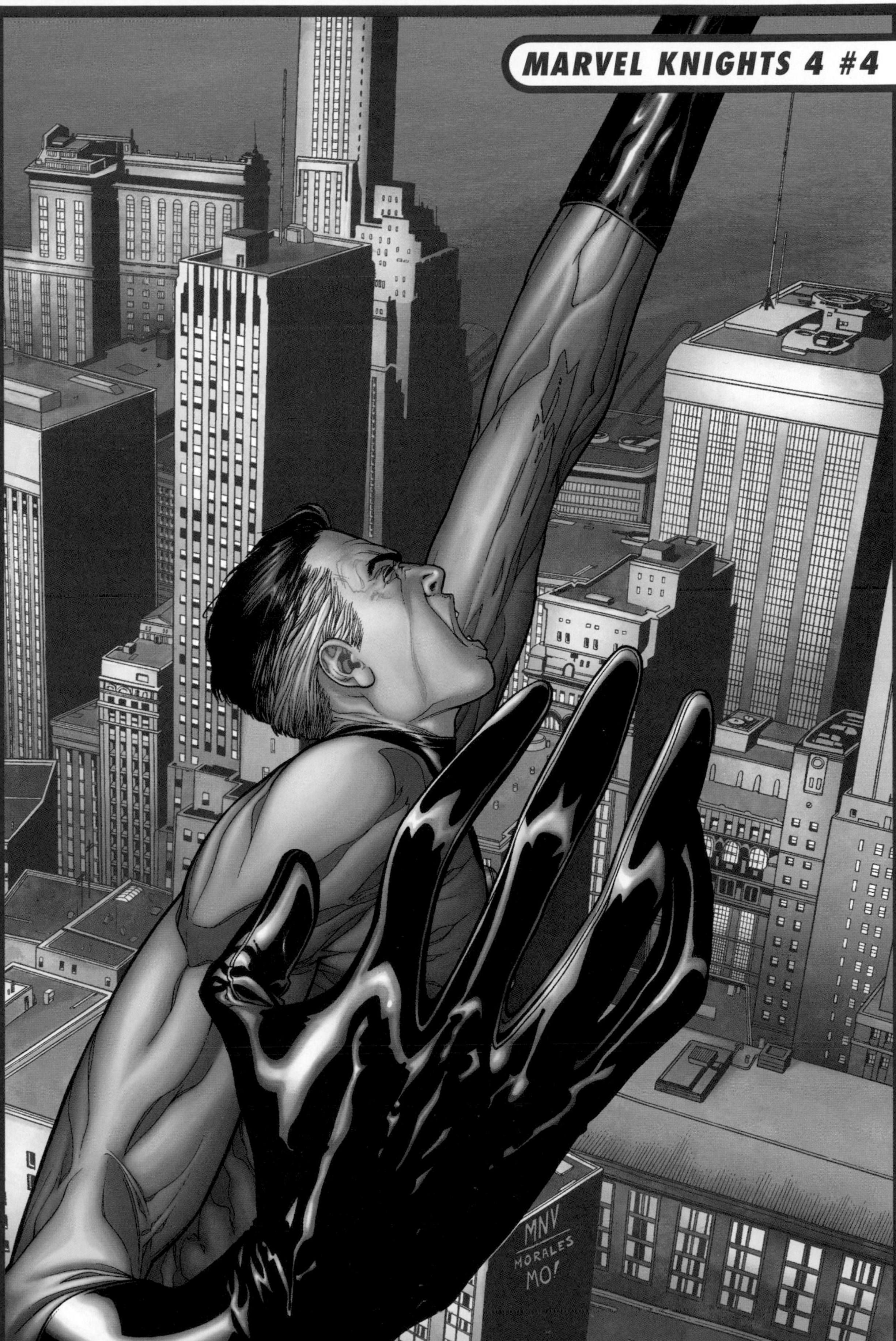
MNV
MORALES
MO!

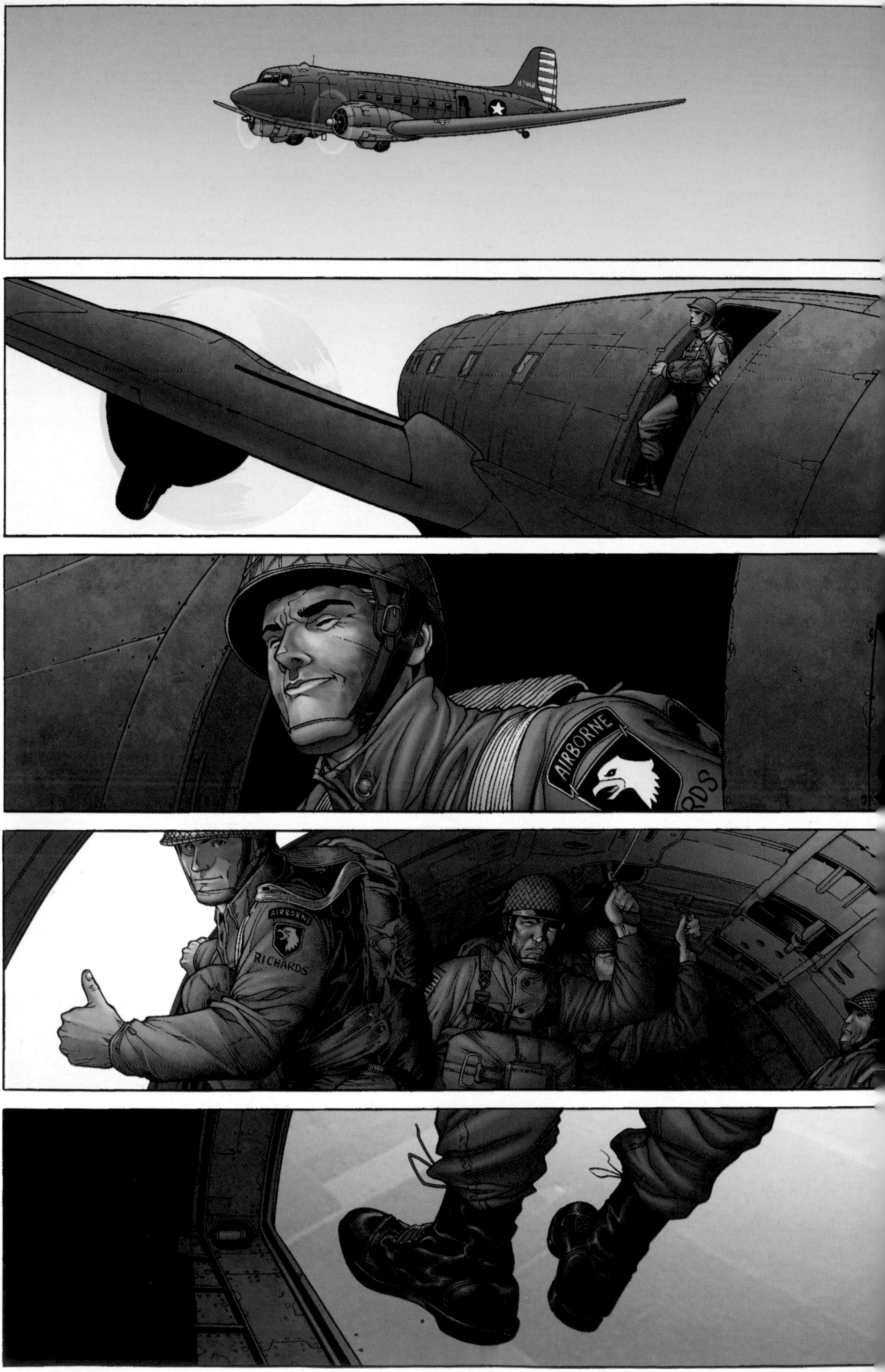
AIRBORNE
AIRBORNE
RICHARDS

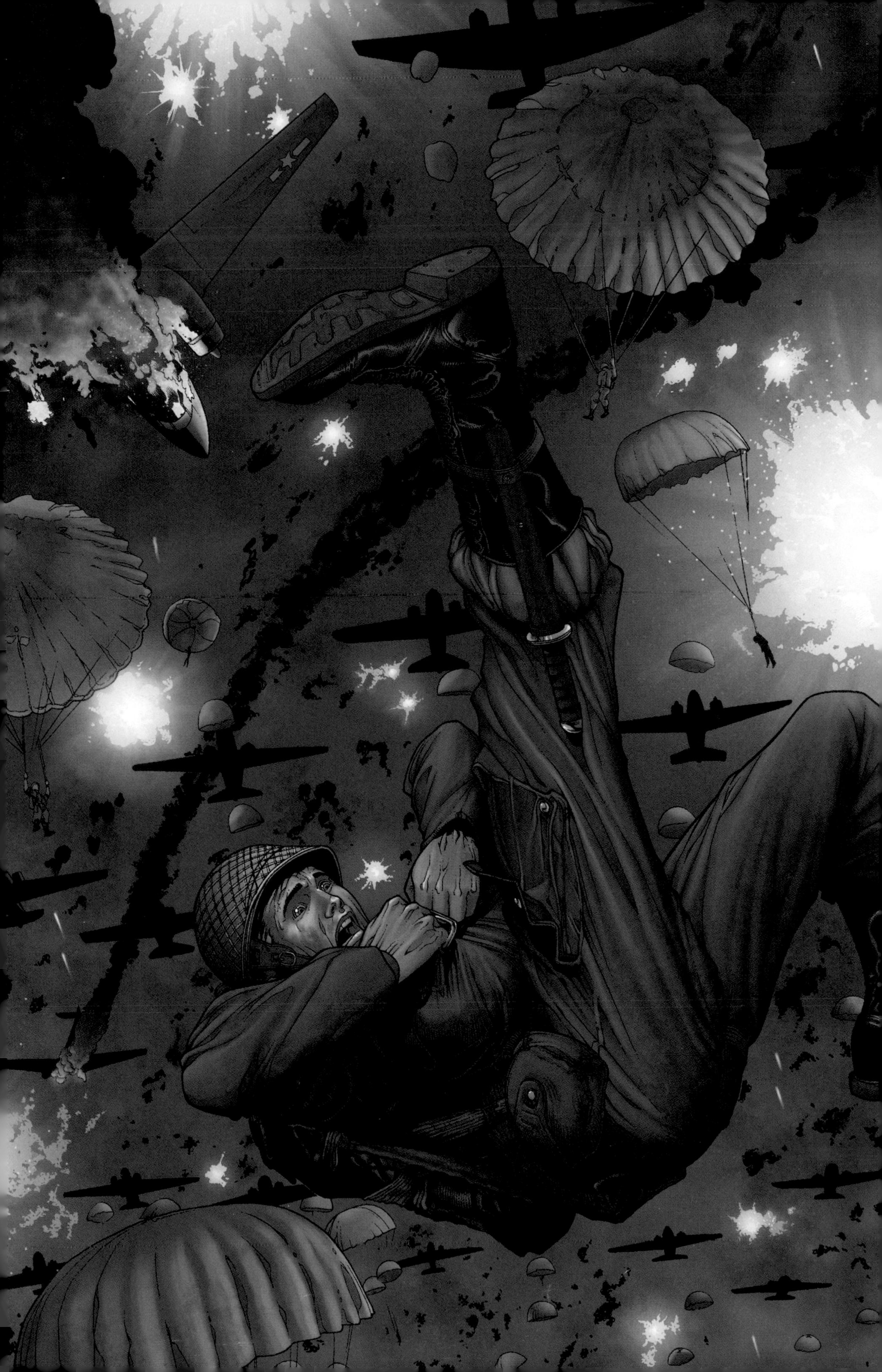

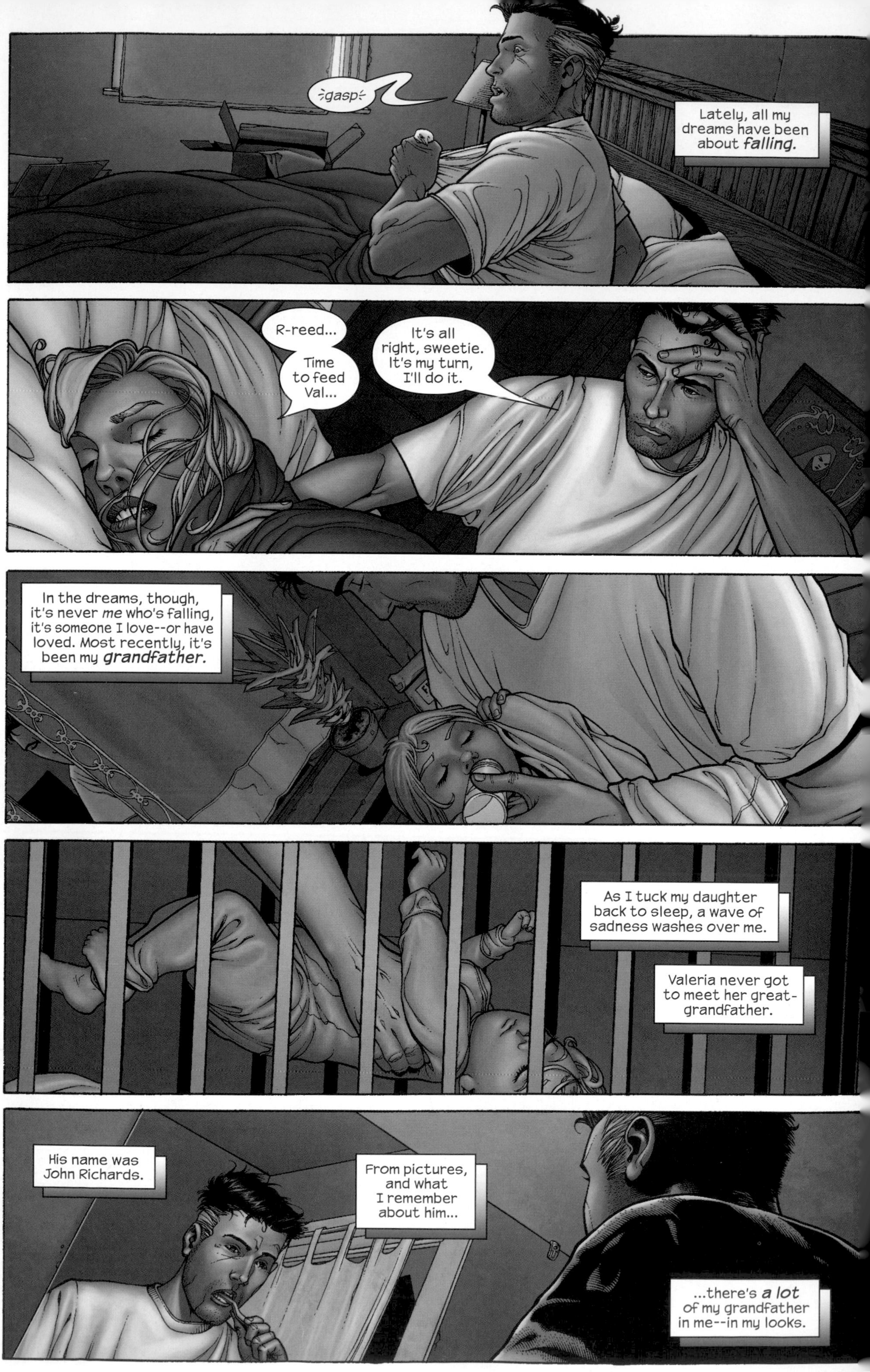

-gasp-
Lately, all my dreams have been about *falling.*
R-reed...
Time to feed Val...
It's all right, sweetie. It's my turn, I'll do it.
In the dreams, though, it's never *me* who's falling, it's someone I love--or have loved. Most recently, it's been my *grandfather.*
As I tuck my daughter back to sleep, a wave of sadness washes over me.
Valeria never got to meet her great-grandfather.
His name was John Richards.
From pictures, and what I remember about him...
...there's *a lot* of my grandfather in me--in my looks.

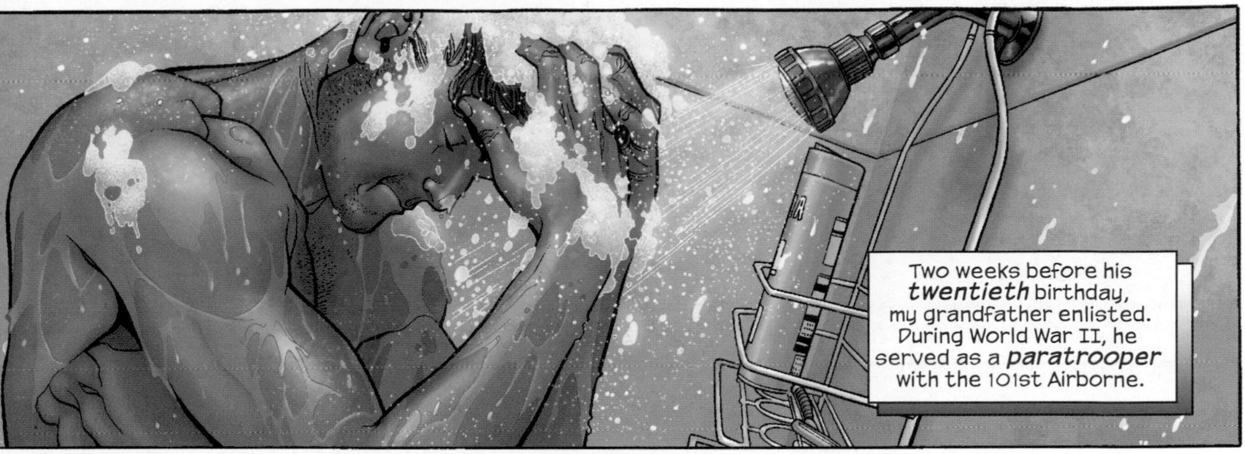
Two weeks before his *twentieth* birthday, my grandfather enlisted. During World War II, he served as a *paratrooper* with the 101st Airborne.

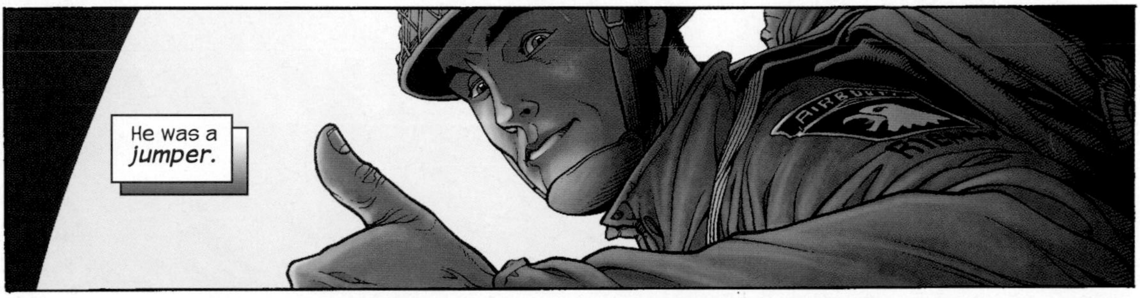
He was a *jumper.*

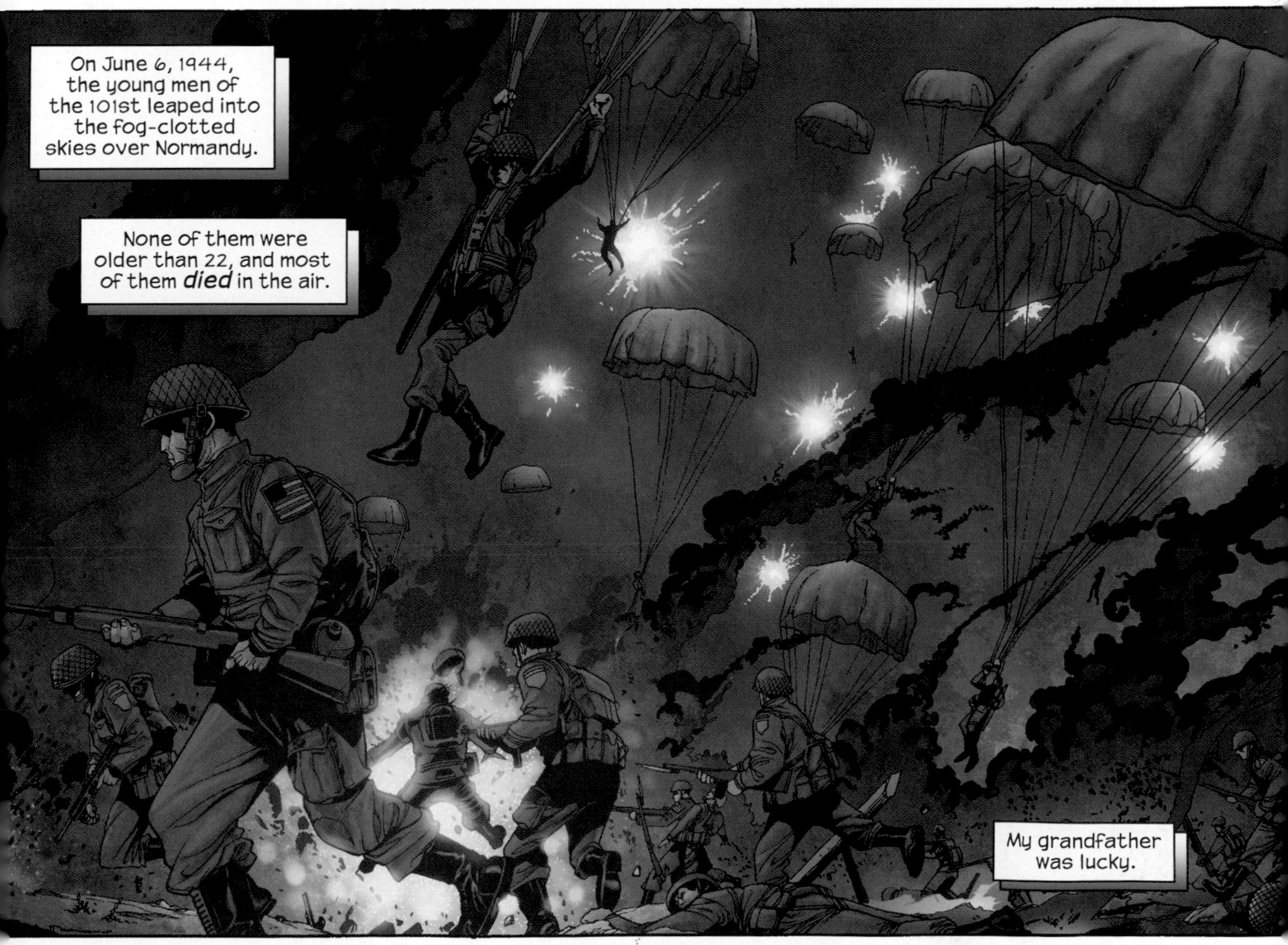
On June 6, 1944, the young men of the 101st leaped into the fog-clotted skies over Normandy.
None of them were older than 22, and most of them *died* in the air.
My grandfather was lucky.

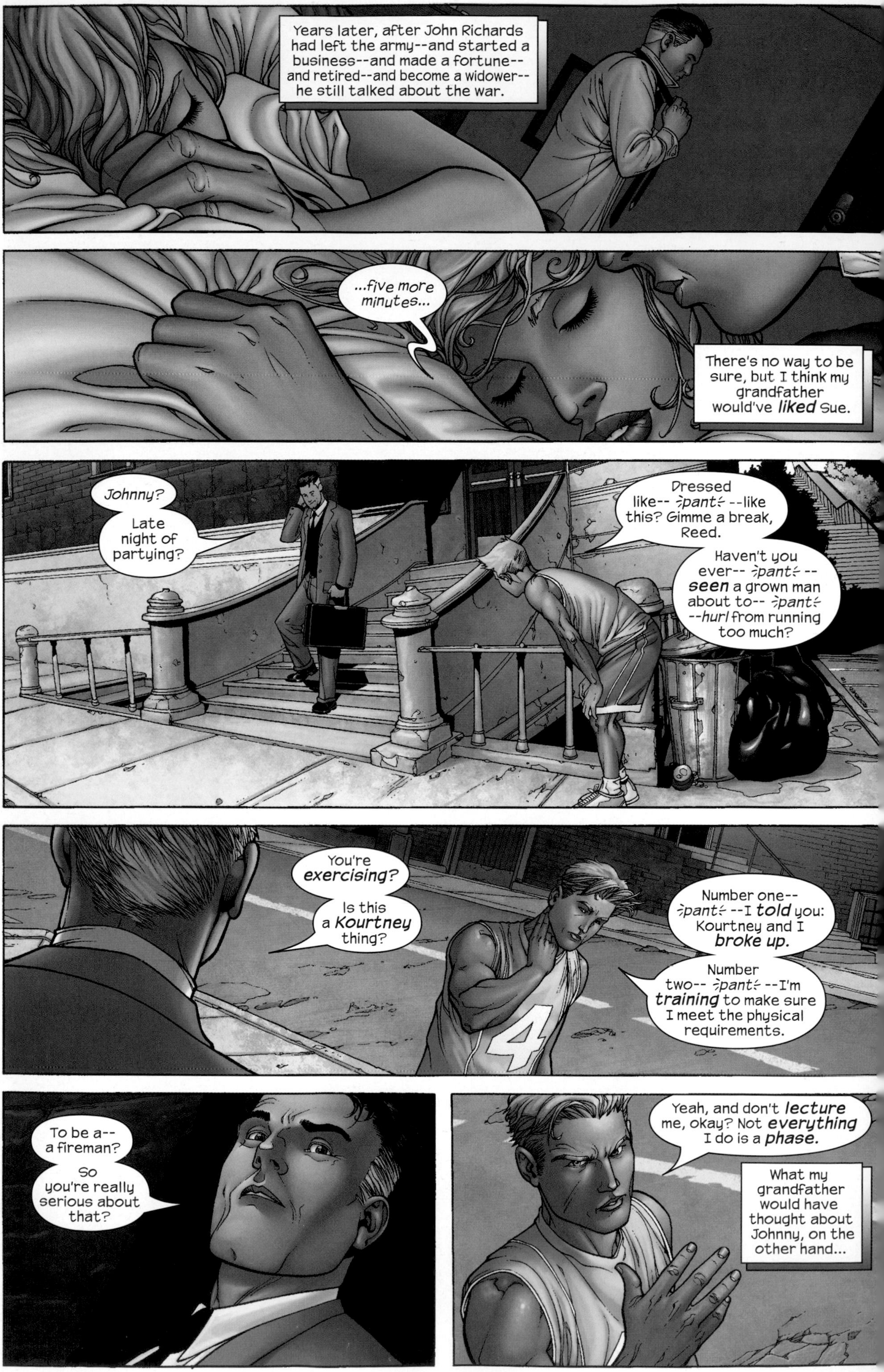
Years later, after John Richards had left the army--and started a business--and made a fortune--and retired--and become a widower--he still talked about the war.
...five more minutes...
There's no way to be sure, but I think my grandfather would've liked Sue.
Johnny?
Late night of partying?
Dressed like-- *pant* --like this? Gimme a break, Reed.
Haven't you ever-- *pant* -- seen a grown man about to-- *pant* --hurl from running too much?
You're exercising?
Is this a Kourtney thing?
Number one-- *pant* --I told you: Kourtney and I broke up.
Number two-- *pant* --I'm training to make sure I meet the physical requirements.
To be a-- a fireman?
So you're really serious about that?
Yeah, and don't lecture me, okay? Not everything I do is a phase.
What my grandfather would have thought about Johnny, on the other hand...

After retiring, my grandfather lived with my parents and me in California. Growing up, I learned most of my *life-lessons* from him.

Lessons in humility...

...and *responsibility*.

I only wish that the *rest* of New York's super hero community would *follow* your lead and make *good* on *their* debts.

...yes, Comptroller Jones.

Of course, they all have *secret identities*, which makes *billing* them impossible.

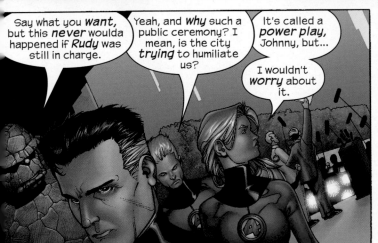

Say what you *want*, but this *never* woulda happened if *Rudy* was still in charge.

Yeah, and *why* such a public ceremony? I mean, is the city *trying* to humiliate us?

It's called a *power play*, Johnny, but...

I wouldn't *worry* about it.

Uh, Mr. Comptroller, what happened to your *pants*?

Susan?

Just trying to keep us off the *front page*, dear.

And I always figured him for a *boxers* kinda guy...

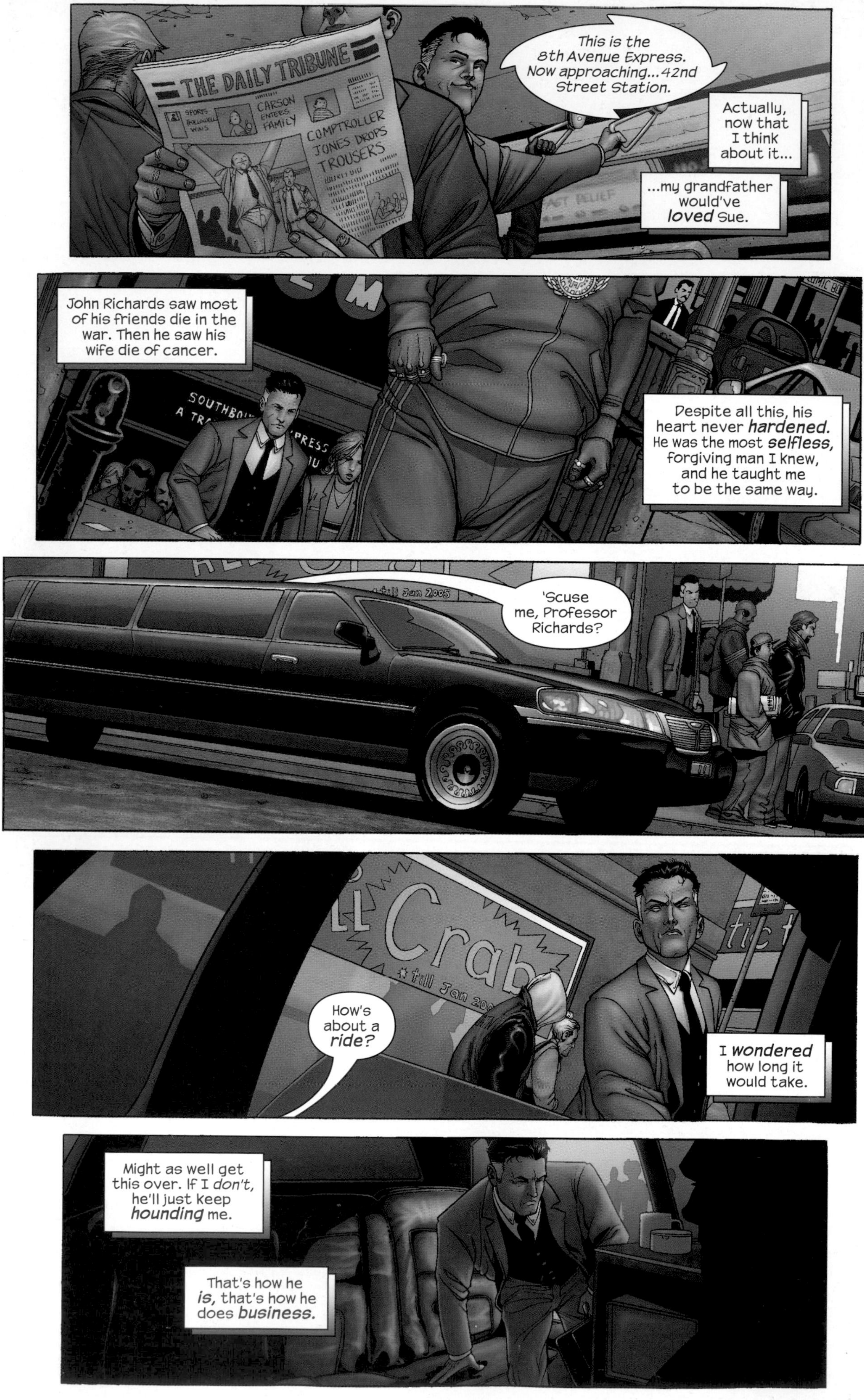
THE DAILY TRIBUNE
SPORTS HOLLOWELL WINS
CARSON ENTERS FAMILY
COMPTROLLER JONES DROPS TROUSERS
This is the 8th Avenue Express. Now approaching...42nd Street Station.
Actually, now that I think about it...
...my grandfather would've *loved* Sue.
John Richards saw most of his friends die in the war. Then he saw his wife die of cancer.
SOUTHBOU
PRESS
Despite all this, his heart never *hardened.* He was the most *selfless,* forgiving man I knew, and he taught me to be the same way.
'Scuse me, Professor Richards?
Crab
till Jan 2005
How's about a *ride?*
I *wondered* how long it would take.
Might as well get this over. If I *don't,* he'll just keep *hounding* me.
That's how he *is,* that's how he does *business.*

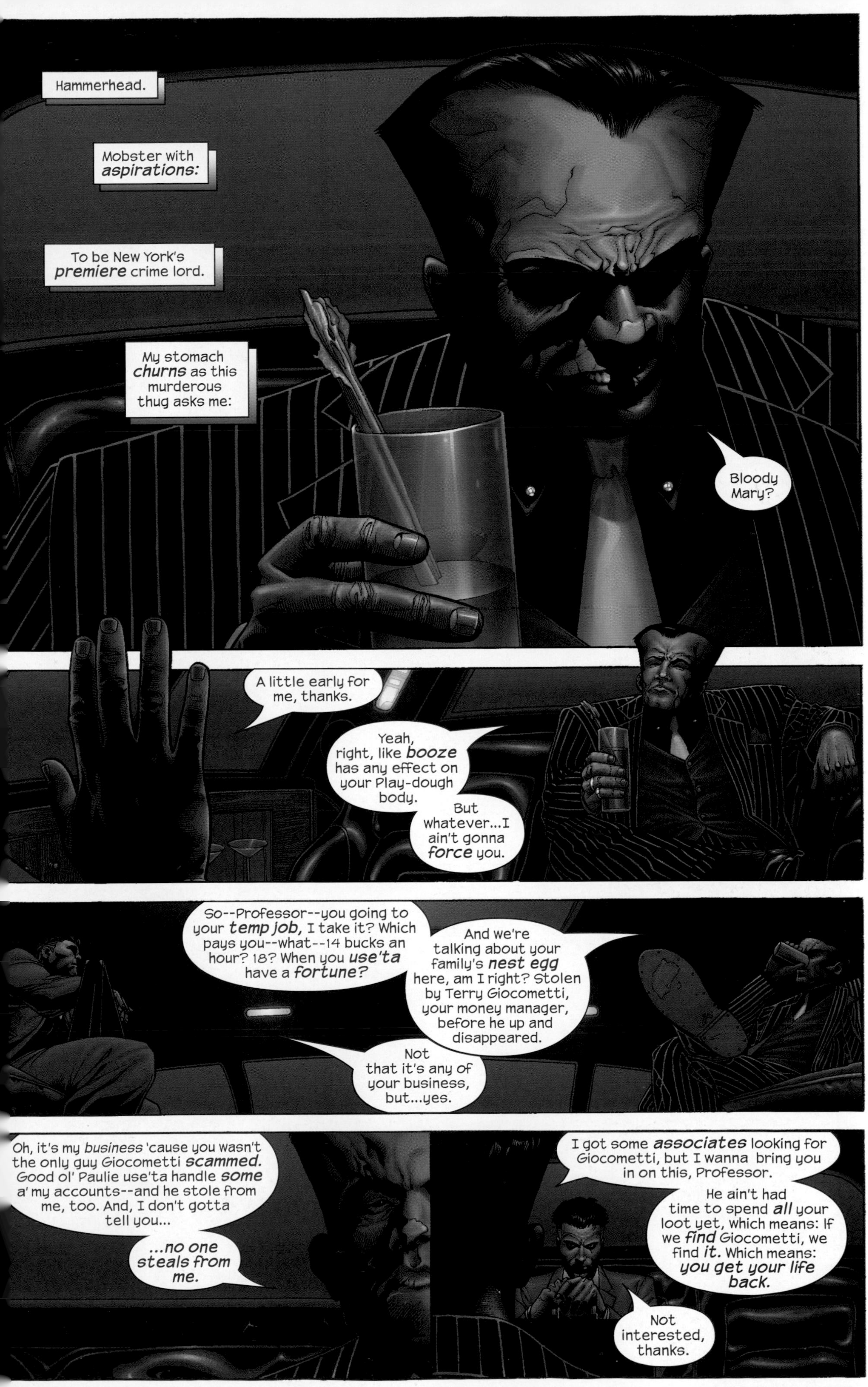

Hammerhead.
Mobster with *aspirations:*
To be New York's *premiere* crime lord.
My stomach *churns* as this murderous thug asks me:
Bloody Mary?
A little early for me, thanks.
Yeah, right, like *booze* has any effect on your Play-dough body.
But whatever...I ain't gonna *force* you.
So--Professor--you going to your *temp job,* I take it? Which pays you--what--14 bucks an hour? 18? When you *use'ta* have a *fortune?*
And we're talking about your family's *nest egg* here, am I right? Stolen by Terry Giocometti, your money manager, before he up and disappeared.
Not that it's any of your business, but...yes.
Oh, it's my *business* 'cause you wasn't the only guy Giocometti *scammed.* Good ol' Paulie use'ta handle *some* a' my accounts--and he stole from me, too. And, I don't gotta tell you...
...no one steals from me.
I got some *associates* looking for Giocometti, but I wanna bring you in on this, Professor.
He ain't had time to spend *all* your loot yet, which means: If we *find* Giocometti, we find *it.* Which means: *you get your life back.*
Not interested, thanks.

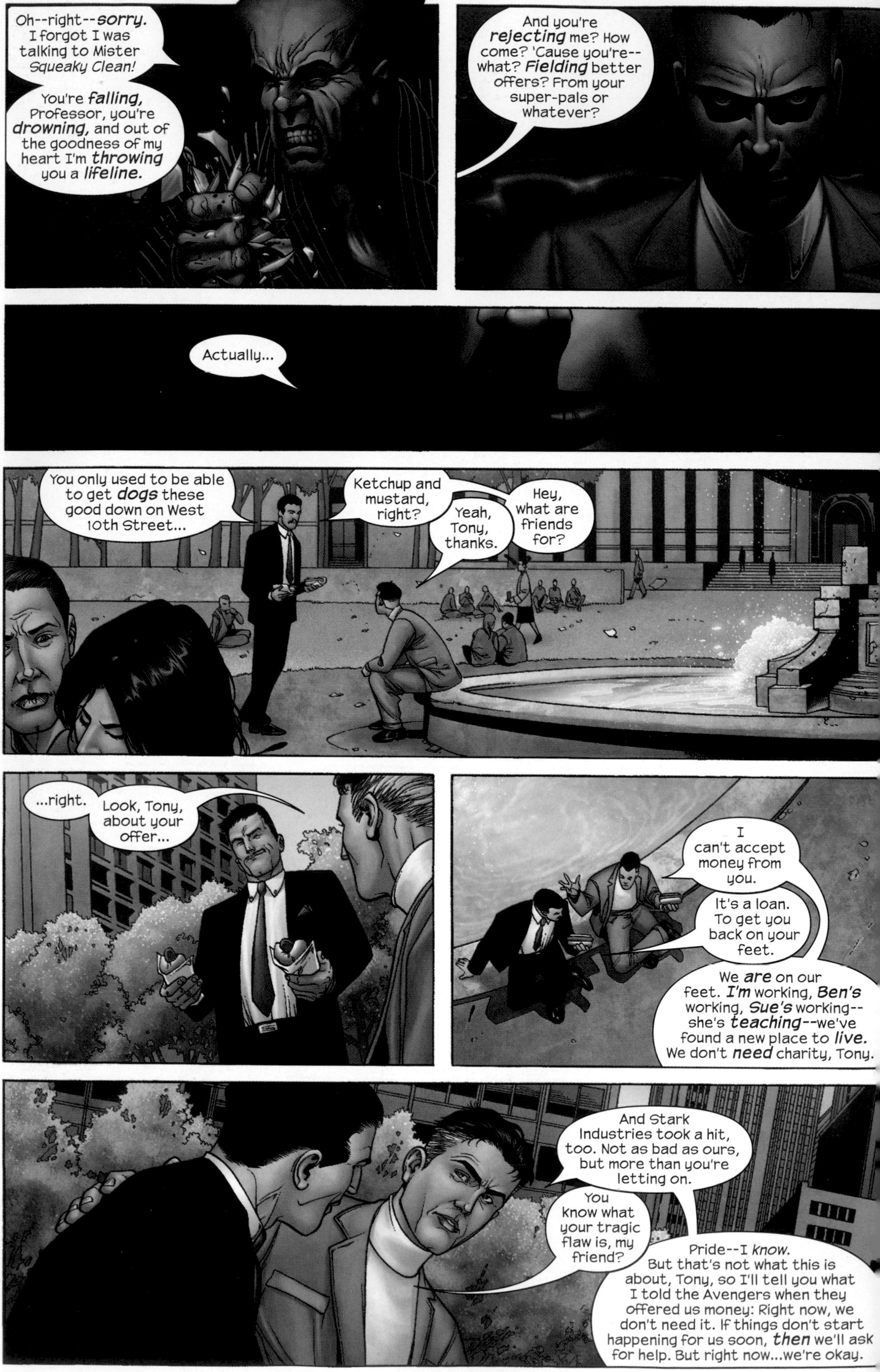
Oh--right--sorry. I forgot I was talking to Mister Squeaky Clean!
You're falling, Professor, you're drowning, and out of the goodness of my heart I'm throwing you a lifeline.
And you're rejecting me? How come? 'Cause you're--what? Fielding better offers? From your super-pals or whatever?
Actually...
You only used to be able to get dogs these good down on West 10th Street...
Ketchup and mustard, right?
Yeah, Tony, thanks.
Hey, what are friends for?
...right.
Look, Tony, about your offer...
I can't accept money from you.
It's a loan. To get you back on your feet.
We are on our feet. I'm working, Ben's working, Sue's working--she's teaching--we've found a new place to live. We don't need charity, Tony.
And Stark Industries took a hit, too. Not as bad as ours, but more than you're letting on.
You know what your tragic flaw is, my friend?
Pride--I know. But that's not what this is about, Tony, so I'll tell you what I told the Avengers when they offered us money: Right now, we don't need it. If things don't start happening for us soon, then we'll ask for help. But right now...we're okay.

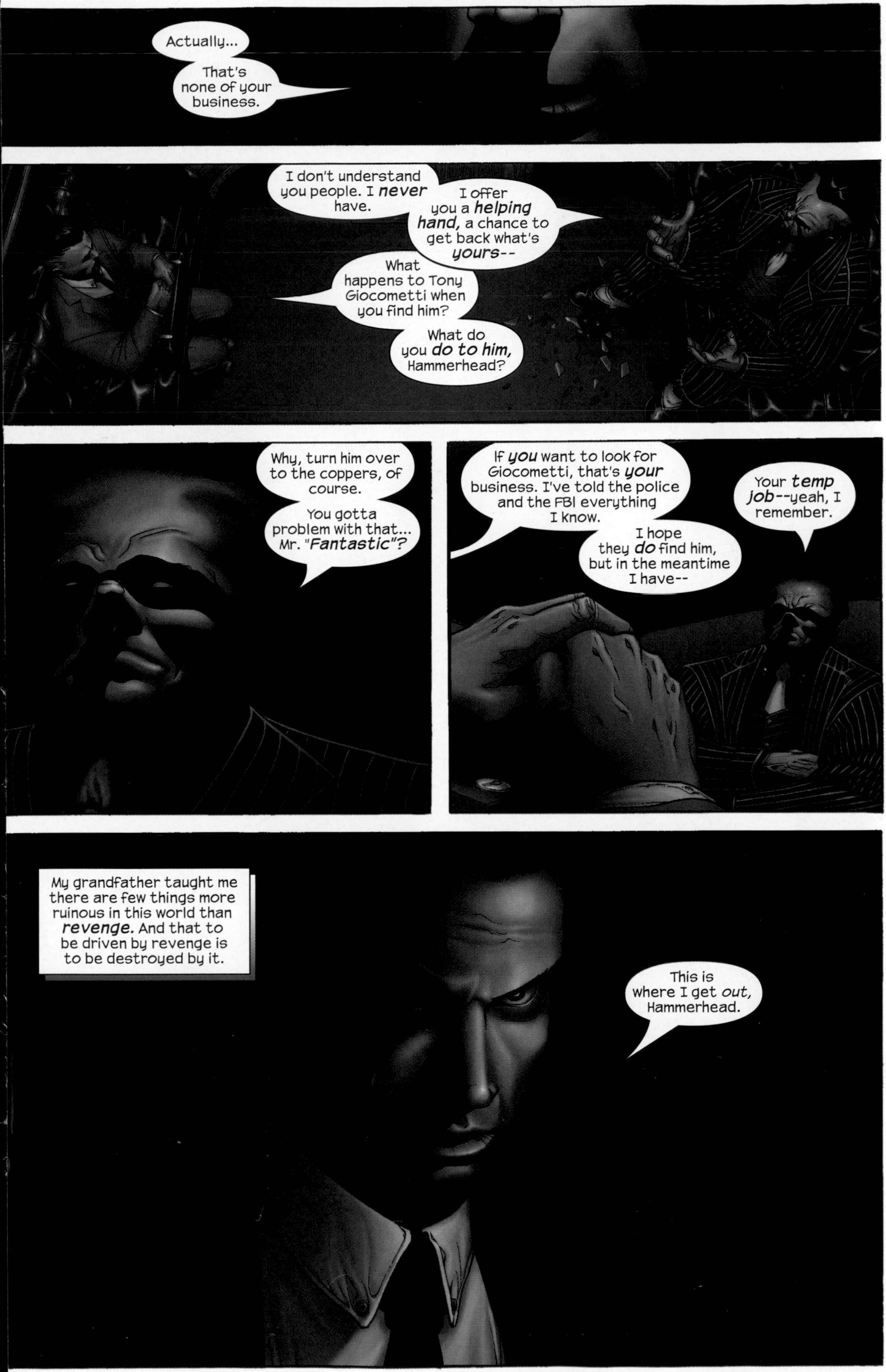
Actually...
That's none of your business.
I don't understand you people. I *never* have.
I offer you a *helping hand,* a chance to get back what's *yours*--
What happens to Tony Giocometti when you find him?
What do you *do to him,* Hammerhead?
Why, turn him over to the coppers, of course.
You gotta problem with that... Mr. "*Fantastic*"?
If *you* want to look for Giocometti, that's *your* business. I've told the police and the FBI everything I know.
I hope they *do* find him, but in the meantime I have--
Your *temp job*--yeah, I remember.
My grandfather taught me there are few things more ruinous in this world than *revenge.* And that to be driven by revenge is to be destroyed by it.
This is where I get *out,* Hammerhead.

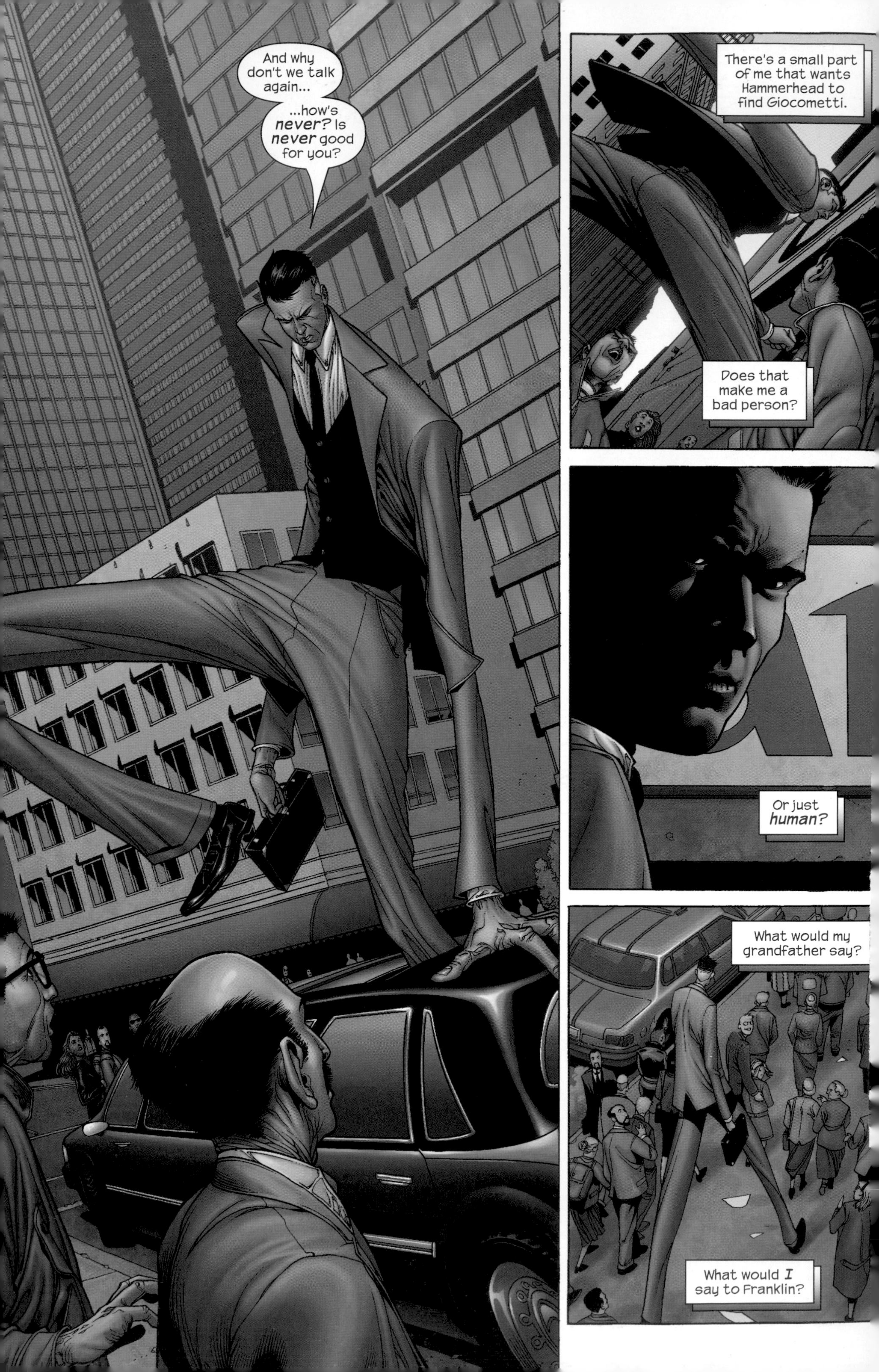
And why don't we talk again...
...how's *never?* Is *never* good for you?
There's a small part of me that wants Hammerhead to find Giocometti.
Does that make me a bad person?
Or just *human?*
What would my grandfather say?
What would *I* say to Franklin?

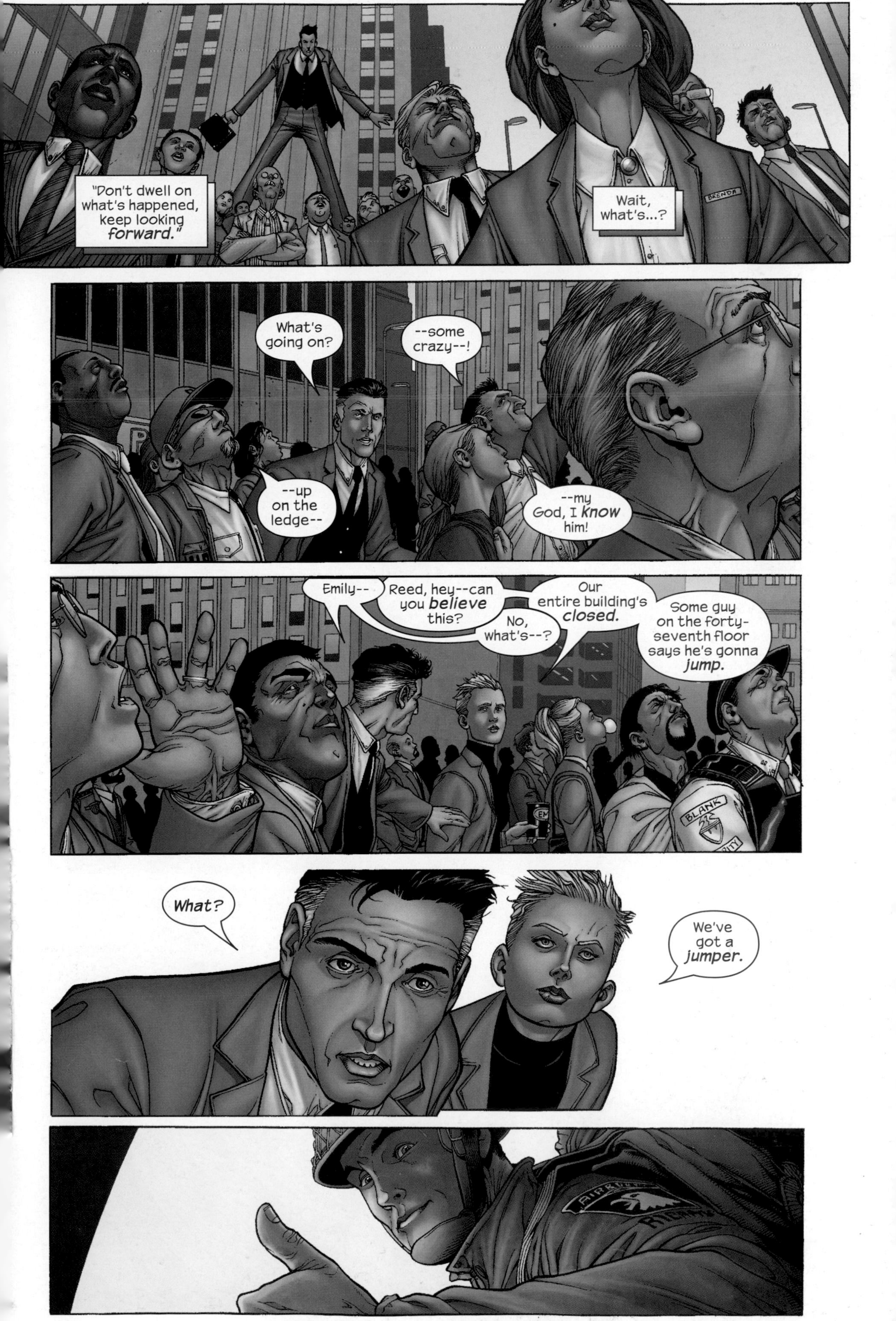
"Don't dwell on what's happened, keep looking forward."
Wait, what's...?
What's going on?
--some crazy--!
--up on the ledge--
--my God, I know him!
Emily--
Reed, hey--can you believe this?
No, what's--?
Our entire building's closed.
Some guy on the forty-seventh floor says he's gonna jump.
What?
We've got a jumper.

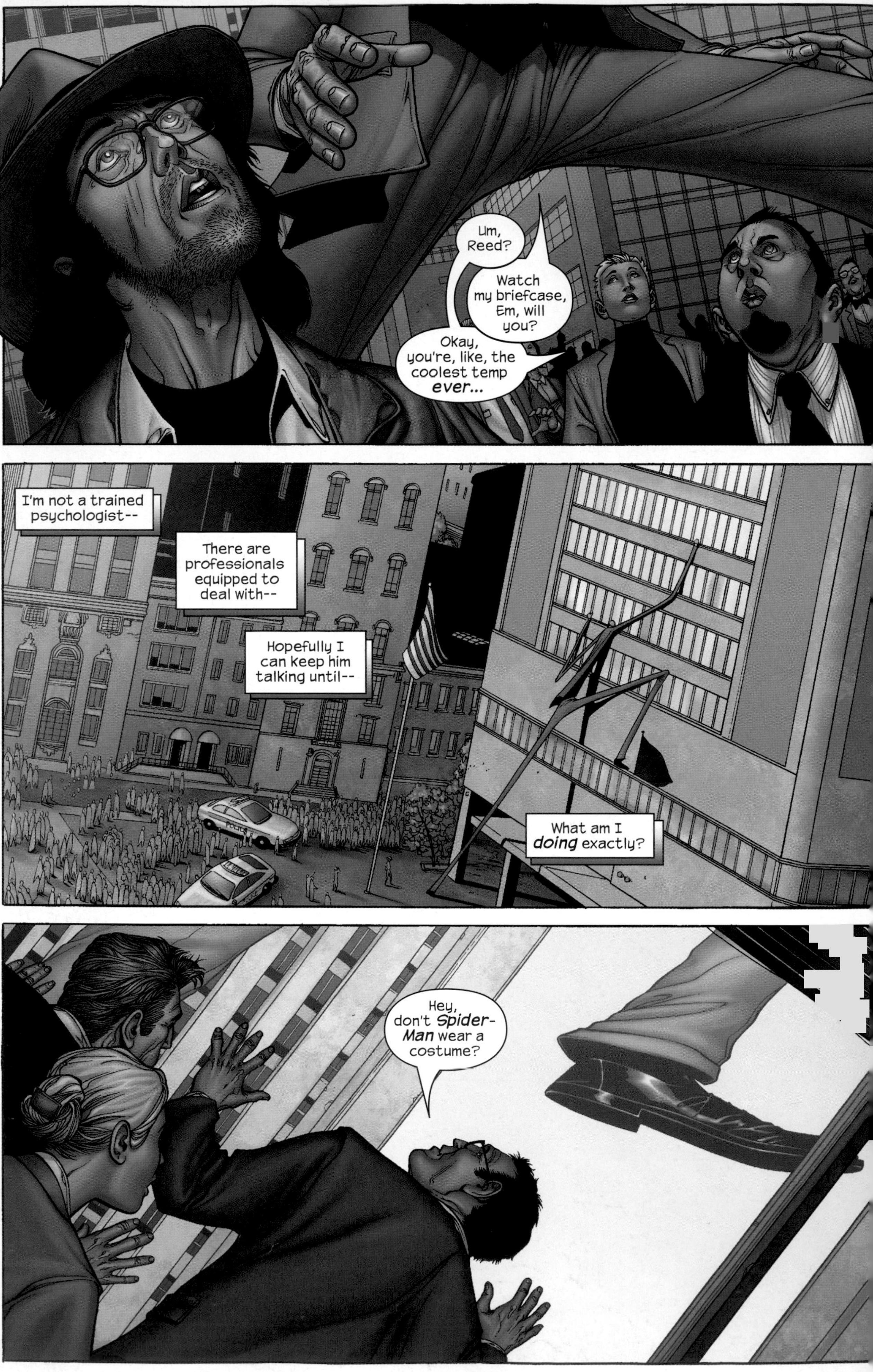
Um, Reed?
Watch my briefcase, Em, will you?
Okay, you're, like, the coolest temp *ever...*
I'm not a trained psychologist--
There are professionals equipped to deal with--
Hopefully I can keep him talking until--
What am I *doing* exactly?
Hey, don't *Spider-Man* wear a costume?

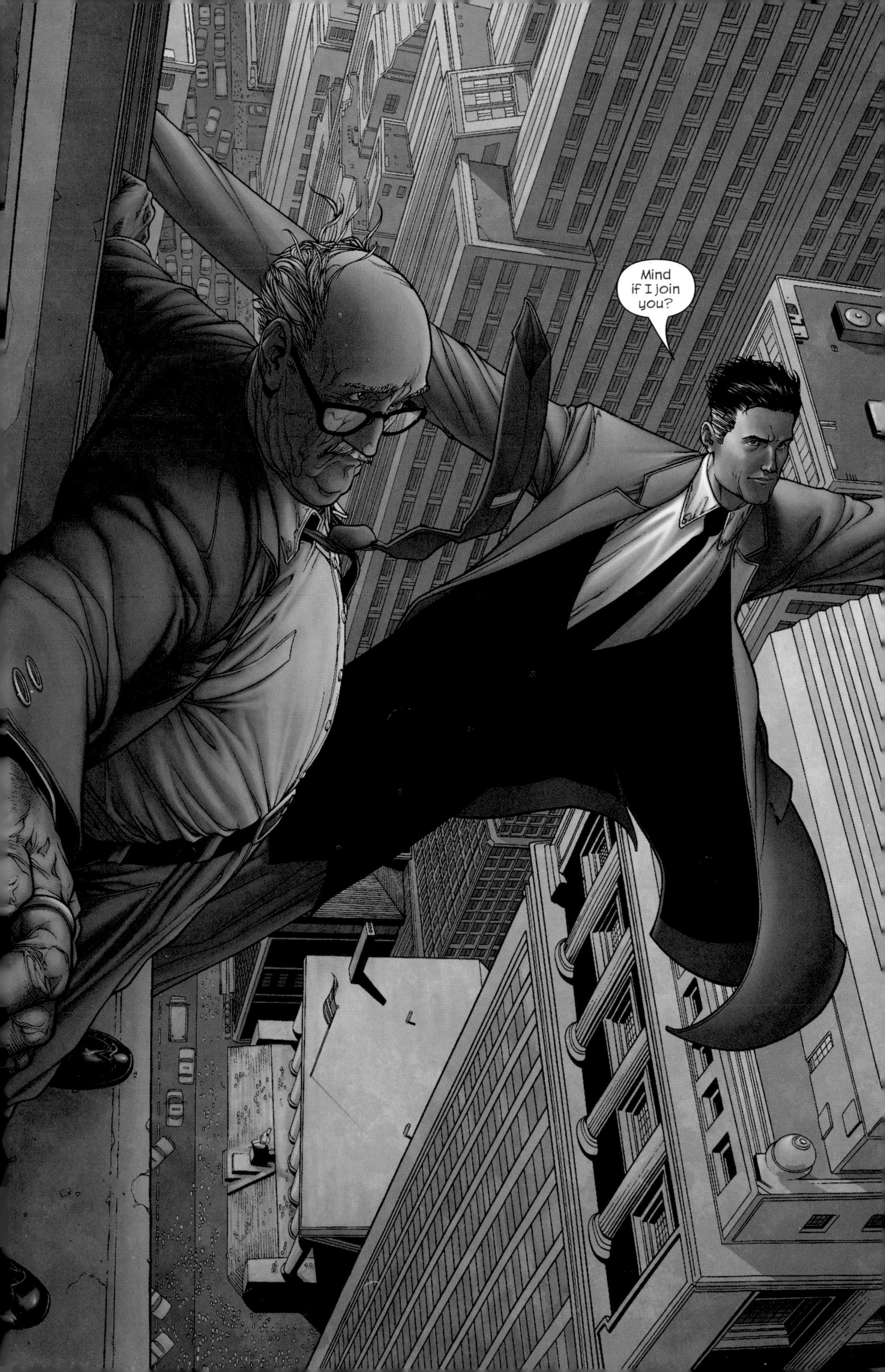
Mind if I join you?

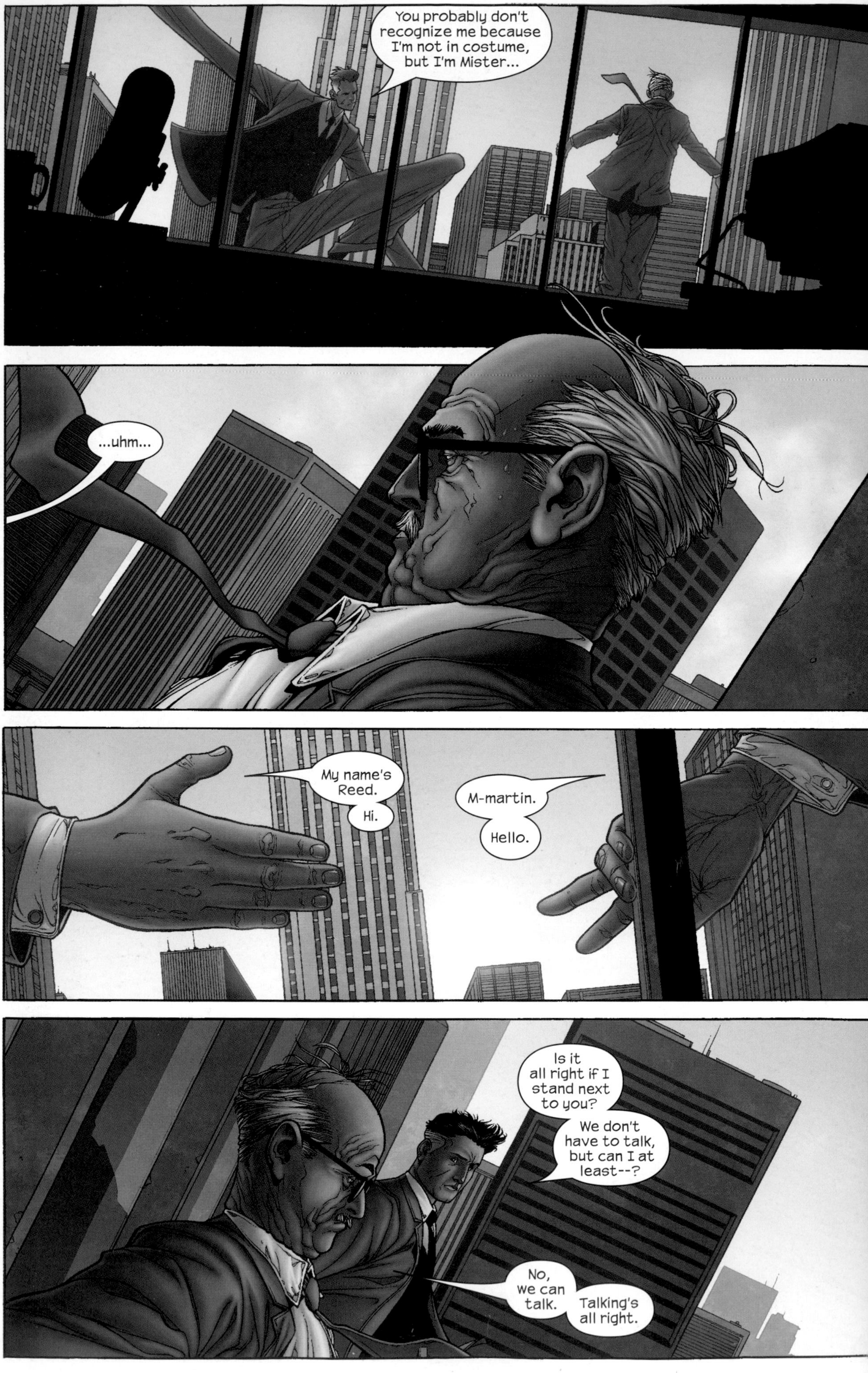
You probably don't recognize me because I'm not in costume, but I'm Mister...
...uhm...
My name's Reed.
Hi.
M-martin.
Hello.
Is it all right if I stand next to you?
We don't have to talk, but can I at least--?
No, we can talk.
Talking's all right.

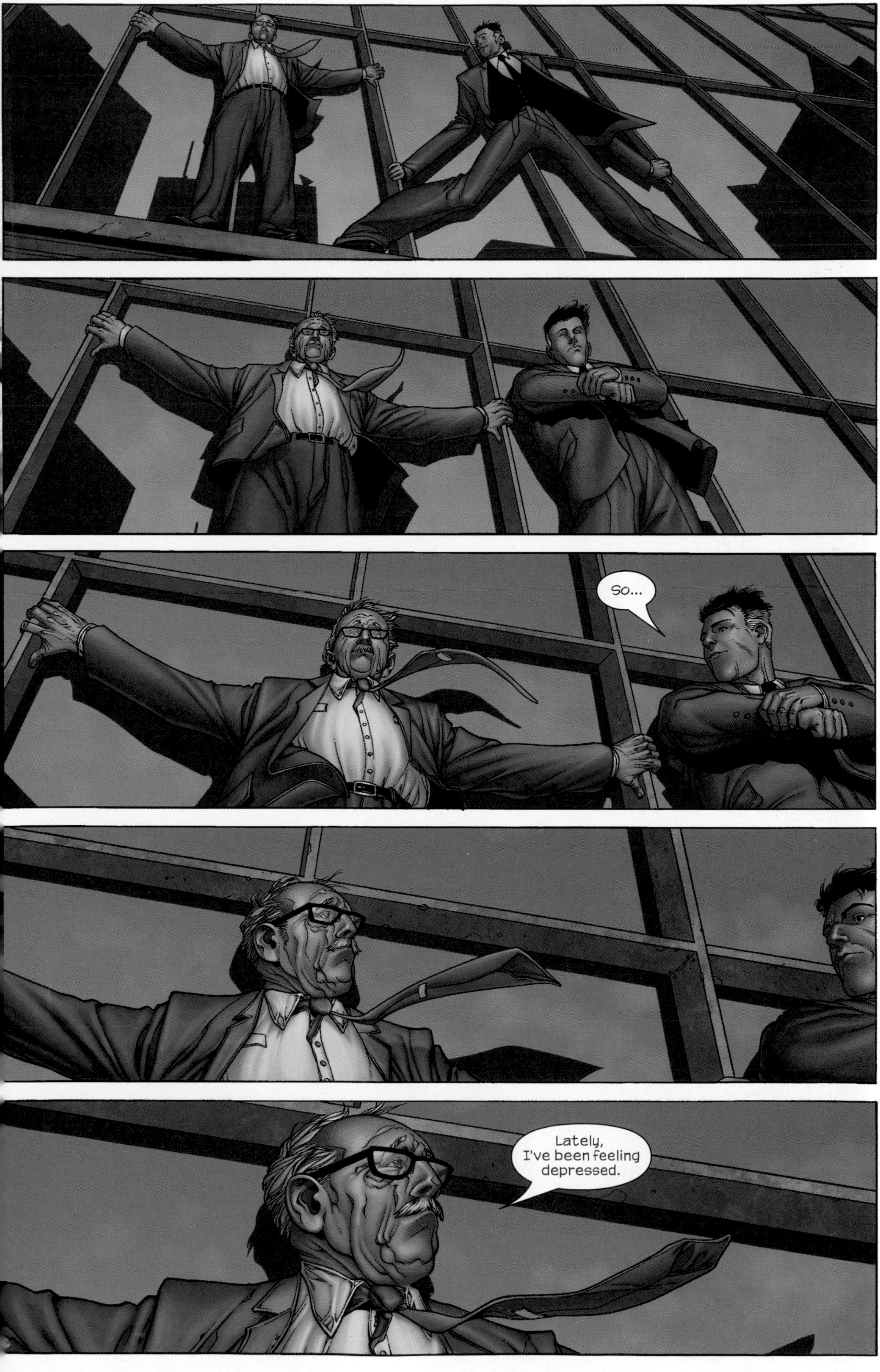
So...
Lately, I've been feeling depressed.

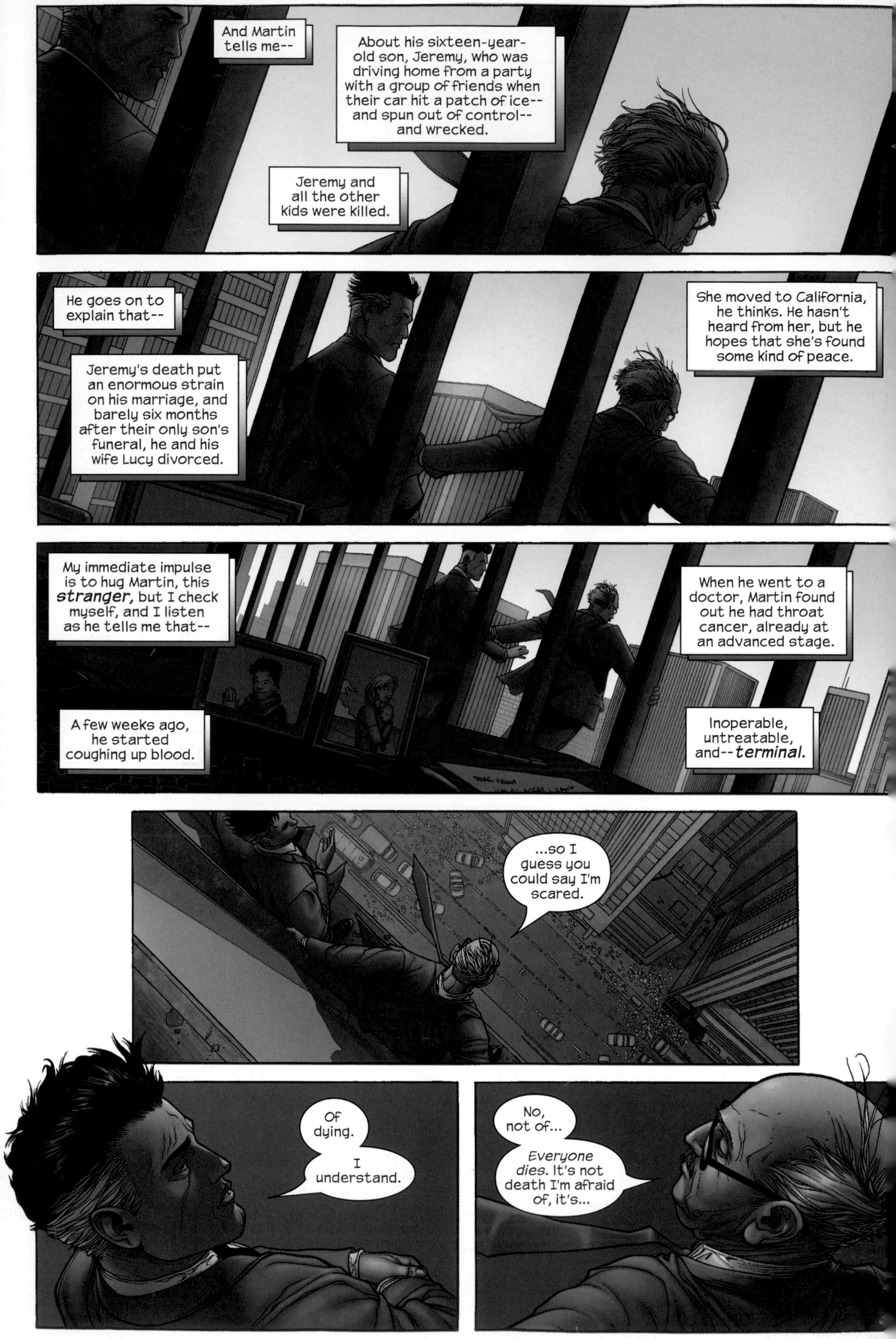

And Martin tells me--
About his sixteen-year-old son, Jeremy, who was driving home from a party with a group of friends when their car hit a patch of ice--and spun out of control--and wrecked.
Jeremy and all the other kids were killed.
He goes on to explain that--
Jeremy's death put an enormous strain on his marriage, and barely six months after their only son's funeral, he and his wife Lucy divorced.
She moved to California, he thinks. He hasn't heard from her, but he hopes that she's found some kind of peace.
My immediate impulse is to hug Martin, this *stranger,* but I check myself, and I listen as he tells me that--
A few weeks ago, he started coughing up blood.
When he went to a doctor, Martin found out he had throat cancer, already at an advanced stage.
Inoperable, untreatable, and--***terminal.***
...so I guess you could say I'm scared.
Of dying.
I understand.
No, not of...
Everyone dies. It's not death I'm afraid of, it's...

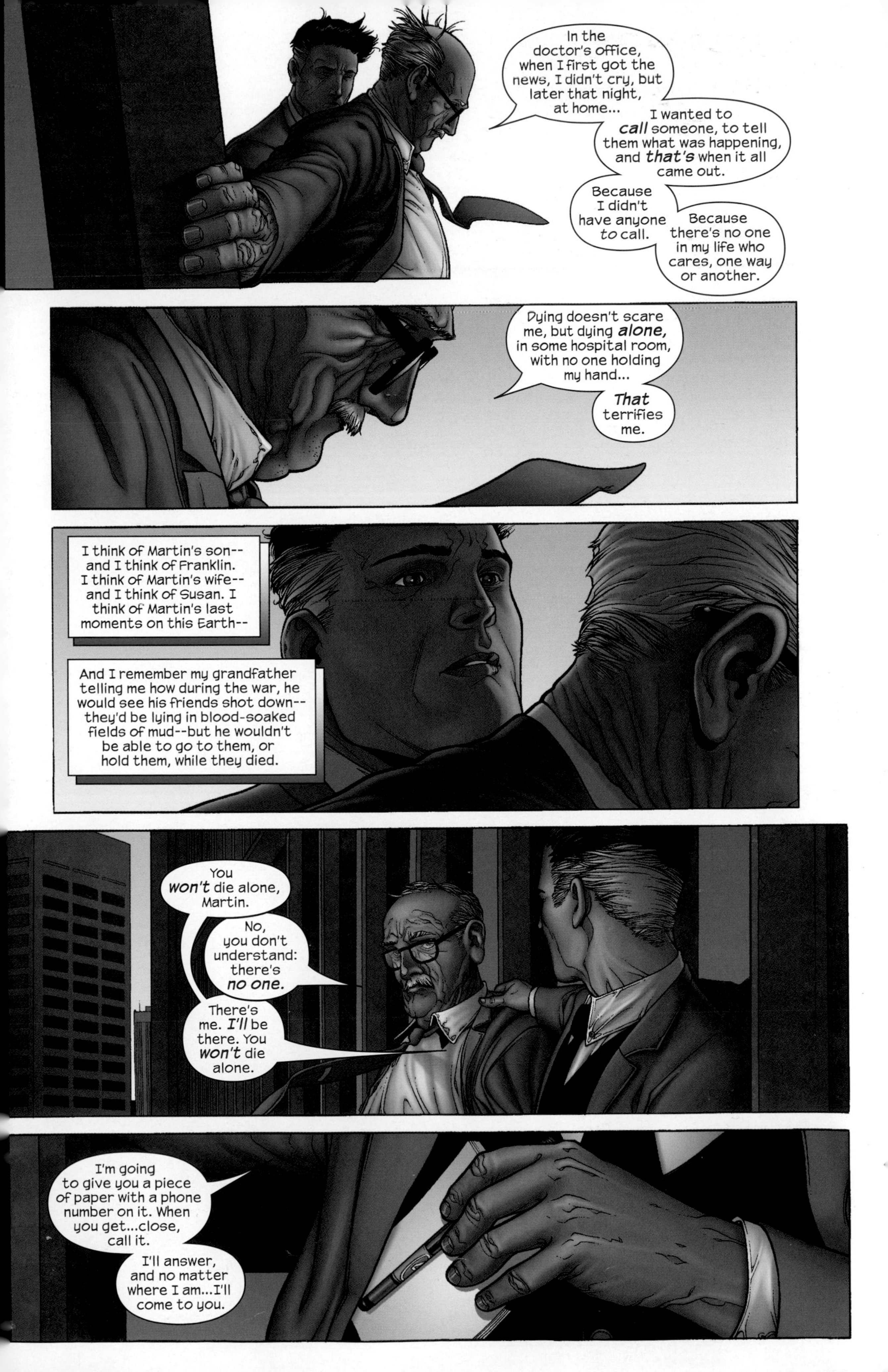

In the doctor's office, when I first got the news, I didn't cry, but later that night, at home...
I wanted to *call* someone, to tell them what was happening, and *that's* when it all came out.
Because I didn't have anyone *to* call.
Because there's no one in my life who cares, one way or another.
Dying doesn't scare me, but dying *alone,* in some hospital room, with no one holding my hand...
That terrifies me.
I think of Martin's son--and I think of Franklin. I think of Martin's wife--and I think of Susan. I think of Martin's last moments on this Earth--
And I remember my grandfather telling me how during the war, he would see his friends shot down--they'd be lying in blood-soaked fields of mud--but he wouldn't be able to go to them, or hold them, while they died.
You *won't* die alone, Martin.
No, you don't understand: there's *no one.*
There's me. *I'll* be there. You *won't* die alone.
I'm going to give you a piece of paper with a phone number on it. When you get...close, call it.
I'll answer, and no matter where I am...I'll come to you.

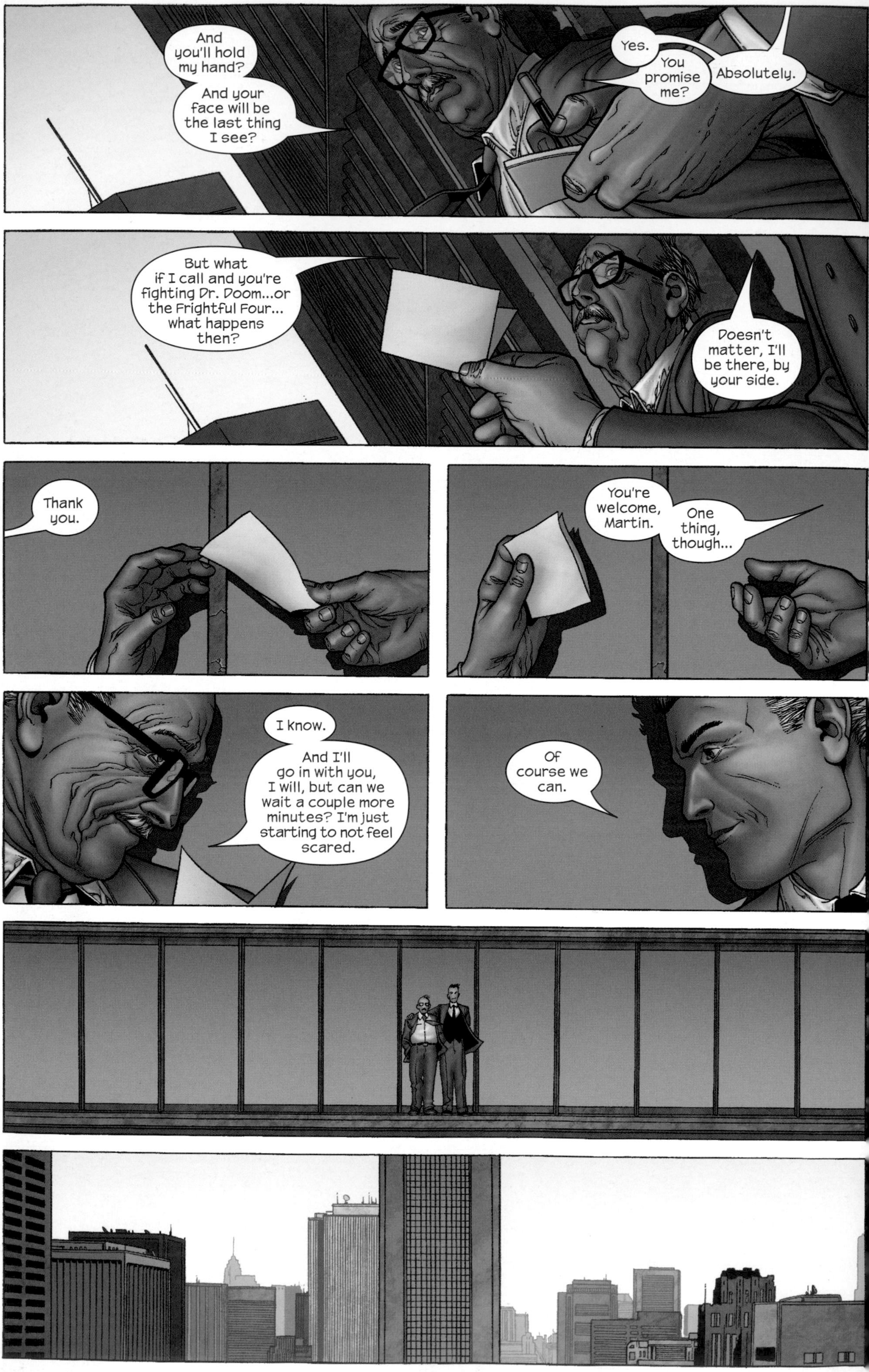
And you'll hold my hand?
And your face will be the last thing I see?
Yes.
You promise me?
Absolutely.
But what if I call and you're fighting Dr. Doom...or the Frightful Four... what happens then?
Doesn't matter, I'll be there, by your side.
Thank you.
You're welcome, Martin.
One thing, though...
I know.
And I'll go in with you, I will, but can we wait a couple more minutes? I'm just starting to not feel scared.
Of course we can.

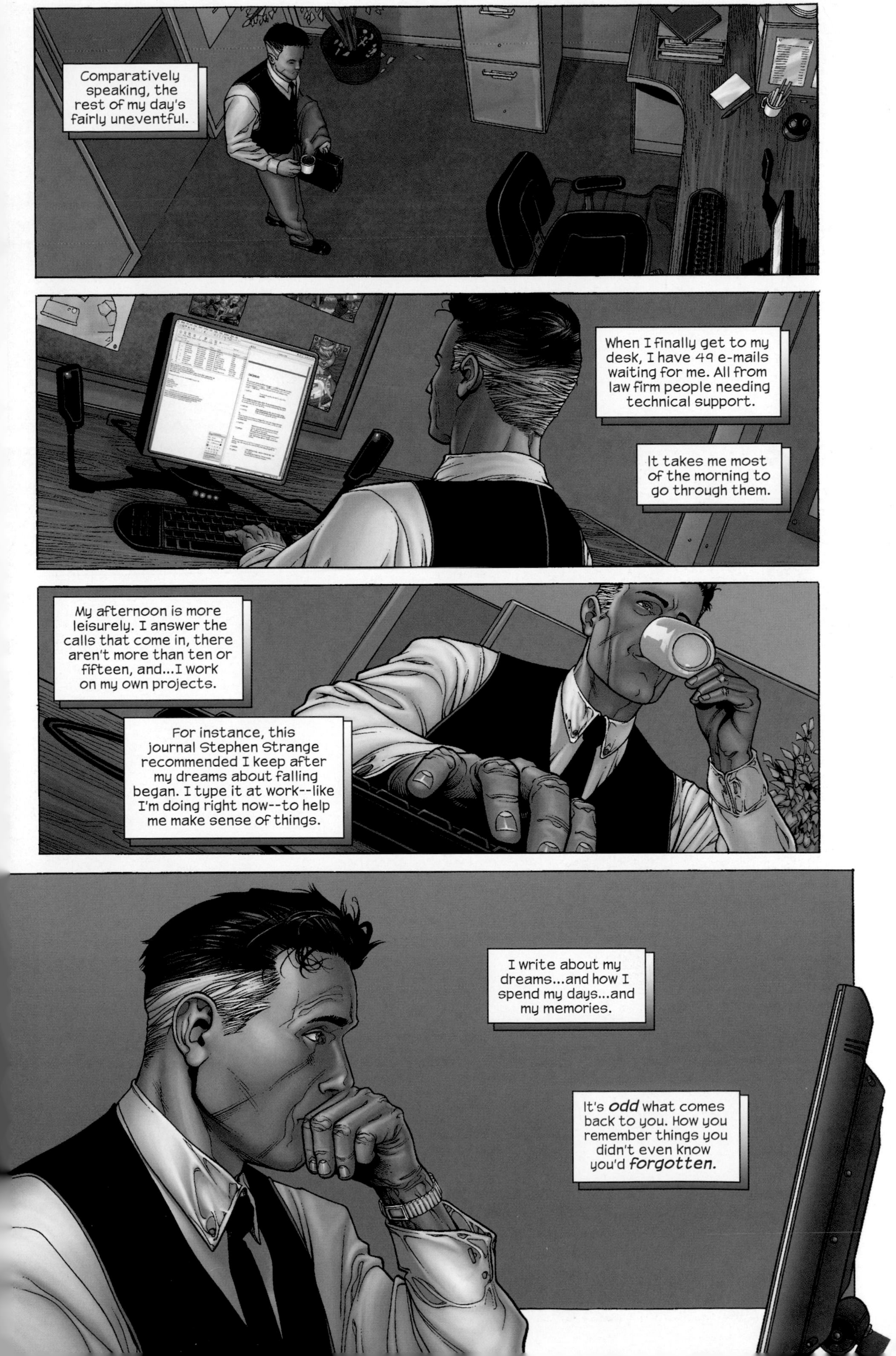
Comparatively speaking, the rest of my day's fairly uneventful.
When I finally get to my desk, I have 49 e-mails waiting for me. All from law firm people needing technical support.
It takes me most of the morning to go through them.
My afternoon is more leisurely. I answer the calls that come in, there aren't more than ten or fifteen, and...I work on my own projects.
For instance, this journal Stephen Strange recommended I keep after my dreams about falling began. I type it at work--like I'm doing right now--to help me make sense of things.
I write about my dreams...and how I spend my days...and my memories.
It's *odd* what comes back to you. How you remember things you didn't even know you'd *forgotten.*

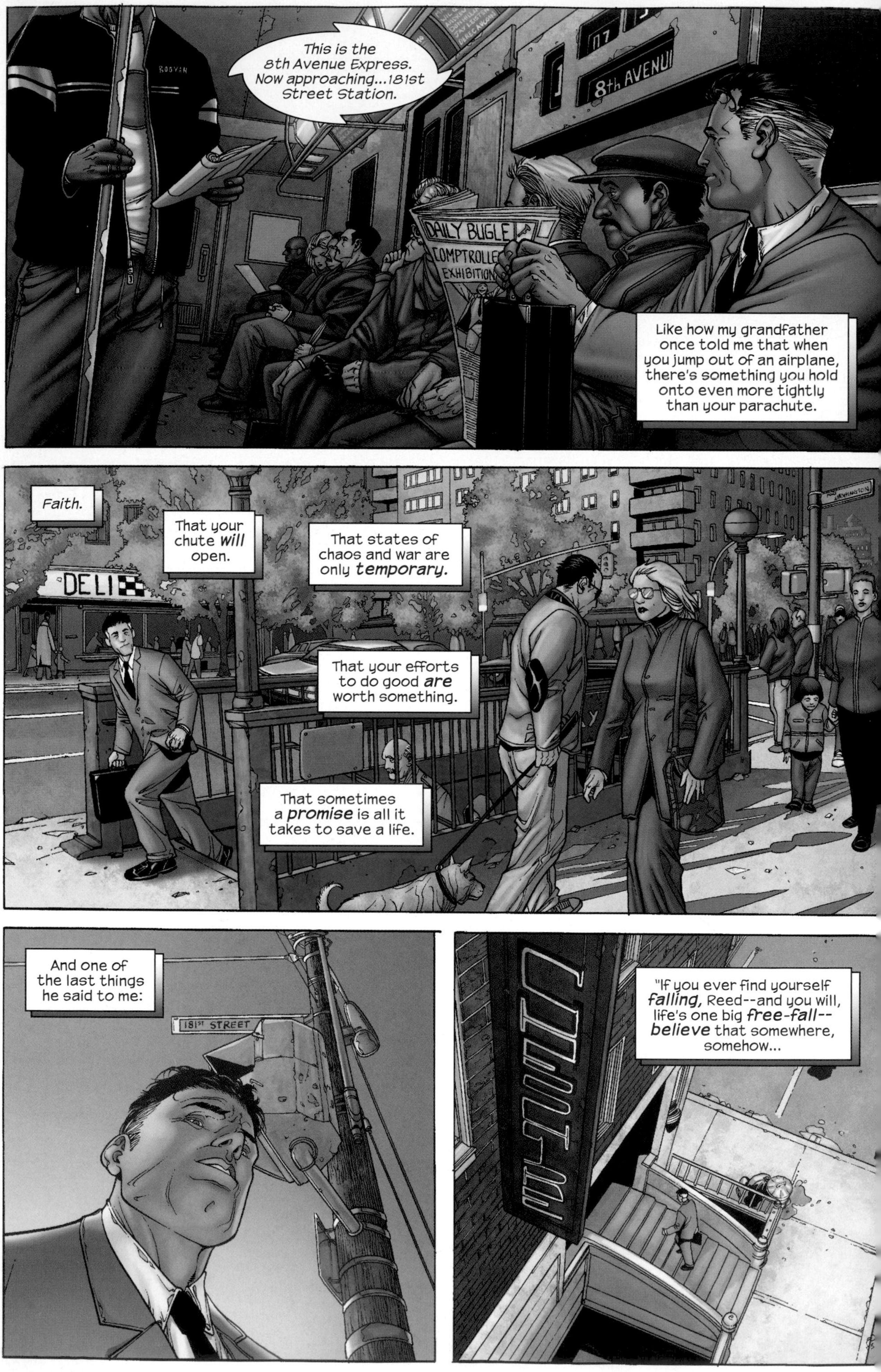

This is the 8th Avenue Express. Now approaching...181st Street Station.
8th AVENU
DAILY BUGLE
COMPTROLLE
EXHIBITION
Like how my grandfather once told me that when you jump out of an airplane, there's something you hold onto even more tightly than your parachute.
Faith.
DELI
That your chute will open.
That states of chaos and war are only temporary.
That your efforts to do good are worth something.
That sometimes a promise is all it takes to save a life.
And one of the last things he said to me:
181ST STREET
"If you ever find yourself falling, Reed--and you will, life's one big free-fall--believe that somewhere, somehow...

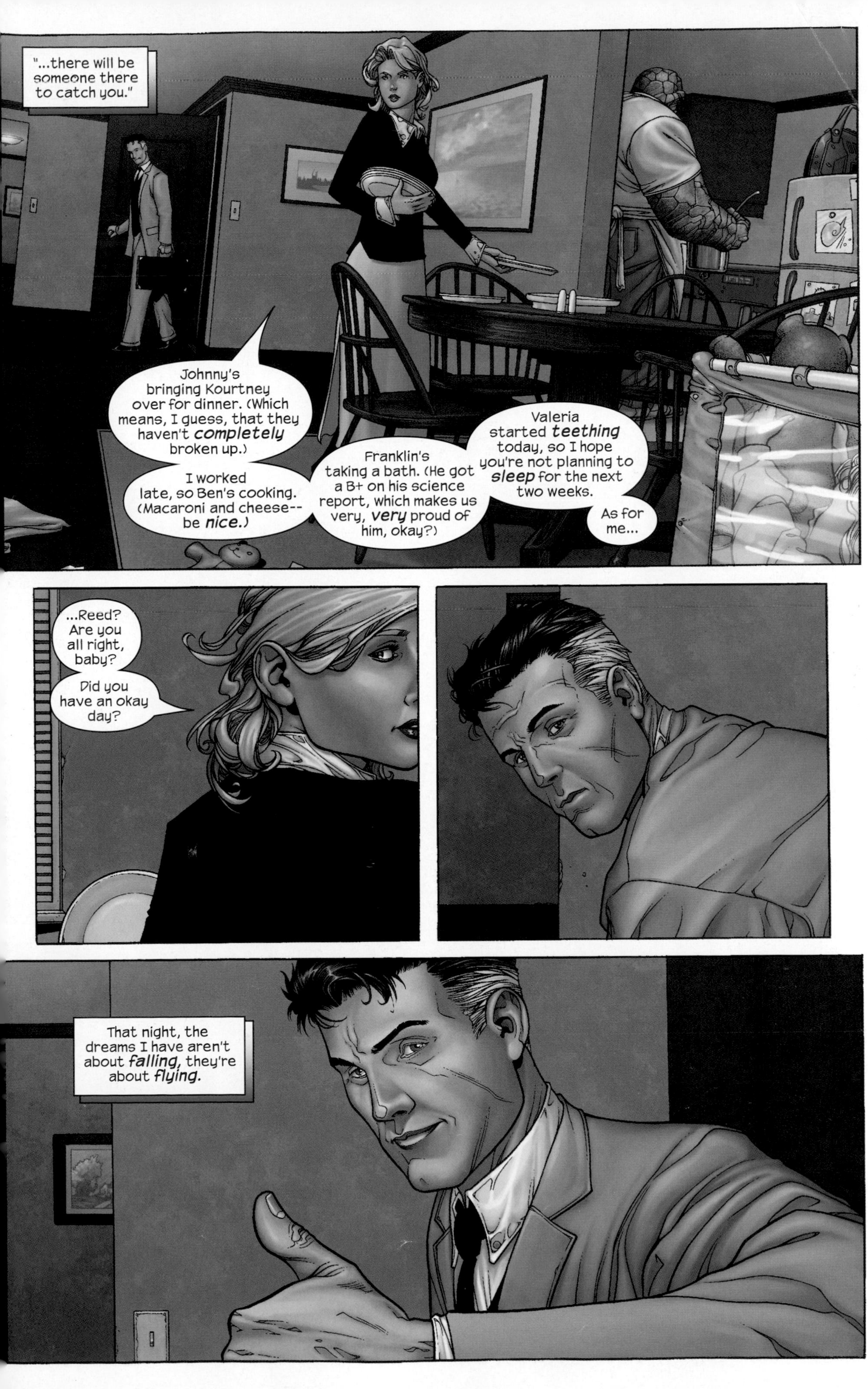
"...there will be someone there to catch you."
Johnny's bringing Kourtney over for dinner. (Which means, I guess, that they haven't *completely* broken up.)
I worked late, so Ben's cooking. (Macaroni and cheese-- be *nice.*)
Franklin's taking a bath. (He got a B+ on his science report, which makes us very, *very* proud of him, okay?)
Valeria started *teething* today, so I hope you're not planning to *sleep* for the next two weeks.
As for me...
...Reed? Are you all right, baby?
Did you have an okay day?
That night, the dreams I have aren't about *falling,* they're about *flying.*

HOMAGE OF COVER TO *FANTASTIC FOUR #1* BY ALEX ROSS

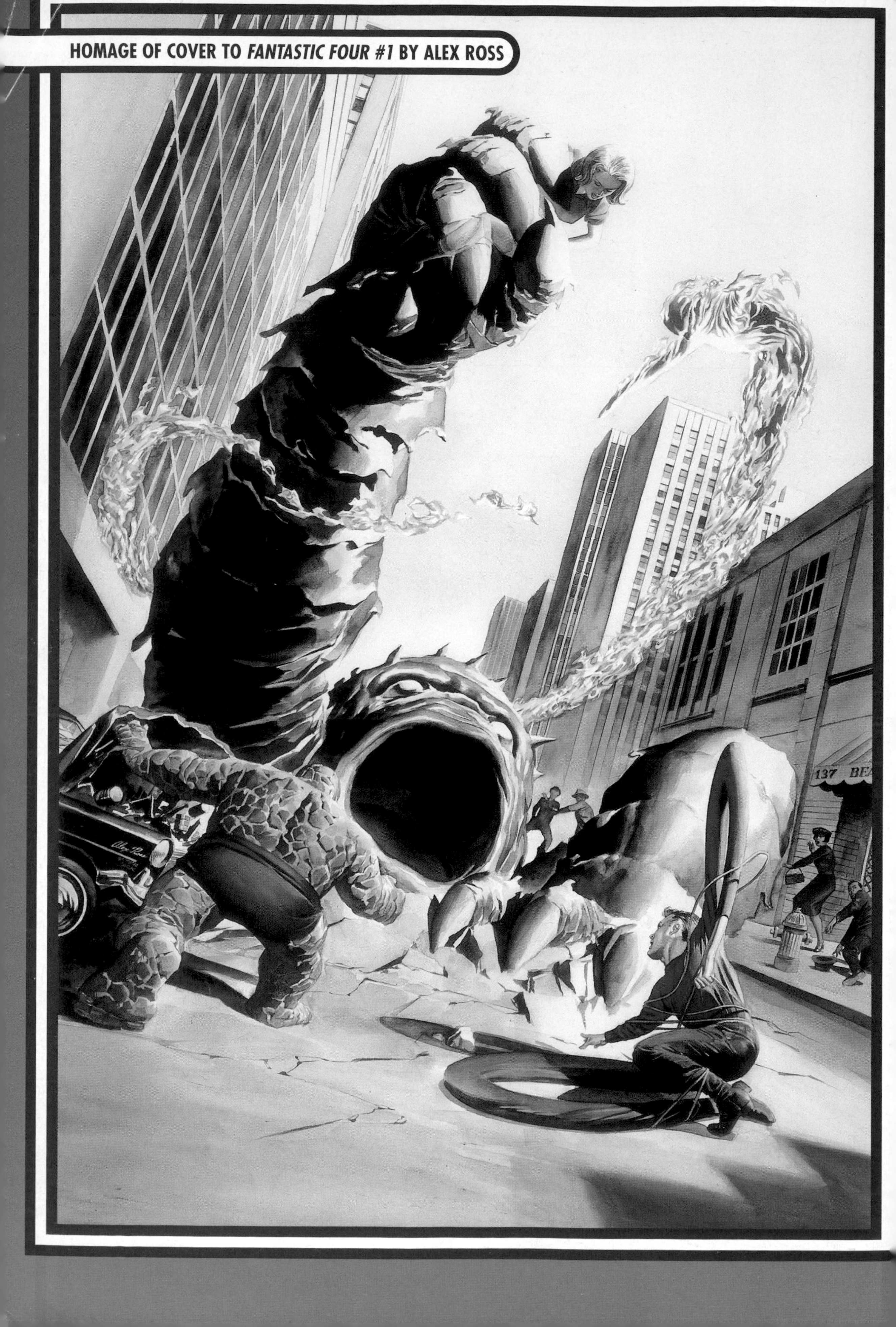
137 BEA

COVER TO *FANTASTIC FOUR VISIONARIES: GEORGE PÉREZ VOL. 1 TPB* BY GEORGE PÉREZ

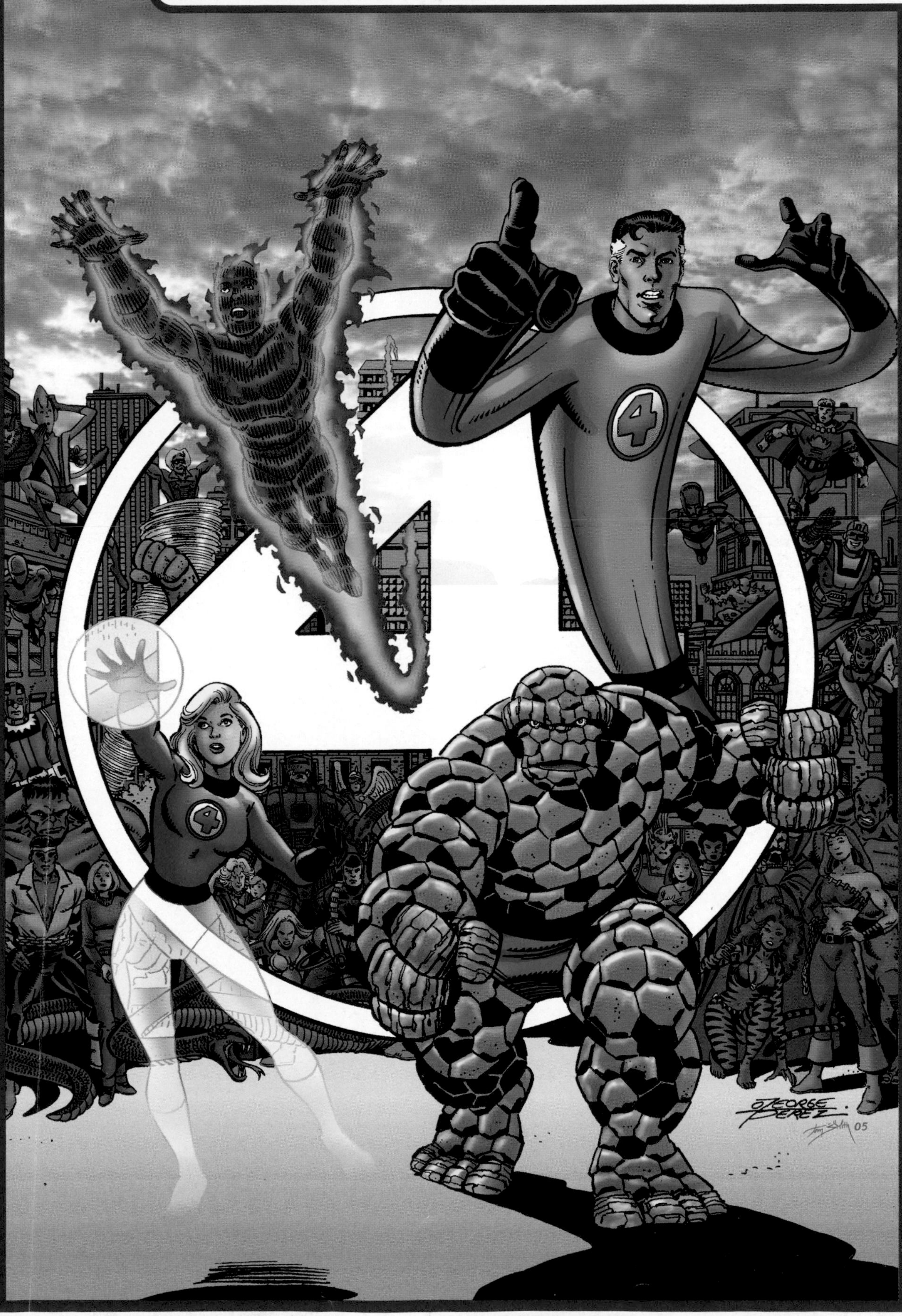

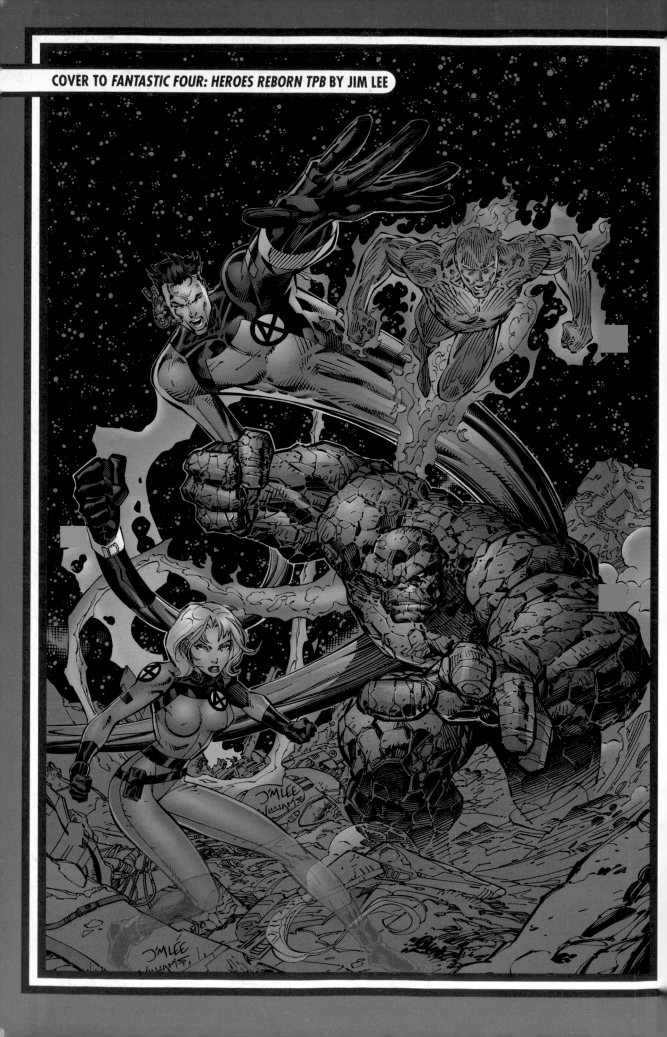

COVER TO *FANTASTIC FOUR: HEROES REBORN TPB* BY JIM LEE

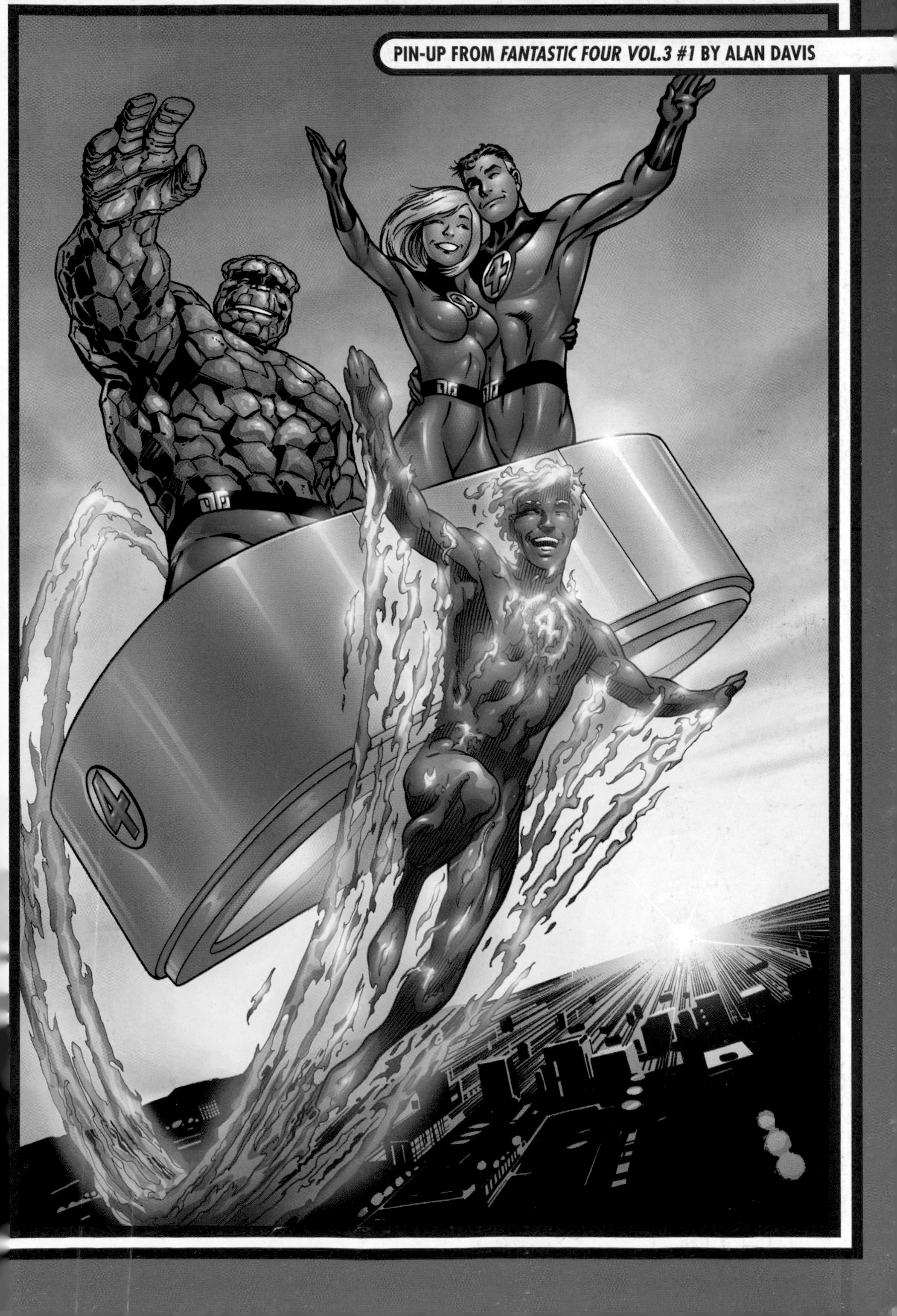

PIN-UP FROM *FANTASTIC FOUR VOL.3 #1* BY ALAN DAVIS

COVER TO *FANTASTIC FOUR VOL. 3 #50* BY BARRY WINDSOR-SMITH

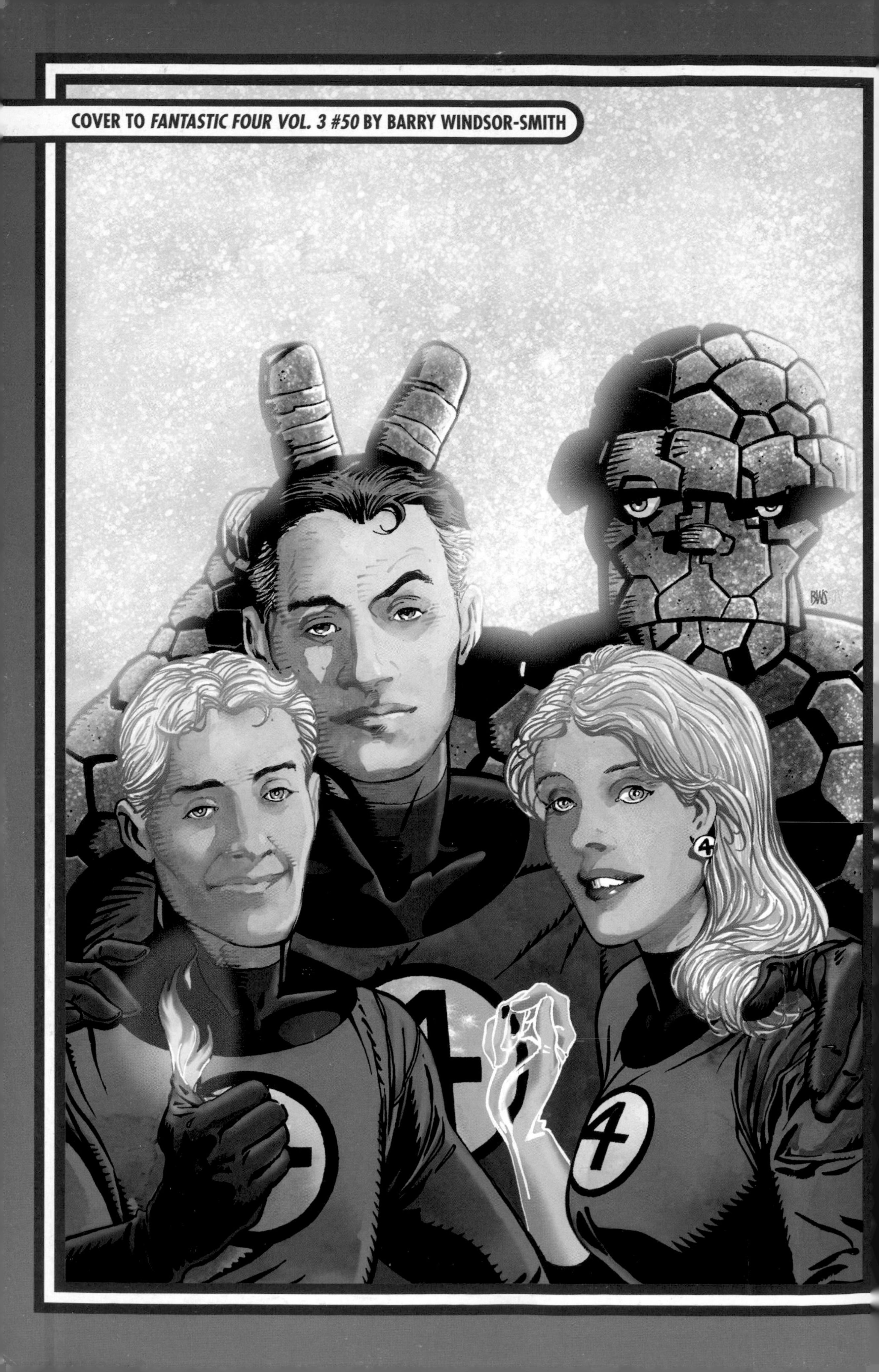
BWS

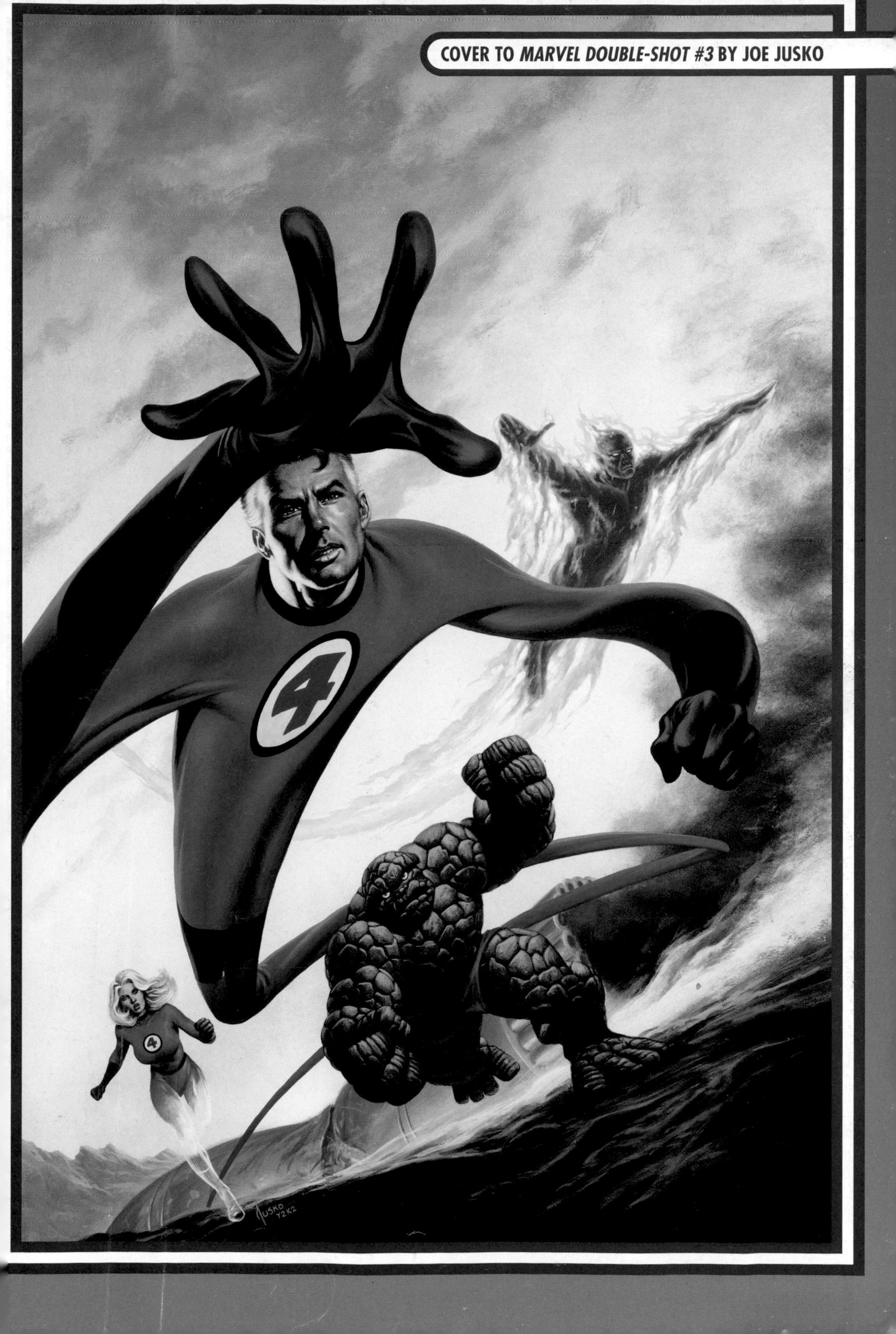

COVER TO *MARVEL DOUBLE-SHOT #3* BY JOE JUSKO

COVER TO THE *OFFICIAL HANDBOOK OF THE MARVEL UNIVERSE: FANTASTIC FOUR 2005*
BY TOM GRUMMETT AND MORRY HOLLOWELL

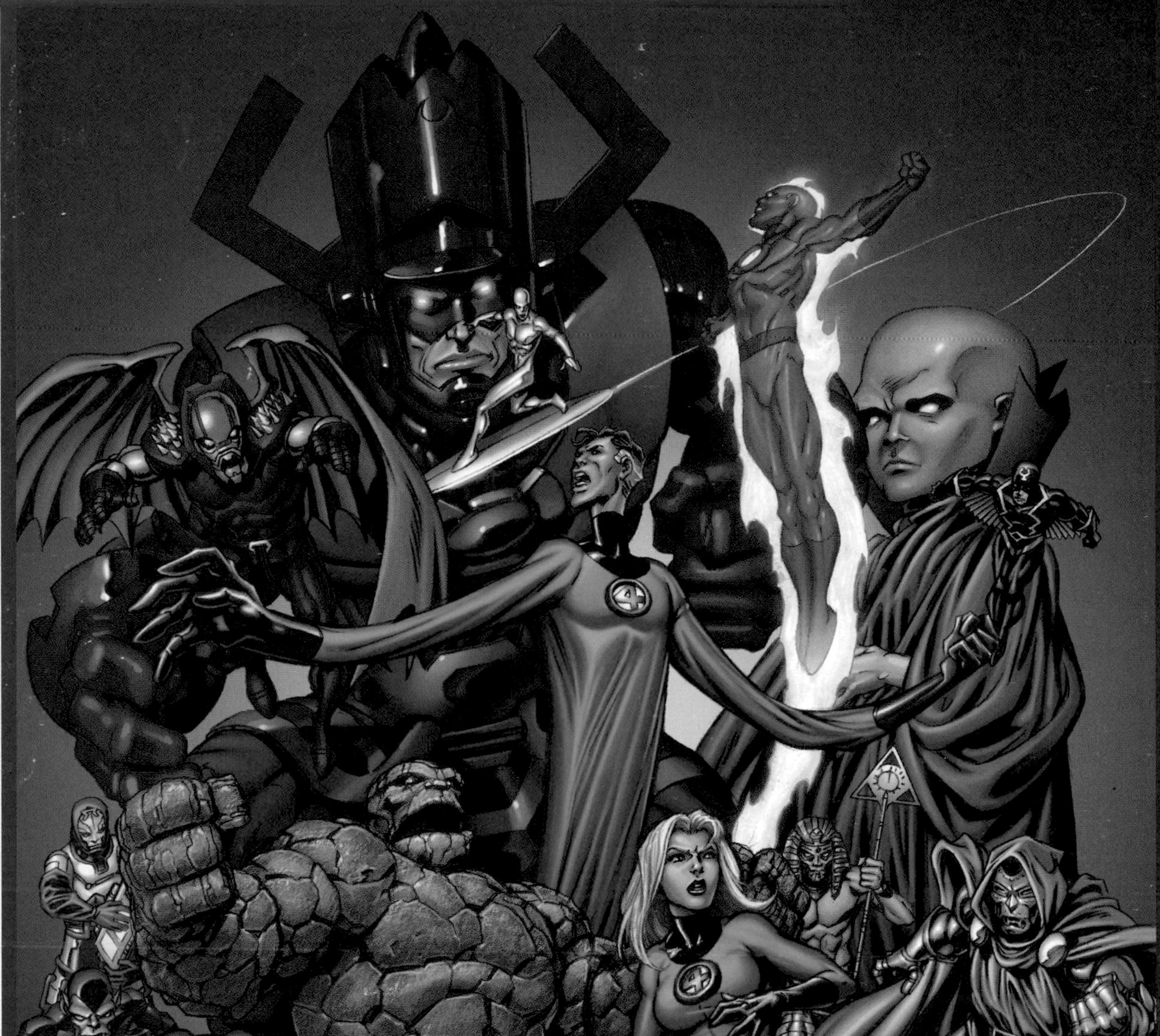